SAP PRESS

SAP PRESS is a joint initiative of SAP and Rheinwerk Publishing. The know-how offered by SAP specialists combined with the expertise of Rheinwerk Publishing offers the reader expert books in the field. SAP PRESS features first-hand information and expert advice, and provides useful skills for professional decision-making.

SAP PRESS offers a variety of books on technical and business-related topics for the SAP user. For further information, please visit our website: *www.sap-press.com*.

Ankisettipalli, Chen, Wankawala
SAP HANA Advanced Data Modeling
2016, 392 pages, hardcover and e-book
www.sap-press.com/3863

Gahm, Schneider, Swanepoel, Westenberger
ABAP Development for SAP HANA (2nd Edition)
2016, 641 pages, hardcover and e-book
www.sap-press.com/3973

Herzig, Heitkötter, Wozniak, Agarwal, Wust
Extending SAP S/4HANA: Side-by-Side Extensions with the SAP S/4HANA Cloud SDK
2018, 618 pages, hardcover and e-book
www.sap-press.com/4655

Paul Hardy
ABAP to the Future (2nd Edition)
2016, 801 pages, hardcover and e-book
www.sap-press.com/4161

SAP HANA® XSA

Francesco Alborghetti, Jonas Kohlbrenner, Abani Pattanayak,
Dominik Schrank, Primo Sboarina

SAP HANA® XSA

Native Development for SAP HANA

Rheinwerk
Publishing

Editor Meagan White
Acquisitions Editor Hareem Shafi
Copyeditor Julie McNamee
Cover Design Graham Geary
Photo Credit Shutterstock.com/83385613/© Ortodox
Layout Design Vera Brauner
Production Kelly O'Callaghan
Typesetting III-Satz, Husby (Germany)
Printed and bound in the United States of America, on paper from sustainable sources

ISBN 978-1-4932-1601-7

1rd edition 2018

Library of Congress Cataloging-in-Publication Data
Names: Alborghetti, Francesco, author.
Title: SAP HANA XSA : native development for SAP HANA / Francesco Alborghetti, Jonas Kohlbrenner, Abani Pattanayak, Dominik Schrank, Primo Sboarina.
Description: First edition. | Bonn : Rheinwerk Publishing, 2018. | Includes index.
Identifiers: LCCN 2018021614 (print) | LCCN 2018022694 (ebook) | ISBN 9781493216024 (ebook) | ISBN 9781493216017 (alk. paper)
Subjects: LCSH: Database design. | Cross-platform software development. | SAP HANA (Electronic resource).
Classification: LCC QA76.9.D26 (ebook) | LCC QA76.9.D26 A44 2018 (print) | DDC 005.74/3--dc23
LC record available at https://lccn.loc.gov/2018021614

Contents at a Glance

PART I Getting Started

1 Introduction to the SAP HANA Development Platform ... 25
2 SAP HANA Development Environment ... 43
3 SAP HANA Development Tools ... 83
4 SAP HANA XS Advanced Architecture ... 119

PART II Developing an Application

5 Defining the Data Model ... 151
6 Developing the Application Layer ... 289
7 Developing a Presentation Layer ... 393

PART III Refining the Application

8 Securing Your Application ... 449
9 Troubleshooting Your Application ... 507
10 Deploying Your Application ... 557

Appendices

A Migrating an SAP HANA XS Application to SAP HANA XS Advanced ... 573
B Additional Resources ... 593
C The Authors ... 595

Dear Reader,

Very few things exactly meet our needs right out of the box. That new cast iron pan? Needs to be scrubbed and then seasoned. Your daughter's new bicycle? Time to add the training wheels and some streamers to the handle bars. Upgraded your coffee table? Don't forget to add anti-slip pads to the feet, and a new coat of stain for the wood would make it match the room perfectly. The same can be said of SAP HANA.

This is where SAP HANA XS Advanced comes in. Between these pages, our expert author team have shown you how to create your own applications that will allow you to get exactly what you need from SAP HANA. Over the past several months they have shown incredible dedication in writing the chapters, reviewing the code, updating for the latest SPS, and ensuring that you'll have the most up-to-date and useful information available.

What did you think about *SAP HANA XSA: Native Development for SAP HANA?* Your comments and suggestions are the most useful tools to help us make our books the best they can be. Please feel free to contact me and share any praise or criticism you may have.

Thank you for purchasing a book from SAP PRESS!

Meagan White
Editor, SAP PRESS

meaganw@rheinwerk-publishing.com
www.sap-press.com
Rheinwerk Publishing · Boston, MA

Contents

Preface 15

PART I Getting Started

1 Introduction to the SAP HANA Development Platform 25

1.1 Business Cases for SAP HANA Applications 25
1.2 SAP HANA Components and Architecture 29
1.2.1 Functional Components 29
1.2.2 Technical Services and Architecture 36
1.3 Application Design Considerations 38
1.4 Summary 40

2 SAP HANA Development Environment 43

2.1 System Landscape 43
2.2 SAP HANA, Express Edition 47
2.2.1 On-Premise Installation Options 48
2.2.2 Installing SAP HANA, Express Edition VM Images 48
2.3 SAP Cloud Appliance Library 54
2.3.1 Registrations 55
2.3.2 SAP HANA, Express Edition Setup 56
2.4 SAP Cloud Platform 60
2.4.1 Registrations 61
2.4.2 Provisioning the SAP HANA Service Instance 61
2.4.3 Enable SAP Web IDE for Full-Stack Development 66
2.5 SAP HANA XS Advanced Organizations and Spaces 69
2.5.1 Organizations and Spaces Overview 69
2.5.2 Organization and Space Management 71

2.6 Git Code Repository 74
2.7 Summary 80

3 SAP HANA Development Tools 83

3.1 Command-Line Client 83
3.1.1 Logon and Setup 85
3.1.2 Application Management 86
3.1.3 Services Management 88
3.1.4 Organizations and Spaces 90
3.1.5 Domains 91
3.1.6 Certificates 92
3.1.7 Routes 93
3.1.8 Buildpacks 94
3.1.9 Runtime Environments and the Blob Store 95
3.1.10 Tasks 96
3.1.11 User Administration 97
3.1.12 Configuration 98
3.1.13 Plug-Ins 99
3.1.14 Other Commands 100
3.2 SAP Web IDE for SAP HANA 101
3.3 SAP HANA Database Explorer 104
3.4 SAP HANA XS Advanced Cockpit 109
3.5 Other SAP HANA Database Development Tools 113
3.5.1 SAP HANA Studio 113
3.5.2 SAP HANA Web-Based Development Workbench 115
3.5.3 SAP HANA Cockpit 116
3.5.4 Postman 117
3.6 Summary 118

4 SAP HANA XS Advanced Architecture 119

4.1 Microservices Architecture 119
4.1.1 Monolithic Architecture 120

4.1.2 Microservices Architecture ... 121

4.2 SAP HANA XS Advanced Architecture ... 122

4.2.1 12-Factor Apps ... 123
4.2.2 Cloud Foundry Basics ... 127
4.2.3 Organization of Applications, Services, and Users ... 129
4.2.4 The Controller ... 130
4.2.5 Deployment and Execution ... 131
4.2.6 Runtime Components and Services ... 133
4.2.7 Platform Services ... 135

4.3 SAP HANA XS Advanced Application Concepts ... 140

4.3.1 Multi-Target Application Concept ... 141
4.3.2 Architecture of a Multi-Target Application in SAP HANA XS Advanced ... 144
4.3.3 Development Workflow for Multi-Target Applications ... 146

4.4 Summary ... 147

PART II Developing an Application

5 Defining the Data Model 151

5.1 Data Model Overview ... 152

5.2 The Demo Application ... 154

5.3 Data Model Design in SAP HANA ... 159

5.3.1 Executing SQL Commands in SAP HANA ... 160
5.3.2 Commonly Used SQL Statements ... 163
5.3.3 Converting an Entity-Relationship Model to a Database Design ... 166
5.3.4 Data Model Using SAP HANA Repository Design-Time Objects ... 182

5.4 SAP HANA Deployment Infrastructure ... 189

5.4.1 HDI Containers ... 190
5.4.2 HDI Technical Users ... 191
5.4.3 HDI Deployer ... 192
5.4.4 Deployment into HDI Container ... 193

5.5 SAP HANA Database Module ... 196

5.5.1 Creating a Multi-Target Application Project ... 197
5.5.2 Creating an SAP HANA Database Module ... 199

5.5.3 Building the SAP HANA Database Module Artifacts 203
5.5.4 Building and Deploying a Multi-Target Application Archive 205

5.6 Core Data Services: The Physical Data Model 208
5.6.1 Editors 208
5.6.2 Entities 211
5.6.3 Data Types and User-Defined Structures 219
5.6.4 Associations 222
5.6.5 Views 224
5.6.6 Extensions 226

5.7 Loading Table Data 228
5.7.1 Using Table Data (.hdbtabledata) 229
5.7.2 Building the .hdbtabledata File 234
5.7.3 Using Table Data Properties (.properties) 235
5.7.4 Generate Time Data 236

5.8 Synonyms and Cross-Schema Access 237

5.9 Virtual Data Model 243
5.9.1 Create Calculation Views 245
5.9.2 Dimension Calculation Views 251
5.9.3 Default Calculation Views 263
5.9.4 Cube Calculation Views with Star Joins 264
5.9.5 Cube Calculation Views 272
5.9.6 Analytic Privileges 274

5.10 SQLScript for Stored Procedures 275
5.10.1 Stored Procedure 276
5.10.2 Table Functions and Scalar Functions 277

5.11 Table Creation without Core Data Services Documents 279

5.12 Other Database Artifacts 281
5.12.1 SAP HANA Database Sequence 281
5.12.2 SAP HANA Database View 282
5.12.3 SAP HANA Database Role 283
5.12.4 List of SAP HANA Deployment Infrastructure Artifacts 286

5.13 Summary 288

6 Developing the Application Layer 289

6.1 Tasks of the Application Layer 290

6.2 Node.js as Application Layer 292

6.2.1 Node.js Module 293

6.2.2 Modules and the Node Package Manager Repository 297

6.2.3 Asynchronous Programming Model 316

6.2.4 Managing Asynchronous Control Flow 320

6.2.5 Exposing Data 330

6.2.6 Accessing the SAP HANA Database 338

6.2.7 Unit Testing a Node.js Module 348

6.3 Java as Application Layer 358

6.3.1 Creating a Java Module to Read Database Content 360

6.3.2 Creating an OData Service to Modify Data 369

6.3.3 Connecting Java Services to an HTML5 Frontend 383

6.4 Summary 391

7 Developing a Presentation Layer 393

7.1 SAPUI5 Frontend Development 394

7.1.1 Application Bootstrapping 395

7.1.2 SAPUI5 Application Structuring 398

7.1.3 Model View Controller 401

7.1.4 Data Binding 404

7.1.5 Routing and Navigation 420

7.2 SAP HANA XS Advanced Application Routing 426

7.2.1 Application Routing Files 426

7.2.2 Application Routes and Destinations 429

7.2.3 SAPUI5 Central Service 431

7.3 Demo Application 436

7.3.1 Create the SAP Fiori Master-Detail Module 437

7.3.2 Demo Application Layout Adjustments 441

7.4 Summary 446

PART III Refining the Application

8 Securing Your Application 449

8.1 SAP HANA XS Advanced Security Concepts 450

8.2 Authorization in SAP HANA XS Advanced 455

8.2.1 Scopes and Attributes 455

8.2.2 Defining Application Security with the Application Security Descriptor 457

8.2.3 SAP HANA XS Advanced User Account and Authorization Service 463

8.2.4 Role Collections 464

8.2.5 Data Control Language 465

8.2.6 Controller Roles 466

8.3 Enable Security in your SAP HANA XS Advanced Application 467

8.3.1 Creating the SAP HANA XS Advanced User Account and Authorization Service 467

8.3.2 Enabling Security for Java Modules 470

8.3.3 Enabling Security for Node.js Modules 472

8.3.4 Enabling Security for SAPUI5 Modules 476

8.3.5 Secure Your Application against Web-Based Attacks 478

8.4 Maintaining Users and Roles in SAP HANA XS Advanced 482

8.4.1 Create Roles in SAP HANA XS Advanced 482

8.4.2 Create an Application User with the Administration Tools 487

8.4.3 Configuring Functional Authorization Checks 489

8.4.4 Configuring Instance-Based Authorization Checks 493

8.5 Assigning HDI Container Roles to Classic Database Users 495

8.5.1 Granting HDI Container Access via Schema Access 496

8.5.2 Granting HDI Container Access via Roles 498

8.6 Default Access Role for HDI Containers 500

8.7 Permissions for Container Objects 503

8.8 Summary 506

9 Troubleshooting Your Application 507

9.1 Debugging 507
- 9.1.1 Debugging Calculation Views 508
- 9.1.2 Debugging Stored Procedures 509
- 9.1.3 Debugging a Node.js Application 510
- 9.1.4 Debugging a Java Application 513
- 9.1.5 Debugging a SAPUI5 Application 515

9.2 Application Logs and Logging 519
- 9.2.1 Logging Data Changes 519
- 9.2.2 Logging Stored Procedure Actions 520
- 9.2.3 SAP HANA XS Advanced Transaction Logs 522
- 9.2.4 Logging in Node.js Applications 523
- 9.2.5 Logging in Java Applications 526

9.3 Database Traces 536
- 9.3.1 Configuring SQL Traces 537
- 9.3.2 Configuring Performance Trace 539

9.4 Performance Optimization 541
- 9.4.1 Execution of SQL Queries on Calculation Views 541
- 9.4.2 Analyze SQL in SAP Web IDE for SAP HANA 542
- 9.4.3 Explain Plan in SAP HANA Studio 547
- 9.4.4 Plan Visualizer in SAP HANA Studio 550

9.5 Summary 555

10 Deploying Your Application 557

10.1 Building the Multi-Target Application Archive 557

10.2 Deployment Process 560
- 10.2.1 Deployment via the SAP Web IDE for SAP HANA 560
- 10.2.2 SAP HANA XS Advanced Command-Line Interface 561

10.3 Transporting SAP HANA XS Advanced Applications 566
- 10.3.1 Manual Transport 566
- 10.3.2 Transport Using the Change and Transport System 567

10.3.3 Continuous Integration ... 568
10.3.4 Outlook: Native Transport ... 569
10.4 Summary ... 570

Appendices 571

A Migrating an SAP HANA XS Application to SAP HANA XS Advanced ... 573
B Additional Resources ... 593
C The Authors ... 595

Index ... 597

Preface

Since SAP HANA was released for the first time in late 2010 (originally presented as *SAP In-Memory Computing Engine*), a lot of things have happened in terms of developing SAP HANA applications.

From the beginning, there was the possibility to create database objects using SQL commands such as schemas, tables, procedures, and so on to create *information models* using the *SAP In-Memory Computing Studio*. While information views were already created in the database repository, other objects, such as schemas and tables, had to be created directly in the database catalog using SQL. Application logic and presentation layers needed to be developed in external systems.

This changed with the release of SAP HANA SPS 5 in late 2012 when *SAP HANA extended application services* was released. For the first time, it was possible to create an application, including data layer, application layer, and presentation layer, entirely on SAP HANA. On top of the tables and views, application logic was written in JavaScript using the *XS engine*, a lightweight application server residing on the SAP HANA database. In addition, the XS Engine was capable of exposing data via a web interface, laying the foundation for web-based frontends using SAPUI5, consuming the exposed data. As for most application objects, a repository object was available, and it was possible to create self-containing applications that allowed the SAP HANA database to evolve into a development platform.

About This Book

In late 2015, the topic of this book, *SAP HANA extended application services, advanced model* (SAP HANA XS Advanced), was released with SPS 11. Based on *Cloud Foundry principles*, the development of native SAP HANA applications became container oriented, where SAP HANA database content, application logic running on Node.js or Java, and web-based presentation layers using, for example, SAPUI5, are now developed and deployed as different modules in one single *multi-target application* (*MTA*).

With every change in the development model, there was also the question about how to transition the development and how to start with the new technologies available. While getting information in the early days of SAP HANA development boiled down to reading the documentation and trial and error (still a very valid approach), today it's more and more difficult to overlook the huge amount of information provided from documentation, videos, tutorials, and courses.

With this book, we want to give you a praxis-oriented work on how to start developing native SAP HANA applications by using the latest available technologies of the SAP HANA platform. This includes both how to use the SAP HANA XS Advanced development model in comparison to the *SAP HANA extended application services, classic model* (SAP HANA XS) development model and also more generic topics, such as how applications architecture changes when being developed for the SAP HANA platform.

Our Demo Scenario

Goethe wrote: "All theory, young friend, is gray. . .," and in keeping with his advice, we'll provide examples throughout the book as we show you how to develop an application.

First, we need a topic to create an application around. In the SAP ecosystem, the SFLIGHT Model is often used as a demo scenario to learn how to write ABAP code, and because this book is also about writing code, we'll use something similar: the Chicken-Wings Airline (see Figure 1)!

Figure 1 Chicken-Wings Airline

We're flying people around the globe with our huge fleet of chicken-piloted airplanes. On board, we serve egg sandwiches, omelets, fried earthworms, and muesli (no chicken wings for trade union reasons, sorry!).

The company hired us to do its first steps on the SAP HANA platform, and we're going to create some applications around the data model, which is built in Chapter 5. Our main entities are airports, planned flights, planes, passengers, and flight bookings.

We're sure you know how our airline business works: in the end, it boils down to getting passengers who booked a flight from one airport to the other with a plane. Even with chicken pilots, it's as easy as that.

One task is to show a list of flights offered by the airline. We'll use the physical data model and expose the flight connections using an OData service that we'll discuss in Chapter 6. The exposed flights will then be displayed by a simple SAPUI5 frontend we create in Chapter 7.

If you wonder where the security is, don't panic—it's everywhere! In Chapter 8, you'll see how to restrict access to data using analytic privileges and attributes in role templates.

Who Should Read This Book

This book has been written to give you practical guidance on how to develop native SAP HANA applications. If you're just starting your development on the SAP HANA platform, planning or blueprinting an application or development project, you'll find a lot of valuable information to get ready. We'll explain basic concepts and give concrete examples that make it easy for you to start.

If you're already familiar with the development of native SAP HANA applications using the SAP HANA Repository, we'll show you how to transition your skills to the SAP HANA XS Advanced development environment and SAP HANA 2.0. We refer to the "classic" way of development here and there, but we're focusing on how to get things to go smoothly using SAP HANA MTAs.

The SAP HANA platform comes with tons of great features and a thousand and one possibilities for native applications. We're sure you understand that we can't discuss all the features in minute detail, but be sure we cover the most important ones. So, if you're already an expert in using the SAP HANA XS Advanced Development Infrastructure (HDI), and you're interested in a deep dive into the single functionalities, you may want to take a look at Appendix B.

Structure of the Book

This book is divided into three major parts: Part I: Getting Started, Part II: Developing an Application, and Part III: Refining the Application.

Part I: Getting Started aims to give you an overview of the more theoretical parts of native SAP HANA development, as follows:

- **Chapter 1: Introduction to the SAP HANA Development Platform**
  First, we introduce you to the SAP HANA platform in general to tackle some basic questions about native SAP HANA development with SAP HANA 2.0 and SAP HANA XS Advanced. For example, we cover in which cases native SAP HANA applications are developed, what to keep in mind during the development, and which parts of the platform are involved.
- **Chapter 2: SAP HANA Development Environment**
  In this chapter, we look at the system landscape we'll use and how it compares to a classic three-tier model. We also explore the various deployment options for the SAP HANA platform, such as the SAP HANA, express edition, or the usage of the SAP Cloud Platform. In the end, we'll discuss the involvement of Git as the development code repository and how to set up the SAP HANA XS Advanced environment on the SAP HANA platform.
- **Chapter 3: SAP HANA Development Tools**
  In this chapter, we discuss the different development tools in use to create a native SAP HANA application, especially the SAP XS Advanced command-line interface (XSA CLI) tools, SAP Web IDE for SAP HANA, and the SAP HANA runtime tools.
- **Chapter 4: SAP HANA XS Advanced Architecture**
  The first part finishes up with an architectural overview of SAP HANA development with SAP HANA XS Advanced. We also discuss concepts such as the Multi-Target Application (MTA), microservices, and the three-tier architecture of a SAP HANA application. Finally, we introduce you to our demo case, which will accompany us throughout the book.

In Part II: Developing an Application, we get to the main part of the book about developing on the SAP HANA platform using the SAP HANA XS Advanced environment, as follows:

- **Chapter 5: Defining the Data Model**
  In this chapter, we take a closer look at how to define the data model of a native SAP HANA application and the differences compared to a traditional normalized data model. We explain the SAP HANA Deployment Infrastructure (HDI), its function to create runtime containers in the database, and how to create them using the SAP Web IDE. Subsequently, we develop the physical data model for our application and add a virtual data model using calculation views. Finally, discuss how to add logic to the data model using stored procedures with SQLScript and how to create unit tests for database objects.

- **Chapter 6: Developing the Application Layer**
  Now that the data model is defined, the focus turns to the application layer. In this chapter, we discuss the different possibilities of using Node.js, Java, or other programming languages on the SAP HANA platform, how to get access to the SAP HANA database, and how to expose data to the outside world.
- **Chapter 7: Developing a Presentation Layer**
  Part II is then rounded out by giving you an introduction into the development of a presentation layer using SAP UI5. You'll see how SAPUI5 works in general and how you can create a frontend that consumes the data exposed by the application layer.

After we have that working, Part III: Refining the Application, focuses on refinement by discussing important topics such as securing and troubleshooting a native SAP HANA application, as follows:

- **Chapter 8: Securing Your Application**
  In this chapter, we focus on the security concepts of the SAP HANA platform and especially those related to SAP HANA XS Advanced. We explain both application layer topics (e.g., the usage of application scopes, attributes, and role collections) and data layer concepts (e.g., analytic privileges, roles, and how to set up cross-container access).
- **Chapter 9: Troubleshooting Your Application**
  Of course, things never work like they should right from the beginning, so this chapter discusses how to debug through the entire application stack, how to add logging to the application, and how to start and use the platform's trace capabilities. We also look at performance optimization principles.
- **Chapter 10: Deploying Your Application**
  Once the development is complete, we discuss how to deploy an application and how to transport it though a system landscape using, for example, SAP HANA application lifecycle management.
- **Appendix A: Migrating an SAP HANA XS Application to SAP HANA XS Advanced**
  As some of you already have SAP HANA applications implemented, we also discuss how to migrate an application or a project from the SAP HANA XS to the SAP HANA XS Advanced development environment in this extra material in the appendix.
- **Appendix B: Additional Resources**
  Here you'll find further reading to help you learn more about SAP HANA XS Advanced and related technologies.

Acknowledgments

Thanks to everyone who finally contributed to this book and made it happen, especially to Johannes Scheerer, Nikolay Valchev, Georgi Vachkov, Klaus Kopecz, Thomas Jung, and the entire SAP HANA organization at SAP for their great support and super valuable inputs. Furthermore, thanks to Trond Strømme for incredible insights into GRA-PPA injected C-containers and for keeping the morale high with plenty of fun every day. Special thanks to my wife Federica, my son Noah, and the entire family for their support during my absence while writing. Thanks to Maximilian Lenkeit for his never-ending help and inspiration; Roberto Messa for outstanding ideas; Felix Diepenbrock for his tremendous support every day; Andreas Pohanka, Alexandra Kumok, and Eleonora Lipovezki for the great time coding in Berlin; and, finally, Hareem Shafi and Meagan White from SAP PRESS for their patience and help. Last but not least, to all you hackers and makers out there: Let's do cool and fun stuff to make this world a bit better every day!

—Jonas

Many thanks, first of all, to Jonas for having involved me in this awesome experience and for his never ending support. Thanks to my colleague Michele Pinton for his clever recommendations on how to structure the content. Thanks to Maximilian Lenkeit for helping me by reviewing my chapter and providing valuable advice. Finally, thanks a lot to my wife Merita and to my daughters Sofia and Martina for all their patience and support.

—Francesco

To my lovely wife Rashmi: You have been the inspiration and force behind every success in my life. This is for you. Thanks to my son Aayan for sacrificing his playtime while I was occupied with this book. Special thanks to my family members Saanta, Bapa, Bou, Dada, and Bhai for their support and blessing. Thanks to my co-authors and the SAP PRESS publishing team, consisting of Hareem Shafi and Meagan White, for their patience and perseverance. Finally, thanks to Arne Harren and Dhirendra Gehlot for their review, feedback, and support. To all the SAP HANA developers out there, I wish you happy learning and success in your project.

—Abani

This book is intended to give developers insights into how to apply the SAP HANA XS Advanced technology in various projects. At this point, it is time to thank Jonas, who initially came up with the idea to create a lively guide and reference book for developers. I am grateful to Thomas Jung and Johannes Scheerer for providing invaluable feedback and advice throughout this project. My further thanks to the SAP colleagues in the SAP Web IDE, SAP HANA application platform, and SAP HANA security product teams for providing guidance and recommendations when implementing SAP HANA XS Advanced. Thanks to my fellow authors for their support and motivation throughout this project. It was a pleasure to work on this project with this committed team. Last, but not least, I'd like to thank the SAP PRESS publishing team, especially Hareem Shafi and Meagan White for their patience and recommendations.

—Dominik

PART I

Getting Started

Chapter 1
Introduction to the SAP HANA Development Platform

With this first look, you'll learn what it means to develop applications with the SAP HANA platform.

Initially released in November 2010, today SAP HANA is a strategic platform to develop and run applications. At its core, SAP HANA is a data management platform and an innovative in-memory database management system that was designed to manage large data volumes efficiently by optimally leveraging the underlying hardware architecture. The SAP HANA platform offers the ability to increase application performance and to enable new applications that weren't possible before.

This chapter provides an introduction to the SAP HANA platform and what it means to develop native SAP HANA applications. We'll first offer an overview of the business case of developing applications with SAP HANA. Next, we'll discuss the components of the SAP HANA platform. Finally, we'll highlight things to consider when designing a native SAP HANA application.

1.1 Business Cases for SAP HANA Applications

Efficiently managing an ever-growing amount of data and an increasing variety of devices, connections, types of data, applications, services, delivery methods, and business needs are just some of the challenges that businesses and organizations face. End users are looking for apps that help them make decisions in real time based on up-to-date data, which might be residing in distributed information systems. The SAP HANA platform implements a novel approach for managing large data volumes. It's designed to process large data volumes in a very performant way by optimally leveraging the available hardware architecture. SAP HANA is a data management and application platform for all types of applications. In this section, we'll highlight the strength of the SAP HANA platform and the business cases to leverage this technology.

SAP HANA is a multiprocessor platform based on a columnar, in-memory, and ACID-compliant (atomicity, consistency, isolation, durability) database that supports mission-critical applications by providing atomicity, consistency, isolation, and durability capabilities:

- **Atomicity**
  This functionality refers to a system that can process a set of transactions entirely or not at all.
- **Consistency**
  This feature takes care that the data is consistent after processing a sequence of different options on the data.
- **Isolation**
  This functionality handles operations on data that are executed in parallel but aren't impacting each other.
- **Durability**
  This capability takes care that the data is persisted after a transaction in a database system. That data that gets persisted also must be guaranteed in case of a system failure.

The SAP HANA in-memory database stores all data that must be retrieved quickly into the main memory, avoiding the expensive operations of swapping and data movements from the disk. The data is mainly saved into columnar tables, which are also referred to as column stores. Columnar tables are optimally suited for analytical applications because they are ideal for parallel processing and provide automatic data compression in SAP HANA.

The default data compression mechanism in the SAP HANA database occurs in column stores because the repeated values in the same column are stored only once and are represented by integer values, and the parallel processing is expedited because each column can be processed by a different processor. Additionally, the SAP HANA database offers advanced compression mechanisms that allow further compression of the data in columns using different compression functions. Advanced algorithms in SAP HANA can automatically determine the optimal compression methods for columns.

SAP HANA fully leverages the advantages of the technological advancements, which make vast amounts of main memory available at low prices, such as high-speed multicore processors, 64-bit operating systems, and robust cache memories to avoid unnecessary accesses to the memory. Different data storage options exist within the

SAP HANA database to save the data in case of system failure and to store nonhot data.

Hot, Warm, and Cold Data

In SAP HANA, the data can be grouped conceptually into hot data (must be frequently obtained), warm data (doesn't have to be accessed so frequently), and cold data (located very rarely and often stored just for legal reasons). The hot data is maintained on main memory in SAP HANA, the warm data is saved on disk, and the cold data can be stored outside of the SAP HANA platform in near-line storage solutions or archived.

With the SAP HANA database, it's often no longer required to preaggregate data for analytical applications as the in-memory storage and available processing power enables end users to directly aggregate data on the fly. This innovation allows a simplification of the data model of applications and enables end users to analyze the data without needing to store the data first. This innovative processing capability ensures that SAP HANA can support both online transaction processing (OLTP) and online analytical processing (OLAP) applications.

The SAP HANA platform can be deployed to both on-premise or in cloud environments. With the SAP HANA on-premise deployment option, a customer takes the responsibility for providing and managing the entire solution but has complete control over the system. In the SAP HANA cloud-based deployment, SAP or a hosting partner manages the SAP HANA system.

In addition to the traditional data types, the SAP HANA system is also capable of managing new data, such as spatial data and unstructured text. Furthermore, the SAP HANA system provides built-in extract, transform, and load (ETL) capabilities, which enables the procurement of data from a variety of data sources, such as remote sources (e.g., other databases), big data stores (e.g., Hadoop), remote Internet of Things (IoT) devices, and data streaming from sensors. Further functionalities of SAP HANA include but aren't limited to text search, text mining, analysis of spatial data, management of networked information, predictive analytics, and analysis of time series data.

The SAP HANA platform allows developers to build full applications by providing application server capabilities. This application server can be leveraged to implement business logic, which offers optimal performance because it's fully optimized for applications that integrate with the SAP HANA database. With the initial releases of

SAP HANA, this application server was called SAP HANA extended application services. Since the SAP HANA 1.0 SP11 release, a new application server architecture is available for the SAP HANA platform called SAP HANA extended application services, advanced model (SAP HANA XS Advanced). SAP HANA XS Advanced allows the development of applications based on the microservices architecture using different programming languages and runtime environments. In this book, we'll focus on the development of applications with the new SAP HANA XS Advanced concept of SAP HANA.

Note

SAP HANA extended application services, advanced model, is often also referred to as SAP HANA XSA or just XSA. In this book, we'll refer to it as SAP HANA XS Advanced. Similarly, SAP HANA extended application services, classic model, is often referred to as SAP HANA XS Classic or XS Classic. We'll refer to it as SAP HANA XS throughout this book.

Figure 1.1 highlights some innovations of the SAP HANA platform.

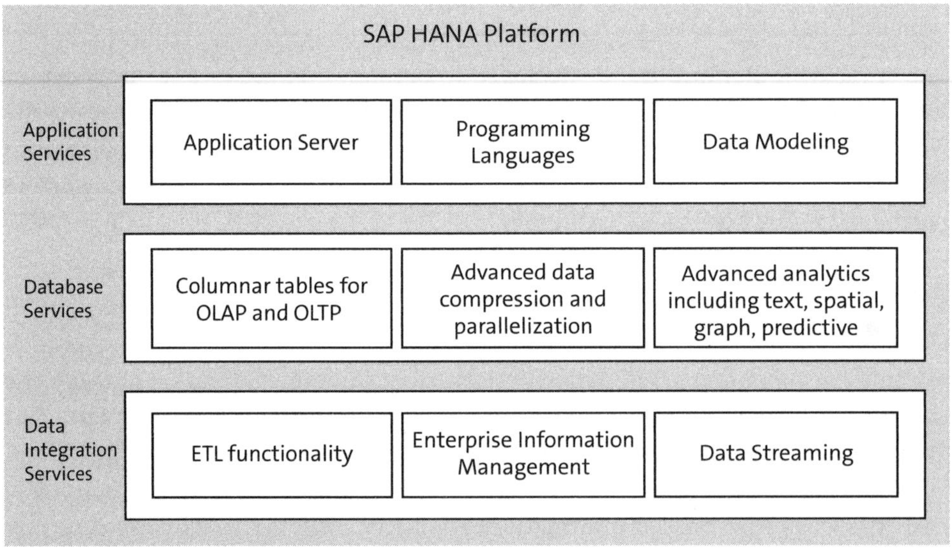

Figure 1.1 Innovations of the SAP HANA Platform

The consolidation of analytical and transactional data in one combined platform not only simplifies the architecture of applications and enables real-time analysis and reporting scenarios in business intelligence (BI) applications, but it also allows the development of new types of applications. With SAP HANA, you can create applications that can both process large data volumes and drill down to the most granular level of the data. Thus, real-time planning or what-if and predictive analysis applications are significant use cases to implement with SAP HANA. In addition, sensor data can be analyzed, which can be especially useful in an IoT application where analyzing the large data volumes generated by sensors is crucial.

Today, SAP HANA is the foundation for many SAP applications and is used to improve the performance of, for example, SAP Business Warehouse (SAP BW), SAP Business Suite, and SAP S/4HANA. SAP S/4HANA is a completely optimized business suite that takes advantage of the capabilities of the SAP HANA platform. SAP HANA as a foundation for SAP applications enables those applications to take advantage of new features such as text analysis, predictive analysis, and big data management, just to name a few examples. The SAP HANA platform facilitates the creation of new applications with both optimal performance and new innovative features that weren't possible before.

1.2 SAP HANA Components and Architecture

The SAP HANA platform is a hybrid database management system that combines several paradigms in one environment. It includes a full relational database management system where individual tables can be stored in memory via columns or rows. The SAP HANA database is built for high-performance applications. All relevant data is kept in main memory. Furthermore, the SAP HANA database provides several programming and modeling options for executing application logic close to the data. This section gives an overview of the functional components of the SAP HANA platform, as well as the primary technical services and architecture of the SAP HANA platform.

1.2.1 Functional Components

The main functional components of the SAP HANA platform can be divided into the following groups:

- Interfaces
- Application services
- Database services
- Data integration services

Figure 1.2 gives an overview of the components of the SAP HANA platform. The components will be discussed in more detail in this section.

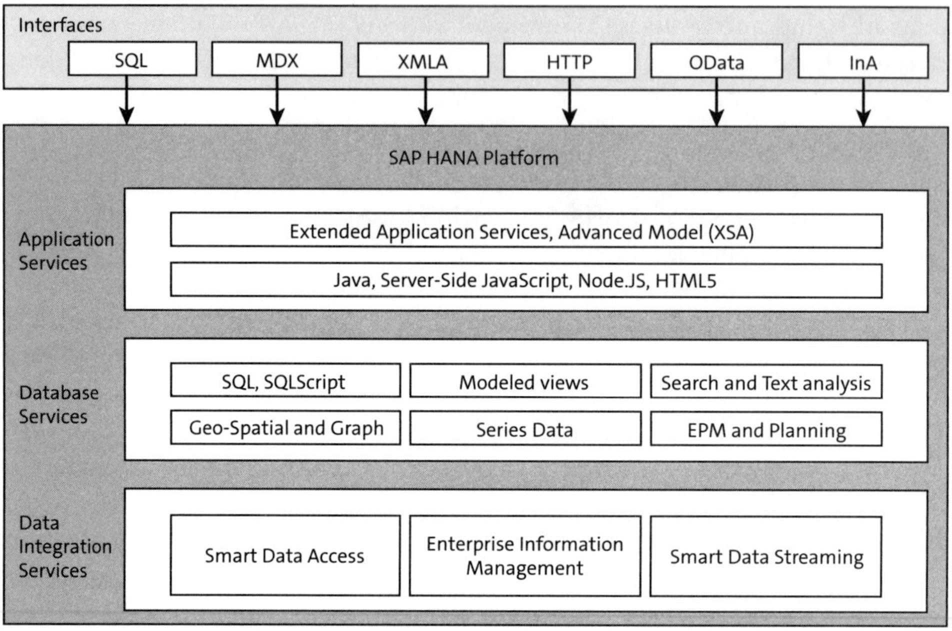

Figure 1.2 Components of the SAP HANA Platform

Interfaces

The SAP HANA platform supports standard interfaces that different types of devices, such as web, mobile, or desktop applications, support to communicate with the SAP HANA platform. The standard interfaces that SAP HANA supports include the following:

- **Structured Query Language (SQL)**
  SQL is a language designed primarily for accessing relational database systems and is the most significant database language in existence. SAP HANA offers several SQL extensions on top of this standard; for example, SAP HANA supports some extended SQL views such as calculation views, which expose results calculated by a procedure or based on a data flow.
- **Multidimensional expressions (MDX)**
  MDX is a de facto standard for querying of multidimensional (OLAP) databases. MDX syntactically resembles SQL, but it incorporates concepts such as cubes, dimensions, hierarchies, and measures. MDX includes a broad set of functions for

statistical analysis, but unlike SQL, MDX has limited Data Definition Language (DDL) or Data Manipulation Language (DML) capabilities. SAP HANA developers create modeled views to expose data via MDX.

- **Hypertext Transfer Protocol (HTTP)**
  HTTP is an application protocol for distributed applications and is the foundation of data communication for web-based applications. The SAP HANA platform includes the SAP HANA XS and SAP HANA XS Advanced server components. SAP HANA XS is a web application server with a server-side JavaScript engine embedded in the database. SAP HANA XS Advanced is a platform for polyglot web applications based on microservices in the cloud and on premise. SAP HANA XS and SAP HANA XS Advanced offer the ability to interact with client applications via HTTP. Developers can use SAP HANA XS and SAP HANA XS Advanced to provide service application programming interfaces (APIs), data, and resources to HTTP clients without the need for an additional application server.
- **XML for Analysis (XMLA)**
  XMLA is an HTTP-based protocol that can be used by clients on any platform to execute MDX statements on the SAP HANA system and retrieve data.
- **Open Data Protocol (OData)**
  OData is a web protocol for querying and updating data. It was published under the Microsoft Open Specification Promise and has been standardized as an industry standard. OData defines operations on resources using HTTP verbs (`GET`, `PUT`, `POST`, and `DELETE`), and it specifies the URI syntax for identifying the resources. Data is transferred over HTTP using the Atom or JavaScript Object Notation (JSON) format. The result set of OData requests can be influenced by specifying query parameters.
- **Information Access (InA)**
  InA is an SAP protocol based on HTTP. The InA protocol is similar to the XMLA interface. It exposes MDX functionalities through a different protocol that is mainly used by SAP applications such as SAP Analytics Cloud or SAP Lumira.

InA interface and SAP HANA XS Advanced

The functionality of the InA interface is available on the SAP HANA XS Advanced platform with the SAP Enterprise Performance Management Multidimensional Services (EPM-MDS) plug-in, which can be installed as of SAP HANA 2.0 SP 01. This plug-in is required by SAP analytical tools such as SAP Analytics Cloud and SAP Lumira to get access to SAP HANA calculation views in SAP HANA XS Advanced. SAP Note 2456225 provides details on where this plug-in can be found and how to install it.

Application Services

The SAP HANA platform offers integrated application server components to build native applications. SAP HANA XS is a layer on top of the SAP HANA database. It provides the platform for running SAP HANA-based web applications. Since SAP HANA SPS 11, a new generation of an SAP HANA XS component is available, as mentioned earlier, called SAP HANA XS Advanced. SAP HANA XS Advanced can run on a separate set of hosts from an SAP HANA system and communicates with the SAP HANA database via SQL. SAP HANA XS Advanced can be installed on dedicated hosts or together with the SAP HANA server on the same host. It's an application platform that supports several programming languages and execution environments, such as Java and server-side JavaScript.

SAP HANA XS Advanced is bundled with SAP HANA so that it's possible to develop and run SAP HANA-based web applications without the need for an additional application server. Furthermore, the SAP HANA XS Advanced runtime embraces a microservices-based architecture and is optimized for the creation of 12-factor applications. This type of design allows the communication across applications via services based on HTTP and facilitates splitting business applications into reusable services. The primary drivers behind the introduction of a microservices-based architecture for SAP HANA XS Advanced include high scalability, being easy to enhance, and the possibility to leverage flexible runtime environments. The advantages and characteristics of a microservices-based design are explained in more detail in Chapter 4, Section 4.1, whereas the 12-factor application principles will be summarized in Chapter 4, Section 4.2.1.

Database Services

The SAP HANA database services support functions for data-intensive processing. The supported functions can be grouped into the following categories:

- **SQL and SQLScript**
  The leading programming language for database applications is SQL. SQL provides functional capabilities for creating, accessing, maintaining, and controlling relational data. SAP HANA extends SQL and offers the possibility to write procedures in the SQLScript programming language. SAP HANA provides SQLScript as the default programming language for writing data flow logic in the form of embedded procedures. SQLScript supports SQL data types and extends this standard with the possibility to define table types. SQLScript also has table variables that can contain internal tables, which can be seen as temporary tables. The results of an SQL

statement or procedure call can be stored in table variables, which can then be used, for example, as the data source in an SQL query. An SQLScript procedure may contain SQL statements, call other procedures, and use if/else statements or loops for control flow. Cursors can be used to iterate through result sets. SQLScript also supports the dynamic execution of SQL statements that are constructed at runtime.

- **Modeled views**
  SAP HANA supports extended SQL views that are generated from design-time objects known as modeled views. Modeled views are design-time definitions, created by application developers with specific modeling tools. An example of a modeled view is a calculation view. The data foundation of a calculation view can include any combination of various sources, such as tables, views of different types, table functions, and virtual tables for accessing remote data. Data can be combined with operations such as joins, unions, projections, aggregations, and star joins between fact tables and dimensional data. Furthermore, complex data models can be created from layers of calculation views. In multidimensional reporting, a calculation view can represent a cube or a dimension, which is used as input for other calculation views. The logic of a calculation view is programmed by applying a visual view editor to create the data flow graph for the view. The advantages of calculation views include but aren't limited to the following:
  - Support for structured and modular abstractions
  - Modeling tools to design complex data flows
  - Additional semantics, such as description texts for attributes, hierarchies, variables, and parameters
  - Modeled views that generate other metadata at deploy-time, which enable access to the views of MDX clients and for generic BI tools
  - Values of columns in the resulting database objects calculated using formulas
- **Search and text analysis**
  SAP HANA offers powerful capabilities for full-text search and text analysis. The text analysis features include the following:
  - Freestyle search: The user doesn't need to know the exact fields to be searched.
  - Linguistic search, fuzzy search, synonyms: Results are found even if there are typing errors, if different linguistic forms of a word are used ("produce" instead of "production"), and if synonyms are used ("purchasing" instead of "buying").
  - Named entity extraction: Texts can be analyzed by extracting entities such as persons, organizations, locations, and products.

  - Ranking of results: You can rank results by a number of criteria so that more relevant results are displayed first.

- **Geo-spatial and graph**
  With the geo-spatial features, it's possible to store geometries in the database and execute spatial functions on them. Spatial functions can also be used in database searches and joins. Thus, SAP HANA supports use cases such as determining the relationship of two geometries; that is, is a geometry contained in another one, or is a geometry within a given distance to another one. This functionality can be used, for example, to find all points of interest along a specific location.

  Furthermore, SAP HANA supports graph database features. Graph structures can be used for semantic queries with nodes, edges, and properties to represent and store data. Efficient processing of graph data is required by various business applications, such as supply chain management, transportation, social media analysis, targeted advertising, and customer sentiment analysis.

- **Time series data**
  A data series is a sequence of data points in successive order. Successive points can be spaced at uniform or nonuniform intervals. For example, hourly temperature measurements were taken at a specific location, the energy consumption was measured by a smart meter, or the oil pressure of an engine recorded. Series data is found in many application domains and different forms. Series data applies to any data set where each element is identified by an attribute that includes both distance and ordering concepts. The most common type of series data has a time stamp associated with each value. These data series are called time series. With recurring measurements, series data can accumulate quickly, so efficient storage is essential. SAP HANA provides improved compression of time stamps by providing additional metadata and built-in functions to support the fast aggregation of data and the generation of time stamp sequences. Furthermore, SAP HANA offers a library of SQL functions to perform necessary processing and analysis of series data.

- **SAP Enterprise Performance Management and planning**
  The SAP Enterprise Performance Management and planning technical platform is used for developing enterprise performance management applications on SAP HANA. It can be used to build applications for planning and simulation of various business aspects, for example, cost, revenue, investment, or sales. This set of functionalities is designed to support the development of SAP HANA-based planning and simulation applications in general. Planning operations can be executed in the database layer for optimal performance.

Integration Services

SAP HANA provides several mechanisms for data provisioning and integration with other data sources:

- **SAP HANA smart data access (SDA)**
  SDA provides data federation capabilities for querying remote data sources from SAP HANA in real time, without creating redundant data copies. SDA allows external data sources to be accessed directly from SAP HANA by defining virtual tables in SAP HANA, which are placeholders pointing to remote data systems. These virtual tables can be used in SQL queries. SAP HANA optimizes these federated queries and sends the relevant parts to the remote system for execution. The results are returned and can be further processed in SAP HANA. SDA supports a variety of source systems, including, SAP HANA, SAP Adaptive Server Enterprise, SAP IQ, SAP Event Stream Processor, SAP SQL Anywhere, SAP MaxDB, SAP Manufacturing Integration and Intelligence (MII), Teradata Database, Oracle, IBM Db2, Microsoft SQL Server, and Hadoop.
- **Enterprise information management (EIM)**
  EIM in SAP HANA includes SAP HANA smart data integration (SDI) and SAP HANA smart data quality (SDQ) features. With these extensions, it's possible to perform data provisioning, replication, transformation, and quality operations in SAP HANA directly, without the need for additional software systems. These functions are available in real time and batch mode. Typical use cases include the following:
  - An external source system provides data to be added into existing SAP HANA tables where the data must be transformed to match the target table structure. Transformations can include address validation, correction and standardization against the official post office data of various countries, converting longitude/latitude geo-coordinates into an address or vice versa, and matching records using multiple rules to identify duplicates.
  - SAP and non-SAP data are integrated into the SAP Cloud Platform for cloud-based applications.
- **SAP HANA streaming analytics**
  SAP HANA streaming analytics integrates consumption data streams and complex event processing from the SAP Event Stream Processor software solution into SAP HANA. SAP HANA streaming analytics adds a high-speed streaming analytics engine to the SAP HANA platform. With this functionality, it's possible to process high-velocity and high-volume streams of messages or events in real time in SAP HANA. Streaming analytics can be applied in real time, as fast as the data arrives,

to turn raw incoming data into useful information. Typical use cases include real-time situation detection. SAP HANA streaming analytics functionalities can instantly detect and respond to situations that warrant immediate attention. One of the primary drivers of this technology is the IoT, where smart devices equipped with sensors are continuously sending vast amounts of information.

1.2.2 Technical Services and Architecture

The SAP HANA system consists of multiple servers that build the SAP HANA platform and enable the functionalities highlighted in the previous section. The following main servers are highlighted in this section:

- **Index server**
  The most important component is the index server, which contains the in-memory data stores and the engines for processing data within SAP HANA. The index server processes incoming SQL or MDX statements in the context of authenticated sessions and transactions.
- **Name server**
  The name server holds the information about the setup and components of an SAP HANA system.
- **XS runtime**
  The XS runtime is the application server infrastructure for native SAP HANA-based web applications. The XS runtime is a default component of the SAP HANA platform and enables a developer to build native applications. The XS runtime is also used to run the web-based tools that come with SAP HANA, for instance, for administration, lifecycle management, and development. As mentioned in the previous section, the SAP HANA XS Advanced architecture was introduced in SAP HANA SPS 11. The SAP HANA XS Advanced runtime consists of several processes for platform services and for executing applications. It runs either on dedicated hosts or together with other SAP HANA components on the same host. The technical architecture is discussed in more detail in Chapter 4, Section 4.2.
- **Extended store server**
  The extended store server provides a high-performance, disk-based column store for huge data volumes up to the petabyte range. Less frequently accessed data, which doesn't need to be kept in main memory, can be put into the extended store. With dynamic tiering, SAP HANA can host vast databases with reduced cost of ownership.

- **Data provisioning server**
  The data provisioning server is part of EIM in SAP HANA. It provides capabilities such as replicating data, transforming data, and performing data quality tasks. It's also possible to create new adapters for different types of data sources with a Software Development Kit (SDK).
- **Streaming cluster**
  The streaming cluster is part of the SAP HANA streaming analytics functionality, which extends SAP HANA with capabilities for consuming data streams and complex event processing.
- **SAP HANA Deployment Infrastructure (HDI) server**
  The HDI server is a separate server process. This service layer of the SAP HANA database simplifies the deployment of SAP HANA database artifacts into containers. The HDI only supports deployment functionalities of database objects; it doesn't include any version-control features nor provide any tools for lifecycle management. HDI was introduced as part of the SAP HANA XS Advanced architecture and will be discussed in more detail in Chapter 4, Section 4.3.
- **Administration tools**
  Web-based administration tools for SAP HANA are available in the SAP HANA cockpit. The cockpit application integrates various tools for administration, monitoring, and software lifecycle management.
- **Development tools**
  SAP Web IDE for SAP HANA is the browser-based development environment for SAP HANA-based applications. It can be used to develop all layers of an application, including user interfaces (UIs), SAP HANA XS Advanced server applications, and SAP HANA database content. It covers various aspects of development, such as editing, modeling, versioning, builds, deployment, and debugging. It's based on SAP HANA XS Advanced and uses an external Git repository for source code management. The SAP HANA Web-Based Development Workbench can be used to develop SAP HANA-based applications for SAP HANA XS. It's still available, but its functions are being migrated to the SAP Web IDE on SAP HANA.
- **Runtime tools**
  The web-based SAP HANA runtime tools contain functions that are needed by both developers and administrators. Examples are the SAP HANA database catalog browser and the SQL Console. Developers typically work with SAP Web IDE for SAP HANA and the SAP HANA database explorer application. We'll introduce the different runtime tools in Chapter 3.

The servers described in this chapter and technical architecture are summarized in Figure 1.3.

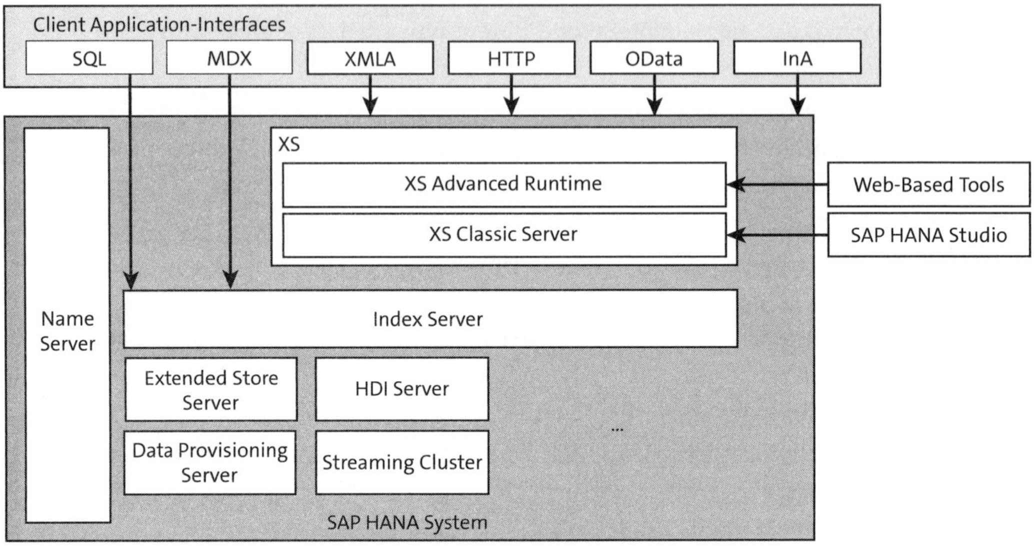

Figure 1.3 Technical Services of the SAP HANA Platform

With all these capabilities, SAP HANA allows all kinds of data to be combined and analyzed within the same database management system. This feature enables developers to create new types of applications, and it reduces complexity and cost, as no separate systems are required for analytical processing, searching, spatial data operations, or graph data processing. With high performance for both read and write operations, the SAP HANA database supports transactional as well as analytical use cases. The SAP HANA XS Advanced service provides the application server components for all native SAP HANA applications and embraces a microservice-based architecture. The characteristics of a microservice-based design are discussed in Chapter 4, Section 4.1.

1.3 Application Design Considerations

SAP HANA extends the traditional database server role, and it functions as a comprehensive platform for the development and execution of business applications. Native SAP HANA applications are executed directly on the SAP HANA platform without relying on an additional runtime component. Thus, applications that require processing of large data volumes are ideal candidates for native SAP HANA applications. In this section, we highlight considerations when designing native SAP HANA applications.

The SAP HANA platform provides several programming and modeling options to execute application logic close to the data and allows developers to create application-specific procedures and models that are run on the SAP HANA platform with fast access to the in-memory data. This functionality is required to make full use of the parallelization and optimization capabilities of SAP HANA. Application development on the SAP HANA platform follows a layered approach.

The layers of a native SAP HANA application include a database, application, and UI layer. The rendering of the UI layer is performed entirely on the client side. The client side can be, for example, a web browser-based application or a mobile application. The UI of native SAP HANA applications is typically created with the SAPUI5 JavaScript library. The server-side procedural logic is implemented with, for example, the Java or Node.js programming environment. Developers can use the server-side control flow logic to provide service APIs, data, and resources to clients, without the need for an additional application server. The server-side control flow logic can access the SAP HANA database directly, which allows developers to take advantage of optimal integration with the SAP HANA database.

This model not only simplifies the architecture of applications but also greatly benefits their performance. The database layer of native SAP HANA applications implements the data model of an application. Furthermore, this layer exposes the data model via database views. The SAP HANA database supports the SQL for creating, accessing, maintaining, controlling, and protecting relational data. SAP HANA extends SQL with specific SQL statements, views, data types, and the possibility to write procedures in the SQLScript language.

In a traditional non-SAP HANA programming model, developers typically process large data volumes outside of the database in the application layer. This application layer implements the control flow and calculation logic of an application and is an external server that isn't integrated with the database layer. This setup results in the nonoptimal movement of data between a database server and the application server where the actual processing of the data takes place in the application server. The flow of large data volumes between a database server and an application server is a bottleneck that often causes performance problems.

In the programming model with SAP HANA, data-intensive logic is processed directly in the database layer, without having to copy large data volumes between the database layer and the application layer. Calculation logic of an application is entirely processed on the database layer, whereas the application layer only processes control flow logic. This concept is also referred to as code push-down and can dramatically improve the performance of applications.

In this book, we'll demonstrate methods to optimally leverage the benefits of SAP HANA by implementing an application that follows the SAP HANA programming model. Figure 1.4 highlights the traditional non-SAP HANA programming model compared to the SAP HANA programming model.

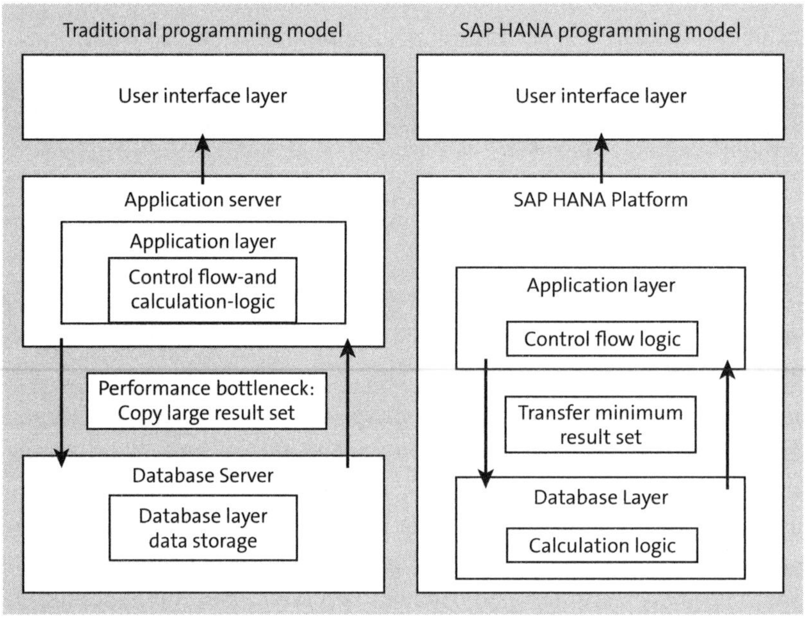

Figure 1.4 Traditional Programming Model Compared to the SAP HANA Programming Model

1.4 Summary

In this chapter, we gave an overview of the SAP HANA in-memory platform and highlighted some of the key functionalities that make this platform unique. SAP HANA allows the efficient management of large data volumes by optimally leveraging the underlying hardware architecture. We discussed the capabilities, such as application services and database services, that help developers when creating business applications. We covered design considerations for developers when building applications on the SAP HANA platform and revealed the components of the SAP HANA platform and its architecture.

In the next chapter, we'll discuss the SAP HANA development environment and will introduce the SAP HANA system landscape to develop SAP HANA XS Advanced applications.

Chapter 2
SAP HANA Development Environment

In this chapter, you'll learn about setting up the SAP HANA development environment in the cloud and/or on premise.

In the previous chapter, you learned the architecture and components of the SAP HANA platform. In this chapter, we'll discuss the installation and configuration of the SAP HANA system as a development environment on premise and in the cloud.

We'll explain how the SAP HANA extended application services, advanced model (SAP HANA XS Advanced) system landscape differs from the traditional SAP landscape and the option of using SAP HANA, express edition as a development system on premise and in the public cloud. We'll also discuss the options to use SAP HANA XS Advanced in the SAP Cloud Platform. Finally, we'll introduce Git as the code repository and outline the steps that organize the development environment into organizations and spaces.

2.1 System Landscape

Traditionally, SAP HANA systems are deployed with a three-tier system landscape made up of the *development* (DEV) tier, *quality* (QAS) tier, and *production* (PRD) tier. Some customers also deploy an extra *preproduction* or *user acceptance* (UAT) tier between the quality and production system. Changes/enhancements or new releases of the application follow the standard DEV-QAS-PRD or DEV-QAS-UAT-PRD transport path, depending on the deployed system landscape, as illustrated in Figure 2.1 ❶. The environments are as follows:

- **Development (DEV)**
  Environment for development of new applications/releases and bug fixes and/or enhancements to the current release of application.
- **Quality (QAS)**
  Environment for end-to-end functional testing and integration testing of applications.

- **Pre-production or user acceptance (UAT)**
  The exact replica of the production system used for pre-production and user acceptance testing. If the customer doesn't have a separate UAT system, pre-production and user acceptance testing is supported in the QAS system.
- **Production (PRD)**
  Productive system used by the customer to execute day-to-day business.

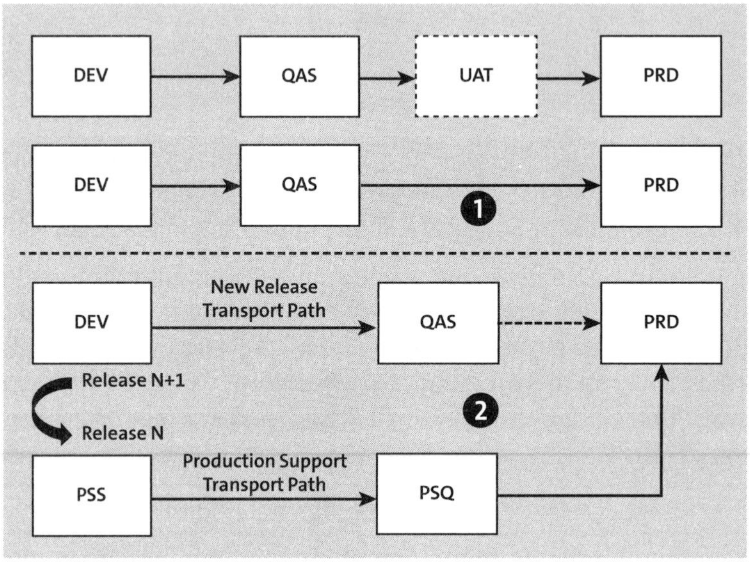

Figure 2.1 SAP N and N+1 System Landscape

Some customers may also adopt a five-tier system landscape, which is also referred to as *N and N+1 system landscape*, where N indicates the current release in production, and N+1 is the new release under development (see Figure 2.1 ❷). The five-tier system landscape offers two separate transport paths, a production support path (PSS-PSQ-PRD), and a new release path (DEV-QAS-PRD). The main advantage of the N+1 landscape is that it enables the development of enhancements/new releases on one landscape while leaving the maintenance landscape free to tackle maintenance work to support day-to-day business.

The built-in SAP HANA Repository is used to keep track of new objects and object changes in the DEV or production support (PSS) systems. These change objects are used in transports to deploy applications to quality and production systems in the landscape. This has served well for application development using traditional waterfall or agile methodology in any type (three-, four-, or five-tier) landscape.

The DevOps methodology has been widely adapted in software development over the past few years to decrease long delivery cycles and to bring development (Dev) and operations (Ops) team closer. DevOps is the union of traditional development and operations as one team with common goals and objectives to facilitate *continuous integration, continuous delivery*, and *continuous deployment* with an emphasis on continuous process improvement, as follows:

- **Continuous integration**
  Continuous integration is a development practice that requires developers to integrate code into a shared repository several times a day. Each code check-in or commit is then verified by an automated build to detect problems early.
- **Continuous delivery**
  Continuous delivery is the practice that requires deployment of codes to production rapidly and safely by delivering every change to a production-like environment and ensuring business applications function as expected through automated regression testing.
- **Continuous deployment**
  Continuous deployment is the practice of automatically deploying every change (that has passed the automated regression tests) to production.

Continuous delivery and continuous deployment are illustrated in Figure 2.2.

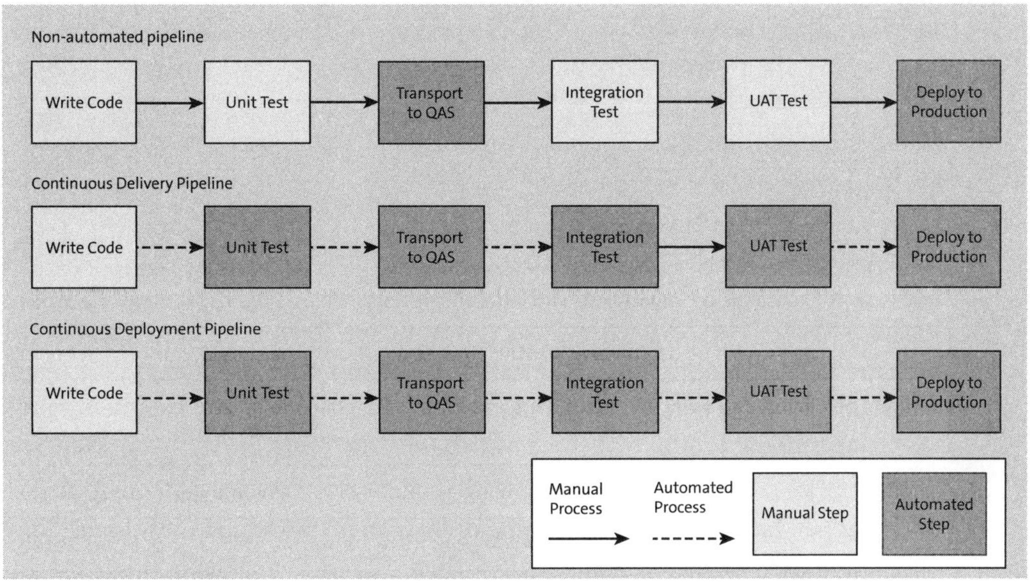

Figure 2.2 DevOps: Continuous Delivery and Continuous Deployment

To support DevOps methodology for software development, SAP HANA XS Advanced supports external source code management tools, such as Git or Gerrit, to be used as a central repository (discussed in Section 2.6) while streamlining the build and deployment process using multi-target application (MTA) archives (*.mtar*) and all-or-nothing deployment.

With SAP HANA XS Advanced, the system landscape can be a simple two-tier landscape (DEV-PRD) with the QA layer provisioned in the DEV landscape or a standard three-tier landscape (DEV-QA-PRD), as illustrated in Figure 2.3. It's also possible to provision additional systems (QA, SIT [system integration testing], UAT, etc.) on demand to support further testing for specific applications, creating a complex system landscape (DEV-QA-SIT-UAT-PRD).

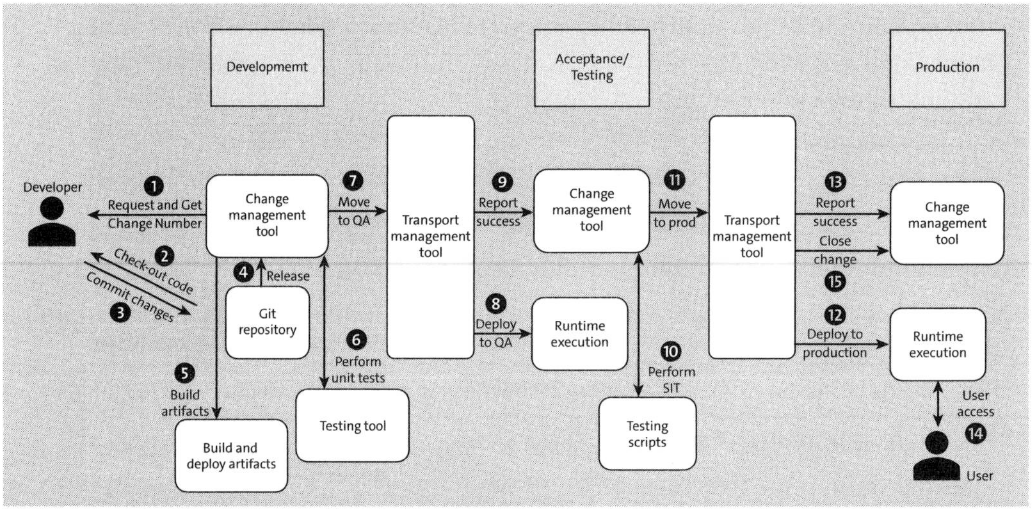

Figure 2.3 Application-Specific Landscape

Because the source code is centrally stored and managed in an external dedicated repository such as Git or Gerrit, the DEV environment can be provisioned on premise or in the cloud. In addition, it can be a shared system within the organization or can be specific to a team or developer. The application can be built based on the committed changes to the central repository, which then can be deployed to any system in the landscape.

Now that you have a fair understanding of the system landscape, let's discuss your options for provisioning a development system.

2.2 SAP HANA, Express Edition

SAP HANA, express edition was officially introduced during SAP TechEd in Las Vegas in September 2016. It's a streamlined version of SAP HANA, optimized to run in computers with minimal hardware configurations, such as personal laptops and desktop systems. It can also be installed and provisioned in public cloud platforms, such as Amazon Web Services (AWS), Microsoft Azure, Google Cloud Platform, and Docker Store.

SAP HANA, express edition comes as a binary installation package for Linux Intel systems and/or as a virtual machine (VM) for any operating systems capable of running a hypervisor, and it can be downloaded free of cost from the SAP website. Developers, startups, and companies can use SAP HANA, express edition to develop, deploy, and run applications in production free of cost up to 32 GB, which can be scaled up to 128 GB for an additional fee.

To efficiently run in a smaller hardware configuration and to support application development in PCs, the following features of the SAP HANA platform have been excluded from SAP HANA, express edition:

- Data warehousing foundation
- Disaster recovery
- Dynamic tiering
- High availability
- Multihosting
- Outward scaling for multiple hosts
- Remote data synchronization
- SAP Solution Manager
- SAP HANA smart data integration (SDI)
- SAP HANA smart data quality (SDQ)
- SAP HANA streaming analytics
- System replication

SAP HANA, express edition can be installed on premise or in the cloud, and the installation and configuration steps are discussed in the following sections.

2.2.1 On-Premise Installation Options

As stated earlier, SAP HANA, express edition is available as a binary installation for Linux and as a VM image for any other operating systems capable of running a hypervisor, as follows:

- **Binary installation for Linux**
  Binary installation packages are available for both SUSE Linux Enterprise Server 11.x or 12 and Red Hat Enterprise Linux 6.x.
- **VM image**
  This VM package offers the simplest setup and is platform-independent so it can be used in Linux, Microsoft Windows, Mac OS, or any other operating system capable of running a hypervisor and with at least 16 GB of RAM. The following hypervisor are supported:
  - VMware Player 7.1
  - VMware Workstation Pro 12.1
  - VMWare Fusion 8.x
  - VMWare Fusion Pro 8.x
  - Oracle VM Virtual Box 5.0.14 or higher

Both the binary installation and VM image options come in two flavors: *server-only package* and *full version package*. The latter includes additional software components, such as SAP HANA cockpit, SAP HANA XS Advanced services, and SAP Web IDE for SAP HANA. We recommend installing the full version package or use the full version VM image to work with the examples discussed in this book. The binary installer and/or the VM image can be downloaded from the SAP HANA, express edition website at *www.sap.com/sap-hana-express*.

2.2.2 Installing SAP HANA, Express Edition VM Images

In this section, we'll discuss the steps to install SAP HANA, express edition 2.0 SPS 3.0 using the VM images. It will install the following:

- A VM running SUSE Linux Enterprise Server (SLES) for SAP Applications 12 SP 2
- An SAP HANA, express edition 2.0 SPS 2.0 instance on the VM with SAP HANA cockpit, SAP HANA XS Advanced services, and SAP Web IDE for SAP HANA preconfigured

Before we proceed with the installation, ensure the following prerequisites are met by the computer to install SAP HANA, express edition:

- At least 8 GB of RAM is required for the *server-only* installation. At least 16 GB of RAM is required (24 GB RAM is recommended) for the *full package* (server plus applications).
- At least two CPU cores (four CPU cores are recommended) are required with virtualization support. For Intel processors, virtualization is a BIOS setting known as either *Intel Virtualization Technology* or *Intel VT*.
- At least 120 GB of storage (Solid State Disk [SSD] recommended) is required.
- A 64-bit Java SE Runtime Enterprise 8 (JRE 8) is installed and running in the machine. JRE 8 can be downloaded from *www.java.com*.

Follow these steps to proceed with the installation:

1. **Install the hypervisor.**
   Hypervisors are software applications used for creating and running VMs. We'll be using VMware Player in our example, which can be downloaded from *www.vmware.com*.
2. **Register.**
   Go to the SAP HANA, express edition web page at *www.sap.com/sap-hana-express*, and register to download the software package. Upon successful registration, select the OS-specific (Windows, Linux, or platform-independent) download manager link under **1A. ON-PREMISE INSTALLATION**. Save the download manager executable.
3. **Download the software using Download Manager.**
   Execute the Download Manager in GUI mode. Select **Linux/x86-64** for **Platform**, **Virtual Machine** for **Image**, and the appropriate **Save** directory. Select **Server + applications virtual machine** option (**Getting Started with SAP HANA, express edition (Virtual Machine Method)** is selected by default), and click the **Download** button, as illustrated in Figure 2.4. A popup message will confirm the successful download.

> **Note**
>
> Additional packages can also be selected, but it's efficient to use the VM's built-in Download Manager.

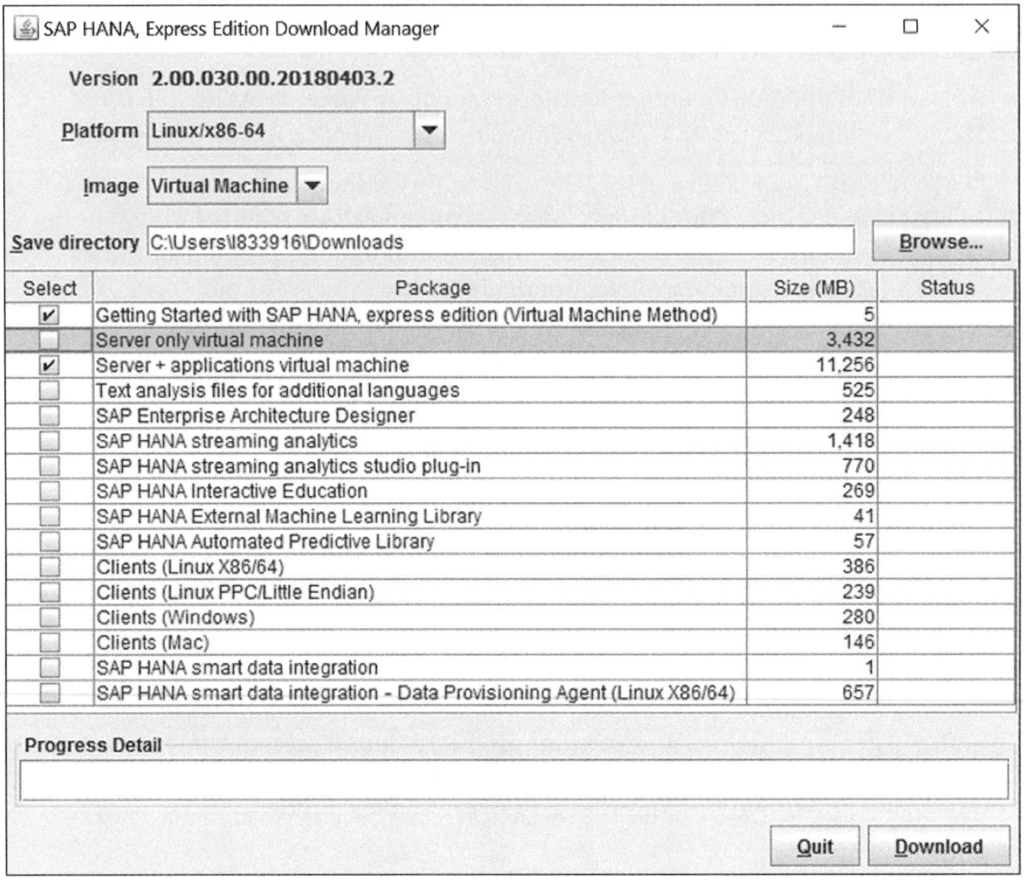

Figure 2.4 SAP HANA, Express Edition Download Manager

4. **Import the open virtual appliance (OVA) file.**
   Start the VMware Player, and select **Open a Virtual Machine** to open the downloaded *OVA hxexsa.ova* file (for **Server + applications virtual machine**). Accept the default options, and import the VM. It will take approximately 5–12 minutes to complete the process.
5. **Turn on the VM and connect.**
   Power on the VM using the **Play** button as shown in Figure 2.5. The IP address of the VM is displayed in the login screen. You'll need to the IP address to configure and connect to your SAP HANA, express edition system. If the IP address isn't shown, power off the VM, and restart it again. Use **Host Name**: **IP address** and **port**: **22** to connect to the VM instance.

Note

If you're using an English QWERTY keyboard, you can continue using the default VM console. However, if you're using another keyboard (German QWERTZ or French AZERTY), you must use a Secure Shell (SSH) client, such as PuTTY. PuTTY can be downloaded free of cost from *www.putty.org*.

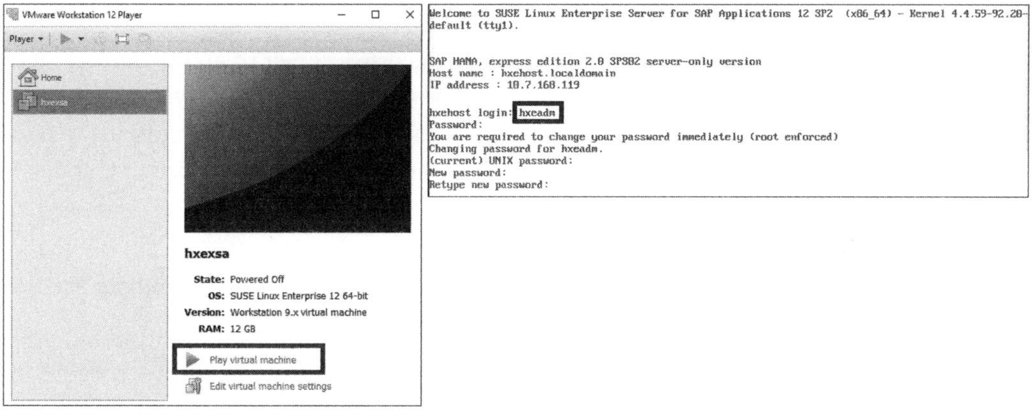

Figure 2.5 SAP HANA, Express Edition VM Login and Setup

6. **Set the user name and password.**
   Use the default user name "hxeadm" and temporary password "HXEHana1" (case sensitive). When prompted to change the temporary password, select a new strong password that complies with the following rules:
   - At least eight characters
   - At least one uppercase letter
   - At least one lowercase letter
   - At least one number
   - Can contain special characters, but not ` (backtick), $ (dollar sign), \ (backslash), ' (single quotation mark), or " (double quotation marks)
   - Can't contain dictionary words
   - Can't contain simplistic or systematic values, such as strings in ascending or descending numerical or alphabetical order

   If the password isn't strong enough, the system will log off, and you'll have to log in again. When prompted, reenter the password to confirm, and change the password Linux OS user password.

7. **Set the master password.**
   The system will then prompt you to change the SAP HANA database master password (i.e., password for the `SYSTEM` user). In our example, because we're installing the server + applications VM, it also changes the password for the `XSA_ADMIN` and `XSA_DEV` users.

   When prompted, select a strong password (it can also be the same as the OS user password), and reenter the password to confirm and change it.

8. **Allow or disallow Internet access.**
   When prompted with **Do you need to use the proxy server to access the internet?**, select **Y** or **N** as appropriate. If you're inside a corporate firewall, you may have to select **Y** and enter the proxy host name, port number, and a comma-separated list of hosts that don't need a proxy, which must include `localhost`, `hxehost`, and `hxehost.localdomain`.

9. **Complete the installation.**
   Select **Y** for the **Wait for the XSA configurations to finish?** to complete the SAP HANA XS Advanced configuration before starting the server.

   Finally, the summary of the configuration before execution will be displayed. Select **Y** when prompted to **Proceed with configuration?**. SAP HANA cockpit and SAP HANA XS Advanced configurations will take around 10 minutes. If the VM goes black, click **VM** or press the `Ctrl` key to wake it up.

   When the installation and configuration is completed, the **Congratulations! SAP HANA, express edition 2.0 is configured** message will be displayed.

Now that the installation is complete, there are some post-installation checks to be done. You need the SAP HANA server host (`hxehost`) IP to connect to the SAP HANA database using client tools. This is the same IP address that was used to connect using the SSH/PuTTY client, and it can be displayed by using the following code in the VM command prompt:

```
/sbin/ifconfig code
```

The `hxehost` IP address is local/private to the VM. To enable applications (e.g., a web browser or SAP HANA Studio) to access the `hxehost` from your laptop, the `hxehost` IP address should be added to the laptop's host file (e.g., *c:\Windows\System32\Drivers\etc\hosts* for Windows and */etc/hosts* for Mac).

For Windows, create an entry with the following format in the *hosts* file and save it:

```
<hxehost IP address>        hxehost
```

For Mac OS or Linux, use the following code in the command prompt:

```
sudo sh - c 'echo <hxehost IP address>    hxehost >> /etc/hosts'
```

The system database of the just installed SAP HANA, express edition instance can be accessed using the following connection parameters in SAP HANA Studio:

- **Hostname**: **hxehost** (or hxehost IP address)
- **Instance Number**: **00**
- **Mode**: **Multiple Container** and **System Database**

You can also check the status of the SAP HANA extended application services, classic model (SAP HANA XS) server by using the following URL in the browser: *http://hxe-host:8090*.

```
hxeadm@hxehost:/usr/sap/HXE/HDB90> xs login -u XSA_ADMIN -p Hanahxe1 -s SAP

API_URL> https://hxehost:39030
USERNAME: XSA_ADMIN
Authenticating...
ORG: HANAExpress
SAPCE: SAP
API endpoint:  https://hxehost:39030 (API version: 1)
User:          XSA_ADMIN
Org:           HANAExpress
Space:         SAP

hxeadm@hxehost:/usr/sap/HXE/HDB90> xs apps

di-cert-admin-ui            STARTED  1/1   16.0 MB   <unlimited> https://hxehost:51026
di-space-provisioning-ui    STARTED  1/1   16.0 MB   <unlimited> https://hxehost:51027
webide                      STARTED  1/1   512 MB    <unlimited> https://hxehost:53075
jobscheduler-db             STARTED  1/1   256 MB    <unlimited>    <none>
jobscheduler=-rest          STARTED  1/1   1.00 GB   <unlimited> https://hxehost:51030

sqlanlz-ui                  STARTED  1/1   128 MB    <unlimited> https://hxehost:51017
hrtt-core                   STARTED  1/1   512 MB    <unlimited> https://hxehost:51018
xsa-admin-backend           STARTED  1/1   1.0 GB    <unlimited> https://hxehost:51020
xsa-admin                   STARTED  1/1   1.0 GB    <unlimited> https://hxehost:51019
sap-portal-services         STARTED  1/1   256 MB    <unlimited> https://hxehost:51021

Cockpit-landscape-svc       STARTED  1/1   128 MB    <unlimited> https://hxehost:51039
cockpit-web-app             STARTED  1/1   512 MB    <unlimited> https://hxehost:51041
cockpit-adminui-svc         STARTED  1/1   128 MB    <unlimited> https://hxehost:51042
cockpit-admin-web-app       STARTED  1/1   128 MB    <unlimited> https://hxehost:51043
di-builder                  STARTED  1/1   256 MB    <unlimited> https://hxehost:51007
```

Figure 2.6 Check SAP HANA XS Advanced Apps

To check the status of SAP HANA XS Advanced applications in the system, use the VM command prompt to connect to the SAP HANA XS Advanced server, as shown in Figure 2.6. We'll use the following commands to connect to the SAP HANA XS Advanced server:

```
xs login -u XSA_ADMIN -p "<password>" -s SAP
```

In this code, `<password>` is the password used to install the SAP HANA database. This will connect to the SAP HANA XS Advanced services and display the following information:

- **ORG: HANAExpress**
- **SPACE: SAP**
- **API endpoint: https://hxehost:39030 (API version: 1)**
- **User: XSA_ADMIN**
- **Org: HANAExpress**
- **Space: SAP**

If the **API Endpoint**, **User**, **Org**, and **Space** are displayed, the SAP HANA XS Advanced installation is working as expected.

The SAP HANA cockpit and SAP Web IDE for SAP HANA are also installed as SAP HANA XS Advanced applications. You can check the status of SAP HANA XS Advanced applications using the following code: `xs apps`. This will display all the SAP HANA XS Advanced applications installed and their execution status, as shown previously in Figure 2.6. Look for the `cockpit-admin-web-app`, `XSA-ADMIN`, and `webide` applications, which should show as `STARTED` with `1/1` instance. Record the URLs of those applications to test them in the browser.

2.3 SAP Cloud Appliance Library

The SAP Cloud Appliance Library (*https://cal.sap.com*) provides an online library of preconfigured SAP solutions that can be deployed in the cloud in minutes and can be used for testing, demoing, training purposes. SAP Cloud Appliance Library doesn't host the solution; rather, the solution instance is hosted by the customer's preferred cloud providers, such as AWS and Azure. All deployed solution instances are easily accessed and managed using the SAP Fiori-based self-service portal.

In the following sections, we'll discuss the steps to configure an SAP HANA, express edition system in an AWS cloud using SAP Cloud Appliance Library.

2.3.1 Registrations

You'll need to register and create an account in SAP Cloud Appliance Library to start using the available preconfigured SAP solution. SAP Cloud Appliance Library is free to try for 30 days, but customers will be charged by the cloud providers based on their usage during this trial period. As the solutions are hosted by cloud providers such as AWS and Azure, you should register and create an account with your preferred cloud provider.

The AWS **Access Key** and **Secret Key** or Azure **Subscription ID** is required to connect your cloud providers to the SAP Cloud Appliance Library account, as shown in Figure 2.7.

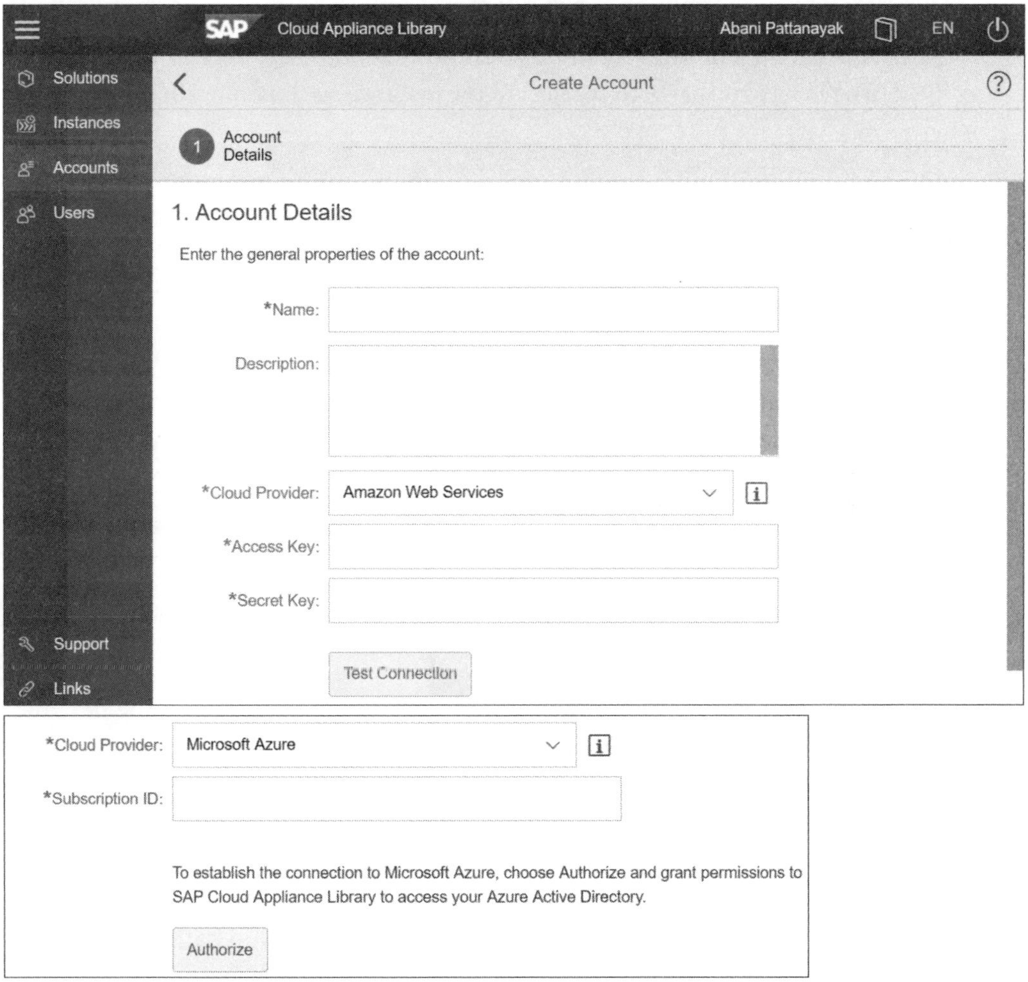

Figure 2.7 Link Cloud Providers

2.3.2 SAP HANA, Express Edition Setup

In the following sections, we'll discuss the steps to set up an SAP HANA, express edition instance in SAP Cloud Appliance Library.

Create Instance

To create an instance of SAP HANA, express edition, navigate to the **Solutions** tab, look for **SAP HANA, Express Edition** and select the **Create Instance** button, as shown in Figure 2.8 ❶.

Select the **Advanced Mode** button to proceed to the next screen to select account details, as illustrated in Figure 2.8 ❷ and ❸.

Select **SAP Cal Default Network** (for Azure) and **ECS-Internet** (for AWS) in the **Network** field to have an external IP to connect to the instance, as illustrated in Figure 2.8 ❹.

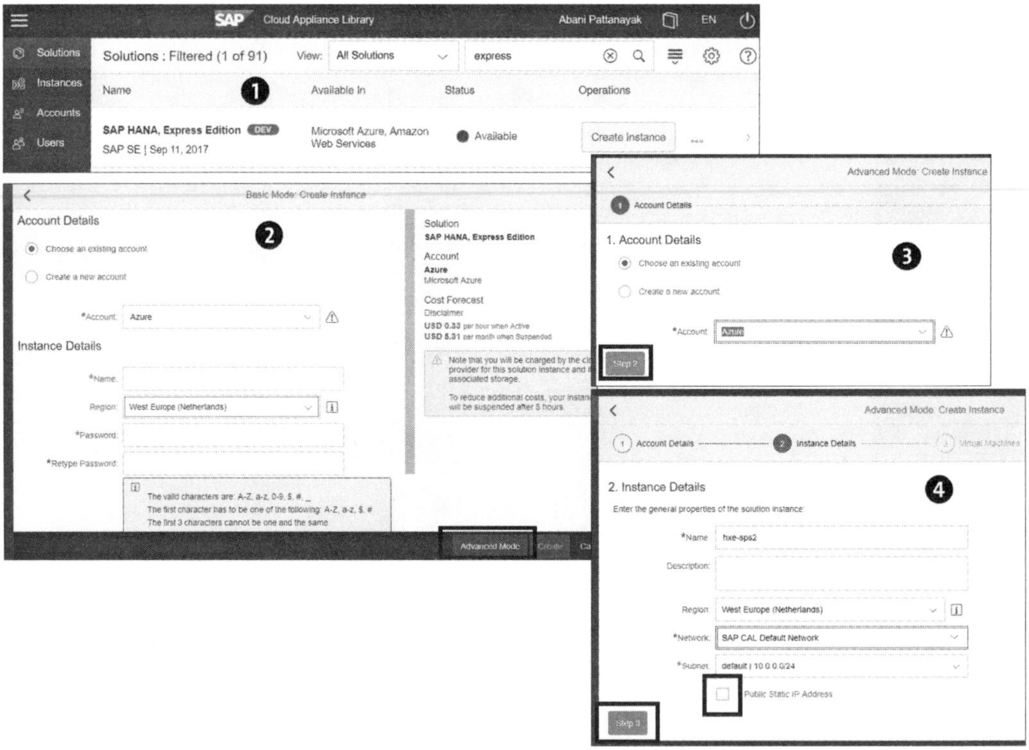

Figure 2.8 Creating an Instance

Review and record the access ports shown in Figure 2.9 ❶. Proceed to the next step to select the SAP HANA master password (for SYSTEM user) and XSA_ADMIN and XSA_DEV user. Make sure the password follows the strong password rules shown in Figure 2.9 ❷.

Proceed to the next screen to select the appropriate scheduling options, as illustrated in Figure 2.9 ❸. Go to the next screen to review the instance details, and click **Create** to create the instance, as shown in Figure 2.9 ❹.

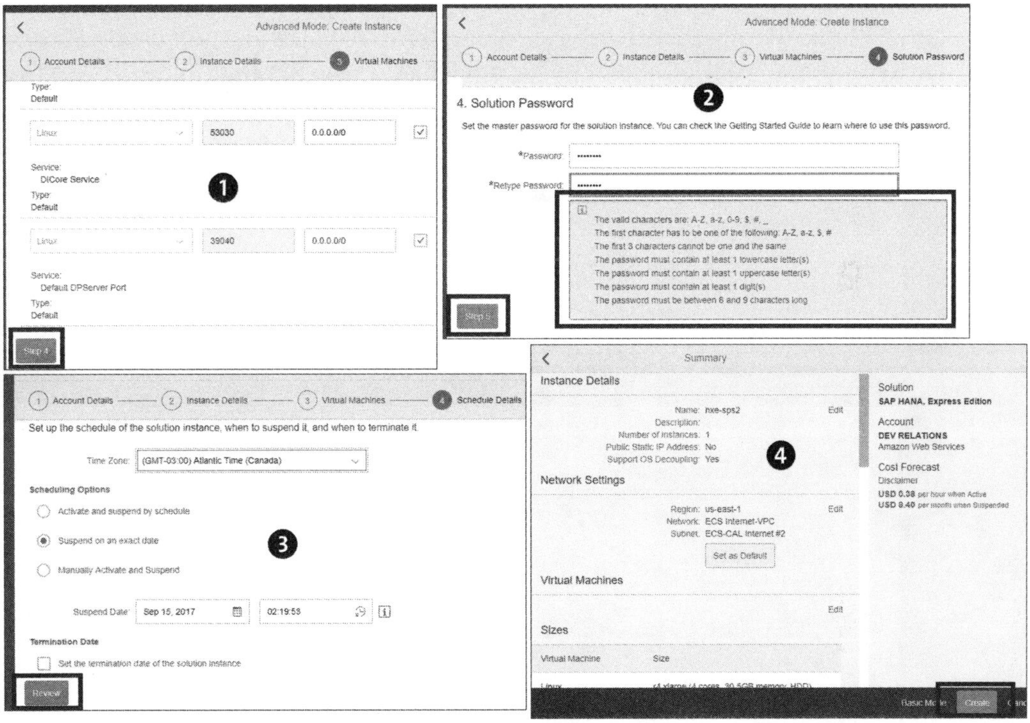

Figure 2.9 Instance Details

The wizard will then display a disclaimer about the usage of SAP HANA, express edition. Upon confirmation, you'll be prompted to store and download the private key. Select **Store** to save the private key details to your instance, and then click **Download** to download it to your local system to connect to the SAP HANA instance using an SSH client such as PuTTY.

It will take around 20–25 minutes to provision and configure the SAP HANA, express edition system in the cloud.

Post-Configuration Checks

When the instance is available and ready for use, it will be displayed in the **Instances** tab. Click on the instance to access its details, record the external IP address, and download the private key, which can be used to connect to the SAP HANA instance from your local computer, as illustrated in Figure 2.10.

Download the *Getting Started Guide* to find details about connecting your SAP HANA, express edition instance, including the SAP HANA database server details (server ID [SID], instance number, database user names, OS user names) and port details of backend services (e.g., port 3*xx*30 for the SAP HANA XS Advanced server and port 5*xx*75 for SAP Web IDE for SAP HANA, where *xx* is the instance number).

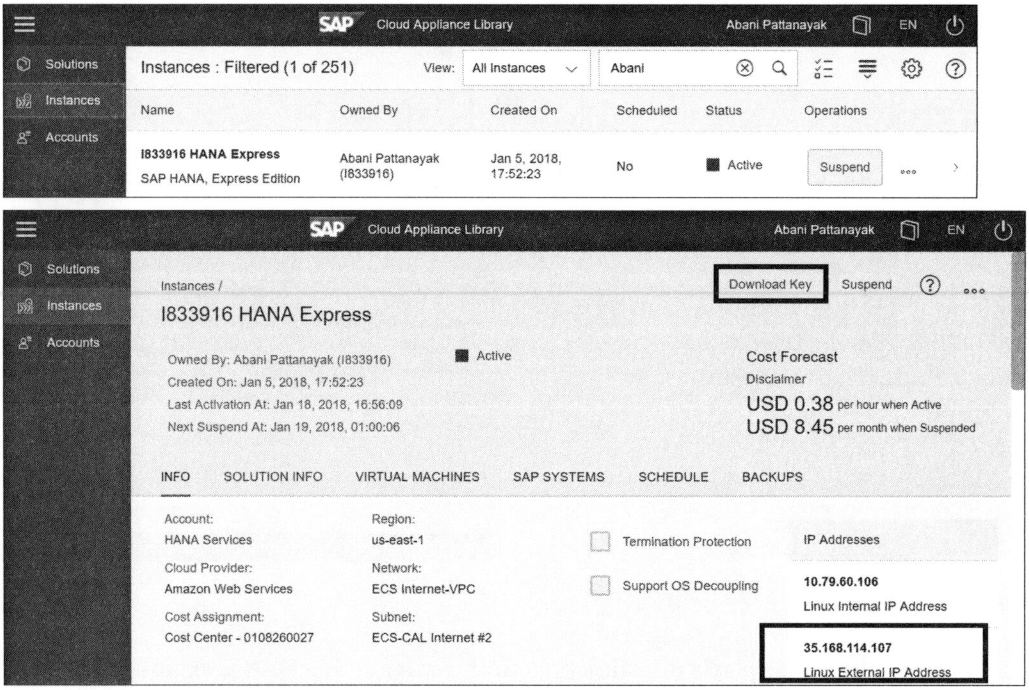

Figure 2.10 SAP CAL Instance Details

To seamlessly access all SAP HANA XS Advanced applications, the `vhcalhxedb` endpoint must be defined in the local systems by adding the external IP address in the laptop's host file (e.g., *c:\Windows\System32\Drivers\etc\hosts* for Windows and */etc/hosts* for Mac OS).

For Windows, create the following entry in the *hosts* file and save it:

```
<IP address>        vhcalhxedb
```

For Mac OS or Linux, use the following code in the command prompt:

```
sudo sh - c 'echo <IP address>    vhcalhxedb >> /etc/hosts'
```

We can then connect to `vhcalhxedb` using SAP HANA Studio, an SSH client (e.g., PuTTY), and a browser to SAP HANA XS Advanced web applications.

Accessing SAP HANA, Express Edition

The downloaded private key file should be converted to a *.ppk* file using key generator tools such as PuTTYgen. Use the generated *.ppk* private key file to authenticate and default the `root` user to connect to the Linux host of the SAP HANA database using SSH tools (e.g., PuTTY).

Use the following commands in the SSH prompt to check the status of the SAP HANA instance. `HXEADM` is the Linux OS user in SAP HANA:

```
su - hxeadm
HDB info
```

If SAP HANA is up, the `SYSTEM` database of the just installed SAP HANA, express edition instance can be accessed using the following connection parameters in SAP HANA Studio:

- **Hostname: vhcalhxedb**
- **Instance Number: 90**
- **Mode: Multiple Container and System Database**

The SAP HANA XS Advanced server (and web dispatcher) status can be checked using the following: *https://vhcalhxedb:3xx30* (where *xx* is the instance number). This will list all available SAP HANA XS Advanced applications and their URLs. For example, the SAP HANA XS Advanced administration console can be accessed using the following: *https://vhcalhxedb:51015*. Similarly, SAP Web IDE for SAP HANA can be accessed using *https://vhcalhxedb:53075*.

The SAP HANA XS Advanced client can be used to connect to the SAP HANA XS Advanced server and check the status of SAP HANA XS Advanced applications such as SAP Web IDE for SAP HANA.

2.4 SAP Cloud Platform

SAP Cloud Platform (formerly SAP HANA Cloud Platform) is an open platform-as-a-service (PaaS) offered by SAP to create new applications or extend existing applications in a secure cloud computing environment. It offers the agility and flexibility to quickly build new or extend existing cloud and on-premise apps (both SAP and non-SAP) with your choice of cloud providers (SAP, AWS, Azure, Google Cloud, etc.) and open and common development languages (Java, Python, JavaScript, Node.js, Cloud Foundry, etc.).

SAP Cloud Platform offers a comprehensive list of services in the area of analytics, business services, data and storage, integration, Internet of Things (IoT), machine learning, mobile services, runtime and containers, software-as-a-service (SaaS) extensions, user experience, and security.

SAP Cloud Platform can be accessed at *https://cloudplatform.sap.com*. It offers a *developer edition* subscription free of cost for evaluation and development purposes that includes the following:

- 1 GB shared SAP HANA
- SAP HANA Cloud Portal
- SAP Web IDE
- SAP Cloud Platform mobile services
- SAP Cloud Platform OData Provisioning

Note

The SAP HANA XS Advanced architecture is loosely based on Cloud Foundry and shares some of its core principles (details about the SAP HANA XS Advanced architecture appear in Chapter 4), so it's possible to develop applications using the SAP HANA XS Advanced environment and run/deploy the applications in the SAP Cloud Platform Cloud Foundry environment.

For SAP HANA XS Advanced application development, subscriptions to the following two services are required:

- SAP HANA service instance
- SAP Web IDE for full-stack development

As of writing this book, the SAP HANA service instance isn't offered as part of the developer edition or trial subscription because it requires at least 16 GB of memory.

In the following sections, we'll discuss provisioning the SAP HANA service instance and SAP Web IDE for full-stack development in SAP Cloud Platform, which can be used as our development environment.

2.4.1 Registrations

You'll need to register and create an account by visiting the SAP Cloud Platform website at *https://cloudplatform.sap.com* and then purchase a subscription for SAP Cloud Platform, starter edition (32 GB or 64 GB) for nonproductive use or any other subscription for productive use.

SAP Cloud Platform offers two environments: Cloud Foundry (infrastructure by AWS, Google Cloud Platform, and Azure) and Neo (infrastructure by SAP). We'll be using the *Cloud Foundry* environment for the SAP HANA service and the Neo environment for the SAP Web IDE, which is discussed in the following sections.

2.4.2 Provisioning the SAP HANA Service Instance

In this section, we'll discuss the steps to provision an SAP HANA service instance in the Cloud Foundry environment of SAP Cloud Platform. The SAP HANA service is fully managed by SAP and offers flexible sizing, elastic scaling, and consumption-based pricing and terms of hosting. At the time of writing this book, it's offered in the cloud AWS or Google Cloud Platform. For more information about features and capabilities of the SAP HANA service instance, refer to online help for SAP HANA service.

Set Up the Cloud Foundry Environment

The SAP HANA service is offered in the Cloud Foundry environment of SAP Cloud Platform. The Cloud Foundry environment needs to be set up before you can instantiate any service.

Log in to the **SAP Cloud Platform Cockpit** screen, and navigate to your Cloud Foundry global account. Create one or more subaccounts to organize resources in your global account. Cloud Foundry needs to be enabled explicitly for each subaccount using the **Enable Cloud Foundry** button in the **Overview** page of the subaccount. In our example, we've created a subaccount called **CF-trial**, details of which are illustrated in Figure 2.11 ❶.

Navigate to the **Spaces** page of your subaccount. Create one or more spaces to organize service instances and applications in your subaccount. In our example, we've created space `CF-trial_space`, details of which are illustrated in Figure 2.11 ❷. Selecting the space changes the navigation menu on the left side. Navigate to the **Services • Service Marketplace** to display a list of services available (see Figure 2.11 ❸).

Click on **SAP HANA Service** (technical name `hana-db`) to display the **Overview** page with additional details and a link to documentation of the service. Navigate to the **Instances** page to display the list of instances provisioned for the service as shown in Figure 2.11 ❹.

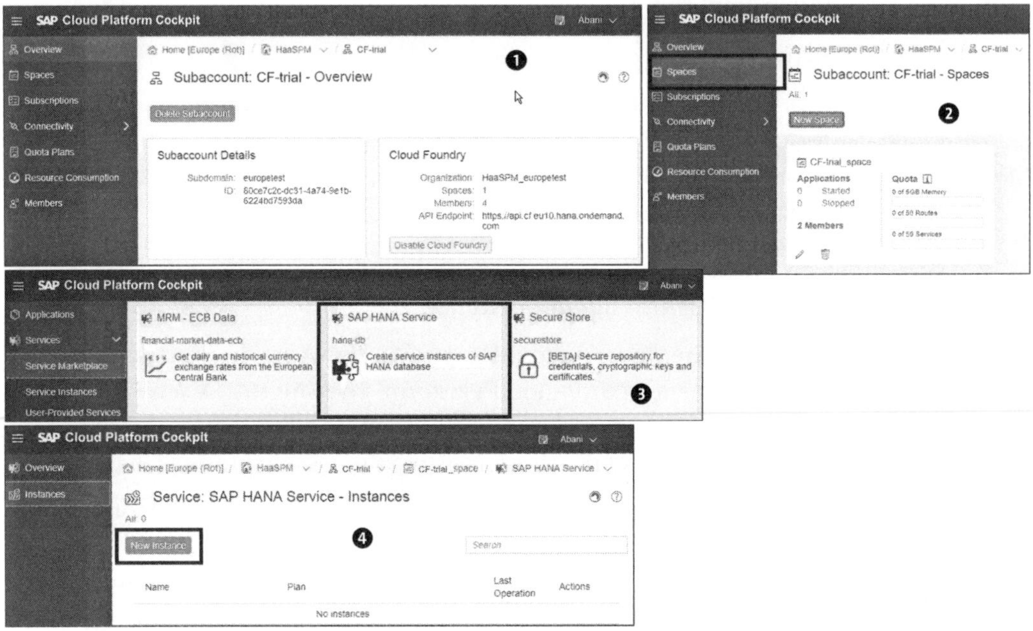

Figure 2.11 Cloud Foundry Environment in SAP Cloud Platform

Create an SAP HANA Service Instance

Click the **New Instance** button to display the new instance wizard for the SAP HANA service as shown in Figure 2.12. There are two plans available for SAP HANA Service: **Standard** (core database features) and **Enterprise** (standard plus additional features, such as predictive, graph, spatial, etc.), as shown in (Figure 2.12 ❶). Select the appropriate service plan based on your business requirement, and click **Next** to proceed.

Specify a password, which will be the password for the system user of the *tenant* database being provisioned. It will actually provision a *system* database and a *tenant* database. As this is an SAP-managed service, the system database is accessed by SAP, whereas the tenant database is secured using the password and is in your control. Select the appropriate memory (in blocks of 16 GB) to provision the tenant database. Because the SAP HANA instance is going to be available across the public Internet, you can effectively control access to your tenant by whitelisting specific IP addresses or allowing open access. Select the appropriate user parameters, and click **Next** to proceed (Figure 2.12 ❷).

Select **Next** to skip this page because we aren't assigning this tenant database to any particular application (Figure 2.12 ❸).

Specify a name for your instance (e.g., "hana_enterprise" for the enterprise version), and click **Finish** to provision the new instance (Figure 2.12 ❹).

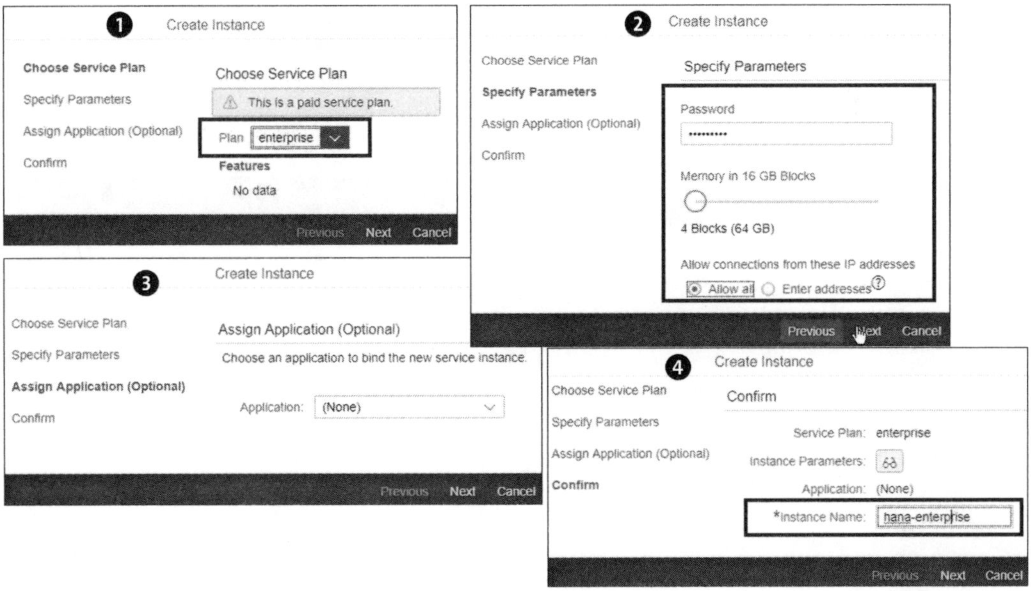

Figure 2.12 Creating an SAP HANA Service Instance

The newly provisioned instance (e.g., `hana_enterprise`) appears, and it may take a few seconds (up to a few minutes) for the system to be ready for use.

You can spin up as many or as few instances as you want and whenever you want using the SAP Cloud Platform cockpit. Because it's a fully managed SAP HANA service, the high availability backups are done by SAP. However, you control what SAP HANA instances you have and when you want to create/delete them to manage the limit in your quota.

Click on the **Open Dashboard** icon to open the **SAP HANA Service Dashboard** screen, which will display critical information about the SAP HANA service instance as illustrated in Figure 2.13 ❶. Record the **ID** of the SAP HANA service instance and **Endpoints** details of the tenant and system database, which will be used to connect using client tools ❷. You can also see where the SAP HANA service is hosted (in our example, it's hosted with AWS) and how much memory is allocated for the instance.

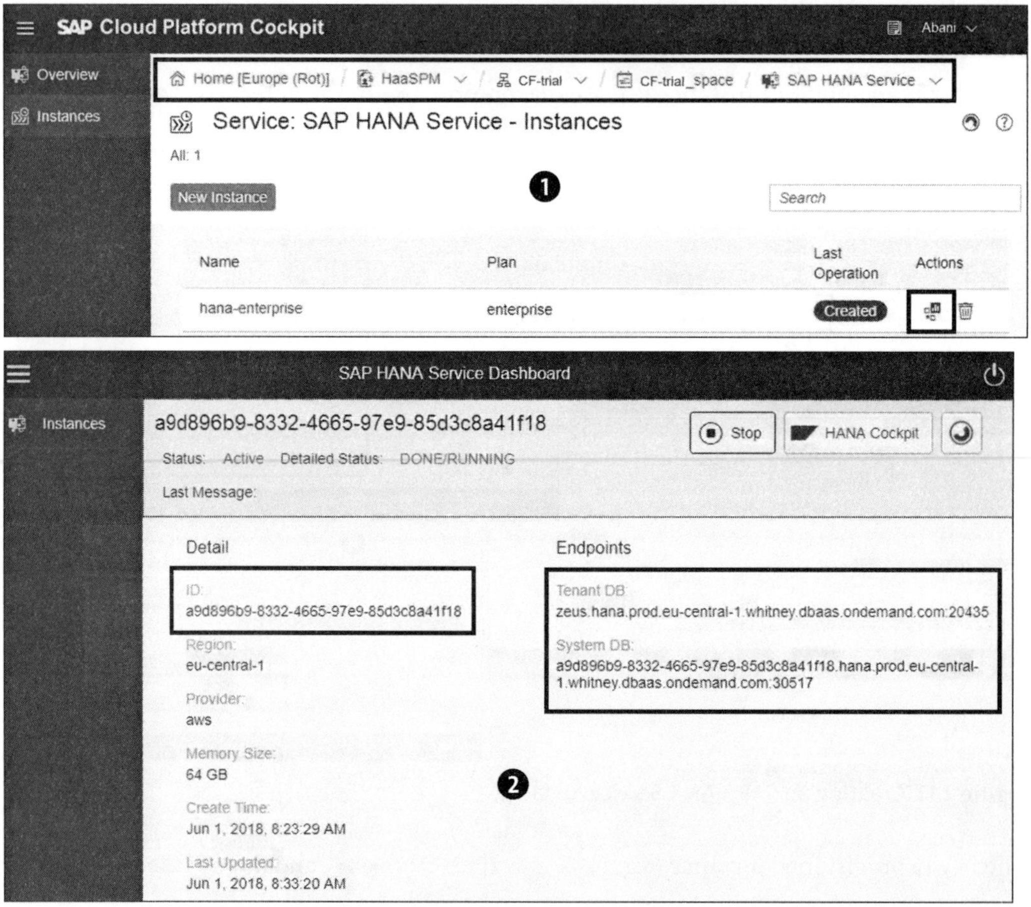

Figure 2.13 SAP HANA Service Dashboard

Accessing the SAP HANA System

Select the **HANA Cockpit** button to open the SAP HANA Platform cockpit of the just-provisioned tenant database in a new browser window. Enter the `SYSTEM` user and the password (used while provisioning the instance) when prompted to authenticate for the SAP HANA cockpit. The **SAP HANA Cockpit** screen offers various options to effectively manage the tenant database, as illustrated in Figure 2.14 ❶. It's recommended to set up one or more individual users with appropriate roles to perform specific tasks and then deactivate the system user to have a secure environment.

Select the **Open SQL Console** button to launch the **SAP HANA Database Explorer** screen to explore the catalog of schemas and execute SQL commands (see Figure 2.14 ❷).

The provisioned tenant database in the Cloud Foundry environment can also be accessed using SAP HANA Studio with the following connection parameters:

- **Hostname**: <endpoint of the tenant database>, for example, `zeus.hana.prod.eu-central-1.whitney.dbaas.ondemand.com`
- **Instance Number**: **00** (not required, default 00 is used)
- **Multiple Container & Tenant Database**: **H00**:<port of the tenant database>, for example, H00:20435

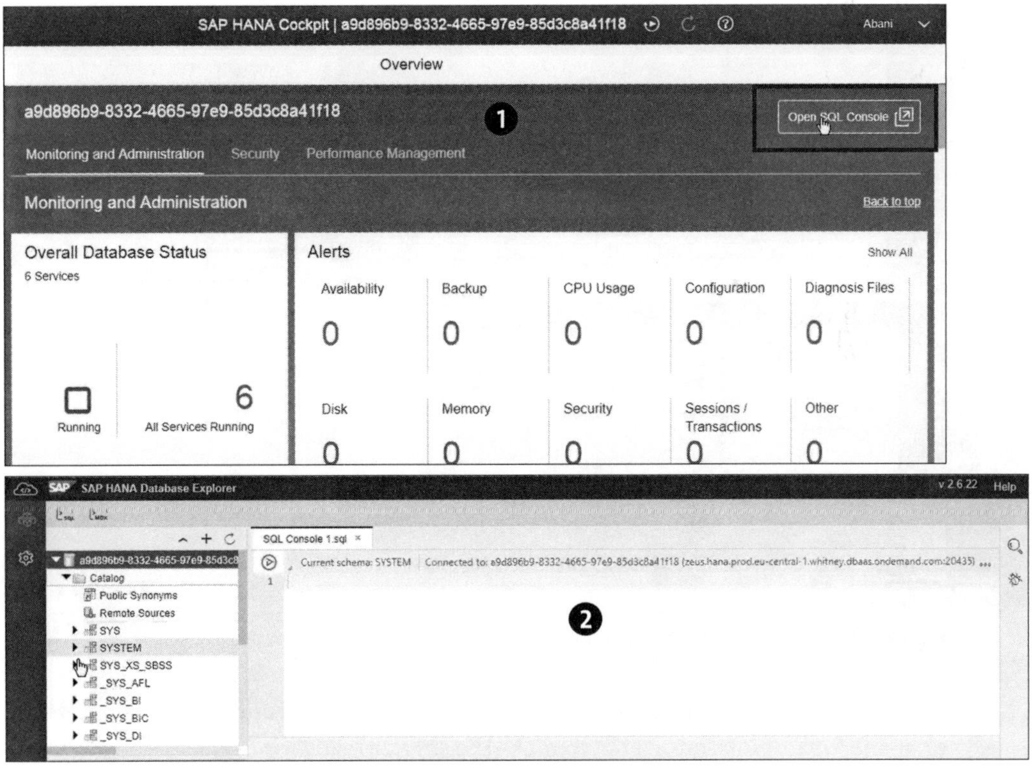

Figure 2.14 Accessing the SAP HANA Service Instance

In the next section, we'll discuss how to enable SAP Web IDE in the SAP Cloud Platform to work with your SAP HANA service instance.

2.4.3 Enable SAP Web IDE for Full-Stack Development

The SAP Web IDE for full-stack development is used to create multi-target applications (MTAs) and build SAP HANA database artifacts such as database tables, views, and procedures in the SAP Cloud Platform environment. The SAP Web IDE is hosted in the Neo environment of SAP Cloud Platform. To use the SAP Web IDE, you must switch to your Neo subaccount (in our example, it's `neo_trial`), as shown in Figure 2.15 ❶.

Navigate to **Services** to display the list of services available for your subaccount in the Neo environment, and select the **SAP Web IDE Full-Stack** service to display details about the service (Figure 2.15 ❷). By default, the service isn't enabled. Select the **Enable** button to enable SAP Web IDE for your subaccount (Figure 2.15 ❸).

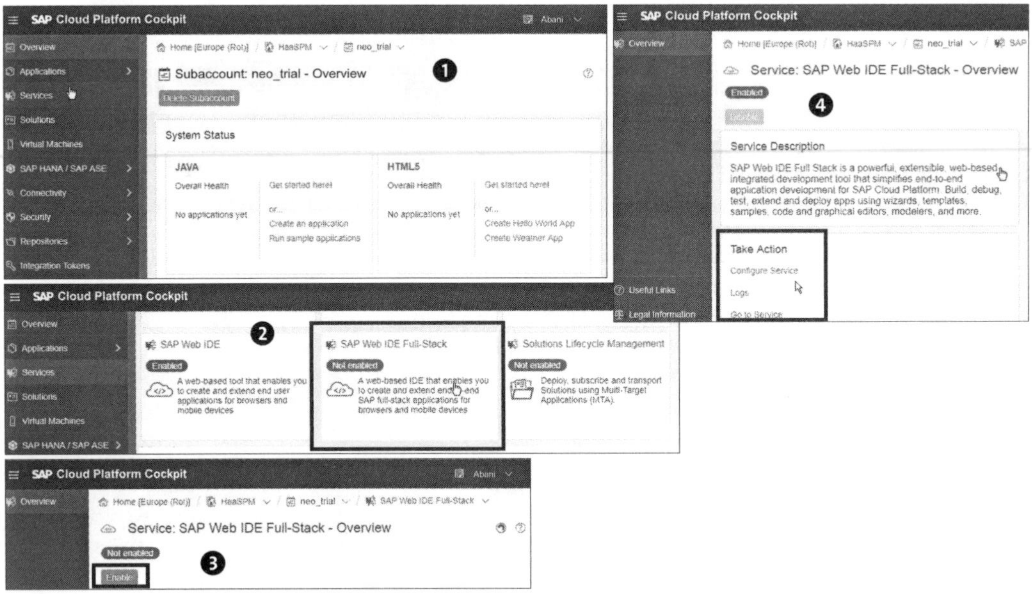

Figure 2.15 Enabling the SAP Web IDE for Full-Stack Development

We need to configure the service and set up users with appropriate roles (e.g., developer and/or administrator, etc.) to make the service ready for users.

Select the **Configure Service** link (Figure 2.15 ❹), select the **DiDeveloper** role, and add one or more users. Similarly, select the **DiAdministrator** role, and add one or more users as illustrated in Figure 2.16 ❶.

We also need to enable principle propagation. To do this, navigate to **Security • Trust**, and explicitly select **Enabled** in the **Principal Propagation** field (Figure 2.16 ❷) instead of using the default setting. Save the changes, and go back to **Services** to launch the SAP Web IDE for full-stack development using the **Go to Service** link (see Figure 2.17 ❶). You can save the URL as a bookmark for easy access.

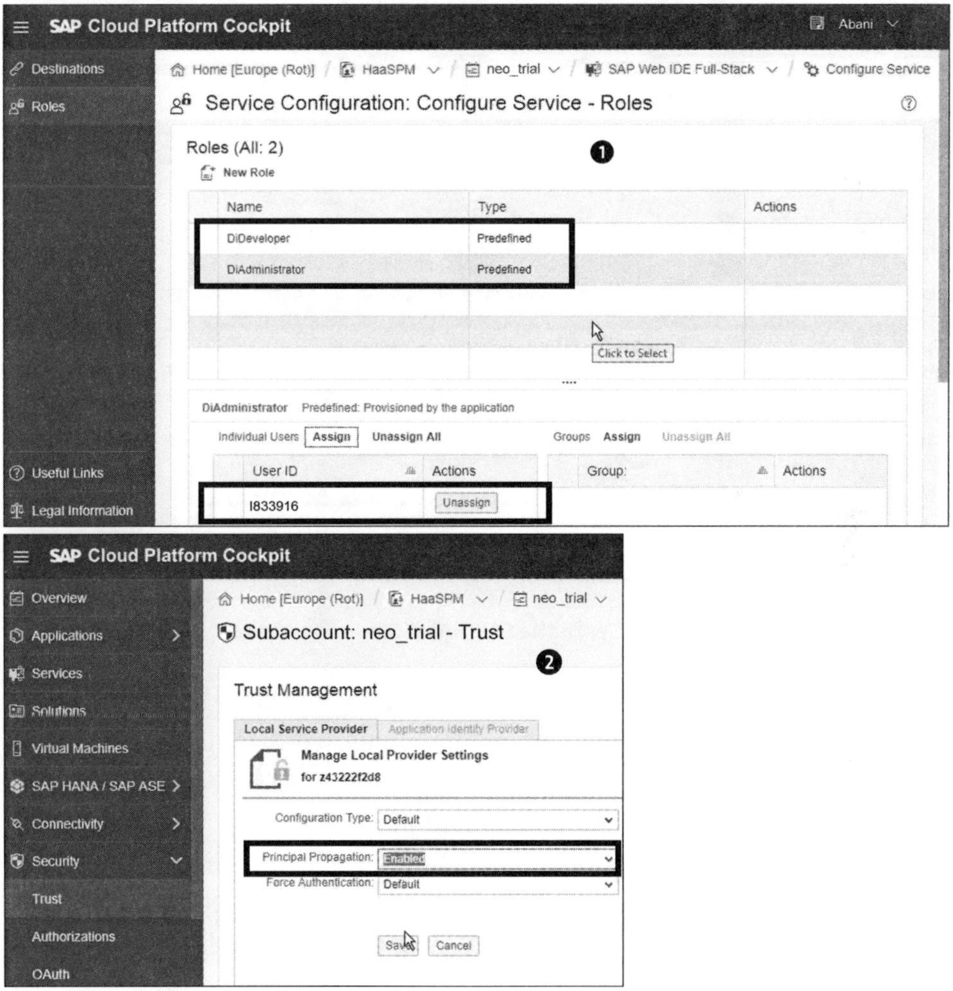

Figure 2.16 Configuring Service Roles

Next, we need to configure the SAP Web IDE to use the SAP HANA service instance we created earlier. In the SAP Web IDE, select the **Preference** icon, and set up the Cloud Foundry endpoint as illustrated in Figure 2.17 ❷.

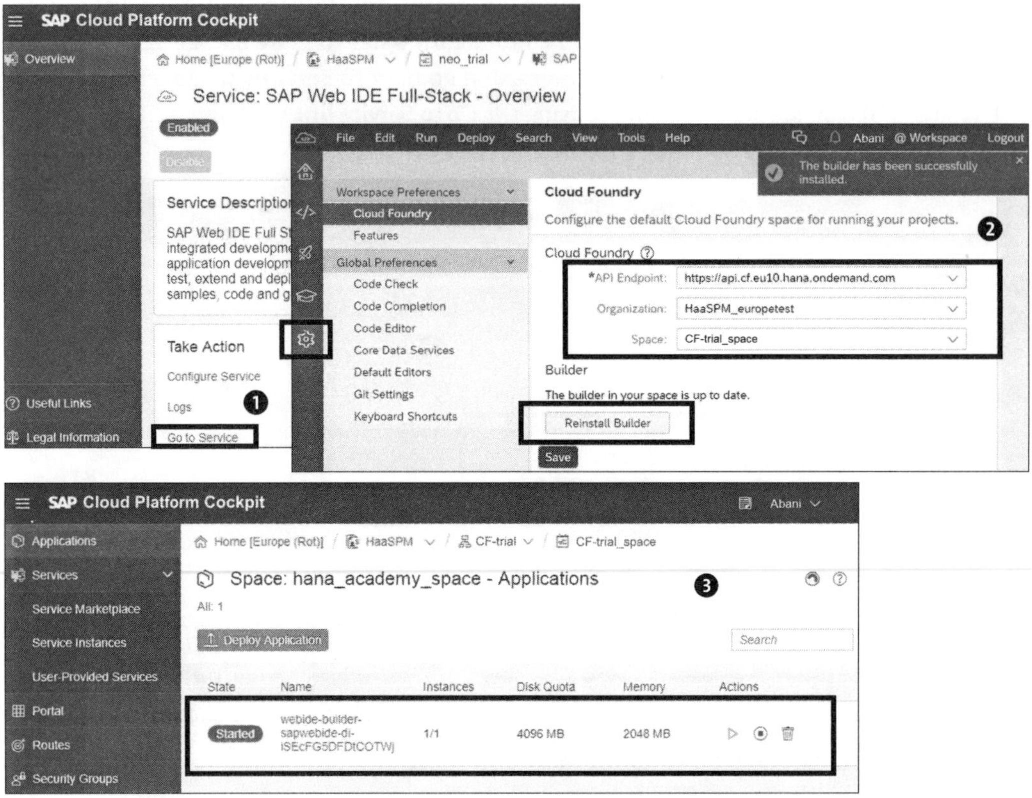

Figure 2.17 Linking SAP Web IDE with the SAP HANA Service Instance

The information for the **Organization** and **API Endpoint** fields is available in the **Overview** page of your Cloud Foundry subaccount as shown earlier in Figure 2.11 ❶, and the **Space** field is the space in which we provisioned the SAP HANA service instance as shown earlier in Figure 2.11 ❷.

Finally, we need to install the builder application that is required to build and deploy applications to our space. To install the builder in your space, select the **Reinstall Builder** button (see Figure 2.17 ❷). Upon successful installation, the builder application will be available in your Cloud Foundry space under **Applications** as illustrated in Figure 2.17 ❸.

With this, the setup of SAP Web IDE for full-stack development is complete, and it's ready for application development.

2.5 SAP HANA XS Advanced Organizations and Spaces

In the following sections, we'll start by providing you with an overview of the concepts behind organizations and spaces in SAP HANA XS Advanced before moving on to the steps you need to take to manage them.

2.5.1 Organizations and Spaces Overview

Applications in an SAP HANA XS Advanced system are deployed and isolated using the concepts of *organizations* and *spaces* with separated OS users to meet the resource requirements of applications.

An *organization* is a development account that one or more developers (*user*) can own and use. All developers in an organization share a resource quota plan, applications, services availability, and custom domains. All resources, applications, spaces, and services in the organization can be managed (and suspended) at the organization level.

Every application and service is scoped to a space, and each organization contains at least one space. A *space* provides users with access to a shared location for application development, deployment, and maintenance.

If there is a need for a group of applications to share system resources used by the same set of end users and to be deployed by the same user, then this group of applications can be deployed to the same space in an SAP HANA XS Advanced environment. Common resources shared by applications in a space can be data storage, user authorizations, and so on.

Depending on the need for shared resources, one or more applications may be deployed in a given space, but an application is always deployed into one and only one space. Each resource (a service instance) required by an application must be available (or created) in the same space, and each service instance must be explicitly banded to the application by the service broker. The service binding entity bears the credentials issued by the service broker, and the execution agent passes these credentials to the bound service instances during start-up.

A user represents a developer or collaborator in the context of SAP HANA XS Advanced. Users can have different roles (manager, auditor, and developer) in different spaces within the organization, governing what level and type of access they have within that space. Finally, a space can be used by several users, and each user/developer may have his own private space as well.

One or more spaces can be grouped together as an organization to manage and administrate collectively. However, the runtime behavior of an application isn't impacted by its organization grouping. For all practical purposes, the runtime behavior and the resource requirements are managed at the space level.

The relationships among organizations, spaces, service instances, and service binding are illustrated in Figure 2.18.

The isolation of spaces is achieved by mapping dedicated OS users for each space, as shown in Figure 2.19. Technically, two or more spaces can also be mapped to a single OS user, and those spaces won't be isolated from each other. Applications running in the same space share all resources, such as data storage, user authorizations, and passwords.

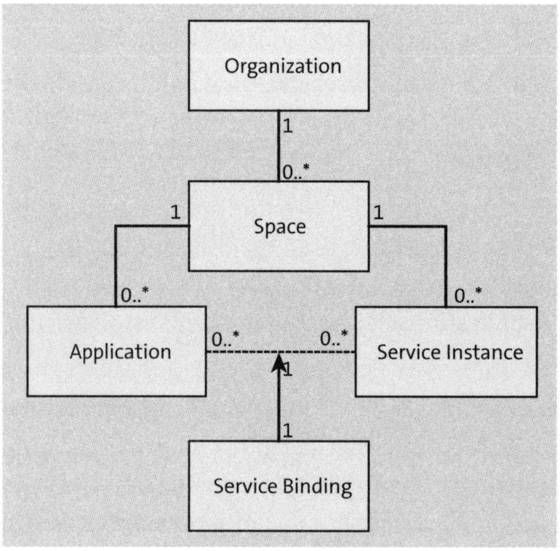

Figure 2.18 Organizations and Spaces

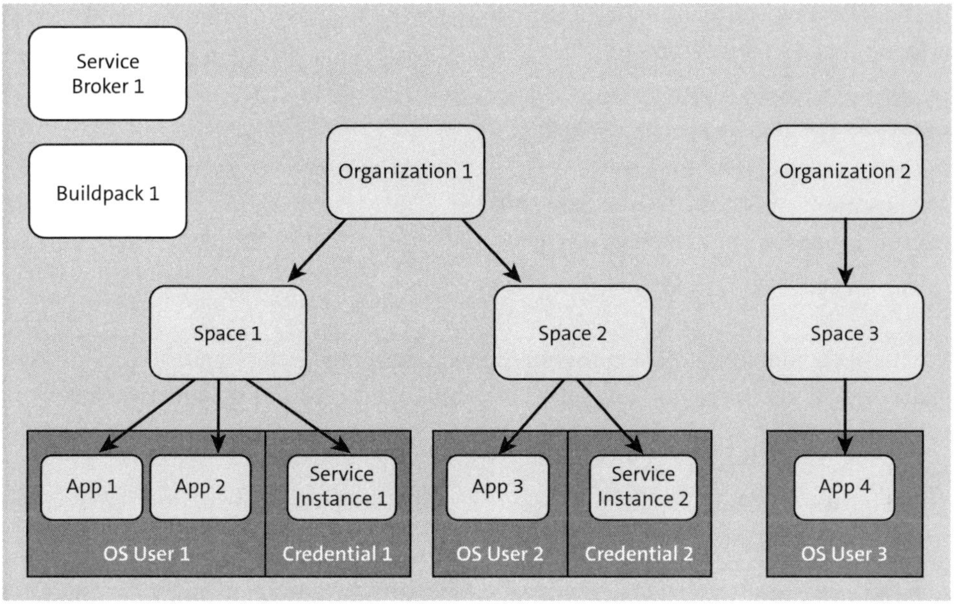

Figure 2.19 OS Level Isolation of Applications

External buildpack processes may or may not have their own dedicated OS user. Application instances and buildpacks in different spaces are only isolated at the OS level if each space is running with a dedicated OS user. From a security perspective, it's important to have isolated spaces with dedicated OS users.

2.5.2 Organization and Space Management

To manage the organization and space for your SAP HANA installation, log in to the SAP HANA XS Advanced administration site. If SAP HANA, express edition is used, SAP HANA XS Advanced administration consolcan be accessed using *https://hxehost:39030* (on premise) or *https://vhcalhxedb:39030*.

Alternatively, if SAP HANA, express edition isn't used, or the ports have been changed, the right URL for the `xsa-cockpit` application can be found using command `xs apps` on the command-line interface (CLI). CLI can be accessed directly on the SSH console on the server, or it can be downloaded using the Download Manager. Log in to the CLI using the `xsa_admin` user (or another user with authorizations to create spaces). The CLI is discussed in detail in Chapter 3.

In the following subsections, we'll explain the steps to create a new space and enable it for application development.

Create Space

In the **XS Advanced Administration** console screen, select the **Organization and Space Management** application to display the list of organizations. In our example, the default organization **HANAExpress** is available (Figure 2.20 ❶). The default can be renamed, and a new organization can be created using the **Create Organization (+)** button.

We'll use the default **HANAExpress** organization to create our space. There are two spaces—**SAP** and **development**—already available under the default **HANAExpress** organization (Figure 2.20 ❷). The **SAP** space is used to deploy all SAP-delivered applications that are part of the SAP HANA XS Advanced infrastructure. Select the **+ Create Space** button to create a space, and provide a suitable space name to proceed (see Figure 2.20 ❸ and ❹).

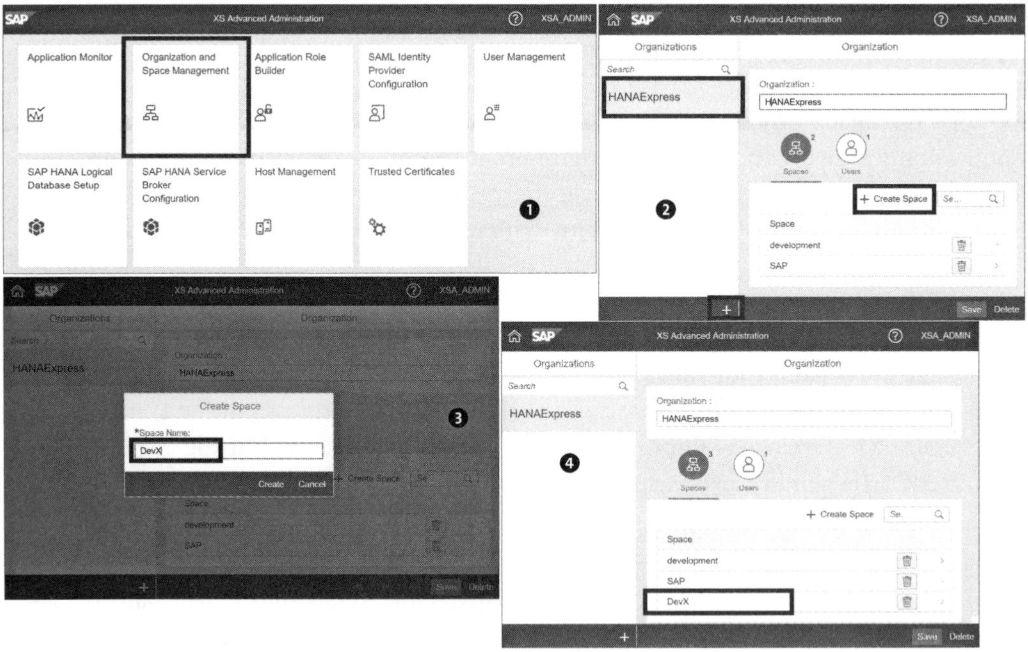

Figure 2.20 Creating a Space

Add Authorized Users

To manage and use the new space just created, users need to be explicitly defined for each space. To do so, click on the new space just created and select the **Users** tab (Figure 2.21 ❶). Select the **Add User** button to select from a list of authorized users and their roles for the space, as shown in Figure 2.21 ❷ and ❸.

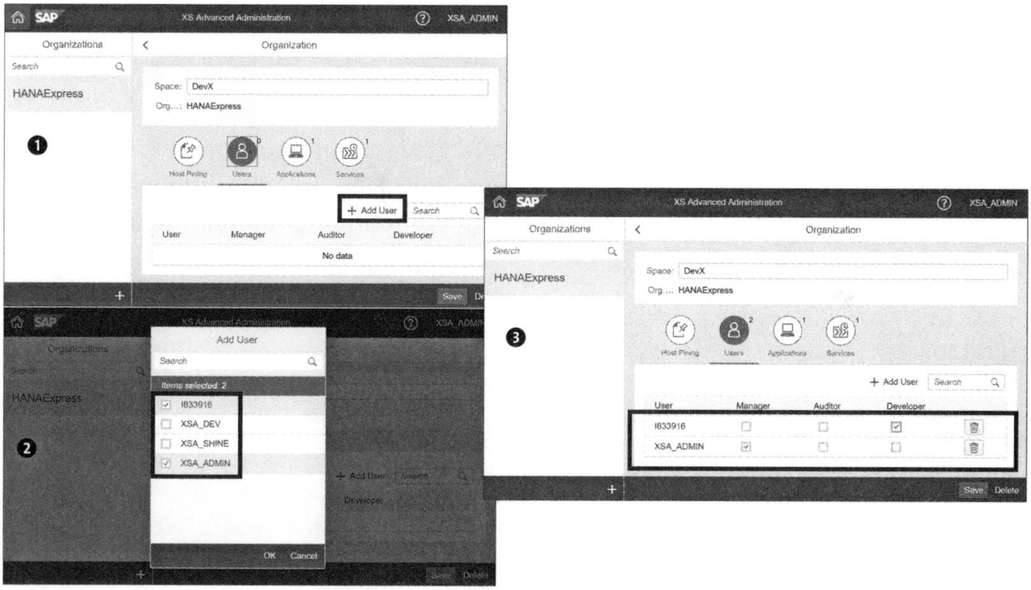

Figure 2.21 Adding Users to a Space

Space Enablement

The new space just created must be explicitly enabled before an SAP HANA XS Advanced application can be deployed in the space. In the **XS Advanced Administration** console screen, select the **Application Monitor** application, and search for app **di-space-enablement-ui** (Figure 2.22 ❶ and ❷). Start the app, if not running. After the application is running and available, launch the URL (in our example, the app is available on *https://vhcalhxedb:51024*) to open the **Space Enablement** tool.

In the **Space Enablement** tool, select the **Enable** button beside the space (Figure 2.22 ❸). The enablement process may take a few minutes to complete the processing and display a success message ❹. Upon successful enablement, the space is ready for use.

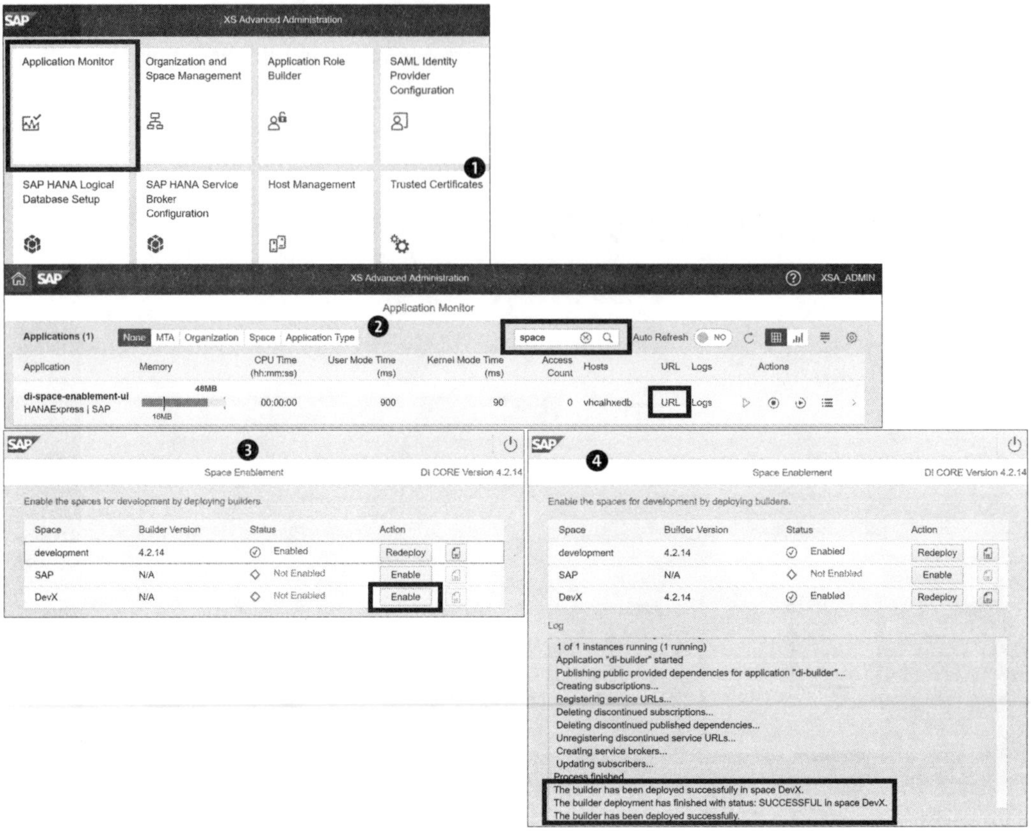

Figure 2.22 Space Enablement

2.6 Git Code Repository

The SAP HANA Repository is available in the SAP HANA system for SAP HANA XS-based development using SAP HANA Studio or the SAP HANA Web-Based Development Workbench. As briefly introduced in Section 2.1, an external source code management tool, such as Git or Gerrit, is used as a central repository for SAP HANA XS Advanced development using SAP Web IDE for SAP HANA.

The Git repository can be hosted in a corporate internal Git/Gerrit installation or a subscription to an external provider such as GitHub, GitLab, or BitBucket. To familiarize yourself with the Git repository, follow along with our example. First, we'll create our Git repository in GitHub with these steps:

1. Log in to your GitHub account, and select **New Repository** to create a repository.
2. Provide the **Repository Name** and **Description**, check the **Initialize This Repository with a README** option, and click the **Create Repository** button. The repository will be created as illustrated in Figure 2.23.
3. Take note of the Git repository URL, which will be used in setting up the SAP HANA XS Advanced project in SAP Web IDE for SAP HANA.

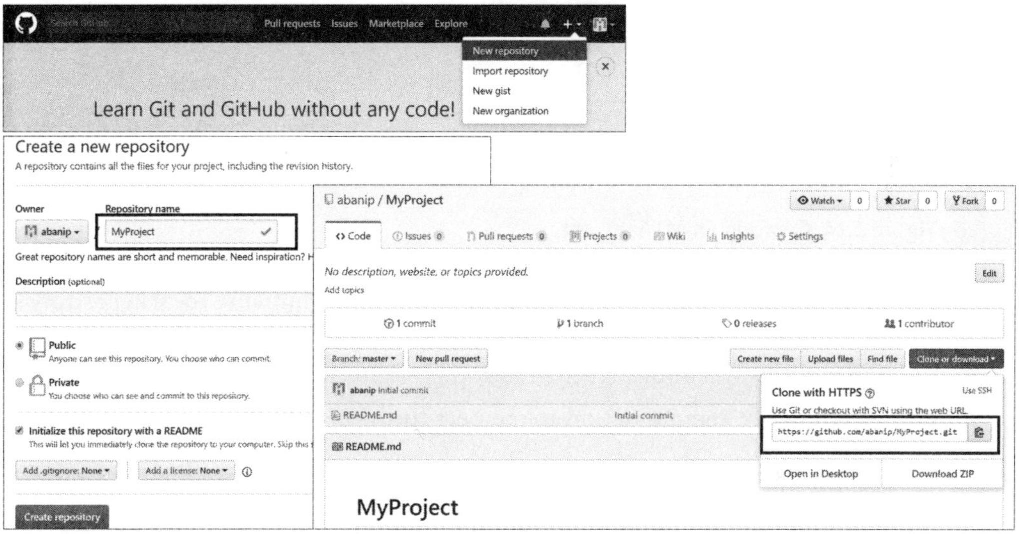

Figure 2.23 Create Git Repository in GitHub

4. Next, begin the project creation by logging in to SAP Web IDE for SAP HANA.
5. Select **File • Project from Template** to select a template for SAP HANA XS Advanced project creation. Choose the **Multi-Target Application Project** template.
6. Provide the **Project Name**, **Application ID**, **Application Version**, **Description**, and **Space** details, and select **Finish** to create the SAP HANA XS Advanced project, as shown in Figure 2.24. The new SAP HANA XS Advanced project will be created and displayed in the SAP Web IDE workspace.

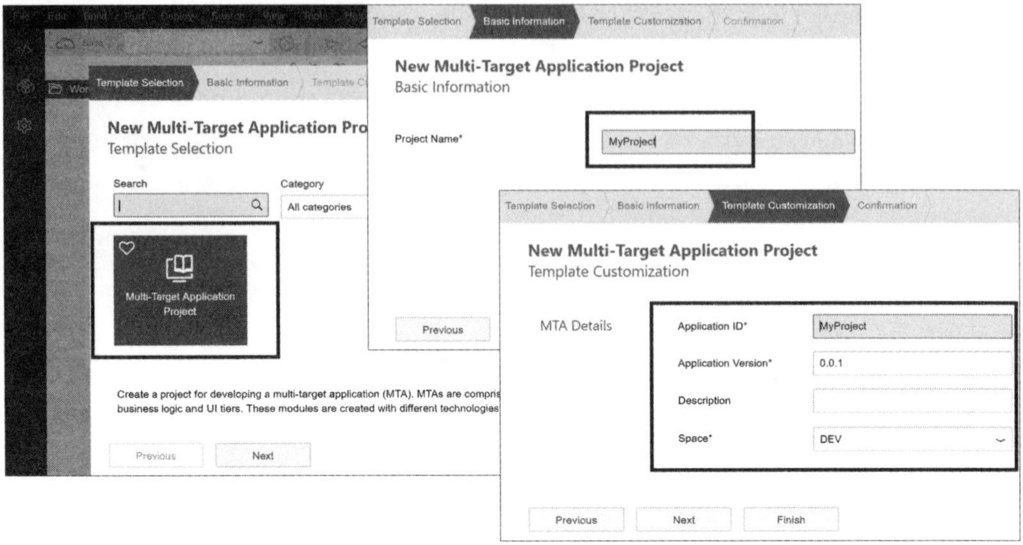

Figure 2.24 Creating an MTA Project

7. To create a local repository for the project, select **Git • Initialize Local Repository** in the context menu shown in Figure 2.25. The successful local repository initialization message will be displayed in the upper-right corner of SAP Web IDE.
8. Select the **Set Remote** option to connect the local repository to the remote Git repository.
9. When prompted, provide the URL of the GitHub repository created earlier. The remote Git server (GitHub in our example) may prompt you to authenticate again to establish the connection.
10. Setting the remote repository automatically does a fetch operation. You should now see the *README.md* file part of the project (the *README.md* file was created during the Git repository creation in GitHub). If the *README.md* file isn't yet pulled (it happens sometimes), select the **Pull** button in the **Git** menu or select **Git • Pull** in the context menu of the project to make sure the local repository has all the files from the remote repository.

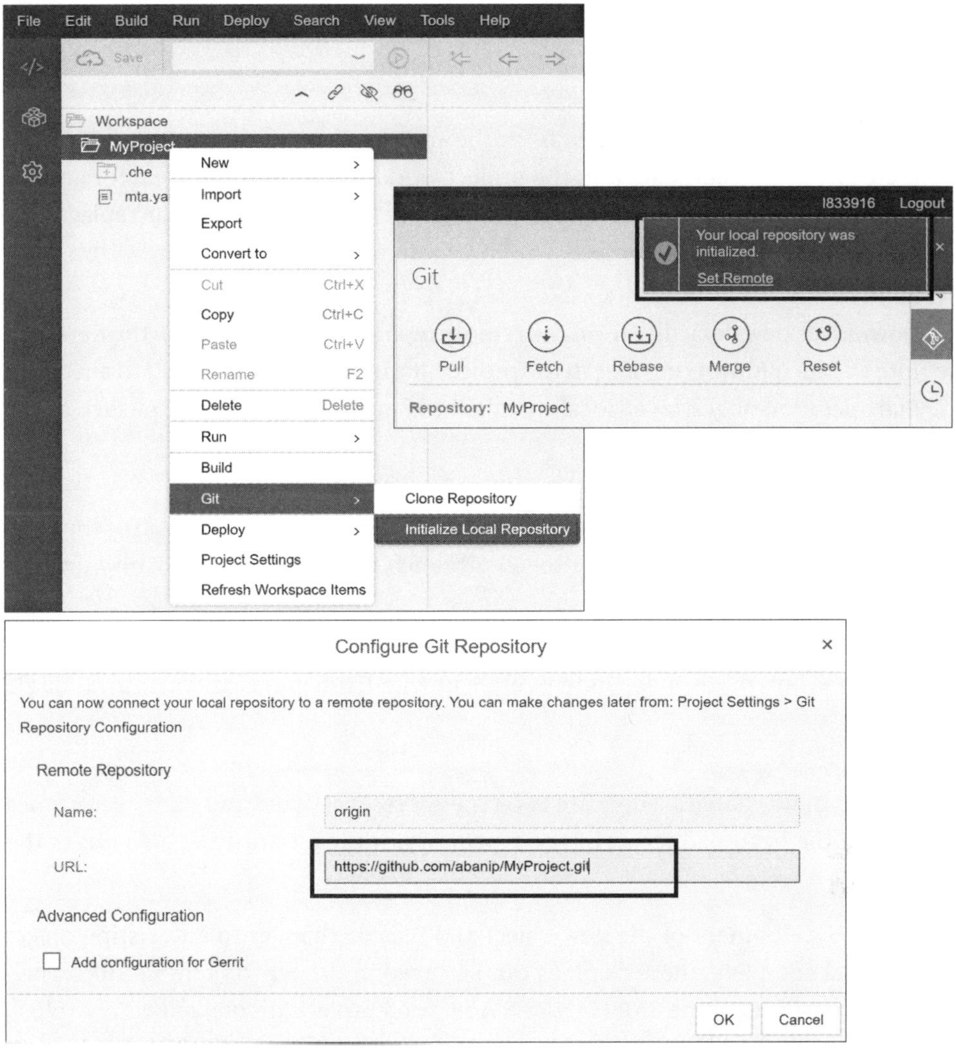

Figure 2.25 Setting Up the Git Repository

> **Note**
>
> Even though both the local and remote Git repositories are in synch at this point, it's a good practice to rebase the repository to establish proper synchronization between the local and remote repositories.

The **Git** pane of SAP Web IDE for SAP HANA has the following five buttons to work with the Git repository.

- **Fetch**
  Downloads only new data/files from the remote repository, but it doesn't integrate any of this new data into the project working files. **Fetch** is great for getting the latest view of the remote repository, and it doesn't override or replace any files/objects of the local project.
- **Pull**
  Downloads new data/files from the remote repository and integrates the new data into the current working files in the project. It's highly recommended to execute a **Pull** operation only after all local changes have been committed and pushed to the remote repository.
- **Rebase**
  Merges another branch into the current working branch and moves all of the local commits that are ahead of the rebased branch to the top of the history on that branch.
- **Merge**
  Takes two or more independent branches and integrates them into a single branch.
- **Reset**
  Used to undo changes. There are two types of resets (**Mixed** and **Hard**). Both types update the head and index of the repository, while a **Hard** reset also resets the working directory.

After the development of the new object and files or changes to an existing object and file are complete, these changes can be saved in the central remote Git repository. The new files in the SAP HANA XS Advanced project are marked with + (plus), and changes are highlighted with * (asterisk), as illustrated in Figure 2.26 ❷.

The new files and changes to existing files are published to the remote repository using the following **Stage** and **Commit & Push** process (see Figure 2.26 ❶), and the log is displayed in the SAP Web IDE console (Figure 2.26 ❹).

After the changes are saved in the remote Git repository, the files in the local project reflect the status with the • (bullet) sign, and files will also be available in the remote Git repository (Figure 2.26 ❸ and ❺, respectively).

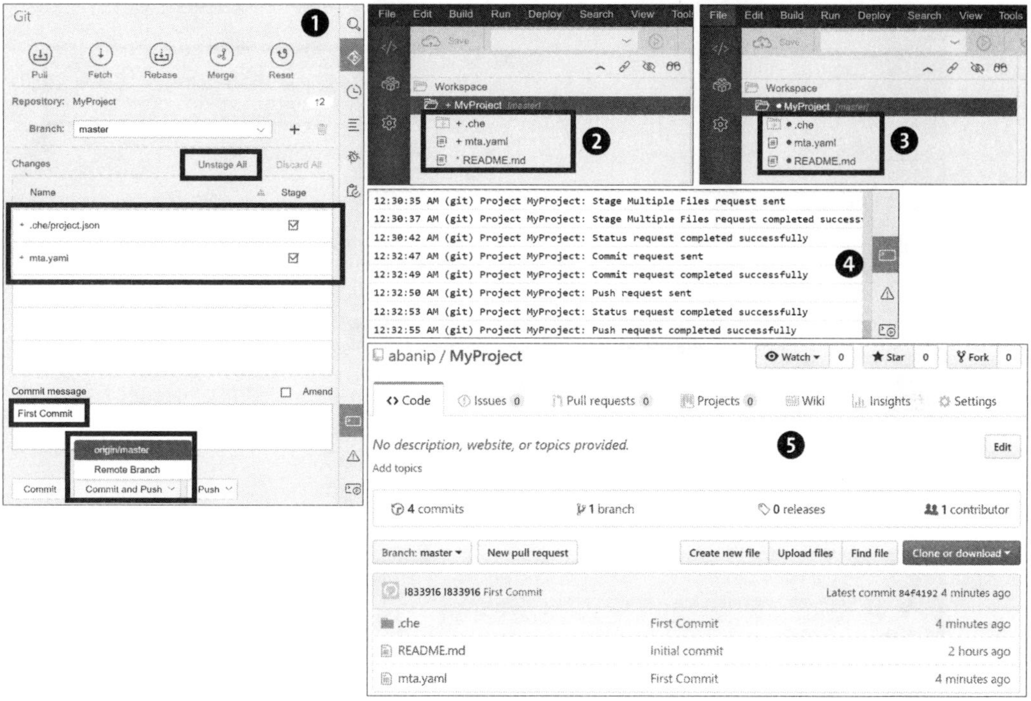

Figure 2.26 Git: Stage, Commit, Push

Finally, if another developer wants to work on your project or if you want to make changes for another project, the remote Git repository of the project can be cloned.

To create a project based on the Git repository, select **File • Git • Clone Repository,** or choose **Git • Clone Repository** in the context menu of the workspace as shown in Figure 2.27. Provide the Git repository **URL**, and select **Clone** to create the project. Upon successful cloning, the successful clone message will be displayed in the upper-right corner of SAP Web IDE. Select the **Create Local Branch** option to create the local repository for the project.

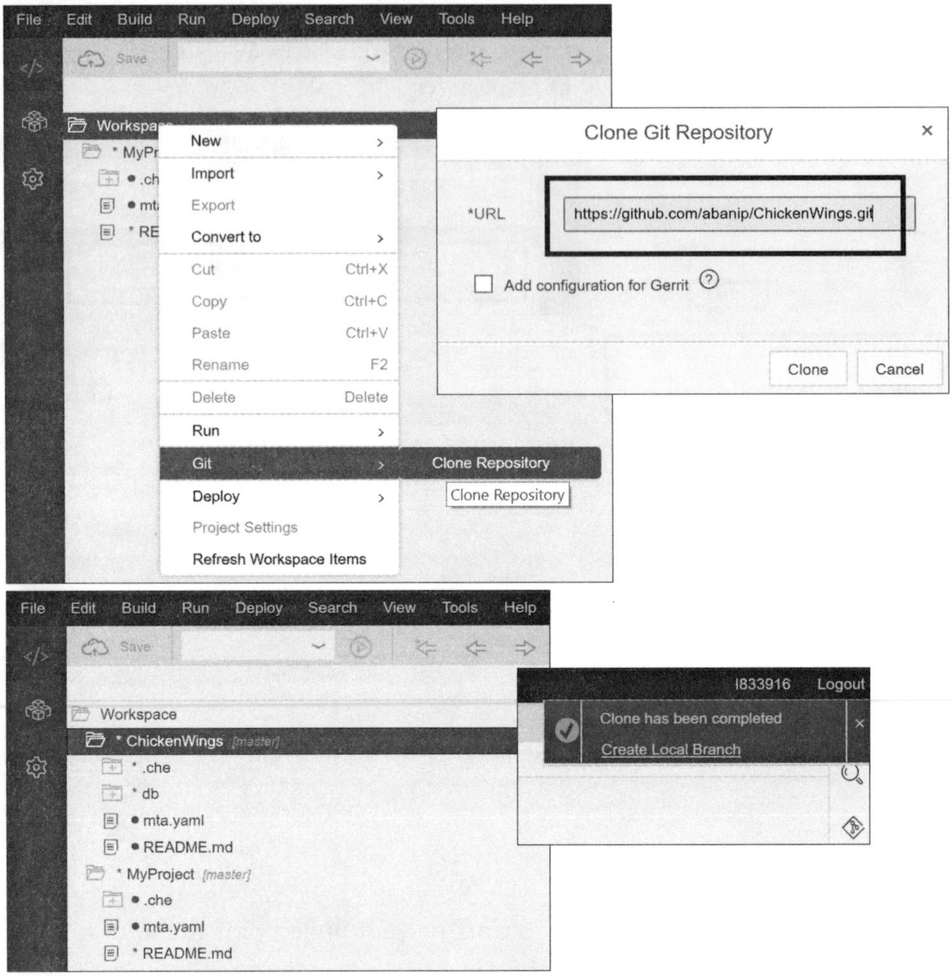

Figure 2.27 Cloning the Git Repository

2.7 Summary

We started this chapter with our discussion on the system landscape of traditional SAP systems and continued with the difference in the system landscape of SAP HANA XS Advanced to support continuous delivery and continuous integration.

Next, we discussed the installation and configuration of SAP HANA, express edition as a development environment in on-premise systems and the AWS public cloud.

You also learned about provisioning the SAP HANA system (including SAP HANA XS Advanced) as a service in the cloud using the SAP Cloud Platform.

We discussed the concept of organizations and spaces to share resources and isolate applications. Finally, we covered using Git as a source code management system and central code repository for SAP HANA XS Advanced development.

In the next chapter, we'll discuss development tools, including SAP HANA XS Advanced command-line interface (XSA CLI), SAP Web IDE for SAP HANA, SAP HANA database explorer, SAP HANA XS Advanced cockpit, SAP HANA Studio, and so on, to develop and administer SAP HANA XS Advanced applications.

Chapter 3
SAP HANA Development Tools

In this chapter, you'll learn about the tools that can be used to develop and administrate applications with the SAP HANA extended application services, advanced (SAP HANA XS Advanced) model.

The SAP HANA platform provides tools for developers and administrators to develop and monitor SAP HANA applications. The tools are designed to improve the productivity of developers and administrators by offering tightly integrated functionalities with the SAP HANA platform. A similar user interface (UI) is provided across the different tools to help end users work with the applications.

This chapter gives an overview of the different tools that help developers and administrators create new applications on the SAP HANA XS Advanced platform, as well as monitor and administrate the platform. We'll first highlight the functionalities and role of the XSA CLI client in the development cycle of an SAP HANA XS Advanced application.

Next, we'll describe the SAP Web IDE for SAP HANA development environment to create new SAP HANA XS Advanced applications. Furthermore, we'll reveal the functionalities of the SAP HANA database explorer, and we'll explain how developers can interact with SAP HANA database objects with this tool. In Section 3.4 of this chapter, we'll introduce the SAP HANA XS Advanced cockpit, which allows you to administrate and monitor the SAP HANA XS Advanced platform. Finally, in Section 3.5 of this chapter, we'll discuss other useful tools when working with the SAP HANA platform.

3.1 Command-Line Client

The SAP HANA XS Advanced platform offers a command-line client tool (XSA CLI client) for developers and administrators to connect with the SAP HANA XS Advanced runtime. The SAP HANA XSA CLI client allows developers and admins to perform administrative tasks such as creating services, starting and stopping applications, reviewing log files, and much more. In this section, we highlight the XSA CLI client activities that developers or administrator can perform. In later chapters, we'll demonstrate the usage of the XSA CLI client to develop and deploy our ChickenWings application.

Getting the XSA CLI client

The XSA CLI client is included in the installation of the SAP HANA XS Advanced platform. However, the XSA CLI client can also be downloaded from the SAP Service Marketplace. Details on the location of the XSA CLI client can be found in the SAP Service Marketplace and how to install the client tool on a computer are explained in SAP Note 2242468.

Developers or administrator of the SAP HANA XS Advanced platform can perform all required activities to deploy and administrate an SAP HANA XS Advanced application with the XSA CLI client. Developers can use the XSA CLI client to maintain the configuration of an SAP HANA XS Advanced application. For example, developers can create the services that are required by an SAP HANA XS Advanced application and maintain those services via the XSA CLI client. Administrators can use the XSA CLI client to create a new organization or space within the SAP HANA XS Advanced platform and configure those components. An action with the XSA CLI client can be initiated with the keyword `xs`. This keyword is followed by a specific `<command>`. Depending on the `<command>`, `[<Arguments>]` and `[<Options>]` can be specified to parameterize a command with the XSA CLI client. Executing a command with the XSA CLI client follows this syntax: `xs <command> [<Arguments>] [<Options>]`.

How to Get Help on a Command

The XSA CLI client includes a help functionality that lists details about the available XSA CLI client functionalities and how to use them. The command `xs help <-a>` will display information about all available XSA CLI client commands. The command `xs help <command>` displays information about a specific command when you replace `<command>` with the name of the command you're researching.

A number of command categories are available in the XSA CLI client, which will be discussed later in this section.

Where to Find More Information and Command-Line Reference

More information on the available commands of the XSA CLI client and supported parameters can be found in the official command-line reference from SAP at *https://bit.ly/2JHkc8H*.

3.1.1 Logon and Setup

The commands of this category support functionalities to log in to the SAP HANA XS Advanced environment, viewing user organization and space targets and setting application programming interface (API) URLs. Table 3.1 lists the available commands.

Command	Action
`login`	Log a user into SAP HANA XS Advanced.
`logout`	Log a user out of SAP HANA XS Advanced.
`target`	Set or view the target SAP HANA XS Advanced organization or space.
`api`	Set or view the API URL of SAP HANA XS Advanced.

Table 3.1 XSA CLI client Login and Setup Commands

The `xs login` command is the first command developers or administrator will execute to connect to the SAP HANA XS Advanced environment. After the user is successfully authenticated, further commands can be triggered with the XSA CLI client. A `username`, `password`, and `API URL` of the SAP HANA XS Advanced platform will be required when running the `xs login` command. When the user is authenticated successfully, the information about the API endpoint, username, name of the default organization, and name of the default space will be displayed in the XSA CLI client. Figure 3.1 ❶ shows the result of the `xs login` command.

This example highlights that the user is now in the SAP HANA organization and the SAP space. To change the target space and organization, developers can run the `xs target` command. The name of the space or organization can be specified as a parameter of the `xs target` command. To navigate to the development space of the SAP HANA XS Advanced platform, developers must run `xs target -s <space name>`. In this command, `<space name>` can be replaced with the name of the actual space on the SAP HANA XS Advanced platform. Figure 3.1 ❷ highlights the results of the `xs target` command.

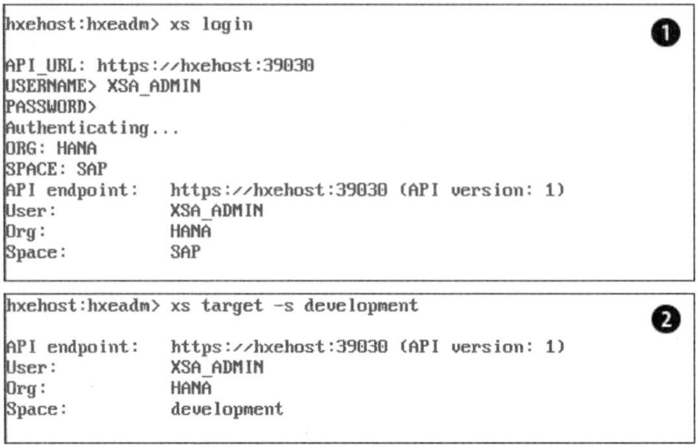

Figure 3.1 Running the xs login and xs target Commands with the XSA CLI Client

3.1.2 Application Management

The commands of the application management category allow developers or administrators to maintain SAP HANA XS Advanced applications such as SAP Web IDE for SAP HANA or custom-built applications. The available functionalities include but aren't limited to listing, deploying, starting, or stopping an SAP HANA XS Advanced application. Table 3.2 lists the available commands.

Command	Action
apps	List all applications available in the current space.
app	Display the status of a specific application.
push	Deploy a new SAP HANA XS Advanced application or update an existing one.
scale	Change or view the application parameters, such as disk-space limit or memory limit.
delete	Delete an SAP HANA XS Advanced application.
delete-app-instances	Delete one or more instances of an SAP HANA XS Advanced application.
rename	Rename an SAP HANA XS Advanced application.

Table 3.2 XSA CLI client Application Management Commands

Command	Action
start	Start an SAP HANA XS Advanced application.
stop	Stop an SAP HANA XS Advanced application.
restart	Restart an SAP HANA XS Advanced application.
restage	Restage an SAP HANA XS Advanced application.
events	Show all recent events related to an SAP HANA XS Advanced application.
files	Print a list of files in a directory or the contents of a file.
logs	List any recent logs of an SAP HANA XS Advanced application.
set-logging-level	Set the logging level of an SAP HANA XS Advanced application.
unset-logging-level	Reset the logging level of an SAP HANA XS Advanced application to its default.
list-logging-levels	List the logging levels that are configured for an SAP HANA XS Advanced application.
env	Show all environment variables set for an SAP HANA XS Advanced application.
Set-env	Set an environment variable for an SAP HANA XS Advanced application.
unset-env	Remove an environment variable for an SAP HANA XS Advanced application.
enable-debugging	Activate the debugging mode for an SAP HANA XS Advanced application.
disable-debugging	Deactivate the debugging mode for an SAP HANA XS Advanced application.
debugging-info	Display details of the configured debugging mode for an SAP HANA XS Advanced application.
java	Retrieve heap-dump or thread-dump information from an SAP HANA XS Advanced Java application.

Table 3.2 XSA CLI client Application Management Commands (Cont.)

Command	Action
nodejs	Retrieve heap-dump or thread-dump information from an SAP HANA XS Advanced Node.js application

Table 3.2 XSA CLI client Application Management Commands (Cont.)

For example, as a developer, run the xs apps command with the XSA CLI client. The program will return the list of applications that are deployed to the current SAP HANA XS Advanced space. Figure 3.2 highlights the results of the xs apps command.

```
hxehost:hxeadm> xs apps

Getting apps in org 'HANA        " / space "development" as XSA_ADMIN...
Found apps:

name                                  requested state   instances   memory   disk          urls
------------------------------------------------------------------------------------------------
di-builder                            STARTED           0/1         256 MB   <unlimited>
                                                                                   https://hxehost:51006
57IjcZ2w7vh85hXIChickenWings-java     STARTED           0/1         512 MB   <unlimited>
                                                                                   https://hxehost:51026
```

Figure 3.2 Running the xs apps Command with the XSA CLI Client

3.1.3 Services Management

The commands of the services management category allow developers or administrators to maintain the services of SAP HANA XS Advanced applications. These services implement a specific functionality and are independently deployable and scalable. A service can be consumed by different SAP HANA XS Advanced applications and form the basis of a microservices-based architecture. The available functionalities include but aren't limited to listing, creating, deleting, or updating the services of SAP HANA XS Advanced applications. Table 3.3 lists the available commands.

Command	Action
marketplace	List available SAP HANA XS Advanced services in the marketplace.
services	List all services in the current SAP HANA XS Advanced space.
managed-service	List all instances of a managed service in the current SAP HANA XS Advanced space,

Table 3.3 XSA CLI client Services Management Commands

Command	Action
create-service	Create a new SAP HANA XS Advanced service.
update-service	Update an existing SAP HANA XS Advanced service.
delete-service	Delete an existing SAP HANA XS Advanced service.
rename-service	Rename an existing SAP HANA XS Advanced service.
bind-service	Bind an SAP HANA XS Advanced service to an application.
unbind-service	Remove the binding between an SAP HANA XS Advanced service and an application.
service-keys	List all service keys for a specified SAP HANA XS Advanced service.
service-key	Displays a service key for an SAP HANA XS Advanced service.
create-service-key	Create a new service key for an SAP HANA XS Advanced service.
delete-service-key	Delete an existing service key for a specified SAP HANA XS Advanced service.
service-brokers	List all available SAP HANA XS Advanced service brokers.
create-service-broker	Create a new SAP HANA XS Advanced service broker.
delete-service-broker	Delete an existing SAP HANA XS Advanced service broker.
Update-service-broker	Update an existing SAP HANA XS Advanced service broker.
Rename-service-broker	Rename an existing SAP HANA XS Advanced service broker.
create-user-provided-service	Create an SAP HANA XS Advanced user-provided service.
update-user-provided-service	Update a user-provided service.

Table 3.3 XSA CLI client Services Management Commands (Cont.)

Command	Action
`register-service-url`	Register a URL for a named SAP HANA XS Advanced service.
`unregister-service-url`	Unregister an SAP HANA XS Advanced service URL.

Table 3.3 XSA CLI client Services Management Commands (Cont.)

For example, developers can run the `xs services` command with the XSA CLI client to get a list of services that are available in the current SAP HANA XS Advanced space. Figure 3.3 highlights the results of the `xs services` command.

```
hxehost:hxeadm> xs services

Getting services in org "HANA" / space "development" as XSA_ADMIN...
Found services:

name                                                service    plan          bound apps
-------------------------------------------------------------------------------------------------
XSA_DEV-tlhvhokcfotj44u4-ChickenWings-hdi-container  hana       hdi-shared    di-builder
                                                                   57Ijc22w7vh85hXIChickenWings-java
authorizationtest-uaa                               xsuaa      default
                                                                   57Ijc22w7vh85hXIChickenWings-java
auditlog                                            auditlog   free
testaudit                                           auditlog   free
                                                                   57Ijc22w7vh85hXIChickenWings-java
```

Figure 3.3 Running the xs services Command with the XSA CLI Client

3.1.4 Organizations and Spaces

Administrators use organization category commands to maintain organizations in the SAP HANA XS Advanced platform. Similarly, the commands in the spaces category are used to maintain spaces in the SAP HANA XS Advanced platform. We introduce the concepts of both organizations and spaces in Chapter 2 where we discuss the SAP HANA development environment. Table 3.4 lists the available commands.

Command	Action
`orgs`	List all defined organizations in the SAP HANA XS Advanced environment.
`create-org`	Create a new SAP HANA XS Advanced organization.
`delete-org`	Delete an SAP HANA XS Advanced organization.

Table 3.4 XSA CLI client Organizations and Spaces Commands

Command	Action
`rename-org`	Rename an SAP HANA XS Advanced organization.
`spaces`	List all defined SAP HANA XS Advanced spaces in the current organization.
`space`	Show details of a specific SAP HANA XS Advanced space.
`create-space`	Create a new SAP HANA XS Advanced space.
`delete-space`	Delete an SAP HANA XS Advanced space.
`rename-space`	Rename an SAP HANA XS Advanced space.
`update-space`	Update the configuration of an SAP HANA XS Advanced space.

Table 3.4 XSA CLI client Organizations and Spaces Commands (Cont.)

For example, developers can run the `xs orgs` command with the XSA CLI client to return the list of organizations available in the SAP HANA XS Advanced environment. Figure 3.4 ❶ highlights the results of the `xs orgs` command. In the same vein, if you run the `xs spaces` command ❷, the program will return the list of spaces available in the current SAP HANA XS Advanced organization.

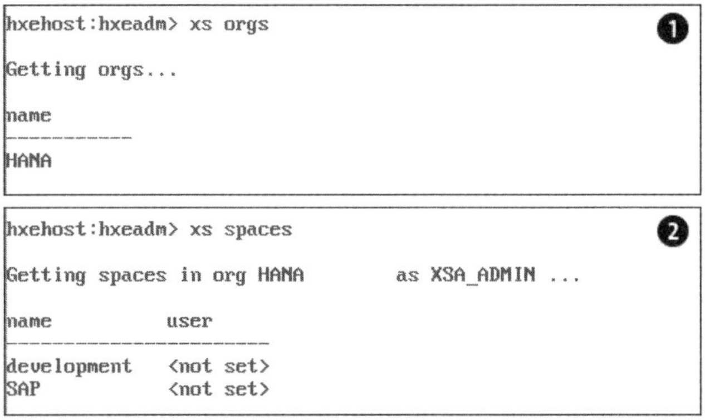

Figure 3.4 Running the xs orgs and xs spaces Commands with the XSA CLI Client

3.1.5 Domains

The commands in the domains category allow administrators to maintain domains of the SAP HANA XS Advanced platform. A domain is the address or hostname of the SAP HANA XS Advanced system. Table 3.5 lists the available commands.

Command	Action
domains	List all domains in the SAP HANA XS Advanced environment.
create-domain	Create a new domain in the SAP HANA XS Advanced environment.
delete-domain	Delete a domain from the SAP HANA XS Advanced environment.
set-certificate	Configure the Secure Sockets Layer (SSL) certificate to be used for a domain in the SAP HANA XS Advanced environment.
delete-certificate	Deletes the SSL certificate used by a domain in the SAP HANA XS Advanced environment.

Table 3.5 XSA CLI client Domains Commands

For example, developers can run the `xs domains` command with the XSA CLI client to return a list of domains registered in the SAP HANA XS Advanced environment. Figure 3.5 highlights the results of the `xs domains` command.

```
hxehost:hxeadm> xs domains

Getting domains...

name      type              org
-----------------------------------
hxehost   shared (default)
```

Figure 3.5 Running the xs domains Command with the XSA CLI Client

3.1.6 Certificates

The commands of the certificates category allow administrators to manage X.509 certificates of the SAP HANA XS Advanced platform. X.509 is a standard for certificates that is used to secure the communication for applications and services. Table 3.6 lists the available commands.

Command	Action
trusted-certificates	Retrieve the list of trusted certificates in the SAP HANA XS Advanced environment.
trust-certificate	Add a trusted X.509 certificate to the SAP HANA XS Advanced environment.

Table 3.6 XSA CLI client Certificates Commands

Command	Action
untrust-certificate	Remove a trusted X.509 certificate from the SAP HANA XS Advanced environment.

Table 3.6 XSA CLI client Certificates Commands (Cont.)

For example, developers can run the `xs trusted-certificates` command with the XSA CLI client to return a list of trusted certificates registered in the SAP HANA XS Advanced environment. Figure 3.6 highlights the results of the `xs trusted-certificates` command.

```
hxehost:hxeadm> xs trusted-certificates

Retrieving the list of trusted certificates as XSA_ADMIN...

Alias: SYSTEM_CERT
------------------------------------------------------------------------
Subject:                  CN=hxehost.localdomain,OU=HXE,OU=HANA SSL
Issuer:                   CN=hxehost.localdomain,OU=HXE,OU=HANA SSL
Valid from:               Tue Apr 03 16:25:22 UTC 2018
Valid until:              Fri Jan 01 00:00:01 UTC 2038
Signature algorithm:      SHA256withRSA
```

Figure 3.6 Running the xs trusted-certificates Command with the XSA CLI Client

3.1.7 Routes

The commands in the routes category allow Administrators or developers to manage application routes of the SAP HANA XS Advanced platform. We explain the concept of routes in Chapter 4 when we reveal the architecture of SAP HANA XS Advanced. Table 3.7 lists the available commands.

Command	Action
routes	List all routes in the current SAP HANA XS Advanced space.
create-route	Create a URL route in an SAP HANA XS Advanced space.
map-route	Assign or change the route assigned to an SAP HANA XS Advanced application.
unmap-route	Remove the URL route assigned to an SAP HANA XS Advanced application.
delete-route	Delete a route from an SAP HANA XS Advanced space.

Table 3.7 XSA CLI client Routes Commands

Developers can run the xs routes command with the XSA CLI client to return the list of routes configured in the current SAP HANA XS Advanced space. Figure 3.7 highlights the results of the xs routes command.

```
hxehost:hxeadm> xs routes

Getting routes in org "HANA" / space "development" as XSA_ADMIN...

host   domain    port    path   type   apps
-------------------------------------------------------------------------
       hxehost   51006   /      HTTP   di-builder
       hxehost   51026   /      HTTP   57IjcZ2w7vh85hXIChickenWings-java
       hxehost   51027   /      HTTP
```

Figure 3.7 Running the xs routes Command with the XSA CLI Client

3.1.8 Buildpacks

The commands in the buildpacks category allow administrators to manage the buildpacks of the SAP HANA XS Advanced platform. We explain the concept of buildpacks in Chapter 4 when we discuss the architecture of SAP HANA XS Advanced. Table 3.8 lists the available commands.

Command	Action
buildpacks	List all available buildpacks in the SAP HANA XS Advanced environment.
create-buildpack	Create a new buildpack in the SAP HANA XS Advanced environment.
update-buildpack	Update an existing buildpack in the SAP HANA XS Advanced environment.
rename-buildpack	Rename an existing buildpack in the SAP HANA XS Advanced environment.
delete-buildpack	Delete an existing buildpack from the SAP HANA XS Advanced environment.

Table 3.8 XSA CLI client Buildpacks Commands

Developers can run the xs buildpacks command with the XSA CLI client to return the list of buildpacks available in the SAP HANA XS Advanced environment. Figure 3.8 highlights the results of the xs buildpacks command.

```
hxehost:hxeadm> xs buildpacks

Getting buildpacks...

buildpacks              version   position   enabled   locked
----------------------------------------------------------------
sap_java_buildpack      1.6.20    1          true
sap_nodejs_buildpack    3.4.3     2          true
sap_python_buildpack    0.2.1     4          true
```

Figure 3.8 Running the xs buildpacks Command with the XSA CLI Client

3.1.9 Runtime Environments and the Blob Store

The commands of the runtime category allow administrators to display, search, update, or delete runtime information for the SAP HANA XS Advanced platform. A runtime environment, for example, Java or Node.js, is responsible for executing application code. The commands of the blob store category, on the other hand, allow administrators to maintain the contents of the blob store for the SAP HANA XS Advanced platform. We explain the concept of runtime environments as well as the blob store in SAP HANA XS Advanced in Chapter 4 when we discuss the platform's architecture. Table 3.9 lists the available commands.

Command	Action
runtimes	List all runtime components in the SAP HANA XS Advanced environment.
runtime	Display information about a specific runtime component in the SAP HANA XS Advanced environment.
create-runtime	Create a new runtime component in the SAP HANA XS Advanced environment.
update-runtime	Update the properties of an existing runtime component in the SAP HANA XS Advanced environment.
delete-runtime	Delete an existing runtime component from the SAP HANA XS Advanced environment.
search-runtime	Search for a runtime component that matches a specified query.
blob-store-info	Show information about the blob store.

Table 3.9 XSA CLI client Runtime Environments and Blob Store Commands

Command	Action
blob-set-list	List all blob sets in the blob store.
blob-list	List all blobs in the blob set.
blob-set-download	Download the content of a blob set as a ZIP file.
blob-store-gc	Start a garbage collection of the blob store.

Table 3.9 XSA CLI client Runtime Environments and Blob Store Commands (Cont.)

For example, developers can run the `xs runtimes` command with the XSA CLI client to return a list of runtimes available in the SAP HANA XS Advanced environment. Figure 3.9 highlights the results of the `xs runtimes` command.

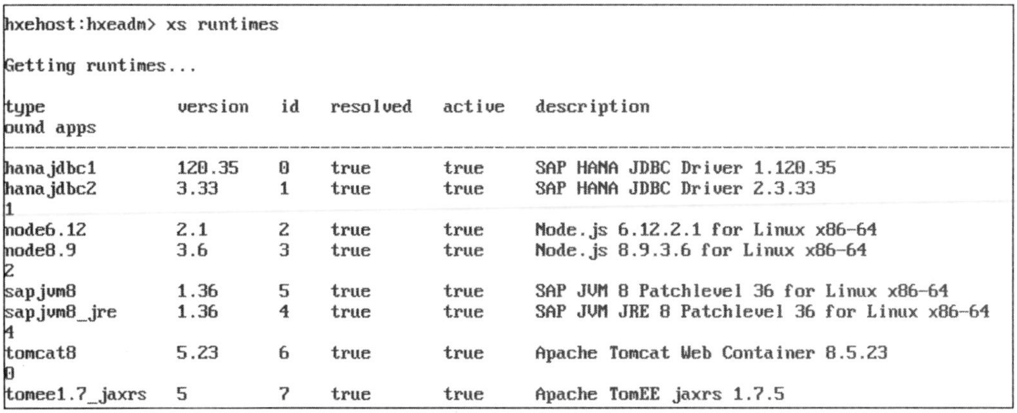
hxehost:hxeadm> xs runtimes
Getting runtimes...
type version id resolved active description
ound apps
hanajdbc1 120.35 0 true true SAP HANA JDBC Driver 1.120.35
hanajdbc2 3.33 1 true true SAP HANA JDBC Driver 2.3.33
1
node6.12 2.1 2 true true Node.js 6.12.2.1 for Linux x86-64
node8.9 3.6 3 true true Node.js 8.9.3.6 for Linux x86-64
2
sapjvm8 1.36 5 true true SAP JVM 8 Patchlevel 36 for Linux x86-64
sapjvm8_jre 1.36 4 true true SAP JVM JRE 8 Patchlevel 36 for Linux x86-64
4
tomcat8 5.23 6 true true Apache Tomcat Web Container 8.5.23
0
tomee1.7_jaxrs 5 7 true true Apache TomEE jaxrs 1.7.5

Figure 3.9 Running the xs runtimes Command with the XSA CLI Client

3.1.10 Tasks

The commands of the tasks category allow Administrators or developers to maintain and manage tasks that are related to SAP HANA XS Advanced applications. A task performs certain actions, for example, administrative actions, for an SAP HANA XS Advanced application. Tasks can be initiated manually or automatically on a given schedule. We explain the role and functionalities of tasks in SAP HANA XS Advanced more in depth in Chapter 6 when discussing the options to develop an application layer in the platform. Table 3.10 lists the available commands.

Command	Action
Tasks	List all tasks configured for an SAP HANA XS Advanced application.
run-task	Run a specified task on an SAP HANA XS Advanced application.
cancel-task	Cancel a specified task on an SAP HANA XS Advanced application.

Table 3.10 XSA CLI Client Tasks Commands

3.1.11 User Administration

The commands of the user administration category allow administrators to maintain users of the SAP HANA XS Advanced platform. Table 3.11 lists the available commands.

Command	Action
Users	List all users in the SAP HANA XS Advanced environment.
purge-users	Delete all users that aren't known to the SAP HANA XS Advanced User Account and Authentication (UAA) service.
space-users	Show SAP HANA XS Advanced space users by role.
set-space-role	Assign a space role to a user.
unset-space-role	Revoke a space role from a user.
org-users	Show organization users by role.
set-org-role	Assign an organization role to a user.
unset-org-role	Revoke an organization role from a user.
Roles	Display all existing application roles.
role-collections	Display a list of all existing application role collections.
role-collection	Display details of a specific application role collection.
create-role-collection	Create a new application role collection.
update-role-collection	Modify an existing application role collection.
assigned-role-collections	Display a list of the application role collections currently assigned to a specific user.

Table 3.11 XSA CLI Client User Administration Commands

Command	Action
`assign-role-collection`	Assign an application role collection to a specific user.
`unassign-role-collection`	Remove an assigned application role collection from a specific user.

Table 3.11 XSA CLI Client User Administration Commands (Cont.)

For example, developers can run the `xs users` command with the XSA CLI client to return the list of users available in the SAP HANA XS Advanced environment. Figure 3.10 ❶ highlights the results of the `xs runtimes` command.

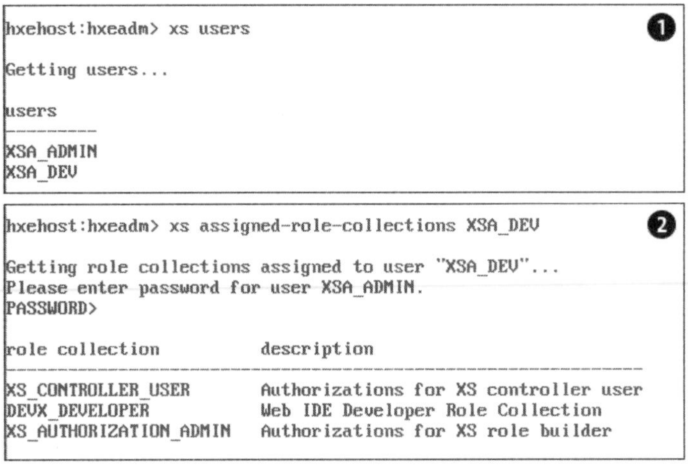

Figure 3.10 Running the xs users and xs assigned-role-collections Commands with the XSA CLI Client

Furthermore, developers can execute the `xs assigned-role-collections <username>` command with the XSA CLI client by replacing the `<username>` with the name of an actual user on the SAP HANA XS Advanced environment. The program will return the role collections that are assigned to the SAP HANA XS Advanced user. Figure 3.10 ❷ highlights the results of the `xs assigned-role-collections` command.

3.1.12 Configuration

The commands of the configuration category allow administrators to maintain environment variables of the SAP HANA XS Advanced platform. Environment variables can be accessed by SAP HANA XS Advanced applications and describe the environment in which the applications run. Table 3.12 lists the available commands.

Command	Action
running-environment-variable-group	Retrieve the contents of an environment variable group.
set-running-environment-variable-group	Create a running environment variable group by passing parameters.
staging-environment-variable-group	Retrieve the contents of the environment variable group.
set-staging-environment-variable-group	Create a staging environment variable group by passing parameters.

Table 3.12 XSA CLI Client Configuration Commands

3.1.13 Plug-Ins

The commands of the plug-ins category allow administrators or developers to install archives and deploy applications on the SAP HANA XS Advanced platform in a flexible way, for example. Table 3.13 lists the available commands.

Command	Action
deploy	Deploy a new SAP HANA XS Advanced application.
bg-deploy	Deploy a new SAP HANA XS Advanced application zero-downtime deployment.
undeploy	Undeploy an existing SAP HANA XS Advanced application.
install	Install a new software component.
uninstall	Uninstall an existing software component.
display-installation-logs	Display logs generated by the Product Installer.
list-components	List all installed software components.
list-products	List all installed products.
mta	Display information about a deployed SAP HANA XS Advanced application.

Table 3.13 XSA CLI Client Plug-Ins Commands

Command	Action
mtas	List all deployed SAP HANA XS Advanced applications.
Mta-ops	List all active operations for SAP HANA XS Advanced applications.
plugins	List all commands that are provided as plug-ins.
download-mta-op-logs	Download the log files for one or more SAP HANA XS Advanced applications.
purge-mta-config	Purge all configuration entries and subscriptions that are no longer valid.
deploy-target	Display information about a target platform for SAP HANA XS Advanced applications.
deploy-targets	List all target platforms for the deployment of SAP HANA XS Advanced applications.
create-deploy-target	Create a target platform for deployment of SAP HANA XS Advanced applications.
update-deploy-target	Update a target platform for a deployment of SAP HANA XS Advanced applications.
delete-deploy-target	Delete a target platform for a deployment of SAP HANA XS Advanced applications.

Table 3.13 XSA CLI Client Plug-Ins Commands (Cont.)

3.1.14 Other Commands

The commands in the other commands category allow administrators to display details of the installed versions of the SAP HANA XS Advanced platform. Table 3.14 lists the available commands.

Command	Action
version	Show the SAP HANA XS Advanced server version information.
help	Access the help feature of the XSA CLI client.
system-info	Show information about the SAP HANA XS Advanced system.

Table 3.14 XSA CLI Client Other Commands

Developers can run the `xs version` command with the XSA CLI client to return server information about the SAP HANA XS Advanced system. Figure 3.11 highlights the results of the `xs version` command.

```
hxehost:hxeadm> xs version

Client version: xs v1.0.82

Server version information:
   name                        = XS Controller
   support                     = http://service.sap.com/message
   build                       = v1.0.82
   version                     = 1
   softwareVersion             = 1.0.82.303870
   contentVersion              = 1.0.82.303870
   overallState                = READY
   user                        = <not set>
   description                 = SAP HANA XS Advanced Runtime
   controllerEndpoint          = https://hxehost:39030
   authorizationEndpoint       = https://hxehost:39032/uaa-security
   loggingEndpoint             = <not set>
   allowDebug                  = true
   acceptEncoding              = gzip, x-gzip
   limits                      = memory: <not set>, apps: <not set>, app uris: <not set>, services
                               set>
   usage                       = memory: <not set>, apps: 44, app uris: 42, services: 40
   databaseType                = HANA_MULTI
   databaseInfo                = HDB 2.00.030.00.1522210459

Registered service URLs:
   deploy-service                       = https://hxehost:51004
   product-installer                    = https://hxehost:51005
   hrtt-service                         = https://hxehost:51009
   hrtt-core                            = https://hxehost:51012
   di-cert-admin-ui                     = https://hxehost:51023
   di-space-enablement-ui               = https://hxehost:51024
   webide                               = https://hxehost:53075
   job-scheduler-service-dashboard      = https://hxehost:51032
   xsa-cockpit                          = https://hxehost:51036
```

Figure 3.11 Running the xs version Command with the XSA CLI Client

Deploying an Application

The role of the XSA CLI client during the deployment of an SAP HANA XS Advanced application will be discussed in Chapter 10 where we'll demonstrate a practical example of the process as well.

3.2 SAP Web IDE for SAP HANA

SAP Web IDE for SAP HANA is a browser-based development environment that can be used to develop SAP HANA XS Advanced applications. SAP Web IDE for SAP HANA provides functionalities that enable developers to create an end-to-end application consisting of a web UI or a mobile UI, business logic, and SAP HANA data models. In this section, we highlight the functionalities of SAP Web IDE for SAP HANA. We'll use SAP Web IDE for SAP HANA extensively throughout this book to demonstrate its capabilities and provide practical examples. For example, we develop the data model of our ChickenWings application in Chapter 5 and develop its application layer in Chapter 6.

SAP Web IDE for SAP HANA supports developers with a variety of features, for example, syntax-aware editors for the creation of application code, and graphical editors for the design and development of data models and calculation views, as well as tools for inspecting, testing, and debugging the source code of an SAP HANA XS Advanced application. SAP Web IDE for SAP HANA supports developers in creating SAP HANA content and models, developing UIs with SAPUI5, and developing business code with Node.js, SAP HANA XS JavaScript (XSJS), or Java. It also integrates with Git version management systems. Developers also benefit from performance analysis tools for SQLScript and calculation views, which are integrated in SAP Web IDE for SAP HANA. This functionality helps developers create the most performant data models and applications. By following a test-driven development approach via an integrated test framework, developers can create and run the unit tests directly in SAP Web IDE for SAP HANA.

Unit Tests in SAP HANA XS Advanced

We discuss the options to develop unit tests with SAP Web IDE for SAP HANA in Chapter 6 when describing how to develop an application layer for SAP HANA XS Advanced.

SAP Web IDE for SAP HANA provides wizards and code templates to help developers get started more quickly and efficiently. The tool automatically updates dependencies between the development and build artifacts. Developers can create, run, and deploy applications directly from SAP Web IDE for SAP HANA.

Access to SAP Web IDE for SAP HANA

Only users of the SAP HANA XS Advanced platform who have the required privileges can access SAP Web IDE for SAP HANA. Developers need the DEVX_DEVELOPER role collection to be allowed access to SAP Web IDE for SAP HANA.

Developers can access SAP Web IDE for SAP HANA through a web browser. The workspace allows developers to create new applications from scratch, create an application from a template via a wizard, clone an application from a Git repository, or import an existing application. SAP Web IDE for SAP HANA offers graphical modelers for data models or calculation views, which enhance the development experience. Developers can create Java or Node.js applications directly in SAP Web IDE for SAP HANA.

Furthermore, the tool offers an integrated debugger, test executions, and source code navigation. Developers also benefit from HTML5, JavaScript, and SAPUI5 syntax assistance. Different applications, such as Java, Node.js, or HTML5, can be started directly from SAP Web IDE for SAP HANA, and developers can build, run, and deploy them here as well. Figure 3.12 displays SAP Web IDE for SAP HANA.

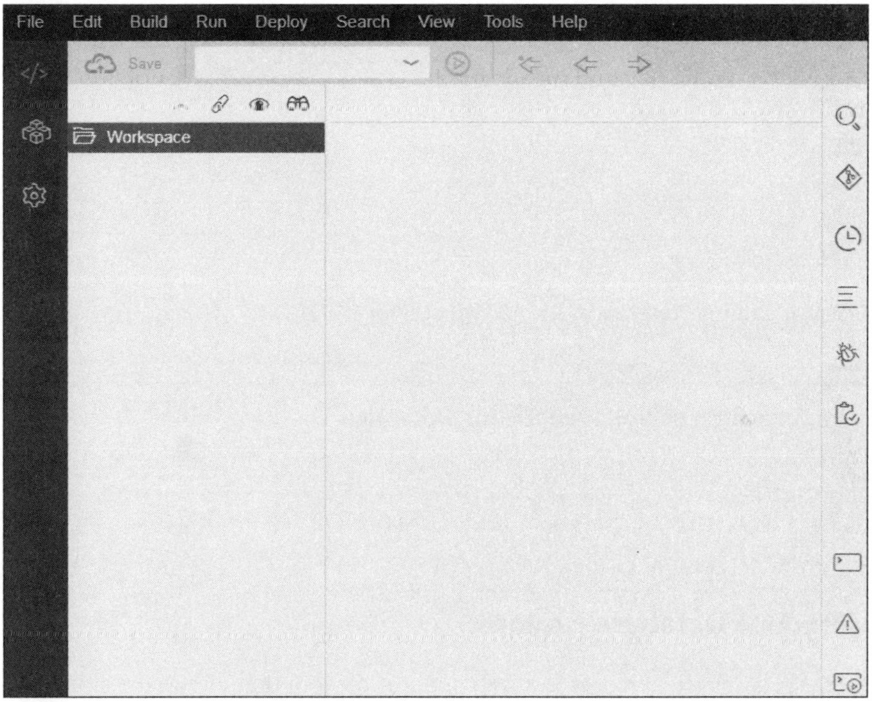

Figure 3.12 SAP Web IDE for SAP HANA

Developers can maintain preferences of SAP Web IDE for SAP HANA by clicking on the preference icon in the left-side menu. A new dialog appears that allows developers to change settings such as **Code Check**, **Code Completion**, **Code Editor**, **Data Preview**, **Git Settings**, and SAP HANA **Modeler** preferences. Figure 3.13 displays the preference settings in SAP Web IDE for SAP HANA.

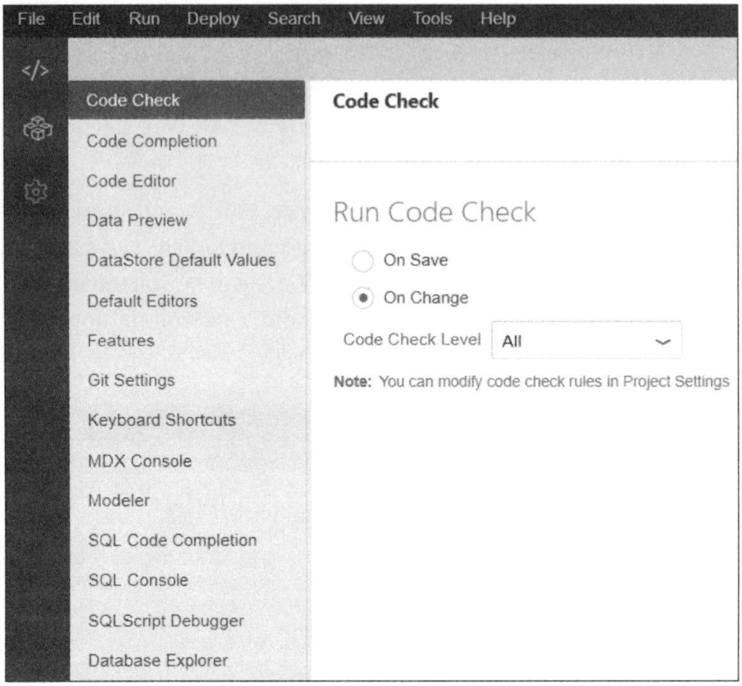

Figure 3.13 Maintaining Preferences in SAP Web IDE for SAP HANA

Further Information on SAP Web IDE for SAP HANA

More information on SAP Web IDE for SAP HANA is available in the central release SAP Note 2510063.

3.3 SAP HANA Database Explorer

The SAP HANA database explorer is a web application tool that allows developers to access and test SAP HANA database objects in SAP HANA XS Advanced applications, as well as access database content from SAP HANA database schemas. We'll use the SAP HANA database explorer in our practical examples throughout this book, for example, when we create the data model for our ChickenWings application in Chapter 5. In this section, we highlight the functionalities of the SAP HANA database explorer.

Developers use the SAP HANA database explorer to view and interact with database content such as calculation views or stored procedures that are part of an SAP HANA XS Advanced application. The tool allows developers to verify the correct deployment of database content, debug stored procedures, and access the database. The SAP HANA database explorer includes the following functionalities:

- **Database catalog browser**
  Developers can browse, view, run, and visualize the content of all types of catalog objects, for example, tables, calculation views, stored procedures, table functions, and synonyms.
- **SQL Console**
  Developers can create SQLScript, run SQL commands, and visualize the content of objects (e.g., stored procedures and table functions) in the SQL Console directly.
- **SQL analyzer**
  Developers can view query plans and analyze the performance of SQL queries.
- **MDX console**
  Developers can create and run multidimensional expression (MDX) queries.
- **SQL debugger**
  Developers can view the call stack and set breakpoints, as well as view and evaluate expressions and variables.

In SAP Web IDE for SAP HANA, developers access the SAP HANA database explorer by clicking on the SAP HANA database explorer icon in the left-side menu. Figure 3.14 highlights the SAP HANA database explorer menu icon in SAP Web IDE for SAP HANA.

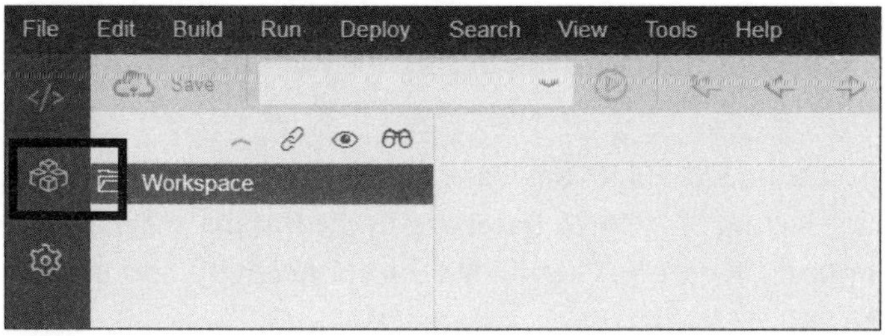

Figure 3.14 Opening the SAP HANA Database Explorer from SAP Web IDE for SAP HANA

The SAP HANA database explorer application opens within SAP Web IDE for SAP HANA. Developers don't have to change the application window to start working with the SAP HANA database explorer. Figure 3.15 displays the SAP HANA database explorer in SAP Web IDE for SAP HANA.

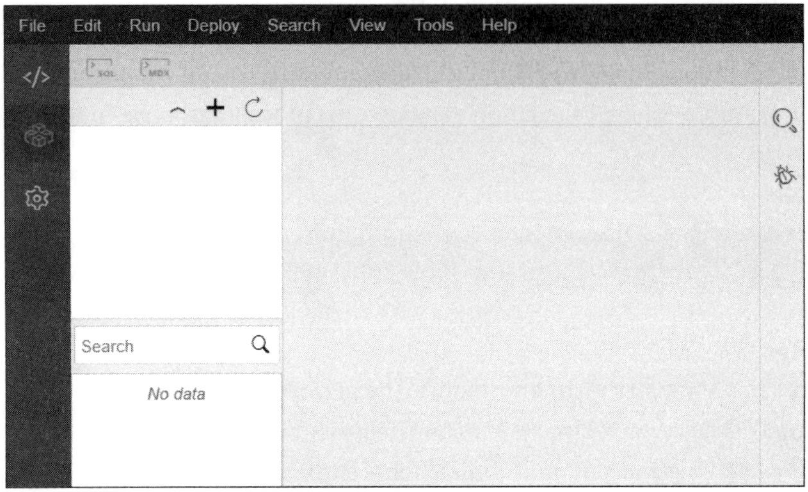

Figure 3.15 SAP HANA Database Explorer

Developers can connect to an SAP HANA database container by clicking on the plus icon + in the menu and then selecting the **HDI Container** option in the **Database Type** dropdown in the dialog that appears. Furthermore, this dialog allows developers to search for SAP HANA database containers to connect. The connectivity to an SAP HANA database container enables developers to browse through database objects of an SAP HANA XS Advanced application. In addition, developers can execute database objects and debug stored procedures and table functions. Figure 3.16 highlights the SAP HANA database explorer application with the connectivity to an SAP HANA database container.

Developers can also connect to an SAP HANA database schema by clicking on the plus icon + in the menu and selecting **SAP HANA Database** in the **Database Type** dropdown in the dialog that appears. Figure 3.17 highlights the connectivity option to an SAP HANA database in the SAP HANA database explorer.

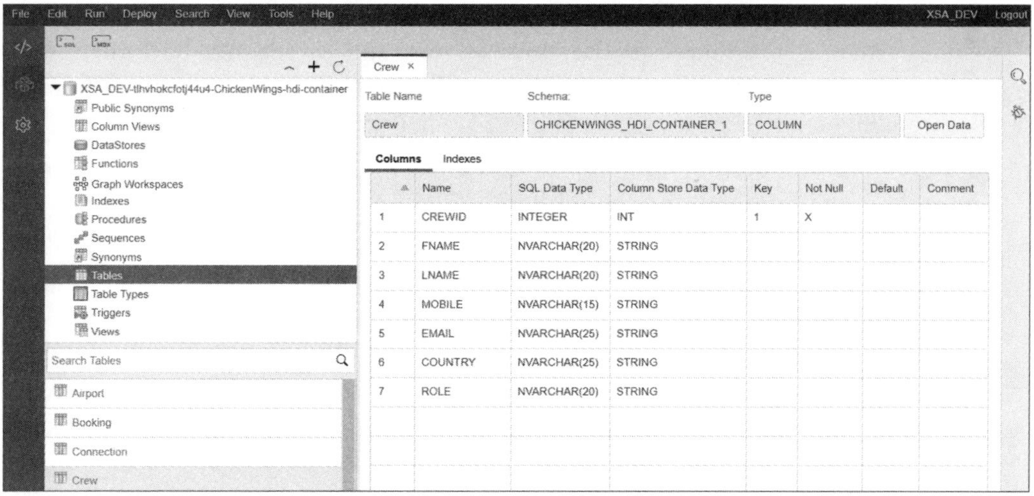

Figure 3.16 Connecting the SAP HANA Database Explorer to an SAP HANA Container

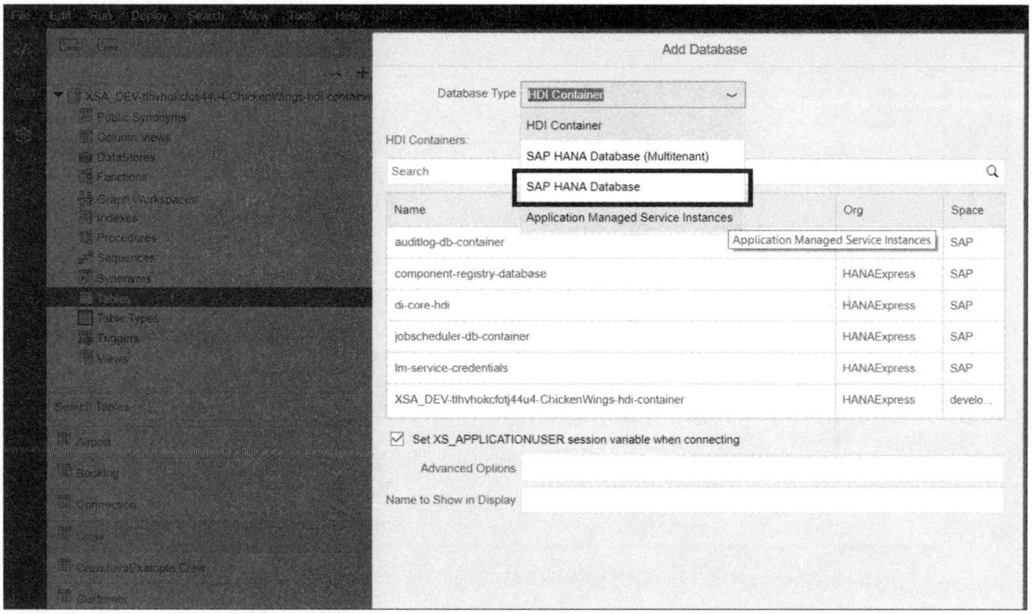

Figure 3.17 Connecting the SAP HANA Database Explorer to an SAP HANA Database

Developers must provide the **Host** and **Instance number** of the SAP HANA database. An SAP HANA database **User** and **Password** are also required to connect. Click on the **OK** button to establish the connectivity to the SAP HANA database (see Figure 3.18).

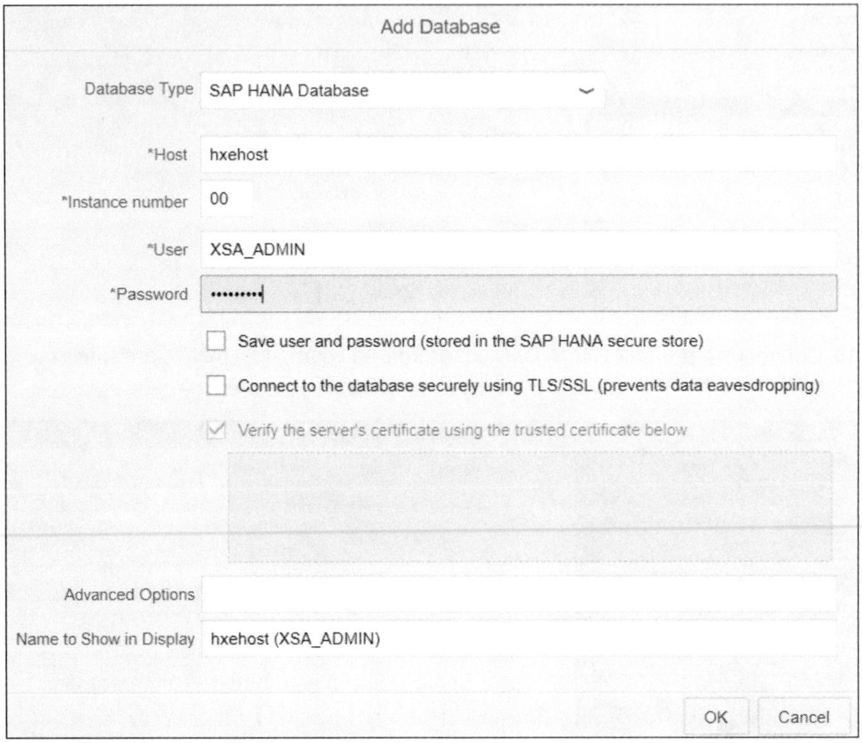

Figure 3.18 Connect SAP HANA Database Explorer to an SAP HANA Container: Add Database

Figure 3.19 highlights the connectivity to an SAP HANA database with the SAP HANA database explorer.

Further Information on the SAP HANA Database Explorer

More information on the SAP HANA database explorer can be found in the central release SAP Note 2373065.

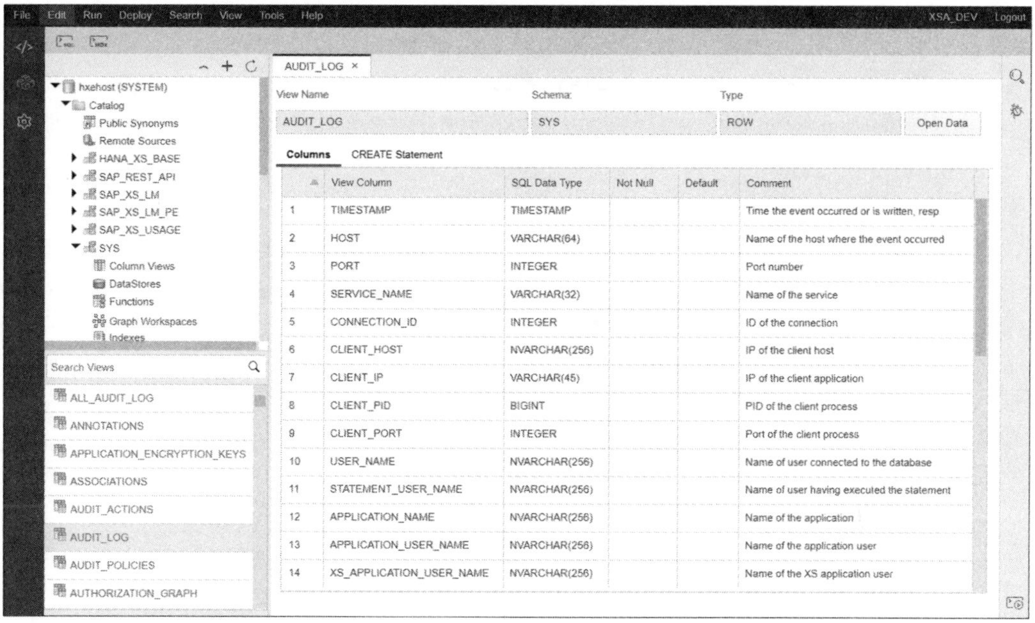

Figure 3.19 Connecting the SAP HANA Database Explorer to an SAP HANA Container

3.4 SAP HANA XS Advanced Cockpit

Administrators and developers use the SAP HANA XS Advanced cockpit to manage the SAP HANA XS Advanced environment and application components. Some administration functionalities enable administrators to maintain and operate the various components of the SAP HANA XS Advanced platform. This section introduces the SAP HANA XS Advanced cockpit. We'll demonstrate its functionalities in other chapters, for example, in Chapter 8, when we reveal the security mechanisms of SAP HANA XS Advanced.

SAP HANA XS Advanced Admin Tool

Note that in previous SAP HANA releases, before SAP HANA 2.0 SPS 03, the SAP HANA XS Advanced Admin tool was used in the SAP HANA XS Advanced platform. However, since the release of SAP HANA 2.0 SPS 03, the SAP HANA XS Advanced Admin tool has been deprecated and replaced with the SAP HANA XS Advanced cockpit. In this book, we'll discuss the relevant administrative functionalities based on the capabilities of the SAP HANA XS Advanced cockpit. Read SAP Note 2609527 for more details regarding these admin tools.

Table 3.15 lists the available functionalities within the SAP HANA XS Advanced cockpit.

Feature	Functionality
Application Monitor	Monitor the system usage of the applications running in the SAP HANA XS Advanced runtime.
Organization and Space Management	Create, list, or delete user organizations and spaces in the SAP HANA XS Advanced runtime.
Application Role Builder	Maintain and manage user roles and role collections in SAP HANA.
SAML Identity Providers Configuration	Configure Security Assertion Markup Language (SAML) Identity Providers (IdP) for SAP HANA XS Advanced applications that use SAML assertions as the login authentication method.
User Management	Create and manage users for SAP HANA XS Advanced applications.
SAP HANA Logical Database Setup	Manage, maintain, and configure SAP HANA logical database for use with SAP HANA XS Advanced applications.
SAP HANA Service Broker Configuration	Manage the mapping of SAP HANA databases to an organization or space.
Host Management	View the list of SAP HANA hosts that are pinned to SAP HANA XS Advanced applications or spaces.
XS Advanced Audit Logs	View all audit logs for any previous operation. In addition, group or filter the audit logs by different criteria such as organization, space, user, and application.
Trusted Certificates	Manage and maintain the certificates used to establish secure and trusted connections between SAP HANA systems and SAP HANA XS Advanced applications.
Job Scheduler Service Dashboard	Create, schedule, and manage long-running operations and jobs in the SAP HANA XS Advanced runtime environment.

Table 3.15 Functionalities of the SAP HANA XS Advanced Cockpit

As shown in Figure 3.20, navigate to **Tools • SAP HANA XS Advanced Cockpit** of SAP Web IDE for SAP HANA to open the **SAP HANA XS Advanced Cockpit** screen in a new web browser tab.

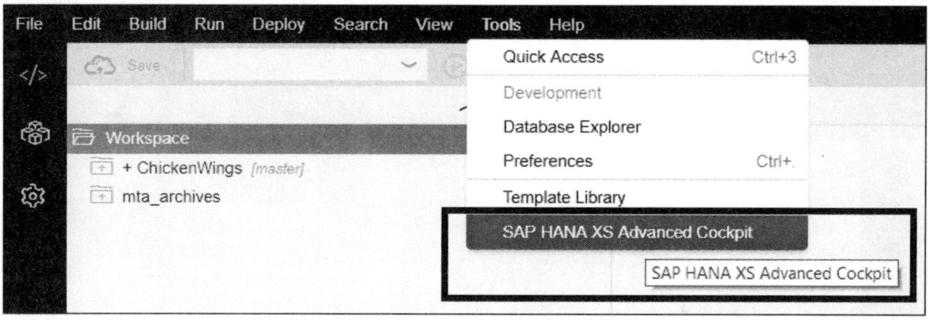

Figure 3.20 Open the SAP HANA XS Advanced Cockpit from SAP Web IDE for SAP HANA

The initial **SAP HANA XS Advanced Cockpit** screen displays the available organizations in the SAP HANA XS Advanced environment (Figure 3.21). Administrators or developers can access the functionalities to configure the SAP HANA XS Advanced platform or applications in this tool. Administrators can click on the name of an organization on the landing page to navigate to the SAP HANA XS Advanced spaces within the organization.

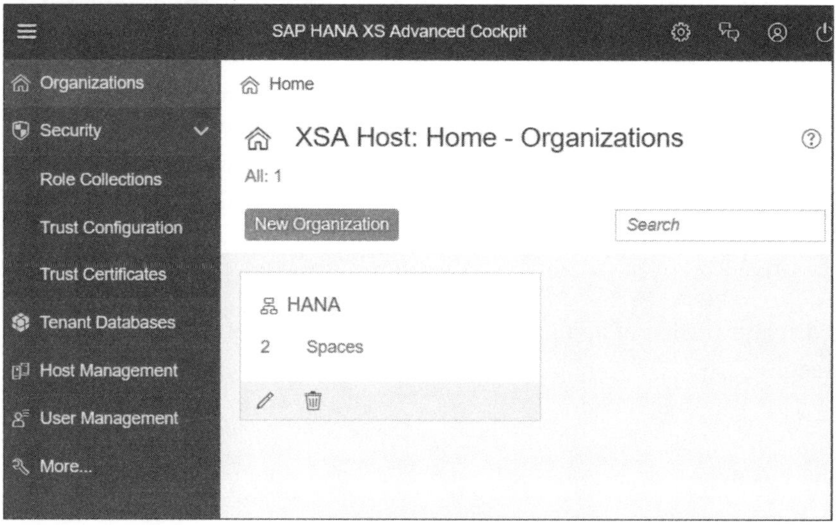

Figure 3.21 SAP HANA XS Advanced Cockpit: Organizations

SAP HANA XS Advanced applications are deployed to a space in the SAP HANA XS Advanced environment, so administrators can navigate between the spaces of an organization in the **SAP HANA XS Advanced Cockpit** screen. Administrators can also display and configure the settings of an SAP HANA XS Advanced application by selecting a space in the **SAP HANA XS Advanced Cockpit** screen (Figure 3.22).

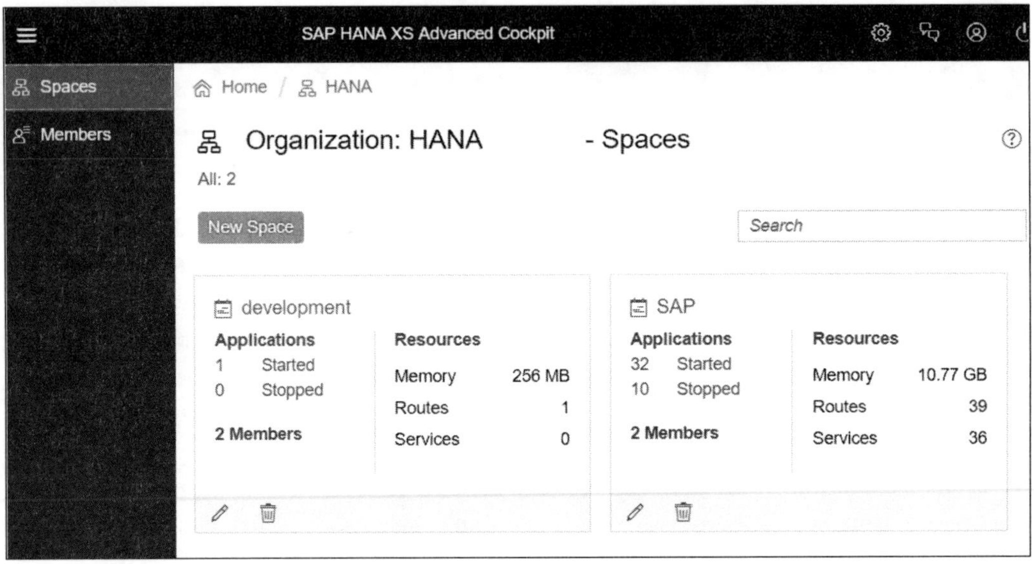

Figure 3.22 Organizations and Spaces in the SAP HANA XS Advanced Cockpit

Administrators can display all available applications within an SAP HANA XS Advanced space by selecting the **Applications** option in the left-side menu of the screen. An overview is provided of all available applications and their statuses. By clicking on an application, administrators can perform administrative tasks, including starting or stopping an application, reviewing application log files, and maintaining security information.

Figure 3.23 displays the list of applications in a space in the **SAP HANA XS Advanced Cockpit** screen.

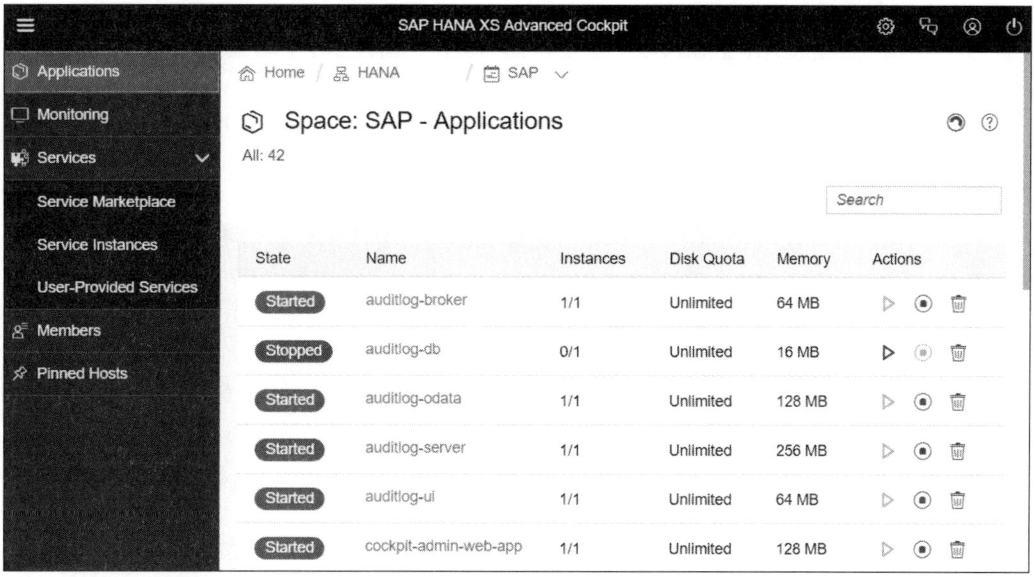

Figure 3.23 Applications in the SAP HANA XS Advanced Cockpit

3.5 Other SAP HANA Database Development Tools

In the previous sections, we gave an overview of the tools of the SAP HANA XS Advanced platform to develop and administrate applications. In this section, we provide an overview of useful tools that were already available before the introduction of the SAP HANA XS Advanced platform that help developers and administrators develop and manage SAP HANA applications.

3.5.1 SAP HANA Studio

Based on the Eclipse development environment, SAP HANA Studio is used for developing native SAP HANA applications. SAP HANA Studio is also used by administrators to administrate and monitor the SAP HANA database. Administrators can view database content such as schemas and tables, administrate the SAP HANA database, and interact with the SAP HANA XS repository. However, SAP HANA Studio can't be used to develop SAP HANA XS Advanced applications; instead, developers must use SAP Web IDE for SAP HANA application for that purpose. Following are the essential perspectives and functionalities of SAP HANA Studio:

- **SAP HANA development perspective**
  This perspective allows developers to create native SAP HANA XS applications but not SAP HANA XS Advanced applications. Developers must work with SAP Web IDE for SAP HANA to create native applications for the SAP HANA XS Advanced platform.
- **SAP HANA Modeler perspective**
  This perspective allows developers to create SAP HANA models for the SAP HANA XS environment. Note that developers must work with SAP Web IDE for SAP HANA to create SAP HANA views on the SAP HANA XS Advanced platform.
- **SAP HANA administration console**
  This functionality enables SAP HANA administrators to manage the SAP HANA database.

Figure 3.24 displays the **SAP HANA Modeler** perspective in the SAP HANA Studio application.

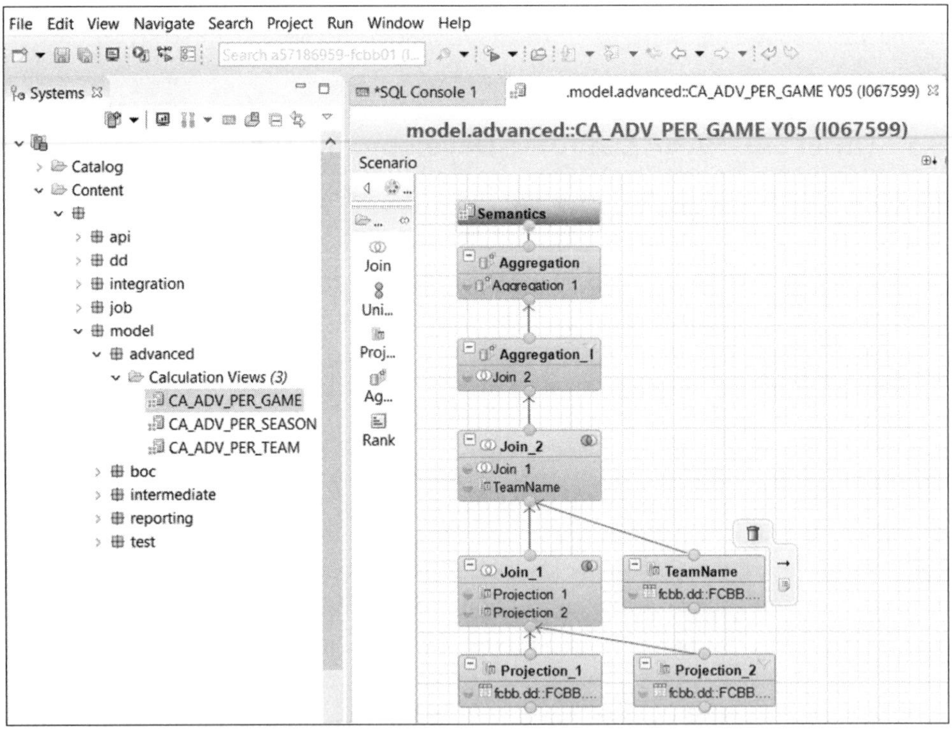

Figure 3.24 SAP HANA Studio: SAP HANA Modeler Perspective

3.5.2 SAP HANA Web-Based Development Workbench

The SAP HANA Web-Based Development Workbench is a web application for the development of native SAP HANA applications and to administrate objects within the SAP HANA Repository. For the development of SAP HANA XS Advanced applications, SAP Web IDE for SAP HANA must be used. In the SAP HANA Web-Based Development Workbench, administrators can view database content such as schemas and tables, administrate the SAP HANA database, and interact with the SAP HANA XS Repository, but they can't develop SAP HANA XS Advanced applications. Instead, developers must use SAP Web IDE for SAP HANA to create new applications on the SAP HANA XS Advanced platform. Developers or administrators can access the SAP HANA Web-Based Development Workbench via a web browser at *https://<host:port>/sap/hana/ide/*. The important functionalities of SAP HANA Web-Based Development Workbench are as follows:

- **Editor**
  This feature allows developers to create native SAP HANA applications in a web-based environment. The tool can be accessed via the following link in a web browser directly: *https://<host:port>/sap/hana/ide/editor*. Note that this tool only allows the creation of SAP HANA XS applications. Developers must work with SAP Web IDE for SAP HANA to create native applications for the SAP HANA XS Advanced platform.
- **Catalog**
  This feature allows developers to interact with SAP HANA database objects such as database schemas, tables, and views. The application can be accessed via the following link in a web browser directly: *https://<host:port>/sap/hana/ide/catalog*.
- **Security**
  The feature enables administrators of SAP HANA to manage SAP HANA database users and create SAP HANA database roles. The tool can be accessed via the following link in a web browser directly: *https://<host:port>/sap/hana/ide/security*. Note that the SAP HANA XS Advanced cockpit must be used to manage the security mechanisms of SAP HANA XS Advanced applications.
- **Traces**
  This feature allows administrators or developers to view SAP HANA database logs directly from a web browser via the following link: *https://<host:port>/sap/hana/ide/trace*.

Figure 3.25 displays the **SAP HANA Web-Based Development Workbench** landing page screen.

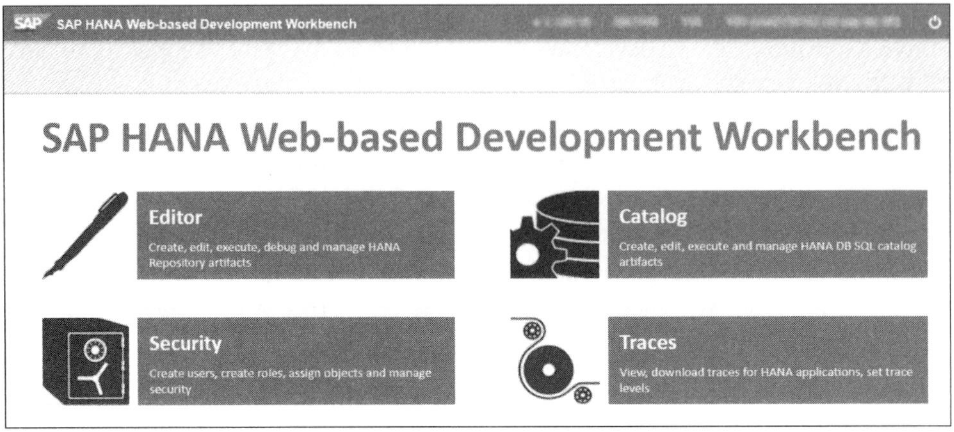

Figure 3.25 SAP HANA Web-Based Development Workbench

3.5.3 SAP HANA Cockpit

The SAP HANA cockpit is a web-based tool for the administration and monitoring of the SAP HANA database. The UI is based on the SAP Fiori UI design. It offers a single point of access to monitor and administrate the SAP HANA database.

Further Information on the SAP HANA Cockpit

Note that the SAP HANA cockpit isn't available out of the box on a SAP HANA system; it needs to be installed first. Furthermore, note that for certain administrative tasks, SAP HANA Studio still might be required. More information on the SAP HANA cockpit and how to install the application can be found in the central release SAP Note 2380291.

The tool can be accessed in a web browser via the following link: *https://<host:port>/sap/hana/admin/cockpit*. Figure 3.26 displays the **SAP HANA Database Administration** cockpit landing page screen.

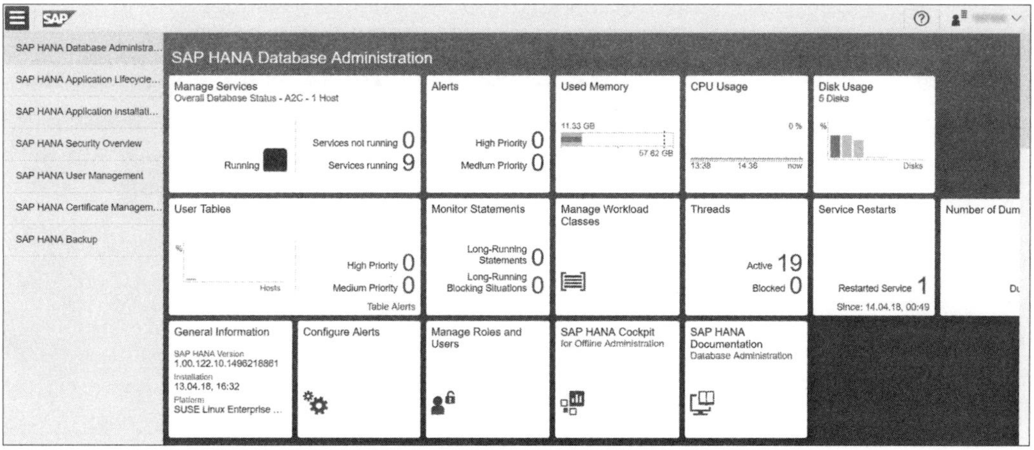

Figure 3.26 SAP HANA Cockpit

3.5.4 Postman

Postman is an extension program of the Google Chrome web browser that helps developers test HTTPS-based APIs. Postman allows developers to send HTTPS requests to APIs and thus enables them to check an API without having to create a separate application or UI. Developers can specify the URL of an API, the HTTPS request mechanism, the authorization mechanism, request headers, and the request body. The Postman tool will send the request to the API and return the result of the API call. We use the Postman application later in this book to test our applications. For example, in Chapter 6, we develop the application layer of the ChickenWings application to test our APIs.

Further Information on Postman

More information on the Postman tool and how to get the tool and be found at *www.getpostman.com*.

Figure 3.27 displays the UI of the Postman application.

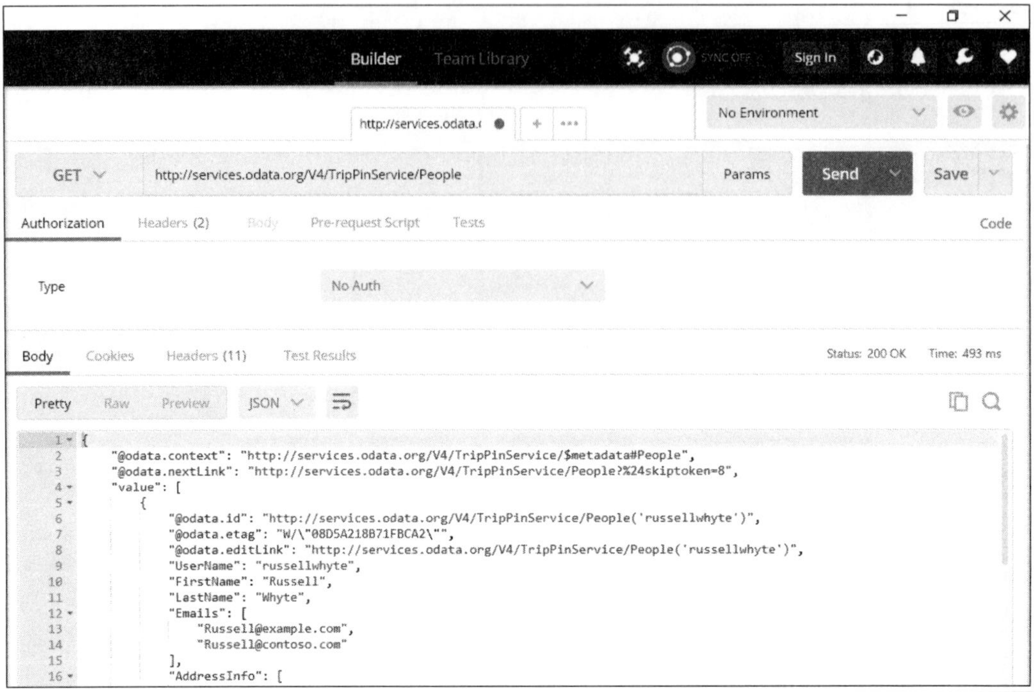

Figure 3.27 Postman Application

3.6 Summary

In this chapter, we introduced the SAP HANA development tools, which we'll use in our practical examples later in the book. We highlighted the relevant tools for administrators, such as the XSA CLI client and the SAP HANA XS Advanced cockpit. Using the SAP HANA XS Advanced administrative tools, administrators can create services, manage applications, configure security, and much more. We introduced the relevant tools for developers as well, such as SAP Web IDE for SAP HANA and the SAP HANA XS Advanced database explorer. The tools provide functionalities that enable developers to create an end-to-end application for the SAP HANA XS Advanced runtime and to access the database objects for SAP HANA XS Advanced applications. Finally, we discussed some additional useful administration and development tools such as SAP HANA Studio, SAP HANA Web-Based Development Workbench, SAP HANA cockpit, and Postman.

In the next chapter, we'll reveal the architecture of SAP HANA XS Advanced applications.

Chapter 4
SAP HANA XS Advanced Architecture

In this chapter, you'll learn about the architecture of the SAP HANA platform, including its new development environment SAP HANA extended application services, advanced model (SAP HANA XS Advanced).

The SAP HANA platform is designed to process large data volumes in a very performant way. The innovations of this new system allow the consolidation of analytical and transactional data in one combined platform. SAP HANA extends the traditional database server role and functions as a comprehensive platform for the development and execution of applications. Since SAP HANA release SPS 11, a new component called SAP HANA extended application services, advanced model (SAP HANA XS Advanced) was introduced in the SAP HANA platform, which enables developers to create applications that are independently deployable and scalable from the SAP HANA database management system.

This chapter highlights the new architecture of SAP HANA XS Advanced and how it extends the possibilities to deliver applications with SAP HANA. We'll first describe the concepts and advantages of a microservices-based architecture and the 12-Factor App principles that led to the SAP HANA XS Advanced innovative platform for developers. In the second section, we'll give an overview of the SAP HANA XS Advanced architecture and discuss the new concept of multi-target applications (MTAs) subsequently.

4.1 Microservices Architecture

The microservices architecture describes an architectural style to develop applications that consists of independent services. These applications typically communicate with services via lightweight mechanisms such as HTTP. A typical characteristic of a microservices-based architecture is that services are built around business capabilities and are independently deployable. One of the predecessors of this architectural style is the monolithic architecture style. While there have been other architecture styles as predecessors of the microservices architecture, we'll highlight the differences with the monolithic architecture style in this section. First, we'll explain the concepts of the monolithic architecture style and highlight the differences and advantages of the microservices architecture style in the second part of this section.

4.1.1 Monolithic Architecture

Applications are built in three main parts according to the monolithic architecture style: a client-side user interface (UI), a server-side application, and a database management system. The UI typically consists of HTML pages rendered in a web browser. The server-side application is a single executable that handles HTTP requests, executes business logic, and retrieves and updates data from the database management system. Changes to this type of application require deploying a new version of the whole server-side application because the application consists of only one executable.

Disadvantages of this architectural style include the scenario of deploying a new version of the application. Even small changes to the server-side application require a complete redeployment of the entire application. Another disadvantage is the scaling requirements of these type of applications. If certain parts of the application require more resources, the entire application must be scaled rather than only the component that requires more resources.

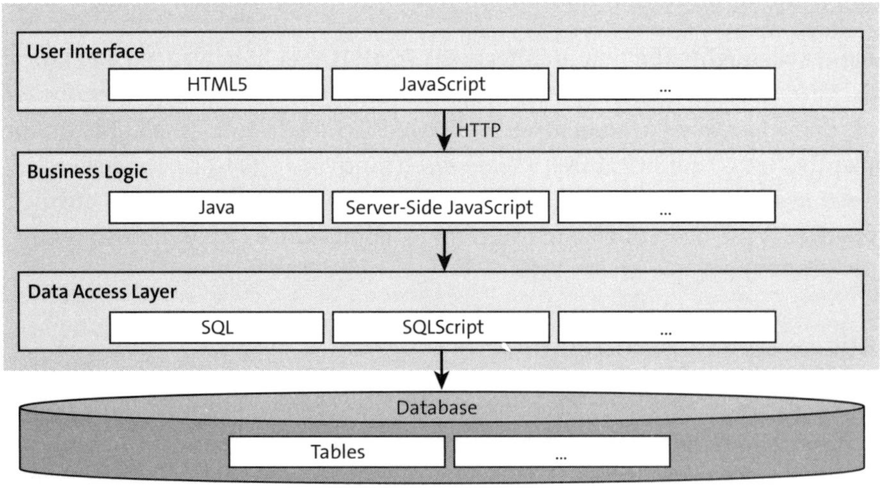

Figure 4.1 Monolithic Architecture

Advantages of the monolithic architecture style include that these systems are rather simple to handle, especially if they don't exceed a certain size of the application. The communication between these components is usually faster and more reliable if it's done in process. Generally speaking, choosing an architecture is usually a trade-off, and the advantages and disadvantages should be evaluated on a case-by-case basis before making the choice for your application. Figure 4.1 highlights a monolithic architecture style-based application.

4.1.2 Microservices Architecture

The limitations of applications that follow the monolithic architecture style have led to the design of the microservices architectural style. This architectural style proposes building applications as suites of services. Furthermore, services should be independently deployable and scalable. The underlying technology of a service is independent from the whole application, allowing for different services to be written in different programming languages and runtime environments. A microservice is a self-contained process that provides a unique business capability. Large applications are a suite of small independent services in the microservices architecture style. Only a very small amount of central management is required for these services. Each microservice runs on its own and communicates with other services using well-defined application programming interfaces (APIs). The key characteristics and advantages of a microservices-based architecture include the following:

- **High scalability**
  Services can be deployed independently to enhance the application performance. For example, the SAP HANA XS Advanced service of the SAP HANA platform can be scaled independently from the SAP HANA database.
- **Resilient to failure**
  Services are independent so that a failure in one service doesn't impact other services and the overall availability of an application.
- **Easy to enhance**
  Microservices-based applications are easier to enhance due to the split in independent services. Typically, these services are organized around business capabilities. Each service implements a specific business functionality. Individual services form a whole application.
- **Flexible runtime technology**
  Services have to be exposed via well-defined APIs. Thus, different applications consume these services via an API. The underlying technology that implements these services is secondary. For example, the SAP HANA XS Advanced service of the SAP HANA platform supports Java or Node.js as execution environments.

- **Independent deployment**
  Services can be updated and deployed independently without having to redeploy an entire application. For example, the SAP HANA XS Advanced runtime of a SAP HANA platform can be updated independently from the SAP HANA database.

A microservices-based architecture provides several technical and organizational advantages compared to a monolithic application architecture. The SAP HANA XS Advanced service of the SAP HANA platform leverages this concept to allow the development of new applications that are independently scalable and thus facilitate agile development and deployment of applications. Chapter 1 discussed the architectural components of SAP HANA XS Advanced in more detail.

Figure 4.2 highlights a microservices-based application architecture.

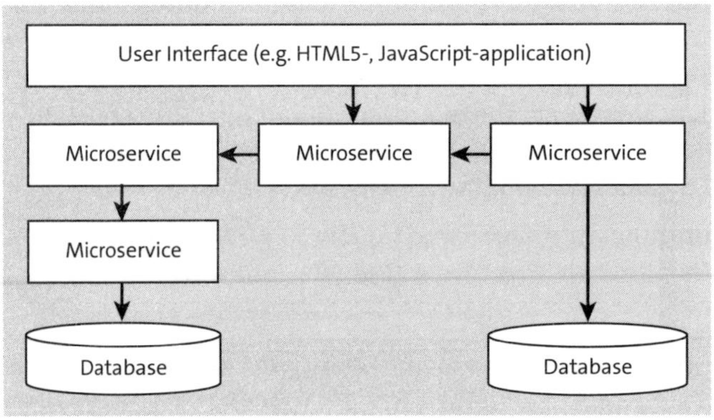

Figure 4.2 Microservices-Based Architecture

4.2 SAP HANA XS Advanced Architecture

The first introduction of the SAP *HANA extended application services, classic model* (SAP HANA XS) with SPS 5 facilitated a lot of the creation of monolithic, self-contained SAP HANA applications, including everything from the data model and the application logic up to the UI. It simplified the overall application architecture by allowing application logic, written in JavaScript, to run in the *XS Engine* of the SAP HANA database without the need for an additional application server. A web-based frontend, for example, using the SAPUI5 libraries, is delivered to the end user via the XS Engine, executed in a web browser, and communicates with the XS Engine of the SAP HANA platform to send and retrieve data. The database evolved to a development platform, which makes it possible to create native SAP HANA applications.

With the shift of the SAP HANA development model to a microservices-based architecture, a lot of progress was made in how native SAP HANA applications are designed and developed. Following the 12-Factor App principles, which we'll present in the next section, the *SAP HANA extended application services, advanced model* (SAP HANA XS Advanced) allowed the creation of *multi-target applications* (MTAs), which consist of multiple microservice applications such as Node.js and Java application logic or HTML5 user frontends (we'll explore these later).

The created application components bring the advantages of a microservices-based architecture, including scalability, flexibility, and robustness, to the native SAP HANA application by isolating every component in its own runtime container that represents a service. Unlike the rather static approach of SAP HANA XS applications, where an application is deployed as a whole, the modules of an SAP HANA XS Advanced application can be managed independently.

Together with the new development model, the architecture of the underlying development platform changed. While the SAP HANA XS environment is a native part of the SAP HANA database and mostly proprietary, the SAP HANA XS Advanced environment is based on the open-source Cloud Foundry platform, which heavily builds on the microservices paradigm we discussed in the previous section.

4.2.1 12-Factor Apps

As mentioned previously, the SAP HANA XS Advanced development model is optimized to facilitate the creation of applications that follow the 12-Factor App principles as is also the case for Cloud Foundry applications. The 12-Factor App principles have been written down by Adam Wiggins in 2011 as a set of best practices, helping developers to create software-as-a-service (SaaS) applications that need to be robust, scalable, and easy to deploy and maintain.

In this section, we discuss the principles briefly and encourage you to review them in detail on the official website at *https://12factor.net/*.

While looking at the architecture in this chapter and the development process later on, you'll recognize the following principles that characterize a 12-Factor App.

Codebase

The usage of a central version management system, such as Git, for the application source code serves several goals. For example, using a central version makes it possible for multiple developers to collaborate on the project, committing their code changes to the repository. From the same codebase, multiple instances reflecting different versions of the development can be deployed, for example, one version for testing with the latest features and one for production with tested and stable functionality.

While we already introduced the usage of Git as the central source code repository for SAP HANA XS Advanced based on SAP HANA development in Chapter 2, you could use any other source code management system as well.

Dependencies

When developing an application, dependencies such as supporting libraries or platform services should be declared explicitly. Doing so allows developers to manage and resolve those dependencies every time the application is deployed without relying on implicitly available (or not available) parts of the target environment.

The management of the dependencies is either done by a dependency manager of the runtime you're developing for, such as npm for node modules, or done manually by including the needed libraries, tools, and so on in the module you're developing.

Configuration

Storing the application's configuration in its environment variables goes a bit in the same direction as the explicit declaration of dependencies by making the configuration independent of the actual environment it runs in. The configuration contains information used by the application, which is usually different between the deployments because, for example, connection information to backing services such as a database isn't the same for a test and a production deployment, credentials or API keys for external services, or other changing values.

Advantages are that the environment variables can be adjusted for every deployment, and you don't risk publishing secret information such as an API key to a public repository if those environment variables are provided during the deployment.

Backing Services

The backing services of your application, such as the persistence database (SAP HANA, PostgreSQL, MySQL, etc.), a queueing service (RabbitMQ), or an email service, are treated like attached resources of the application. The services are loosely coupled via the applications configuration, which makes it possible to exchange the actual service instances that are used without the need to change the application code. This is the case, for example, when a specific backing service instance is configured during the application deployment or if a backing service needs to be replaced during the runtime of the application because it becomes unavailable.

Build, Release, Run

A 12-Factor App strictly separates the different phases into build, release, and run:

- **Build**
  This phase is either triggered directly by the developer or automatically in a continuous integration setup. It resolves the declared dependencies we introduced before and creates an executable application out of the source code.
- **Release**
  During this phase, the configuration for the target environment is added to the executable application, which is then ready to run.
- **Run**
  This phase includes the actual execution of the application in the target environment and its management. As the execution is usually automated, the application can be (re)started and scaled by the target environment.

Processes

To easily scale an application during the runtime and increase robustness, the application should be designed to be executed as one or more stateless, shared-nothing processes. As the process, being stateless, doesn't rely on information available only locally but handles data storage via an attached backing service, additional processes can be started or existing ones restarted if there is a process failure or the need to handle more user requests.

Port Binding

As stated before, a 12-Factor App is designed to be independent and can run standalone. The single processes therefore don't rely on external components, which make it possible to access the application. Instead, the application binds to a port in the environment it's running in and listens for incoming requests. On the system, a routing layer is usually established, which directs incoming requests using the publicly available hostname to the actual port where the application is listening.

Using the port binding, the application itself can also be used as a service for other applications that just need to declare a dependency.

Concurrency

The processes we talked about before are the foundation of applications' ability to scale. If the processes run as shared-nothing, their concurrency can be easily implemented, which makes it then possible to start additional processes when the applications load rises.

Disposability

Disposability of application processes means that it should be possible to start and stop them in a short amount of time, which makes it easier to dynamically scale the whole application depending on the number of requests coming in.

If new processes are needed to respond to a rising number of requests, they should be operative in as little time as possible. It may also be necessary to start processes on a different physical machine after a hardware failure.

Regarding shutdown, the time is less important than a graceful shutdown of the process. After it receives a shutdown signal, the process should first refuse new requests from the port it has been bound to, then finish the currently executing job, and return any remaining jobs to the queue where another process can pick them up. In addition to the graceful shutdown, the processes should also be robust against sudden failure as they can occur after a hardware or power failure.

Dev/Prod Parity

The principle to keep the individual runtime environments as similar as possible serves different goals. On one hand, using the same backing services in development, test, and production makes it more likely that a successfully tested application also runs in production. On the other hand, it's easier to reproduce issues that occur in the production environment. As for the code commits, the single deploys should be rather small to make it easier to investigate issues.

The dev/prod parity doesn't stop at the application code but is also seen as part of a continuous integration and Dev/Ops strategy. This means to shorten the time a developed piece of code gets deployed and used productively, which is supported by the Dev/Ops approach, where the developers themselves are responsible or at least heavily involved in the operation of their application.

Logs

The log information produced by the application makes it possible for developers and administrators to monitor its behavior. To write log information, the application should use the standard output method of the respective runtime instead of explicitly handling its own log writing. Doing so, the log information can be treated differently in the single runtime environments.

For a development deploy, the developer can simply watch the application's output stream, whereas in a production environment, the log information could be collected and saved. Of course, to be useful, the application must provide extensive information about what's going on.

Admin Processes

In the production environment, it's usually necessary to run administrative tasks from time to time, such as health checks or data migrations. Instead of manually executing these tasks step by step, they should be automated, for example, by a script that is then started in the target environment if necessary. The automated task should also be part of the codebase to provide a history and be deployed together with the application to the target environment where it's finally executed.

4.2.2 Cloud Foundry Basics

To understand the components of SAP HANA XS Advanced, let's take a look at the foundation of the microservices-based architecture of Cloud Foundry.

Cloud Foundry is a container-based application platform designed for distributed web applications that follow the 12-Factor App principles introduced earlier. The open-source PaaS is maintained by the Cloud Foundry Foundation, whose members include SAP, IBM, and its founder Pivotal (formerly part of VMware). Initially developed to support Java as a programming language, it now supports many different runtimes, including Node.js, Java, and .NET.

In comparison to infrastructure-as-a-service (IaaS), which provides virtual or physical processing power, storage, and network, Cloud Foundry provides a platform with services (e.g., load balancing and scaling) and APIs on which applications can be built, deployed, and run.

Most of the Cloud Foundry concepts and components can be found just the same in SAP HANA XS Advanced. Technically, we need to distinguish between the SAP HANA-based adaptation of the Cloud Foundry concepts, SAP HANA XS Advanced, and the Cloud Foundry-based SAP Cloud Platform, which integrates with SAP HANA XS Advanced (see Figure 4.3).

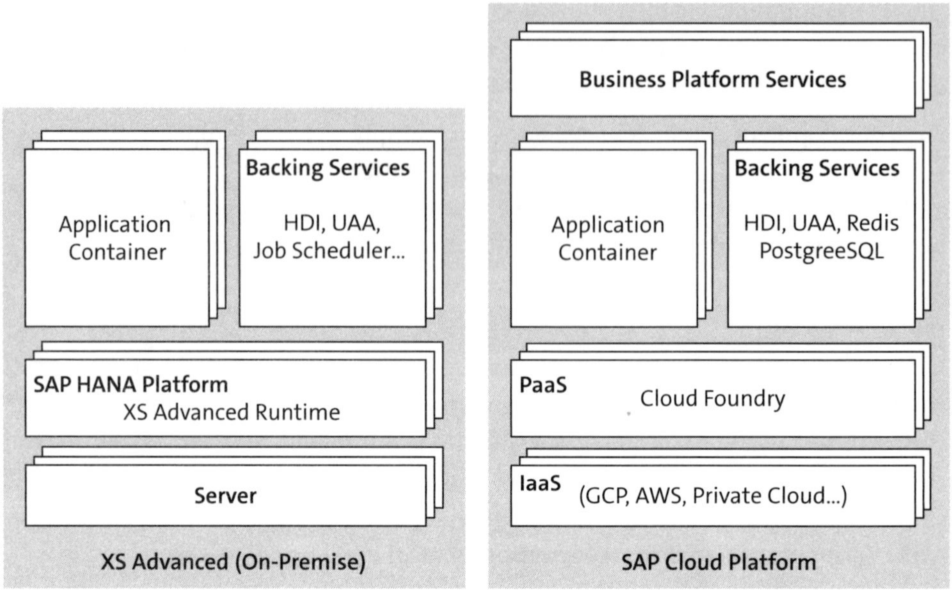

Figure 4.3 SAP HANA XS Advanced On-Premise and SAP Cloud Platform

The Cloud Foundry environment of the SAP Cloud Platform, which has been publicly available since May 2017, runs the actual Cloud Foundry open-source PaaS as its foundation and adds SAP specific extensions to it. The extensions include, for example, the tight integration of the SAP HANA database using the SAP HANA Deployment Infrastructure (HDI), which can be used as a persistence service for the developed applications. HDI will be explained in detail in Chapter 5.

For on-premise SAP HANA installations, SAP implemented central Cloud Foundry APIs to achieve compatibility between both worlds. Native SAP HANA applications built with SAP HANA XS Advanced are implemented once and can then be deployed on-premise as well as in the cloud without major modifications.

In an on-premise setup, the SAP HANA XS Advanced server is part of the SAP HANA installation and fully integrated into the platform by means of operation and administration. The server is part of SAP HANA and integrated into its backup and high-availability infrastructure. It can also be monitored using the SAP HANA tools.

In the SAP Cloud Platform, SAP HANA is a separate service, which can be used by applications to leverage its capabilities, but it's optional. Developers can also choose other backing services, such as a PostgreSQL or MongoDB instance, to manage an application's persistency.

4.2.3 Organization of Applications, Services, and Users

Cloud Foundry and SAP HANA XS Advanced implement an internal organization and space structure, as shown in Figure 4.4. At the top, the Cloud Foundry or SAP HANA XS Advanced instance is accessible via an API endpoint URL. You use this URL, for example, when you connect with the command-line interface (CLI) to the server.

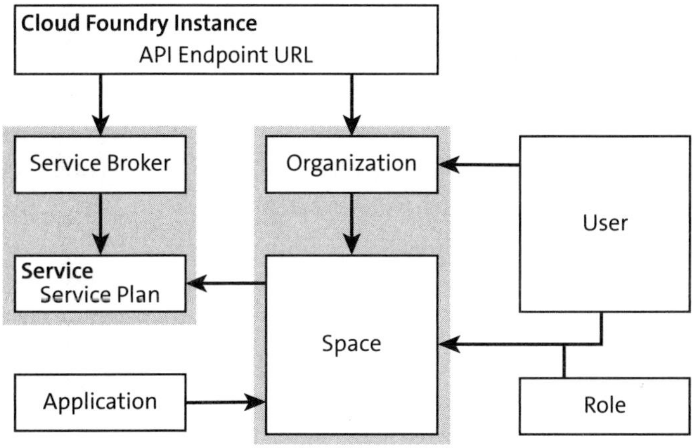

Figure 4.4 Organization of Cloud Foundry/SAP HANA XS Advanced

An instance can host one or more *organizations*. A standard organization is created during the installation of the SAP HANA XS Advanced components on-premise or during the setup of the SAP Cloud Platform account.

The organization itself contains one or more *spaces*, which host applications and services. Spaces are created according to their usage types. They can be used to separate, for example, development streams or even development, test, and production environments.

Users in Cloud Foundry or SAP HANA XS Advanced always belong to an organization. Regarding a specific space, users can be vested with roles such as manager or developer. Chapter 8 will go into further details regarding the security concepts.

For every space, there are *services* available that can be consumed. SAP HANA XS Advanced offers, for example, a scheduling service, file system storage, and HDI as a service. For each service, *service plans* define special configurations, according to which they are provided. The SAP HANA service, for example, can be provided as an HDI container on a shared database, as a plain database schema, or as an access to the SAP HANA secure store—making it a kind of service flavor or specific configuration.

Before a service can be consumed, a *service instance* must be created by the service's *service broker* according to one of the service plans. The service instance is then bound to the application that wants to consume it. For each offered service on the platform, there is a service broker registered at a Cloud Foundry or SAP HANA XS Advanced instance.

We'll take a closer look at the available services in Section 4.2.7.

4.2.4 The Controller

The one keeping track of and managing all the spaces, applications, and services is the *platform controller*. The *platform controller* is the central component of SAP HANA XS Advanced (XS Controller) and Cloud Foundry (Cloud Controller), which manages the organizations, spaces, applications, services, and so on and stores them in the system database. The controller also provides the representational state transfer (REST) API endpoint to access the system, for example, via the CLI xs for SAP HANA XS Advanced and cf command on Cloud Foundry. The CLI was described in further detail previously in Chapter 3.

When you deal with a SAP HANA XS Advanced system, the endpoint URL on which you reach the controller depends on whether the system is configured for port-based routing or hostname-based routing. The routing decision is usually made during the installation of the SAP HANA XS Advanced component. For a productive system, it's recommended to use hostname-based routing because the access URLs are more user friendly than in a system for port-based routing. The downside of hostname-based routing is a slight overhead for maintaining a separate URL for every application in your network. This is why for development and sandbox systems, port-based routing is usually chosen.

To find out how your system is configured, the easiest way is to try to connect to the controller with your web browser. The controller will only respond to one or the other URL.

For port-based routing it's assembled as follows: *https://<hostname>:3<instanceNo>30*. So if your SAP HANA system has the hostname hana.chickenwings.corp, and the instance number of the installation is 0, you reach the controller under *https://hana.chickenwings.corp:30030*. Note that the instance number must be double digits; in this case, it's 00.

In your browser, you should see the screen shown in Figure 4.5, which also holds a list of links to important components on the right.

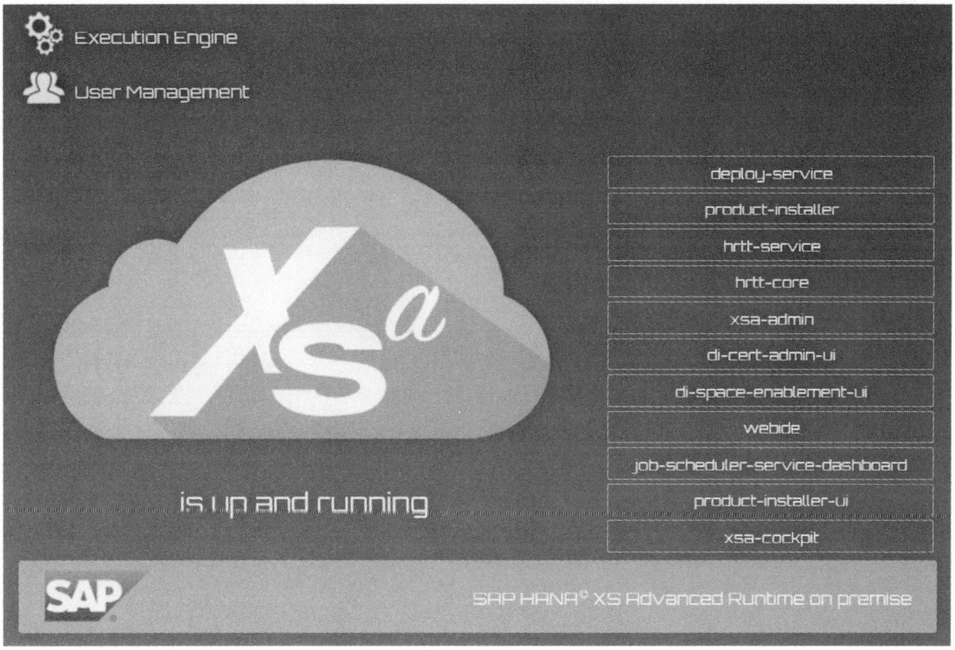

Figure 4.5 SAP HANA XS Advanced Controller

For hostname-based routing instead, the API endpoint is reached using *https://api.<hostname>:3<instanceNo>33*. So, in our example, it would translate to *https://api.chickenwings.corp:30033*.

To access the cloud controller of the SAP Cloud Platform instead, you use the API endpoint URL, which you find in the SAP Cloud Platform cockpit that depends on the region your account is assigned to. The datacenter for Europe in Frankfurt, for example, is reached via *https://api.cf.eu10.hana.ondemand.com*.

If you send push, start, or stop commands for an application, you're communicating those commands to the controller via its API. We'll now take a closer look at how those commands work and what they do on the platform.

4.2.5 Deployment and Execution

Before a Cloud Foundry/SAP HANA XS Advanced application can be executed, it needs to be deployed. The deployment phases are *push*, *stage*, and *run*, as shown in Figure 4.6, each of which will be discussed in the following sections.

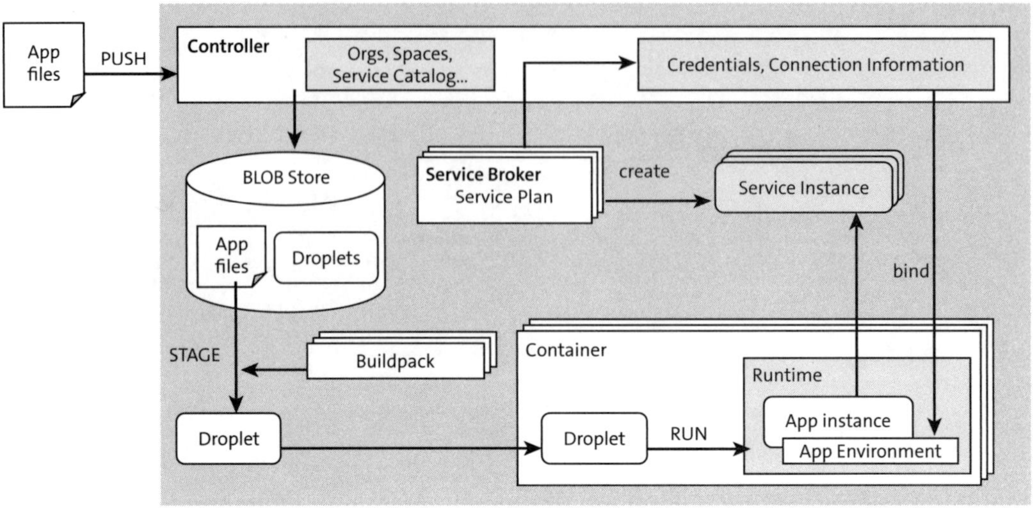

Figure 4.6 Deployment and Execution of an Application

Push

After the development of the application is completed, the deployment is initiated by using the push command of the Cloud Foundry or the SAP HANA XS Advanced CLI, which starts the upload of the application files to the platform. What exactly is uploaded differs between the different runtime languages. For a Node.js application, this includes, for example, source files and configuration files; for a Java application, a *.war* archive is included. Once uploaded, the files are stored in the platform's central *blob store*.

The blob store is designed to hold binary files. In addition to the application code, it also contains the platform's *buildpacks* and *droplets*, which we'll introduce in just a second. For SAP HANA XS Advanced, the blob store is reseeding on the SAP HANA database in the SYS_XS_RUNTIME schema. For Cloud Foundry, the kind of storage used depends on the configuration.

It's important to notice that the command differs depending on whether you create a single application or you develop an MTA, which in fact consists of multiple single applications in one project. Standard Cloud Foundry applications must be "pushed" to the platform and will result in one running application. In addition, for SAP HANA XS Advanced, single applications can be developed and "pushed" to the platform.

If you decide to develop a full-stack application using SAP's MTAs, which we'll explore further in the next section, you use the deploy command. Because the MTA is a kind of container to group multiple smaller applications, a `push` command will be issued behind the scenes for every module/single application in your MTA. For the XSA CLI tools, the `deploy` command is available per default. For the Cloud Foundry CLI tools, a plug-in must be installed first to support the deployment of MTAs.

Stage

After the application files are uploaded to the platform and stored in the blob store, the application must run through the staging process to be started. The staging process converts the files into an executable entity by using buildpacks—collections of scripts to support the specific target runtime of the application—which is an integral part of the platform's multilanguage support. For SAP HANA XS Advanced, there is currently out-of-the-box support for JavaScript running on Node.js and for Java running on Tomcat. In Cloud Foundry, there is also support for Ruby, Hypertext Preprocessor (PHP), or Go.

The right buildpack for the application is determined by the platform controller or specified explicitly together with the push command. If the right buildpack is found, the application sources are converted into a self-contained and ready-to-run application archive called a *droplet*. The conversion process is highly dependent on the target runtime and might include compilation steps, dependency resolution, and/or the addition of files and artifacts to the application.

After the droplet has been built, it's released and stored in the blob store.

Run

From the blob store, the platform controller is now able to create a new droplet instance and hand it over to the responsible execution runtime. In the created droplet, commands have been embedded to start the application instance. Finally, the platform controller advises the responsible execution runtime to execute the start command of the application instance.

If necessary, this process can be repeated to create multiple instances of the droplet to, for example, respond to an increasing load on the application.

4.2.6 Runtime Components and Services

Now that we have a ready-to-run application, let's look at the components involved during runtime, as shown in Figure 4.7.

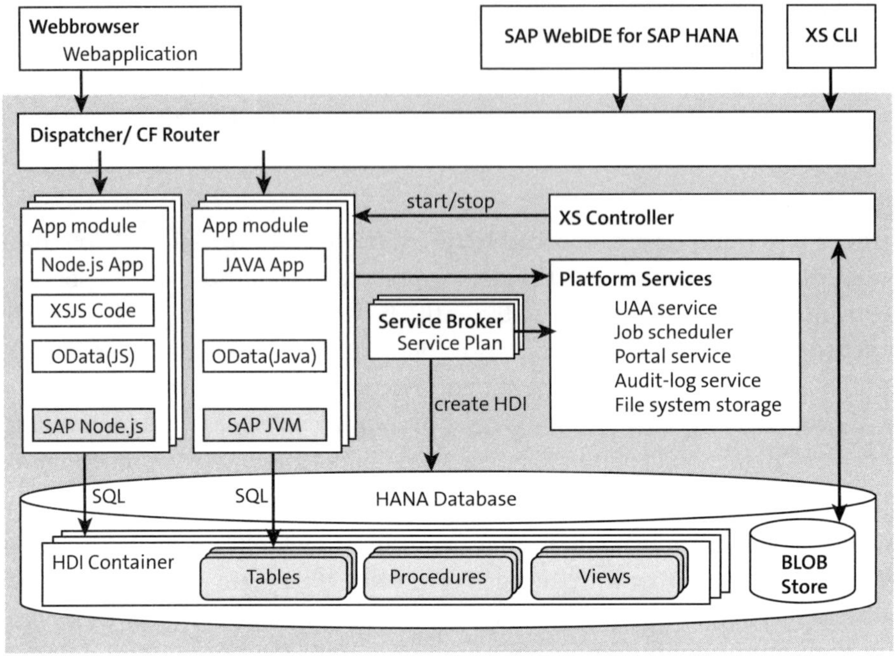

Figure 4.7 SAP HANA XS Advanced Runtime Components

Dispatcher

Every HTTP(s) request to the controller, applications, or platform services first goes through the dispatcher, which also serves as a load balancer and reverse proxy for the whole system. For SAP HANA XS Advanced, the *SAP Web Dispatcher* of the SAP HANA system provides this functionality; on the SAP Cloud Platform, it's the *Cloud Foundry Router*.

As discussed earlier, depending on the setup of the system, applications are either accessed by providing an application-specific subdomain (hostname-based routing) or by specifying its assigned port number together with the system's hostname (port-based routing). For hostname-based routing, the dispatcher matches the subdomain of an incoming request to the internal port number on which the targeted application runs and routes the request accordingly.

> **Note**
>
> The dispatcher isn't only used for requests coming from outside the system but also for requests between applications and services.

Application Router

If an MTA with different modules has been developed, you need to provide a single entry point for the end user. To achieve this, every MTA should use its own application router. The application router is a Node.js component provided by SAP that can be configured by the developer. It can be seen as a dispatcher on the application level, which is configurable by the developer.

First of all, the application router is responsible to bring together the different modules of the MTA under one umbrella by redirecting the incoming requests to the responsible runtime container, for example, the Node.js or Java runtime. Static content, such as the files of an HTML5 module, is delivered directly by the application router.

In the application configuration file *xs-app.json*, *routes* to the different microservices/modules of the application are created. We'll discuss the configuration details in more detail in Chapter 7.

Another task of the application router is to provide proxy functionalities for the application that are used to integrate other microservices, web APIs, or backend systems into the application. A defined route can refer to a *destination*, which contains the remote address to be used for a request.

The application router also plays an important role when securing an application. It takes care of authenticating users with the *User Account and Authentication Service (UAA)*. The different routes can then be secured with the information from the logged-on user's profile, which is also forwarded from the application router to the backend modules in the form of a *JSON Web Token (JWT)*. Subsequently, it's important that the backend module is checking the JWT security information for additional authorization checks.

The router also provides protection against cross-site request forgery attacks and can manage URL rewriting. The security aspects will be discussed further in Chapter 8.

4.2.7 Platform Services

When developing an SAP HANA XS Advanced or Cloud Foundry application, you can make use of the platforms' backing services. As explained before, service brokers are taking care of creating a service instance according to a service plan bound to the application that wants to make use of it.

The service binding can be done either manually via the CLI or automatically when you define the binding in the *mta.yaml* file of your MTA. During the service binding, the credentials to the service instance are stored in the environment variable `VCAP_`

SERVICES of the application instance it's bound to. This can include, for example, a URL, user name and password, or a service key. The application instance can read this information and connect to the service.

> **Note**
> Service bindings can only be created within one space. If the application needs to consume external services, user-provided services are used.

The available services in a space can be found at the SAP Service Marketplace, which is accessible via the xs marketplace or cf marketplace command.

For SAP HANA XS Advanced, the following service brokers are currently available:

- UAA (xsuaa)
- SAP HANA Services (hana)
- Job Scheduler service (jobscheduler)
- File-system storage (fs-storage)
- Audit-log service (auditlog)
- Portal services (portal-services)

The following sections will introduce them briefly.

User Account and Authentication Service

The *UAA* (XSUAA) has been added by SAP to both the Cloud Foundry environment of SAP Cloud Platform and SAP HANA XS Advanced to facilitate authentication and authorization tasks.

As already explained, the application router uses this service to secure access to the application parts it manages. Before a user can access a secured route for which he must be logged on, the application router redirects to the XSUAA service for authentication. After the user logged in successfully, the XSUAA service issues an *OAuth access token* for the user's session, which is used for subsequent requests and related authorization tasks.

The user is now logged on to the system (authenticated), but for the requested resource, additional privileges are needed to access it (authorization). In this case, the OAuth access tokens construct of *scopes* and *attributes* is used to check if the user has the necessary permissions. A scope is usually a component of an application to which access needs to be controlled, such as userProfile, email, calendar, or tasks in an email provider application. The attributes would then define the level of access to the defined attributes, for example, `readOnly`, `readWrite` for the user profile, or `send` for the emailing part of the application.

The authorization information can now either be used to secure a specific route, which is served by the application router directly, or to make custom checks inside of a runtime container.

In the first case, the authorization checks are configured in the application configuration file *xs-app.json* of the HTML5 module. The application router will check automatically for the existence of a specific security scope in the user's profile and grant or deny access to the resource the route is pointing to.

To do security checks inside an application module, the session information, such as OAuth tokens and scopes, is forwarded by the application router to the target runtime and can be accessed there.

In Chapter 8, we'll see in detail how to secure an application with the `XSUAA` service.

SAP HANA Services

Because SAP HANA XS Advanced is based on the SAP HANA platform, the SAP HANA Services provide the primary persistence services when developing for an on-premise system. For the Cloud Foundry environment on the SAP Cloud platform, SAP HANA is available among other persistence services (e.g., PostgreSQL).

Depending on the needs of your application, the SAP HANA Service Broker offers the following service plans to access the database:

- **HDI container: `hdi-shared`**

  For every service instance with the `hdi-share` service plan, an HDI container is created on the database. This container is basically a database schema generated for each individual service instance. Dedicated technical database users, which are used to access the container schema, ensure the isolation from other HDI containers and the rest of the database. This strict isolation makes it possible, for example, to deploy the same application multiple times or in different versions using the same SAP HANA database. However, it also implies that access from one container to another isn't possible by default. If cross-container access is needed, it must be enabled explicitly.

  The container content, such as database tables, stored procedures, and calculation views, is created in a declarative way. During the development phase, you create a SAP HANA database module (HDB module) as part of the MTA that contains the database design-time artifacts. When you subsequently deploy the application, the HDB module's definition files are pushed as part of an HDI Deployer application that is generated for your project. This HDI Deployer application is then bound to the HDI container service instance and deploys your defined artifacts into that container using the provided technical users.

As pointed out before, the generated credentials are accessible for other modules of your MTA through their `VCAP_SERVICES` environment variable if you've defined a dependency. In the next chapter, we'll explore in detail how to design and create the database artifacts.

- **Schema on the SAP HANA database: `schema`**
  Using the `schema` service plan, a plain schema on the database is provided without the HDI. This can be used if the application that consumes the service handles the creation of database artifacts itself.
- **Connection to the SAP HANA Secure Store: `securestore`**
  The `securestore` service plan provides a service instance that makes it possible for the bound application to access the SAP HANA Secure Store. Using the service instance, it's possible to read, write, and remove encrypted key/value pairs on the database. The access happens either directly using the provided stored procedures or via the `@sap/xsa-securestore` module for a Node.js application.

Job Scheduler Service

The Job Scheduler service allows a planned and/or repetitive execution of application parts and is available on the Cloud Foundry environment of the SAP Cloud Platform and the SAP HANA XS Advanced runtime.

After the service instance has been created and bound to the application, it can be configured to execute an HTTP call to any web service you provide. The configuration happens either via the Job Scheduler's API or its UI and contains the necessary parameters, such as the action (web service URL), an HTTP method, and the desired schedule.

Recurring schedules can be defined either via a fixed execution interval, that is, a fixed time at which the job is executed once a day, or by using a cron expression for maximum control over the job schedule. Additionally, the scheduler allows one-time executions by specifying an execution point in time.

The scheduled web-service calls can be done synchronously or asynchronously, depending on what's best suited to the nature of the service you want to schedule. Synchronous jobs are preferred when the executed logic is returning a result in a short time, whereas an asynchronous call is used to trigger long-running tasks.

4

File-System Storage

SAP HANA XS Advanced provides file-system storage for applications that require direct access. When a file-system storage service instance is created, a directory will be mounted to it that is then available for read/write operations. This information is accessible in the application's environment variables that the file-system storage service instance has been bound to.

Audit-Log Service

The audit-log service enables applications to write messages to an audit-log trail that isn't sharing the same persistence as the application itself. This allows you to log security-relevant events such as access to sensitive information and executed configuration changes without the possibility to be modified again by the application.

To use the audit log, a service instance must be created and bound to the application. For Java and Node.js modules, libraries are available to facilitate the creation of audit-log messages.

Portal Service

The SAP portal service provides an SAP Fiori launchpad running in the SAP HANA XS Advanced environment. The SAP Fiori launchpad can be defined as the entry portal for SAP Fiori apps that are built with SAPUI5. The end users connect to the SAP Fiori launchpad and select an application they want to start. These applications are organized in tiles, as shown in Figure 4.8.

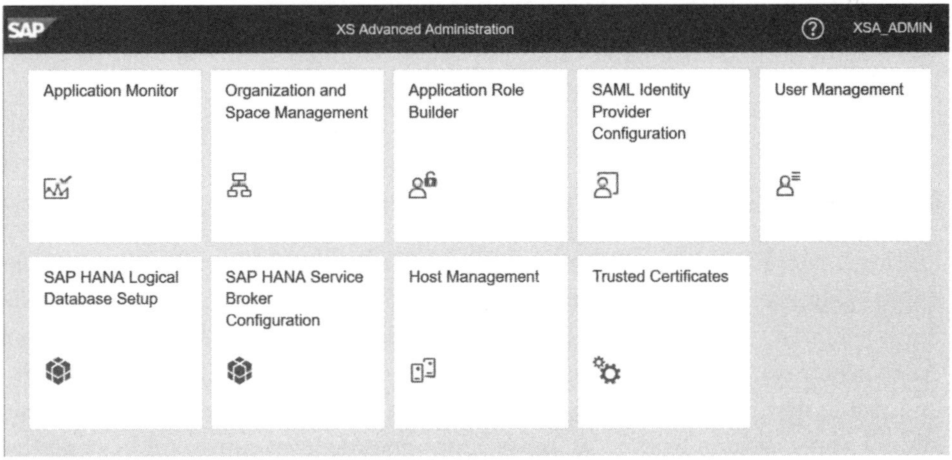

Figure 4.8 Launchpad with Applications Organized as Tiles

User-Provided Services

Now that you've seen an overview of some of the available platform services, we'll look at the *user-provided services*, which are also sometimes referred to as *user-defined services*.

User-provided services are used to make services available that aren't part of the same space and organization your application will run in. For example, if you want to use an API that requires authentication or you need to connect to a database that isn't within your SAP HANA XS Advanced or SAP Cloud Platform environment, a created user-provided service instance will hold the necessary information, such as hostname, user name, and password, and can be bound to your application. The information you provided while creating the service instance is then available to your application via the environment variables.

For creation, you use the xs cups or cf cups command. You can then provide a JSON object, which can contain any information you want to be provided by the service instance.

A user-provided service is also involved if you need to break out of your HDI container to access, for example, data from a different schema or container. As a result of the strict container isolation, the technical user of your HDI container doesn't have the necessary privileges on the objects you want to access and can't grant himself the necessary rights to do so. So the idea is to utilize a user that instead has the required access privileges and can grant them to your container user. This user's credentials are used to create a user-provided service that is subsequently leveraged to grant access to the objects outside of your container.

You'll learn how to create and make use of user-defined services in the following chapters.

4.3 SAP HANA XS Advanced Application Concepts

End users interact with an application typically via a single access point, for example, a web application. However, there can be a complex network of dependent components behind a single access point that form a whole application. Such a component could be, for example, a database system, a server-side process, or an HTML5 front-end, just to name a few. Typically, a developer of such an application has the responsibility for a certain subset of these components. The components could be developed using different programming languages and be executed on different runtime environments. However, they should all follow a common lifecycle from development to deployment. As stated previously, SAP introduced the term MTAs for applications that are composed of multiple components. Each component can be identified as a separate microservice that together forms one application.

In this section, we'll first explain the concept and characteristics of MTAs and, second, the architecture of an MTA within SAP HANA XS Advanced. Third, we'll reveal the typical development workflow of creating an MTA in SAP HANA XS Advanced.

4.3.1 Multi-Target Application Concept

SAP started the concept of MTAs with the introduction of SAP HANA XS Advanced. Each MTA consists of one or more modules that all share a common lifecycle for development and deployment. These modules can be written in different technologies and can be deployed to different target runtime platforms. Trends in a microservices-based architecture led to the development of applications constructed out of multiple decoupled modules, which is in line with the backing services principle of a 12-Factor App. Thus, an MTA is logically a single application, consisting of multiple related and interdependent parts that can be developed using different technologies or programming paradigms with a single lifecycle, which are then coupled together.

MTA addresses deployment challenges by isolating the developer from target-specific native tools via a target-independent application model. An MTA supports the declaration of resources on which an application depends at runtime or deployment time. These resources can be components of the application or even external services. This makes an MTA flexibly deployable. Furthermore, it's possible to declare configuration variables that allow you to distinguish different deployments of an application as it's foreseen by the config principle of a 12-Factor App.

A typical MTA in SAP HANA XS Advanced consists of a Node.js module that serves as the UI with programming interfaces and processes user requests. This frontend part of an application is the only part that end users will interact with. However, server-side backend processing also might be required. This can be achieved by providing either Java backend services, SAP HANA XS JavaScript (XSJS), or Node.js backend services. A common requirement is to persist data in a database using a backing service. In the context of MTA on SAP HANA XS Advanced or Cloud Foundry on the SAP Cloud Platform, data can be persisted in the SAP HANA database via database service providers. When the MTA components are designed to adhere to the concurrency principle of a 12-Factor App, they can be independently scaled based on the resource requirements. In any case, the system resources for a service can be configured.

User Account and Authentication Service

The SAP HANA XS Advanced central UAA service can be leveraged within an MTA if an application has authentication and authorization requirements. A developer doesn't need to reimplement, for example, the authentication logic within an application but can rather reuse the standard service, which is provided by the SAP HANA XS Advanced runtime.

The concept of an MTA and the relationship to other components and external services is summarized in Figure 4.9.

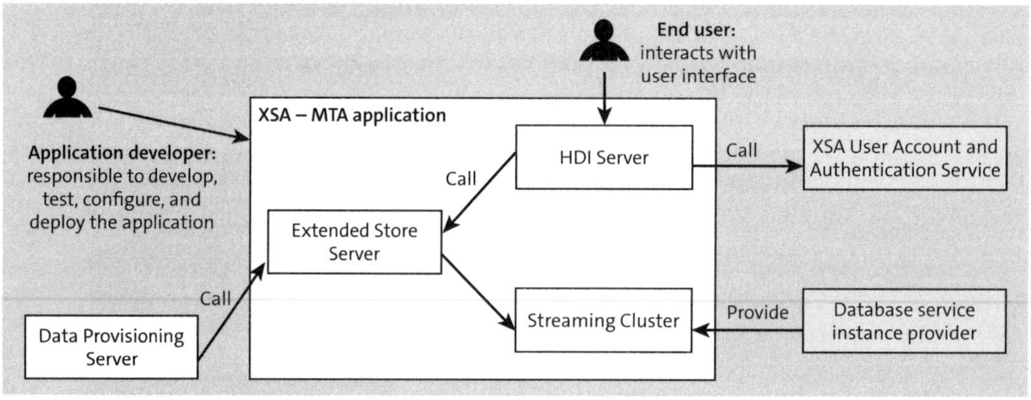

Figure 4.9 MTA Concept

There are four configuration elements of an MTA that ensure its successful deployment across different landscapes:

- **MTA development descriptor**
  An MTA development descriptor is used to describe the modules of the application, their dependencies, and required and exposed interfaces within the MTA specification. The MTA deployment descriptor or development descriptor is one file (*mta.yaml*) within an MTA that describes all its components following the YAML format. In this file, the resources on which the application depends at runtime or deployment time are described. Key elements in the MTA specification are as follows:
  - **Global elements**
    An MTA descriptor has global elements, such as an identifier and a version, that uniquely identify it. MTAs contain modules that provide elements and require

elements that are exposed by other modules. Resources are anything required to run the application that aren't contained inside the MTA itself.

- **Module properties**
  Module properties are key/value pairs that are made available to a module at runtime.
- **Resources**
  A resource is a component within an MTA that is required by a module of the MTA at runtime or deployment time but isn't provided inside the MTA. The resource dependency is described within the MTA descriptor. A typical example of a required resource is a relational database.

- **MTA deployment descriptor**
  The MTA deployment descriptor is an enhanced MTA development descriptor that contains prerequisites for the deployment, such as necessary system resources. The file *mtad.yaml* is used by the MTA deployer for the actual deployment. The deployment descriptor is either created manually or generated by SAP Web IDE for SAP HANA.
- **MTA deployer**
  The MTA deployer is a tool that consumes a description of the MTA model and translates it into target-specific native commands for provisioning runtime containers, creating and binding resources, and installing, running, and updating application modules. This service is also called the deploy service.
- **MTA archive**
  An MTA is delivered and distributed in the form of an MTA archive. This archive is used to deploy an application that comprises multiple modules in one deployment operation. An MTA archive contains all the application modules to be deployed. The archives have the file extension *.mtar*. This archive follows the ZIP file format, which means the content can be viewed and updated with standard tools.

An application developer uses development tools to create the components of an MTA that implement the business logic of an application. The MTA development descriptor is used to describe the modules of the application, their dependencies, and required and exposed interfaces. All modules of an MTA and the MTA deployment descriptor can be compiled into one MTA archive. Only the MTA archive file will be deployed to other environments.

An administrator optionally augments the MTA model in the deployment descriptor with an extension descriptor and uses the MTA deployer to initiate the deployment. Extensions are required if, for example, certain details aren't known yet or if certain configurations are different per environment. Examples include proxy information, memory requirements, and URLs, to name a few.

One way to author and build the different source modules of an MTA is to use MTA-aware tools such as SAP Web IDE, managing all MTA source modules as a single MTA project. Another option is the MTA Build tool, which allows the generation of MTA archives in a continuous integration pipeline, as illustrated in Figure 4.10.

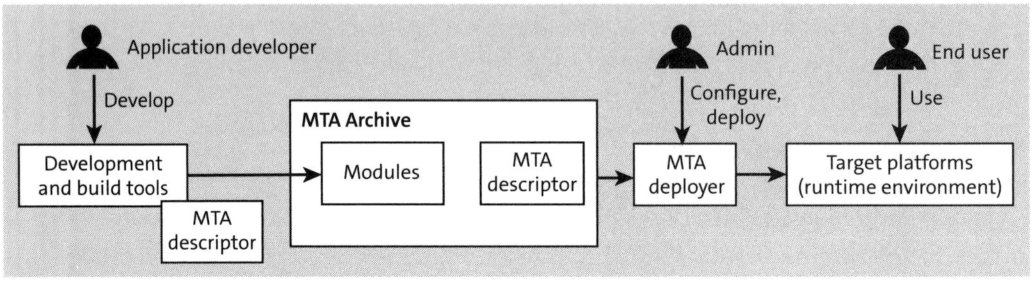

Figure 4.10 MTA Development Lifecycle

4.3.2 Architecture of a Multi-Target Application in SAP HANA XS Advanced

An MTA consists of multiple modules that can be developed using different programming languages and runtime environments. These microservice-type applications are developed using SAP Web IDE for SAP HANA. This browser-based development tool facilitates the development of an MTA. SAP Web IDE for SAP HANA is the central tool for developers to develop, test, and build SAP HANA XS Advanced applications. When creating a new MTA, developers first need to define the relevant space for the application. The space should be dedicated to a certain project in the SAP HANA XS Advanced environment. Business logic is implemented within modules in an MTA. Today, SAP HANA XS Advanced supports the creation of HTML5, Java, Node.js, or SAP HANA database modules. A SAP HANA database module can consist of table definitions via Core Data Services (CDS), calculation views, stored procedures, or table functions, just to name a few examples.

User-provided services enable developers to leverage resources that aren't directly part of an MTA's modules. Examples of such external services include a SAP HANA database schema that isn't part of the SAP HANA XS Advanced application, an external web service, or the central UAA service. As mentioned in Section 1.3, every SAP HANA XS Advanced application has a dedicated container to which database artifacts are deployed. For example, tables or views that belong to an application are deployed to this container. This also means that SAP HANA database schemas that aren't part of the application, for example, will need to be accessed via a user-provided service and a synonym definition in the SAP HANA XS Advanced application. When discussing the data model of our application in Chapter 5, we'll cover the options to access data from a SAP HANA database schema that isn't part of the application.

The source code of an SAP HANA XS Advanced application is managed with an external version management system following the codebase principle of 12-Factor Apps. Git is the recommended version control system for SAP HANA XS Advanced because SAP Web IDE for SAP HANA offers an integration option with Git. Developers, for example, have the option to connect to existing Git repositories via the SAP Web IDE for SAP HANA, clone these repositories, and push source code changes to the external Git repository. SAP also offers an on-premise Git server with Gerrit.

The application is built (compiled and packaged) to an **.MTAR* archive (MTA archive) after the development is completed. The archive is then deployed using either the deploy functionality of the XSA CLI or the respective function of SAP Web IDE for SAP HANA. Required SAP HANA XS Advanced services of the application that can't be resolved automatically, such as the user-provided service for SAP HANA database schema access, need to be deployed before deploying the **.MTAR* archive of the SAP HANA XS Advanced application. However, there is also the option to define user-provided services in the MTA descriptor configuration file as well. The concept is summarized in Figure 4.11.

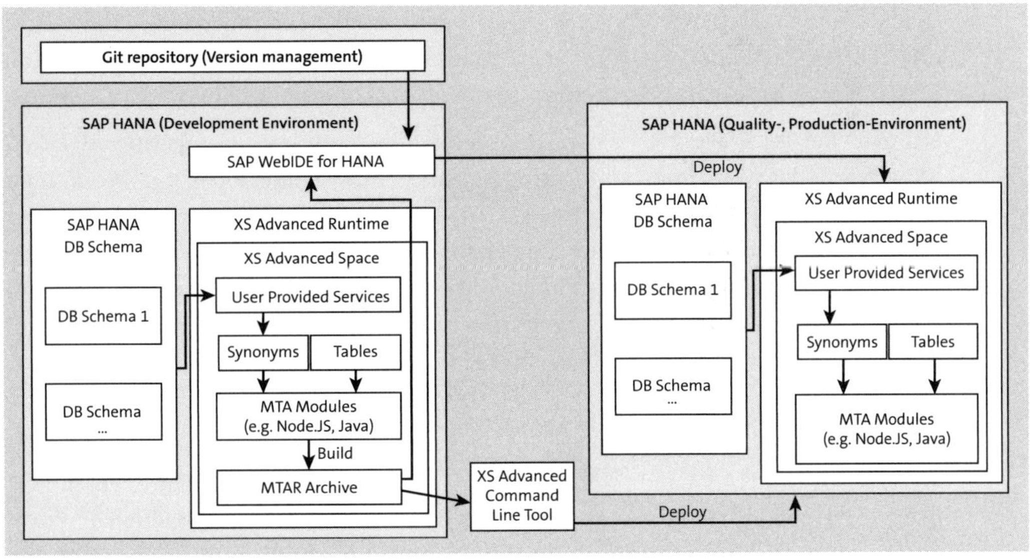

Figure 4.11 Architecture of an MTA with SAP HANA XS Advanced

4.3.3 Development Workflow for Multi-Target Applications

Developers are recommended to work with SAP Web IDE for SAP HANA and a version control system to develop MTAs for the SAP HANA XS Advanced environment. As stated previously, Git is the recommended version control system for SAP HANA XS Advanced because SAP Web IDE for SAP HANA offers a tight integration.

A Git repository can be hosted by a cloud platform provider (e.g., GitHub, Git on the SAP Cloud Platform, or SAP's on-premise Git server Gerrit), or a dedicated server infrastructure for Git repositories can be set up in a customer landscape. It's strongly recommended to have a Git repository available before starting to develop an MTA for SAP HANA XS Advanced to leverage the full capabilities of the Git version control system.

When starting a project, developers need to clone the Git repository in SAP Web IDE for SAP HANA first to start the development after the Git repository has been set up. The setup of the Git repository is typically performed outside the SAP Web IDE for SAP HANA environment. The required setup procedure depends on the Git repository provider system. The development of an SAP HANA XS Advanced application can start after cloning the Git repository in SAP Web IDE for SAP HANA. A developer can start to create new modules in SAP HANA XS Advanced or modify existing ones. The changes within an SAP HANA XS Advanced application need to be pushed regularly to the central Git repository. The Git repository supports the scenario that multiple developers work with one Git repository and push and pull code changes from one central Git repository. After several developers perform changes on the same files, it might be necessary to do some merges. Git also supports this type of scenario.

SAP Web IDE for SAP HANA is used to develop new modules, compile the SAP HANA XS Advanced application, and perform tests. Thus, a developer can work independently on a new feature of an SAP HANA XS Advanced application without impacting other developers. The source code changes become visible for other developers only when the new source code changes are pushed to the Git repository from SAP Web IDE for SAP HANA. A Git pull operation needs to be performed by the other developers to get the latest source code changes into their SAP Web IDE for SAP HANA environment.

An SAP HANA XS Advanced application is compiled via the build functionality in SAP Web IDE for SAP HANA and packaged into an MTA archive file after the development of an SAP HANA XS Advanced application is completed. The archive is then deployed using either the deploy functionality of the XSA CLI tool or the respective function of SAP Web IDE for SAP HANA. Figure 4.12 highlights the steps that are performed by a developer in SAP Web IDE for SAP HANA. The deployment of an **.MTAR* is the final step after an SAP HANA XS Advanced application gets deployed to a new SAP HANA XS Advanced environment. This deployment can be performed either via the XSA CLI tool or via SAP Web IDE for SAP HANA.

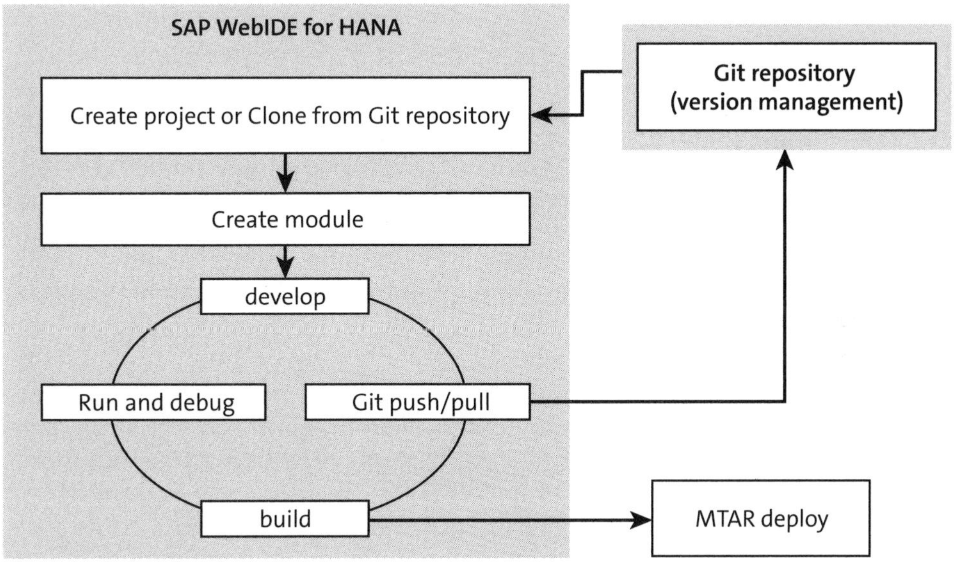

Figure 4.12 Development Workflow of an MTA with SAP HANA XS Advanced

4.4 Summary

In this chapter, we described how the new architecture of SAP HANA XS Advanced extends the capabilities of the SAP HANA database and thus enables the development of new applications that are independently deployable and scalable from the SAP HANA database management system. One of the critical concepts of SAP HANA XS Advanced is a microservices-based architecture. We described this architecture style and the 12-Factor App principles that form the foundation of SAP HANA XS Advanced. Furthermore, we revealed the SAP HANA XS Advanced architecture and its components. Finally, we described the new concept of MTAs and how developers leverage this concept to build SAP HANA XS Advanced applications.

In the next chapter, we'll set the basis of our practical SAP HANA XS Advanced application by discussing the data model and describing the capabilities to create a data model with SAP HANA XS Advanced.

PART II

Developing an Application

Chapter 5
Defining the Data Model

In this chapter, you'll learn the concepts, approach, and steps to build the physical and virtual data model for your SAP HANA extended application services, advanced model (SAP HANA XS Advanced) application.

In the previous chapter, you learned about the architecture and components of the SAP HANA XS Advanced platform. We also discussed the basic principles of building three-tier applications and how it relates to the microservices architecture in SAP HANA XS Advanced using the multi-target application (MTA). In this chapter, we'll discuss the concepts, approach, and steps to build the data model or database layer of the application. We'll take a closer look at how to define the data model of a native SAP HANA application and the differences to a traditional normalized data model. We'll discuss the approach to create the physical data model from entity relationships and proceed to create the database tables using SAP HANA SQL. We'll also briefly introduce the design-time definition of database objects with SAP HANA Repository.

Next, we'll discuss the SAP HANA Deployment Infrastructure (HDI) and its function to create runtime containers in the database. We'll explain how the SAP HANA database module (HDB module) can be used to create runtime objects (tables, views, calculation views, procedures, etc.) using design-time artifacts. We'll explain the use of Core Data Service (CDS) to build physical data models and HDB artifacts to load sample data (comma-separated value [CSV] files) to database tables.

We'll then dive in to creating virtual data models using SAP HANA calculation views to report on top of the physical data model. We'll explain various types of calculation views and their use to build multidimensional models and analytic privileges to secure the data model. In contrast to graphical calculation views, we'll look at building complex business logic using table functions and stored procedures with SQLScript. We'll also discuss best practices for developing good procedures.

Finally, we'll conclude the chapter by discussing other HDI-supported artifacts that can be used to build data models or database artifacts.

5.1 Data Model Overview

A *data model* is a logical representation of data structures of any application that are required to store and retrieve business information efficiently. The data structures include data objects or *entities*, the relationships between the data objects, and the rules of interactions between the data objects.

Entities are physical or abstract things, which have a business meaning in the context of the business application being developed. They can be physical (e.g., a customer, a building, or a part of an automobile), or they can be abstract (e.g., a purchase or a meeting). *Attributes* are used to describe an entity. For example, a customer entity may be described by customer number, name, address, and phone number attributes. Entities are described by at least two attributes. One or more attributes (referred to as *key attributes*) are used to uniquely identify each occurrence of an entity. In the preceding example, the customer number attribute uniquely defines each customer.

Data models also define the relationship between two or more entities. For example, in an online retailer, the customer and products entities are related to each other because customers can buy certain products, and the relationship between products and customer is represented as the order placed by the customer.

In addition to the relationship between entities, the *cardinality* of the relationship must be documented in a data model. Cardinality describes "how many" of one entity is related to "how many" of another entity. For example, a customer can buy many products and a product can also be bought by many customers. Cardinality between two entities can be one-to-many (1:n, 1..1:1..n, or 0..1:0..n), many-to-one (n:1, 0..n:1..1, or 1..n:0..1), or many-to-many (m:n, 0..m:0..n, or 1..m:1..n). Many-to-many (m:n) relationships must be avoided in a data model. These relationship can be resolved using two one-to-many (1:n) relationships. For example, a many-to-many (m:n) relationship between customers and products is resolved by the one-to-many (1:n) relationship between a customer and orders, plus the one-to-many (1:n) relationship between a product and orders.

Note that relationships between entities can be optional (0..1:0..n) or mandatory (1..1:1..n). For example, the relationship between order and product is mandatory because an order can't exist without products. However, the relationship between order and promotion is optional because there can be orders without promotions (coupons or discounts).

An *entity-relationship (ER)* diagram depicts a graphical representation of entities and their relationship in a business application. Figure 5.1 illustrates the ER diagram for our example. ER diagrams are specific to business applications and are independent of the database used.

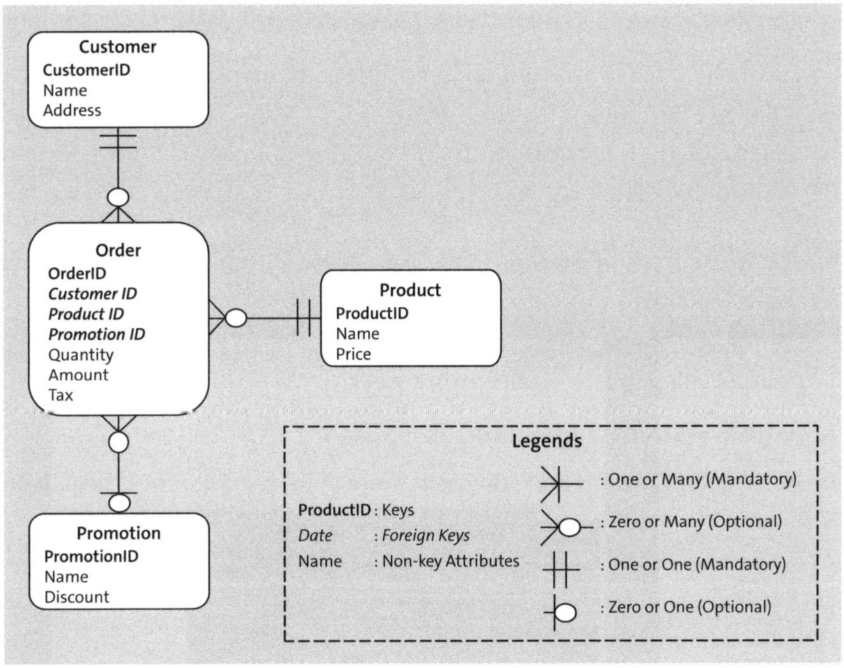

Figure 5.1 ER Diagram

The entities in an ER diagram are converted to database tables when designing the physical data model for a business application.

The process of organizing the tables and table columns in the database is called *normalization*. The idea is to design a database with each table exclusively for one specific purpose, and columns for that specific purpose should be included in the respective tables. There are multiple forms of normalizations, but the *first normal form (1NF)*, *second normal form (2NF)*, and *third normal form (3NF)* are the most common. These forms are progressive; that is, for a table to be in 3NF, it must satisfy the rules of 3NF, 2NF, and 1NF as well. The three normalization forms are as follows (the quotes are from E. F. Codd, 1971):

- **1NF**
  "A relation is in first normal form if and only if the domain of each attribute contains only atomic (indivisible) values, and the value of each attribute contains only a single value from that domain."

So, to qualify for 1NF, the information is stored in a relational table, each table column contains atomic (single) values, and there are no repeating groups of columns.

- **2NF**
  "A relation is in 2NF if it's in 1NF and no nonprime attribute is dependent on any proper subset of any candidate key of the relation."

  So, to qualify for 2NF, the table must be in 1NF, and all the nonkey columns depend on the table's primary key.
- **3NF**
  "A relation is in 3NF if it's in 2NF and every nonprime attribute of the relation is nontransitively dependent on every key of the relation."

  So, to qualify for 3NF, the table must be in in 2NF, and all of its nonkey columns can't be transitively dependent on the primary key.

There are three main reasons to normalize a database:

- To minimize data duplications and efficiently store data to reduce the size of database tables
- To avoid and/or minimize data modification challenges (insert, update, and delete anomalies)
- To simplify data access (select and sort queries)

However, there are times when it isn't worth the time and effort to fully normalize a database simply because a single business transaction may have to touch/modify multiple tables and hence significantly reduce the throughput of the application. In addition, it may take significant resources and time to summarize or aggregate data for management or operational reporting in a highly normalized database. Therefore, there may be a need to denormalize the database tables to meet certain application performance standards. In a high-volume scenario, aggregates or summarized tables are created to enable faster data access and improve the response time of application.

With innovation in database technology and overall reduced storage cost, data modeling in 2NF (or even 1NF) may be good enough for accuracy and performance of the database application.

5.2 The Demo Application

In the Preface, we briefly introduced you to the demo application that will be used throughout this book. To explain the key concepts of native application development, we'll be building an airline management application for a fictitious airline named *Chicken-Wings* (Figure 5.2). This application is loosely based on the SAP Flight Model application available in all SAP ABAP installations.

Figure 5.2 Chicken-Wings Airline

The scope of our ChickenWings airline management application covers the following functional areas:

- **Available flights**
  The application displays the list of available flight connections for a given day in tabular form or on a geographical map. This display can be specific to a date and origin and/or destination airport. This feature will be used to display arrival/departure flight information at the airport.
- **Ticket booking**
  Flights with departure only six months into the future should be available for booking. The application has options for airline customers to search available flights on a given date from specific origin and destination airports. It must have options to sort the flight connections based on time of departure, duration of the flight, and price of a ticket. Customers should be able to select and reserve vacant seats on economy, business, or first class.
- **Alternate airport**
  Customers must have options to find and select an alternate origin or destination airport within a certain distance (say 100 km). The idea is to use the alternate airport to find alternate flight connections for a cheaper price and/or a more convenient departure time.
- **Booking history**
  The application should display the past and future reservations for the logged-in customer, with the option to cancel a future reservation. A reservation cancellation

must free up the canceled seat for other customers. Customers' travel history must include the geographical miles traveled by the customer.

- **Connection management**
  Airline management must have the option to add new flight connections for a future departure (including today) and cancel a future flight connection (at least one hour before departure). A flight cancellation must trigger notification for flight crews and customers.
- **Flight status update**
  Airline staff should have the option to update the status of the flight.
- **Pricing ticket**
  The application will have business logic to adjust the ticket price based on the flight date and number of available seats.
- **Reporting**
  There must be analytical reports, including occupancy, profitability of flights, flight routes, and frequent flying customers.
- **Pilot cockpit/flight status (optional)**
  Current flight status will be provided with estimated arrival and departure status, including current geographical locations and nearby airports for emergency landing.

At a high level, the flight management application for Chicken-Wings Airline has the following entities:

- `Airport`
  Describes the airport with attributes such as airport code, name of the airport, city, country, time zone, and geographical coordinates.
- `Plane`
  Describes the airplane details with attributes such as registration number, registration date, model, manufacturer, year and type of aircraft, maximum seating capacity, and configured economy, business, and first-class seats.
- `Customer`
  Describes the passenger details, such as customer ID, first name, last name, mobile number, email, country, and frequent flyer status.
- `Crew`
  Describes the flight crew details, including crew ID, first name, last name, mobile number, email, country, and role/job (pilot, service director, etc.).

- `Pricing Calendar`
  Seasonal calendar details used to determine ticket pricing with attributes such as date, pricing rate (standard or peak), and season.
- `Seat`
  Describes the seat details for a particular plane model, including seat number, class (economy or business), and type (isle or window).
- `Connection`
  Describes the list of connections offered by the airline with attributes such as flight number, origin airport, destination airport, scheduled departure time, scheduled arrival time, distance in miles, service start date, service end date, standard price for economy class, peak price for economy class, standard price for business class, peak price for business class, standard price for first class, and peak price for first class.
- `Flight`
  Describes the flight details on a specific date with attributes of flight number, departure date, actual departure time, actual arrival time, pilot, co-pilot, crew 1, crew 2, crew 3, crew 4, aircraft/plane, and flight status (schedule, delayed, canceled, departed, and arrived).
- `Booking`
  Describes the flight booking details, including flight number, departure date, seat number, customer, base price, book price, surcharge/fees, discounts, tax, total amount, mode of payment, and check-in status.

The ER diagram of the ChickenWings flight management application is illustrated in Figure 5.3.

Let's discuss the relationship between the entities in our sample use cases. A `Connection` (e.g., CW-101) is defined as a scheduled flight from one airport to another, and there may be multiple connections between two airports, resulting in a many-to-one (0..n:1..1) relationship between the `Connection` entity and `Airport` (origin) and another many-to-one (0..n:1..1) relationship between the `Connection` entity and `Airport` (destination) entity. The `Connection` entity has a mandatory relationship with the `Airport` (origin or destination) entity, and for every connection, there must be one and only one airport as the origin airport and as the destination airport (see Figure 5.3). Therefore, a connection can't exist without an origin airport, whereas an airport can exist without any connections.

Multiple *flights* may be offered (a maximum of one per day) for a connection, whereas it's possible to have connections without a scheduled flight (a brand-new connection being planned or a connection no longer available for booking). There is a many-to-one (0..n:1..1) mandatory relationship between the Flight entity and Connection entity because for every flight, there must be one and only one connection. The Connection entity has a one-to-many optional relationship with the Flight entity and a connection can exist without any scheduled flight.

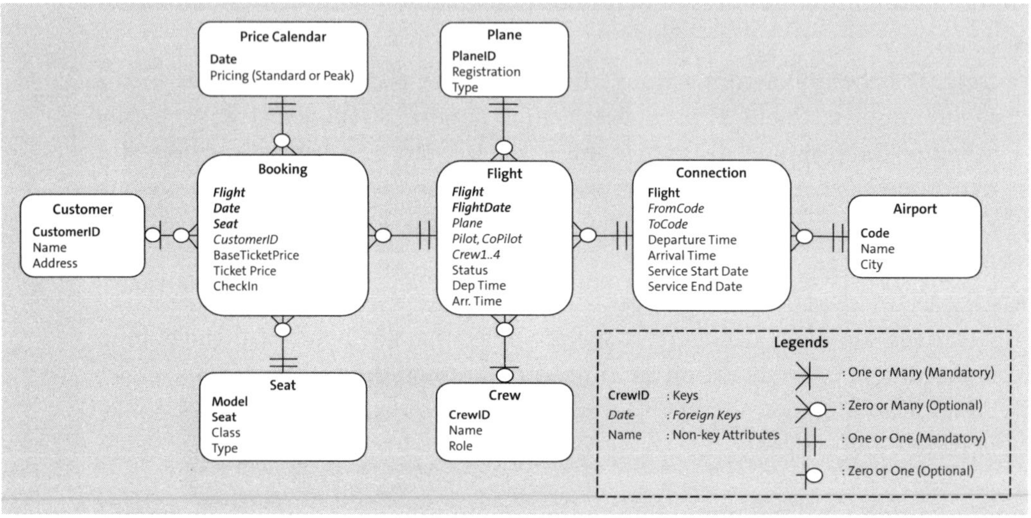

Figure 5.3 ChickenWings Application ER Diagram

Similarly, the Flight entity has a many-to-one (0..n:1..1) mandatory relationship with the Plane entity, and there has to be one and only one plane for every scheduled flight. However, the Plane entity has a one-to-many optional relationship with the Flight entity, so a plane can exist without any flight.

There is a many-to-many (m:n) relationship between Crew and Connection, which has been resolved by using the Flight entity. The Flight entity has a many-to-one (0..n:0..1) optional relationship with the Crew entity on Pilot, Co-pilot, Crew 1, Crew 2, Crew 3, and Crew 4 attributes independent of each other. Therefore, a flight can be defined without crew assignments.

A customer can book multiple seats on a flight, and there can be many customers on a flight. This many-to-many (m:n) relationship between Customer and Flight entities has been resolved with the Booking entity. The Booking entity has a many-to-one (n:1) relationship with the Customer, Flight, Seat, and Price_Calendar entities. The relationship between Booking and Flight entities is mandatory (0..n:1..1), whereas the reverse relationship (between Flight and Booking entities) is optional because there may be no bookings on a future flight. A seat must be assigned for every booking, so the Booking entity has a mandatory many-to-one (0:n:1..1) relationship with the Seat entity. The Booking entity has an optional many-to-one (0..n:0..1) relationship with the Customer entity because there can be vacant/available seats not yet booked by any customer. The Customer entity also has an optional one-to-many (0..1:0..n) relationship with the Booking entity because there can be (new) customers who haven't booked any seats yet. Finally, the Booking entity has a mandatory many-to-one (0..n:1..1) relationship with the Price_Calendar entity because bookings can't me made without pricing details.

5.3 Data Model Design in SAP HANA

SAP HANA is an atomicity, consistency, isolation, durability (ACID)-compliant, in-memory columnar database that supports high-speed transactions along with advanced analytics with a subsecond response.

SAP HANA supports ANSI standard SQL syntax, as well as procedural programming language SQLScript based on ANSI SQL-92 to create database stored procedures, functions, and so on. SAP HANA supports Data Definition Language (DDL) to define database objects (CREATE, ALTER, DROP, etc.), Data Manipulation Language (DML) to read and manipulate data sets (SELECT, INSERT, UPDATE, DELETE), and Data Control Language (DCL) for access control (GRANT, REVOKE, CREATE/ALTER/DROP USER/ROLE). It also supports SQL statements for transaction management (COMMIT, ROLLBACK, SET TRANSACTION, LOCK TABLE), system management (ALTER SYSTEM), and session management (CONNECT, SET SCHEMA, SET/UNSET SESSION).

ANSI SQL

SQL is a language used to define, access, manipulate, and manage data structures in a relational database. SQL is based on the concept of processing a set of records with a single command and consists of the DDL, DML, and DCL, as just mentioned.

The body of the International Electrotechnical Commission (IEC) and the International Organization for Standardization (ISO) collaborated with national standards bodies such as American National Standards Institute (ANSI) to unify SQL for best practices and created specific standards for database query languages. SQL became an ANSI standard in 1986 and an ISO standard in 1987.

Most relational database systems support the ANSI-92 SQL standard (SELECT, INSERT, UPDATE, DELETE, and WHERE) but also have their own proprietary extensions to the SQL standard.

Like any other relational database, data models in SAP HANA can be created using SQL statements. In the next four sections, we'll introduce various SAP HANA tools to execute SQL commands; discuss commonly used SQL statements to create database tables, views, and procedures; and interact with data in the database objects. We'll also explain the approach to convert the ER diagram of our sample application (developed in the preceding section) to database tables using SQL statements and SAP HANA Repository design-time objects.

5.3.1 Executing SQL Commands in SAP HANA

SAP HANA Studio or SAP Web IDE for SAP HANA can be used to connect to SAP HANA and execute SQL commands in *SQL Console*. These development tools are discussed in Chapter 3.

To access the SQL Console in SAP HANA Studio, select the SAP HANA system in the **Systems** view, and choose **Open SQL Console** in the context menu or from the SQL icon in the toolbar, as illustrated in Figure 5.4.

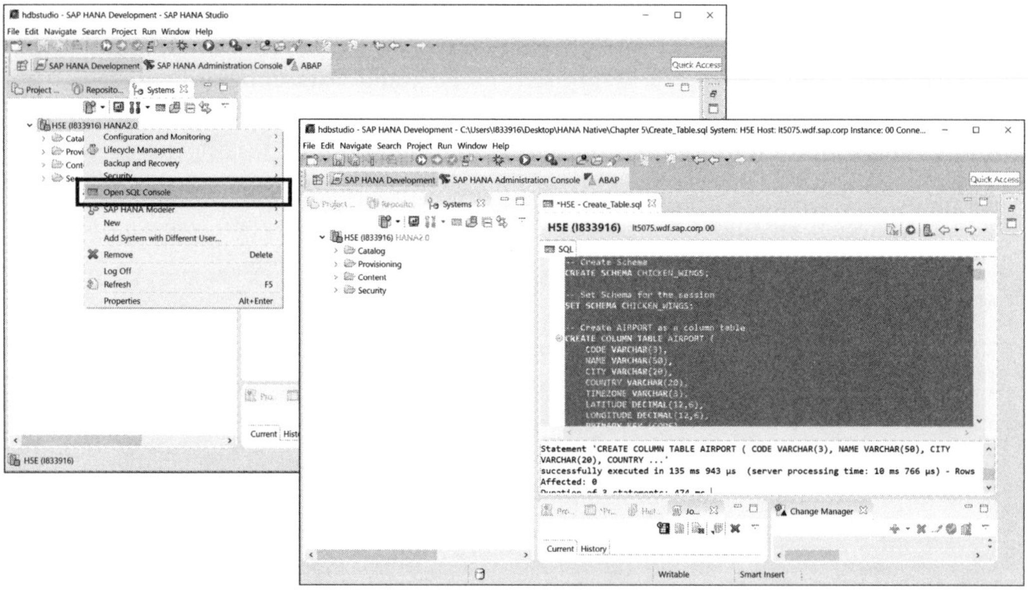

Figure 5.4 SQL Console in SAP HANA Studio

To access the **Database Explorer** in SAP Web IDE for SAP HANA, select the **Tools • Database Explorer** menu item or select the icon. To access the SQL Console in SAP

HANA database explorer, select the SAP HANA system, and then choose the **Open SQL Console** menu item in the context menu or from the SQL icon in the toolbar, as illustrated in Figure 5.5.

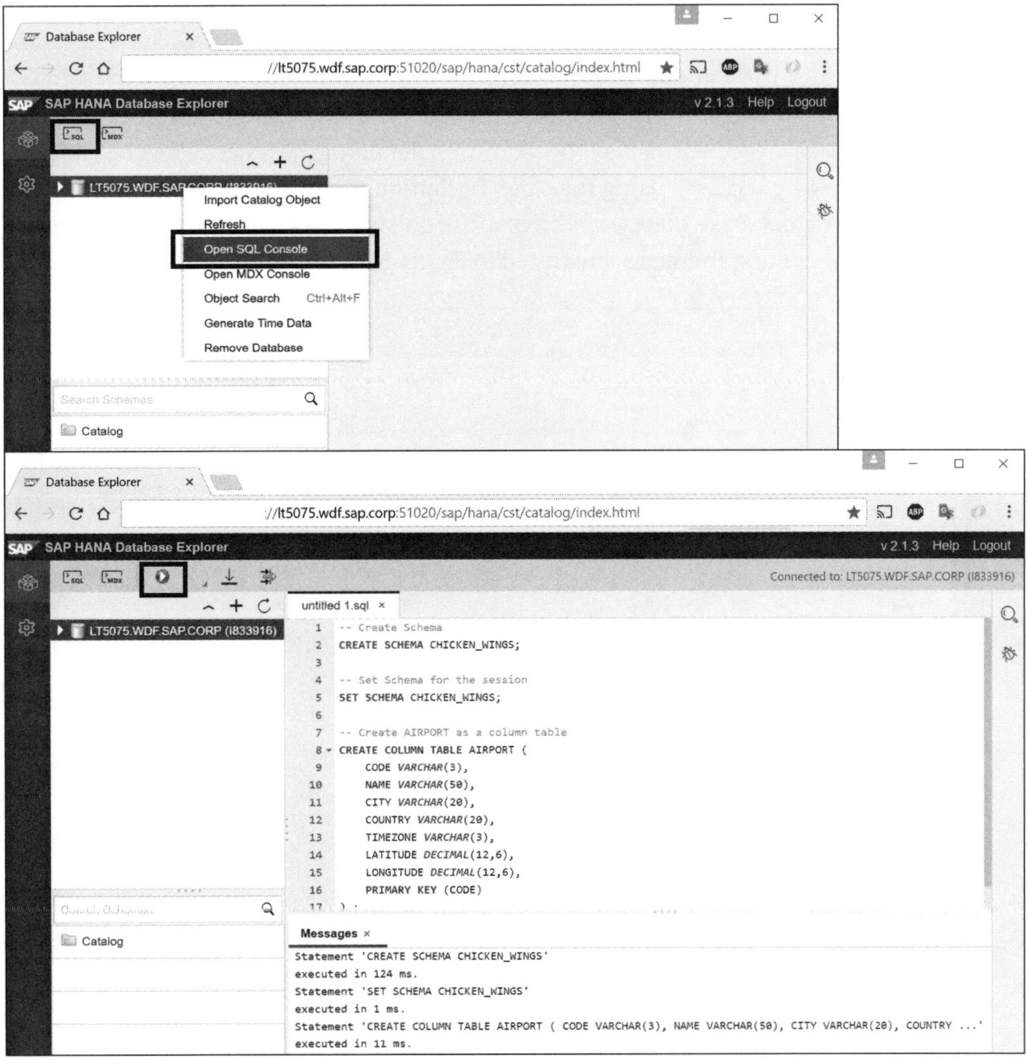

Figure 5.5 SQL Console in SAP HANA Database Explorer

In the SQL Console, specify SQL commands to define and modify the structure of SAP HANA database objects (DDL), query and modify table contents (DML), and manage rights (DCL). To execute one or more SQL statements, select the appropriate SQL statements in the SQL Console and click on the **Execute** button in SAP HANA Studio (**Run** button in SAP HANA database explorer). The execution status and error messages (if any) are also displayed in the SQL Console.

In SAP HANA Studio, the database objects defined in the SAP HANA system can be viewed under the **Catalog** folder. Different database objects are organized into a folder structure according to their database schema and object types. Double-clicking on a database object will display the definition details of the object. The object definition can also be accessed using the **Open Definition** menu item in the context menu. Content of a database object can be displayed using the **Open Data Preview** menu item in the context menu, as illustrated in Figure 5.6.

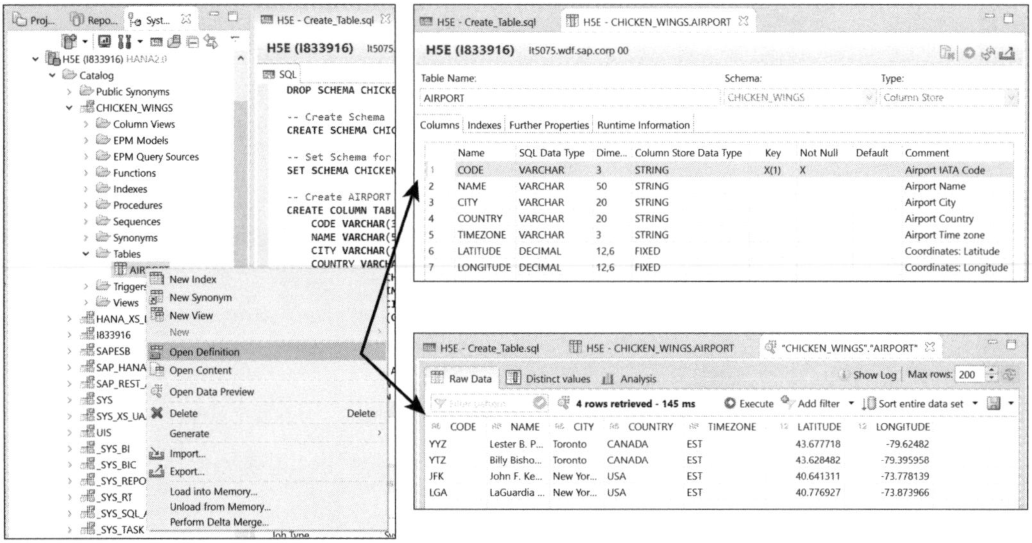

Figure 5.6 Database Objects in SAP HANA Studio

Similarly, in SAP HANA database explorer, the database objects defined in the SAP HANA system can be viewed under the **Catalog** folder. Database objects are organized into different categories under each schema. Selecting a category will display the list of objects in the display area below. Double-clicking on a database object will display the definition details of the object. The object definition can also be accessed using the **Open** menu item in the context menu. Content of a database object can be displayed using the **Open Data** menu item in the context menu, as illustrated in Figure 5.7.

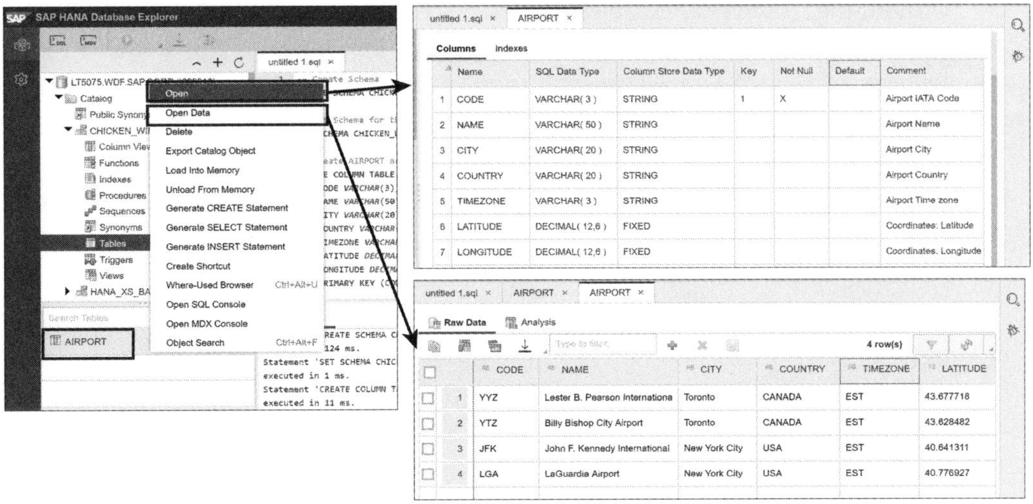

Figure 5.7 Database Objects in SAP HANA Database Explorer

5.3.2 Commonly Used SQL Statements

Some of the commonly used SQL statements to define SAP HANA tables are discussed in the following sections. Refer to SAP HANA SQL and System Views Reference guide (*https://bit.ly/2sR5K4u*) for the complete list of SQL statements supported by SAP HANA.

CREATE SCHEMA

`CREATE SCHEMA` creates a new schema in the database. The syntax for this statement is as follows:

```
CREATE SCHEMA <schema_name> [OWNED BY <user_name>]
```

In this syntax, <schema_name> specifies the schema name, and <user_name> specifies the name of the schema owner. If <user_name> is omitted, the current user is the owner of the schema. An example of this syntax in action is as follows:

```
CREATE SCHEMA CHICKEN_WINGS;
```

SET SCHEMA

`SET SCHEMA` changes the current schema for the session. When schema is set for a session, objects in the specified schema (i.e., tables, views, etc.) can be referenced without the schema name. Objects in other schemas have to be referenced with the schema name, for example, MY_SCHEMA.MY_TABLE. The syntax for this statement is as follows:

```
SET SCHEMA <schema_name>
```

In this syntax, <schema_name> specifies the name of the schema. An example of this syntax in action is as follows:

```
SET SCHEMA CHICKEN_WINGS;
```

CREATE TABLE

CREATE TABLE creates a new table in the database. The syntax for this statement, in its simplest form, is as follows:

```
CREATE [<table_type>] TABLE <table_name> (
<column_name> <data_type>,
<column_name> <data_type>,...
PRIMARY KEY (<column_name>,<column_name>..))
```

In this syntax, <table_type> defines the type of table storage organization such as COLUMN, ROW, HISTORY COLUMN, and so on. The default value is ROW. We'll be using COLUMN tables for defining our data model.

In addition, <table_name> and <column_name> specify the name of the table and columns to be created, respectively. The <table name> and <column_name> attributes are case sensitive if specified using double quotes (e.g., "Airport" instead of Airport).

Next, <data_type> specifies the data type of the columns in the table. Commonly used data types are INTEGER, NVARCHAR(x), DECIMAL(p,s), DATE, TIME, and so on. Refer to the SAP HANA SQL and System Views Reference guide for a complete list of supported data types. An example of this syntax in action is as follows:

```
CREATE COLUMN TABLE AIRPORT (
CODE NVARCHAR(3),
NAME NVARCHAR(50),
CITY NVARCHAR(20),
PRIMARY KEY (CODE));
```

COMMENT ON

COMMENT ON adds or removes a comment to an object in the database. The syntax for this statement is as follows:

```
COMMENT ON <object_type> <object_name> IS <comment>
```

In this syntax, <object_type> specifies the type of object, that is, table, view, or column; <object_name> specifies the name of the object to add the comment to; and <comment> specifies the comment itself. If NULL is specified, then any existing comment is dropped. An example of this syntax in action is as follows:

```
-- Comment on 'Airport' Table
COMMENT ON TABLE AIRPORT is 'Airport Details';
-- Comment on 'CODE' Column of 'AIRPORT' table
COMMENT ON COLUMN AIRPORT.CODE is 'Airport IATA Code';
```


ALTER TABLE

ALTER TABLE alters the definition of a table, that is, to add/drop table columns, create/drop constraints such as foreign keys, and so on. The syntax to add a foreign key constraint is as follows:

```
ALTER TABLE <table_name> ADD CONSTRAINT <constraint_name>
FOREIGN KEY
(<referencing_column_name> [{,<referencing_column_name>}...])
REFERENCE (<table_name>(<referenced_column_name>[{,<referenced _column_
name>}...]);
```

An example of this syntax in action is as follows:

```
-- AIRPORT.CODE is referenced from CONNECTION.FROMAP column
ALTER TABLE CONNECTION ADD CONSTRAINT FK_CONNECTION_AIRPORT_FROM
FOREIGN KEY (FROMAP) REFERENCES AIRPORT(CODE)
```

INSERT INTO

INSERT INTO adds a record to a table, and the syntax is as follows:

```
INSERT INTO <table_name> [<column_list>] VALUES (
<column_value>, <column_value>, ...)
```

In this syntax, the optional <column_list> specifies the list of columns for which values are provided. If <column_list> isn't provided, values must be provided for all columns. In addition, <column_value> specifies the value for each column.

An example of this syntax in action is as follows:

```
INSERT INTO AIRPORT VALUES ('YYZ','Lester B. Pearson International',
'Toronto','CANADA','EST',43.677718,-79.624820);
```

SELECT

SELECT retrieves information from the database table, and the syntax in its simplest form is as follows:

```
SELECT <column_name> [,column_name, column_name] FROM <table_name>;
```

In this syntax, <column_name> specifies the list of columns to retrieve data from the <table_name> table. An example of this syntax in action is as follows:

```
-- Retrieves data for all columns
SELECT * FROM AIRPORT;
-- Retrieves data for selected columns
SELECT CODE, NAME, CITY, COUNTRY FROM AIRPORT;
```

5.3.3 Converting an Entity-Relationship Model to a Database Design

With support of the ANSI-92 SQL standard, data models can be created in SAP HANA like any other relational database. In addition, SAP HANA has the following advantages over traditional relational databases for designing efficient data models:

- **Denormalization**
  SAP HANA supports both row-based and column-based tables. In a column table, all values in a column are stored together, so access to individual data elements (e.g., employee name) is significantly faster than traditional row-store tables. Column tables can use dictionary and other compression techniques to store data efficiently, and this compression enables even faster columnar operations. In addition, due to dictionary compression, the size of the column is based on the number of unique values in the column, as opposed to the number of records in the tables. Therefore, columns with all null values or columns with values populated for a few rows have virtually no impact on the overall size of the column table. This has a significant positive influence in the data model design, as denormalization can be used to improve read (SELECT) performance without comprising the write (INSERT) performance and size of the database table.
- **Indices on each column**
  Because column tables employ some form of dictionary compression techniques to efficiently store and retrieve data, the dictionary at each column acts as an

index for each column, which eliminates the need for an index on a column table to enable data access.

- **No need for aggregate tables**
  With SAP HANA column tables, columnar aggregation operations such as `SUM`, `MIN`, `MAX`, and `AVG` are significantly faster than row store tables. With SAP HANA, all data is stored in memory (RAM), which gives the CPUs quick access to data for processing. SAP HANA comes as an appliance with multicore CPUs, multiple CPUs per board, and multiple boards per server—all running in parallel to provide serious computational power and virtually eliminate the need for preaggregated tables.
- **Design-time and runtime objects**
  Starting with SAP HANA SP 05, SAP HANA supports SAP HANA extended application services, classic model (SAP HANA XS)-based design-time definition of the objects (`.hdbschema`, `.hdbtable`, etc.), which creates the corresponding runtime objects (schema, tables, etc.) when activated. The SAP HANA XS-based developments are discussed in Section 5.3.4.

  Starting with SAP HANA 1.0 SP 11, SAP introduced further enhancements to the design-time definition and deployment on the SAP HANA XS Advanced infrastructure, which is the focus of this book. The design-time definition of the objects can be used for change management, effective version control, and simplified deployment processes.

Based on the advantages just outlined, SAP HANA provides significant flexibility in designing truly agile data models to meet business requirements. We'll still follow the normalization approach to store the data efficiently, but our primary focus is ease of accessing data vs. avoiding redundancy to minimize storage cost.

Now that you have a basic understanding of creating SAP HANA persistence models using SAP HANA SQL and SAP HANA XS design-time objects, let's proceed to define the data model for our sample use case. In the SAP HANA database, as in other relational databases, an entity is represented as a table with fixed number columns, but it can have any number of rows.

The ER diagram of the ChickenWings application was illustrated earlier in Figure 5.3. In this section, we'll discuss the process to convert each entity in the ER diagram to database tables in the SAP HANA database. As a starting point, all entities in the ER diagram will be converted to database tables, and we'll simplify the structure by applying standard rules of normalization (where applicable).

AIRPORT Table

The structure of the AIRPORT table is {Code + Name, City, County, Timezone, Coordinates} where the Code attribute is the primary key. To store data efficiently and simplify data access, the AIRPORT table should meet 3NF. For the AIRPORT table to be in 3NF, it must satisfy the rules of 3NF, 2NF, and 1NF as well:

- **Check for 1NF**
  All attributes except Coordinates are atomic in nature; that is, each of them contains a single value. We'll split the Coordinate attribute into two separate Longitude and Latitude attributes for the AIRPORT table to qualify for 1NF.
- **Check for 2NF**
  To satisfy 2NF, all nonkey attributes must be dependent on the primary key. The attributes Country and Timezone are dependent upon the City attribute as opposed to Code. So, the AIRPORT the table isn't in 2NF. To satisfy 2NF, it must be split into two tables, that is, AIRPORT {Code + Name, City, Latitude, Longitude} and City {City, Country, Timezone}, as illustrated in Figure 5.8.

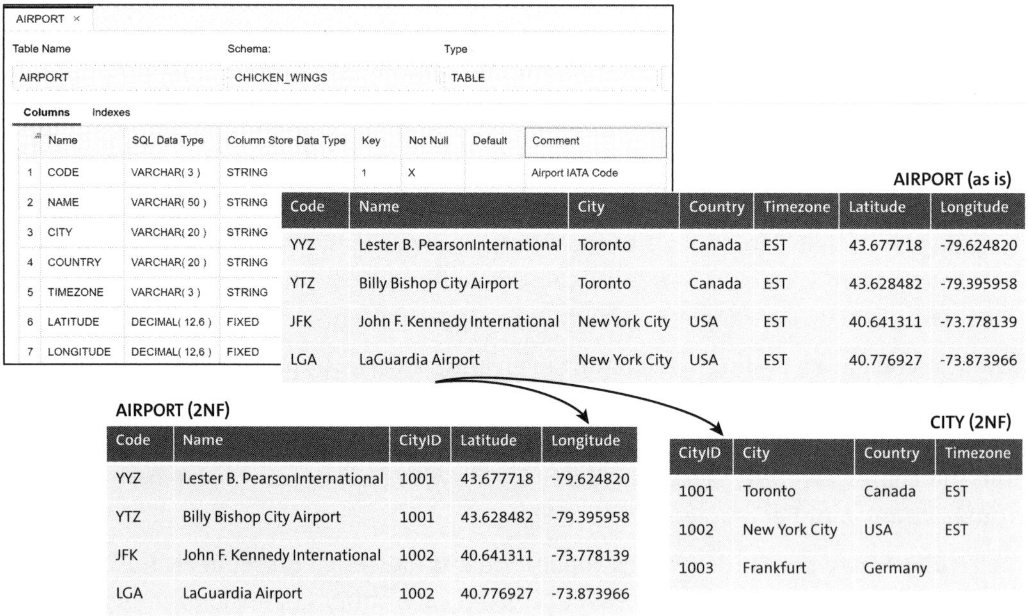

AIRPORT ×

Table Name	Schema:	Type
AIRPORT	CHICKEN_WINGS	TABLE

Columns | Indexes

	Name	SQL Data Type	Column Store Data Type	Key	Not Null	Default	Comment
1	CODE	VARCHAR(3)	STRING	1	X		Airport IATA Code
2	NAME	VARCHAR(50)	STRING				
3	CITY	VARCHAR(20)	STRING				
4	COUNTRY	VARCHAR(20)	STRING				
5	TIMEZONE	VARCHAR(3)	STRING				
6	LATITUDE	DECIMAL(12,6)	FIXED				
7	LONGITUDE	DECIMAL(12,6)	FIXED				

AIRPORT (as is)

Code	Name	City	Country	Timezone	Latitude	Longitude
YYZ	Lester B. PearsonInternational	Toronto	Canada	EST	43.677718	-79.624820
YTZ	Billy Bishop City Airport	Toronto	Canada	EST	43.628482	-79.395958
JFK	John F. Kennedy International	NewYork City	USA	EST	40.641311	-73.778139
LGA	LaGuardia Airport	New York City	USA	EST	40.776927	-73.873966

AIRPORT (2NF)

Code	Name	CityID	Latitude	Longitude
YYZ	Lester B. PearsonInternational	1001	43.677718	-79.624820
YTZ	Billy Bishop City Airport	1001	43.628482	-79.395958
JFK	John F. Kennedy International	1002	40.641311	-73.778139
LGA	LaGuardia Airport	1002	40.776927	-73.873966

CITY (2NF)

CityID	City	Country	Timezone
1001	Toronto	Canada	EST
1002	New York City	USA	EST
1003	Frankfurt	Germany	

Figure 5.8 AIRPORT Table

However, for our use case, it doesn't make sense to split the AIRPORT table because the volume of the data set is very small, and keeping all the fields together in one table will simplify data access. Data entry to the AIRPORT table (as is) can be effectively managed by the user interface (UI).

The AIRPORT table can be defined using the SQL code in Listing 5.1.

```
-- Create AIRPORT as a column table
CREATE COLUMN TABLE AIRPORT (
CODE NVARCHAR(3),
NAME NVARCHAR(50),
CITY NVARCHAR(20),
COUNTRY NVARCHAR(20),
TIMEZONE NVARCHAR(3),
LATITUDE DECIMAL(12,6),
LONGITUDE DECIMAL(12,6),
PRIMARY KEY (CODE)
);
-- Comments on the Table
COMMENT ON TABLE AIRPORT is 'Airport Details';
COMMENT ON COLUMN AIRPORT.CODE is 'Airport IATA Code';
COMMENT ON COLUMN AIRPORT.NAME is 'Airport Name';
COMMENT ON COLUMN AIRPORT.CITY is 'Airport City';
COMMENT ON COLUMN AIRPORT.COUNTRY is 'Airport Country';
COMMENT ON COLUMN AIRPORT.TIMEZONE is 'Airport Time zone';
COMMENT ON COLUMN AIRPORT.LATITUDE is 'Coordinates: Latitude';
COMMENT ON COLUMN AIRPORT.LONGITUDE is 'Coordinates: Longitude';
```

Listing 5.1 Defining the AIRPORT Table

PLANE Table

The structure of the PLANE table is {RegNo + Model, Manufacturer, Year, Type, RegDate, MaxSeat, Economy, Business, FirstClass}, where the RegNo attribute is the primary key. To store data efficiently and simplify data access, the PLANE table should meet 3NF. For the PLANE table to be in 3NF, it must satisfy the rules of 3NF, 2NF, and 1NF:

- **Check for 1NF**
  Because all attributes are atomic in nature, and there are no repeating attributes, the PLANE table is in 1NF.
- **Check for 2NF**
  To satisfy 2NF, all nonkey attributes must be dependent on the primary key RegNo field. However, the attributes Manufacturer, Type, and MaxSeat (maximum number

of seats) are dependent upon the `Model` attribute as opposed to `RegNo` (plane registration number). Therefore, these fields can be split into a separate `MODEL` table {`Model` + `Manufacturer, Type, MaxSeat`}, as illustrated in Figure 5.9. The as-is `PLANE` table doesn't qualify for 2NF.

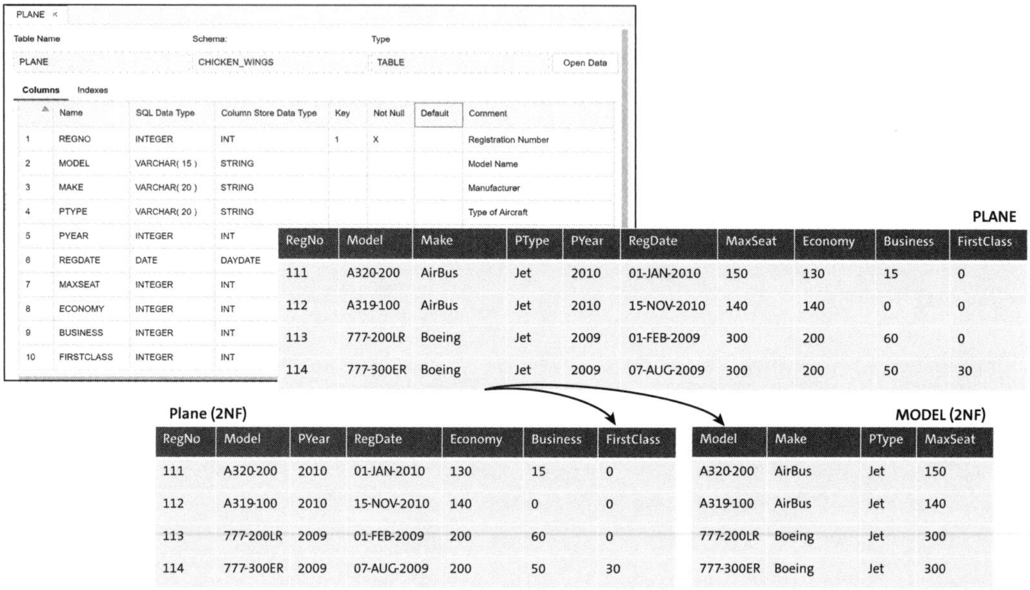

PLANE ×

Table Name: PLANE | Schema: CHICKEN_WINGS | Type: TABLE | Open Data

Columns | Indexes

	Name	SQL Data Type	Column Store Data Type	Key	Not Null	Default	Comment
1	REGNO	INTEGER	INT	1	X		Registration Number
2	MODEL	VARCHAR(15)	STRING				Model Name
3	MAKE	VARCHAR(20)	STRING				Manufacturer
4	PTYPE	VARCHAR(20)	STRING				Type of Aircraft
5	PYEAR	INTEGER	INT				
6	REGDATE	DATE	DAYDATE				
7	MAXSEAT	INTEGER	INT				
8	ECONOMY	INTEGER	INT				
9	BUSINESS	INTEGER	INT				
10	FIRSTCLASS	INTEGER	INT				

PLANE

RegNo	Model	Make	PType	PYear	RegDate	MaxSeat	Economy	Business	FirstClass
111	A320-200	AirBus	Jet	2010	01-JAN-2010	150	130	15	0
112	A319-100	AirBus	Jet	2010	15-NOV-2010	140	140	0	0
113	777-200LR	Boeing	Jet	2009	01-FEB-2009	300	200	60	0
114	777-300ER	Boeing	Jet	2009	07-AUG-2009	300	200	50	30

Plane (2NF)

RegNo	Model	PYear	RegDate	Economy	Business	FirstClass
111	A320-200	2010	01-JAN-2010	130	15	0
112	A319-100	2010	15-NOV-2010	140	0	0
113	777-200LR	2009	01-FEB-2009	200	60	0
114	777-300ER	2009	07-AUG-2009	200	50	30

MODEL (2NF)

Model	Make	PType	MaxSeat
A320-200	AirBus	Jet	150
A319-100	AirBus	Jet	140
777-200LR	Boeing	Jet	300
777-300ER	Boeing	Jet	300

Figure 5.9 PLANE Table

However, it doesn't make sense to split the `PLANE` table for our use case, as keeping all the fields together in one table will simplify data access. The `PLANE` table can be defined using the SQL code in Listing 5.2.

```
-- Create PLANE as a column table
CREATE COLUMN TABLE PLANE (
REGNO INTEGER,
MODEL NVARCHAR(15),
MANUFACTURER NVARCHAR(20),
TYPE NVARCHAR(20),
YEAR INTEGER,
REGDATE DATE,
MAXSEAT INTEGER,
ECONOMY INTEGER,
```

```
BUSINESS INTEGER,
FIRSTCLASS INTEGER,
PRIMARY KEY (REGNO)
) ;

-- Comments
COMMENT ON TABLE PLANE is 'Plane Details';
COMMENT ON COLUMN PLANE.REGNO is 'Registration Number';
COMMENT ON COLUMN PLANE.MODEL is 'Model Name';
COMMENT ON COLUMN PLANE.MANUFACTURER is 'Manufacturer';
COMMENT ON COLUMN PLANE.TYPE is 'Type of Aircraft';
COMMENT ON COLUMN PLANE.YEAR is 'Year of Manufacture';
COMMENT ON COLUMN PLANE.REGDATE is 'Registration Date';
COMMENT ON COLUMN PLANE.MAXSEAT is 'Maximum Seating Capacity';
COMMENT ON COLUMN PLANE.ECONOMY is 'No of Economy Class Seats';
COMMENT ON COLUMN PLANE.BUSINESS is 'No of Business Class Seats';
COMMENT ON COLUMN PLANE.FIRSTCLASS is 'No of First Class Seats';
```

Listing 5.2 Defining the PLANE Table

Customer Table

The structure of the CUSTOMER table is {CustID + FName, LName, Mobile, Email, Country, FlyerID}, where the CustID attribute is the primary key. To store data efficiently and simplify data access, the CUSTOMER table should meet 3NF. For the CUSTOMER table to be in 3NF, it must satisfy the rules of 3NF, 2NF, and 1NF as well:

- **Check for 1NF**
  Because all attributes of the CUSTOMER table are atomic in nature, and it doesn't have repeating attributes, the CUSTOMER table is in 1NF.
- **Check for 2NF**
  Because all nonkey attributes of the CUSTOMER table are dependent on the primary key CustID, it's also in 2NF.
- **Check for 3NF**
  Because there is no transitive relation between the attributes of the CUSTOMER table, it's also in 3NF.

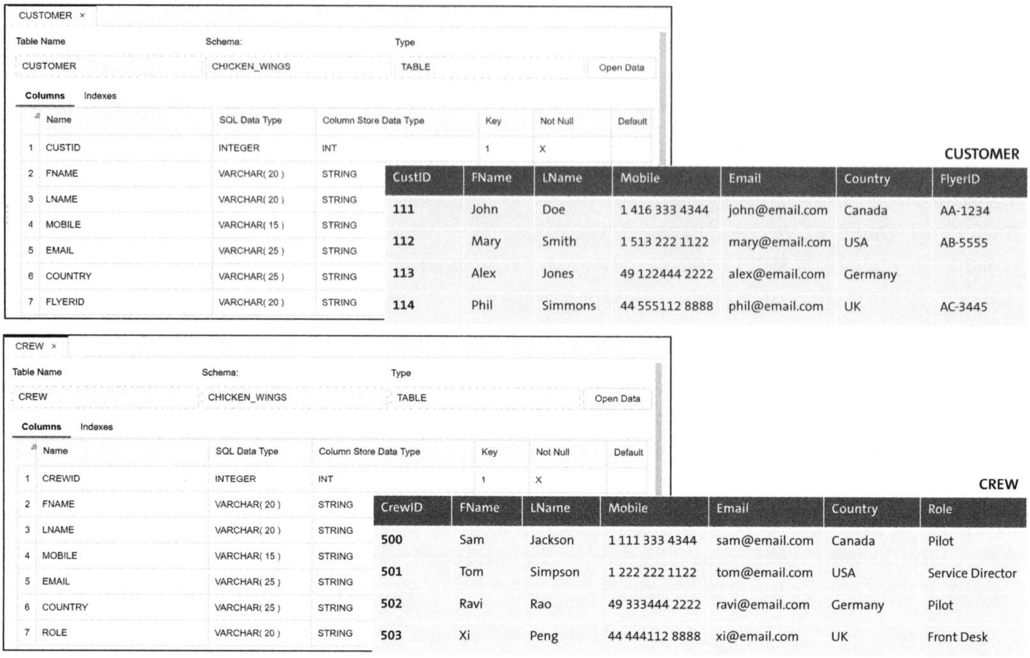

CUSTOMER

CustID	FName	LName	Mobile	Email	Country	FlyerID
111	John	Doe	1 416 333 4344	john@email.com	Canada	AA-1234
112	Mary	Smith	1 513 222 1122	mary@email.com	USA	AB-5555
113	Alex	Jones	49 122444 2222	alex@email.com	Germany	
114	Phil	Simmons	44 555112 8888	phil@email.com	UK	AC-3445

CREW

CrewID	FName	LName	Mobile	Email	Country	Role
500	Sam	Jackson	1 111 333 4344	sam@email.com	Canada	Pilot
501	Tom	Simpson	1 222 222 1122	tom@email.com	USA	Service Director
502	Ravi	Rao	49 333444 2222	ravi@email.com	Germany	Pilot
503	Xi	Peng	44 444112 8888	xi@email.com	UK	Front Desk

Figure 5.10 CUSTOMER and CREW Table

The structure of the CUSTOMER table is illustrated in Figure 5.10, and it can be defined using the SQL code in Listing 5.3.

```
-- Create CUSTOMER as a column table
CREATE COLUMN TABLE CUSTOMER (
CUSTID INTEGER,
FNAME NVARCHAR(20),
LNAME NVARCHAR(20),
MOBILE NVARCHAR(15),
EMAIL NVARCHAR(25),
COUNTRY NVARCHAR(25),
FLYERID NVARCHAR(20),
PRIMARY KEY (CUSTID)
) ;
-- Comments
COMMENT ON TABLE CUSTOMER is 'Customer Details';
COMMENT ON COLUMN CUSTOMER.CUSTID is 'Customer ID';
```

```
COMMENT ON COLUMN CUSTOMER.FNAME is 'First Name';
COMMENT ON COLUMN CUSTOMER.LNAME is 'Last Name';
COMMENT ON COLUMN CUSTOMER.MOBILE is 'Mobile/Cell Number';
COMMENT ON COLUMN CUSTOMER.EMAIL is 'Email';
COMMENT ON COLUMN CUSTOMER.COUNTRY is 'Country of Residence';
COMMENT ON COLUMN CUSTOMER.FLYERID is 'Frequent Flyer ID';
```

Listing 5.3 Defining the CUSTOMER Table

Crew Table

The structure of the CREW table is {CrewID + FName, LName, Mobile, Email, Country, Role}, where CrewID is the primary key. Like the CUSTOMER table, the CREW table is also in 3NF.

The structure of the Crew table is illustrated in Figure 5.10, shown previously, and it can be defined using the SQL code in Listing 5.4.

```
-- Create CREW as a column table
CREATE COLUMN TABLE CREW (
CREWID INTEGER,
FNAME NVARCHAR(20),
LNAME NVARCHAR(20),
MOBILE NVARCHAR(15),
EMAIL NVARCHAR(25),
COUNTRY NVARCHAR(25),
ROLE NVARCHAR(20),
PRIMARY KEY (CREWID)
) ;
-- Comments
COMMENT ON TABLE CREW is 'CREW Details';
COMMENT ON COLUMN CREW.CREWID is 'Crew ID';
COMMENT ON COLUMN CREW.FNAME is 'First Name';
COMMENT ON COLUMN CREW.LNAME is 'Last Name';
COMMENT ON COLUMN CREW.MOBILE is 'Mobile/Cell Number';
COMMENT ON COLUMN CREW.EMAIL is 'Email';
COMMENT ON COLUMN CREW.COUNTRY is 'Country of Residence';
COMMENT ON COLUMN CREW.ROLE is 'Job/Role of Crew';
```

Listing 5.4 Defining the CREW Table

PRICE_CALENDAR Table

The structure of the PRICE_CALENDAR table is {CDate + Rate, Season}, where CDate is the primary key. Like the CUSTOMER table, the PRICE_CALENDAR table is also in 3NF.

The structure of the PRICE_CALENDAR table is illustrated in Figure 5.11, and it can be defined using the SQL code in Listing 5.5.

```
-- Create PRICE_CALENDAR as a column table
CREATE COLUMN TABLE PRICE_CALENDAR (
CDATE DATE,
RATE NVARCHAR(10),
SEASON NVARCHAR(20),
PRIMARY KEY (CDATE)
) ;
-- Comments
COMMENT ON TABLE PRICE_CALENDAR is 'Price Calendar';
COMMENT ON COLUMN PRICE_CALENDAR.CDATE is 'Date';
COMMENT ON COLUMN PRICE_CALENDAR.RATE is 'Standard or Peak Rate for Pricing';
COMMENT ON COLUMN PRICE_CALENDAR.SEASON is 'Season used for Pricing';
```

Listing 5.5 Defining the PRICE_CALENDAR Table

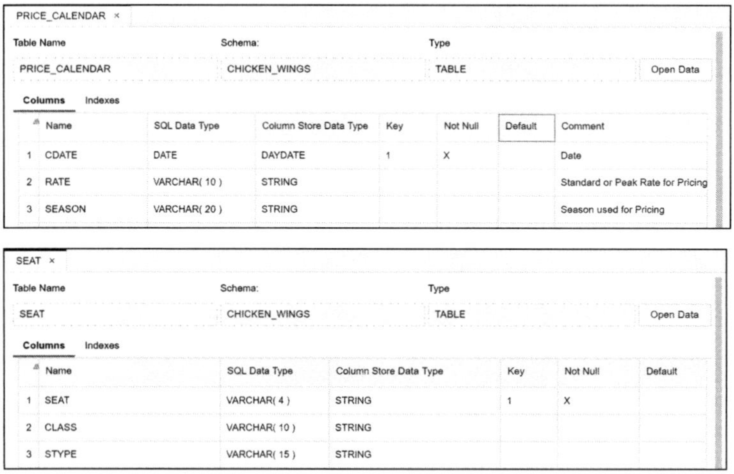

PRICE_CALENDAR ×

Table Name	Schema:		Type				
PRICE_CALENDAR	CHICKEN_WINGS		TABLE				Open Data

Columns   Indexes

	Name	SQL Data Type	Column Store Data Type	Key	Not Null	Default	Comment
1	CDATE	DATE	DAYDATE	1	X		Date
2	RATE	VARCHAR(10)	STRING				Standard or Peak Rate for Pricing
3	SEASON	VARCHAR(20)	STRING				Season used for Pricing

PRICE_CALENDAR

CDate	Rate	Season
31-DEC-2017	Peak	Holiday
01-JAN-2017	Standard	Holiday
02-JAN-2017	Peak	Holiday
03-JAN-2017	Standard	Regular

SEAT ×

Table Name	Schema:		Type				
SEAT	CHICKEN_WINGS		TABLE				Open Data

Columns   Indexes

	Name	SQL Data Type	Column Store Data Type	Key	Not Null	Default
1	SEAT	VARCHAR(4)	STRING	1	X	
2	CLASS	VARCHAR(10)	STRING			
3	STYPE	VARCHAR(15)	STRING			

SEAT

Seat	Class	Type
1A	Business	Window
1B	Business	Isle
11D	Economy	Isle
11E	Economy	Middle
11F	Economy	Window

Figure 5.11 PRICE_CALENDAR and SEAT Tables

SEAT Table

The structure of the SEAT table is {Seat + Class, Type}, where Seat is the primary key. Like the CUSTOMER table, the SEAT table is also in 3NF.

The structure of the SEAT table is illustrated in Figure 5.11, shown previously, and it can be defined using the SQL code in Listing 5.6.

```
-- Create SEAT as a column table
CREATE COLUMN TABLE SEAT (
    MODEL NVARCHAR(10),
SEAT NVARCHAR(4),
    CLASS NVARCHAR(10),
    STYPE NVARCHAR(15),
    PRIMARY KEY (MODEL, SEAT)
) ;
-- Comments
COMMENT ON TABLE SEAT is 'Seat Details';
COMMENT ON COLUMN SEAT.MODEL is 'Model ID';
COMMENT ON COLUMN SEAT.SEAT is 'Seat Number';
COMMENT ON COLUMN SEAT.CLASS is 'Class of Seat: Economy, Business';
COMMENT ON COLUMN SEAT.STYPE is 'Type of Seating: Window/Isle';
```

Listing 5.6 Defining the SEAT Table

CONNECTION Table

The structure of the CONNECTION table is {Flight + FromAP, ToAP, DepT, ArrT, DepT, ArrT, Miles, SStartD, SEndD, ESPrice, EPPrice, BSPrice, BPPrice, FSPrice, FPPrice}, where Flight is the primary key. To store data efficiently and simplify data access, the CONNECTION table should meet 3NF. For the CONNECTION table to be in 3NF, it must satisfy the rules of 3NF, 2NF, and 1NF as well:

- **Check for 1NF**
  Because all attributes of the CONNECTION table are atomic in nature, and it doesn't have repeating attributes, the CONNECTION table is in 1NF.
- **Check for 2NF**
  The nonkey attribute Miles is dependent on FromAP (from airport) and ToAP (to airport), so the CONNECTION table isn't in 2NF.

However, the CONNECTION table as-is meets our functional requirements. The structure of the CONNECTION table is illustrated in Figure 5.12, and it can be defined using the SQL code in Listing 5.7.

```
--Create CONNECTION as a column table
CREATE COLUMN TABLE CONNECTION (
FLIGHT NVARCHAR(6),
FROMAP NVARCHAR(3),
TOAP NVARCHAR(3),
DEPT TIME,
ARRT TIME,
MILES INTEGER,
SSTARTD DATE,
SENDD DATE,
ESPRICE DECIMAL(12,2),
EPPRICE DECIMAL(12,2),
BSPRICE DECIMAL(12,2),
BPPRICE DECIMAL(12,2),
FSPRICE DECIMAL(12,2),
FPPRICE DECIMAL(12,2),
PRIMARY KEY (FLIGHT)
) ;
-- Foreign Key to Airport
ALTER TABLE CONNECTION ADD CONSTRAINT FK_CONNECTION_AIRPORT_FROM
FOREIGN KEY (FROMAP) REFERENCES AIRPORT(CODE);
ALTER TABLE CONNECTION ADD CONSTRAINT FK_CONNECTION_AIRPORT_TO
FOREIGN KEY (TOAP) REFERENCES AIRPORT(CODE);
-- Comments
COMMENT ON TABLE CONNECTION is 'Connection Details';
COMMENT ON COLUMN CONNECTION.FLIGHT is 'Flight Number';
COMMENT ON COLUMN CONNECTION.FROMAP is 'Origin Airport';
COMMENT ON COLUMN CONNECTION.TOAP is 'Destination Airport';
COMMENT ON COLUMN CONNECTION.DEPT is 'Departure Time';
COMMENT ON COLUMN CONNECTION.ARRT is 'Arrival Time';
COMMENT ON COLUMN CONNECTION.MILES is 'Distance in Miles';
COMMENT ON COLUMN CONNECTION.SSTARTD is 'Service Start Date';
COMMENT ON COLUMN CONNECTION.SENDD is 'Service End Date';
COMMENT ON COLUMN CONNECTION.ESPRICE is 'Economy Class Standard Price';
COMMENT ON COLUMN CONNECTION.EPPRICE is 'Economy Class Peak Price';
```

```
COMMENT ON COLUMN CONNECTION.BSPRICE is 'Business Class Standard Price';
COMMENT ON COLUMN CONNECTION.BPPRICE is 'Business Class Peak Price';
COMMENT ON COLUMN CONNECTION.FSPRICE is 'First Class Standard Price';
COMMENT ON COLUMN CONNECTION.FPPRICE is 'First Class Peak Price';
```

Listing 5.7 Defining the CONNECTION Table

CONNECTION ×

Table Name	Schema:	Type
CONNECTION	CHICKEN_WINGS	TABLE

Columns Indexes

	Name	SQL Data Type	Column Store Data Type	Key	Not Null	Default	Comment
1	FLIGHT	VARCHAR(6)	STRING	1	X		Flight Number
2	FROMAP	VARCHAR(3)	STRING				Origin Airport
3	TOAP	VARCHAR(3)	STRING				Destination Airport
4	PLANEID	INTEGER	INT				Aircraft ID
5	DEPT	TIME	SECONDTIME				Departure Time
6	ARRT	TIME	SECONDTIME				Arrival Time
7	MILES	INTEGER	INT				Distance in Miles
8	SSTARTD	DATE	DAYDATE				Service Start Date
9	SENDD	DATE	DAYDATE				Service End Date
1	ESPRICE	DECIMAL(12,2)	FIXED				Economy Class Standard Price
1	EPPRICE	DECIMAL(12,2)	FIXED				Economy Class Peak Price
1	BSPRICE	DECIMAL(12,2)					
1	BPPRICE	DECIMAL(12,2)					
1	FSPRICE	DECIMAL(12,2)					
1	FPPRICE	DECIMAL(12,2)					

CONNECTION

Flight	FromAP	ToAP	PLane ID	DepT	ArrT	Miles	SStartD	SEndD	ESPrice	EPPrice	BSPrice	BPPrice	FSPrice	FPPrice
CW111	YYZ	JFK	111	0800	0930	500	01-JAN-2010	31-DEC-9999	300	500	500	800	700	1000
CW222	YYZ	FRA	112	1000	2300	4000	10-JAN-2010	30-AUG-2014	900	1200	1300	1700	1500	2000
CW333	JFK	LHR	113	0600	2100	3500	22-MAR-2010	31-DEC-9999	900	1200	1300	1700	1500	2000
CW444	LHR	YYZ	114	1500	1800	3600	15-MAY-2011	30-JUN-2017	800	1100	1200	1600	1400	1900

Figure 5.12 CONNECTION Table

FLIGHT Table

The structure of the FLIGHT table is {Flight, Date + PlaneID, Pilot1, Pilot2, Crew1, Crew2, Crew3, DepT, ArrT, Status, ESPrice, EPPrice, BSPrice, BPPrice}, where the combination of Flight and Date is the primary key.

All attributes of the FLIGHT table are atomic in nature; however, Pilot1, Pilot2, Crew1, Crew2, and Crew3 are repeating attributes. Hence, the FLIGHT table isn't in 1NF. We can create a FLIGHT_CREW table for these attributes to make the FLIGHT(1nf) table compatible for 1NF. However, we'll choose to keep the FLIGHT table denormalized to simplify data access.

The structure of the FLIGHT table is illustrated in Figure 5.13, and it can be defined using the SQL code in Listing 5.8.

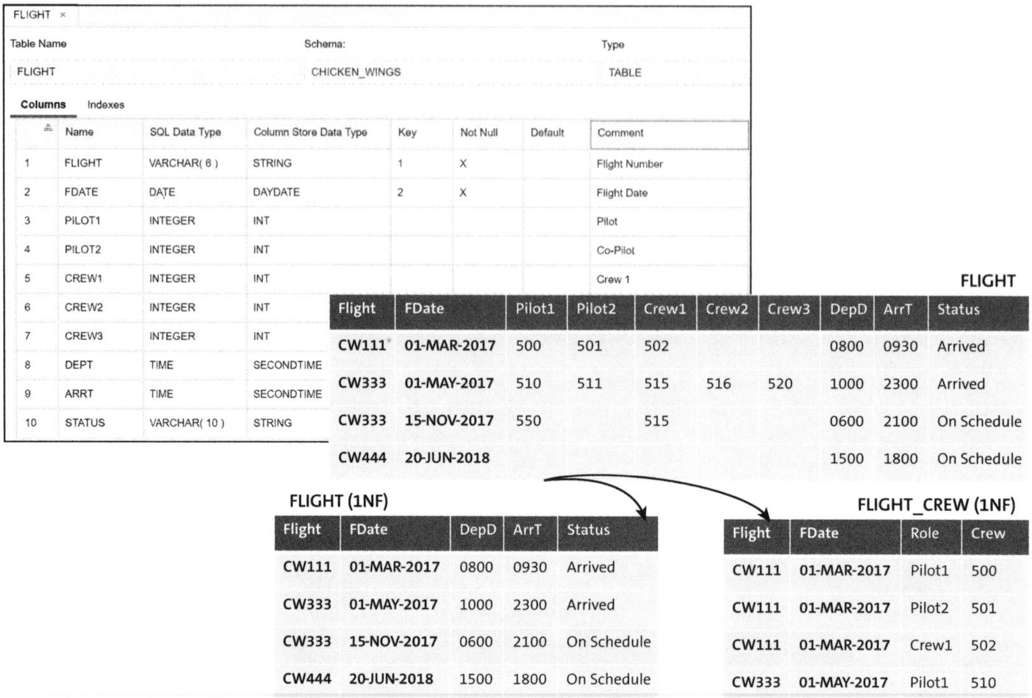

FLIGHT ×

Table Name	Schema:	Type
FLIGHT	CHICKEN_WINGS	TABLE

Columns | Indexes

	Name	SQL Data Type	Column Store Data Type	Key	Not Null	Default	Comment
1	FLIGHT	VARCHAR(6)	STRING	1	X		Flight Number
2	FDATE	DATE	DAYDATE	2	X		Flight Date
3	PILOT1	INTEGER	INT				Pilot
4	PILOT2	INTEGER	INT				Co-Pilot
5	CREW1	INTEGER	INT				Crew 1
6	CREW2	INTEGER	INT				
7	CREW3	INTEGER	INT				
8	DEPT	TIME	SECONDTIME				
9	ARRT	TIME	SECONDTIME				
10	STATUS	VARCHAR(10)	STRING				

FLIGHT

Flight	FDate	Pilot1	Pilot2	Crew1	Crew2	Crew3	DepD	ArrT	Status
CW111	**01-MAR-2017**	500	501	502			0800	0930	Arrived
CW333	**01-MAY-2017**	510	511	515	516	520	1000	2300	Arrived
CW333	**15-NOV-2017**	550		515			0600	2100	On Schedule
CW444	**20-JUN-2018**						1500	1800	On Schedule

FLIGHT (1NF)

Flight	FDate	DepD	ArrT	Status
CW111	**01-MAR-2017**	0800	0930	Arrived
CW333	**01-MAY-2017**	1000	2300	Arrived
CW333	**15-NOV-2017**	0600	2100	On Schedule
CW444	**20-JUN-2018**	1500	1800	On Schedule

FLIGHT_CREW (1NF)

Flight	FDate	Role	Crew
CW111	**01-MAR-2017**	Pilot1	500
CW111	**01-MAR-2017**	Pilot2	501
CW111	**01-MAR-2017**	Crew1	502
CW333	**01-MAY-2017**	Pilot1	510

Figure 5.13 FLIGHT Table

```
CREATE COLUMN TABLE FLIGHT (
FLIGHT NVARCHAR(6),
FDATE DATE,
PLANEID INTEGER,
PILOT2 INTEGER,
PILOT2 INTEGER,
CREW1 INTEGER,
CREW2 INTEGER,
CREW3 INTEGER,
DEPT TIME,
ARRT TIME,
STATUS NVARCHAR(10)
PRIMARY KEY (FLIGHT, FDATE)
) ;
-- Foreign Key to Connection
ALTER TABLE FLIGHT ADD CONSTRAINT FK_FLIGHT_CONNECTION
FOREIGN KEY (FLIGHT) REFERENCES CONNECTION(FLIGHT);
```

```
-- Foreign Key to CREW
ALTER TABLE FLIGHT ADD CONSTRAINT FK_FLIGHT_PLANE
FOREIGN KEY (PLANEID) REFERENCES PLANE(REGNO);
ALTER TABLE FLIGHT ADD CONSTRAINT FK_FLIGHT_CREW_PILOT1
FOREIGN KEY (PILOT1) REFERENCES CREW(CREWID);
ALTER TABLE FLIGHT ADD CONSTRAINT FK_FLIGHT_CREW_PILOT2
FOREIGN KEY (PILOT2) REFERENCES CREW(CREWID);
ALTER TABLE FLIGHT ADD CONSTRAINT FK_FLIGHT_CREW_CREW1
FOREIGN KEY (CREW1) REFERENCES CREW(CREWID);
ALTER TABLE FLIGHT ADD CONSTRAINT FK_FLIGHT_CREW_CREW2
FOREIGN KEY (CREW2) REFERENCES CREW(CREWID);
ALTER TABLE FLIGHT ADD CONSTRAINT FK_FLIGHT_CREW_CREW3
FOREIGN KEY (CREW3) REFERENCES CREW(CREWID);
-- Comments
COMMENT ON TABLE FLIGHT is 'Flight Details';
COMMENT ON COLUMN FLIGHT.FLIGHT is 'Flight Number';
COMMENT ON COLUMN FLIGHT.FDATE is 'Flight Date';
COMMENT ON COLUMN FLIGHT.PLANEID is 'Aircraft ID';
COMMENT ON COLUMN FLIGHT.PILOT1 is 'Pilot';
COMMENT ON COLUMN FLIGHT.PILOT2 is 'Co-Pilot';
COMMENT ON COLUMN FLIGHT.CREW1 is 'Crew 1';
COMMENT ON COLUMN FLIGHT.CREW2 is 'Crew 2';
COMMENT ON COLUMN FLIGHT.CREW3 is 'Crew 3';
COMMENT ON COLUMN FLIGHT.DEPT is 'Actual Departure Time';
COMMENT ON COLUMN FLIGHT.ARRT is 'Actual Arrival Time';
COMMENT ON COLUMN FLIGHT.STATUS is 'Flight Status';
```

Listing 5.8 Defining the FLIGHT Table

BOOKING Table

The structure of the BOOKING table is {Flight, Date, Model, Seat + CustID, StdPrice, BookPrice, Fees, Tax, CheckIn}, where the combination of Flight, Date, Model, and Seat is the primary key.

However, as you've noticed, the BOOKING table has more than one purpose: (1) it has the list of seats available for booking or already booked; (2) it has the payment information; and (3) it has the customer check-in information. In a traditional database design, these three data sets should be stored in separate tables. However, for our use case, we're storing them all in one denormalized table for easy access. To store data efficiently and simplify data access, the BOOKING table should meet 3NF. For the BOOKING table to be in 3NF, it must satisfy the rules of 3NF, 2NF, and 1NF as well:

- **Check for 1NF**
  All attributes of the BOOKING table are atomic in nature, and there are no repeating attributes. Hence the BOOKING table is in 1NF.
- **Check for 2NF**
  The Total field is dependent on nonkey fields such as Book Price, Fees, Tax, and Discount. However, these fields are measures (as opposed to attributes), so the BOOKING table is in 2NF.
- **Check for 3NF**
  Because there is no transitive relation between the attributes of the BOOKING table, it's also in 3NF.

The structure of the BOOKING table is illustrated in Figure 5.14, and it can be defined using the SQL code in Listing 5.9.

```
-- Create BOOKING as a column table
CREATE COLUMN TABLE BOOKING (
    FLIGHT NVARCHAR(6),
    FDATE DATE,
    MODEL NVARCHAR(10),
    SEAT NVARCHAR(4),
    CUSTID INTEGER,
    STDPRICE DECIMAL(12,2),
    BOOKPRICE DECIMAL(12,2),
    FEES DECIMAL(12,2),
    DISCOUNT DECIMAL(12,2),
    TAX DECIMAL(12,2),
    TOTAL DECIMAL(12,2),
    PAYMENT DECIMAL(12,2),
    CHECKIN NVARCHAR(1),
    STATUS NVARCHAR(10),
    PASSENGER NVARCHAR(20),
PRIMARY KEY (FLIGHT, FDATE, MODEL, SEAT)
) ;
-- Foreign Key to FLIGHT
ALTER TABLE BOOKING ADD CONSTRAINT FK_BOOKING_FLIGHT
FOREIGN KEY (FLIGHT,FDATE) REFERENCES FLIGHT(FLIGHT,FDATE);
-- Foreign Key to SEAT
ALTER TABLE BOOKING ADD CONSTRAINT FK_BOOKING_SEAT
    FOREIGN KEY (MODEL, SEAT) REFERENCES SEAT(MODEL, SEAT);
-- Foreign Key CUSTOMER
```

```
ALTER TABLE BOOKING ADD CONSTRAINT FK_BOOKING_CUSTOMER
    FOREIGN KEY (CUSTID) REFERENCES CUSTOMER(CUSTID);
-- Comments
COMMENT ON TABLE BOOKING is 'BOOKING Details';
COMMENT ON COLUMN BOOKING.FLIGHT is 'Flight Number';
COMMENT ON COLUMN BOOKING.FDATE is 'Flight Date';
COMMENT ON COLUMN BOOKING.CUSTID is 'Customer ID';
COMMENT ON COLUMN BOOKING.SEAT is 'Seat Number';
COMMENT ON COLUMN BOOKING.STDPRICE is 'Base Price';
COMMENT ON COLUMN BOOKING.BOOKPRICE is 'Booking Price';
COMMENT ON COLUMN BOOKING.FEES is 'Surcharges/Fees';
COMMENT ON COLUMN BOOKING.DISCOUNT is 'Discount';
COMMENT ON COLUMN BOOKING.TAX is 'Tax';
COMMENT ON COLUMN BOOKING.TOTAL is 'Total Amount Charged';
COMMENT ON COLUMN BOOKING.PAYMENT is 'Mode of Payment';
COMMENT ON COLUMN BOOKING.CHECKIN is 'Check-in Status';
COMMENT ON COLUMN BOOKING.STATUS is 'Booking Status';
COMMENT ON COLUMN BOOKING.PASSENGER is 'Passenger Name';
```

Listing 5.9 Defining the BOOKING Table

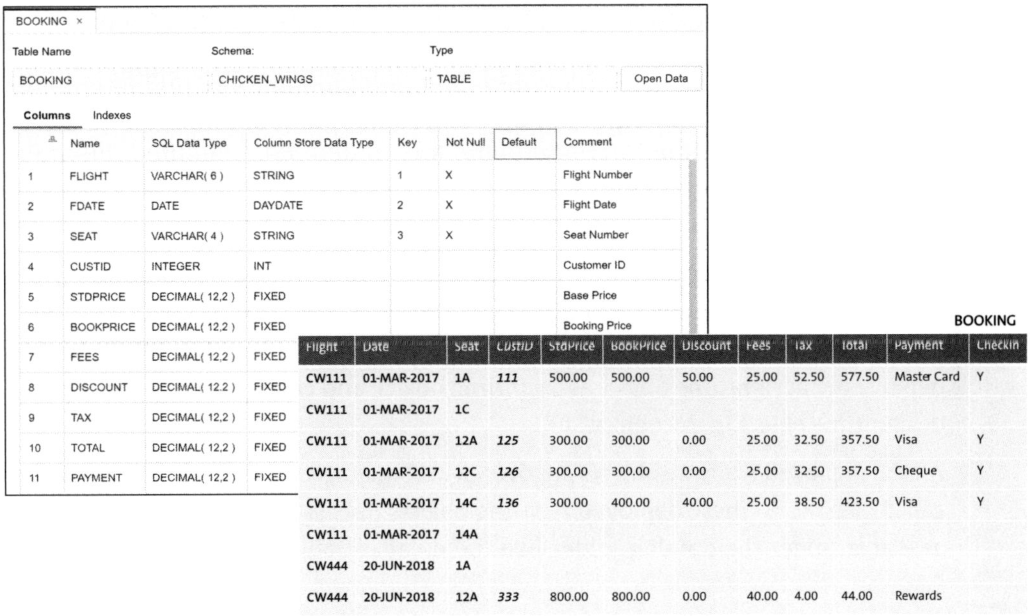

BOOKING ×

Table Name: BOOKING | Schema: CHICKEN_WINGS | Type: TABLE | Open Data

Columns | Indexes

	Name	SQL Data Type	Column Store Data Type	Key	Not Null	Default	Comment
1	FLIGHT	VARCHAR(6)	STRING	1	X		Flight Number
2	FDATE	DATE	DAYDATE	2	X		Flight Date
3	SEAT	VARCHAR(4)	STRING	3	X		Seat Number
4	CUSTID	INTEGER	INT				Customer ID
5	STDPRICE	DECIMAL(12,2)	FIXED				Base Price
6	BOOKPRICE	DECIMAL(12,2)	FIXED				Booking Price
7	FEES	DECIMAL(12,2)	FIXED				
8	DISCOUNT	DECIMAL(12,2)	FIXED				
9	TAX	DECIMAL(12,2)	FIXED				
10	TOTAL	DECIMAL(12,2)	FIXED				
11	PAYMENT	DECIMAL(12,2)	FIXED				

BOOKING

Flight	Date	Seat	CustID	StdPrice	BookPrice	Discount	Fees	Tax	Total	Payment	Checkin
CW111	01-MAR-2017	1A	111	500.00	500.00	50.00	25.00	52.50	577.50	Master Card	Y
CW111	01-MAR-2017	1C									
CW111	01-MAR-2017	12A	125	300.00	300.00	0.00	25.00	32.50	357.50	Visa	Y
CW111	01-MAR-2017	12C	126	300.00	300.00	0.00	25.00	32.50	357.50	Cheque	Y
CW111	01-MAR-2017	14C	136	300.00	400.00	40.00	25.00	38.50	423.50	Visa	Y
CW111	01-MAR-2017	14A									
CW444	20-JUN-2018	1A									
CW444	20-JUN-2018	12A	333	800.00	800.00	0.00	40.00	4.00	44.00	Rewards	

Figure 5.14 BOOKING Table

In this section, we designed the data model for our sample application and created the database tables using SQL in SAP HANA. In the next section, we'll look at a new flexible approach to generate database objects using SAP HANA Repository design-time objects.

5.3.4 Data Model Using SAP HANA Repository Design-Time Objects

Starting with Support Package Stack (SPS) 5 for both SAP HANA XS Advanced and SAP HANA XS, design-time object definition was introduced to SAP HANA. A design-time object definition can be for a project, package, schema, table, procedure data model, and so on, and these are stored in the SAP HANA Repository and deployed as runtime objects during activation.

Using design-time definitions of the persistence model has several advantages:

- They often provide a higher level of abstraction and a more powerful language than plain SQL, and sometimes several database objects are created from a single design-time file.
- They are easier to understand, analyze, and compare.
- Design-time files can be versioned in a source code management system and be used to ship database content from development to production or to customers.

SAP HANA XS enables you to create database schemas, tables, views, and sequences as design-time files in the SAP HANA Repository, and these design-time objects will create the corresponding runtime objects (i.e., database schemas, tables, views, procedures and sequences, etc.) when activated/deployed.

The SAP HANA Repository is the main component of the design-time environment to store and manage all design-time objects. During the activation process, the repository saves the previously active version to the object history, validates/compiles/deploys the design-time object as a runtime object, and creates a new version of the design-time object in the object.

All the deployed runtime objects are owned and managed by a special database user called `_SYS_REPO`. These deployed runtime objects (tables, views, procedure, etc.) are available under the **Catalog** folder like the database objects created using SQL. In addition to defining various database objects, design-time objects can also be used to import data into the previously defined table structures.

All repository files, including your view definition, can be transported (along with tables, schemas, and sequences) to other SAP HANA systems, for example, in a delivery unit. A delivery unit is the medium SAP HANA provides to enable you to assemble all your application-related repository artifacts together into an archive that can be easily exported to other systems.

In SAP HANA Studio, the design-time objects can be created using the *SAP HANA development perspective*. Navigate to the appropriate package in the repository view, and create a new design-time objects using the **Database Table** template to define a database table. Define the table, and click on the **Activate SAP HANA Development Object** button to create the runtime (i.e., database table) object from the design-time definition. Upon successful activation, the database table will be available under the **Catalog** folder, as shown in Figure 5.15. To define the runtime objects uniquely, the package location is automatically appended to the name of the runtime table.

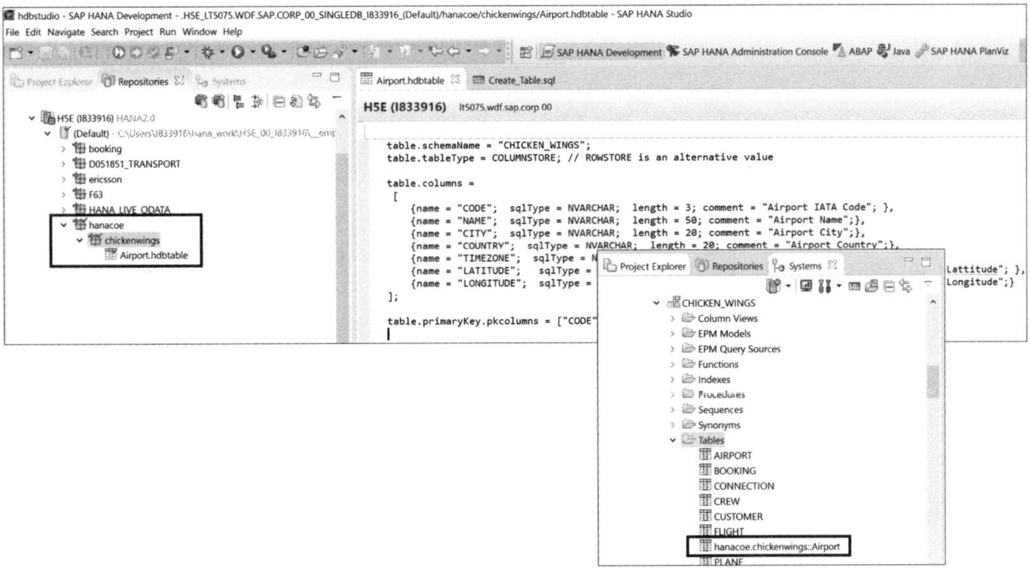

Figure 5.15 Design-Time Objects in SAP HANA XS

SAP HANA XS supports various design-time definitions as listed in Table 5.1.

File Type	Description
`.hdbschema`	Define a design-time schema and maintain the schema definition in the repository; the transportable schema has the file extension *.hdbschema*, for example, *MYSCHEMA.hdbschema*.
`.hdbsynonym`	Define a design-time synonym and maintain the synonym definition in the repository; the transportable synonym has the file extension *.hdb-synonym*, for example, *MySynonym.hdbsynonym*.
`.hdbtable`	Define a design-time table and maintain the table definition in the repository; the transportable table has the file extension *.hdbtable*, for example, *MYTABLE.hdbtable*.
`.hdbstructure`	Define the structure of a database table in a design-time file in the repository; you can reuse the table-structure definition to specify the table type when creating a new table. The transportable structure has the file extension *.hdbstructure*, for example, *MyTableType.hdbstructure*.
`.hdbview`	Define a design-time view and maintain the view definition in the repository; the transportable view has the file extension *.hdbview*, for example, *MYVIEW.hdbview*.
`.hdbsequence`	Define a design-time sequence and maintain the sequence definition in the repository; the transportable sequence has the file extension *.hdbse-quence*, for example, *MYSEQUENCE.hdbsequence*.
`.hdbti`	Define data-provisioning rules (extension *.hdbti*) that enable you to import data from comma-separated values (*.csv*) files into SAP HANA tables using the SAP HANA XS table-import feature. The complete configuration can be included in a delivery unit and transported between SAP HANA systems. Note the *.hdbti* files are meant for constant data (sample data) that isn't modified at runtime. However, these data sets can be modified using subsequent DML statements.

Table 5.1 SAP HANA XS Repository File Types

Some of the commonly used SAP HANA XS design-time definitions to create tables and views are discussed in the following sections.

.hdbschema File

To create a schema called <new_schema>, create a design-time definition file *<new_schema>.hdbschema* with the following contents:

```
schema_name = "NEW_SCHEMA";
```

An example of a valid transportable schema-definition file for CHICKENWINGS schema (*CHICKENWINGS.hdbschema*) will contain the following:

```
schema_name = "CHICKENWINGS";
```

During the activation process, the schema CHICKENWINGS will be created, if it doesn't exist in the database. After activation, the schema object (e.g., CHICKENWINGS) is only visible in the catalog to the _SYS_REPO user. To enable other users to view the newly created schema in SAP HANA Studio's Modeler perspective, the SELECT privilege on the schema must be explicitly granted.

The following SQL procedure should be executed to grant SELECT access on the new schema to any user:

```
call _SYS_REPO.GRANT_SCHEMA_PRIVILEGE_ON_ACTIVATED_CONTENT('select',
'CHICKENWINGS','<username>');
```

.hdbtable File

A design-time definition file *<new_table>.hdbtable* should be created to define a new database table. The syntax of the *<new_table>.hdbtable* in its simplest form is shown in Listing 5.10.

```
table.schemaName = "SCHEMA_NAME";     // Schema should exist
table.temporary = true or false;
table.tableType = COLUMNSTORE or ROWSTORE;
table.loggingType - LOGGING or NOLOGGING;
table.columns = [
{name = "Col1"; sqlType = NVARCHAR; nullable = false; length = 20; comment =
 "dummy comment";},
{name = "Col2"; sqlType = INTEGER; nullable = false;},
{name = "Col3"; sqlType = NVARCHAR; nullable = true; length =
 20; defaultValue = "Defaultvalue";},
{name = "Col4"; sqlType = DECIMAL; nullable = false; precision = 2; scale =
 3;}];
```

```
table.indexes = [
{name = "MYINDEX1"; unique = true; order = DSC; indexColumns = ["Col2"];},
{name = "MYINDEX2"; unique = true; order = DSC; indexType = B_
TREE; indexColumns = ["Col1", "Col4"];}];
table.primaryKey.pkcolumns = ["Col1", "Col2"];
```

Listing 5.10 Syntax of .hdbtable Artifact

In this syntax, each item is defined as follows:

- `schemaName`
  Name of the schema where the table will physically exist.
- `temporary`
  Used to define a temporary table. Temporary tables are session-specific, so only the owner session of the temporary table is allowed to `INSERT/READ/TRUNCATE` the data. As the name suggests, temporary tables are temporary in nature; that is, they exist only for the duration of the session, and data from the local temporary table is automatically dropped when the session is terminated.
- `tableType`
  Type of table. SAP HANA supports both `ROWSTORE` and `COLUMNSTORE` tables.
- `logging`
  Specifies the logging option for the table. `LOGGING` is enabled by default. `NO LOGGING` means the definition of the table is persistent and globally available, but data is temporary and global.
- `columns`
  Defines the column structure with the following attributes:
  - `name`: Column name.
  - `sqlType`: SQL data type.
  - `nullable`: Boolean. Allows a null value.
  - `length`, `scale`, and `precision`: As appropriate based on the data type.
  - `default value`: Default value for the column.
  - `comment`: Comments on the column.
- `primaryKey.pkcolumns`
  Defines the primary keys of the table.
- `indexes`
  Defines the index on the table with the following attributes:

- `name`: Index name.
- `unique`: Boolean. Unique value.
- `type`: Type of Index `B_TREE` or `CPB_TREE`.
- `order`: Order of the index—`ASC` or `DESC`.

An example of a valid transportable table-definition file for table `AIRPORT` (*Airport.hdbtable*) is shown in Listing 5.11.

```
table.schemaName = "CHICKENWINGS";
table.tableType = COLUMNSTORE;
table.columns =
[
    {name = "CODE";  sqlType = NVARCHAR;  length = 3; comment =
 "Airport IATA Code"; },
    {name = "NAME";  sqlType = NVARCHAR;  length = 50; comment =
 "Airport Name";},
    {name = "CITY";  sqlType = NVARCHAR;  length = 20; comment =
 "Airport City";},
    {name = "COUNTRY";  sqlType = NVARCHAR;  length = 20; comment =
 "Airport Country";},
    {name = "TIMEZONE";  sqlType = NVARCHAR;  length = 3; comment =
 "Airport Timezone";},
    {name = "LATITUDE";   sqlType = DECIMAL; precision = 12; scale =
 6; comment = "Coordinates: Latitude"; },
    {name = "LONGITUDE";  sqlType = DECIMAL; precision = 12; scale =
 6; comment = "Coordinates: Longitude";}
];
table.primaryKey.pkcolumns = ["CODE"];
```

Listing 5.11 Defining AIRPORT Table with .hdbtable Artifact

.hdbview

A design-time definition file *<new_view>.hdbview* should be created to define a new SQL view. The syntax of the *<new_table>.hdbview* in its simplest form is as follows:

```
schema="SCHEMA_NAME";     //Schema should exist
query="<SELECT_QUERY>";
depends_on=["Table1", "Table2"];  //Tables should exist
```

An example of a valid transportable SQL view definition file (*DepartureAirport.hdbview*) is shown in Listing 5.12.

```
schema="CHICKENWINGS";
query="SELECT T1.FROMAP, T2.CITY, T2.COUNTRY FROM CHICKENWINGS.\
" hanacoe.chickenwings::Connection\" AS T1 LEFT JOIN CHICKENWINGS.\
"hanacoe.chickenwings::Airport\" AS T2 ON T1.FROMAP = T2.CODE";
depends_on=[
"hanacoe.chickenwings::Connection", " hanacoe.chickenwings::Airport"];
```

Listing 5.12 Example of .hdbview Artifact

.hdbsequence

A design-time definition file *<new_sequence>.hdbsequence* should be created to define a sequence. The syntax of the *<new_sequence>.hdbsequence* in its simplest form is shown in Listing 5.13.

```
schema="SCHEMA_NAME";     //Schema should exist
start_with= <start_value>;
maxvalue= <max_value>;
nomaxvalue=false;
minvalue= <min_value>;
nominvalue=true;
cycles= false;
reset_by= "<SELECT_QUERY>";
depends_on=["TABLE1", "TABLE2"];
```

Listing 5.13 Syntax of .hdbsequence Artifact

An example of a valid transportable sequence definition file (*CrewId.hdbsequence*) is shown in Listing 5.14.

```
schema= "CHICKENWINGS";
start_with= 100;
maxvalue= 999;
nomaxvalue=false;
minvalue= 1;
nominvalue=true;
cycles= false;
reset_by= "SELECT IFNULL(MAX(CREWID), 0)+1
```

```
FROM \"hanacoe.chickenwings::Crew\"";
depends_on=["hanacoe.chickenwings::Crew"];
```

Listing 5.14 CrewId Sequence Using the .hdbsequence Artifact

5.4 SAP HANA Deployment Infrastructure

Starting with SAP HANA SPS 11, SAP introduced SAP HANA XS Advanced with the option of using the Git or GitHub repository (external to SAP HANA) to store and manage the design-time objects and the concept of schema-less development using the *SAP HANA Deployment Infrastructure (HDI)*.

The HDI is a service layer of the SAP HANA database that simplifies the deployment of database objects using declarative design-time artifacts, ensures consistent deployments by guaranteeing that multiple objects are deployed in the right sequence based on their dependencies, and implements a transactional all-or-nothing deployment. HDI manages development of pure database artifacts to store and provision data. This service includes a family of consistent design-time artifacts (`.hdbcds`, `.hdbview`, `.hdbprocedure`, etc.) for all key database features that describe the target (runtime) state of database artifacts (tables, views, procedures, etc.). These artifacts are modeled, staged (uploaded), built, and deployed into SAP HANA to create runtime database objects. The all-or-nothing transactional deployment model with implicit dependency management significantly simplifies development, maintenance, and deployment of database objects.

In addition, HDI introduces an isolation concept using *HDI containers* on the database level, which is based on database schemas and the schema-level security concept. All development objects within the scope of HDI exist within an HDI container. From the database perspective, an HDI container is a normal database schema that manages its contained objects. Therefore, all objects within the scope of an HDI container exist in the same database schema, and access to all database objects in the design-time is strictly managed via the HDI container (no direct access to the underlying database schema). Upon a successful build (i.e., activation of the design-time artifacts), the generated runtime database objects can be accessed (using business intelligence [BI] tools) like any other database objects referencing the database schema. The HDI container isn't visible (i.e., doesn't play a role) while accessing the runtime objects. The HDI container upgrades/regenerates existing runtime artifacts when their corresponding design-time artifacts are modified.

In design time, there is no need (also forbidden) for specifying schema names to access the database objects in SQL statements or modeling artifacts. The HDI container abstracts the physical database schema and provides schema-less development and security isolation. Any number of HDI containers can be defined within a SAP HANA database and are technically implemented using different database schemas. The same objects can also be deployed multiple times into different HDI containers in the same SAP HANA database. Several instances of the same application (i.e., same or different versions of the same software product) can be deployed on one SAP HANA database, which is one of the key benefits and arguments for the schema-free data model. Depending on the database connection, SAP HANA XS Advanced apps can be automatically set up with a `SET SCHEMA <container>` to enable schema-free runtime access.

SAP HANA information models (e.g., calculation views) are no longer deployed to a single central schema such as `_SYS_BIC`; these models are placed in a container-specific schema like any other development objects.

In the following sections, we'll discuss the technical implementations of HDI containers of database schemas and technical users in the SAP HANA database and the deployment/creation of database runtime objects in HDI containers using HDI Deployer.

5.4.1 HDI Containers

An HDI container is implemented using a set of database schemas and container-specific technical users. Each HDI container is composed of two containers, that is, a *design-time container (DTC)* and a *runtime container (RTC)*, as illustrated in Figure 5.16.

The DTC (database schema) is used to store the design-time definitions of the catalog objects, additional metadata (e.g., dependencies between the objects), plug-in metadata, and application programming interface (API) procedures required for the deployment process. The DTC doesn't provide direct access to its database storage; it contains metadata that can only be accessed via the HDI API. The physical schema name in the database will be `<container>#DI`.

The RTC (database schema) stores the deployed runtime objects such as tables, views, procedures, and so on. This schema is used by the application user to perform database operations. The physical schema name in the database will be `<container>`.

In the context of SAP HANA XS Advanced, the SAP HANA Service Broker is used to create and destroy these containers. Note that there are other use cases without SAP HANA XS Advanced (e.g., ABAP or SQL-based scenarios) where containers aren't created by the SAP HANA Service Broker.

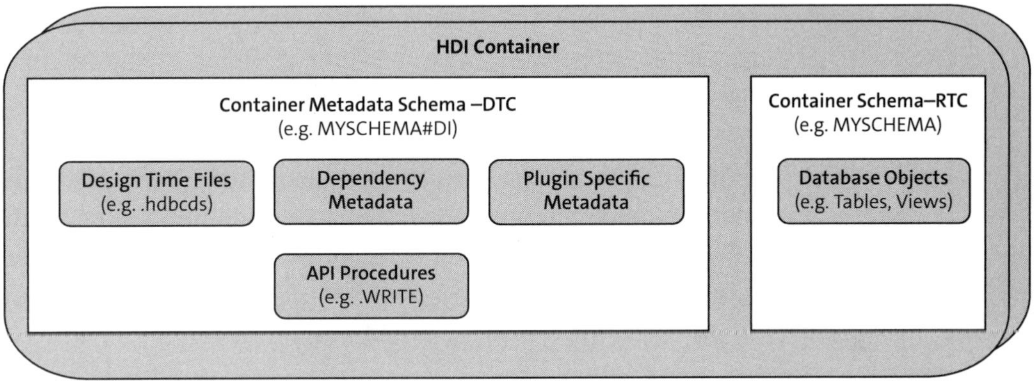

Figure 5.16 HDI Container Schema

5.4.2 HDI Technical Users

HDI uses several container-specific technical users to separate the different container-related tasks such as creating the schemas, triggering deployment, and creating application database objects.

When a container is created, a special container-specific deployment user (the container's `<container>#DI` user, i.e., deployment user) is created, which owns the design-time definitions, plug-in metadata, and API procedures required for the deployment process.

The container schema is created with a special container-specific technical system user (the container's schema owner, i.e., `<container>` user), whereas the application database objects are created with a special technical system user (the container's `<container>#00` user, i.e., object owner) during the deployment process. Unless explicitly granted, the `#00 user` user has no access to the metadata schema and especially not to the HDI API procedures. This prevents an application procedure with definer mode security from getting unwanted access to metadata and the deployment API.

Application users need access privileges only on the container schema. The SAP HANA XS Advanced applications connect to HDI containers using the container-specific application users <container>_<GUID>_DT and <container>_<GUID>_RT users when executing database logic.

As discussed, HDI containers are isolated from each other using schema-level access privileges. Cross-container access at the database level is prevented by default, but it can be enabled by explicitly granting the necessary privileges.

Access to container database objects can be given to other SAP HANA database users by assigning container-specific roles such as the global <container>::access_role role or any other role deployed to the container.

The container-specific (#00) technical user only has access to its local container objects. Access to foreign objects is enabled via synonyms and must be explicitly granted to the #00 user by the technical owner of the foreign schema, as illustrated in Figure 5.17. Access to system tables, such as DUMMY, or views in system schemas (e.g., SYS) are enabled using synonyms in the HDI container.

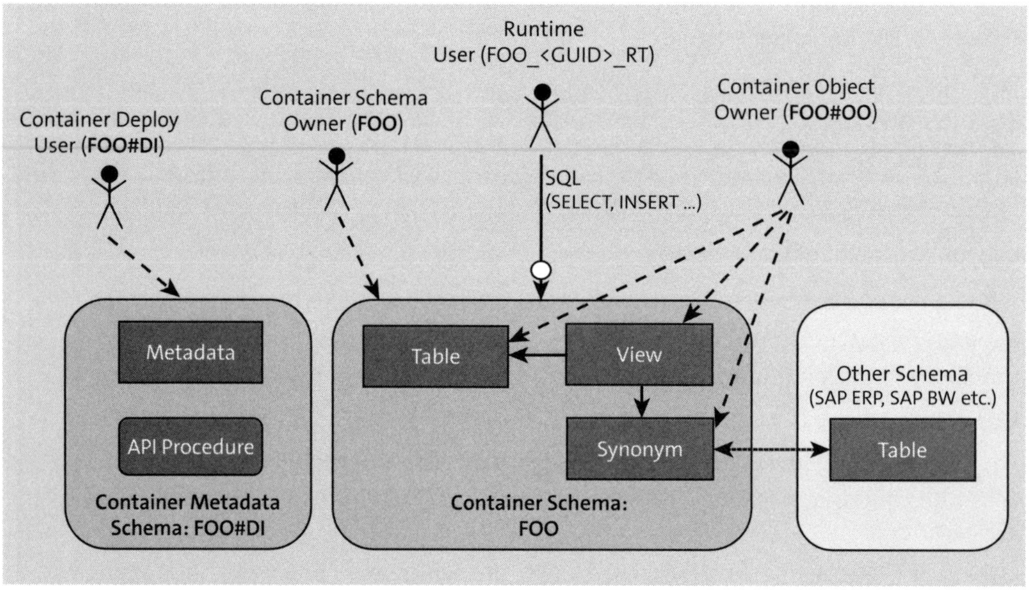

Figure 5.17 Container-Specific Technical Users

5.4.3 HDI Deployer

The *HDI Deployer* is an application part of the SAP HANA XS Advanced infrastructure used to deploy HDI design-time artifacts to the respective HDI containers. When an

MTA is deployed, the HDI Deployer application is pushed first to "prepare" the SAP HANA persistence and make sure the HDI container is ready for use.

Deployment into an HDI container is done in two steps. In the first step, the design-time artifacts are uploaded (WRITE process) into the metadata schema. In the second step, the content in the metadata schema is deployed (MAKE process) as new objects or changes to existing objects in the container schema.

The uploaded design-time artifacts are organized in virtual file systems and appear as hierarchical folders containing files at the API level. For each HDI container, there are two virtual file systems: *deployed file system* and *work file system*. The deployed file system contains the design-time files that reflect the currently deployed state of the container schema. The newly uploaded (WRITE process) design-time files (for new objects or changes to existing objects) are part of the work file system representing the future state (after deployment). When the MAKE operation deploys a folder in the work file system to the database, the contained design-time files are promoted to the deployed file system, and the corresponding database objects are created or changed in the container schema. The database objects are generated from the design-time artifacts via HDI plug-ins. Operations such as uploading and downloading design-time files or triggering deployment are invoked by calling container-specific API procedures, which are generated when the container is created. These API procedures are created in the container metadata schema.

5.4.4 Deployment into HDI Container

Deployment of design-time artifacts into an HDI container is illustrated in Figure 5.18. The key components of the HDI architecture are HDI API, HDI client, SQL processor, HDI server, and HDI plug-ins, as follows:

- **HDI API**
  HDI API is used to manage the HDI container and its contents. The HDI APIs have been implemented using two sets of SQL stored procedures, as follows:
  - System-wide: The system-wide container management API contains procedures for creating and dropping containers. Starting with SAP HANA 2 SPS 00, containers can be grouped via container groups where a corresponding group-level management API restricts the management operations (create/drop, configure, etc.) to the set of containers in the specific group. These procedures are available under the `_SYS_DI#<group>` schema. The `SYS_DI` schema contains the system-wide management APIs and the APIs of the default group.

  - Container-specific: Each HDI container has container-specific API procedures for uploading, listing, and retrieving design-time objects (WRITE, READ, LIST), for deploying uploaded design-time objects (MAKE), and for granting/revoking access (GRANT, REVOKE) to/from the container's schemas and API.

- **HDI client**
  HDI clients use HDI APIs to interact with HDI containers to access database services. Common examples of HDI clients are HDI command-line clients, the development environment (SAP Web IDE for SAP HANA), and SAP HANA XS Advanced applications with database services.

- **SQL processor**
  The SQL processor is responsible for preparing and executing SQL statements in the SAP HANA database.

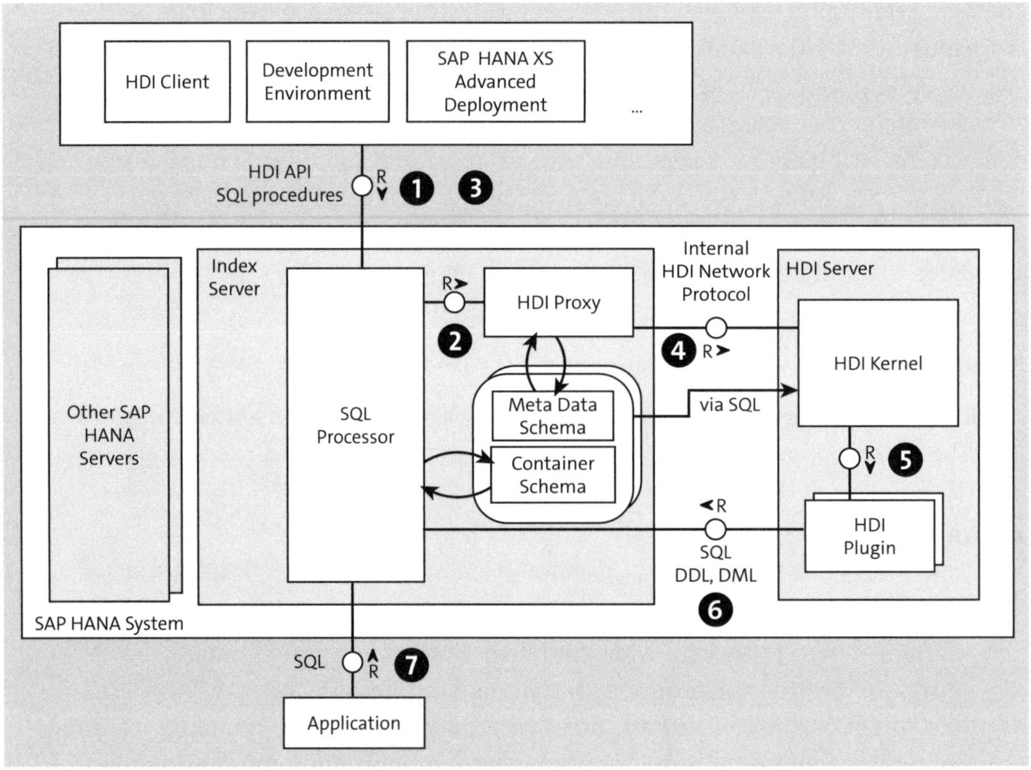

Figure 5.18 HDI Architecture

- **HDI server**
  There is one HDI server in each SAP HANA database (or one HDI server for each tenant database in a multitenant system). The HDI server is responsible for reading the file metadata and executing HDI plug-ins for deployment.
- **HDI plug-ins**
  HDI plug-ins are available for interpreting different types of design-time files. Supported file types include definitions of tables, views, virtual tables, functions, virtual functions, procedures, triggers, sequences, graph workspaces, roles, analytical privileges, replication tasks, Core Data Service (CDS) files, and table content. The assignment of plug-ins to file types isn't hard-coded but is specified in a configuration file deployed into the HDI container.

The deployment process is executed using the following key steps (see Figure 5.18):

❶ The HDI client uploads the design-time files to the HDI container by calling the container-specific WRITE procedure.

❷ The SQL processor in the SAP HANA index server delegates the execution to the HDI proxy library, which writes the files to the virtual work file system in the container metadata schema.

❸ After all files are uploaded, the HDI client calls the MAKE API procedure to trigger the actual deployment for the specified set of virtual files and folders.

❹ The call is again dispatched to the HDI proxy, which delegates the call to the HDI server to read the files from the metadata schema. The HDI kernel in the HDI server invokes the HDI plug-ins for the different types of design-time files.

❺ The HDI plug-ins interpret the design-time files, extract dependency information, and generate the SQL statements needed to create the database objects.

❻ The HDI kernel evaluates the dependency information, determines the right deployment order, and executes the plug-ins to apply the changes in the container schema via SQL. This process is managed as a separate database all-or-nothing transaction using the container's #00 user. In case of an error, the entire transaction is rolled back (either by the database or by the HDI kernel, depending on the kind of error).

❼ After a successful deployment, the database objects are available for application use.

5.5 SAP HANA Database Module

Typically, business applications have several components, such as database, business logic layer, data exchange interfaces, frontend logics, and static web contents. Because all these components are part of the same business applications and have dependencies for deployment, these components should be developed, packaged, configured, and deployed together. SAP introduced the concept of multi-target applications (MTAs) to manage the development of modern business applications.

An MTA comprises one or more modules with contents for multiple distinct runtime environments. Each module in the MTA is a separate SAP HANA XS Advanced microservice application with a different runtime environment to be deployed in the target deployment platform.

The MTA deployment descriptor file contains the lists of MTA modules, their technical type, dependencies, and required parameters. The MTA deployment descriptor is used to deploy modules in the right order by managing the interdependencies and setting up the connections required between the modules.

Each module in an MTA archive has its own folder. The mapping of folders to modules is described in an MTA manifest file. The following base-level folders may be available as part of a SAP HANA XS Advanced MTA:

- *web/*
  Folder for static web content and application router configuration.
- *java/*
  Folder for a Java application.
- *js/*
  Folder for a Node.js application or SAP HANA XS JavaScript application.
- *db/*
  Folder for the SAP HANA database artifacts (HDB module).

The database persistence in SAP HANA XS Advanced is organized as an HDB module. It's a collection of SAP HANA design-time database artifacts, such as entities (tables), views, procedures, synonyms, roles, column views, and so on. Deployment of these database objects using HDI is based on a container model where each container corresponds to one database schema. Except for the references to external database objects, the database persistence of an application is self-contained, and the database module contains all required design-time files for creating the persistence inside the container's database schema.

We've discussed the technical implementation of HDI containers and the deployment of artifacts into HDI containers. In the following subsections, we'll provide detailed, step-by-step instructions to create the database module for our sample application using the HDB module in an MTA project and deploy the application into the SAP HANA XS Advanced infrastructure.

5.5.1 Creating a Multi-Target Application Project

SAP Web IDE for SAP HANA is the main development tool for application development in SAP HANA XS Advanced. To develop our business application and create the database objects, we need to first create an MTA project.

Use the following steps to create a new MTA project in SAP Web IDE for SAP HANA:

1. In the development view, select **New • Project from Template** in the context menu of the **Workspace** folder, or select **File • New • Project from Template**.
2. Select the **Multi-Target Application Project** template, and click **Next** to proceed to the **Basic Information** screen.
3. Provide a **Project Name,** and select **Next** to proceed to the **Template Customization** screen.
4. Provide the **Application Version** (default "0.0.1") and **Description** (optional), select **Space** (as advised by your administrator) in SAP HANA XS Advanced for running the project, and then click **Finish** to create the project in your workspace (see Figure 5.19).
5. This will create a folder *<project_name>* (e.g., *ChickenWings*) under the **Workspace** and contain a *mta.yaml* file describing the project. The *mta.yaml* file contains the project-based configuration settings and will be updated as new modules are added to the project.
6. Create a local repository for the project, and then select **Git • Initialize Local Repository** in the context menu. The successful local repository initialization message will be displayed in the upper-right corner of the SAP Web IDE.
7. (Optional): To link the local repository to an external Git repository, select the **Set Remote** option, and provide the external Git repository URL, as shown in Figure 5.20. (Git setup was discussed in Chapter 2, Section 2.6.)

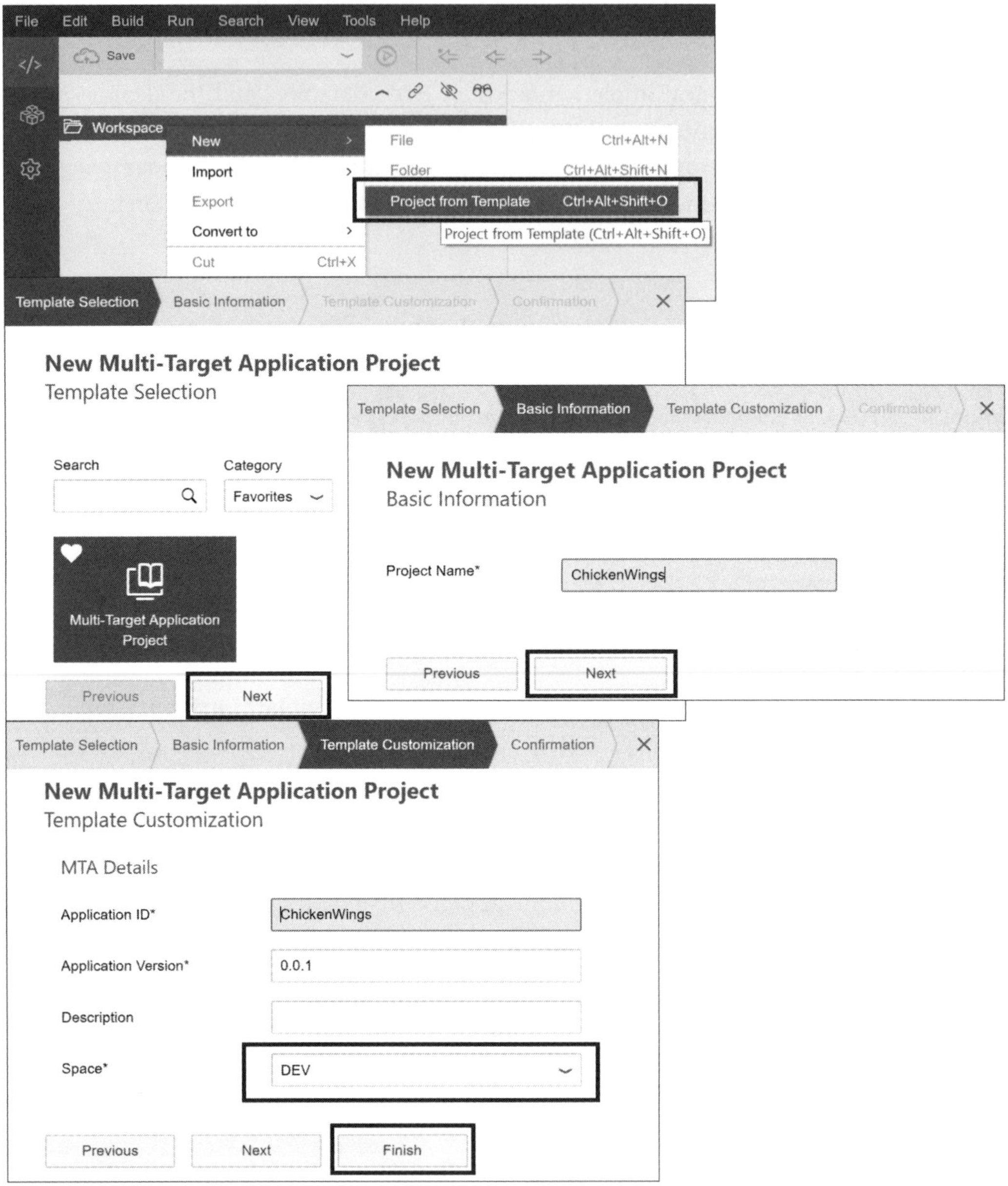

Figure 5.19 Creating an MTA Project

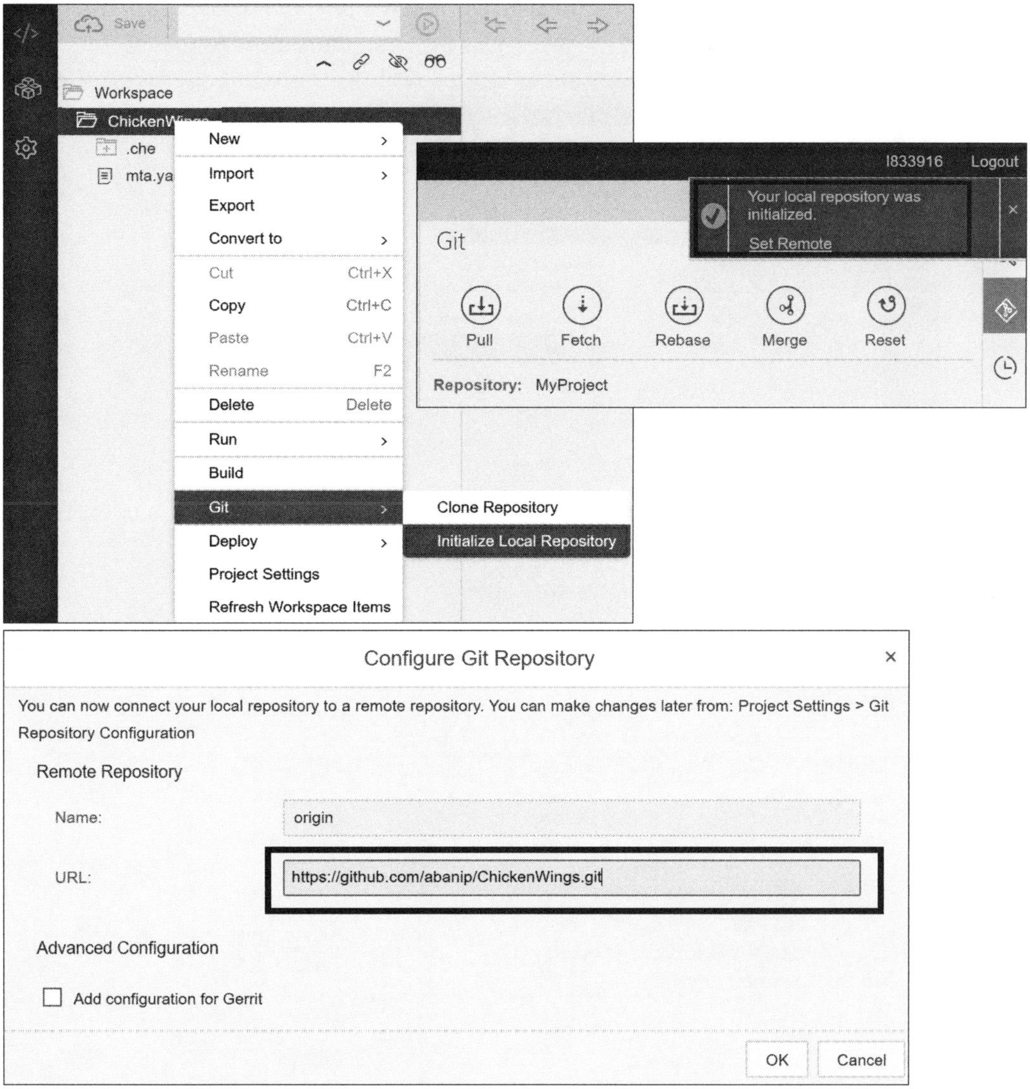

Figure 5.20 Using GitHub as the Repository

5.5.2 Creating an SAP HANA Database Module

An HDB module is required to create database artifacts required for the application. Use the following steps to add a new HDB module to the MTA project:

1. In the context menu of the Project, select **New • SAP HANA Database Module** to add a new HDB module to the project, as illustrated in Figure 5.21.

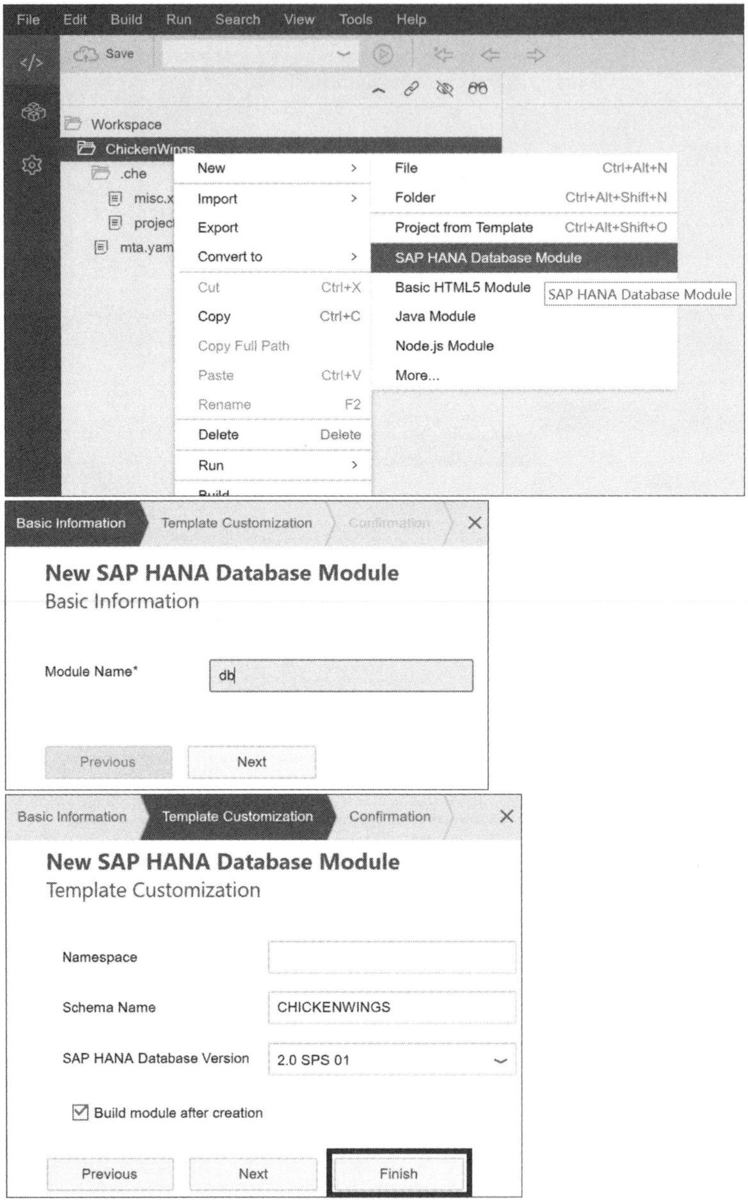

Figure 5.21 Creating a New HDB Module

2. Provide the **Module Name,** and select **Next** to proceed to the **Template Customization** screen.
3. Provide a **Namespace, Schema Name**, and **SAP HANA Database Version**. Note that if a namespace is provided, all runtime objects will be qualified with the namespace provided in the target schema, for example, `Namespace.ObjectName`. The namespace can be blank to create objects without namespace qualification. Select the **Build module after creation** checkbox to build the container schemas immediately. Select **Finish** to proceed.
4. The just created HDB module will be created part of the MTA project, as illustrated in Figure 5.22

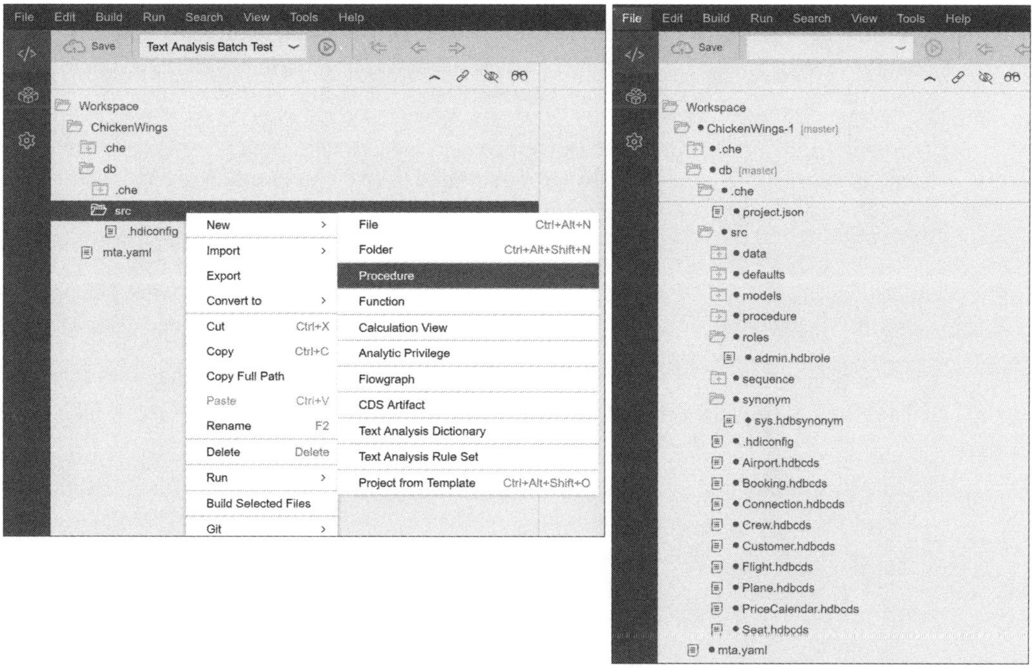

Figure 5.22 HDB Folder Structure

5. As specified, a new *db* folder for the HDB module is created in the MTA project with a subfolder *src* to host design-time database artifacts. The *src* folder has an *.hdconfig* file (hidden by default), which lists the supported design-time database artifact file types and their corresponding plug-in details. To display the hidden files, select **View • Show Hidden Files** in the menu of SAP Web IDE for SAP HANA.

6. The definition of the *mta.yml* file is also updated to include the HDB module definition.
7. From the context menu of the *src* folder, select **New • Choose one of the available artifacts**. The list of available artifacts is given in Table 5.2.

Artifacts	Instructions
File	Create a file with an appropriate extension to develop any artifact supported by SAP HANA XS Advanced and use a text editor.
Procedure (*.hdbprocedure*)	Choose **Procedure**, and enter the file name to create a database procedure. The new artifact is added to the module and opens in a dedicated code editor.
Function (*.hdbfunction*)	Choose **Function**, and enter the file name to create database functions. The new artifact is added to the module and opens in a dedicated code editor
Flowgraph (*.hdbflowgraph*)	Choose **Flowgraph**, and then enter a name. The new artifact is added to the module and the Flowgraph editor opens. New nodes (e.g., aggregation, filter, joins, etc.) can be placed on the canvas and configured to meet data transformation requirements.
Analytic privilege (*.hdbanalyticprivilege*)	Choose **Analytic Privilege**, and enter a name and label. The new artifact is added to the module and opens in the dedicated editor.
HDB CDS artifact (*.hdbcds*)	Choose **CDS Artifact**, enter a name, and choose the editor (graphical or text). The new artifact is added to the module and opens in the chosen editor.
Calculation view (*.hdbcalculationview*)	Choose **Calculation View,** enter a name and label, and select the type and category. The new artifact is added to the module and opens in the calculation view editor. New nodes (e.g., aggregation, projections, join, union, minus, intersection, rank, graph node, etc.) can be placed on the canvas and configured to model business logic.
Virtual table (*.hdbvirtualtable*)	Choose **Virtual Table**, and enter a file name to create the virtual table. The new artifact is added to the model and opens in a dedicated editor for configuration.
Text analysis dictionary (*.hdbtextdict*)	Choose **Text Analysis Dictionary**, and enter a name. The name can be with or without the file extension. A text editor will open for the new dictionary file with an XML template automatically populated.

Table 5.2 HDB Artifacts

Artifacts	Instructions
Text analysis rule set (*.hdbtextrule*)	Choose **Text Analysis Rule Set**, and enter a name with or without the file extension. A text editor will open for the new rule set file.

Table 5.2 HDB Artifacts (Cont.)

8. Various design-time database artifacts can be created and organized into separate folders to improve readability, as shown in Figure 5.22. As an example, we're using the following folder structure:
   - *data*: CDS artifacts to create database tables.
   - *defaults*: To define default roles with all required accesses for the SAP HANA XS Advanced application.
   - *ext1*, *ext2*, and so on: To define extensions to extend the data model for future changes.
   - *function*: Artifacts to create database functions.
   - *models*: Calculation views to create SAP HANA virtual models.
   - *privilege*: Artifacts to define analytic privileges for securing data in calculation views.
   - *procedure*: Artifacts to create database procedures.
   - *roles*: To define specific technical roles with limited access for foreign technical users from other applications.
   - *samples*: Sample data (*.csv* and *.hdbtabledata*) for the database tables.
   - *sequence*: Artifacts to create database sequences for the tables.
   - *synonym*: Artifacts to create database synonyms for external (to container) tables in any other schema (`_SYS_BI` or `SAPERP` schema).

5.5.3 Building the SAP HANA Database Module Artifacts

During the development process, the **Build** step is used to generate runtime database objects from the HDI design-time artifacts. It supports either one-object-at-a-time creation (build selected files) or all-objects-at-once creation (build at the module level).

To generate the runtime database object, select the design-time artifact, and choose **Build Selected Files** from the context menu, or select **Build Selected Files** from the menu in SAP Web IDE for SAP HANA. Upon a successful build, the runtime database objects will be available in the HDI container and can be accessed using SAP HANA database explorer, as shown in Figure 5.23.

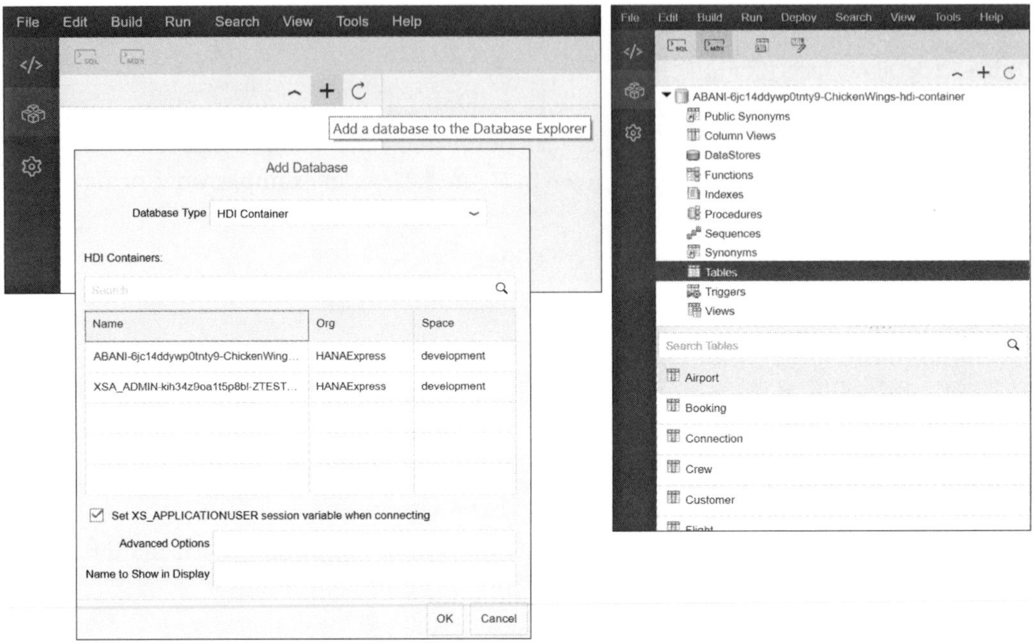

Figure 5.23 HDB Container Objects in SAP HANA Database Explorer

Definitions of the (already built) runtime database objects can be changed by changing and building the corresponding design-time artifacts. However, if a design-time artifact is deleted from the project, the corresponding runtime database object will remain in the container schema. These orphaned runtime database objects must be explicitly undeployed using an *undeply.json* file as part of the HDB module. The structure of the *undeploy.json* file is shown in Listing 5.15.

```
File Name: undeploy.json
[
  "src/data/Airport.hdbcds",
  "src/view/CloseAirport.hdbview"
]
```

Listing 5.15 undeploy.json

As discussed in Section 5.4, the HDI container for HDB modules will create multiple database schemas and technical users. The generated runtime objects will be available in the container schema (e.g., CHICKENWINGS_1). In addition, two additional container schemas are also created, that is, container metadata schema xxx#DI (e.g., CHICKENWINGS_1#DI) and object owner user schema xxx#OO (e.g., CHICKENWINGS_1#OO). The xxx#DI (e.g., CHICKENWINGS_1#DI) contains the metadata tables and API procedures, as shown in Figure 5.24. The xxx#OO schema (e.g., CHICKENWINGS_1#OO) doesn't contain database objects.

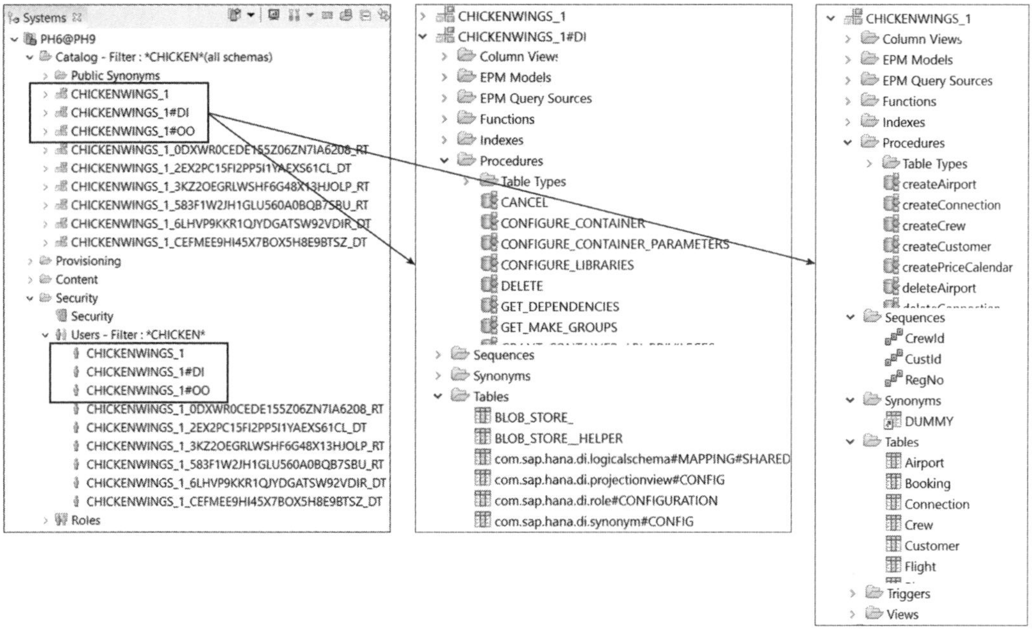

Figure 5.24 HDB Container Schemas and Technical Users

A few other technical users for the HDI container in the format of XXX_GUID_RT (e.g., CHICKENWINGS_1#XXXXXX_DT) and XXX_GUID_RT (e.g., CHICKENWINGS_1#XXXXXX_RT) are also created. These technical users are used by various SAP HANA XS Advanced applications such as SAP Web IDE for SAP HANA and SAP HANA database explorer. These technical users are automatically created and destroyed.

5.5.4 Building and Deploying a Multi-Target Application Archive

In a typical customer implementation project, there will be multiple developers working on the same project. Each developer will work in their own HDI container to develop project artifacts, and those artifacts will be checked in to the central Git repository upon completion. The central Git repository will have the finalized version of all artifacts developed as part of the project implementation. To test and verify completeness of the project, all artifacts must be packaged as a *.mtar* file and deployed as an application (see Figure 5.25).

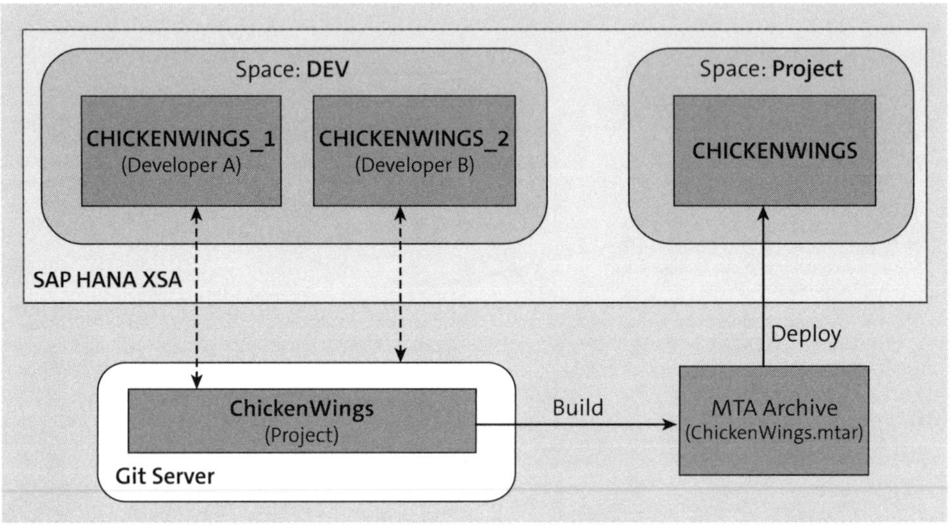

Figure 5.25 Developer Containers and Deployment Container

Before we proceed to build the MTA archive, the local Git repository must be refreshed with the latest content from the remote Git repository. Rebuild the HDB module (i.e., *db* folder) to regenerate all the runtime database objects as a final validation. Upon successful completion, proceed to build the MTA archive.

To build the MTA archive in SAP Web IDE for SAP HANA, select the project (i.e., **ChickenWings**), and choose **Build** from the context menu, as shown in Figure 5.26. The build process will generate the *Project_version.mtar* (e.g., `ChickeWings_0.0.1.mtar`) under the *mta_archive* folder per the name and version specification in the *mta.yaml* file.

For DevOps/automation, SAP Web IDE for SAP HANA isn't used to create the MTA archive; instead, the command-line tool MTA archive builder is used to create the MTA archive based on the source code in the Git repository.

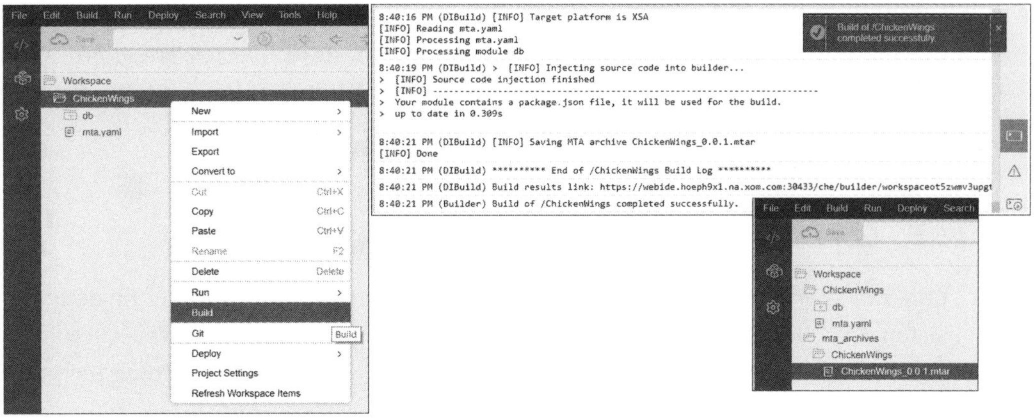

Figure 5.26 Building the MTA Archive

To deploy an MTA archive, choose **Deploy • Deploy to XS Advanced** from the context menu of the MTA archive (e.g., **ChickenWings_0.0.1.mtar**), and select the **Organization** and **Space** of the target SAP HANA XS Advanced environment, as shown in Figure 5.27. The deployment process may take a few seconds to a few minutes depending on the number of artifacts that are part of the MTA archive.

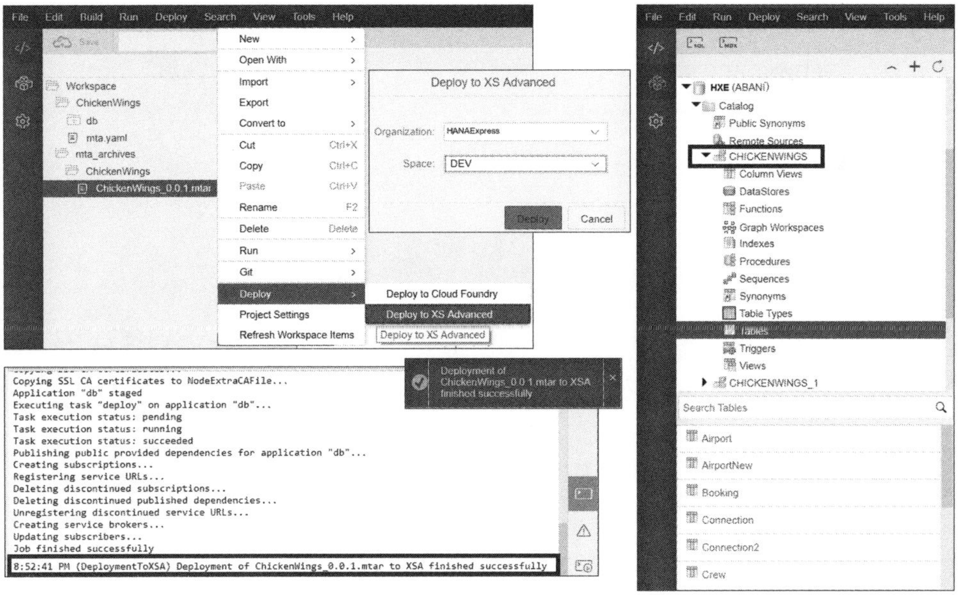

Figure 5.27 Deploying the MTA Archive

Upon successful deployment the project container is available for use. To access the database objects of the deployed container, the user must be assigned appropriate container role. The default container role is Container::access_role (i.e., `ChickenWings::access_role`).

5.6 Core Data Services: The Physical Data Model

Core Data Services (CDS) was introduced in SAP HANA 1.0 SP 06 to define data persistence in SAP HANA using design-time artifacts. CDS offers an infrastructure to define and consume semantically rich data models (specifically enriching technical definitions with semantics such as annotations and associations vs. SQL statements such as `CREATE TABLE` and `CREATE VIEW`). The DDL of CDS allows you to define database tables, database views, and data types by wrapping the according native SAP HANA SQL statements and enriching them with semantical properties.

The CDS syntax and its implementation has evolved since its introduction; specifically, there are some incompatible changes and additions between CDS syntax with SAP HANA XS and SAP HANA XS Advanced. In this section, we'll discuss CDS editors and the CDS syntax for SAP HANA XS Advanced to create the following:

- CDS entities (tables)
- CDS data types and user-defined types
- CDS associations (between entities)
- CDS views
- CDS extensions

5.6.1 Editors

To create and add a CDS document to the HDB module, select **New • CDS Artifact** in the context menu of the *src* folder to add a new calculation view to the HDB module (Figure 5.28).

SAP Web IDE for SAP HANA has two editors to define data-persistence objects in CDS documents (*.hdbcds*) using the DDL-compliant CDS syntax: CDS text editor and CDS graphical editor.

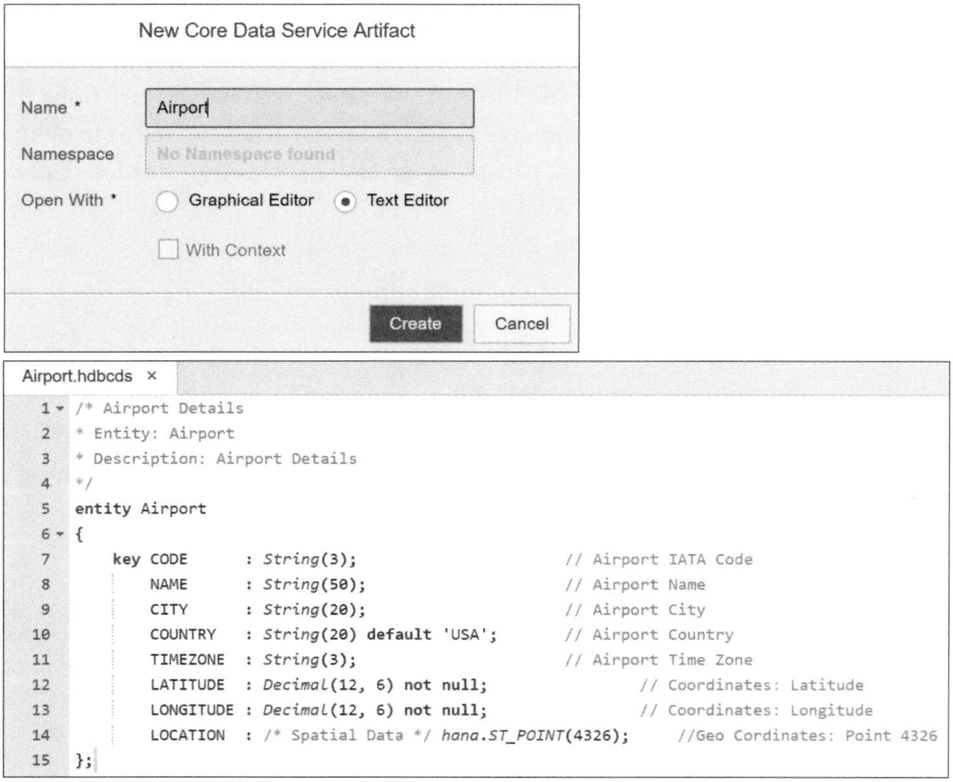

Figure 5.28 CDS Code Editor

CDS Text Editor

The CDS text editor can be opened using **Open With • Code Editor** in the context menu of an *.hdbcds* document. The CDS text editor supports syntax highlighting for keywords and assigned values, and it offers code completion by providing a list of suggestions for keywords, as shown in Figure 5.28. Double slash (//) and forward slash with asterisk (/*..*/) are used for single line and multiline comments, respectively. The CDS text editor parsers checks and validates syntax errors as the code is written. Errors are also shown in the **Problems** view of SAP Web IDE for SAP HANA. Semantic errors are generated during the build process and displayed in the **Console** tab.

CDS Graphical Editor

The CDS graphical editor can be opened by double-clicking or using **Open With • Graphical Editor** in the context menu of an *.hdbcds* document. The CDS graphical editor is used to design and develop database artifacts graphically with little or no coding, and the CDS source code is generated when the model is built.

The CDS graphical editor can be used to create entities, contexts, associations (to internal and external entities), structured types, and scalar types, as well as to define technical configurations (indexes, partitions, groupings, etc.) for entities (Figure 5.29).

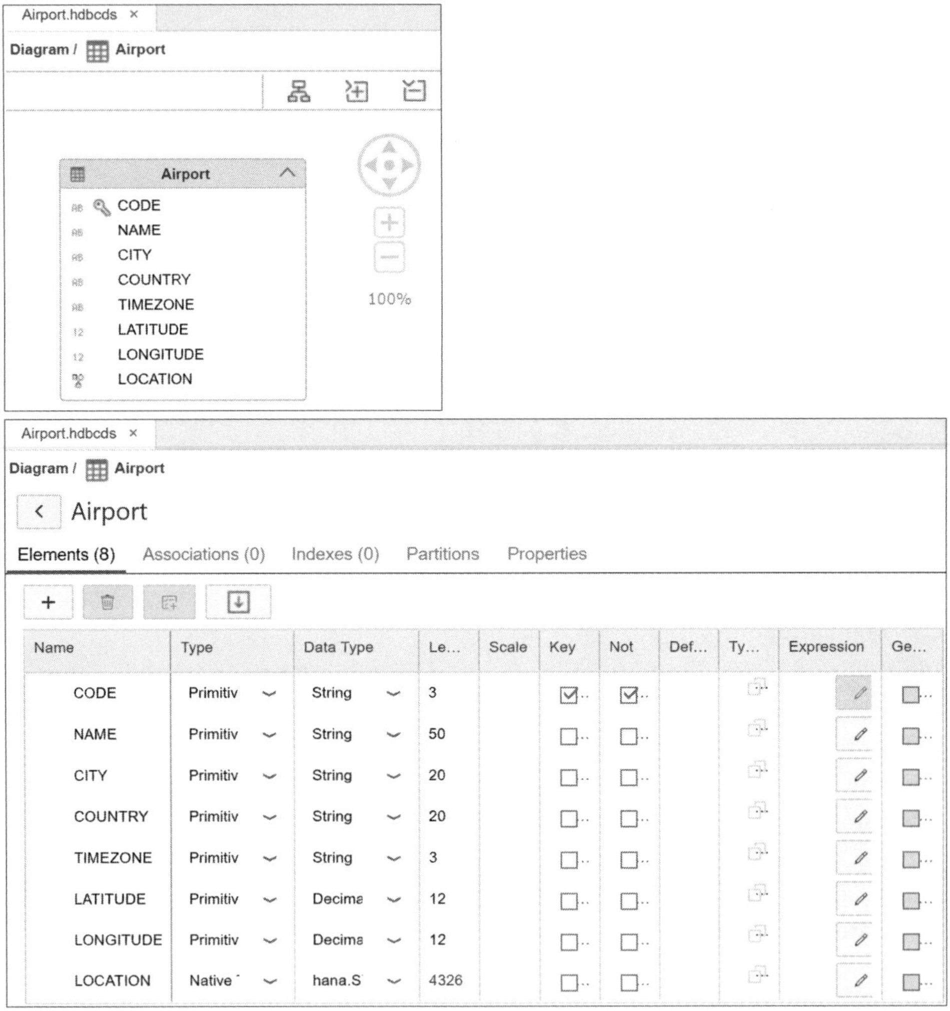

Figure 5.29 Graphical CDS Editor

5.6.2 Entities

Starting with SAP HANA 2.0 SPS 01, a single CDS document can be used to define multiple top-level artifacts (entities and contexts), and the name of the CDS document can be anything. In earlier releases, only one top-level artifact (namespace or entity) could be part of one CDS document, and the name of the CDS document had to match the name of the top-level artifact. Note that we can define multiple entities under one namespace, but the name of the namespace is added to the generated object's (table or view) name as `<namespace>.<entity>`.

In our example, we've created one CDS document (*tables.hdbcds*) to define all our entities (database tables). A CDS entity when deployed creates a database table, which is available under **Catalog • Container Schema • Tables**. The structure of the single CDS document with all entities is shown in Listing 5.16.

File Name: /src/tables.hdbcds

```
/*
* Data Type Definition
*/
type NameT        : String(20);
type PhoneT        : String(15);
type EmailT        : String(30);
type CityT        : String(20);
type CountryT        : String(25);
type CodeT        : String(3);
type FlightT        : String(6);
type PriceT        : Decimal(12,2);
type ModelT        : String(10);
type SeatT        : String(4);

/*
* Structure definition
* technical structure to be used in all entities
* to store last changed timestamp and last changed by user
*/
type ChangeT {
    USER: String(20);        //Changed by User
    TIMESTAMP: UTCTimestamp;
};
```

```
entity Airport {
    key CODE      : String(3);        // Airport IATA Code
        NAME      : String(50);     // Airport Name
        CITY      : CityT;            // Airport City
        COUNTRY   : CountryT     default 'USA'; // Airport Country
        TIMEZONE  : String(3);        // Airport Time Zone
        LATITUDE  : Decimal(12, 6) not null; // Coordinates: Latitude
        LONGITUDE : Decimal(12, 6) not null; // Coordinates: Longitude
        LOCATION  : /* Spatial Data */ hana.ST_POINT(4326)
                  = new ST_
POINT ('POINT ('||LONGITUDE || ' ' || LATITUDE || ')',4326); //
Geo Coordinates: Point 4326
        CHANGE    : ChangeT; // Technical Columns
}
technical configuration {
    column store;        //Column Table
    auto merge;            //Enable auto merge
    unload priority 5;  //Standard settings
    group type app group subtype ChickenWings group name master;
};

//Plane Details
entity Plane
{
    key REGNO      : Integer;             //Registration Number
        MODEL      : String(10);        //Model Name
        MANUFACTURER       : String(20);        //Manufacturer
        TYPE       : String(20);        //Type of Aircraft
        YEAR       : Integer;             //Year of Manufacture
        REGDATE       : LocalDate;          //Registration Date
        MAXSEAT    : Integer;             //Maximum Seating Capacity
        ECOSEAT    : Integer;             //No of Economy Class Seats
        BUSSEAT    : Integer;             //No of Business Class Seats
        FIRSEAT    : Integer;             //No of First Class Seats
        CHANGE       : ChangeT;     //Last Change Timestamp and User
}
technical configuration {
    column store;        //Column Table
    auto merge;            //Enable auto merge
```

```
    unload priority 5;  //Standard settings
    group type app group subtype ChickenWings group name master;
};

// Crew Details
entity Crew
{
    key CREWID  : Integer;             //Customer ID
        FNAME   : NameT;            //First Name
        LNAME   : NameT;            //Last Name
        MOBILE  : PhoneT;            //Mobile/Cell Number
        EMAIL   : EmailT;            //Email
        COUNTRY : CountryT;            //Country of Residence
        ROLE    : String(20);        //Job/Role of Crew
        CHANGE    : ChangeT;    //Last Change Timestamp and User
}
technical configuration {
    column store;         //Column Table
    auto merge;             //Enable auto merge
    unload priority 5;  //Standard settings
    group type app group subtype ChickenWings group name master;
};

//Customer Details
entity Customer
{
    key CUSTID  : Integer;             //Customer ID
        FNAME   : NameT;            //First Name
        LNAME   : NameT;            //Last Name
        MOBILE  : PhoneT;            //Mobile/Cell Number
        EMAIL   : EmailT;            //Email
        COUNTRY : CountryT;         //Country of Residence
        FLYERID : String(20);        //Frequent Flyer ID
        CHANGE    : ChangeT;    //Last Change Timestamp and User
}
technical configuration {
    column store;         //Column Table
    auto merge;             //Enable auto merge
    unload priority 5;  //Standard settings
```

```
    group type app group subtype ChickenWings group name master;
};

//Seat Details
entity Seat
{
    key MODEL    : ModelT;              //Plane Model
    key SEAT    : SeatT;              //Seat Number
        CLASS    : String(10);          //Class of Seat: Economy, Business
        STYPE    : String(15);          //Type of Seating: Window/Isle
        CHANGE    : ChangeT;    //Last Change Timestamp and User
}
technical configuration {
    column store;        //Column Table
    auto merge;            //Enable auto merge
    unload priority 5;  //Standard settings
    group type app group subtype ChickenWings group name master;
};

//Price Calendar
entity PriceCalendar
{
    key CDATE    : LocalDate ;         //Date
        RATE    : String(10);         //Standard or Peak Rate for Pricing
        SEASON    : String(20);         //Season used for Pricing
        CHANGE    : ChangeT;    //Last Change Timestamp and User
}
technical configuration {
    column store;        //Column Table
    auto merge;            //Enable auto merge
    unload priority 5;  //Standard settings
    group type app group subtype ChickenWings group name master;
};

//Connection Details
entity Connection
{
    key FLIGHT    : FlightT;              //Flight Number
        FROMAP    : CodeT;              //Origin Airport
```

```
        TOAP     : CodeT;              //Destination Airport
        DEPT     : LocalTime;          //Scheduled Departure Time
        ARRT     : LocalTime;          //Scheduled Arrival Time
        SSTARTD     : LocalDate;          //Service Start Date
        SENDD     : LocalDate;          //Service End Date
        ESPRICE     : PriceT;              //Economy Class Standard Price
        EPPRICE     : PriceT;              //Economy Class Peak Price
        BSPRICE     : PriceT;              //Business Class Standard Price
        BPPRICE     : PriceT;              //Business Class Peak Price
        FSPRICE     : PriceT;              //First Class Standard Price
        FPPRICE     : PriceT;              //First Class Peak Price
        MILES     : Integer;             //Distance in Miles
        CHANGE     : ChangeT;    //Last Change Timestamp and User
        // Associations
        _FromAirport  : association[*, 0..1] to Airport
            on _FromAirport.CODE = FROMAP;
        _ToAirport    : association[*, 0..1] to Airport
            on _ToAirport.CODE = TOAP;
}
technical configuration {
    column store;         //Column Table
    auto merge;             //Enable auto merge
    unload priority 5;  //Standard settings
    group type app group subtype ChickenWings group name master;
};

//Flight Details
entity Flight
{
    key FLIGHT     : FlightT;              //Flight Number
    key FDATE     : LocalDate;          //Flight Date
        PLANE     : Integer;             //Plane RegNo
        PILOT1     : Integer;             //Pilot
        PILOT2     : Integer;             //Co-Pilot
        CREW1     : Integer;             //Crew 1
        CREW2     : Integer;             //Crew 2
        CREW3     : Integer;             //Crew 3
        DEPT     : LocalTime;          //Actual Departure Time
        ARRT     : LocalTime;          //Actual Arrival Time
```

```
        STATUS     : String(10);        //Flight Status
        CHANGE     : ChangeT;     //Last Change Timestamp and User
        // Associations
        _Connection     : association[*, 0..1] to Connection
            on _Connection.FLIGHT = FLIGHT;
        _Plane            : association[*, 0..1] to Plane
            on _Plane.REGNO = PLANE;
        _Pilot1         : association[*, 0..1] to Crew
            on _Pilot1.CREWID = PILOT1;
        _Pilot2         : association[*, 0..1] to Crew
            on _Pilot2.CREWID = PILOT2;
        _Crew1          : association[*, 0..1] to Crew
            on _Crew1.CREWID = CREW1;
        _Crew2          : association[*, 0..1] to Crew
            on _Crew2.CREWID = CREW2;
        _Crew3          : association[*, 0..1] to Crew
            on _Crew3.CREWID = CREW3;
}
technical configuration {
    column store;        //Column Table
    auto merge;            //Enable auto merge
    unload priority 5;  //Standard settings
    group type app group subtype ChickenWings group name master;
};

//Booking Details
entity Booking
{
    key FLIGHT    : FlightT;        //Flight Number
    key FDATE     : LocalDate;         //Flight Date
    key MODEL     : ModelT;            //Plane Model
    key SEAT      : ModelT;         //Seat Number
        CUSTID    : Integer;        //Customer ID
        STDPRICE  : PriceT;         //Base Price
        BOOKPRICE : PriceT;         //Book Price
        FEES      : PriceT;         //Surcharges/Fees
        DISCOUNT  : PriceT;         //Discount
        TAX       : PriceT;         //Tax
        TOTAL     : PriceT;         //Total Amount Charged
```

```
        PAYMENT   : String(15);      //Mode of Payment CREDIT, CASH, POINTS
        STATUS    : String(10);         //Booking Status Hold/Confirmed/
Available
        PASSENGER : String(20);      //Name of the Passenger
        CHECKIN   : String(1);         //Check-in Status
        CHANGE      : ChangeT;  //Last Change Timestamp and User
        // Associations
        _Flight   : association[*, 0..1] to Flight {FLIGHT,FDATE};
        _Seat     : association[*, 0..1] to Seat {MODEL, SEAT};
        _Customer : association[*, 0..1] to Customer {CUSTID};
}
technical configuration {
    column store;        //Column Table
    auto merge;            //Enable auto merge
    unload priority 5;  //Standard settings
    group type app group subtype ChickenWings group name transaction;
};
```

Listing 5.16 CDS Entity Structure

The elements of an entity can be defined using *native data types* (e.g., Integer, String) as well as user-defined data (e.g., CityT, CountryT) definitions. It also supports element definition using spatial data types (hana.ST_POINT and HANA.ST_Geometry). The following entity modifiers are also available to influence the behavior:

- key
  Specifies the element as the primary key or part of the primary key of the entity.
- null or not null
  Specifies if the element can have NULL values or not. Elements defined as key can't have NULL values.
- default <literal_value>
  Specifies the default value for the element. The default value is inserted in the database tables if the value isn't specified by an INSERT SQL statement. The literal_value must be specified using native data types.
- generated always as <expression>
  The value of the element is computed per the <expression>, and the value is inserted/updated to the database table during the INSERT/UPDATE operation. It's supported only for column tables.

- generated [always/ by default] as identity (start with m increment by n)
  Specifies an identity column with the starting value m and increments by n for subsequent rows. If the element is defined with always, the value is always generated, whereas for by default, the value is generated by default (i.e., when not specified).
- calculated always as <expression>
  The value of the element is computed per the <expression>. The element isn't stored/materialized at the record level but is computed during a SELECT operation.
- Calculated fields (= <expression>)
  The value of the element is calculated per the expression, which can be any SQL function. It can be a simple calculation, such as = elementA + elementB, or not so simple, such as = new ST_POINT ('POINT ('||LONGITUDE || ' ' || LATITUDE || ')',4326). However, the calculated element can't be part of the primary key or part of any *associations* (discussed in Section 5.6.4), and no index can be defined on a calculated column.

The technical configuration (row/column tables, partitions, etc.) of the generated database tables can be specified using the technical configuration settings. The syntax of these technical settings is very similar to the corresponding clauses in the CREATE TABLE SQL statement described here:

- store (storage type)
  Defines as a row store or column store table.
- index
  Indexes can be generated for a particular element to enable faster access. Data access is significantly faster with SAP HANA column tables, so indexes aren't required for most common scenarios.
- full index
  Specifies full-text index settings for the generated table to enable full-text searches for the specified column.
- partition by
  Specifies partition settings of the generated table. SAP HANA supports *multilevel partitioning* of tables with HASH, RANGE, and ROUND ROBIN options.

  By default, external changes to tables are lost during redeployment. However, existing external partitioning specifications can be preserved using partition by keeping existing layout.
- migration disabled
  Specifies the migration setting. If migration is disabled for a table, changing data

type of an element or dropping an element (later) isn't allowed. However, adding new elements to an entity is possible.

- `group type XXX group subtype YYY group name ZZZ`
  Defines the grouping setting for the generated tables. Tables with the same group name are placed on the same host, or first-level partitions are placed on the same table for partitioned tables in a distributed system. Tables with grouping settings are included in the `SYS.TABLE_GROUPS` table.
- `unload priority`
  Specifies the unload priority of the generated table. Tables are unloaded from memory based on a least recently used (LRU) algorithm. Possible options are `0 (cannot be unloaded)` to `9 (earliest unload)`.
- `auto merge or no auto merge`
  Specifies the auto merge option for the generated table. SAP HANA automatically triggers a delta merge operation for tables with auto merge enabled.

Global temporary tables can be defined using temporary keywords as part of the entity definition, such as `temporary entity Airport`.

5.6.3 Data Types and User-Defined Structures

CDS supports the SAP HANA native data types listed in Table 5.3 for defining entities, user-defined types, and user-defined structures.

Name	SAP HANA Data Types	Comments
`String (n)`	`NVARCHAR`	Max value of *n* is 5000.
`LargeString`	`NCLOB`	
`Binary(n)`	`VARBINARY`	
`LargeBinary`	`BLOB`	
`Integer`	`INTEGER`	Signed 32-bit integer.
`Integer64`	`BIGINT`	Signed 64-bit integer.
`Decimal(p, s )`	`DECIMAL(p, s)`	Max value of *p* and *s* is 34.
`DecimalFloat`	`DECIMAL`	

Table 5.3 CDS Primitive Data Types

Name	SAP HANA Data Types	Comments
BinaryFloat	DOUBLE	
LocalDate	DATE	
LocalTime	TIME	
UTCDateTime	SECONDDATE	
UTCTimestamp	TIMESTAMP	
Boolean	BOOLEAN	

Table 5.3 CDS Primitive Data Types (Cont.)

User-defined data types, on the other hand, are module- or document-specific data types created for consistent element/column definition. User-defined data types can reference native data or other user-defined data types.

In our example shown in Listing 5.16, the element COUNTRY is part of multiple entities (Airport, Crew, and Customer), and the user-defined data type CountryT : String(25) is used to ensure the data types and length of the COUNTRY element remains consistent in all entities.

The elements and user-defined data types must be unique in the context they are defined; that is, we can't define an element as CountryT : CountryT. Therefore, a consistent naming convention must be followed to distinguish them.

A structure data type consists of a list of attributes, all of which can be of different data types and can reference both native and other user-defined data types.

In our example in Listing 5.16, the structure ChangeT is used in all entities to define two technical columns (CHANGE.USER and CHANGE.TIMESTAMP) to track data changes in the generated tables.

Elements can also be defined when referencing an individual attribute of a structure, for example, NAME : type of ChangeT.USER.

User-defined structures generate table types runtime objects when deployed and are available under **Catalog • Container Schema • Procedure • Tables Types**.

To reuse the user-defined structures in multiple CDS documents, a separate CDS document (e.g., CWTypes.hdbcds) can be created to define one or more structures (BaseT and myChangeT), as shown in Listing 5.17.

File Name: /src/CWTypes.hdbcds

```
context CWTypes {

    type BaseT {
         NameT         : String(20);
         PhoneT    : String(15);
         EmailT    : String(30);
         CityT         : String(20);
         CountryT     : String(25);
         CodeT         : String(3);
         FlightT    : String(6);
         PriceT    : Decimal(12,2);
         ModelT    : String(10);
         SeatT         : String(4);
    };

    type myChangeT {
        USER: String(20);          //Changed by User
        TIMESTAMP: UTCTimestamp;
    };

};
```

Listing 5.17 External User-Defined Structure

The external structures can then be referenced in multiple CDS documents. We've added a new entity called `AirportNew` with the same structure as that of `Airport` but referencing the `CWTypes` structure, as shown in Listing 5.18.

File Name: /src/Tables.hdbcds

```
/* Reference to external structures */
using CWTypes.BaseT;
using CWTypes.myChangeT;

/* Define Entity */
entity AirportNew {
    key CODE      : type of BaseT.CodeT;     // Airport Code
        NAME      : String(50);              // Airport Name
        CITY      : type of BaseT.CityT;     // Airport City
```

```
        COUNTRY   : type of BaseT.CountryT default 'USA';
        TIMEZONE  : String(3);              // Time Zone
        LATITUDE  : Decimal(12, 6) not null;  // Latitude
        LONGITUDE : Decimal(12, 6) not null;     // Longitude
        LOCATION  : /* Spatial Data */ hana.ST_POINT(4326)
                    = new ST_
POINT ('POINT ('||LONGITUDE || ' ' || LATITUDE || ')',4326); //
Geo Coordinates: Point 4326
        CHANGE    : myChangeT; // Technical Columns
}
technical configuration {
    column store;          //Column Table
    auto merge;          //Enable auto merge
    unload priority 5;       //Standard settings
    group type app group subtype ChickenWings group name master;
};
```

Listing 5.18 AirportNew Entity with External Structures

5.6.4 Associations

CDS associations are used to define relationships between entities and are defined along with the entity definition. There are two types of CDS associations: *managed* and *unmanaged*.

Managed Associations

The relationship to the target entity is part of the element definition in managed associations. The syntax to define a managed association is as follows:

```
Association [ <cardinality> ] to <targetEntity> [ <forwardLink> ]
```

For example, the `FROMAP` (`Origin Airport`) element of the `Connection` entity is defined with association to the `Airport` entity in Listing 5.19 as follows:

```
FROMAP    : association[*, 1] to Airport {CODE}; //Origin Airport
```

This will create a field/column `FROMAP.CODE` in the generated `Connection` table, as shown in Figure 5.30.

Unmanaged Associations

An unmanaged association is created based on existing elements of the source and target entities. Because they aren't part of the element definition, no fields are created in the target table. An unmanaged association is created based on the join condition. The syntax to define an unmanaged association is as follows:

```
Association [ <cardinality> ] to <targetEntity> <unmanagedJoin>
```

For example, the _ToAirport unmanaged association to Connection is defined in Listing 5.19 as follows:

```
_ToAirport : association[*, 1] to Airport
             on _ToAirport.CODE = TOAP;
```

As shown in Figure 5.30, there will be no field generated for the _ToAirport association.

The type of the relationship (to-one, to-many, or one-to-one) can be specified using cardinality in an association. Both source and target cardinality can be specified as [maxs, min .. max], where maxs denotes the source cardinality and min..max denotes the target cardinality. If no cardinality is specified, the default cardinality [0..1] is assumed for target.

```
entity Connection
{
    key FLIGHT : FlightT;             //Flight Number
        //Managed Association - Origin Airport
        FROMAP : association[*, 1] to Airport {CODE};
        TOAP    :  CodeT;     //Destination Airport
        DEPT    : LocalTime;     //Scheduled Departure Time
        ARRT    : LocalTime;         //Scheduled Arrival Time
        SSTARTD    : LocalDate;     //Service Start Date
        SENDD        : LocalDate;         //Service End Date
        ESPRICE    : PriceT;      //Economy Class Standard Price
        EPPRICE    : PriceT;      //Economy Class Peak Price
        BSPRICE    : PriceT;      //Business Class Standard Price
        BPPRICE    : PriceT;      //Business Class Peak Price
        FSPRICE    : PriceT;      //First Class Standard Price
        FPPRICE    : PriceT;      //First Class Peak Price
        MILES        : Integer;     //Distance in Miles
     CHANGE     : ChangeT;     //Change Timestamp and User
```

```
    // Unmanaged Associations
    _ToAirport    : association[*, 1] to Airport
        on _ToAirport.CODE = TOAP;
}
```

Listing 5.19 Managed and Unmanaged Associations

Table Name	Schema:	Type
Connection	CHICKENWINGS_1	TABLE

Columns Indexes

	Name	SQL Data Type	Column Store Data Type	Key	Not Null
1	FLIGHT	NVARCHAR(6)	STRING	1	X
2	TOAP	NVARCHAR(3)	STRING		
3	DEPT	TIME	SECONDTIME		
4	ARRT	TIME	SECONDTIME		
5	SSTARTD	DATE	DAYDATE		
6	SENDD	DATE	DAYDATE		
7	ESPRICE	DECIMAL(12,2)	FIXED		
8	EPPRICE	DECIMAL(12,2)	FIXED		
9	BSPRICE	DECIMAL(12,2)	FIXED		
10	BPPRICE	DECIMAL(12,2)	FIXED		
11	FSPRICE	DECIMAL(12,2)	FIXED		
12	FPPRICE	DECIMAL(12,2)	FIXED		
13	MILES	INTEGER	INT		
14	CHANGE.USER	NVARCHAR(20)	STRING		
15	CHANGE.TIMESTAMP	TIMESTAMP	LONGDATE		
16	FROMAP.CODE	NVARCHAR(3)	STRING		

Figure 5.30 Result of Associations in a Table

5.6.5 Views

One or more SQL views can be created using the CDS view definition based on the `SELECT` statement as shown in Listing 5.20. This is the equivalent of the `CREATE VIEW` SQL statement.

Upon deployment, the generated SQL database view (OpenSeat) will be available under **Container Schema • Views** (see Figure 5.31 ❶).

```
//CDS View: Creates database View
view OpenSeats
as SELECT FROM Booking
{
        FLIGHT,
        FDATE,
        COUNT(SEAT) as TOTAL_SEATS
} WHERE STATUS = 'AVAILABLE'
  GROUP BY FLIGHT,
         FDATE
  HAVING COUNT(SEAT) > 2
  ORDER BY FLIGHT ASC, FDATE DESC
;

//CDS View with Parameters: Creates database table function
view OpenSeats2 with parameters P_DATE : LocalDate
as SELECT FROM Booking
{
        FLIGHT,
        FDATE,
        COUNT(SEAT) as TOTAL_SEATS
} WHERE STATUS = 'AVAILABLE'
    AND FDATE = :P_DATE
  GROUP BY FLIGHT,
         FDATE
  HAVING COUNT(SEAT) > 2
  ORDER BY FLIGHT ASC, FDATE DESC
;
```

Listing 5.20 OpenSeats and OpenSeats2 CDS Views

A CDS view can also be defined with parameters to select data dynamically based on the input parameter. A CDS view with parameters (e.g., OpenSeats2) will actually generate a database table function under **Container Schema • Functions** (see Figure 5.31 ❷).

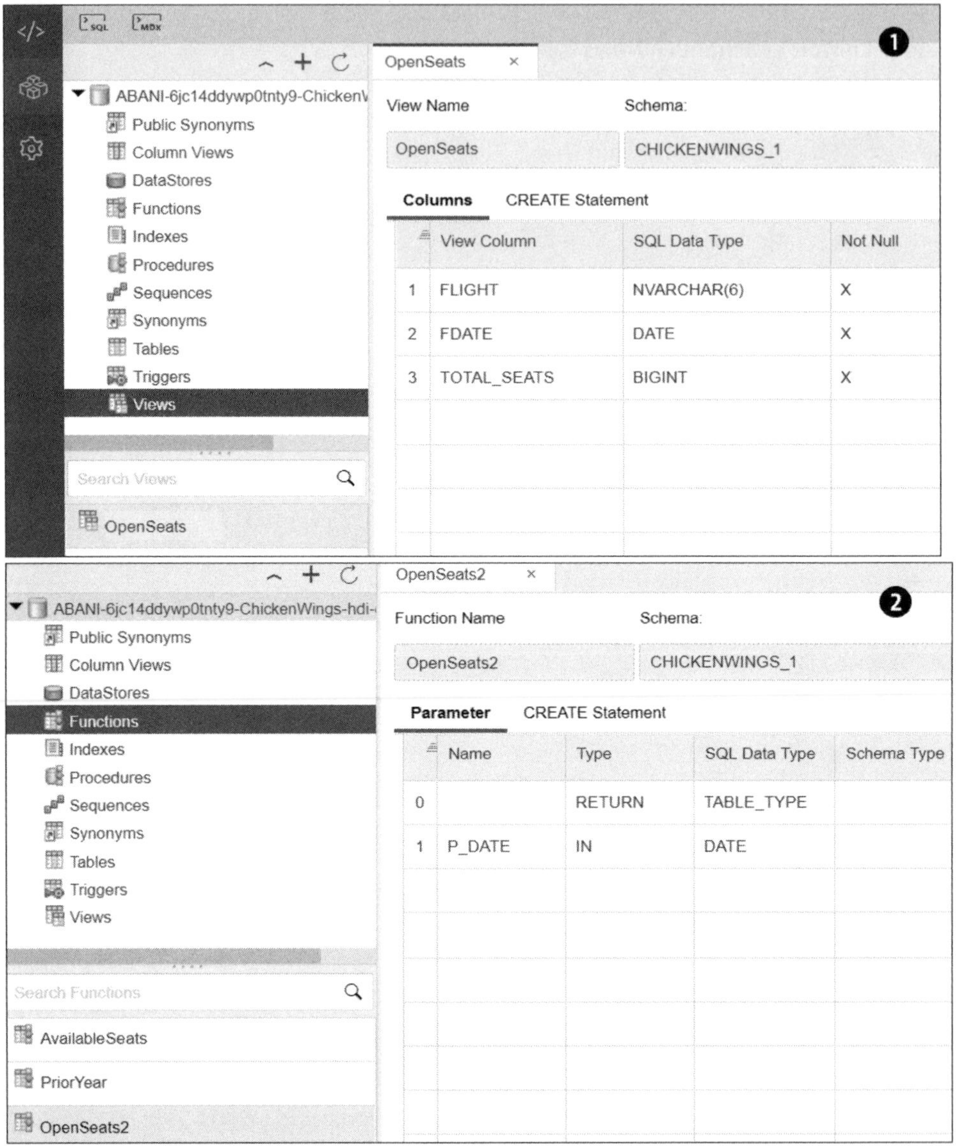

Figure 5.31 OpenSeats SQL View

5.6.6 Extensions

CDS extensions are used to extend an existing CDS model by adding new properties to existing CDS artifacts without modifying the original source files. The extensions are packaged separately and can be deployed as enhancements on top of an existing deployment. Multiple independent extension packages can be defined and deployed on an existing application. The build process will generate one object based on the effective combined definition of both the original and the extension, and the generated object will be available in the container schema. The following types of extensions are supported:

- Adding new elements to entities and structure types
- Adding new select items/elements to views
- Adding new entities/views/structures to a context
- Adding technical configurations to entities
- Adding new annotations to entities and entity elements

However, there are certain restrictions for CDS extensions, including the following:

- The extension of CDS artifacts must be defined in a separate package.
- Multiple extensions of the same entity can't be defined in one package. However, one entity can be extended in multiple extension packages.

To illustrate the concept, we'll add a new field called `INTERNATIONAL` to denote whether an airport offers international connections. To extend the `AIRPORT` entity, follow these steps:

1. Create a new folder (e.g., `ext1`) for the extension.
2. Create two new CDS artifacts (`package.hdbcds`) and (`db.hdbcds`) in the `ext1` folder to define the package and entity extensions as shown in Listing 5.21.
3. Upon deployment of the two new CDS artifacts, the new field `INTERNATIONAL` will be available in the `AIRPORT` table, as illustrated in Figure 5.32.

Filename: /src/ext1/package.hdbcds

```
package ext1;
```

Filename: /src/ext1/db.hdbcds

```
in package ext1;
using Airport;
extend entity Airport with {
    INTERNATIONAL: Boolean;
}
```

Listing 5.21 AIRPORT Entity with CDS Extension

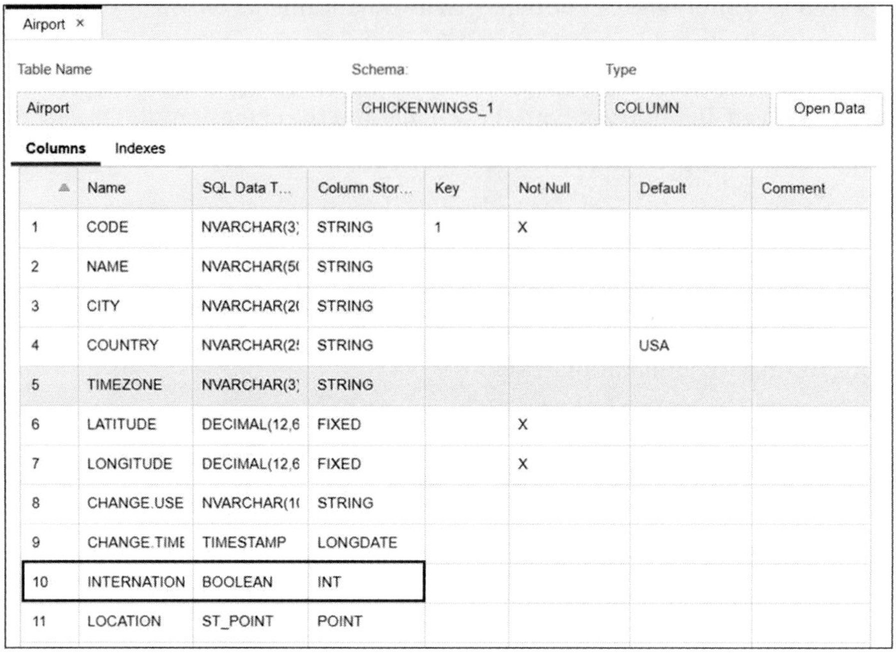

	Name	SQL Data T...	Column Stor...	Key	Not Null	Default	Comment
1	CODE	NVARCHAR(3;	STRING	1	X		
2	NAME	NVARCHAR(5(	STRING				
3	CITY	NVARCHAR(2(	STRING				
4	COUNTRY	NVARCHAR(2!	STRING			USA	
5	TIMEZONE	NVARCHAR(3;	STRING				
6	LATITUDE	DECIMAL(12,6	FIXED		X		
7	LONGITUDE	DECIMAL(12,6	FIXED		X		
8	CHANGE.USE	NVARCHAR(1(	STRING				
9	CHANGE.TIME	TIMESTAMP	LONGDATE				
10	INTERNATION	BOOLEAN	INT				
11	LOCATION	ST_POINT	POINT				

Figure 5.32 CDS Entity Extension

For more details on CDS extensions, refer to SAP HANA Core Data Services Reference Guide at *http://help.sap.com*.

5.7 Loading Table Data

You may need to prepopulate data to certain application tables during application deployment. This can be done by manually creating entries after the database tables are created or by executing one or more stored procedures to create the entries in database tables. In both scenarios, it requires manual intervention during deployment. The data creation/loading process can also be automated using design-time artifacts (*.hdbtabledata* and *.csv*) supported by SAP HANA XS Advanced. This process is meant for configuration tables (and not meant to prepopulate sample data into productive tables), as the data is deleted and inserted on the next deployment. In addition, SAP HANA XS Advanced also supports data import from *.properties* files into database tables managed by HDI; for example, the translated texts/labels used in calculation views are uploaded using the *.properties* file.

In the following sections, we'll discuss the syntax of *.hdbtabledata* and *.properties* files, which can be used to load data into HDI tables. We'll also discuss the tools available in SAP Web IDE for SAP HANA to generate time-dimension data for our application.

5.7.1 Using Table Data (.hdbtabledata)

The table data plug-in (.`hdbtabledata`) can be used to load data from other files (e.g., *.csv* files) to database tables managed by HDI. The data in the *.csv* file is uploaded to the target database table (specified in table data artifacts) during the deployment process. Because the table data plug-in has ownership of the data, runtime modification of the data in the target table is overwritten during the subsequent deployment of the table data artifact.

The table data plug-in information is available in the *.hdiconfig* file of the HDI container, as shown in Listing 5.22.

```
"hdbtabledata" : {
"plugin_name" : "com.sap.hana.di.tabledata
},
"csv" : {
    "plugin_name" : "com.sap.hana.di.tabledata.source"
}
```

Listing 5.22 Plug-In Details for .hdbtabledata and .csv Artifacts

The table data design-time definition follows JavaScript Object Notation (JSON) syntax, as shown in Listing 5.23.

File Name: /src/data/Table.hdbtabledata

```
{
  "format_version": 1,
  "imports":
  [
    {
    "column_mappings": {
      "tableCol1": 1,
      "tableCol2": "csvCol4",
      "tableCol3": {"type": "constant", "value": Constant"},
      "tableCol4": {
        "type": "function",
        "name": "range",
```

```
    "parameters": {
    "increment_by": "1",
    "start_with": "1"
    }
  },
  "tableCol5": {
    "type": "function",
    "name": "decodeBase64String",
    "parameters": {
    "column_name": "csvCol2"
    }
    }
  },
"import_settings": {
    "import_columns": [
    "tableCol1",
    "tableCol2",
    "tableCol3"
    ],
"include_filter": [
    { "tableCol1" : "de", // ( "de" and "X" )
    "tableCol4": "X"}
    ],
"exclude_filter": [
    { "tableCol1" : "de", // ( "de" and "10" )
    "tableCol3": "10"}
    ]
},

"source_data": {
    "data_type": "CSV",
    "file_name": "com.sap.hana.example.data::data.csv",
    "has_header": true,
    "no_data_import": false,
    "delete_existing_foreign_data": false,
    "dialect": "HANA", // optional
    "type_config": {
        "delimiter": ","
    }
},
"target_table" : "com.sap.hana.example::TABLE"
```

```
  }
  ]
}
```

Listing 5.23 .hdbtabledata Syntax

As shown in Listing 5.23, the `imports` property defines the key components of the table data definition and has the following attributes:

- `target_table`
  Mandatory. Specifies the name of the target database table to load data. The target database table must physically exist in the same HDI container. It can't refer to a synonym or to a database table in another schema.
- `source_data`
  Describes the structure of the data file (*.csv*) to be used for the data load. It has the following attributes:
  - `Data_Type`: Mandatory. Describes the type of the data file to be used in the data import. Only *.csv* and *.properties* files are supported.
  - `file_name`: Mandatory. Specifies the name of the data file.
  - `has_header`: Optional. Boolean flag indicating if the data file has a header record.
  - `no_data_import`: Optional. Default value is `false`. Boolean flag indicating that the data file won't be imported and the undeploy call won't delete entries from the target table.
  - `delete_existing_foreign_data`: Optional. Boolean flag indicating if the existing data in the target table has to be deleted during deployment.
  - `type_config`: Optional. Data parser configuration to match the data file format. Some of the common attributes are as follows:
    - `delimeter`: Record delimiter character. The default value is comma (,).
    - `do_escape`: Flag to enable escaping. Default is `false`.
    - `escape_character`: Escape character. Default value is backslash (\).
    - `do_quote`: Flag to enable quoting. Default is `true`.
    - `quote_character`: Quoting character for records. Default value is quote (").
  - `dialect`: Optional. Default value is `HANA`.
- `import_settings`
  Mandatory. Specifies the target table columns and filters for the data that is inserted into the target table.

- import_columns: Mandatory. Defines the list of relevant columns of the target table for data import.
- include_filter: Optional. Defines the filter to restrict the data set from the source file.
- exclude_filter: Optional. Defines the filter to restrict the data set from the source file. If both include_filter and exclude_filter are specified, exclude_filter is applied first.

- column_mappings

  Describes the mapping of each of the relevant target table columns (as specified in the import_columns) to the data specified in the source_data section.

  The column_mappings attribute is mandatory except in one case where the data file has a header record and the column names and column orders are identical to that of the target table. The following types of column mappings are supported:

  - Position mapping: "tableCol1": 1. TableCol1 of the target table is mapped to the first column of the source CSV file.
  - Column mapping: "tableCol2": "CODE". TableCol2 is mapped to the column *CODE* of the source CSV file.
  - Constant mapping: "tableCol3": {"type": "constant", "value": "XYZ"}. TableCol3 is mapped to a fixed value XYZ.
  - Range mapping: "tableCol4": {"type": "function", "name": "range", "parameters": {"increment_by": "1", "start_with": "1"}}. TableCol4 is mapped to a constant sequence starting with 1 and increasing by 1 for each row.
  - Function mapping: "tableCol5": {"type": "function", "name": "decodeBase64String", "parameters": {"column_name": "CODE"}}. TableCol5 is mapped to the output of the decodeBase64String function based on the value of column CODE of the source CSV file.

Two simple examples (*Airport.hdbtabledata* and *Airport.csv*) are shown in Listing 5.24 and Listing 5.25, respectively.

```
Example: /src/data/Airport.hdbtabledata
{
    "format_version": 1,
    "imports": [{
    "target_table": "Airport",
    "source_data": {
    "data_type": "CSV",
        "file_name": "Airport.csv",
```

```
        "has_header": false,
        "dialect": "HANA",
        "type_config": {
        "delimiter": ","
        }
    },
    "import_settings": {
    "import_columns": [
        "CODE",
        "NAME",
        "CITY",
        "COUNTRY",
        "TIMEZONE",
        "LATITUDE",
        "LONGITUDE"]
    },
    "column_mappings": {
        "CODE": 2,
        "NAME": 3,
        "CITY": 4,
        "COUNTRY": 5,
        "TIMEZONE": 6,
        "LATITUDE": 7,
        "LONGITUDE": 8
        }
    }]
    }
```

Listing 5.24 Sample Airport.hdbtabledata

Example: /src/data/Airport.csv

```
1,YYZ,Lester B. Pearson International, Toronto,CANADA,EST,43.677718,-
79.624820,0101000000C078060DFDE753C08CF4A276BFD64540
2,YTZ,Billy Bishop City Airport, Toronto,CANADA,EST,43.628482,-
79.395958,0101000000C078060DFDE753C08CF4A276BFD64540
3,JFK,John F. Kennedy International, New York City,USA,EST,40.641311,-
73.778139,0101000000C078060DFDE753C08CF4A276BFD64540
4,LGA,LaGuardia Airport, New York City,USA,EST,40.776927,-
73.873966,0101000000C078060DFDE753C08CF4A276BFD64540
```

Listing 5.25 Sample Airport.csv

5.7.2 Building the .hdbtabledata File

To upload the data in the CSV file to the runtime database object, select the `.hdbtabledata` and `.csv` artifacts, and choose **Build Selected Files** from the context menu (or select **Build Selected Files** from the SAP Web IDE for SAP HANA menu).

Upon a successful build, the imported data will be available in the runtime database objects. This can be verified using SQL statements in the SAP HANA database explorer tool, as illustrated in Figure 5.33.

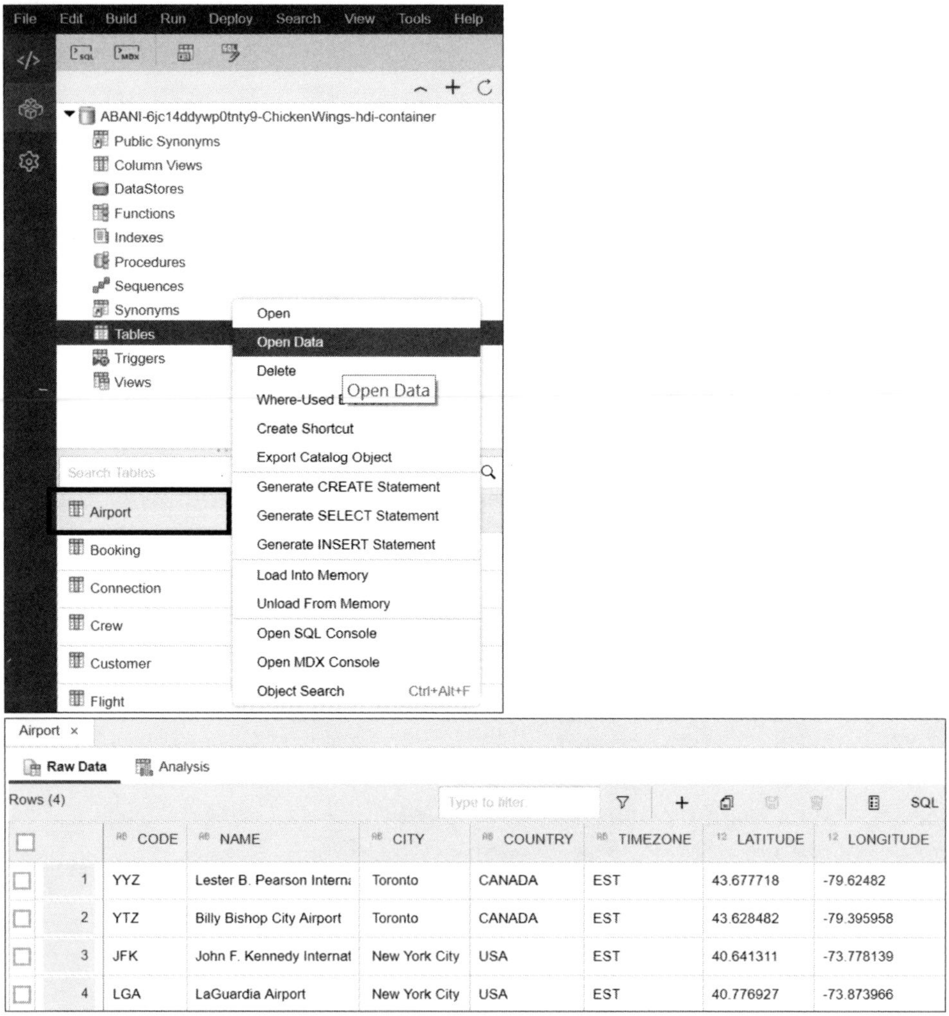

Figure 5.33 Data Loading Using .hdbtabledata

5.7.3 Using Table Data Properties (.properties)

The table data properties plug-in is used to import data from the *.properties* file into database tables managed by HDI. Translated texts or labels used in calculation views are stored in a special database-internal `"_SYS_BI"."BIMC_DESCRIPTIONS"` table. The `target_table` value `"#BIMC_DESCRIPTIONS"` must be used to deploy translated texts for calculation views.

The table data properties plug-in information is available in the *.hdiconfig* file of the HDI container as listed in Listing 5.26. The table data properties plug-in can also be used to load *.tags* files.

```
"properties" : {
    "plugin_name" : "com.sap.hana.di.tabledata.properties"
},
"tags" : {
    "plugin_name" : "com.sap.hana.di.tabledata.properties"
},
```

Listing 5.26 Plug-In Details for .properties and .tags Artifacts

The syntax of table data properties design-time definition is shown in Listing 5.27.

```
File Name: /src/data/VIEWNAME_en_US.properties
#!tabledata
#{
# "target_table" : "#BIMC_DESCRIPTIONS",
# "column_mappings" : {
#     "OBJECT" : { "type" : "constant",
#             "value" : "name.space::VIEWNAME" },
#     "LANGUAGE" : { "type" : "function",
#             "name" : "extractLanguageCodeFromFileName",
#             "parameters": { "file_name": "OBJECT"} },
#     "KEY" : 1,
#     "VALUE" : 2
# }
#}
# Note: The table data header ends on the first empty line or
# earlier on the second occurrence of the !tabledata marker
# Note: Format of .properties entries:
##
# <metadata for translation process>
```

```
# <key>=<value>
#
# XCOL, 120
KEY_1=First Key
# XCOL, 120
KEY_2=Second Key
# XCOL, 120
PARAMETER_1=Parameter One
# XCOL, 120
CUSTOMERS_HIERARCHY=CUSTOMERS Hierarchy
```

Listing 5.27 .properties File Syntax

As shown here, the target table, additional constant values, and column mappings are provided using the `!tabledata` header. The `extractLanguageCodeFromFileName` function is used to extract the language code (`en_US`) information from the *.properties* file name.

5.7.4 Generate Time Data

The date/time data is required in almost all applications to record time details of business transactions. It's also used to navigate/analyze business transactions through dates or attributes of dates such as months, quarters, years, fiscal periods, fiscal years, holidays, and so on.

Starting with SAP HANA 2.0 SP 03, SAP Web IDE for SAP HANA generates time data as a local table in the HDI container. It significantly simplifies maintenance of time data in an application versus using central external time dimension tables such as `_SYS_BI.M_TIME_DIMENSION`, which impacts all applications deployed in the SAP HANA database. Time data can be generated for both Gregorian and fiscal calendars to meet business requirements.

To generate time data, select **Modeling Actions • Maintain Time Tables** in the context menu of the HDB module (e.g., `db`) in the project as illustrated in Figure 5.34. Select the **Gregorian** or **Fiscal** calendar option, then select the appropriate time period, that is, **Month**, **Week**, **Year**, and finally choose the **Time** checkbox (with **Day**, **Hour**, **Minute**, or **Second** granularity). Check the **Generate Data After Creation** checkbox, and provide the **From year**, **To Year**, and **First Day of Week** details. Select the **Generate** button to continue creating the time dimension table as a CDS artifact (e.g., `M_TIME_DIMENSION.hdbcds` for our Gregorian time).

Because the **Generate Data After Creation** option is selected, the build process will kick in to generate the time dimension table (e.g., `M_TIME_DIMENSION`) and generate the data for the selected time period. The generated table and data can be verified using the SAP HANA database explorer, as shown in Figure 5.34.

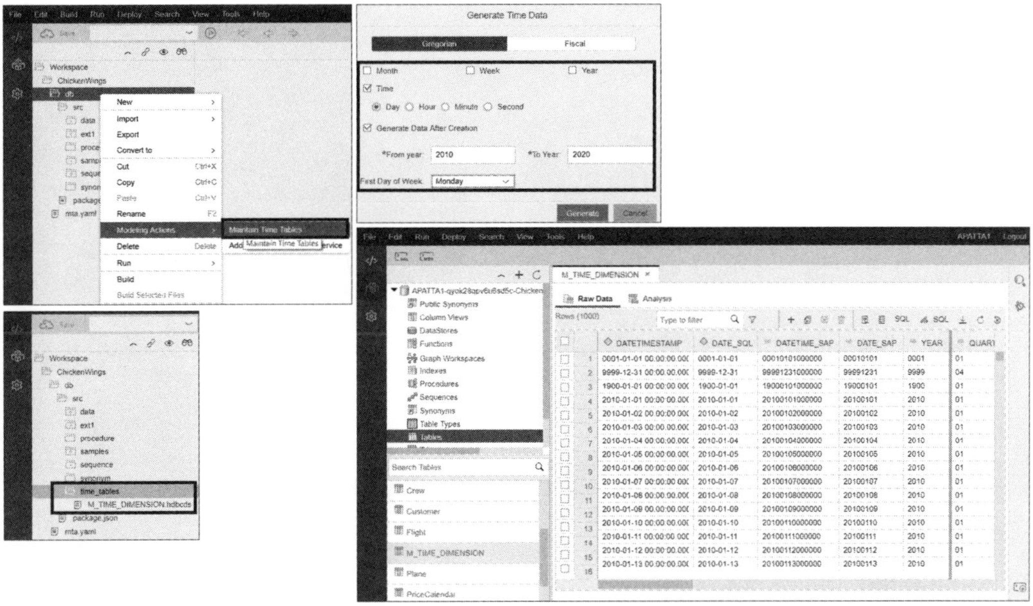

Figure 5.34 Generating Time Data

5.8 Synonyms and Cross-Schema Access

With HDI, all objects are local to the HDI container. However, you can access objects in another HDI container schema or objects in a database schema (e.g., `_SYS_BI`, `SAPERP`, etc.) using synonyms. Synonyms are created using the `.hdbsynonym` artifact.

First, we need to create a synonym for the `SYS.DUMMY` table, which is used in SQLScript. To define a synonym, create a new file artifact with the *.hdbsynonym* extension (e.g., *sys.hdbsynonym*) in the *src/synonym* folder The *.hdbsynonym* file can be opened using the graphical synonym editor to define synonyms, or the code shown in Listing 5.28 can be used in the file editor. For a multitenant database, the tenant database (e.g., `"database": "HXE"`) should be used to define the synonym.

Upon deployment, the **DUMMY** synonym will be available under the **Synonyms** folder of the container schema, as shown in Figure 5.35.

Filename: src/synonym/sys.hdbsynonym

```
{
  "DUMMY": {
    "target": {
      "object": "DUMMY",
      "schema": "SYS",
    }
  }
}
```

Listing 5.28 sys.hdbsynonym for DUMMY

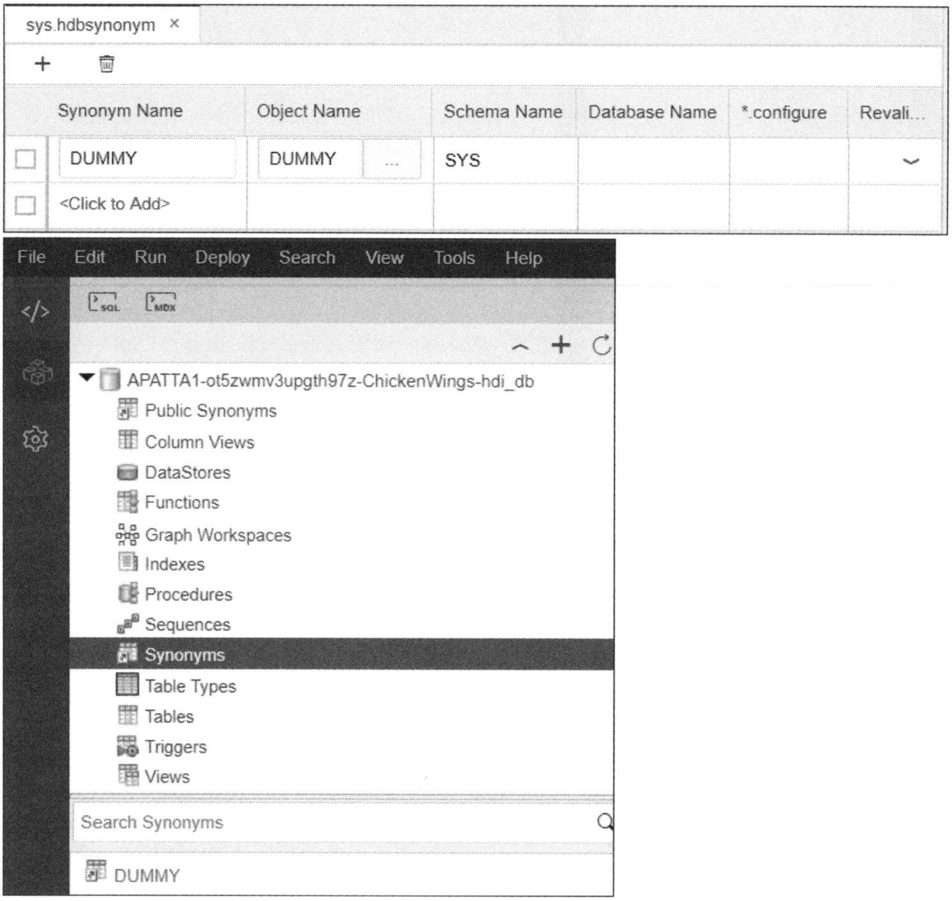

Figure 5.35 Synonym Editor

To enable access to external schema (e.g., SAPERP, SAPBW, _SYS_BI, etc.) objects from an HDI container, data access must be provisioned for the HDI object owner (<container>#OO) user and HDI container application (<container>_<GUID>_RT) user. To demonstrate this, we'll enable access to the calendar or time dimension tables available in the _SYS_BI schema.

Follow these steps to enable cross-schema access for an HDI container.

1. Define a user with appropriate access (at least SELECT WITH GRANT OPTION) on the external schema (e.g., _SYS_BI or SAPERP, etc.). It's recommended to have absolute minimal access for this user.
2. Create a user-provided service CROSS_SCHEMA_SYS_BI using XSA CLI. (The XSA CLI tool was discussed in Chapter 3.) Use the following commands to log in:

   ```
   xs api https:<host_name>:3<instance>30 --skip-ssl-validation
   xs login -u <user_name> -p <password> -s <dev_space>
   ```

   Use the cups command to create a user-provisioned service (CROSS_SCHEMA_SYS_BI) for accessing the _SYS_BI schema:

   ```
   xs cups CROSS_SCHEMA_SYS_BI -p "{\"host\":\"<host_name>\",\"port\":\
   "3<instance>15\",\"user\":\"<user_name>\",\"password\":\"<password>\",\"driver\
   ":\"com.sap.db.jdbc.Driver\",\"tags\":[\"hana\"] , \"schema\" : \"_SYS_BI\" }"
   ```

Note

The port can be 3xx15 or 3xx13, where xx is the instance number. You can find the right port by running xs apps or netstat in the OS console.

3. Add the user-provided service as a resource to the MTA project in SAP Web IDE for SAP HANA.
4. Open the *mta.yaml* file using the MTA editor, and define a new resource, for example, **CrossSchemaSysBi** with **Type org.cloudfoundry.existing-service** and parameters **Key**: **service-name** and **Value**: **CROSS_SCHEMA_SYS_BI** (name of the user-provided service created earlier), as shown in Figure 5.36.
5. Add the newly defined resource as a dependency for the HDB module (Figure 5.36). To avoid hard-coding the user-provided service in object definitions, an alias **hdb-sys-bi-service** is defined with **key**: **hdb-sys-bi-service** and **service**: **~{sys-bi-service-name}**.
6. The structure of the *mta.yml* is updated in the previous step and should look like the code in Listing 5.29. Note that the TARGET_CONTAINER properties for the HDI container is added to the *mta.yaml* file. If it's missing for some reason, enter it.

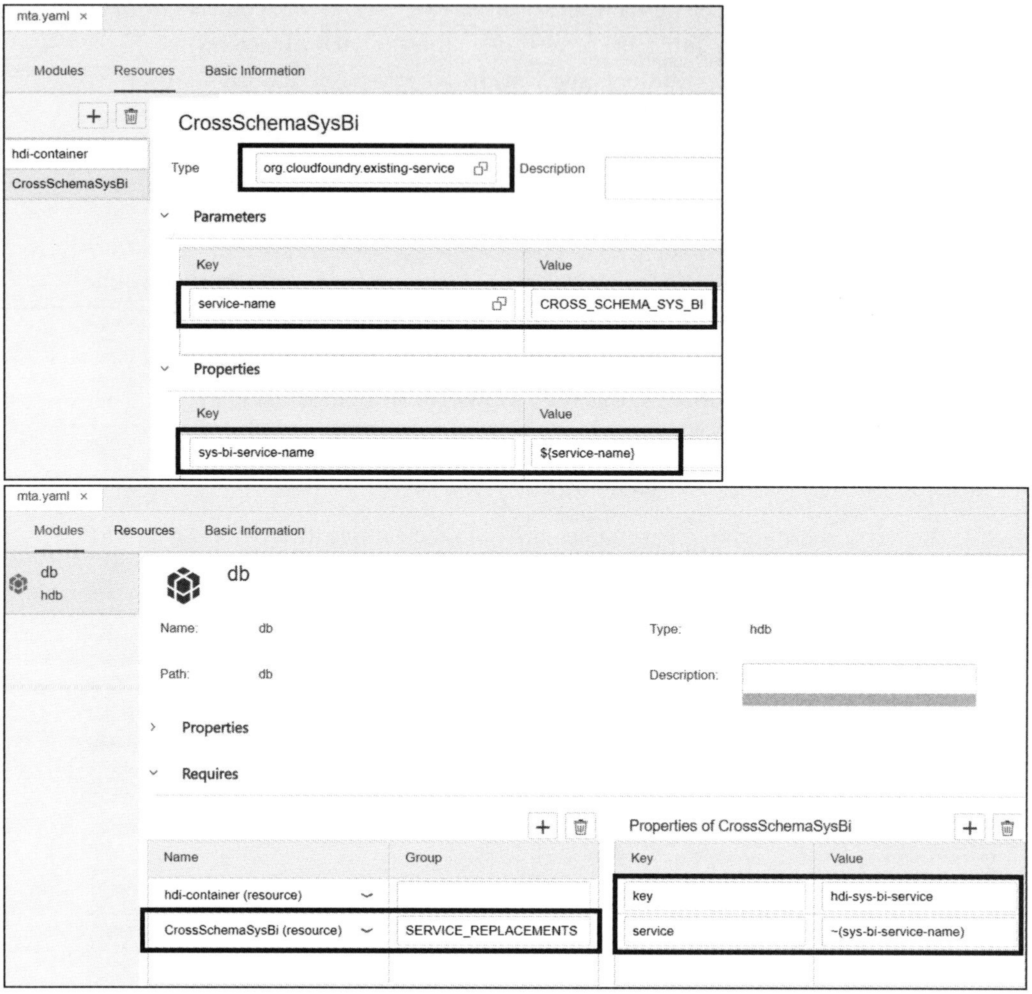

Figure 5.36 Configuring mta.yaml

Filename: mta.yaml

```
ID: ChickenWings
_schema-version: '2.0'
version: 0.0.1
modules:
 - name: db
   type: hdb
   path: db
```

```
    requires:
     - name: hdi-container
       properties:
         TARGET_CONTAINER: ~{hdi-container-name}

     - name: CrossSchemaSysBi
       group: SERVICE_REPLACEMENTS
       properties:
         key: hdi-sys-bi-service
         service: ~{sys-bi-service-name}

resources:
 - name: hdi-container
   parameters:
     config:
         schema: ChickenWings
   properties:
      hdi-container-name: ${service-name}
   type: com.sap.xs.hdi-container

 - name: CrossSchemaSysBi
   type: org.cloudfoundry.existing-service
   parameters:
     service-name: CROSS_SCHEMA_SYS_BI
   properties:
     sys-bi-service-name: ${service-name}
```

Listing 5.29 Structure of mta.yaml

7. Grant access on the CROSS_SCHEMA_SYS_BI service (using its alias hdb-sys-bi-service) to object owner and application user by creating a sysbi.hdbgrants artifact, as shown in Listing 5.30.

   In our example, both the object owner and application user have similar access, that is, only read-only (SELECT) access. It's also possible to give write access (INSERT/UPDATE/DELETE) to the object owner.

```
Filename: /cfg/sys_bi.hdbgrants
{
  "hdi-sys-bi-service": {
    "object_owner": {
      "schema_privileges":[
```

```
          { "reference":"_SYS_BI",
            "privileges_with_grant_option":["SELECT"]
            }
        ]
      },
      "application_user": {
        "schema_privileges":[
          { "reference":"_SYS_BI",
            "privileges":["SELECT"]
            }
        ]
      }
    }
  }
```

Listing 5.30 hdbgrants for the External Schema

8. Create one or more synonyms (e.g., **M_TIME_DIMENSION** for **_SYS_BI.M_TIME_DIMENSION**) for the objects in the external schema using the graphical synonym editor with the **CROSS_SCHEMA_SYS_BI** service, as shown in Figure 5.37.

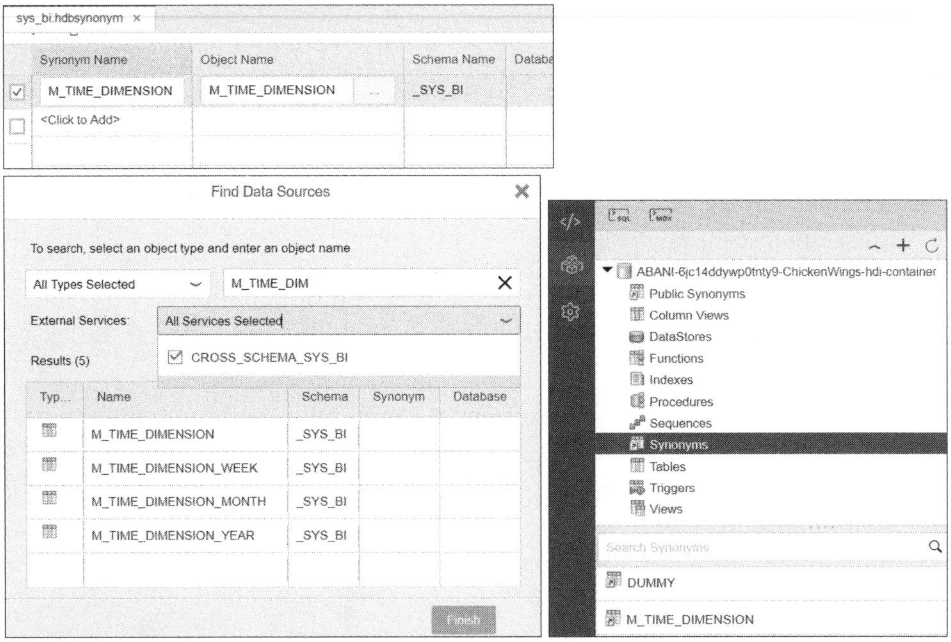

Figure 5.37 Synonym for Cross Schema Objects

9. Build the HDB module (i.e., *db* folder). Upon a successful build, the **M_TIME_DIMENSION** synonym is available in the container schema.

5.9 Virtual Data Model

Virtual data models are created in SAP HANA to explore and analyze data in the context of a business scenario. This involves refining, slicing, summarizing, and combining one or more data sets on the fly to model business requirements. SAP HANA virtual data models (also called information models) are built using calculation views, table functions and analytic privileges,, and so on.

Virtual data models consist of three types of calculation views based on their usage, as illustrated in Figure 5.38:

- **Dimension view**
  These views are used to model dimensions in the business case. A dimension represents a logical entity in business analysis, for example, customer, crew, airport, and so on. Attributes are properties (e.g., name, email, country, etc.) used to describe a dimension. The collection of dimensions represents the master data in the system. Dimension calculation views are used to create dimension views.
- **Analysis or multidimensional (cube) view**
  These views are used to model tangible transactions or interactions between two or more dimensions, which are represented by *measures or key figures* in the *fact table*. A multidimensional (cube) view has one fact table joined to two or more dimension views, with the fact table at the center forming the *star schema*. A *cube type* calculation view with a *star join* is used to model multidimensional views.
- **Reporting or business view**
  This view combines one or more multidimensional views, dimension views, and other reporting views to implement additional business logic using a combination of projection, aggregation, join, union, and rank operations. Note that there may be multiple layers of business views stacked on top of one another to implement complex business logic. A cube type calculation view (without a star join) is used to model these views.

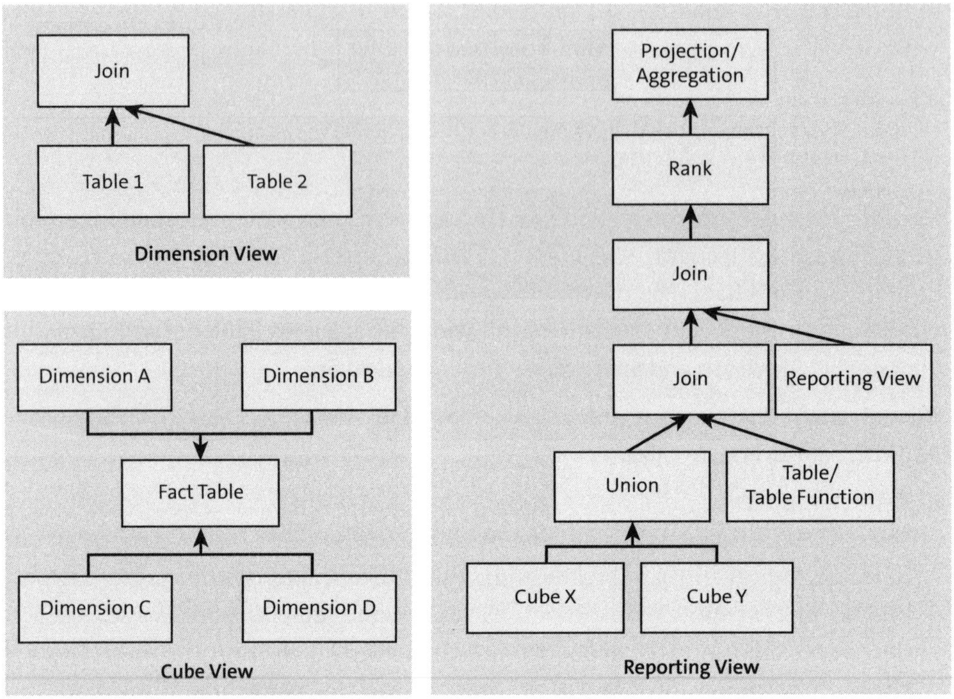

Figure 5.38 Virtual Data Model

Advantages of SAP HANA information models are as follows:

- SAP HANA information views are optimized to take full advantage of the underlying SAP HANA engines (Online Analytical Processing [OLAP] Engine, Join Engine, and Calculation Engine).
- SAP HANA information models are optimized for join and column pruning for faster query execution (unnecessary columns and table joins are eliminated from the query execution plan).
- SAP HANA information models automatically generate additional metadata, which is leveraged by BI frontend tools such as SAP Lumira, SAP Analysis for Microsoft Office, and so on.

In the following sections, we'll discuss the approach and steps to create virtual data models using default, dimension, and cube calculation views, as well as secure data in the virtual data model using analytic privileges.

5.9.1 Create Calculation Views

Follow these steps to create a dimension calculation view:

1. In the context menu of the **models** folder, select **New • Calculation View** to add a new calculation view to the HDB module (see Figure 5.39).

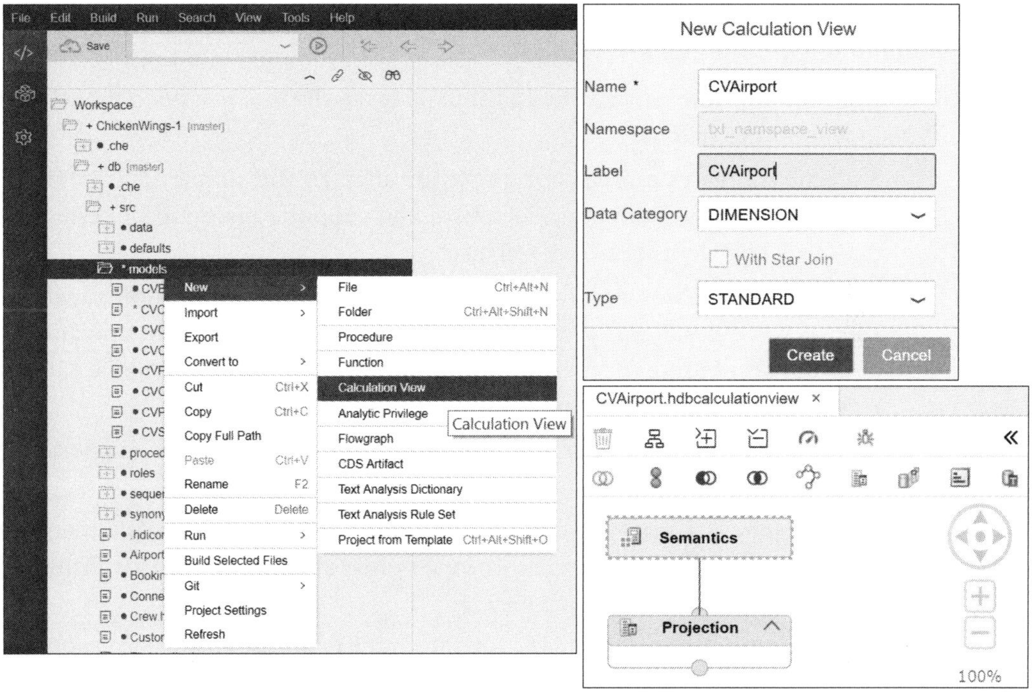

Figure 5.39 Creating a Calculation View

2. Provide a **Name** and **Label** for the calculation view. Select an appropriate value for **Data Category** and **Type**:
   - **Data Category**: As discussed earlier there are three types of calculation views. **DIMENSION** and **CUBE** options are selected to model respective types of calculation views, whereas **DEFAULT** is selected to model any other calculation views (reporting or business view, etc.).
   - **Type**: This option is available only for dimension calculation views. **Time** type dimension views are a special kind of view to model time/date dimensions. Generation of time data was discussed in Section 5.7.4.
   - **With Star Join**: This checkbox is available for cube type calculation views to model a star schema.

3. Click the **Create** button to display the canvas to build the calculation view.
4. The new calculation view editor will be launched with the **Semantics** node and default **Aggregation** or **Projection** node, depending on the data category (**Aggregation** for cubes and **Projection** for others) of the calculation view. The default node type can also be changed by selecting the appropriate option (**Switch to**) in the context menu of the node. Drag one or more nodes from the tool palette to continue building the calculation view.
5. The calculation view canvas offers a list of nodes in the tool palette to model data set operations as follows:
   - **Projection**: Creates a projection list (equivalent to the simple SELECT <field_list>) from the underlying data source and supports restricting/filtering the data set (equivalent to the WHERE clause).
   - **Aggregation**: Creates aggregation (equivalent to SQL aggregation functions such as SUM, AVG, MIN, and MAX with GROUP BT clause). Distinct count operation is also supported using counters. It also supports restricting/filtering the data set (equivalent to the WHERE clause).
   - **Join** and **Star-Join**: Enables matching of two data sets. SAP HANA supports the following types of joins in the graphical modeler.
     - **Inner join**: Returns only the matching rows from both data sets if there is a match in the joining columns. An inner join is always executed for all queries executed on the calculation view.
     - **Left outer join**: Returns all the rows from the left data set and corresponding matching records from the right data set. Rows without any match on the right side will have null values. Left outer joins are efficient during query execution because left outer joins are performed only if columns from the right-side data set are explicitly requested by the query. Therefore, when no column is requested from the right-side data set, the join isn't executed during query execution.
     - **Right outer join**: Returns all the rows from the right-side data set and corresponding matching records from the left side. Rows without any match on the left side will have null values. The runtime behavior of right outer joins is similar to that of left outer joins; that is, the join won't be performed if no field is selected from the left side. However, functionally, some columns from the left side are always selected. Hence, the right outer joins are always performed during query execution. Therefore, if the scenario can be modeled

using both a left outer join and a right outer join, it's recommended to use the left outer join.

- **Referential join**: Behave like inner joins, so if the columns are selected from both sides of the joins during query execution and behave like outer joins, columns are selected only from one side of the join.
- **Text join**: Used for multilingual reporting and can read language-dependent text/labels based on the logged-on user's language settings (**E**, **D**, or **F**, with the internal input parameter `$$language$$`). Technically, text joins behave like inner joins with a restricted language column.

Cardinality of the joins should be set for efficient join execution and must reflect the actual data relationship to avoid incorrect results and/or low performance. Cardinality settings can be left blank if the underlying data relationship is unknown. In this case, the SAP HANA optimizer will automatically determine cardinality during query execution. Possible options for cardinality settings are 1:1 (one-to-one), N:1 (many-to-one), 1:N (one-to-many), and m:n (many-to-many).

- **Non Equi Join**: Used to create join conditions with various comparisons or unequal operators (<, >=, !=, etc.) on several columns.
- **Minus**: Equivalent of the SQL `MINUS` operator and returns all rows from the first data set that don't exist in the second data set when the structures of the two data sets are the same (same number of columns and compatible data types of columns). Technically, the `MINUS` operator selects all rows from the first data set and then discards all records that appear in the second data set.
- **Intersect**: Equivalent of SQL `INTERSECT` operator and returns all rows from the first data set that exist in the second data set when the structures of the two data sets are the same (same number of columns and compatible data types of columns).
- **Union**: Equivalent of SQL `UNION ALL` operator and combines the first and second data set when the structures of the two data sets are the same (same number of columns and compatible data types of columns).
- **Rank**: Returns the top/bottom *N* records from a data set by partitioning the records based on the partition columns and ordering based on the order columns. The **Dynamic Partition Elements** checkbox enables dynamic selection of columns from the partition columns based on columns requested by the query during execution.

   - **Graph Node**: Helps model different kinds of networks and linked data to depict relationships visually. It also executes one of the available actions on a graph workspace and provides the output as a table.
   - **Table Function**: Enables SAP HANA table functions (`.hdbtablefunction`) as data sources. Table functions are read-only user-defined functions that can access one or more parameters and return exactly one results table. We'll discuss SAP HANA table functions in Section 5.10.2.
   - **Hierarchy Function**: Used for SAP HANA hierarchy functions in the calculation.
   - **Anonymization**: Used to anonymize calculation view output.
6. Select **Add Data Source** or the button in the context menu of the node to add data sources to the calculation view. Then proceed to the **Mapping** on the details pane to select output columns.
7. Select the **Draw Connection** button (on the context of the node) to drag and connect to another node or the default **Aggregation/Projection** node to complete the view and select output columns.
8. Select the **Semantics** node, and define attributes/measures and their properties in the **Columns** tab. Use the **Hierarchy** and **Parameter** tabs to define hierarchies and parameters, respectively. In addition, properties of the calculation view can be edited in the **View Properties** tab.

   The following list of properties is set to manage the runtime behavior of the calculation view, as shown in Figure 5.40:
   - **Run with**: Identifies the appropriate authorization for executing the calculation view. Options are **Definer's Rights** (authorizations of the user who created the calculation view) and **Invoker's Rights** (authorizations of the current user executing the query).
   - **Default Client**: Enables data restriction/filtration based on a **Fixed Client** or the **Session Client**. The **Cross Client** option doesn't filter any data.
   - **Apply Privileges**: Enables data access restrictions using SQL analytic privileges. We'll discuss data access control using SQL analytic privileges in Section 5.9.6.
   - **Default Member**: Identifies the default member for all hierarchies defined in the calculation view.
   - **Count Star Column**: By default, the internal `row.count` column is used to serve the result of `SELECT COUNT(*)` queries. The property enables selection of another column as the count star column.

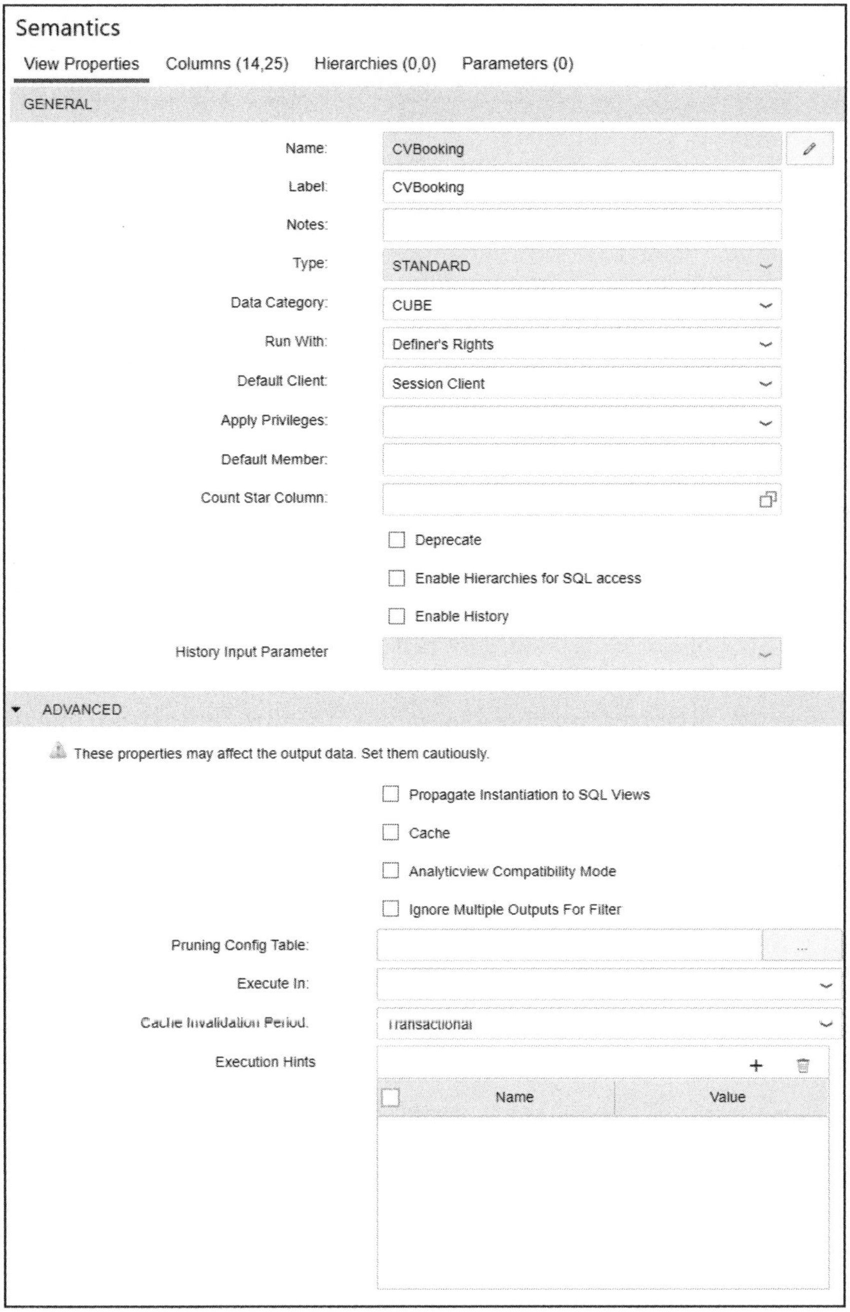

Figure 5.40 Calculation View Properties

- **Deprecate**: Deprecates a calculation view to discourage others from using it in other modeler objects.
- **Enable Hierarchies for SQL access**: Only relevant for cube calculation views with star joins and enables SQL access to shared hierarchies (from dimension views).
- **Enable History** and **History Input Parameter**: Enables time travel queries for calculation views using history tables for the **History Input Parameter**.

The following additional advanced properties can be set to influence the execution and performance of the calculation view:

- **Propagate Instantiation to SQL Views**: Relevant for consumption of the calculation view in another SQL view or CDS view. Refer to SAP Note 1764658 for further details.
- **Cache**: Enables and disables the SAP HANA cache for the calculation view. The SAP HANA cache can be configured to improve query performance in specific scenarios.
- **Cache Invalidation Period**: Determines the time interval (**Daily** or **Hourly**) to invalidate or remove the cached content.
- **Analyticview Compatibility Mode**: By default, all joins with N:M cardinality (irrespective of join types) are performed during query execution. However, this property can be used to ignore joins with N:M cardinality when no columns are selected from the right side of the join.
- **Ignore Multiple Outputs for Filter**: Used in situations when one node is consumed by two nodes. If separate filters were used in the two consumer nodes, those two filters will be combined using a logical AND and then applied on the shared node.
- **Pruning Config Table**: Relevant for calculation views using the **Union** node.
- **Execute in**: Determines if the calculation view will be executed in the context of the SQL Engine or the Column Engine. Refer to SAP Note 1857202 for further details.
- **Execution Hints**: Specify SAP HANA execution hints to instruct optimizer to use a specific access path to execute the query on the calculation view.

9. After the calculation view development is completed, build the calculation view. Upon a successful build, the view will be available in the column view folder of the container schema.
10. The data in the calculation view can be previewed and analyzed using the **Data Preview** context menu, as shown in Figure 5.41.

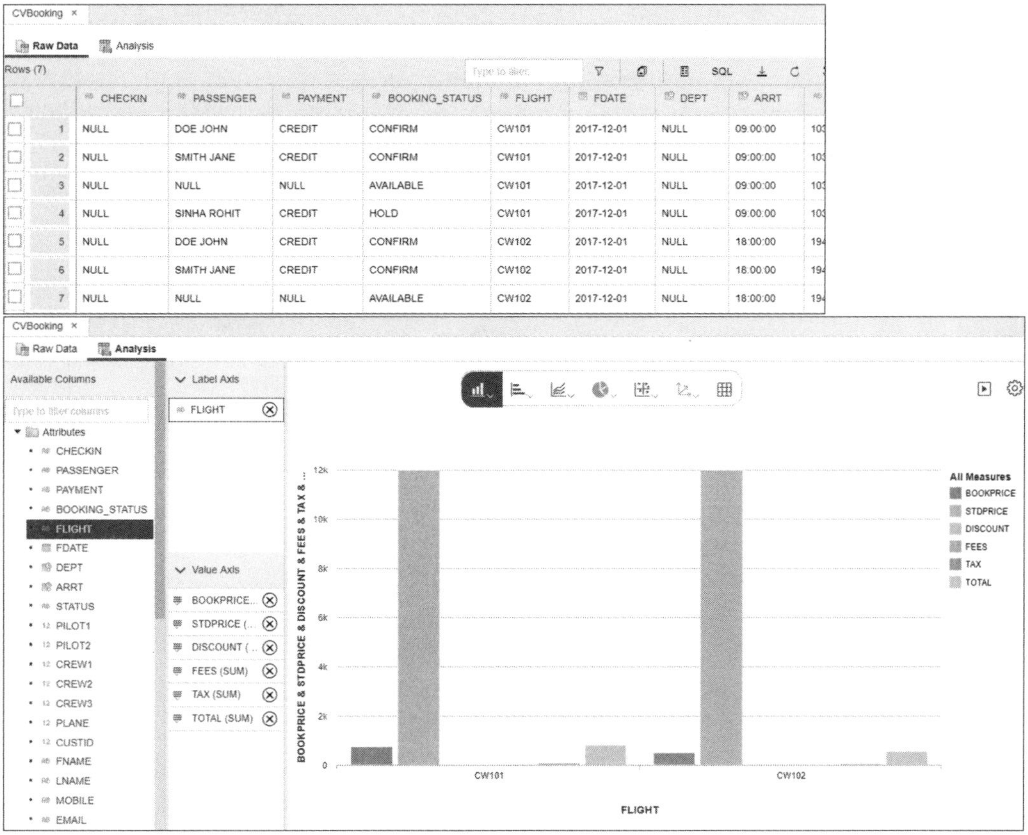

Figure 5.41 Calculation View Data Preview

5.9.2 Dimension Calculation Views

Dimension views are created to model the logical entities involved in the business scenario. One dimension view needs to be created for each dimension.

In this section, we'll discuss the steps to create dimension calculation views. As an example, let's start with a simple dimension calculation view with one data source.

CVAirport Calculation View

The **CVAirport** dimension calculation view is illustrated in Figure 5.42.

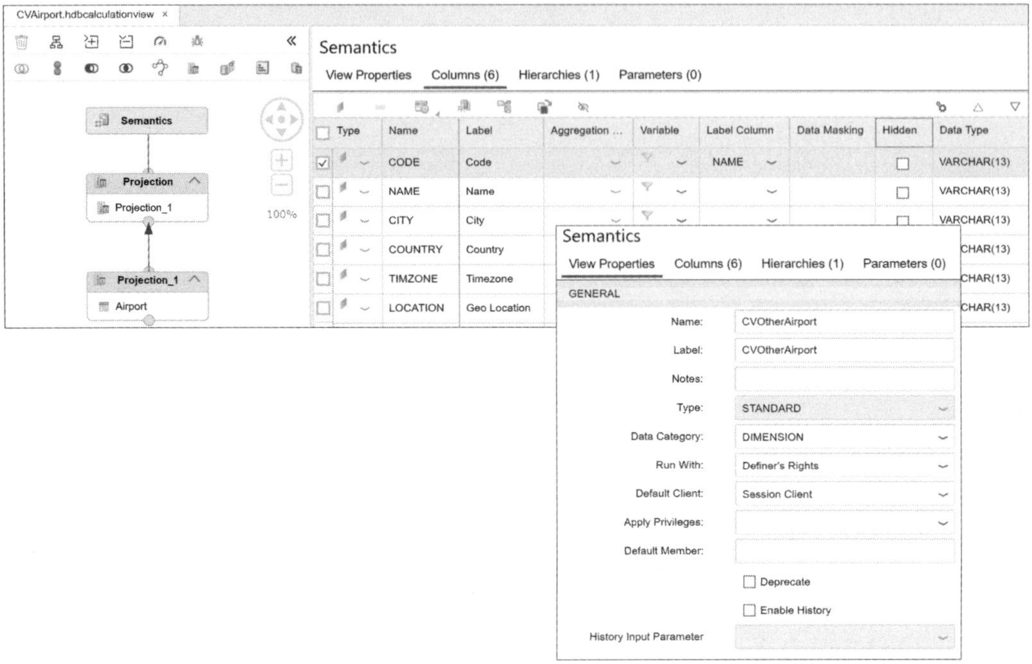

Figure 5.42 Airport Dimension View

Dimension calculation views have **Projection** as the default final node. The **Airport** dimension view has the `Airport` table as the only data source with **CODE**, **NAME**, **CITY**, **COUNTRY**, **TIMEZONE**, and **LOCATION** (geo spatial) columns selected using a projection node (**Projection_1**). Note that the nodes in calculation views can be renamed to provide unique names in the context of the calculation view. The projection node provides the option to define additional restrictions/filters and create additional calculated columns; however, for the **Airport** dimension view, no filter has been defined. Because there is no filter defined in **Projection_1**, we could have directly added the `Airport` table as the data source in the default **Projection** node, eliminating the need for adding the **Projection_1** node.

Functionally, an airport (`CODE`) belongs to one `CITY`, and one `CITY` belongs to one `COUNTRY`. This relation can be expressed using a *hierarchy*. We can build a hierarchy named **Geography**, as illustrated in Figure 5.43.

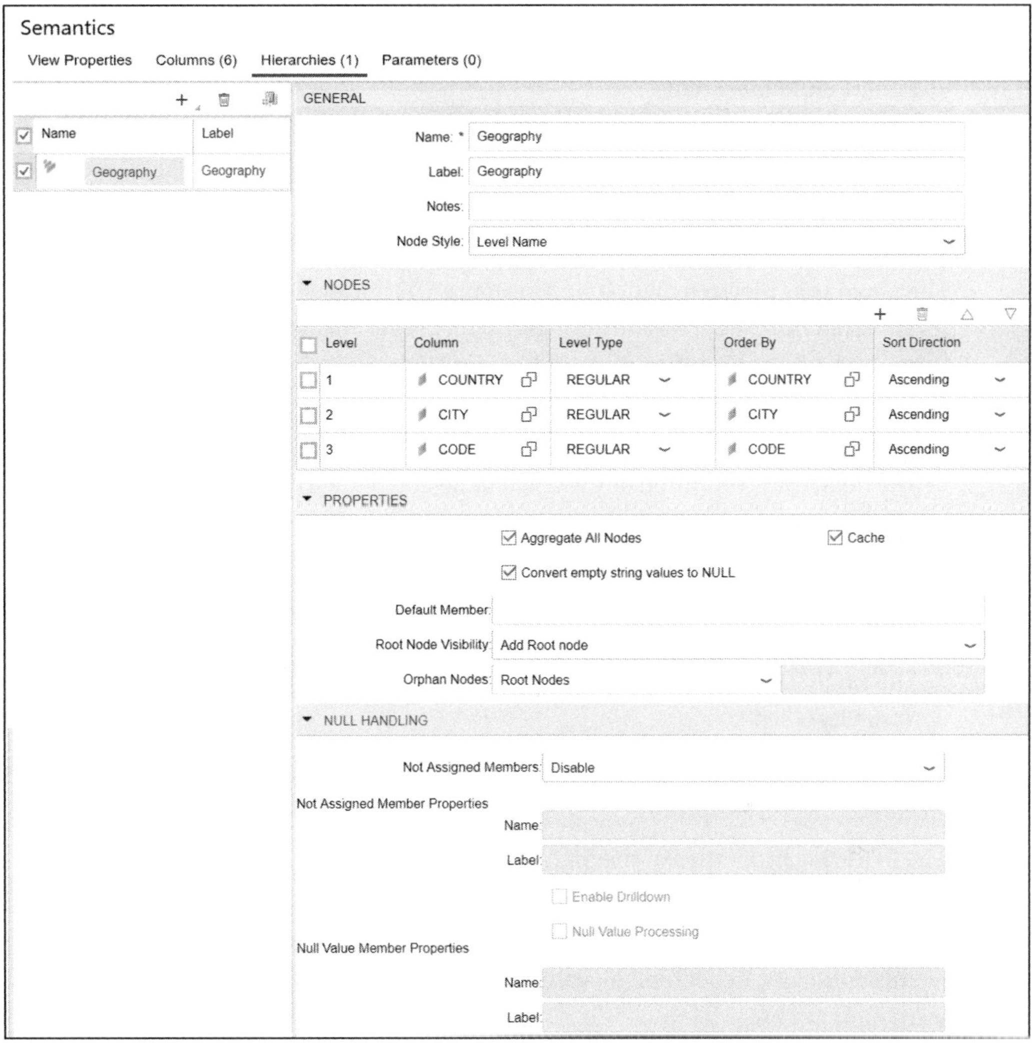

Figure 5.43 Hierarchy in the Airport Dimension View

SAP HANA supports two types of hierarchies in calculation views:

- **Level hierarchy**
  Level hierarchies consists of one or more fixed levels and are used for data aggregation. Hierarchy nodes at a level roll up to the next higher level in a many-to-one relationship, hierarchy nodes at the next level roll up into the next higher level, and so on, until they reach the highest level. Because a level hierarchy has a rigid

structure, the root node or child nodes can be accessed in a defined order only. The attributes for different levels are sourced from different columns.

- **Parent-child hierarchy**
  A parent-child hierarchy can be built if there is a parent-child relationship between two attributes of a dimension, and the hierarchy structure is based on a self-join on the parent column of the data set. The number of levels in the hierarchy isn't fixed and is driven by the values in the data set.

The **Geography** hierarchy illustrated in Figure 5.43 is a level hierarchy. To create a new level hierarchy, click the **+** button, and select **Level Hierarchy**. Provide a **Name** and **Label**, and select the appropriate option for **Node Style**. The node style determines the unique node ID, and it has three possible options:

- **Level Name**
  The node ID is composed of the level name and node name, for example, **[Level 3]. "JFK"**.
- **Name Only**
  The node ID is composed of the level name alone, for example, **"JFK"**.
- **Name Path**
  The node ID is composed of the full path of the node, for example, **"USA"."New York City"."JFK"**.

For our sample case, the data set in the **CITY** column is unique, so we can select any of the preceding three options.

The following properties of the hierarchy can also be set:

- **Aggregate All Nodes**
  This option should be checked if there is a value posted on the aggregation node. If this option isn't checked, the value will be calculated for the aggregate nodes.
- **Default Member**
  This option is used to set a default member for the multidimensional expressions (MDX) clients.
- **Root Node Visibility**
  Two options are available to select if the root node should be displayed: **Add Root Node** and **Do Not Add Root Node**.
- **Orphan Nodes**
  These options are used to set the behavior of orphan nodes (nodes with no parents or higher levels):

- **Root Nodes**: Show orphan nodes as root nodes.
- **Errors**: Stop processing and show an error.
- **Ignore**: Ignore orphan nodes.
- **Step Parents**: Show orphan nodes under the stepparent node. The stepparent node must exist in the hierarchy and must be at the root level.

The behavior of **Null Value Processing** and **Not Assigned Members** in the hierarchy can also be set using appropriate options in the **Not Assigned Members** dropdown list: **Enable**, **Disable**, and **Auto Assign**. Select **Enable** to customize the display.

The definition of the calculation view is stored in XML format, and the graphical editor generates the XML definition as the calculation view is built. Open the calculation view in the code editor to see the XML contents. The XML contents of `CVAirport` are shown in Listing 5.31. Changes to the calculation view can be made using the code editor or the graphical calculation view editor.

File: src/model/CVAirport.hdbcalculationview

```
<?xml version="1.0" encoding="UTF-8"?>
<Calculation:scenario xmlns:xsi="http://www.w3.org/2001/XMLSchema-
instance" xmlns:Calculation="http://www.sap.com/ndb/
BiModelCalculation.ecore" xmlns:Dimension="http://www.sap.com/ndb/
BiModelDimension.ecore" id="CVAirport" applyPrivilegeType="NONE" dataCategory=
"DIMENSION" dimensionType="STANDARD" schemaVersion="3.0" defaultClient=
"$$client$$" outputViewType="Projection" cacheInvalidationPeriod=
"NONE" enforceSqlExecution="false">
<descriptions defaultDescription="CVAirport"/>
<localVariables/>
<variableMappings/>
<dataSources>
  <DataSource id="Airport">
    <resourceUri>Airport</resourceUri>
  </DataSource>
</dataSources>
<calculationViews>
  <calculationView xsi:type="Calculation:ProjectionView" id="Projection_1">
    <viewAttributes>
      <viewAttribute id="CODE">
        <descriptions defaultDescription="CODE"/>
      </viewAttribute>
```

```
      <viewAttribute id="NAME">
        <descriptions defaultDescription="NAME"/>
      </viewAttribute>
      <viewAttribute id="CITY">
        <descriptions defaultDescription="CITY"/>
      </viewAttribute>
      <viewAttribute id="COUNTRY">
        <descriptions defaultDescription="COUNTRY"/>
      </viewAttribute>
      <viewAttribute id="TIMEZONE">
        <descriptions defaultDescription="TIMEZONE"/>
      </viewAttribute>
      <viewAttribute id="LOCATION">
        <descriptions defaultDescription="LOCATION"/>
      </viewAttribute>
    </viewAttributes>
    <calculatedViewAttributes/>
    <restrictedViewAttributes/>
    <input node="Airport">
      <mapping xsi:type="Calculation:AttributeMapping" target="CODE" source=
"CODE"/>
      <mapping xsi:type="Calculation:AttributeMapping" target="NAME" source=
"NAME"/>
      <mapping xsi:type="Calculation:AttributeMapping" target="CITY" source=
"CITY"/>
      <mapping xsi:type="Calculation:AttributeMapping" target=
"COUNTRY" source="COUNTRY"/>
      <mapping xsi:type="Calculation:AttributeMapping" target=
"TIMEZONE" source="TIMEZONE"/>
      <mapping xsi:type="Calculation:AttributeMapping" target=
"LOCATION" source="LOCATION"/>
    </input>
  </calculationView>
</calculationViews>
<inlineHierarchy xsi:type="Dimension:LeveledHierarchy" id=
"Geography" aggregateAllNodes="true" orphanedNodesHandling="ROOT_
NODES" rootNodeVisibility="ADD_ROOT_NODE" withRootNode="true" nodeStyle=
"LEVEL_NAME_ENFORCED" cacheEnabled="true" cycleHandling=
"BREAKUP" emptyValueIsNull="true">
```

```
  <descriptions defaultDescription="Geography"/>
  <unassignedMemberProperties mode="FALSE"/>
  <levels>
    <level levelAttribute="COUNTRY" levelType="MDLEVEL_TYPE_REGULAR" order=
"1" orderAttribute="COUNTRY" sortDirection="ASC"/>
    <level levelAttribute="CITY" levelType="MDLEVEL_TYPE_REGULAR" order=
"2" orderAttribute="CITY" sortDirection="ASC"/>
    <level levelAttribute="CODE" levelType="MDLEVEL_TYPE_REGULAR" order=
"3" orderAttribute="CODE" sortDirection="ASC"/>
  </levels>
</inlineHierarchy>
<logicalModel id="Projection_1">
  <attributes>
    <attribute id="CODE" order="1" displayAttribute=
"false" attributeHierarchyActive="false">
      <descriptions defaultDescription="Code"/>
      <keyMapping columnObjectName="Projection_1" columnName="CODE"/>
    </attribute>
    <attribute id="NAME" order="2" displayAttribute=
"false" attributeHierarchyActive="false">
      <descriptions defaultDescription="Name"/>
      <keyMapping columnObjectName="Projection_1" columnName="NAME"/>
    </attribute>
    <attribute id="CITY" order="3" displayAttribute=
"false" attributeHierarchyActive="false">
      <descriptions defaultDescription="City"/>
      <keyMapping columnObjectName="Projection_1" columnName="CITY"/>
    </attribute>
    <attribute id="COUNTRY" order="4" displayAttribute=
"false" attributeHierarchyActive="false">
      <descriptions defaultDescription="Country"/>
      <keyMapping columnObjectName="Projection_1" columnName="COUNTRY"/>
    </attribute>
    <attribute id="TIMEZONE" order="5" displayAttribute=
"false" attributeHierarchyActive="false">
      <descriptions defaultDescription="Timezone"/>
      <keyMapping columnObjectName="Projection_1" columnName="TIMEZONE"/>
    </attribute>
    <attribute id="LOCATION" order="6" displayAttribute=
```

```
"false" attributeHierarchyActive="false">
      <descriptions defaultDescription="Geo Location"/>
      <keyMapping columnObjectName="Projection_1" columnName="LOCATION"/>
    </attribute>
  </attributes>
  <calculatedAttributes/>
  <baseMeasures/>
  <calculatedMeasures/>
  <restrictedMeasures/>
</logicalModel>
<layout>
  <shapes>
    <shape expanded="true" modelObjectName="Output" modelObjectNameSpace=
"MeasureGroup">
      <upperLeftCorner x="92" y="112"/>
      <rectangleSize width="140"/>
    </shape>
    <shape expanded="true" modelObjectName="Projection_
1" modelObjectNameSpace="CalculationView">
      <upperLeftCorner x="92" y="217"/>
      <rectangleSize height="30" width="140"/>
    </shape>
  </shapes>
</layout>
</Calculation:scenario>
```

Listing 5.31 CVAirport XML Definition

Upon a successful build, two column views **CVAirport** and **CVAirport/hier/Geography** (for the hierarchy) will be available under the **Column View** folder in the container schema.

As shown in Listing 5.32, the `CVAirport` column view has the DB-internal representation of a `CALCULATION SCENARIO`.

```
CREATE CALCULATION SCENARIO "CHICKENWINGS_1"."CVAirport" USING '[{"__
CalculationNode__": true,"name": "Airport","operation": {"__AnyDSNodeData__
": true,"source": "CHICKENWINGS_1:Airport"},"attributeVec": [{"__Attribute__
": true,"name": "CODE","role": 1,"datatype": {"__DataType__
": true,"type": 83,"sqlType": 37,"sqlLength": 3},"attributeType": 0},{"__
```

Attribute__": true,"name": "NAME","role": 1,"datatype": {"__DataType__
": true,"type": 83,"sqlType": 37,"sqlLength": 50},"attributeType": 0},{"__
Attribute__": true,"name": "CITY","role": 1,"datatype": {"__DataType__
": true,"type": 83,"sqlType": 37,"sqlLength": 20},"attributeType": 0},{"__
Attribute__": true,"name": "COUNTRY","role": 1,"datatype": {"__DataType__
": true,"type": 83,"sqlType": 37,"sqlLength": 20},"attributeType": 0},{"__
Attribute__": true,"name": "TIMEZONE","role": 1,"datatype": {"__DataType__
": true,"type": 83,"sqlType": 37,"sqlLength": 3},"attributeType": 0},{"__
Attribute__": true,"name": "LATITUDE","role": 1,"datatype": {"__DataType__
": true,"type": 66,"length": 12,"scale": 6,"sqlType": 34,"sqlLength": 12},"att
ributeType": 0},{"__Attribute__
": true,"name": "LONGITUDE","role": 1,"datatype": {"__DataType__
": true,"type": 66,"length": 12,"scale": 6,"sqlType": 34,"sqlLength": 12},"att
ributeType": 0},{"__Attribute__
": true,"name": "LOCATION","role": 1,"datatype": {"__DataType__
": true,"type": 104,"length": 4326,"sqlType": 75,"sqlLength": 8},"attributeTyp
e": 0}]},{"__CalculationNode__": true,"name": "Projection_1","inputVec": [{"__
Input__": true,"name": "Airport","mappingVec": [{"__Mapping__
": true,"type": 1,"target": "CODE","source": "CODE","length": 0},{"__Mapping__
": true,"type": 1,"target": "NAME","source": "NAME","length": 0},{"__Mapping__
": true,"type": 1,"target": "CITY","source": "CITY","length": 0},{"__Mapping__
": true,"type": 1,"target": "COUNTRY","source": "COUNTRY","length": 0},{"__
Mapping__
": true,"type": 1,"target": "TIMEZONE","source": "TIMEZONE","length": 0},{"__
Mapping__
": true,"type": 1,"target": "LOCATION","source": "LOCATION","length": 0}]}],"o
peration": {"__ProjectionOpNodeData__": true},"attributeVec": [{"__Attribute__
": true,"name": "CODE","role": 1,"datatype": {"__DataType__
": true,"type": 83,"sqlType": 37,"sqlLength": 3},"attributeType": 0},{"__
Attribute__": true,"name": "NAME","role": 1,"datatype": {"__DataType__
": true,"type": 83,"sqlType": 37,"sqlLength": 50},"attributeType": 0},{"__
Attribute__": true,"name": "CITY","role": 1,"datatype": {"__DataType__
": true,"type": 83,"sqlType": 37,"sqlLength": 20},"attributeType": 0},{"__
Attribute__": true,"name": "COUNTRY","role": 1,"datatype": {"__DataType__
": true,"type": 83,"sqlType": 37,"sqlLength": 20},"attributeType": 0},{"__
Attribute__": true,"name": "TIMEZONE","role": 1,"datatype": {"__DataType__
": true,"type": 83,"sqlType": 37,"sqlLength": 3},"attributeType": 0},{"__
Attribute__": true,"name": "LOCATION","role": 1,"datatype": {"__DataType__
": true,"type": 104,"length": 4326,"sqlType": 75,"sqlLength": 8},"attributeTyp

```
e": 0}],"debugNodeDataInfo" :  {"__DebugNodeDataInfo__
": true,"nodeName": "Projection_1"}},{"__CalculationNode__
": true,"name": "finalNode","isDefaultNode": true,"inputVec": [{"__Input__
": true,"name": "Projection_1","mappingVec": [{"__Mapping__
": true,"type": 1,"target": "CODE","source": "CODE","length": 0},{"__Mapping__
": true,"type": 1,"target": "NAME","source": "NAME","length": 0},{"__Mapping__
": true,"type": 1,"target": "CITY","source": "CITY","length": 0},{"__Mapping__
": true,"type": 1,"target": "COUNTRY","source": "COUNTRY","length": 0},{"__
Mapping__
": true,"type": 1,"target": "TIMEZONE","source": "TIMEZONE","length": 0},{"__
Mapping__
": true,"type": 1,"target": "LOCATION","source": "LOCATION","length": 0}]}],"o
peration": {"__ProjectionOpNodeData__": true},"attributeVec": [{"__Attribute__
": true,"name": "CODE","role": 1,"datatype": {"__DataType__
": true,"type": 83,"sqlType": 37,"sqlLength": 3},"description": "Code","attrib
uteType": 0},{"__Attribute__": true,"name": "NAME","role": 1,"datatype": {"__
DataType__
": true,"type": 83,"sqlType": 37,"sqlLength": 50},"description": "Name","attri
buteType": 0},{"__Attribute__": true,"name": "CITY","role": 1,"datatype": {"__
DataType__
": true,"type": 83,"sqlType": 37,"sqlLength": 20},"description": "City","attri
buteType": 0},{"__Attribute__
": true,"name": "COUNTRY","role": 1,"datatype": {"__DataType__
": true,"type": 83,"sqlType": 37,"sqlLength": 20},"description": "Country","at
tributeType": 0},{"__Attribute__
": true,"name": "TIMEZONE","role": 1,"datatype": {"__DataType__
": true,"type": 83,"sqlType": 37,"sqlLength": 3},"description": "Timezone","at
tributeType": 0},{"__Attribute__
": true,"name": "LOCATION","role": 1,"datatype": {"__DataType__
": true,"type": 104,"length": 4326,"sqlType": 75,"sqlLength": 8},"description"
: "Geo Location","attributeType": 0}],"debugNodeDataInfo" :  {"__
DebugNodeDataInfo__": true,"nodeName": "Projection"}},{"__Variable__
": true,"name": "$$client$$","typeMask": 512,"usage": 0,"isGlobal": true},{"__
Variable__
": true,"name": "$$language$$","typeMask": 512,"usage": 0,"isGlobal": true}]'
;
CREATE COLUMN VIEW "CHICKENWINGS_1"."CVAirport" WITH PARAMETERS (indexType=11,
      'PARENTCALCINDEXSCHEMA'='CHICKENWINGS_1',
     'PARENTCALCINDEX'='CVAirport',
```

```
    'PARENTCALCNODE'='finalNode')
;
COMMENT ON VIEW "CHICKENWINGS_1"."CVAirport" is 'CVAirport'
;
COMMENT ON COLUMN "CHICKENWINGS_1"."CVAirport"."CODE" is 'Code'
;
COMMENT ON COLUMN "CHICKENWINGS_1"."CVAirport"."NAME" is 'Name'
;
COMMENT ON COLUMN "CHICKENWINGS_1"."CVAirport"."CITY" is 'City'
;
COMMENT ON COLUMN "CHICKENWINGS_1"."CVAirport"."COUNTRY" is 'Country'
;
COMMENT ON COLUMN "CHICKENWINGS_1"."CVAirport"."TIMEZONE" is 'Timezone'
;
COMMENT ON COLUMN "CHICKENWINGS_1"."CVAirport"."LOCATION" is 'Geo Location'
```

Listing 5.32 DDL of the CVAirport Column View

CVConnection Calculation View

The **CVConnection** dimension calculation view is illustrated in Figure 5.44. The **Connection** table is the primary data source with additional attributes (departure and arrival airport details) sourced from two instances of the **CVAirport** calculation view.

The **FROMAP** column of **P_Connection** is joined (**J_Departure**) to the **CODE** column of the **CVAirport** view using a left outer join with N:1 cardinality. Similarly, the **TOAP** column of **J_Departure** is joined (**J_Arrival**) to the **CODE** column of another instance of **CVAirport** using a left outer join with N:1 cardinality.

A calculation column **CC_DISTANCE** is defined in the **Calculated Column** tab to calculate the spatial distance between the departure and arrival airport, as shown in Figure 5.44. The **Data Type** of **CC_DISTANCE** is **Integer** with the **Label** of **Distance in KM**. The spatial distance is computed using the `ST_Distance` function with the following expression:

```
ST_Distance("FR_LOCATION","TO_LOCATION" , 'Kilometer')
```

In this expression, the `FR_LOCATION` and `TO_LOCATION` columns are of spatial data type `ST_Point`.

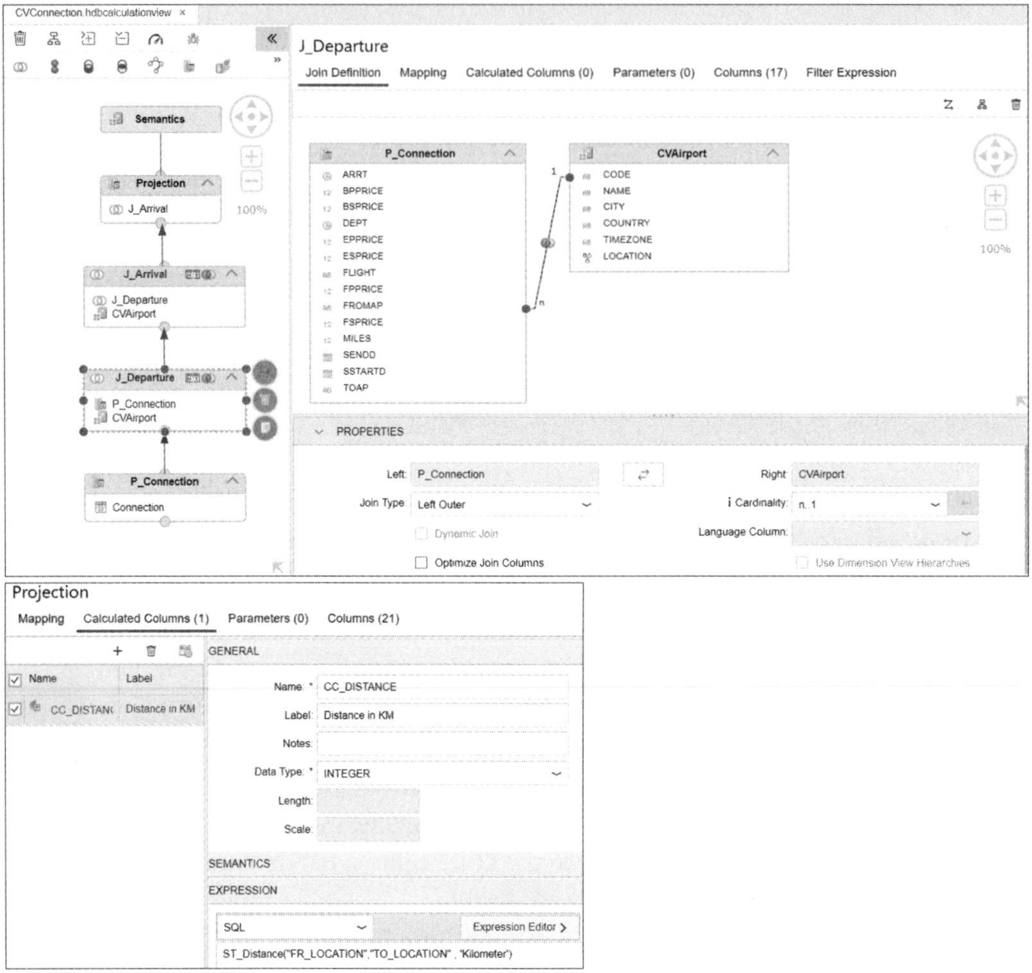

Figure 5.44 CVConnection Calculation View

CVPriceCalendar Calculation View

This is a special kind of dimension calculation view (type **Time**) that represents the pricing calendar dimension. The **CVPriceCalendar** calculation view is illustrated in Figure 5.45.

The **PriceCalendar** table is used as the primary data source (**Rate** and **Season**) with additional attributes (calendar details **Week**, **Month**, **Quarter**, **Year**, etc.) sourced from the **M_TIME_DIMENSION** synonym pointing to the **M_TIME_DIMENSION** table in the

_SYS_BI schema. (We discussed the topic of cross-schema data access using synonyms in Section 5.8.)

The **CDATE** column of **P_PriceCalendar** is joined to the **DATE_SQL** column and the **P_TIME** projection using a left outer join with 1:1 cardinality.

Figure 5.45 CVPriceCalendar Dimension View

5.9.3 Default Calculation Views

The default calculation view is the generic form of calculation view that is very similar to the dimension calculation view with default **Projection** node.

The **CVConnection** default calculation view shown in Figure 5.46 is a report view or business view with a very specific purpose, that is, to find alternate airports within 100 KM. It uses a spatial join (`Within Distance predicate`) between two instances of `CVAirport`.

A calculation column CC_DISTANCE is defined to calculate the spatial distance between the original and alternate airport using the ST_Distance function.

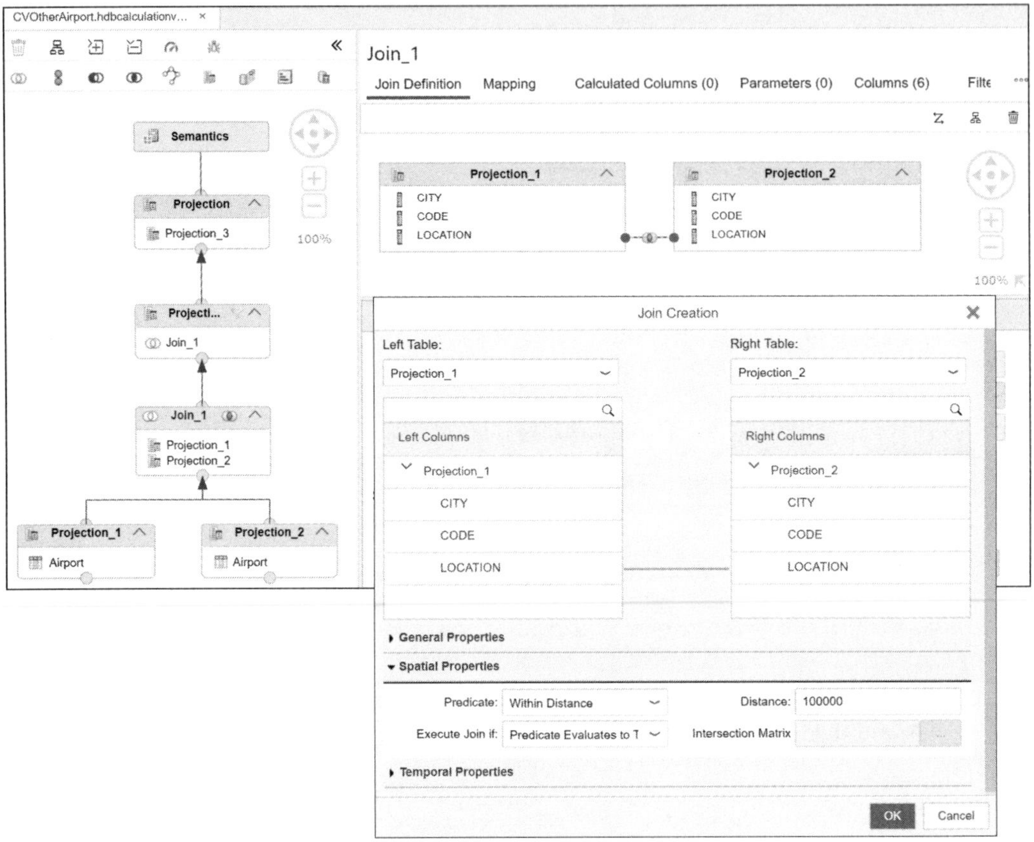

Figure 5.46 OtherAirport Calculation View

5.9.4 Cube Calculation Views with Star Joins

Cube calculation views are used to model multidimensional analysis and may include combinations of attributes, calculated and restricted columns, input parameters, and variables. There are two types: *cube calculation views* and *cube calculation views with star join*. An aggregation node is the default node of the cube calculation view, whereas the star join is the default node of the cube calculation view with star join.

The calculation view with star join is discussed in this section with the **CVBooking** view as an example (see Figure 5.47).

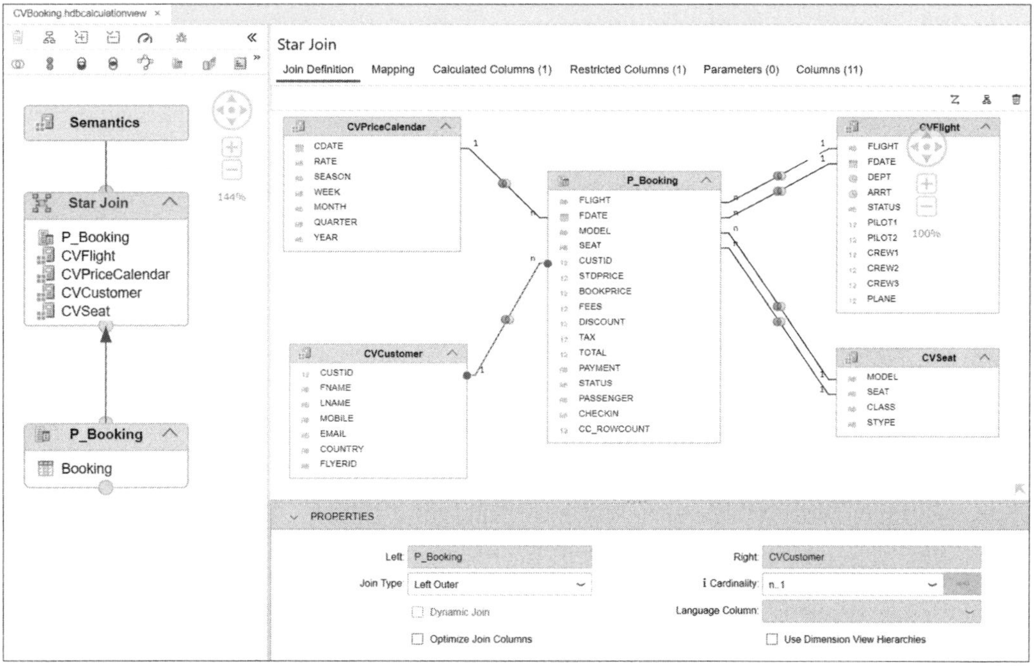

Figure 5.47 CVBooking CubeView

The cube calculation view will have one fact table as part of the data foundation joined to one or more dimension views forming the star schema in its simplest form. The three key components of a star join calculation view are as follows:

- **Data foundation**
  The projection node `P_Booking` with `BOOKING` table forms the data foundation of the `CVBooking` calculation view. For other scenarios, the data foundation may use another calculation view with complex business logic involving multiple data sources. If the data foundation is composed of more than one data source, the measures or key figures should come from the data source with the highest granularity.

- **Star join**
  The projection node `P_Booking` is connected to the `Star Join` node to serve as the data foundation and is joined to one or more dimension views forming the star

schema (see Figure 5.47). The joins between the data foundation and dimension views are independent of each other; that is, the join type and cardinality of each of the joins can be set independently.

In addition, the following properties in each join can be defined:

- **Dynamic Join**: If the join between the two data sets (in this case, data foundation and dimension view) are based on more than one column, the join will be executed only on the columns requested by the query. The join column not requested by the query during runtime won't be participating in the join.

- **Language Column**: This is used to select the language column to be referenced by the text join.

- **Optimize Join Columns**: By default, all joining columns (even if not requested by the query) are retrieved during query execution. By selecting this option, the joining columns won't be retrieved unless columns from the right-side data set are explicitly requested by the query.

- **Semantics**

  The semantics is the final node of all types (dimension, cube, or default) of calculation views and is used to define the semantics of the output columns. The semantics of the output columns such as **Column Type** (for attributes or measures), **Aggregation Type** (for measures), **Label Column** (for attributes), **DATA Masking**, and **Conversion Functions** can be defined as shown in Figure 5.48.

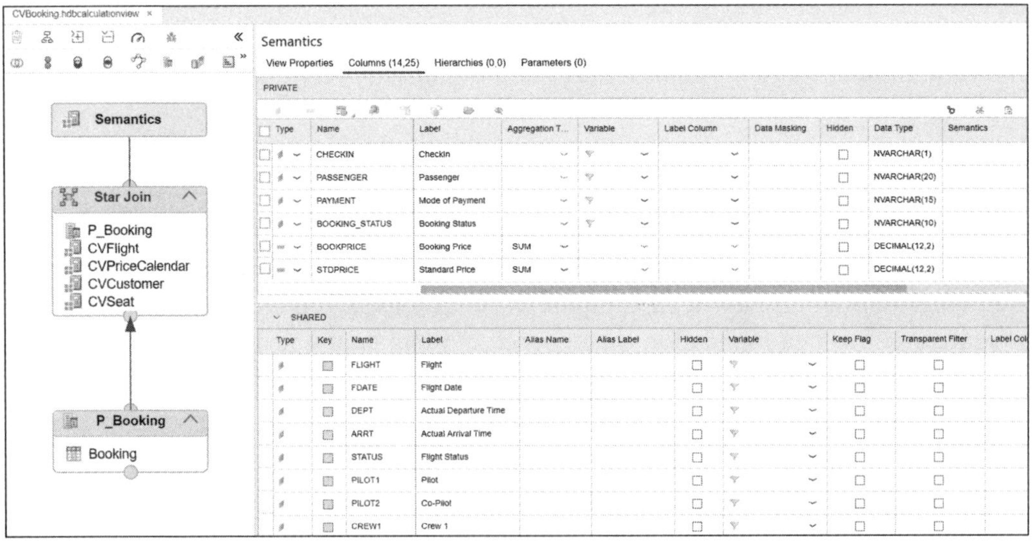

PRIVATE

Type	Name	Label	Aggregation T...	Variable	Label Column	Data Masking	Hidden	Data Type	Semantics
	CHECKIN	Checkin						NVARCHAR(1)	
	PASSENGER	Passenger						NVARCHAR(20)	
	PAYMENT	Mode of Payment						NVARCHAR(15)	
	BOOKING_STATUS	Booking Status						NVARCHAR(10)	
	BOOKPRICE	Booking Price	SUM					DECIMAL(12,2)	
	STDPRICE	Standard Price	SUM					DECIMAL(12,2)	

SHARED

Type	Key	Name	Label	Alias Name	Alias Label	Hidden	Variable	Keep Flag	Transparent Filter	Label Col
		FLIGHT	Flight							
		FDATE	Flight Date							
		DEPT	Actual Departure Time							
		ARRT	Actual Arrival Time							
		STATUS	Flight Status							
		PILOT1	Pilot							
		PILOT2	Co-Pilot							
		CREW1	Crew 1							

Figure 5.48 Cube Calculation View Columns

The calculation view editor has multiple tabs to configure and enable functionality specific to the calculation view being modeled. These features are relevant for all types (cube, dimension, and default) of calculation views and can be defined at various nodes (e.g., **Projection**, **Aggregation**, **Intersection**, etc.) in calculation views. Following are some of these key features used in our star join calculation views:

- **Calculated Columns**

  New attributes and/or measures for the cube can be created in the **Calculated Columns** tab. To create a calculated column, select the **Calculated Column** option from the context menu of the **+ (Add)** button.

  Select **Name**, **Label**, **Column Type** (**Attribute** or **Measure**), and **Data Type** for the calculated column, as illustrated in Figure 5.49 ❶.

  The calculation formula can be built using the expression editor with available columns, other calculated columns, restricted columns, input parameters, and a list of available functions.

  In this example, the **Extra Charges** (**CC_EXTRA_CHARGE**) is calculated as the difference of the booking price (**BOOKPRICE**) and standard price (**STDPRICE**) of the airline ticket. The following properties can also be set to influence the behavior of the calculated column:

  - **Hidden**: Used to make the calculated column invisible to MDX clients. These hidden fields will remain available for use in other calculation views.
  - **Enable client side aggregation**: Applicable to **Measures** only to select a client-side aggregation function (e.g., `SUM`, `MIN`, `COUNT`, etc.).
  - **COUNTER**: Distinct counters are a special kind of measure that can be created using the **Counters** option from the context menu of the **+ (Add)** button. Select the appropriate column from data foundation or dimension views, as shown in Figure 5.49 ❷.

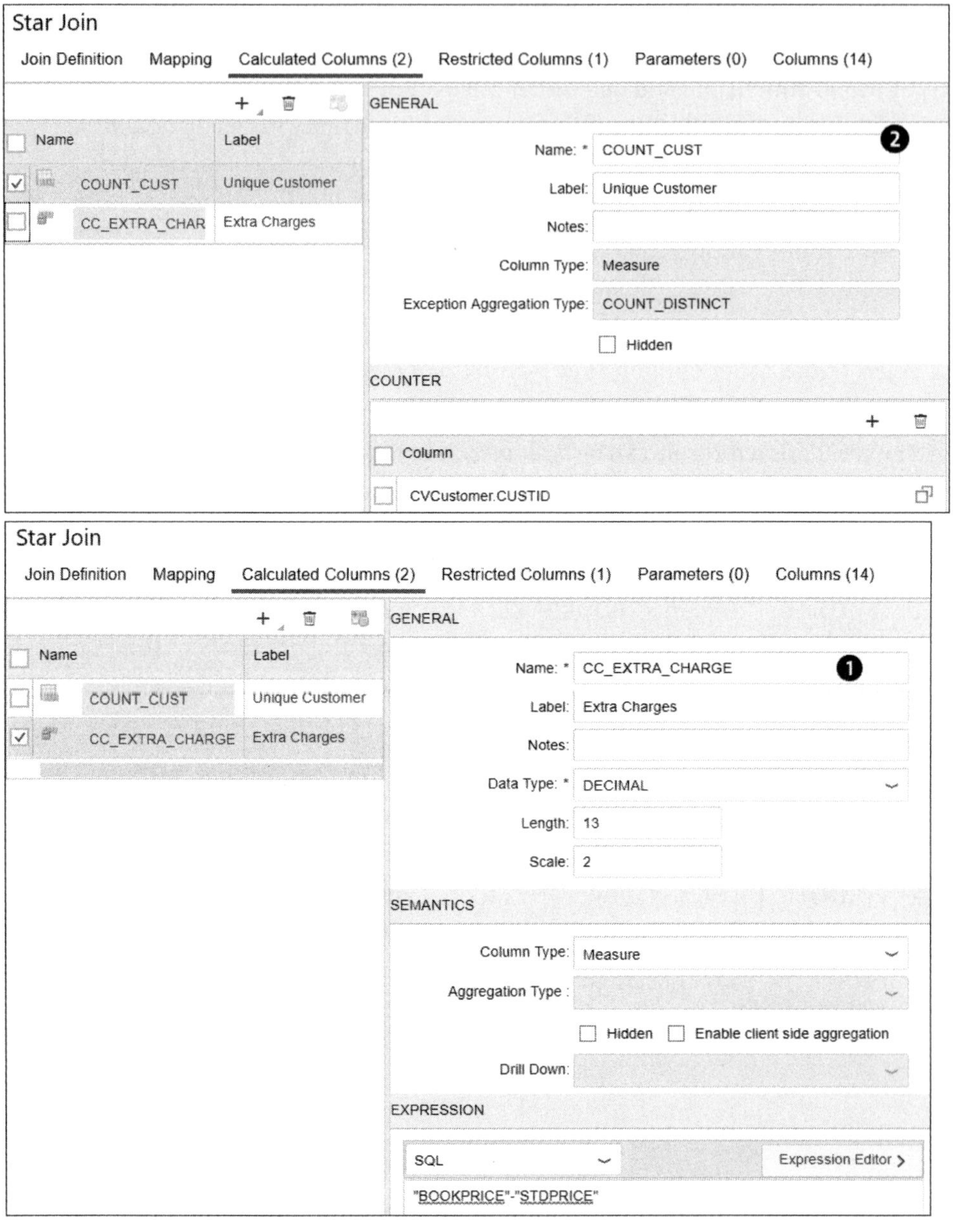

Figure 5.49 Calculated Columns and Counters

As an example, the number of unique customers (**COUNT_CUST**) is calculated as the distinct count of Customer ID (**CVCustomer.CUSTID**).

Keep in mind that the distinct count operations are significantly more expensive to compute compared to a simple count (or any other aggregation operation). The distinct count is a two-step computation process; in the first step, a dictionary must be created to store all the unique values, and the aggregation function (i.e., count) is applied in the second step.

- **Restricted Columns**
  Restricted columns are measures based on attribute restrictions.

  New restricted measures can be created in the **Restricted Columns** tab by selecting the **+ (Add)** button. Select **Name**, **Label**, and **Column Restriction**, as shown in Figure 5.50. The restriction can also be defined using an expression.

  The restricted measure number of open seats (**RES_OPEN_SEAT**) is based on the row count (**CC_ROWCOUNT**) measure where `BOOKING_STATUS = 'AVAILABLE'`.

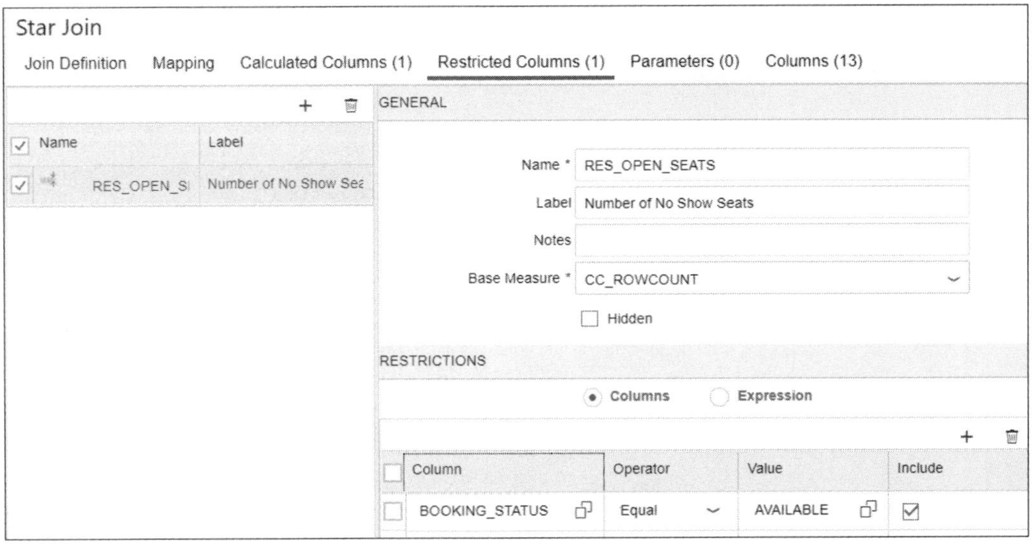

Figure 5.50 Restricted Columns

- **Parameters**
  The two types of parameters available in all types of calculation views are *variable* and *input parameters*, which can be defined using the **Parameters** tab:
  - Variables are used for filtering the data in the output node and hence are bound to columns for filtering using `WHERE` clauses. Technically, variables aren't known

to the SAP HANA engines; they are only meant for frontend tools, such as Data Preview and MDX clients to pass `WHERE` clauses during execution. The following types of variables are supported:

- **Single Value**: Filter based on a single value.
- **Interval**: Filter based on start and end values of an interval.
- **Range**: Filter based on operators such as **Greater Than** or **Less Than**.

As an example, we've defined a variable to filter on the **Flight Number (FLIGHT)** column in Figure 5.51.

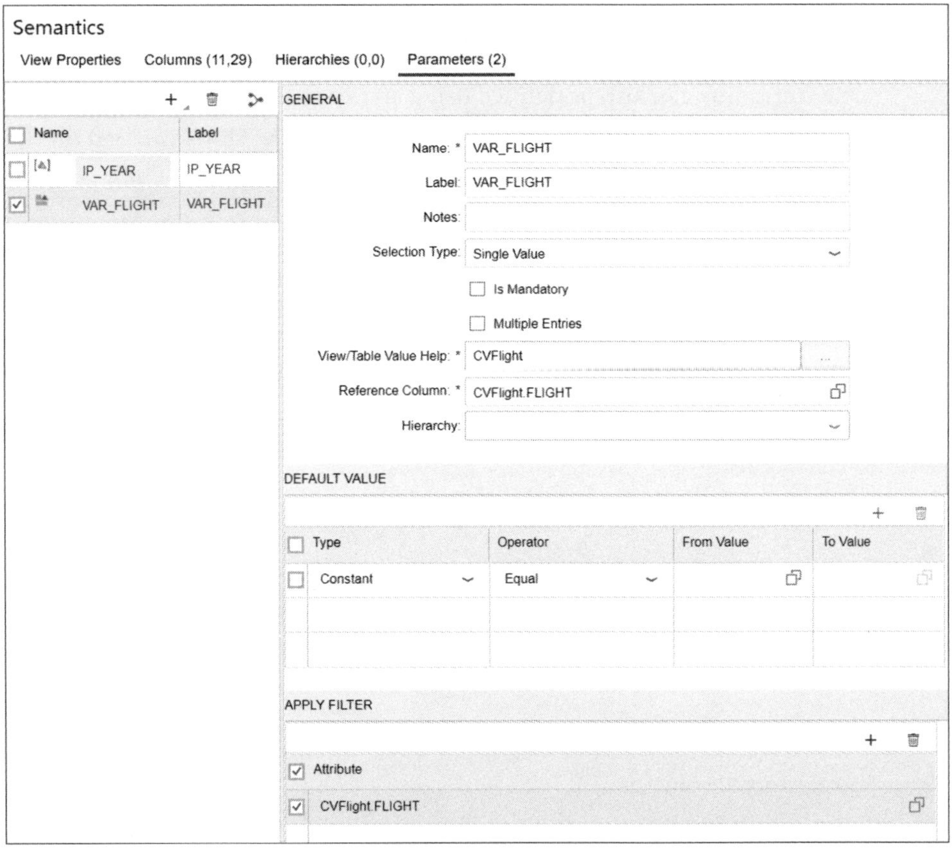

Figure 5.51 Variables

– Input parameters can be used for filtering in **Projection** and **Aggregation** nodes and can also be used in expression of **Calculated Columns** and **Restricted Columns**. Therefore, input parameters are versatile and not limited to just filtering data sets. They can be used to provide intelligence to control the behavior of the entire model. Unlike variables, input parameters are part of the calculation view and known to SAP HANA engines as placeholders in the model. As an example, we've defined an input parameter **IP_YEAR** (year). The following types of input parameters are supported:

- **Direct**: Free form (enter any value), as illustrated in Figure 5.52 ❶.
- **Column**: Select one of the values from the distinct list of values of a column ❷.
- **Static List**: Select one of the values from a static list of values defined during design time.
- **Derived From Procedure/Scalar Function**: The value is read from a procedure or scalar function ❸. This can be used to derive values based on complex business logic.
- **Derived From Table**: Read values from a predefined table ❹. The values in the table can be refreshed independently of the calculation view.

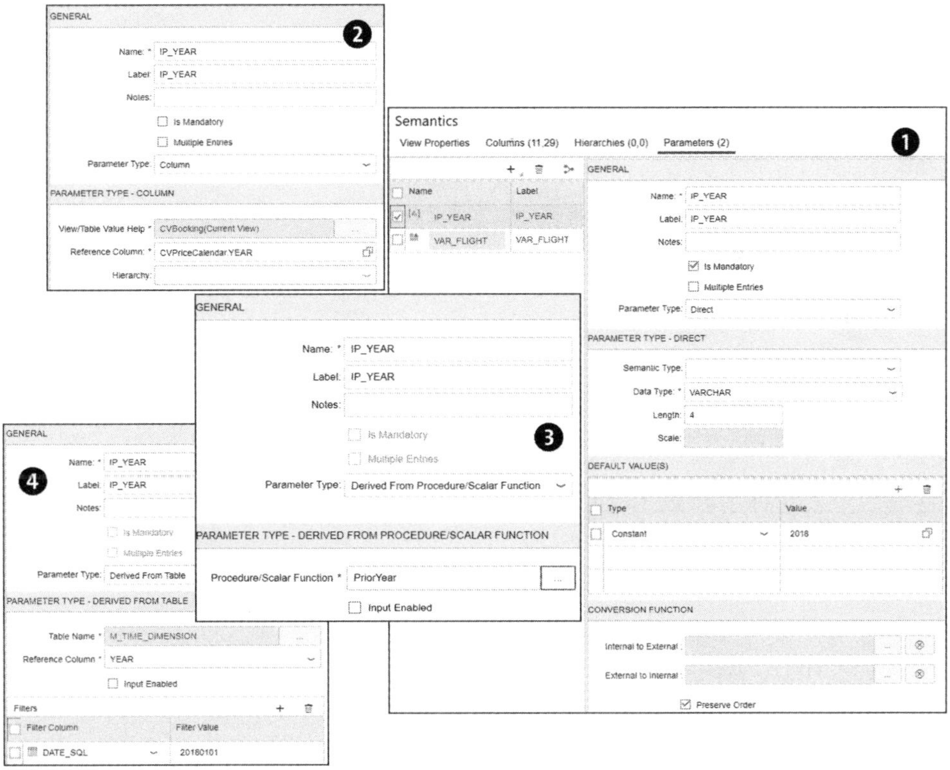

Figure 5.52 Input Parameters

5.9.5 Cube Calculation Views

As discussed earlier, the aggregation node is the default node for cube calculation views. Cube calculation views are used to model additional business logic on top of other calculation views and data sources. It's also used for multidimensional analysis and may include combinations of attributes, calculated and restricted columns, input parameters, and variables.

The **CVCompare** calculation view is illustrated in Figure 5.53 as an example. The **CVCompare** view takes two input parameters—current year (**IP_CY**) and prior year (**IP_PY**)—and is modeled for a year over year scenario. The same approach can be used to combine and compare two similarly structured data sets, for example, *plan vs. actual*.

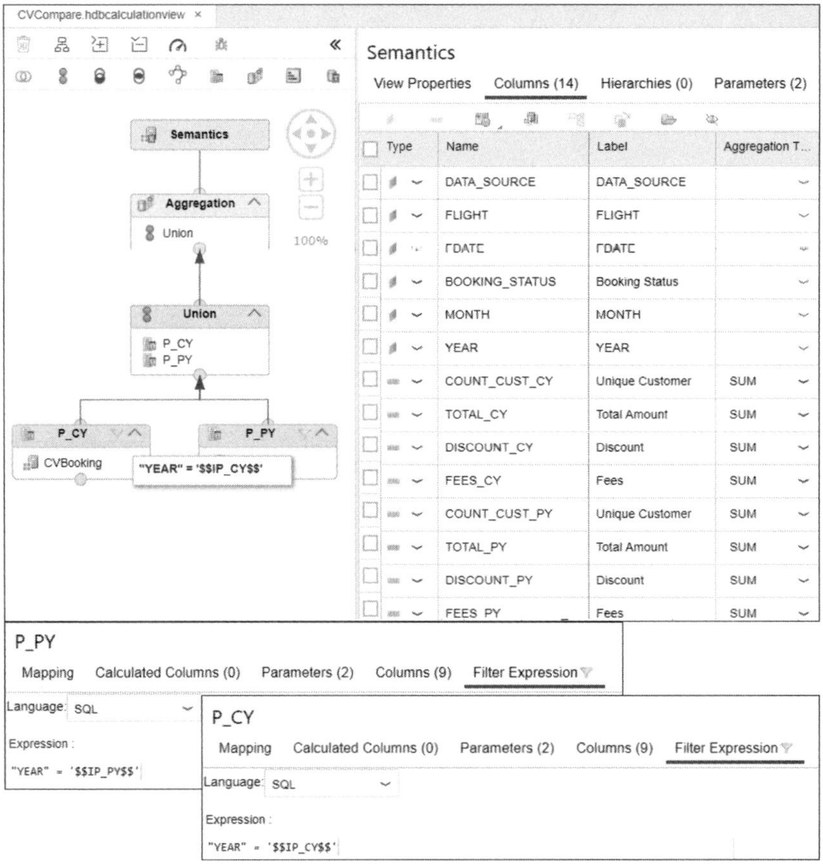

Figure 5.53 CVCompare Calculation View

Projection **P_CY** is filtered using **IP_CY** to represent the current year data set. Likewise, projection **P_PY** is filtered using **IP_PY** and represents the prior year's data set.

These two data sets are then combined using a **Union** node, as illustrated in Figure 5.54. A constant column **DATA_SOURCE** is defined with constant values **CY** and **PY** for **P_CY** and **P_PY** nodes, respectively. This constant column **DATA_SOURCE** can be used for model pruning during query execution.

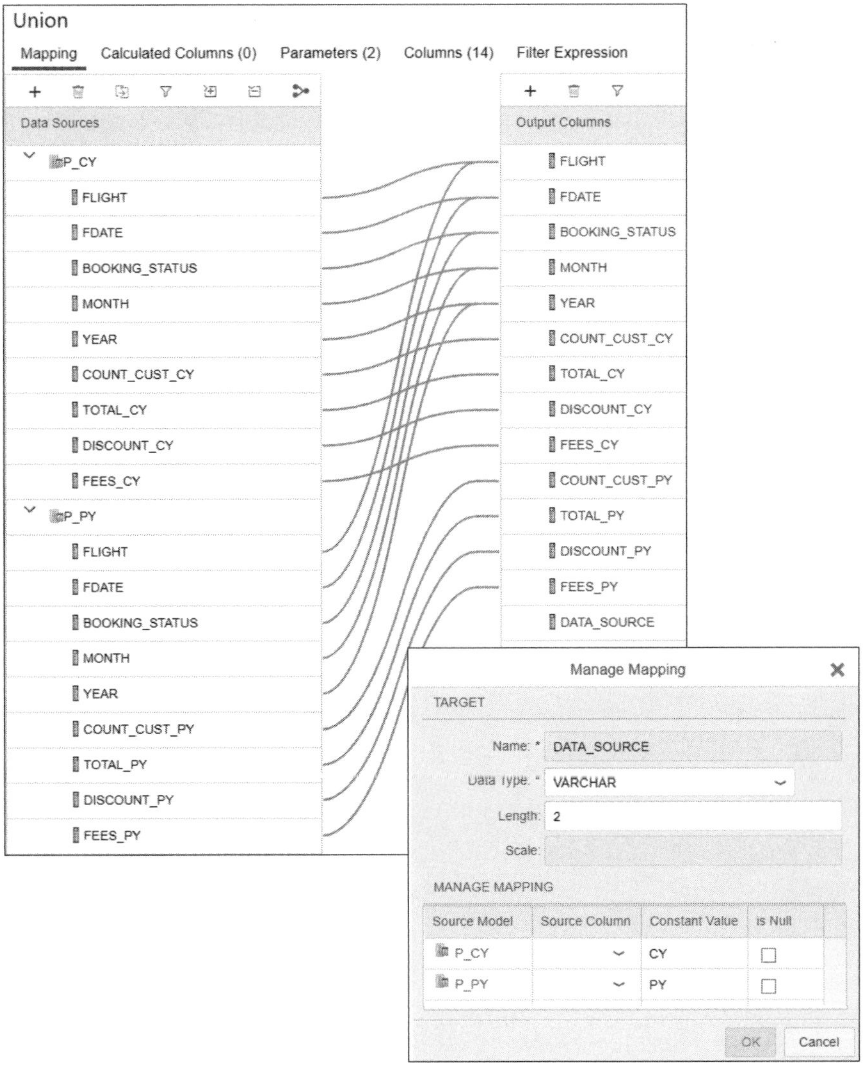

Figure 5.54 Union Node

For example, a query with WHERE DATA_SOURCE = 'CY' will only invoke the P_CY projection node. The other half of the model with the P_PY projection node won't be engaged during query execution. The behavior will be similar in reverse order for a query with WHERE DATA_SOURCE = 'PY'. For a query with no WHERE clause or WHERE DATA_SOURCE in ('CY','PY'), both sides of the model will be engaged.

5.9.6 Analytic Privileges

In the past few sections, we discussed the process of building virtual data models using calculation views. In this section, we'll model *analytic privileges* to secure/restrict the data in the calculation views. Standard database object privileges (SELECT, EXECUTE, etc.) provide access control only at the object level, so users have either full access to an object or no access at all. Analytical privileges, on the other hand, provide access control on the row-level data set of a calculation view, which is critical from a business perspective. Analytical privileges can be used to manage data security based on logged-on user's attributes (i.e., organization, department, etc.) and display relevant business data that is based on the user's role and line of business.

Analytical privilege can be created using .hdbanalyticalprivilege design-time artifacts. Select **New • Analytic Privilege** in the context menu of the **privilege** folder to add a new analytic privilege to the HDB module.

As an example, the **CustomerBooking** analytic privilege is defined for the **CVBooking** calculation view, as shown in Figure 5.55. This can be used to restrict the display of booking information for the logged-in customer.

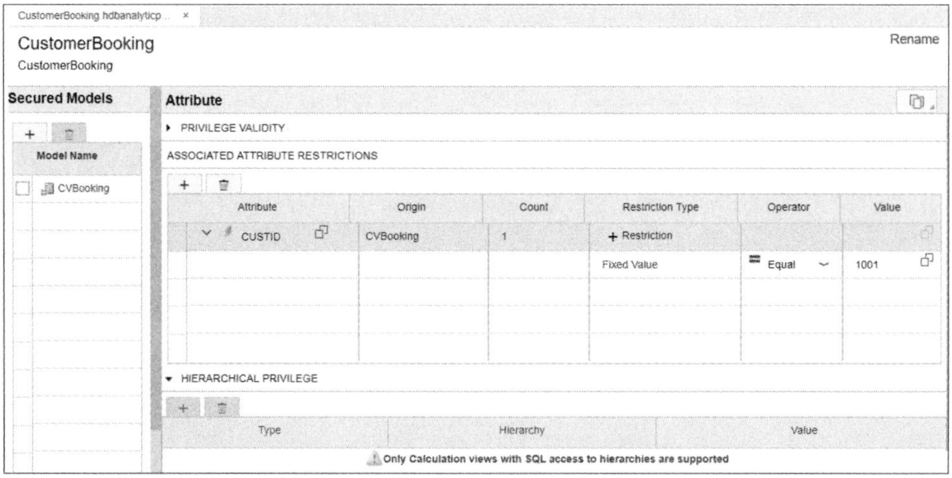

Figure 5.55 Analytic Privileges

Note

The **Apply Privilege** setting must be set to **SQL Analytic Privilege** before an analytic privilege can be defined on a calculation view.

5.10 SQLScript for Stored Procedures

SAP HANA virtual data models using calculation views are very efficient in analyzing massive amounts of data in real time. Graphical calculation view modeling can be used to model very complex business logic, but there will be scenarios where scripting is needed. As discussed earlier, SQLScript can be used to define table functions, which can be used in graphical calculation views.

Application development is more than just analysis of data. It also involves complex business logic for recording business transactions. The idea is to push the data-intensive application logic to the database.

Conceptually, SAP HANA SQLScript is related to stored procedures as defined in the SQL standard, but SQLScript is designed to provide superior optimization possibilities. SQLScript is a collection of extensions to SQL that includes the following:

- **Data extensions**
  Table type definitions without database tables.
- **Functional extensions**
  Table and scalar functions to perform complex data flows.
- **Procedural extensions**
  Stored procedures to implement imperative logic.

We'll discuss the creation of stored procedures, table functions, and scalar functions to implement complex business logic in the following subsections.

Best Practices for SQLScript

It's essential that the SQLScript code used in stored procedures, table functions, or scalar functions exploit the parallelism in the SAP HANA database for better performance. Refer to the SAP HANA SQLScript Reference Guide at *https://bit.ly/2Igm7wg* for details.

5.10.1 Stored Procedure

SQL procedures can be used to implement imperatives to model complex business transactions and transformations. Procedures can be created using the `.hdbprocedure` design artifact.

To create a table function, click the **procedure** folder, and select **New • Procedure** from the context menu to add a new procedure to the HDB module.

The SQLScript code for a simple `CreateAirport` procedure is shown in Listing 5.33. This is used to add a new airport code to the `AIRPORT` master data table.

File Name: /src/procedure/CreateAirport.hdbprocedure

```
PROCEDURE "CreateAirport" (
    IN im_code NVARCHAR(3),
    IN im_name NVARCHAR(50),
    IN im_city NVARCHAR(20),
    IN im_country NVARCHAR(20),
    IN im_timezone NVARCHAR(3),
    IN im_latitude DECIMAL(12,6),
    IN im_longitude DECIMAL(12,6),
    OUT ex_error NVARCHAR(100))
LANGUAGE SQLSCRIPT SQL
SECURITY DEFINER AS
BEGIN
    -- Declare variables
    declare noc integer;

    -- Check if the entry exists
    select count(im_code) into noc
    from "Airport"
    where "CODE" = im_code;

    -- Raise an Error
    if :noc > 0 then
        ex_error := 'ERROR: Airport ' || :im_code || ' already exists!';

    -- Insert the Record
    else
        insert into "Airport" values (
        im_code,
        im_name,
```

```
        im_city,
        im_country,
        im_timezone,
        im_latitude,
        im_longitude,
        new ST_POINT ('POINT ('|| im_longitude || ' ' || im_
latitude || ')',4326)
        );
    end if;

END
```

Listing 5.33 CreateAirport Procedure

The procedure plug-in information available in the *.hdiconfig* file of the HDI container is as follows:

```
"hdbprocedure" : {
"plugin_name" : "com.sap.hana.di.procedure"
}
```

5.10.2 Table Functions and Scalar Functions

Table functions are read-only, user-defined functions to implement complex business logic using SQLScript, and they return exactly one results table as output. Table functions can access one or more parameters to compute the result set.

Table functions can be created using `.hdbfunction` design-time artifacts. To create a table function, click the **function** folder, and select **New • Function** from the context menu to add a new function to the HDB module.

The SQLScript code for the `AvailableSeats` table function is shown in Listing 5.34. As shown, the ticket price is being computed based on the seat availability on the flight.

File Name: /src/function/AvailableSeats.hdbfunction

```
FUNCTION "AvailableSeats" (IP_FLIGHT NVARCHAR(6), IP_DATE DATE)
       RETURNS TABLE (FLIGHT NVARCHAR(6), FDATE DATE, SEAT NVARCHAR(4), PRICE
DECIMAL(13,2), SEAT_CLASS NVARCHAR(10), SEAT_TYPE NVARCHAR(15))
       LANGUAGE SQLSCRIPT
       SQL SECURITY DEFINER AS
BEGIN
```

```
    DECLARE factor DECIMAL(6,2);

    --Calculate the Price factor based on occupancy
    SELECT 2-SUM(CASE WHEN STATUS = 'AVAILABLE' THEN 1 ELSE 0 END)/COUNT(SEAT)
    INTO factor
    FROM "Booking"
    WHERE FLIGHT = :IP_FLIGHT AND FDATE = :IP_DATE
    ;

    --Compute the Resultset
    result = SELECT a.FLIGHT, a.FDATE, a.SEAT, a.STDPRICE*:factor as PRICE,
        b.ClASS as SEAT_CLASS, b.STYPE as SEAT_TYPE
    FROM "Booking" as a INNER JOIN "Seat" as b
        ON a.MODEL = b.MODEL and a.SEAT = b.SEAT
    WHERE a.FLIGHT = :IP_FLIGHT AND a.FDATE = :IP_DATE
    AND a.STATUS = 'AVAILABLE'
    ;

    return :result;

END;
```

Listing 5.34 AvailableSeats Table Function

A scalar function is a read-only, user-defined function that takes one or more input parameters and uses SQLScript to compute one or more scalar outputs. Scalar functions with exactly one output can be used to provide value to input parameters. Scalar functions are also created using an `.hdbfunction` design-time artifact.

An example of the `PriorYear` scalar function is shown in Listing 5.35.

```
File Name: /src/function/PriorYear.hdbfunction
FUNCTION "PriorYear" ( )
       RETURNS PRIOR_YEAR NVARCHAR(4)
       LANGUAGE SQLSCRIPT
       SQL SECURITY INVOKER AS
BEGIN

 SELECT year(now())+1
 INTO PRIOR_YEAR
 FROM dummy;
```

```
-- The following code instead of the above SQL statement
-- will also work fine
 -- PRIOR_YEAR := YEAR(NOW())+1;

END;
```

Listing 5.35 PriorYear Scalar Function

The function plug-in information is available in the *.hdiconfig* file of the HDI container, as follows:

```
"hdbfunction" : {
"plugin_name" : "com.sap.hana.di.function"
}
```

5.11 Table Creation without Core Data Services Documents

In addition to CDS entity definition (.hdbcds), HDBTable definition (.hdbtable and .hdbdropcreatetable) is also supported in SAP HANA XS Advanced for defining database tables. The HDBTable syntax for defining database base tables is quite similar to SAP HANA SQL DDL, so developers with SQL backgrounds will be comfortable using the HDTable syntax.

Note

The .hdbtable artifact in SAP HANA XS Advanced is different from the design-time table definition (.hdbtable) in the context of SAP HANA XS as discussed in Section 5.3.4.

Any and all features of SAP HANA SQL DDL (CREATE TABLE) are supported in the SAP HANA XS Advanced HDBTable definition, whereas only a subset of those features is available when defining tables using CDS. However, multiple entities can be defined in one CDS artifact, and CDS associations can be leveraged to define the relationships between entities in one place. Although associations between database tables are also supported using the HDBTable definition, only tables can be defined in each artifact.

There are two plug-ins (.hdbtable and .hdbdropcreatetable) available to create table artifacts in SAP HANA XS Advanced. The .hdbtable plug-in uses a data migration component to transform an already deployed version of the table into the new structure and copies the existing data into the new structure. The .hdbdropcreatetable plug-in doesn't support data migration and creates the table as the new structure after dropping the last deployed table.

The table plug-in information is available in the *.hdiconfig* file of the HDI container as shown in Listing 5.36.

```
"hdbtable" : {
    "plugin_name" : "com.sap.hana.di.table"
},
"hdbdropcreatetable" : {
    "plugin_name" : "com.sap.hana.di.dropcreatetable"
},
"hdbconstraint" : {
"plugin_name" : "com.sap.hana.di.constraint"
},
```

Listing 5.36 Plug-ins for .hdbtable, .hdbdropcreatetable, and .hdbconstraint

The syntax of HDBTable (.hdbtable) in SAP HANA XS Advanced is similar to SAP HANA SQL DDL (CREATE TABLE) without the CREATE clause, as shown in Listing 5.37.

```
File Name: /src/data/CUSTOMER.hdbtable
COLUMN TABLE CUSTOMER (
    CUSTID INTEGER COMMENT 'Customer ID',
    FNAME NVARCHAR(20) COMMENT 'First Name',
    LNAME NVARCHAR(20) COMMENT 'Last Name',
    MOBILE NVARCHAR(15) COMMENT 'Mobile/Cell Number',
    EMAIL NVARCHAR(25) COMMENT 'Email',
    COUNTRY NVARCHAR(25) COMMENT 'Country of Residence',
    FLYERID NVARCHAR(20) COMMENT 'Frequent Flyer ID',
    PRIMARY KEY (CUSTID)
)
WITH ASSOCIATIONS
(
JOIN FREQUENT_FLYER
AS
TO_FREQUENT_FLYER
ON FLYERID = FREQUENT_FLYER.ID
)
COMMENT 'Customer Details'
```

Listing 5.37 SAP HANA XS Advanced .hdbtable Syntax

As shown here, association to other tables is also supported in HDBTable. However, HDBTable also has certain restrictions versus the CREATE TABLE SQL statement as follows:

- Specifying the table type (ROW or COLUMN) is mandatory.
- Creation of the HISTORY table isn't supported.
- A table can't be created that references another table (TABLE TABLE_X like TABLE_Y) or a SELECT SQL query (TABLE TABLE_X as SELECT[..] FROM TABLE_B).
- Creation of flexible tables (e.g., WITH SCHEMA FLEXIBILITY clause) isn't supported.
- Creation of named constraints isn't supported. However, foreign key constraints can be defined as separate .hdbconstraint artifacts.

The syntax for .hdbconstraint is similar to the following ALTER TABLE SQL statement:

File Name: /src/data/NEW_CONSTRAINT.hdbconstraint

```
CONSTRAINT NEW_CONSTRAINT
ON TABLE_X
FOREIGN KEY (FIELD) REFERENCES TABLE_Y (FIELD) ON UPDATE CASCADE
```

In this syntax, NEW_CONSTRAINT is the constraint name on TABLE_X with the foreign key relationship with TABLE_Y.

5.12 Other Database Artifacts

In this section, we'll discuss some of the other SAP HANA XS Advanced artifacts that can be used to create database sequences, views, and security roles. We'll also provide the complete list of SAP HANA XS Advanced supported objects.

5.12.1 SAP HANA Database Sequence

A database sequence can be created using the .hdbsequence design-time artifact. The .hdbsequence artifact uses a DDL-style syntax that is similar to SQL command CREATE SEQUENCE but without the leading CREATE. The RESET BY query (optional, if defined) is executed during deployment to set the sequence to its start value.

The sequence plug-in information is available in the *.hdiconfig* file of the HDI container, as follows:

```
"hdbsequence" : {
  "plugin_name" : "com.sap.hana.di.sequence",
  "plugin_version": "2.0.0.0"
}
```

The structure of the sample *CrewId.hdbsequence* file is shown in Listing 5.38.

```
File Name: /src/sequence/CrewId.hdbsequence
SEQUENCE "CrewId"
INCREMENT BY 1 START WITH 1001
MINVALUE 1 MAXVALUE 9999
NO CYCLE
RESET BY
SELECT IFNULL(MAX(CREWID), 0)+1
FROM "Crew"
```

Listing 5.38 CrewId HDB Sequence

5.12.2 SAP HANA Database View

A database view or SQL view can be created using the HDB view definition based on the SELECT statement. This is equivalent to the CREATE VIEW SQL statement. The HDB view definition will generate the database view similar to that of the CDS view described in Section 5.6.5. To generate the same OpenSeat SQL view, the syntax of HDB views is shown in Listing 5.39.

The view plug-in information is available in the *.hdiconfig* file of the HDI container as follows:

```
"hdbview" : {
  "plugin_name" : "com.sap.hana.di.view",
  "plugin_version": "2.0.0.0"
}
```

Upon a successful build, the generated SQL view (**OpenSeats3**) will be available under **Catalog • Views** of the HDB container.

```
--HDB View: Create SQL View
VIEW "OpenSeats3" as
SELECT
    FLIGHT,
    FDATE,
```

```
    COUNT(SEAT) as TOTAL_SEATS
FROM "Booking"
WHERE STATUS = 'AVAILABLE'
GROUP BY FLIGHT, FDATE
HAVING COUNT(SEAT) > 2
ORDER BY FLIGHT ASC, FDATE DESC;
```

Listing 5.39 OpenSeats3 HDB View

5.12.3 SAP HANA Database Role

A *role* is a collection of privileges that is used to secure the data and the system in SAP HANA. A *privilege* is an authorization to carry out certain operations (e.g., `SELECT`, `DELETE`, etc.) on certain objects. There are privileges at the object, schema, and system level to define roles. One or more roles can be assigned to a user or to another role.

A runtime role can be created using the `.hdbrole` design-time artifact. The *.hdbrole* file must follow the JSON syntax and specify one or more privileges or other roles to define the role.

The structure of the *.hdbrole* file may have the following properties:

- `"role"`
  Mandatory. The root of the JSON data structure.
- `"name"`
  Mandatory. The name of the role to be generated.
- `"global_roles"`
  Optional. A role can include valid global roles, that is, roles created without any schema, such as `DATA ADMIN` or `MODELING`. For example:

  ```
  "global_roles": ["MODELING","DATA ADMIN"]
  ```

- `"schema_roles"`
  Optional. A role can include other schema roles referencing the local schema. For example:

  ```
  "schema_roles": [
    {
    "schema": "Schema_XXX",
    "names": ["Role_YYY", "Role_ZZZ"]
    }
  ]
  ```

- "system_privileges"
  Optional. A role can include system privileges such as CATALOG READ or USER ADMIN. For example:

  ```
  "system_privileges": ["CATALOG READ", "USER ADMIN"]
  ```

- "schema_privileges"
  Optional. A role can include privileges referencing another schema. The "schema" entry is optional. If omitted, the privilege is assigned on the local container schema. For example:

  ```
  "schema_privileges": [
    {
    "schema": "Schema_XXX",
    "privileges": ["INSERT", "UPDATE"],
    "privileges_with_grant_option": ["SELECT"]
    }
  ]
  ```

- "object_privilege"
  Optional. A role can include privileges on the local container schema objects. For example:

  ```
  "object_privileges": [
    {
    "name": "Table_XXX",
    "type": "TABLE"
    "privileges": ["INSERT", "UPDATE"],
    "privileges_with_grant_option": ["SELECT"]
    }
  ]
  ```

- "schema_analytic_privileges"
  Optional. A role can include schema-local analytic privileges. The "schema" entry is optional. If omitted, the analytic privilege is assigned on the local container schema. For example:

  ```
  "schema_analytic_privileges": [
    {
    "schema": "Schema_XXX",
    "privileges": ["AP_YYY"],
  ```

```
    "privileges_with_grant_option": ["AP_ZZZ"]
    }
  ]
```

The plug-in for role and role configuration is available in the *.hdiconfig* file of the HDI container as follows:

```
"hdbrole" : {
  "plugin_name" : "com.sap.hana.di.role",
  "plugin_version": "2.0.0.0"
}
```

The structure of the sample *admin.hdbrole* file is shown Listing 5.40.

```
File Name: /src/roles/admin.hdbrole
-- HDB View: Creates database SQL View
{
    "role":{
        "name": "admin",
        "schema_privileges": [{
           "privileges": ["SELECT METADATA",
                          "SELECT CDS METADATA",
                          "SELECT",
                          "INSERT",
                          "EXECUTE",
                          "DELETE",
                          "UPDATE",
                          "CREATE TEMPORARY TABLE",
                          "TRIGGER"
           ]
        }],
        "schema_analytic_privileges":[
        {
        "privileges": ["CustomerBooking"]
        }]
      }
}
```

Listing 5.40 admin HDB Role

5.12.4 List of SAP HANA Deployment Infrastructure Artifacts

We discussed development of some of the common HDI artifacts in this chapter. The complete list of artifacts supported by HDI is available in the *.hdiconfig* file of the HDI container listed in Table 5.4.

Artifact	Description
txt,*	All other file types not explicitly defined deployed as is
Csv	Data file for a table import (also hdbtabledata)
Hdbafllangprocedure	Definition of a language procedure for an application function library (AFL)
Hdbanalyticprivilege	XML-based analytic privileges
Hdbcalculationview	Calculation view
Hdbcds	CDS entities
Hdbconstraint	Constraint on database tables
Hdbdropcreatetable	Database table database (also hdbtable)
Hdbfulltextindex	Full text index
Hdbfunction	Database function
Hdbgraphworkspace	Graph work space resource
Hdbindex	Table index
Hdbmrjob	Hadoop map-remote job
Jar	Optional mapping for direct access to Hadoop files
Hdblibrary	Library resource
Hdbprocedure	Database procedure
Hdbprojectionview	Projection view
hdbprojectionviewconfig	Configuration file for a projection view
hdbpublicsynonym	Public database synonym
Hdbresultcache	Result cache

Table 5.4 Supported HDI Artifacts

Artifact	Description
Hdbrole	Database roles
Hdbroleconfig	Configuration of database privileges (and other roles) to be included in a database role
Hdbsearchruleset	Search configurations for built-in search procedure
Hdbsequence	Database sequence
Hdbsynonym	Database synonym
Hdbsynonymconfig	Configuration file for a database synonym
Hdbstatistics	Statistics definition file
Hdbstructuredprivilege	Analytic or structured privileges
Hdbtable	Database table (see hdbdropcreatetable)
Hdbtabledata	Data-import operation for a database table (also *.csv*)
Hdbtabletype	Table type
Hdbtextconfig	Customization of the options used for text analysis
Hdbtextdict	Specification of the custom entity types and entity names to be used with text analysis
Hdbtextrule	Specification of the rules (patterns) for extracting complex entities and relationships using text analysis
hdbtextinclude	Definition of the rules to be used in one or more extraction rule sets for top-level text analysis
hdbtextlexicon	Definition of the lists of words used in one or more top-level text analysis rule sets
hdbtextminingconfig	Customization of the features and options used for text mining
hdbtrigger	Database trigger
hdbview	SQL view
hdbvirtualfunction	Virtual database function

Table 5.4 Supported HDI Artifacts (Cont.)

Artifact	Description
hdbvirtualfunctionconfig	Configuration file for a virtual function
hdbvirtualprocedure	Virtual database procedure
hdbvirtualprocedureconfig	Configuration file for the virtual database procedure
hdbvirtualtable	Virtual table
hdbvirtualtableconfig	Configuration file for virtual tables

Table 5.4 Supported HDI Artifacts (Cont.)

5.13 Summary

In this chapter, we started with the difference between SAP HANA and traditional databases regarding building normalized data models and then continued our discussion on creating data models from entity-relationship (ER) diagrams. We discussed the tools and steps to create database tables using SAP HANA SQL and SAP HANA Repository design-time objects.

Next, we introduced the SAP HANA Deployment Infrastructure (HDI), its function to create runtime containers in the database, and the SAP HANA database (HDB) module to create database runtime objects (tables, views, calculation views, procedures, etc.) using design-time artifacts. You also learned about CDS (`.hdbcds` artifacts) to build physical data models and `.hdbtabledata` artifacts to load sample data (*.csv* files) to application tables.

We continued our discussion on creating virtual data models using SAP HANA calculation views to report on top of the physical data model. You learned about various types of calculation views to build multidimensional models and analytic privileges to secure the data model. In contrast to graphical calculation views, we also discussed building complex procedural business logic using table functions and stored procedures with SQLScript.

Finally, we concluded the chapter with a discussion on other HDI-supported artifacts to various database objects.

In the next chapter, we'll discuss building the application layer to expose data from the data model to the frontend UI using the different technologies of Node.js, Java, XSODATA, and so on supported by SAP HANA XS Advanced.

Chapter 6
Developing the Application Layer

In this chapter, we'll add the application layer to the data model that has been developed previously. We'll discuss the different possibilities of using Node.js, Java, or other programming languages on the SAP HANA platform, how to get access to the SAP HANA database, and how to expose data to the outside world.

In the previous chapter, we highlighted how to set up and build a data model. We discussed the data model of our Chicken-Wings Airline, which is the basis for the application layer that we're going to develop in this chapter. The role of the application layer is to add business logic to the application and expose the underlying data model to the user interface (UI), which we're going to develop in Chapter 7. The application layer is the link between the data model and the UI. In this chapter, we'll discuss application services in depth and will reveal how to expose the data from the data model to a frontend UI. The SAP HANA extended application services, advanced model (SAP HANA XS Advanced) platform allows the creation of an application layer using different technologies, such as Node.js, Java, and XSODATA. We'll highlight the various technical options to develop the application layer and develop the application layer of our Chicken-Wings Airline by using the different supported technologies of SAP HANA XS Advanced to demonstrate the concepts of these techniques.

In Section 6.1, we'll introduce the general tasks of an application layer and the role of an overall SAP HANA XS Advanced application. In Section 6.2, we'll demonstrate the development of Node.js modules with SAP HANA XS Advanced. We'll highlight the different concepts and options that a Node.js module offers and explain the capabilities by implementing the workflow of booking a seat on a plane for our Chicken-Wings Airline. SAP HANA XS Advanced also supports the creation of Java modules out of the box. Thus, application layer logic is written in the Java programming language. We'll reveal these concepts in Section 6.3 and show a practical example of maintaining crew information for our Chicken-Wings Airline. We'll introduce the capabilities of creating OData services with the Java runtime of SAP HANA XS Advanced to read, insert, update, and delete data from tables.

6.1 Tasks of the Application Layer

A key benefit of SAP HANA XS Advanced native SAP HANA applications is its tight integration with the SAP HANA database, enabling optimal application performance. No additional software or server component is required to develop native SAP HANA applications. All the necessary technologies and services are available directly within the SAP HANA XS Advanced runtime and can be used by developers in their applications. Nevertheless, as already highlighted in Chapter 4, it's also possible to deploy the SAP HANA XS Advanced platform separately from the SAP HANA database.

This functionality allows the application layer of SAP HANA XS Advanced to be scalable independently from the SAP HANA database while still benefiting from the optimal integration offered by the SAP HANA XS Advanced runtime with the SAP HANA database. One of the primary attributes of native SAP HANA XS Advanced applications is that server-side application objects are solely exposed via the HTTP using a microservices application programming interface (API). As highlighted in Chapter 4, a microservices-based architecture serves the purpose of being able to share services across applications efficiently and even enables the development of new applications constructed from these services. SAP HANA XS Advanced acts as application server, web server, and development platform. It's integrated into the SAP HANA platform and can be scaled independently from the SAP HANA database, enabling the design of highly efficient architectures.

The central concept of the programming model of SAP HANA XS Advanced applications is that those apps are created purely with server-side technologies. The server-side technologies are directly executed on the SAP HANA XS Advanced runtime and can leverage a broad set of functionalities and services that are optimized for applications that integrate with the SAP HANA database.

As described in Chapter 5, database development objects in SAP HANA are SQLScript procedures, calculation views, or table functions, just to name a few examples. Those database artifacts can be accessed by server-side SAP HANA XS Advanced technologies, such as Node.js, directly. Furthermore, the SAP HANA XS Advanced runtime provides a list of APIs and services that allow access to the SAP HANA database. Those APIs are available for the different runtime technologies of SAP HANA XS Advanced (e.g., Node.js and Java).

The following primary concepts apply when developing the application layer of an SAP HANA XS Advanced application:

- All development artifacts are compiled and executed within a specific runtime container of the application that SAP HANA XS Advanced generates. This runtime container can be a Node.js runtime or Java runtime, for example.
- A Git repository stores the source code of application layer artifacts outside of the SAP HANA XS Advanced runtime and manages the versions of the source code as well.
- Server-side technologies, such as Node.js or Java, implement the application logic.
- The rendering of a UI (e.g., web browser or mobile app) happens solely on the client-side.

Although all server-side parts of an SAP HANA XS Advanced application are deployed and executed on the SAP HANA XS Advanced runtime, an application consists of the following three layers:

- **Database layer**
  Records of the database layer are accessed via the SQL interface. Furthermore, the logic of SAP HANA XS Advanced applications is deployed on the database layer to ensure optimal performance when processing large amounts of data.
- **Application layer**
  The control flow logic of an SAP HANA XS Advanced application gets defined via server-side JavaScript via the Node.js runtime or the Java runtime. Thus, SAP HANA XS Advanced acts as a lightweight application server. HTTP is used to consume resources of an SAP HANA XS Advanced application. Specific APIs are available that allow accessing SAP HANA database objects and exposing them via interfaces such as OData.
- **Presentation layer**
  Typically, the presentation layer of an SAP HANA XS Advanced application gets developed with the HTML5 framework SAPUI5. On the client-side, a web browser or mobile application renders the UI.

The programming model of an SAP HANA XS Advanced application allows the optimal combination of the database layer and application layer of an application. Both layers support powerful integration options while remaining independently scalable and deployable. This programming model facilitates an optimal architecture and uses all advantages of the SAP HANA in-memory database technology. Figure 6.1 summarizes the layers of an SAP HANA XS Advanced application.

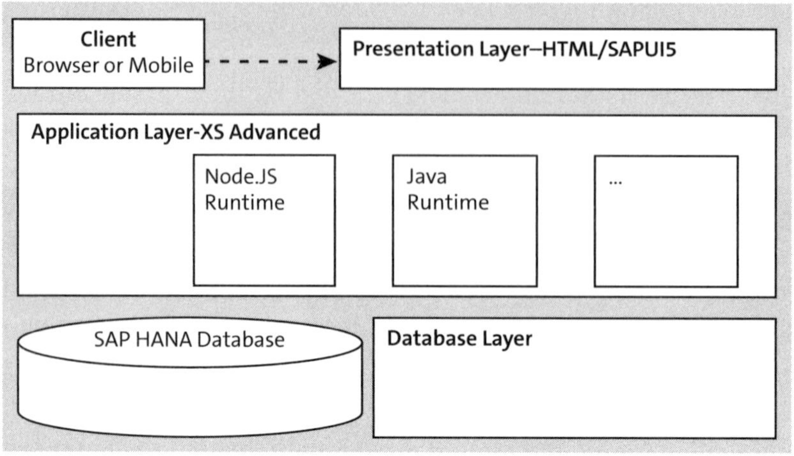

Figure 6.1 Layers of an SAP HANA XS Advanced Application

6.2 Node.js as Application Layer

Node.js is one of the available programming languages to control the flow of data between the frontend and the SAP HANA database. It focuses on the ability to run scalable network applications that are written in JavaScript. You can download the latest version to run it on your own machine and find the documentation at *http://nodejs.org*. In most cases, Google's V8 JavaScript engine is used to execute the code, as in the Google Chrome web browser, with one important difference: it's not running in a client but in a server environment.

In a client-side environment, for example, a web browser running the SAPUI5 interface we'll build later, JavaScript is primarily used to manipulate the displayed web page, to interact with the user through UI controls, and to send requests to a backend system. In the server-side environment, the main goal is to listen to incoming client requests and react to them after doing some processing, such as evaluating the request payload and reading information from the database accordingly.

In the next sections, we'll give you the tools to start coding your Node.js application layer. First we're going to create a Node.js module with SAP Web IDE for SAP HANA and dive into the different files of the module and their functions. After that, we'll take a closer look at how to create reusable node modules and which modules SAP delivers together with the platform. Furthermore, we discuss the asynchronous programming model and how to manage it using promises and the Async library.

In addition, a very important subject that we cover for application development is how to expose data to a consuming frontend and in which way the database can be accessed to retrieve data from it. The Node.js discussion is then closed by examining how to create unit tests for the developed code.

6.2.1 Node.js Module

To give you an idea what this looks like, let's create the node module of our multi-target application (MTA) before we go into more detail:

1. From the context menu of the project, select **New • Node.js Module**, and follow the creation wizard, as shown in Figure 6.2.
2. Provide a **Module Name**. We'll use "js" for the example backend services. Especially for the Node.js module, we recommend using only lowercase letters to be in line with the node package manager (npm) guidelines for node packages.
3. For the **Module settings** in the subsequent step, provide a **Version** number, a **Description**, and the name of the **Main JS file**.
4. Finally, confirm the module creation.

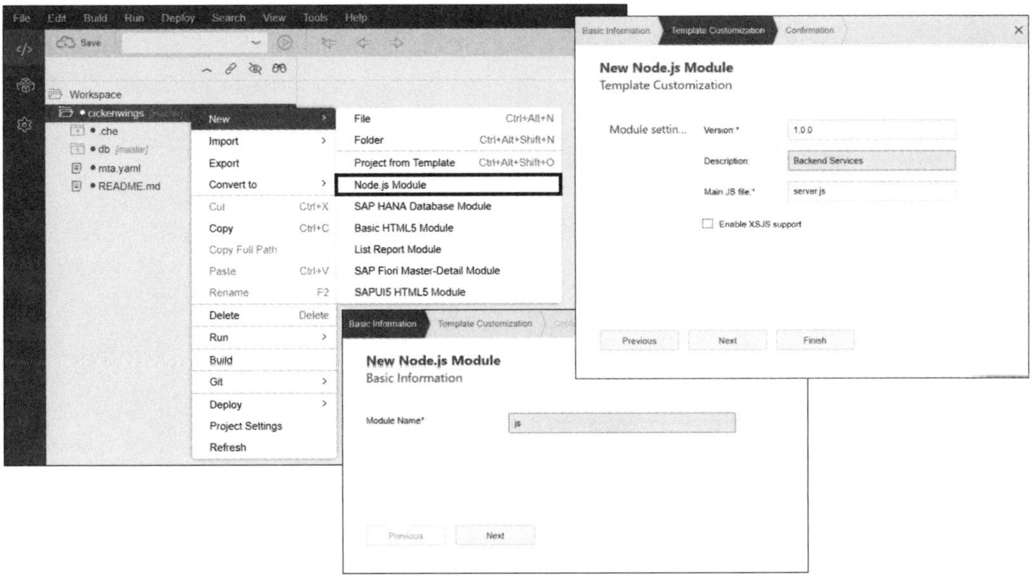

Figure 6.2 Node.js MTA Module Creation

After the module is created, click on the module folder (*js*, in this case), and click the **Run** button in the toolbar. At the bottom of the screen, the Run Console will open, showing you the progress of the build and start processes. Once finished successfully, you'll find the URL that points to the node module in the run console header, as shown in Figure 6.3.

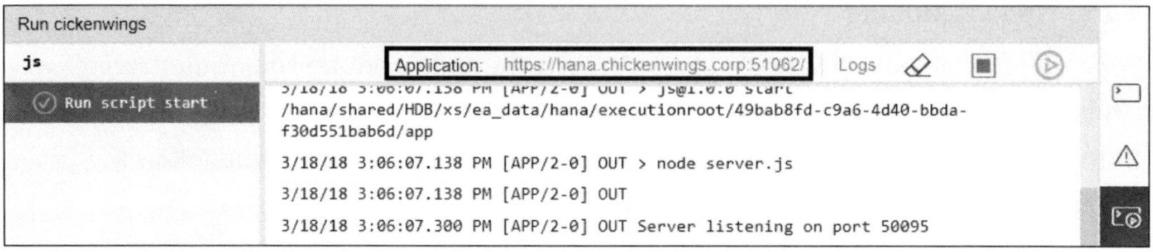

Figure 6.3 SAP Web IDE for SAP HANA Run Console

You can navigate directly to the node module, which will open in a new browser window where you should see the world-famous sentence, "Hello World." In our example, we actually want that to be "Hello Chicks!", so let's look at the created files shown in Figure 6.4 and where we can change that standard sentence.

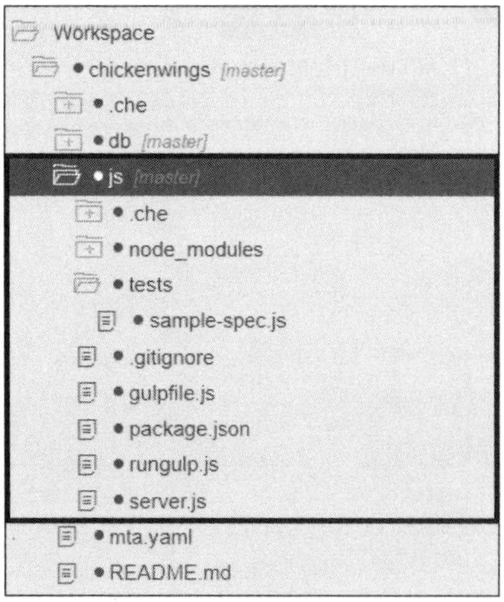

Figure 6.4 Node.js Module Package Structure

The entry point to see what's going on in a node package is the *application package descriptor* file: *package.json*, as shown in Listing 6.1.

```
{
  "name": "js",
  "version": "1.0.0"
  "description": "Backend Services",
  "dependencies": {},
  "devDependencies": {
    "gulp": "3.9.1",
    [...]
  },
  "main": "server.js",},
  "engines": {
    "node": "8.x"
  },
  "scripts": {
    "start": "node server.js",
    "test": "node ./node_modules/gulp/bin/gulp test",
    "test-coverage": "node ./node_modules/gulp/bin/gulp test-coverage"
}
```

Listing 6.1 Application Package Descriptor: package.json

The most important fields are actually `name` and `version`; without them, the node module wouldn't be able to build. Other applications can add a dependency to the node module via its name and the specified version number. The name can be prefixed with a namespace as is the case for the @sap modules. And, of course, the **Description** is where you're supposed to put something meaningful.

The *package.json* file also contains the dependencies of our module in the `dependencies` section, which is currently empty. Here we define the node modules our application uses together with the needed version. There is also a `devDependencies` section that works equivalent to the `dependencies` section, with the only difference that the declared dependencies will only be needed when running in the development environment. In our example, you can find the `gulp` package, which is used to run our unit tests. The declared node modules are downloaded during the build process from the npm repository and placed in the *node_modules* folder. You'll learn more about node modules and versioning later in Section 6.2.2.

In the `engines` section, you specify on which version of the node our module is meant to run. For SAP HANA XS Advanced, it's important that an available runtime version is used here. The available versions can be looked up using the XS command-line interface (CLI) command `xs runtimes`, which returns all installed runtimes on the connected server.

The property `main` points to the modules main file relative to the root folder. When the module is required, this file's export objects will be returned. This is especially important if you plan to publish your node module to an npm registry.

The `scripts` section of the *package.json* file is very important because it contains the `start` script, which is executed when the node module is executed. In the preceding example, you can see that when running the `js` module, the *server.js* file is executed because it was specified during the module creation.

Besides the `start` script, it contains the `test` and `test-coverage` scripts, which run the module's unit tests and collect the test coverage, respectively. When started, the tests in the *tests* subfolder are executed, and the results are shown in the SAP Web IDE.

More aboutpackage.json

For more information about *package.json*, consult the specifications at *https://docs.npmjs.com/files/package.json*.

Connected to the test infrastructure, you can see the *gulpfile.js* and *rungulp.js* files. They basically contain the configuration for the unit test execution and code coverage collection. In Section 6.2.7, you'll learn how to make use of that in detail and how to run the tests.

Finally, the *server.js* file is started as we discovered in the *package.json* file. The example in Listing 6.2 is what you find after the creation of a plain node module with SAP Web IDE.

```
/*eslint no-console: 0*/
"use strict";

var http = require("http");
var port = process.env.PORT || 3000;

http.createServer(function (req, res) {
  res.writeHead(200, {"Content-Type": "text/plain"});
  res.end("Hello World\n");
```

```
}).listen(port);

console.log("Server listening on port %d", port);
```

Listing 6.2 server.js File Generated by the Node.js Module Wizard

What happens is that we first import the `http` module (more about node modules in just a second) using the `require` function.

Next, we need to look into the node application's environment variables to retrieve the port number that the application has been bound to. You remember that we discussed in Chapter 4 how every application pushed to the SAP HANA XS Advanced or Cloud Foundry environment is bound to a specific port that is available through the application's environment variables. This is also in line with the principles port binding and configuration of a 12-Factor App.

After that, we use the HTTP module's `createServer` method, passing a function that is invoked every time a request is sent to the created HTTP server. Inside, we simply respond (`res`) to every incoming request (`req`) with a happy "Hello Chicks!".

Finally, we invoke the `listen` function of the created server instance to tell it on which port to listen for the incoming requests. Without doing that, the execution of the *server.js* file would simply terminate without a chance for us to invoke a request to it.

You'll see in Section 6.2.3 how the requests are handled technically by the node server.

6.2.2 Modules and the Node Package Manager Repository

In Listing 6.2, we used a node core module (`http`) to respond to incoming HTTP requests. One of the strengths of Node.js is the organization of reusable libraries as "modules." Let's first look at how node modules are created and organized in general before introducing some of the SAP-delivered node modules.

Node.js Modules and Node Package Manager Repository Overview

When developing bigger applications, it's a good practice to modularize code that can be reused in different parts of the application or even in other applications.

Depending on the complexity of the module and your own preference, you can either create a single, file-based module or a more extensive folder-based module.

While a file-based module is basically a *.js* file containing the code, a folder-based module might need a bit more organization: you either create a *package.json* file inside the folder that defines the main module containing your code or use the file named *index.js*, which is loaded by default when the *package.json* file is missing.

The *package.json* file would look like Listing 6.3.

```
{
  "name": "flight-recorder",
  "main": "./flight-recorder.js"
}
```

Listing 6.3 The Module's package.json File

In both cases, the module code is stored in a *.js* file. By default, the content of that module is private and can't be accessed from the outside unless explicitly allowed. To make a function or attribute of the module public, it needs to be added to the `module.exports` object of the module, which is available by default. Let's see what an example module (Listing 6.4) looks like and how it's used (Listing 6.5).

```
module.exports.isAlive = true;
module.exports.log = function(message) {
  console.log(`i FlightRecorder ${message}`);
};
[...]
```

Listing 6.4 Module flight-recordert.js

```
const flightRecorder = require("./flight-recorder");
if (flightRecorder.isAlive) {
  flightRecorder.log("Hurray, still alive!");
}
```

Listing 6.5 Usage Example of the flight-recorder Module

Additionally, a common technique is to replace the default `module.exports` object with a function that creates a clear, primary API for the module. Additional functions, attributes, and so on can be added as shown in Listing 6.4 to provide, for example, a more sophisticated API to the module like Listing 6.6.

```
module.exports = function(message) {
  console.log(`i FlightRecorder ${message}`);
};
```

```
module.exports.error = function(message) {
  console.error(`e FlightRecorder ${message}`);
};
```

Listing 6.6 flight-recorder.js

Using the FlightRecorder module would look like Listing 6.7.


```
const flightRecorder = require("./flight-recorder");
flightRecorder("Reached cruising altitude");
flightRecorder.error("No internet connection available");
```

Listing 6.7 Usage Example of the Changed flight-recorder.js

So, in the first *flight-rectoder.js* module example, we added the attribute isAlive and the function log() to the exports object, which is returned when the module is loaded using the require function and therefore is public, that is, available to be used. In the second example, require returns the anonymous function we've exported, containing also the added error function.

The require function itself expects the path to the module you would like to load and the module name without the file extension. Node.js will automatically search for a file ending with *.js*, *.json*, or *.node* for a file-based module or for a folder-based module with the same name. You can provide an absolute path, starting from the server's root folder, which begins with "/". For a local module, it makes more sense to provide a relative path, starting with "./" for the directory of the requiring code or "../" to start at the parent directory.

Most times, you'll actually see that only the module name is passed, without one of the prefixes just mentioned. In that case, Node.js will first search among the core modules, such as for the http module in the earlier Hello World! example. If nothing is found there, the search continues in the *node_modules* folder of the application, which is the standard directory *npm*. The npm installs modules that come from a module repository.

If we think back to Chapter 4, Section 4.2.1, one of the 12-Factor App principles is to declare the dependencies of our module. For the node application, this happens in the *package.json* file, which is located in the root folder and looks similar to Listing 6.8.

```
{
  "dependencies": {
    "@sap/hdbext": "4.7.2",
    "@sap/xsenv": "^1.2.9",
```

```
    [...]
  },
  "devDependencies": {
    "gulp": "~3.9.1",
    [...]
  }
  [...]
}
```

Listing 6.8 Dependencies in the package.json File

During the build process of the node module, the npm of the node buildpack will download and install the modules with the specified version. As you can see in Listing 6.8, the version isn't necessarily fixed. The npm uses semantic versioning to allow you to specify the allowed version of the packages to be used.

The version number is divided into three parts—the major version, the minor version, and the patch version—as follows:

```
<major_version>.<minor_version>.<patch_version>
```

While a fixed version number such as 4.7.2 or =4.7.2 or a starting point such as > 1.0.0 or <= 2.3.1 are quite self-explanatory, in many modules, you can see notations like ^ or ~, which are explained in Table 6.1.

Semantic Version	Explanation
1.2.3 / =1.2.3	Exact version; default if nothing is specified
<1.2.3	Less than 1.2.3
<=1.2.3	Less than or equal to 1.2.3
>1.2.3	Greater than 1.2.3
>=1.2.3	Greater than or equal to 1.2.3
>1.2.3 <=2.3.4	Range: Greater than and less than or equal to
1.2.3 || >=2.3.4 <3.0.0	Exactly 1.2.3 or (greater than or equal to and less than)
1.X / 1.x / 1.*	Any minor version of 1 (e.g., 1.2.3 or 1.9)
~1.2.3	Allows patch level changes: >=1.2.3 <1.3.0

Table 6.1 Semantic Versioning Syntax Overview

Semantic Version	Explanation
`~1.2`	Allows patch level changes; equivalent to 1.2.x
`~1`	Allows minor version changes: >=1.0.0 <2.0.0; equivalent to 1.x
`^1.2.3`	The most left nonzero digit remains unchanged: >=1.2.3 <2.0.0
`^0.0.3`	Allows only 0.0.3
`latest`	Refers to the newest available version

Table 6.1 Semantic Versioning Syntax Overview (Cont.)

The notations in Table 6.1 are just the tip of the iceberg of what is possible using semantic versioning. For more details, check out the official documentation at *https://docs.npmjs.com/misc/semver.*

A tool that can help you verify version expressions, the npm semver calculator, can be found at *https://semver.npmjs.com/.*

Dependency Hell

Bear in mind that modules can themselves contain dependencies that are downloaded into the module's own subfolder structure. On the one hand, this helps to resolve the dependency hell by allowing a specific module to be installed in different versions if required by different modules without blocking each other. On the other hand, you can easily end up having hundreds of modules in your build application, so we highly recommend keeping an eye on the dependencies because they can make your application suddenly huge in terms of size and complex to audit.

If you created the node module as described earlier, open the *node_modules* folder and be blown away by the number of packages already downloaded!

As previously mentioned, the npm will download the required packages. Let's see where they are coming from.

First, with the installation of SAP Web IDE for SAP HANA in your SAP HANA XS Advanced environment, there comes a local npm repository that works as a proxy for caching requests and for providing special SAP node modules. When we look at the installed applications in the SAP space of our environment, we can see the **di-local-npm-registry**, as shown in Figure 6.5.

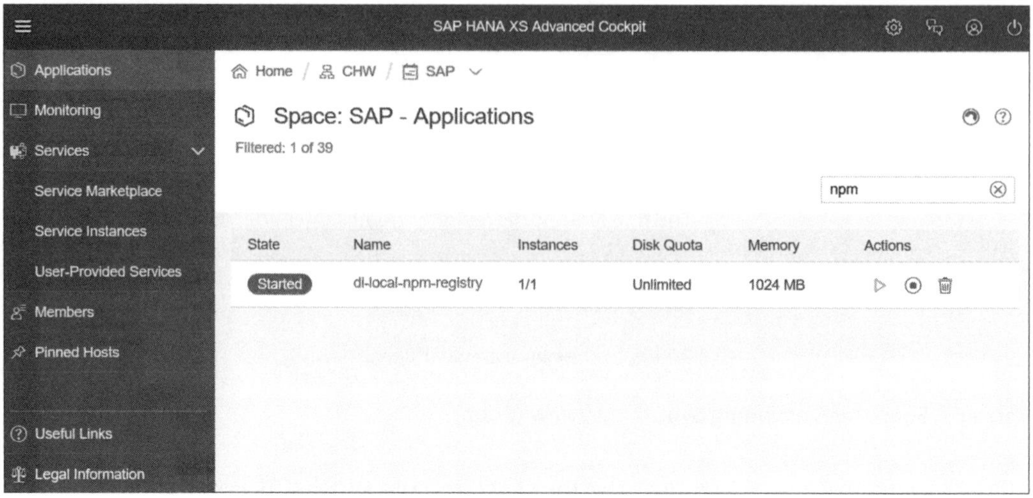

Figure 6.5 Local npm Registry in the SAP Space

You can actually access the internal npm repository, which also acts as a cache for public modules, to see the available modules. If you know the name of a module, you can access the information as follows:

https://<di-local-npm-registry>/<package_name>

To access the `@sap/hdbext` module, it would look like this:

https://hana.chickenwings.corp:51033/@sap%2Fhdbext

If the node package that has to be pulled into your application isn't found in the local repository, there are two other possibilities for the npm to retrieve the packages from an upstream repository:

- By default, the SAP upstream repository is configured for SAP Web IDE for SAP HANA, which is reached by the npm at *https://npm.sap.com*. From there, the SAP node packages and their dependencies are distributed.
- The second option is to configure a custom npm repository of your choice, which can, for example, be done during the installation of SAP Web IDE for SAP HANA. This might either be a repository of your organization or a public one such as *www.npmjs.com/*, where the npm will finally try to search for the modules.

If you want to install the SAP-distributed packages locally, you need to add the following entry in your *.npmrc* file:

```
@sap:registry=https://npm.sap.com
```

By doing so, the SAP-delivered Node.js modules, which are all prefixed with @sap, are fetched.

SAP-Delivered Node.js Modules

To make our developer life easier, SAP provides a bunch of Node.js libraries distributed either via the SAP npm repository or via a download from the SAP Service Marketplace.

We'll now introduce a selection of the most commonly used modules, as listed in Table 6.2. The full list of modules, which is constantly growing, can be found in the SAP HANA Developer Guide. They can all be obtained from the SAP npm repository.

Module Name	Function
@sap/approuter	Application router
@sap/hana-client	SAP HANA database driver
@sap/hdbext	SAP HANA database client with convenience functions
@sap/hdi-deploy	SAP HANA Deployment Infrastructure (HDI), Deploy App
@sap/textanalysis	SAP HANA Text Analysis API
@sap/textbundle	Text Internationalization helper
@sap/xsenv	Application environment variables and services
@sap/xsjs	SAP HANA XS Compatibility Layer
@sap/xssec	SAP HANA XS Advanced Container Security API

Table 6.2 SAP-Delivered Node.js Modules

Application Router: @sap/approuter

As explained in Chapter 4, the entry point for business applications is a dedicated application router that can be configured by the application developer. The main tasks, besides the role as the application's single entry point, are to authenticate users before they can access a route, to deliver static content such as images and HTML pages, and to act as a proxy for requests to other services.

You'll learn more about the configuration of the application router in Chapter 7.

SAP HANA Database Client: @sap/hana-client

The hana-client is the SAP HANA database client for Node.js, which communicates directly with the native SAP HANA libraries. It provides the necessary functions to manage database connections and to execute queries, as shown in Listing 6.9.

```
const hana = require("@sap/hana-client");
const hanaConfig = {
  host: "hana.chickenwings.corp",
  port: 30015,
  uid: "HARALD",
  pwd: "easter"
};

const connection = hana.createConnection();

connection.connect(hanaConfig, (connectionError) => {
  if (connectionError) {
    return console.error(connectionError);
  }
  connection.exec("SELECT * FROM DUMMY", (queryError, result) => {
    if (queryError) {
      return console.error(queryError);
    }
    console.log(`Dummy value: ${result[0].DUMMY}`);
    connection.disconnect();
  });
});
```

Listing 6.9 Connect to the Database Using @sap/hana-client

In principle, you can use only the hana-client in your Node.js application, but we recommend having a look at the hdbext module, which provides some neat convenience functions in addition.

Database Client Convenience Functions: @sap/hdbext

The hdbext SAP HANA database client for Node.js is maybe the most important node module when you develop a Node.js application that runs on the SAP HANA platform. It extends the functionality of the publicly available hdb module with, for example, a middleware for the Node.js Express module and the possibility to load stored procedures directly into your JavaScript code. For the future, it's planned to replace the usage of the hdb module with the hana-client library.

Because Section 6.2.6 is dedicated to explaining how to access the SAP HANA database from a Node.js application, we won't go into details here.

SAP HANA Deployment Infrastructure Deployer: @sap/hdi-deploy

In Chapter 4, we briefly introduced the functions of the HDI Deployer application when we talked about the SAP HANA services and how an HDI container is populated with the database design-time artifacts. In Chapter 5, you also learned how to create database artifacts using the `HDB` module of an MTA.

By looking at that created HDB module, you notice artifacts, such as the *package.json* file shown in Listing 6.10, that are usually used for Node.js modules. Here you also find the dependency to the `@sap/hdi-deploy` module and the `start` command, which is executed after the module is deployed:

```
{
  "name": "deploy",
  "dependencies": {
    "@sap/hdi-deploy": "3.3.0"
  },
  "scripts": {
    "start": "node node_modules/@sap/hdi-deploy/deploy.js"
  }
}
```

Listing 6.10 package.json File with Application Router Start Command

The Deploy app is expecting the SAP HANA design-time artifacts in the *src* subfolder of the module. For example, an *.hdbtable* file is used to create a database table, or an *.hdbcalculationview* file is used for a modeled calculation view. The *cfg* folder, instead, can contain optional configuration files for the Deploy app, such as *.hdbgrants* files, which are used to break out of the created container. For more details, see Chapter 5.

SAP HANA-Based Text Analysis: @sap/textanalysis

The `@sap/textanalysis` library provides an interface to the SAP HANA text analysis function. It's basically a convenience function to call the `TA_ANALYZE` stored procedure to process unstructured data. It can be used to do linguistic analysis on free text such as extracting features or performing sentiment analysis. We found it especially useful for projects in the chatbot area, where free user input needs to be evaluated.

The module only exposes the `analyze()` function, with the following signature:

```
analyze(values, client, onComplete)
```

The `values` object will be mapped to the stored procedure's input parameters. You can provide any of the parameters using the JSON format as in Listing 6.11.

```
let values = {
DOCUMENT_BINARY: null,
DOCUMENT_TEXT: "An egg a day keeps the doctor away!",
LANGUAGE_CODE: "EN",
MIME_TYPE: null,
TOKEN_SEPARATORS: null,
LANGUAGE_DETECTION: null,
CONFIGURATION_SCHEMA_NAME: null,
CONFIGURATION: "LINGANALYSIS_FULL",
RETURN_PLAINTEXT: 0
};
```

Listing 6.11 Values Passed to the Text Analysis Procedure

Table 6.3 provides you an overview of the possible parameters.

Parameter Name	Parameter Use
DOCUMENT_BINARY	A binary document, that is, Word, PDF, and so on.
DOCUMENT_TEXT	Document as plain text, XML, or HTML.
LANGUAGE_CODE	Fixes the language code of the document if you don't want to use the language detection feature; otherwise, leave empty and set the LANGUAGE_DETECTION parameter.
MIME_TYPE	Fixes the mime type for DOCUMENT_TEXT, that is, text/plain, text/xml, or text/html. If empty, automatic detection is used. Binary documents are always detected automatically.
TOKEN_SEPARATORS	List of characters that separate tokens in the document. If empty, the default set is used.
LANGUAGE_DETECTION	A list of language codes to be used for detection. If empty, the LANGUAGE_CODE field must be passed.
CONFIGURATION_SCHEMA_NAME	Schema name for the location of the configuration; blank if standard configuration.

Table 6.3 Parameters for the TA_ANALYZE Procedure

Parameter Name	Parameter Use
CONFIGURATION	Name of the configuration, for example, EXTRACTION_CORE or EXTRACTION_CORE_VOICEOFCUSTOMER, to be loaded; default is LINGANALYSIS_FULL.
RETURN_PLAINTEXT	If set to 1, the document's plain text is returned in the PLAINTEXT return parameter.

Table 6.3 Parameters for the TA_ANALYZE Procedure (Cont.)

After preparing the values, you need to create a connection to the database, as the client object is used to send the text analysis request to the database. Then you can pass the parameter's object and the client to the analyze function, providing a callback method for the results with the following structure:

```
done(err, parameters, rows)
```

Per the callback convention in Node.js, the first parameter is filled in case of errors. The parameters argument will contain the procedure's output parameter PLAINTEXT if you require it by setting the parameter RETURN_PLAINTEXT to 1.

The rows parameter contains the result of the text analysis, which includes information such as the extracted token, its stem, and its occurrence in the text.

A complete example would look like Listing 6.12.

```
const hdbext = require("@sap/hdbext");
const textAnalysis = require("@sap/textanalysis");

const hanaConfig = {
    host: "hana.chickenwings.corp",
    port: 30015,
    user: "HARALD",
    password: "easter"
};

const values = {
    DOCUMENT_BINARY: null,
    DOCUMENT_TEXT: "The flight was good, thank you very much for all the ...
chicken!",
```

```
    LANGUAGE_CODE: "EN",
    MIME_TYPE: null,
    TOKEN_SEPARATORS: null,
    LANGUAGE_DETECTION: null,
    CONFIGURATION_SCHEMA_NAME: null,
    CONFIGURATION: "EXTRACTION_CORE_VOICEOFCUSTOMER",
    RETURN_PLAINTEXT: 0
};

hdbext.createConnection(hanaConfig, (error, client) => {
    if (error){
        return console.error("Error connection to DB", error);
    }
    textAnalysis.analyze(values, client, (error, parameters, rows) => {
        if (error){
            return console.error("Error executing TextAnalysis", error);
        }
        console.log(rows);
    });
});
```

Listing 6.12 Text Analysis Example

Note

If you want more information about the SAP HANA text analysis capabilities, check out the SAP HANA Text Analysis Developer Guide at *http://help.sap.com/hana* and the SAP HANA Academy tutorials or the Text Analysis course on OpenSAP. You can find the links in Appendix B.

Internationalization: @sap/textbundle

Text bundles are originally a SAPUI5 concept to make it easy to provide a frontend in different languages. For each language you want to support, a UTF-8 formatted *.properties* file is created following this naming convention:

```
<Prefix>_<Languagecode>[_<Countrycode>].properties
```

To give a practical example, a *.properties* file could contain the following:

```
i18n.properties => original texts
i18n_en.properties => generic english
i18n_de_DE.properties => german for Germany
i18n_de_AT.properties => german for Austria
```

Note

Note that you need to provide one file without a language and country code for the library to work.

The content of a text bundle is a simple key value format and looks like the following for *i18n.properties*:

```
title=Flight Booking
options=You have {0} menu options for flight {1}.
```

For *i18n_de_DE.properties*, it looks like this:

```
title=Flug Buchen
options=Sie haben {0} Menüoptionen für Flug {1}.
```

After you've created the language files, the single text values can be retrieved using the `.getText(<textKey>[, <placeholders>])` method of the `textbundle` module. The function expects the text key as first parameter and eventual placeholder values in an array as second parameter, as shown in Listing 6.13.

```
const path = require("path");
const { TextBundle } = require("@sap/textbundle");

let bundle = new TextBundle(path.resolve(__dirname, "./i18n/i18n"), "en");
console.log(bundle.getText("title"));
console.log(bundle.getText("options", [5, "ChickenWings 0815"]));
bundle = new TextBundle(path.resolve(__dirname, "./i18n/i18n"), "de_DE");
console.log(bundle.getText("title"));
console.log(bundle.getText("options", [5, "ChickenWings 0815"]));
```

Listing 6.13 Text Bundle Usage

As a result, you'll see the following text in the console:

Flight Booking
You have 5 menu options for flight ChickenWings 0815.
Flug Buchen
Sie haben 5 Menüoptionen für Flug ChickenWings 0815.

Application Environment Variables: @sap/xsenv

The xsenv module provides an easy way to access and manage the application's environment variables. It's most used to retrieve the services that have been bound to the application to connect to them. The service binding for an application is either done manually using the xs bind-service command or automatically when you define the binding in the *mta.yaml* file of your MTA. (For more information, see Chapter 4, Section 4.3.1.)

Services can be retrieved using the getServices(<service query>) function, which expects a *service query* object as parameter and returns the matching services.

The service query object itself contains one or more keys under which the requested service is returned with a corresponding search criterion. The search criterion can either be a single string to match the service name, an object to match more than one service attribute, or a function, which returns true if a service matches. Let's look at Listing 6.14.

```
const xsenv = require("@sap/xsenv");

const services = xsenv.getServices({
    query1: "cickenwings-hdi-container",
    query2: {
        name: " cickenwings-hdi-container"
    },
    query3: {
        name: " cickenwings-hdi-container",
        label: "hana",
        tag: "hana",
        plan: "hdi-shared"
    },
    query4: (service) => {
        return service.credentials.host === "hana.chickenwins.corp";
    }
});

console.log(`Query 1 Host: ${services.query1.host}`);
```

```
console.log(`Query 2 Port: ${services.query2.port}`);
console.log(`Query 3 User: ${services.query3.user}`);
console.log(`Query 4 Password: ${services.query4.password}`);
```

Listing 6.14 Example of Retrieving Services from the Application Environment

As you may have noticed, we include four service queries in the `getServices` call that target the same HDI container service to show you the different options you have to realize a query.

Query 1 and query 2 are actually the same, meaning that if you only provide a string as query, it searches for an exact match on the service instance name as in query 2.

> **Note**
>
> During development with SAP Web IDE for SAP HANA, it's difficult to match your service by name because they are prefixed with a developer-specific workspace identifier to allow multiple deployments of the same application.

Query 3 adds all attributes you can include in a query object, that is, `name`, `label`, `tag`, and `plan`. The service label corresponds to the service name you can see when using the `xs marketplace` command. `name`, `plan`, and `tag`, instead, are related to the service instance and can be looked up by using the `xs service <serviceName>` command for a specific service you want to search for.

Query 4 finally uses a function to iterate over all services that are bound to the application. The function should return `true` if its logic detects a matching service. The advantage here is that you can create more complex queries, and, more importantly, you can access all attributes of a service. In the example given in Listing 6.14, we search for an SAP HANA connection to a specific host.

The `getServices()` call will return the service instance credentials using the code in Listing 6.15.

```
{
    "hana1": {
        "schema": "CHICKENWINGS",
        "hdi_password":"secret",
        "password": "supersecret",
        "tenant_name": "HDB",
        "driver": "com.sap.db.jdbc.Driver",
        "port": "30015",
```

```
        "host": "hana.chickenwings.corp",
        "db_hosts": [{
            "port": 30015,
            "host": " hana.chickenwings.corp "
        }],
        "hdi_user": "SBSS_...",
        "user": "SBSS_...",
        "url": "jdbc:sap://hana.chickenwings.corp:30015…"
    },
    "<key2>": …
}
```

Listing 6.15 Example Result of a Service Query

SAP HANA XS Compatibility Layer: @sap/xsjs

If you've already done some native SAP HANA development with the SAP HANA extended application services, classic model (SAP HANA XS), you know, for example, how convenient it is to expose database tables or calculation views as an OData service with minimal effort.

The good news is that we can include the `xsjs` node module and use the compatibility layer to still use `xsodata` and `xsjs` artifacts in a node module of our application.

The easiest way to create a node module with the XSJS compatibility layer is to use the wizard in SAP Web IDE for SAP HANA, as follows:

1. From the context menu of the project, select **New • Node.js Module**.
2. Provide a **Module Name**. We'll use "xsjs" for the simple OData backend services.
3. In **Module settings**, make sure you select the **Enable XSJS Support** checkbox.
4. Finally, confirm the module creation.

Let's look at the *server.js* file in Listing 6.16 and see what the differences are to a plain Node.js module.

```
var xsjs  = require("@sap/xsjs");
var xsenv = require("@sap/xsenv");
var port  = process.env.PORT || 3000;

var options = {
    anonymous : true, // remove to authenticate calls
    redirectUrl : "/index.xsjs"
};
```

```
// configure HANA
try {
    options = Object.assign(options, xsenv.getServices({ hana: {tag: "hana"} }));
} catch (err) {
    console.log("[WARN]", err.message);
}

// configure UAA
try {
    options = Object.assign(options, xsenv.getServices({ uaa: {tag: "xsuaa"} }));
} catch (err) {
    console.log("[WARN]", err.message);
}

// start server
xsjs(options).listen(port);

console.log("Server listening on port %d", port);
```

Listing 6.16 server.js with XSJS Compatibility Layer Option Enabled

The example consists basically of three parts:

1. The `@sap/xsjs` and `@sap/xsenv` modules are imported, and the port to which the service should be bound is determined.
2. The configuration object for the `xsjs` application is set up, which includes the location of a default file (`redirectUrl`) and the possibility to access the `xsjs` server without authentication (`anonymous`). Additionally, the root folders can be defined, which contain the *xsjs* and *xsodata* files. Per default, the `xsjs` server expects the directory *lib* to contain those files, but you can use the parameter `rootDir` to set another one or `rootDirs` to pass an array with more than one directory.

   Besides the parameters, the `xsjs` module expects several services to be configured. In the example, the credentials for the `hana` service and the `xsuaa` service are retrieved using the `xsenv` module and added to the configuration object. In addition, the configuration object can contain the keys `mail` and `jobs`, which are filled with the service credentials for the mail server and the credentials of the xs-jobscheduler service, respectively.
3. The `xsjs` server is created and started to listen to the port which was defined before (`xsjs(options).listen(port)`).

Under the hood, the `xsjs` module is based on the `express` module, which is a framework to create node web applications and is used to provide the web server functionality. The `xsjs` server will then deliver the files that are placed in the directory defined earlier (in our case, *lib*), as shown in Figure 6.6.

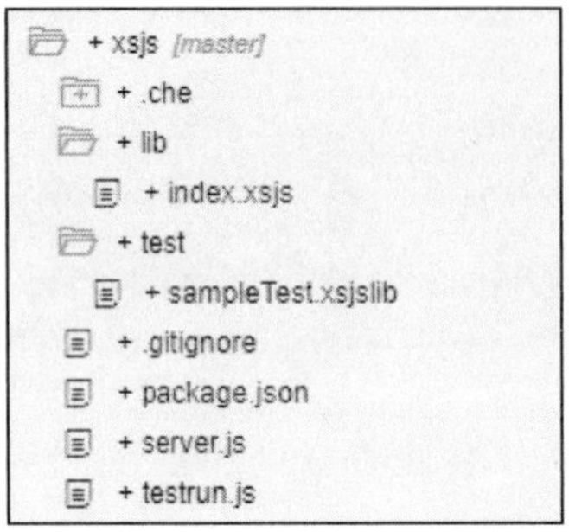

Figure 6.6 Structure of a Node Module with XSJS Support

So if you run the node module, the *index.xsjs* file is delivered automatically.

We'll take a more detailed look at how to create XSODATA services to expose data from the database in Section 6.2.5.

Container Security Application Programming Interface: @sap/xssec

The `xssec` library allows you to add authentication and authorization checks to a node module that are provided by the platform's User Account and Authentication (UAA) service. On one hand, it's possible to make sure that a user must log on before accessing the desired node resource (authentication), and, on the other hand you can check that the authenticated user has the necessary privileges for a specific resource (authorization). Listing 6.17 shows an example of how this can be achieved.

```
const http = require("http");
const xssec = require("@sap/xssec");
const xsenv = require("@sap/xsenv");

const services = xsenv.getServices({ uaa: "ChickenUAA" });
const port = process.env.PORT || 3000;

http.createServer((req, res) => {
    const authToken = req.headers.authorization;
    if (!authToken || !authToken.startsWith("Bearer")) {
        res.writeHead(403);
        res.end();
```

```
        return;
    }
    const securityToken = authToken.substr(7);
    xssec.createSecurityContext(securityToken, services.uaa, (error,
securityContext) => {
        if (error) {
            res.writeHead(403);
            res.end();
            return;
        }

        res.writeHead(200, { "Content-Type": "text/plain" });
        res.end(`Successfully authenticated as ${securityContext.userInfo.
logonName}`);

    });

}).listen(port);
```

Listing 6.17 Usage of the @sap/xssec Library

To use the container security API when receiving a request, we first need to extract the JSON Web Token (JWT) from the request header. The token is provided by the UAA service after a user is logged in to the platform, which usually happens through the application router. The application router then forwards the request together with the token to our node module where we can pass it to the `xssec` library to retrieve the related security information. It's important to pass the plain token to the `createSecurityContext()` function, so we need to remove the "`Bearer`" prefix from the header content.

After calling the `createSecurityContext()` method, we need to check if the authentication token could be successfully resolved to a security scope so we can tell if a user was authenticated by the system.

> **Note**
>
> Further authorization checks can be done with the `checkScope()` and `getAttribute()` methods. We'll discuss them further in Chapter 8.

An easier way to consume the container security API is by using a ready-made authentication strategy for `passport`, an Express authentication middleware. We'll take a closer look at the Express framework later. For the time being, just consider how the `JWTStrategy` provided by the `xssec` library is passed to `passport` and finally plugged in to the Express app. For every incoming request, the successful authentication will be automatically checked by the framework using the code in Listing 6.18.

```
const express = require("express");
const passport = require("passport");
const { JWTStrategy } = require("@sap/xssec");
const xsenv = require("@sap/xsenv");

const services = xsenv.getServices({ uaa: "ChickenUAA" });
const port = process.env.PORT || 3000;

const app = express();

passport.use(new JWTStrategy(services.uaa));

app.use(passport.initialize());
app.use(passport.authenticate("JWT", { session: false }));

app.get("/securityExpress/", (req, res) => {
    res.send(`Successfully authenticated as ${req.user.id}`);
});

app.listen(port, () => {
    console.log(`Expecting trouble at port ${port}`);
});
```

Listing 6.18 Container Security API Express Middleware

In Chapter 8, you'll learn more detail regarding how the SAP HANA XS Advanced security framework works and how it's used in the various application parts. In particular, we'll see how roles and scopes are defined to implement fine-grained access control.

6.2.3 Asynchronous Programming Model

Now that we've discussed the way modules work in Node.js and which SAP modules are available, let's dive a bit deeper into how Node.js works and how it implements the asynchronous programming model.

Let's first consider Listing 6.19, which is used to access the SAP HANA database in a *synchronous* way, using the XSJS compatibility layer.

```
try {
  const connection = $.hdb.getConnection();
  let result = connection.executeQuery("SELECT * FROM DUMMY");
  $.trace.info("Dummy value: " + result[0].DUMMY);
} catch(error) {
  $.trace.error(error);
}
```

Listing 6.19 Synchronous SAP HANA Database Access via the XSJS Compatibility Layer

In this context, synchronous means that the statements are executed one after the other, and we can rely on the fact that the processed statement is finished before the next one gets started, which may pick up results from the previous one.

In Listing 6.19, the creation of the database connection as well as the query execution happen synchronously, so we can be sure that the query result is available when we invoke the tracing function. We can also say that the `getConnection` and `executeQuery` method invocations are *blocking*, as they block the program execution until they come back with the desired result. This is exactly what you would expect and what you're used to from other programming languages, right?

Now, if we look at the execution timeline of Listing 6.19 in Figure 6.7, we can see that from a resource perspective, it's not very effective to block the execution each time we need to interact with another resource.

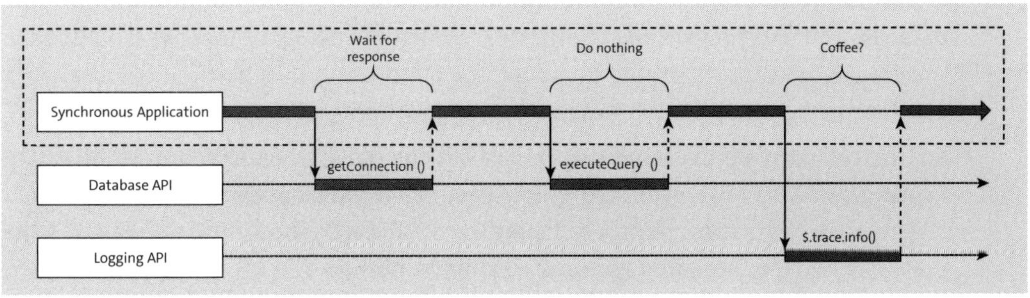

Figure 6.7 Synchronous, Blocking Execution

Particularly for applications that expect a high concurrent load, such as web applications, the synchronous processing blocks system resources that could be used for another request. A common approach to solve this problem is the creation of multiple threads to enable the system to handle more requests in parallel, for example, similar to writing a Java application.

Node.js, however, is single threaded and therefore approaches the concurrency problem with a mostly nonblocking programming model. Let's see how that works next.

In anticipation of Section 6.2.4, let's look at Listing 6.20, which can be used in Node.js to make a SELECT statement to the SAP HANA database using an asynchronous, nonblocking API.

```
const hdbext = require("@sap/hdbext");
const xsenv = require("@sap/xsenv");
const services = xsenv.getServices({ hanaConfig: { tag: "hana" } });
hdbext.createConnection(services.hanaConfig, (connectionError, client) => {
    if (connectionError) {
        return console.error(connectionError);
    }
    client.exec("SELECT * FROM DUMMY", (queryError, result) => {
        if (queryError) {
            return console.error(queryError);
        }
        console.log(`Dummy value: ${result[0].DUMMY}`);
    });
});
```

Listing 6.20 Asynchronous SAP HANA Database Access via hdbext

If we execute Listing 6.20, we first require the necessary node libraries to make the database call and prepare the connection configuration. After that, we only invoke the createConnection() method, passing the connection information and a callback function using the arrow (=>) notation, and our current execution terminates.

So, the program we executed didn't wait for the database connection to be established, much less for a result being retrieved from the database. We instead passed the instructions on how to proceed after the database connection was created to the createConnection() method within the callback method.

The callback method is executed by the createConnection() function, as soon as it has established a database connection or the connection creation failed for some reason. Depending on the result, either the error or the client parameter of the callback method is populated.

If the connection was successfully created, we use the returned client object to execute a query (client.exec(...)). Again, the execution of the createConnection() callback method doesn't wait for the database to respond but "delegates" that by passing another callback method with the instructions to output the response to the console (`console.log(…)`).

When looking at the execution timeline shown in Figure 6.8, you can see that the execution of the main application isn't blocked when making a call to an asynchronous resource. Instead of waiting for a response, other tasks could be done in the meantime.

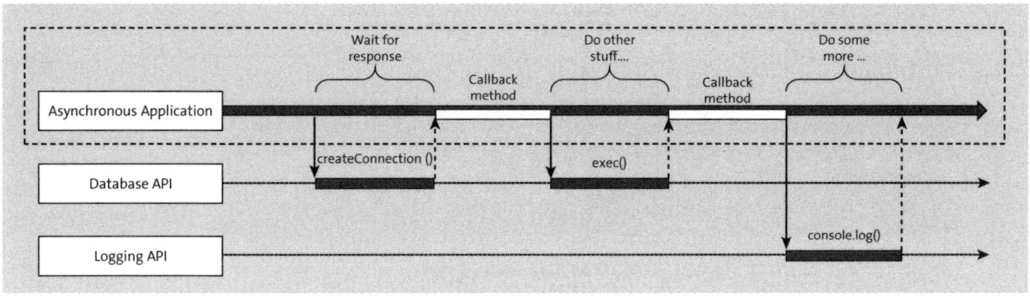

Figure 6.8 Asynchronous, Nonblocking Execution

To generalize the concept we just explained, let's see how the application execution works in the Node.js event loop, which is shown in Figure 6.9:

1. If an application requests an I/O operation such as the database call in the preceding example, a new event is pushed to the event queue together with the callback method. After finishing its operation, control is given to the event loop.
2. The event loop processes the requests in the event queue and starts the desired input/output (I/O) operation.
3. After the I/O operation is complete, the event loop will hand over control to the requesting application and execute the callback method that was passed with the request.
4. After the callback method is executed, control is returned again to the event loop, which can pick up the next request from the event queue.
5. If there are no events left in the queue, the node program terminates.

Loop

The callback logic executed in step 3 could itself request an I/O operation that results in another event in the queue and a callback method that could itself request an I/O operation.

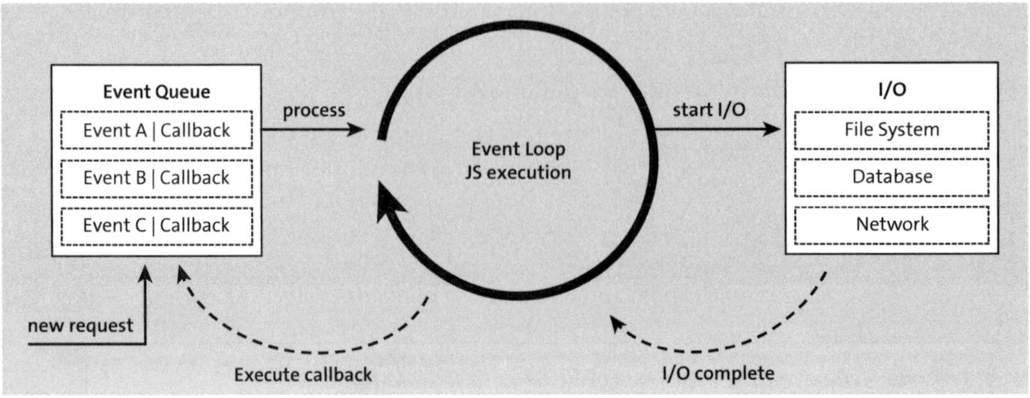

Figure 6.9 Node.js Event Loop

6.2.4 Managing Asynchronous Control Flow

Now that you understand how the asynchronous programming model of Node.js works, we'll look at some techniques to handle the asynchronous control flow.

As discussed before, in Node.js, we can call an asynchronous function to pass a callback method to be invoked after the work of the asynchronous function is done. As the calling program doesn't wait until the callback method is executed, we can actually start many of those asynchronous function calls, as shown in Figure 6.10, which will then run in parallel. Usually, you can't tell which one finishes first.

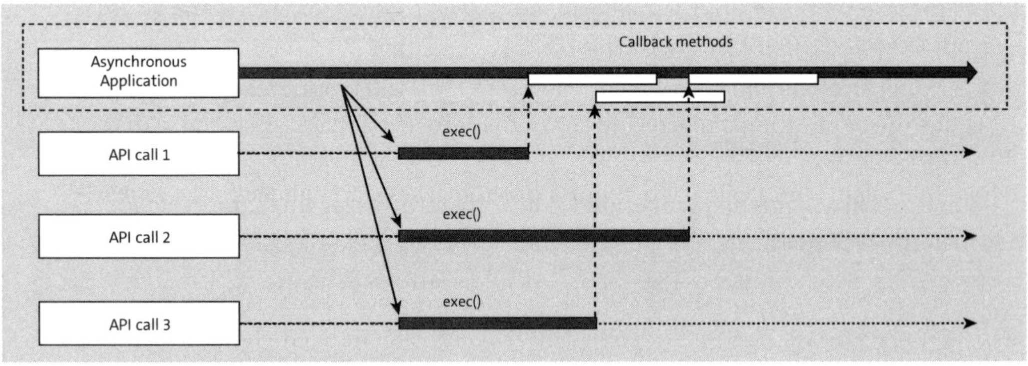

Figure 6.10 Parallel Processing of Asynchronous Functions

This behavior leads to the question of how to orchestrate the different function calls if they are independent, but the program logic can only proceed after all of them are processed, for example, if you do parallel database calls and want to send them in a single response.

Another scenario occurs when the asynchronous function calls are depending on each other, as shown in Figure 6.11, meaning that they can't be processed in parallel but need to be started sequentially.

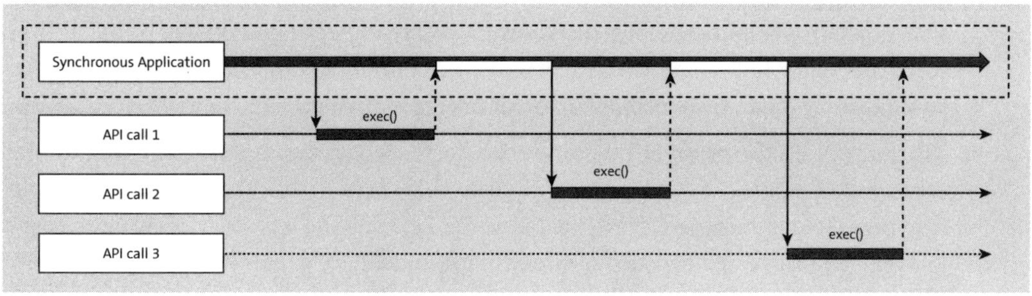

Figure 6.11 Parallel Processing of Asynchronous Functions

This can be achieved by starting the second function call in the callback method of the first one, and so on; however, the more sequential steps you have to process, the more complex and difficult to maintain it gets, as evidenced in Listing 6.21.

```
exec( (error, result) => {
  exec( (error, result) => {
    exec( (error, result) => {
      exec( (error, result) => {
        ...
      }
    }
  }
}
```

Listing 6.21 Callback Hierarchy

Let's see how we can handle these two cases in a more elegant way. We first look at promises, which can be found natively supported by Node.js, and then we'll consider the Async library, a node module that needs to be installed.

Promises

Promises have been introduced to the JavaScript (also known as ECMAScript) specification in version ES6 from 2015. Even though being a relatively new feature (considering that JavaScript was first standardized in 1997), it can be used in Node.js since version 0.12, and many of the available node modules added support for it, too. Even if a module doesn't yet support promises, such as the majority of the SAP-provided libraries at the time of writing this book, they can easily be "promisified" using a library such as bluebird. We'll see how to do this in the following section.

A promise is basically an object that is returned if you call an asynchronous function. This object represents the promised result you're expecting at a later point in time from the requested operation. The promise can either be *fulfilled* if the operation was successful, or it can be *rejected* if an error occurred instead.

After we obtain the promise object, we can decide what happens after the request has completed by passing a callback method to the `promise.then()` function. That function takes two parameters, `onFulfilled` and `onRejected`, so we can react to both cases. For the error case, you can also use the function `catch()`, which is executed in case of failure.

Now, let's first look how we can transform the example in Listing 6.22 of a synchronous execution using promises.

```
const hdbext = require("@sap/hdbext");
const xsenv = require("@sap/xsenv");
const services = xsenv.getServices({ hanaConfig: { tag: "hana" } });
hdbext.createConnection(services.hanaConfig, (connectionError, client) => {
  if (connectionError) {
    return console.error(connectionError);
  }
  client.exec("SELECT COUNT(LNAME) AS TROUBLEMAKERS FROM \"CVBooking\" WHERE
\"LNAME\" LIKE '%FOX%'", (queryError, result) => {
    if (queryError) {
      return console.error(queryError);
    }
    if (result[0].TROUBLEMAKERS > 0) {
      return console.log("Mr. HUNTER, please proceed immediately to gate 42!
Mr. HUNTER please.");
    } else {
      console.log("Boarding completed!");
    }
  });
});
```

Listing 6.22 Database Call without Using Promises

The first step in Listing 6.22 is to create a database connection (`hdbext.createConnection()`). After the connection is established, a SQL query can be sent (`client.exec()`) in the second step, and, as soon as the result arrives, it can be processed in the third step. Because the steps depend on the result of the prior step, they need to be executed sequentially. Here, this is simply achieved by starting the query execution in the callback method, which was passed to the `createConnection()` function, and the result evaluation is done in the `exec()` callback method.

Now, this is only a small example with two callback methods, but you can easily imagine a program with much more database interaction and a lot of concatenated callback methods getting confusing very quickly. Another drawback is the fact that you need to handle errors in every callback method and deal with overlapping variable names of, for example, the `error` variable.

To solve this sequential execution of callbacks using promises, we first need to "promisify" the `@sap/hdbext` library, as there is currently no support for promises out of the box.

Promisifying an Application Programming Interface

The node module `bluebird` is one of the most used libraries to easily add support for promises to other node modules. Doing so usually consists of using the following code:

```
const hdbext = require("@sap/hdbext");
const Promise = require("bluebird");
Promise.promisifyAll(hdbext);
```

By calling the `promisifyAll()` function on a node module, the bluebird library will iterate over all methods it finds and try to create a promisified version. To work correctly, the functions you're interested in must comply with the Node.js convention to expect a callback method as its last parameter (`function(param1, param2, callback)`) and execute the callback method with the error object as a first argument and the success object as second (`callback(error, success)`). The converted functions have the same name as the original function, except the `Async` suffix, and return a promise instead of accepting a callback method directly.

Unfortunately, it can happen that libraries have some functions that return more than just the error and success parameters to the callback method as is the case, for example, when loading stored procedures with the `@sap/hdbext` library. In those cases, we need to make use of the bluebird `multiArgs` parameter when promisifying the respective function. If this parameter is set, the promise callback method will return an array containing all the parameters provided by the callback.

Sequential Processing

Listing 6.23 shows an adapted example of a database call from Listing 6.22 using promises.

```
const hdbext = require("@sap/hdbext");
const xsenv = require("@sap/xsenv");
const services = xsenv.getServices({ hanaConfig: { tag: "hana" } });

const Promise = require("bluebird");
Promise.promisifyAll(hdbext);

hdbext.createConnectionAsync(services.hanaConfig)
  .then((client) => {
    return client.execAsync("SELECT COUNT(LNAME) AS TROUBLEMAKERS FROM
\"CVBooking\" WHERE \"LNAME\" LIKE '%FOX%'");
  })
  .then((result) => {
    if (result[0].TROUBLEMAKERS > 0) {
      console.log("Mr. HUNTER, please proceed immediately to gate 42! Mr.
HUNTER please.");
    } else {
      console.log("Boarding completed!");
    }
  })
  .catch((error) => {
    return console.error(error);
  });
```

Listing 6.23 Database Call Using Promises

We now use the `createConnectionAsync()` method, which returns a promise to connect to the database. The callback method to execute the database query isn't passed to that method anymore but to the `.then()` function of the promise, which will be called after the promise is fulfilled.

In the first callback function, we now need to return the promise created by the `execAsync()` method call, and we can again use the `.then()` function to define what happens after the result is ready.

Parallel Processing

Using promises, it's also very easy to handle parallel API calls, as shown in Listing 6.24. The native JavaScript `Promise` as well as the `bluebird` library provide the method `Promise.all(<promises>)`, which itself returns a promise. That promise will resolve when all of the promises in the passed array have been resolved. If one of the grouped promises rejects, the whole promise will reject. Another option is to use the `Promise.race(<promises>)` function, which will resolve as soon as one of the grouped promises resolves.


```
const hdbext = require("@sap/hdbext");
const xsenv = require("@sap/xsenv");
const services = xsenv.getServices({ hanaConfig: { tag: "hana" } });

const Promise = require("bluebird");
Promise.promisifyAll(hdbext);

hdbext.createConnectionAsync(services.hanaConfig)
  .then((client) => {
    return Promise.all([
      client.execAsync(
      "SELECT COUNT(LNAME) AS FOXES FROM \"CVBooking\" WHERE \"LNAME\" LIKE
'%FOX%'"
      ),
      client.execAsync(
        "SELECT COUNT(LNAME) AS WOLVES FROM \"CVBooking\" WHERE \"LNAME\" LIKE
'%WOLF%'"
      )
    ]);  })
  .then((results) => {
    const totalBadGuys = results[0][0].FOXES + results[1][0].WOLVES;
    if (totalBadGuys > 0) {
      console.log(
        "Ladies and Gentlemen, we unfortunately have to cancel the flight
because of missing crew members."
      );
    } else {
      console.log("Boarding completed!");
    }
  })
```

```
  .catch((error) => {
    return console.error(error);
  });
```

Listing 6.24 Waiting for Two Parallel Database Calls

To use the Promise.all() or Promise.race() function, we first start the database queries and collect the returned promises in the array dbCalls. We then simply pass the array to the function Promise.all(), which creates again a promise that is returned.

We can add the callback method to handle the successful execution of both database queries to the promise chain. You can see that an array is passed to the callback method that contains the results of both database queries, and we can properly process them further. The results are always returned in the same order the promises were collected into the array.

Further Information about Promises

You now should have a good overview about promises and how they can help to structure your asynchronous program flow. If you want to dig a bit deeper, you can find more information and additional functions in the bluebird API documentation (*http://bluebirdjs.com/docs/api-reference.html*) or the documentation of the built-in JavaScript Promise object (*https://developer.mozilla.org/en-US/docs/Web/JavaScript/Reference/Global_Objects/Promise*).

Async Library

Another possibility to manage asynchronous control flow is the usage of the async module for Node.js. While we'll look at how we can implement sequential and parallel execution, the async module offers a lot of additional functionalities to manage your control flow as, for example, a limited parallel execution.

Sequential Processing

To execute a process flow that has dependent asynchronous API calls, the Async library provides the function waterfall(<tasks>[,<callback()]). It expects an array with functions to be executed one after the other, providing the output of an executed function as input for the next function in the list. The functions in the array are expected to accept a callback method as the last parameter, which refers to the next function in the task list. Inside the function logic, you call this method whenever you

want to proceed to the next function, providing first a possible error and then the results you want to pass to the next function, for example, `next(null, results)`. If you return an error, the execution of the task list will be stopped, and the main callback function (`callback()`) will be executed with the error. If everything runs smoothly, the main callback will be executed with the result of the last function in the task list.

Our example would look like Listing 6.25.


```
const hdbext = require("@sap/hdbext");
const xsenv = require("@sap/xsenv");
const services = xsenv.getServices({ hanaConfig: { tag: "hana" } });

const async = require("async");

async.waterfall([
  (next) => {
    hdbext.createConnection(services.hanaConfig, next);
  },
  (client, next) => {
    client.exec(
      "SELECT COUNT(LNAME) AS TROUBLEMAKERS FROM \"CVBooking\" WHERE
\"LNAME\" LIKE '%FOX%'",
      next
    );
  },
  (result, next) => {
    if (result[0].TROUBLEMAKERS > 0) {
      next(null, "Mr. HUNTER, please proceed immediately to gate 42! Mr. HUNTER
please.");
    } else {
      next(null, "Boarding completed!");
    }
  }
],
(error, result) => {
  if (error) {
    console.error("Mayday, Mayday!", error);
  } else {
```

```
    console.log(result);
  }
});
```

Listing 6.25 Database Call Using Async's Waterfall Method

We first fill the task list array, starting with the createConnection() method. The callback method of createConnection()will be called as expected by waterfall with an error as the first argument and the database client as the second argument so we can directly pass the next callback to createConnection(). After the database connection is created, the client object is passed to the next function where we execute the database query and use **next** again as the query callback. In the last function, we then evaluate the query results and return the output to the main callback method where it's logged to the console. If an error occurs in one of the steps, the main callback is called immediately and logs the error.

Parallel Processing

If we want to execute several database queries or asynchronous API calls in parallel, the Async library provides the parallel(<tasks>[, <callback()>]) function, which is used in Listing 6.26. In principle, you use it exactly like the waterfall() function, but the tasks are executed in parallel, and the results are only passed to the main callback method.

```
const hdbext = require("@sap/hdbext");
const xsenv = require("@sap/xsenv");
const services = xsenv.getServices({ hanaConfig: { tag: "hana" } });

const async = require("async");

async.waterfall([
  (next) => {
    hdbext.createConnection(services.hanaConfig, next);
  },
  (client, next) => {
    async.parallel([
      (done) => {
        client.exec(
          "SELECT COUNT(LNAME) AS FOXES FROM \"CVBooking\" WHERE \"LNAME\"
LIKE '%FOX%'",
```

```
          done
        );
      },
      (done) => {
        client.exec(
          "SELECT COUNT(LNAME) AS WOLVES FROM \"CVBooking\" WHERE \"LNAME\"
LIKE '%WOLF%'",
          done
        );
      }
    ],
    next
    );
  },
  (results, next) => {
    const totalBadGuys = results[0][0].FOXES + results[1][0].WOLVES;
    if (totalBadGuys > 0) {
      next(null, "Ladies and Gentlemen, we unfortunately have to cancel the
flight because of missing crew members.");
    } else {
      next(null, "Boarding completed!");
    }
  }
],
(error, result) => {
  if (error) {
    console.error("Mayday, Mayday!", error);
  } else {
    console.log(result);
  }
});
```

Listing 6.26 Two Parallel Database Calls Using Async's Parallel Method

When doing the database calls, we pass them in an array to the `async.parallel()` function. Each database call will execute the callback method `done` after the result is available. When both database queries are returned, the `parallel()` function's callback `next` is executed, which will pass the query results as an array to the next function of the sequential execution list where it's evaluated.

Further Information about the Async Library

As mentioned in the beginning, the Async library provides many more functions to manage asynchronous program flows. It's possible, for example, to restrict the number of queries executed in parallel using the `parallelLimit()` function. If you want to dive deeper into the API, we recommend the API reference (*https://caolan.github.io/async/index.html*).

6.2.5 Exposing Data

Now that we've explored how Node.js works, let's discuss how we can expose data to the next layer. With Node.js, there are several possibilities, but as we need to provide data to a SAPUI5 frontend, the most suitable options are to create a custom endpoint, which provides JSON data; create an endpoint using the OData protocol, or create a web-socket connection. Let's first look at how to expose an OData service and subsequently how a representational state transfer (REST) service is built using the `express` module.

Exposing Data as OData

The Open Data Protocol (OData) is a standard that defines best practices for building and consuming RESTful APIs. The SAPUI5 library uses the OData model as the primary way to fetch data from the application backend and bind it to the UI controls on the screen.

Using SAP HANA XS Advanced, we currently have the choice between two implementations of the OData protocol that can directly expose database objects: the XSJS-based XSODATA v2 and the Java-based OData v4.

In general, we recommend using the Java-based OData v4 because it's much more convenient to expose data, especially when you've created your data model using CDS, as described in Chapter 5. You'll see how that works in Section 6.3. However, depending on your application's architecture, you might not want to add an additional Java module, so you can still use `xsodata` to easily expose tables and views to a SAPUI5 frontend. SAPUI5 actually supports both versions of OData.

Let's jump to the Node.js module we created earlier with XSJS support. We can directly add an OData service to it by adding a *.xsodata* file like the one in Listing 6.27 to the *lib* folder or the folder we specified in the `rootDir` parameter.

```
service {
    "Airport" as "Airports"
    with ( "CODE","NAME","CITY","COUNTRY","TIMEZONE","LATITUDE","LONGITUDE");
}
```

Listing 6.27 flightBooking.xsodata

First, we just expose the `AIRPORT` table and create an alias `as "Airports"` under which the table is available in the OData service. Finally, we specify which attributes of the table are getting exposed by passing a list after the `with` keyword.

> **Database Object Name**
>
> The object name in the OData definition file must be the exact same name as in the database container. In our case, it's simply "Airport", but it might be that there is a prefix if you use a context or a namespace when defining the database objects. It's best to look up the object's name in SAP HANA database explorer and copy it to the OData definition file.

After building and running the `xsjs` module, we're now able to access the OData service using the following URL:

https://hana.chickenwings.corp:<port>/flightBooking.xsodata?$format=json

As the `xsodata` implementation only supports the JSON format, we need to add the `$format=json` parameter to the URL to not run into an error. As a response, we see the entity sets that are exposed by the service, as shown in Figure 6.12.


```
{
  - d: {
      - EntitySets: [
            "Airports"
        ]
    }
}
```


Figure 6.12 XSODATA Entity Sets

Now, compared to other libraries or services to expose information as OData with only the code written above, we already get a bunch of functionality for free such as the ability to perform the following:

- Retrieve all entries of the table AIRPORT: flightBooking.xsodata/Airports
- Refer to an entry by its key: flightBooking.xsodata/Airports('BER')
- Filter the entries: flightBooking.xsodata/Airports?$filter=COUNTRY eq 'GERMANY'
- Order the results: flightBooking.xsodata/Airports?$orderby=CODE desc
- Paging with $top and $skip: flightBooking.xsodata/Airports?$top=3&$skip=3
- Entry count: flightBooking.xsodata/Airports/$count
- Select specific attributes: /flightBooking.xsodata/Airports?$select=CODE,COUNTRY

By default, the OData service also allows you to CREATE, UPDATE, and DELETE data in the exposed database tables besides the read access. If you want to restrict these possibilities, you can specify the code in Listing 6.28 in the xsodata definition.

```
service  {
    "Airport" as "Airports"
    with ( "CODE","NAME","CITY","COUNTRY","TIMEZONE","LATITUDE","LONGITUDE")
        create forbidden
        update forbidden
        delete forbidden;
}
```

Listing 6.28 XSODATA Service with Restricted CREATE, UPDATE, DELETE

Another strength of OData services in general is the ability to create associations between objects that work like joins in the database. This makes it easy to access information from associated objects when requesting data from the OData service.

First, we need to add the additional entity Connection and the associations between the airport attributes and the Airport entity using the code in Listing 6.29.

```
"Connection" as "Connections"
with ("FLIGHT", "FROMAP", "TOAP", "DEPT", "ARRT")
navigates ("ConnectionFromAirport" as "FromAirport", "ConnectionToAirport" as
"ToAirport")
    create forbidden
    update forbidden
    delete forbidden;

association "ConnectionFromAirport"
    principal "Connections"("FROMAP") multiplicity "1"
```

```
    dependent "Airports"("CODE") multiplicity "1";
association "ConnectionToAirport"
    principal "Connections"("TOAP") multiplicity "1"
    dependent "Airports"("CODE") multiplicity "1";
```

Listing 6.29 Association between Connection and Airport

Now, we can see the associations when accessing the `Connections` entity `/flightBooking.xsodata/Connections`, as shown in Figure 6.13.

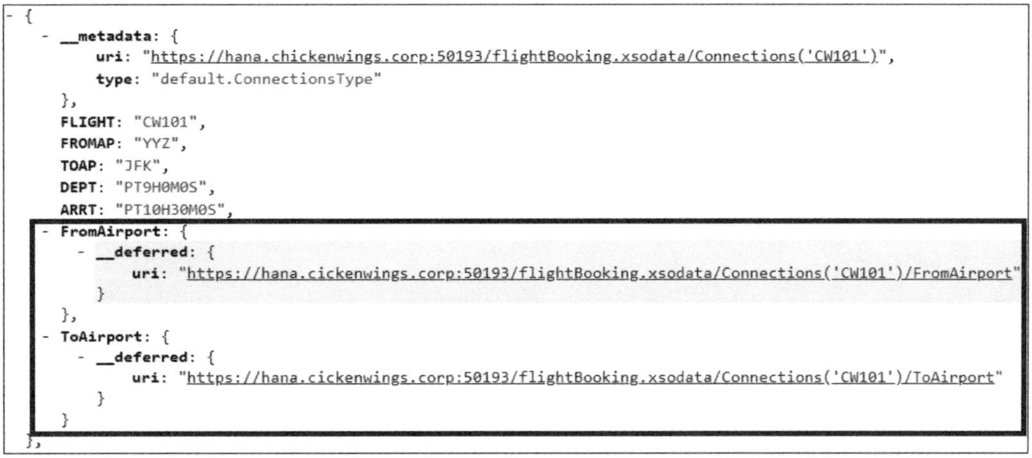
- {
- __metadata: {
uri: "https://hana.chickenwings.corp:50193/flightBooking.xsodata/Connections('CW101')",
type: "default.ConnectionsType"
},
FLIGHT: "CW101",
FROMAP: "YYZ",
TOAP: "JFK",
DEPT: "PT9H0M0S",
ARRT: "PT10H30M0S",
- FromAirport: {
- __deferred: {
uri: "https://hana.cickenwings.corp:50193/flightBooking.xsodata/Connections('CW101')/FromAirport"
}
},
- ToAirport: {
- __deferred: {
uri: "https://hana.cickenwings.corp:50193/flightBooking.xsodata/Connections('CW101')/ToAirport"
}
}
},

Figure 6.13 XSODATA Associations

By default, the association in an entry only contains the identifier of the referenced object, in this case, the airports of the connection. The attributes of the airport can either be retrieved with a new request to the OData service using the identifier, or we can use the `$expand` parameter when doing the initial request to automatically include the airport attributes `/flightBooking.xsodata/Connections?$expand=FromAirport,ToAirport`, as shown in Figure 6.14.

Further Information about XSODATA

The shown features of the XSODATA services are just the tip of the iceberg. If you want to learn more, we suggest the SAP HANA Developer Guide and the OData website at *http://odata.org*. The SAP HANA Interactive Education (SHINE) application for SAP HANA XS Advanced also provides more examples of using XSODATA functions.

```
- {
    - __metadata: {
          uri: "https://hana.cickenwings.corp:50193/flightBooking.xsodata/Connections('CW101')",
          type: "default.ConnectionsType"
      },
      FLIGHT: "CW101",
      FROMAP: "YYZ",
      TOAP: "JFK",
      DEPT: "PT9H0M0S",
      ARRT: "PT10H30M0S",
    - FromAirport: {
        - __metadata: {
              uri: "https://hana.cickenwings.corp:50193/flightBooking.xsodata/Airports('YYZ')",
              type: "default.AirportsType"
          },
          CODE: "YYZ",
          NAME: "Lester B. Pearson International",
          CITY: "Toronto",
          COUNTRY: "CANADA",
          TIMEZONE: "EST",
          LATITUDE: "43.677718",
          LONGITUDE: "-79.624820"
      },
    + ToAirport: {…}
  },
```


Figure 6.14 XSODATA Expanded Associations

Express Framework

Another option to provide a REST API to our node module is the use of the Express framework at *http://expressjs.com*. We've already seen that the `@sap/xssec` module provides a middleware for Express applications to implement authentication and authorization for every defined route. Let's start to modify the *server.js* file of the `js` module we created earlier to see how the Express framework can be used to provide a web API to the SAPUI5 application we'll create in the next chapter or to other applications in general. The steps we'll take will be covered in the following sections.

Create an Express Application

To create an Express application, we first need to require the `express` library and create the application instance using the following exposed `express()` function:

```
const express = require("express");
const app = express();
```

Now we can define the routes on which the express application should respond. The `app` object therefore provides a function for each HTTP method (e.g., `GET` or `POST`), which can be registered at a route or path.

Add a Route Path

If we want to react to GET requests that are sent to the application's root URL "/", we add the following to the code:

```
app.get("/", (request, response) => {
   response.send("Hello Chicks!");
});
```


The route methods expect the actual path they should register to as the first argument. In the simplest case, the path is a fixed string such as "/" for the application's root or "/flightAnnouncment"; however, it can also be a regular expression, such as the following that matches every route finishing with -eggs with, for example, boiled-eggs:

```
app.get(/.*-eggs$/, (request, response) => {
  response.send("Hands off my eggs!");
});
```

There is also the option to include predefined parameters in the route by adding a colon ":" prefixed string to it, as shown in Listing 6.30. These parameters are later available in the request object's params attribute.

```
app.get("/departure/:to", (request, response) => {
  if (request.params.to === "HOME") {
    return response.send("Harry, start the engines!");
  }
  response.send("Sorry, no food, no flight!");
});
```

Listing 6.30 Defining Route Parameters

Registering to a route's POST request is a working equivalent to the GET requests by using the post() method instead, as shown in Listing 6.31.

```
app.post("/flightStatus", (request, response) => {
    if (request.body.departure === "NCE") {
        return response.json({ flightStatus: "strike" });
    }
    response.json({ flightStatus: "onTime" });
});
```

Listing 6.31 Registering to a Route's POST Request

There is one extra thing you need to take care of to be able to access a request's payload/body: the application must be explicitly configured to parse the incoming payload. Express provides out-of-the-box support for JSON payload and URL-encoded data as it's sent from a web form. As we're expecting data to be sent from the SAPUI5 frontend, the best choice is to use the JSON option. The JSON middleware needs to be registered as follows:

```
app.use(express.json());
```

The `express.json([options])` function can be passed an object with several parameters to refine the behavior when parsing a JSON payload. By default, the parameter `type` is set to `application/json`, which means only requests sending the header `content-type = application/json` will be considered valid. In addition, the size `limit` for the payload is set to `100kb`, and the option `strict` is enabled, which only accepts JSON arrays and objects as payload. You can find more details here: *http://expressjs.com/en/4x/api.html#express.json*.

After mounting the `express.json()` middleware, the content of the request is available in the variable `request.body`, which is passed to the route's callback method.

Data Validation

Beware—the route parameters and request payloads aren't validated or sanitized in any way! You need to make sure to only process valid user input by, for example, using the `express-validator` middleware (*https://github.com/ctavan/express-validator*).

Add a Path Callback

The second argument of the route method is a callback function that is executed when the specified route is matched. The callback method should provide an argument for the `request` and the `response` objects, which are used to retrieve the request parameters, headers, payload, and so on, as well as to send the response.

It's also possible to register multiple callbacks at one route, which will be executed in order. It's then important to provide an additional argument, `next`, as shown in Listing 6.32, which is used by the first callback to invoke the next registered one, and so on.

```
app.get("/flightAnnouncement",
  (request, response, next) => {
    console.log("Captain: Steeeeeeeeve!!!!!!");
    next();
  },
  (request, response) => {
    console.log("Co-pilot: Why is it always me???");
    response.send("Hello, this is your first officer speaking!");
  }
);
```

Listing 6.32 Handing Over Control from One Path Callback to the Next

The request object contains, among others, the headers, params, and query object that contain key/value pairs. The params object contains the corresponding values of the route parameters, prefixed with the colon ":", which have been defined. The query object instead contains what is known as HTTP query parameters. For a GET request, query parameters are passed as follows:

/queryParameter?<parameter>=<value>

Finally, the response object is used to send back a reply to the requestor. As you've seen in many of the examples earlier in this chapter, the simplest way to return something is to use the response.send(<message>) method, which will send a response of type text/html if you pass a string value or application/json if you pass a JavaScript object or array. For our example, we chose the method response.json() to explicitly send a JSON response.

You can also set the HTTP status code before sending a response with the following construct:

```
response.status(403).send("You don't have a ticket! Start washing dishes...");
```

If you just need to send an empty response with a status code, you can use the method end() instead of send() or json().

Application Port Listening

Finally, we need to tell the application on which port to listen for incoming requests. First, we determine the application port from the environment variables, and then we can register the Express application to it, as follows:

```
const port = process.env.PORT || 3000;
app.listen(port, () => {
    console.log(`Expecting troubles at port ${port}`);
});
```

Mount Middleware

Many node modules, such as `@sap/xssec` and `@sap/hdbext`, provide an Express middleware to make their functionality easily accessible in the Express request–response cycle.

A middleware is basically a function that is executed before our request callback methods. It has access to the `request` and `response` objects and can manipulate them to, for example, provide additional attributes to the `request` object.

To add a middleware to the Express application, the `app.use([<path>,] <callback()>[, <callback()>])` method is used. If you don't specify the `path` parameter, the middleware is mounted to every route in the application.

For examples, see the next section where we discuss how to use the `@sap/hdbext` middleware to connect to the SAP HANA database or the earlier `@sap/xssec` example.

> **Further Information about the Express Framework**
>
> Again, we can't write about all the features of the Express framework here, so to get a deeper look, you can consult the project's web page with guides and documentation: *http://expressjs.com/*.

6.2.6 Accessing the SAP HANA Database

Now we want to look a little bit deeper into how it's possible to connect with our node program to the SAP HANA database to read and write data and to execute stored procedures. As mentioned in Section 6.2.2, we'll take a closer look at the `@sap/hdbext` here to make use of its convenience functions.

Connecting

Before we can send any query to the database, a connection must be established, providing the library one or more hosts to connect to and the SQL port number, which, for SAP HANA, is composed of `3<Instancenumber>15` and the user name plus password. We can hard-code the connection configuration or read the configuration from the application's environment variables. To see how that works, let's first see how to generally connect to the database using the code in Listing 6.33.

```
const hdbext = require("@sap/hdbext");
const hanaConfig = {
    host: "hana.chickenwings.corp",
    port: 30015,
    user: "PLASSO",
    password: "hattner"
};
hdbext.createConnection(hanaConfig, (connectionError, client) => {
  if (connectionError) {
    return console.error(connectionError);
  }
  client.exec("SELECT * FROM DUMMY", (queryError, result) => {
    if (queryError) {
      return console.error(queryError);
    }
    console.log(`Dummy value: ${result[0].DUMMY}`);
  });
});
```

Listing 6.33 Simple Database Connection

In the simplest case, we only use the `@sap/hdbext` library to establish the connection. The credentials are provided to the `createConnection()` function and a callback method, which gets executed after the connection is established, and we can execute a database query.

Additionally, the configuration can be extended using the parameters in Table 6.4 to influence the connection.

Parameter	Effect
`autoCommit`	Boolean: default is `true`
`isolationLevel`	Setting the session isolation level to `READ_COMMITTED`, `REPEATABLE_READ`, or `SERIALIZABLE`.
`locale`	String: Session language code, such as `ru`, `fr`, or `zh`

Table 6.4 Additional Connection Parameters

Parameter	Effect
schema	String: Session default schema name
session	Object: Key/value pairs that will be available in the database session variables

Table 6.4 Additional Connection Parameters (Cont.)

In the next sections, we'll show how to connect to a database container that is bound to the application via its environment variables, briefly look at connection pooling, and finally discuss how to use the Express middleware provided by the @sap/hdbext module to easily include database calls into an Express REST application.

Connecting to a Bound Database Container

As stated, we probably want to run the code of Listing 6.33 not only in our development environment but also later in production, so it's better to abstract the database credentials and store them in the application's environment variables as suggested by the 12-Factor App principle of configuration. The code also becomes reusable, and you don't risk committing the credentials to a public code repository too easily. Another thing to keep in mind is that following the preceding example, you don't get access to the tables in the database module of our MTA because you connect directly to the database using the credentials of your developer user. So, the easiest thing to do is to wire the database container to the node module in the *mta.yaml* file using the code in Listing 6.34.

```
modules:
[...]
- name: js
  [...]
   requires:
     - name:
[...]
resources:
 - name: hdi-container
```

Listing 6.34 Add Another Module as Dependency to the mta.yaml File

Because the HDI container is called hdi-container, we can just reference it in the requires section of our node module. The result is that during the deployment of the

MTA, the database module's credentials get injected into the node module's environment variables and can be retrieved.

Let's change the example slightly to use the @sap/xsenv library to read the connection credentials from the environment and count the number of airports currently in the database using the code in Listing 6.35.

```
const hdbext = require("@sap/hdbext");
const xsenv = require("@sap/xsenv");
const services = xsenv.getServices({ hanaConfig: { tag: "hana" } });
hdbext.createConnection(services.hanaConfig, (connectionError, client) => {
  if (connectionError) {
    return console.error(connectionError);
  }
  client.exec("SELECT COUNT(CODE) AS AIRPORTS FROM \"Airport\"",
    (queryError, result) => {
    if (queryError) {
      return console.error(queryError);
    }
    console.log(`Number of Airports: ${result[0].AIRPORTS}`);
  });
});
```

Listing 6.35 Connecting to the MTA Database Container

Connection Pooling

Connections to the database can be pooled to avoid the continuous creation of new connections to the database.

First, the connection pool needs to be initialized using the `hdbext.getPool(<hanaConfig>[, <poolConfig>]);` function. The `hdbext` library implements the `generic-pool` module (*https://github.com/coopernurse/node-pool*) and can be configured with options such as the minimum and maximum numbers of connections.

When a connection is needed, it can be retrieved using the `acquire(<callback(error, client)>)` function of the pool instance.

If the connection is no longer needed, it should be released back to the pool using either the `release(<client>)` function of the pool or the `client.close()` or `client.disconnect()` functions. Listing 6.36 shows how everything is tied together.

```
const hdbext = require("@sap/hdbext");
const xsenv = require("@sap/xsenv");
const services = xsenv.getServices({ hanaConfig: { tag: "hana" } });

const pool = hdbext.getPool(services.hanaConfig);

pool.acquire((poolError, client) => {
  if (poolError) {
    return console.error(poolError);
  }
  client.exec("SELECT COUNT(CODE) AS AIRPORTS FROM \"Airport\"",
    (queryError, result) => {
    if (queryError) {
      return console.error(queryError);
    }
    console.log(`Number of Airports: ${result[0].AIRPORTS}`);
    pool.release(client);
  });
});
```

Listing 6.36 Using a Pooled Database Connection

Express Middleware

For web applications using the Express framework, the hdbext library provides a middleware that enables easy access to a pooled connection when a request is sent to the application.

The function `hdbext.middleware(<hanaConfig>[, <poolConfig>])` must be mounted to the Express application, as shown in Listing 6.37, which automatically creates the connection pool using the given SAP HANA connection configuration.

```
const hdbext = require("@sap/hdbext");
const xsenv = require("@sap/xsenv");
const services = xsenv.getServices({ hanaConfig: { tag: "hana" } });const
express = require("express");
const port = process.env.PORT || 3000;

const app = express();
```

```
app.use(hdbext.middleware(services.hanaConfig));

app.get("/", (request, response) => {
    request.db.exec("SELECT COUNT(CODE) AS AIRPORTS FROM \"Airport\"",
    (queryError, result) => {
        if (queryError) {
            response.send(500, queryError);
            return console.error(queryError);
        }
        response.send(`Number of Airports: ${result[0].AIRPORTS}`);
    });
});

app.listen(port, () => {
    console.log(`Expecting trouble at port ${port}`);
});
```

Listing 6.37 Using the hdbext Middleware for Express

The functions to execute database queries and to load procedures are available in the `request.db` object when a request is sent to the Express application.

Executing a Database Query

After the successful connection to the database container, we can use the `exec()` method to directly fire an SQL query and pass a callback function to handle the result, as follows:

```
client.exec(<query> [,<options>], callback(error, rows))
```

As you might have deduced from the preceding example in Listing 6.37, the query response is returned as an array. Every array element represents a record or row in the response and contains an object with attributes which are named after the result columns. These attributes contain the actual result values. The following example shows first the database query, the returned result in Table 6.5, and finally the described JavaScript structure you work with in Listing 6.38.

```
select "CODE", "NAME", "CITY", "COUNTRY"
from "Airport"
```

Code	Name	City	Country
FRA	Frankfurt Airport	Frankfurt	GERMANY
MUC	Munich Airport	Munich	GERMANY
BER	Berlin Brandenburg Airport	Berlin	GERMANY
MXP	Milan-Malpensa Airport	Milan	ITALY
FCO	Leonardo da Vinci-Fiumicino Airport	Rome	ITALY

Table 6.5 Query Results

Listing 6.38 shows the JavaScript object that is returned by the `exec()` call. As you can see, accessing the records is straightforward.

```
result: [
  {
    CODE: "FRA",
    NAME: "Frankfurt Airport",
    CITY: "Frankfurt",
    COUNTRY: "GERMANY"
  },
  {
    CODE: "MUC",
    NAME: "Munich Airport",
    CITY: "Munich",
    COUNTRY: "GERMANY"
  },
  [...]
]
```

Listing 6.38 Format of the Result Returned by exec()

Calling a Database Procedure

Calling a database procedure with the `@sap/hdbext` library is very convenient because we can load the procedure using the `loadProcedure()` function from the database. The function's callback method will receive a method with the signature of the stored procedure and can be called directly from the node program.

Let's load the procedure in Listing 6.39 into our module.

```
PROCEDURE "GetAirportsNearby" (
    IN CENTER NVARCHAR(100),
    IN MAX_DISTANCE INTEGER,
    OUT CLOSEST NVARCHAR(3),
    OUT AIRPORTS TABLE(
        CODE NVARCHAR(3),
        NAME NVARCHAR(50)
    )
)
   LANGUAGE SQLSCRIPT
   SQL SECURITY INVOKER
   READS SQL DATA AS
BEGIN

    AIRPORTS= SELECT
        "CODE", "NAME"
        FROM "Airport"
        WHERE "LOCATION"
            .ST_WithinDistance(new ST_Point(:CENTER, 4326), :MAX_
DISTANCE, 'kilometer') = 1
        ORDER BY "LOCATION"
            .ST_Distance(new ST_Point(:CENTER, 4326), 'kilometer');

    CLOSEST = :AIRPORTS."CODE"[1];
END
```

Listing 6.39 GetAirportsNearby SAP HANA Stored Procedure

The procedure will use the location data stored in the table `Airports` to find all airports within a given range (`maxDistance`) from a starting point (`center`) and return them as a table variable. In addition, the code of the closest airport is returned as a scalar variable.

As you can see in Listing 6.40, the first thing we do is again to create the database connection, but then we use the function `loadProcedure(<client>, <schema>, <procedure>, <callback>)` to retrieve a JavaScript equivalent of the database stored procedure. In our example, we leave the schema name empty to use the database container's default schema.

Afterward, we use the returned function, which expects an object with the input parameters of the stored procedure as the first argument and expects a callback method as the second argument, which has the error object in case something went wrong during the procedure call as the first parameter, an object holding all scalar variables returned from the procedure as the second parameter, and one object per returning table variables of the procedure as the third parameter.

```
const hdbext = require("@sap/hdbext");
const xsenv = require("@sap/xsenv");
const services = xsenv.getServices({ hanaConfig: { tag: "hana" } });
hdbext.createConnection(services.hanaConfig, (connectionError, client) => {
    if (connectionError) {
        return console.error(connectionError);
    }
    hdbext.loadProcedure(client, "", "GetAirportsNearby", (loadError,
storedProcedure) => {
        if (loadError) {
            return console.error(loadError);
        }
        storedProcedure({
            CENTER: "Point(48.7534183 8.2418817)",
            MAX_DISTANCE: 200
        },
        (callError, parameters, airports) => {
            if (callError) {
                return console.error(callError);
            }
            console.log(`Closest Airport: ${parameters.CLOSEST}`);
            console.log(airports);
        });
    });
});
```

Listing 6.40 Loading and Calling a SAP HANA Stored Procedure

In Section 6.2.4, we used promises to simplify the asynchronous program flow but only had a look at simple methods that could be promisified easily. As loading a stored procedure is a bit special due to the fact that it returns more than one result parameter, Listing 6.41 shows how this is done.

```
const hdbext = require("@sap/hdbext");
const xsenv = require("@sap/xsenv");
const services = xsenv.getServices({ hanaConfig: { tag: "hana" } });
const Promise = require("bluebird");
Promise.promisifyAll(hdbext);
hdbext.createConnectionAsync(services.hanaConfig)
  .then((client) => {
    return hdbext.loadProcedureAsync(client, "", "GetAirportsNearby");
  })
  .then((storedProcedure) => {
    const storedProcedureAsync = Promise.promisify(storedProcedure, {
multiArgs: true });
    return storedProcedureAsync({
      CENTER: "Point(48.7534183 8.2418817)",
      MAX_DISTANCE: 200
    });
  })
  .then((result) => {
    console.log(`Closest Airport: ${result[0].CLOSEST}`);
    console.log(result[1]);
  })
  .catch((error) => {
    return console.error(error);
  });
```

Listing 6.41 Procedure Call Using Promises

After the stored procedure is loaded using the `loadProcedure()` function, the returned JavaScript method is promisified using the `multiArgs` parameter. Doing so, we can include the loaded procedure in out promise chain and evaluate the results after they are available. The procedure results are available in an array (`results`), which is passed to the callback method. The order of the stored procedure return parameters is exactly the same as in the results array, meaning that the first element (`[0]`) contains the scalar parameters, and the second element (`[1]`) contains the table variable.

6.2.7 Unit Testing a Node.js Module

Unit testing is the process that verifies individual portions of code (units) to confirm that they behave as expected. This is important when new functionalities are added because it ensures that no side effects on the existing code base are generated.

When you develop a Node,js module in the SAP HANA XS Advanced programming model, unit testing is performed using *Jasmine* (*https://jasmine.github.io*). Jasmine is probably the most-used testing framework for JavaScript. A Jasmine test consists of a JavaScript function that identifies the test suite and a set of inner functions that represent the unit test specifications (*specs*).

When you create a new Node.js module with SAP Web IDE for SAP HANA, by default, it creates a folder called *tests* with a sample test suite implementation, as shown in Listing 6.42.

```
describe("sample test suite", function() {

    beforeEach(function() {
    });

    it("not ok", function() {
        expect(0).toBe(1);
    });
});
```

Listing 6.42 Sample Test Suite Generated by SAP Web IDE for SAP HANA

The outermost `describe` function defines the test suite and takes two arguments:

- A name for the test suite
- A function with the test suite implementation

Inside the `describe` implementation function, you can define the unit tests or specs by calling the `it` function, which expects two arguments as well:

- A name for the spec
- A function that defines the spec

You can think of the test suite like a sentence ("describe this test as something") and the test units as predicates of this sentence ("we expect it to do this thing").

Let's now explore how the tests are executed and where to retrieve the results.

Testing Your Node.js Module

To run the unit test in your module, you first need to create a new run configuration for it. As discussed in Section 1.2.1, we make use of the `test` script from the *package.json* file of our module:

1. Open the context menu of the node module, and choose **Run • Run Configurations**.
2. Click on the **Add +** button on the top of the configuration list to add a **Node.js Test** configuration.
3. In the created configuration, choose **Start with package.json script**, and point to the `test` script.
4. After clicking the **Save and Run** button, the results appear in the **Test Results** panel on the right side of the SAP Web IDE.

You can run the unit tests of your Node.js module from the context menu of the module by selecting **Run • Run Configurations**.

In the modal view, you can define a new configuration by selecting the **Add +** button and then choosing **Node.js Test • Run script test**, as shown in Figure 6.15.

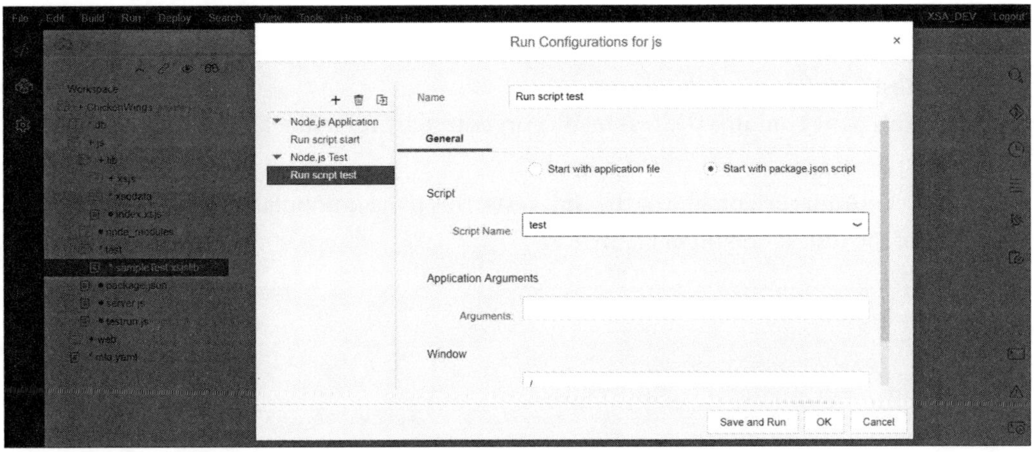

Figure 6.15 Run Configuration: Modal View

Evaluating Your Testing Results

As soon as the test run is complete, test results are available on the right side of SAP Web IDE for SAP HANA, as shown in Figure 6.16.

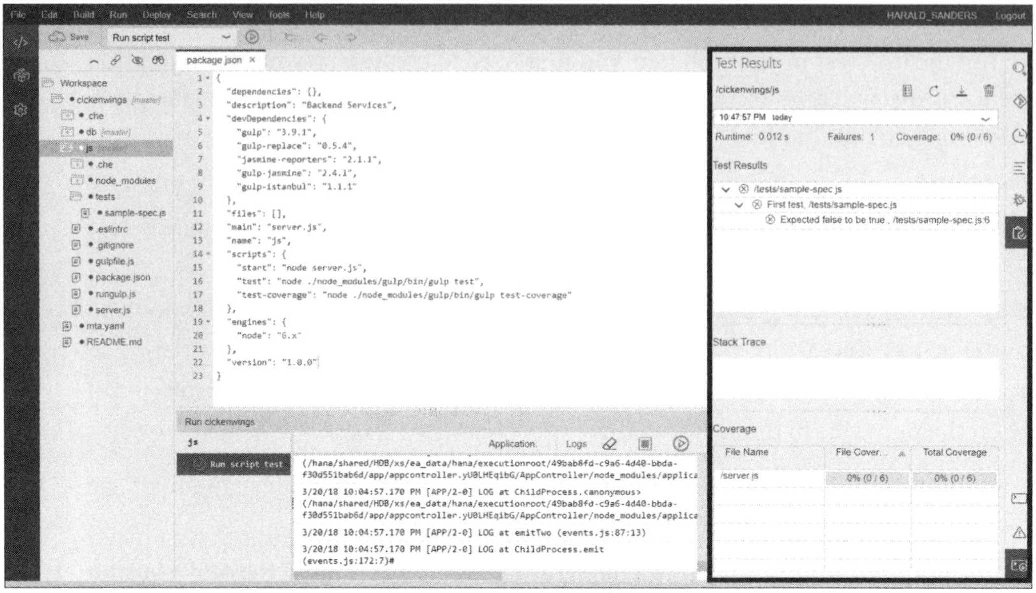

Figure 6.16 Test Results in SAP Web IDE for SAP HANA

As we can see, the test results are displayed in three panes:

- **Test Results**
  This pane contains the test results organized by test suite and unit test.
- **Stack Trace**
  When you click on one of the unit tests, this pane is populated with the stack trace of the test, as shown in Figure 6.17.

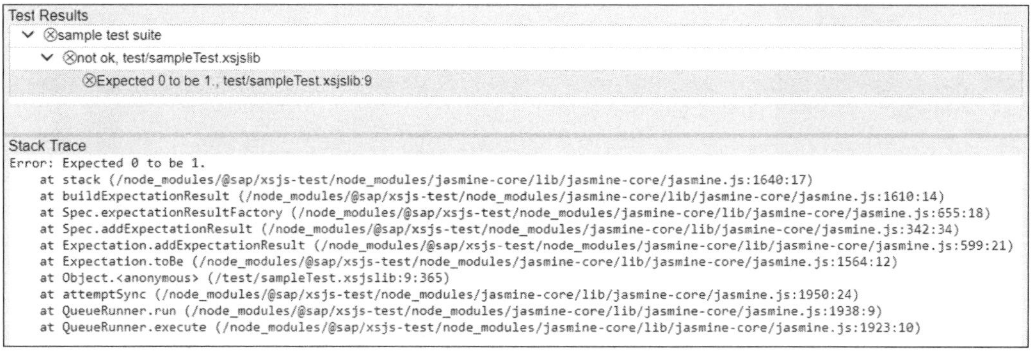

Figure 6.17 Stack Trace Pane of Test Results

- **Coverage**
  This pane displays the coverage of the unit tests of this run. You can decide if you want to display the test coverage in the editor pane by clicking the **Settings** button at the top right and selecting the **Show Code Coverage in Editor** checkbox, as shown in Figure 6.18.

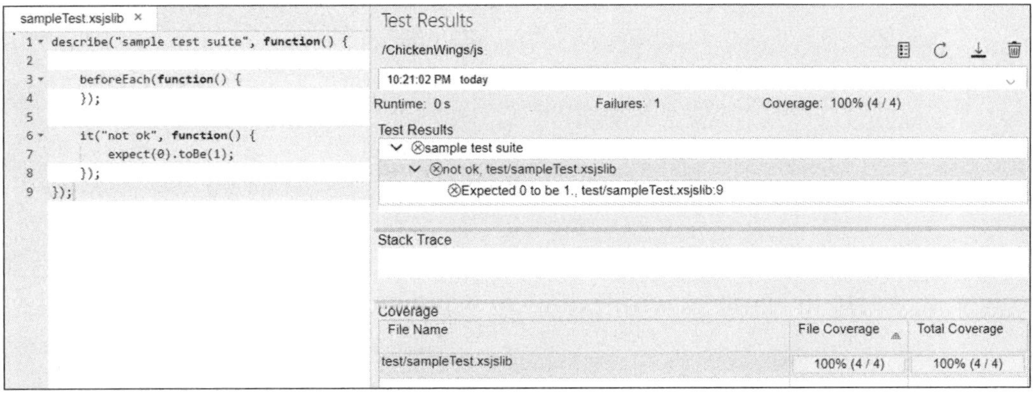

Figure 6.18 Showing Code Test Coverage in the Editor

Matchers

In the sample unit test that SAP Web IDE for SAP HANA generates, the test is performed by the following function:

```
it("not ok", function() {
        expect(0).toBe(1);
});
```

The function `expect` creates Jasmine *expectations*, which takes a variable of any type that represents the *actual value* of the expectation and is chained to a *matcher* function that compares the actual value with an expected value or condition. The result of the actual value and expected value/condition comparison is a Boolean value that determines the test result.

Jasmine provides a set of matcher functions that we can use when we define the unit test. Table 6.6 lists the current available matchers.

Matcher	Description
`toBe(expected)`	Expect the actual value to be equal (===) to the expected value.
`toBeCloseTo(expected, precision)`	Expect the actual value to be within a specified precision of the expected value.
`toBeDefined()`	Expect the actual to be defined (not equal to `undefined`).
`toBeFalsy()`	Expect the actual value to be `false`.
`toBeGreaterThan(expected)`	Expect the actual value to be greater than the expected value.
`toBeGreaterThanOrEqual(expected)`	Expect the actual value to be greater than or equal to the expected value.
`toBeLessThan(expected)`	Expect the actual value to be less than the expected value.
`toBeLessThanOrEqual(expected)`	Expect the actual value to be less than or equal to the expected value.
`toBeNaN()`	Expect the actual value to be not a number (NaN).
`toBeNegativeInfinity()`	Expect the actual value to be a negative `infinity` value.
`toBeNull()`	Expect the actual value to be `null`.
`toBePositiveInfinity()`	Expect the actual value to be a positive `infinity` value.
`toBeTruthy()`	Expect the actual value to be `truthy`.
`toBeUndefined()`	Expect the actual value to be `undefined`.
`toContain(expected)`	Expect the actual value to contain a value.
`toEqual(expected)`	Expect the actual value to be equal to the expected value (using the `deepEqual` function).

Table 6.6 Jasmine Standard Matchers

Matcher	Description
`toHaveBeenCalled()`	Expect the actual spy to have been called. The actual value is a Jasmine spy that tracks calls to a function and its arguments.
`toHaveBeenCalledBefore(expected)`	Expect the actual spy to have been called before the expected spy.
`toHaveBeenCalledTimes(expected)`	Expect the actual spy to have been called the expected number of times.
`toHaveBeenCalledWith()`	Expect the actual spy to have been called with the expected arguments.
`toHaveClass(expected)`	Expect the actual value to be a Document Object Model (DOM) element that has the expected class.
`toMatch(expected)`	Expect the actual value to match the expected regular expression.
`toThrow(expected)`	Expect a function to throw the expected object.
`toThrowError(expected, message)`	Expect a function to throw the expected error and message.
`toThrowMatching(predicate)`	Expect a function to throw something matching the predicate (a function that takes the thrown exception and returns a Boolean whether it matches or not).

Table 6.6 Jasmine Standard Matchers (Cont.)

Jasmine also provides some shared functions for executing some code before and after the unit tests, as follows:

- `beforeAll`
  Run some setup code before all test specs.
- `beforeEach`
  Run some setup code before each spec.
- `afterAll`
  Run some teardown code after all specs.

- `afterEach`
  Run some teardown code after each spec.

Choosing Code to Test

In the previous sections, you've seen how you can define unit tests and how to run them, but one typical question that arises when you start to use unit tests regards what they should cover.

There is one development approach called *test-driven development* (*https://martinfowler.com/bliki/TestDrivenDevelopment.html*) that says you should write your unit tests even before the real implementation code is written. The development lifecycle should consist of four main phases:

- Write the tests.
- Run the tests and check that they fail.
- Write the code.
- Rerun the tests and check that they are successful.

All development process should iterate on those four steps to ensure that robust code is written. As an example, let's assume that we want to add a new service to our application that manages the baggage reservation of a flight booking. To do so, we'll start by defining an empty service that provides these methods:

- `isEmpty`
  Return a Boolean if the baggage list is empty.
- `add`
  Add a new baggage to the baggage list.
- `remove`
  Remove a baggage from the baggage list.

In the Node.js module, we'll create a new file called *baggage.xsjslib*, for instance, in directory *lib/xsjs*, with the empty service implementation, as shown in Listing 6.43.

```
function isEmpty() {
return true;
}
function add(type) {
```

```
}
function remove(id) {
}
```

Listing 6.43 Baggage Service Definition

Before starting with the service implementation, we'll define the unit tests for the service logic we're going to implement. In our case, we're assuming this behavior:

- At the beginning, the baggage list is empty.
- When the user adds a baggage, the service should return an ID for the added baggage, and the list should not be empty anymore.
- When the user removes the baggage, the baggage list should be empty again.

We'll change the default test suite, as shown in Listing 6.44, to provide these unit tests.

```
$.import("xsjs", "baggage");

describe("baggage test suite", function() {

    var baggage = $.xsjs.baggage,
        newBaggage;

    it("starts empty", function() {
        expect(baggage.isEmpty()).toBeTruthy();
    });

    it("add a new baggage", function() {
        newBaggage = baggage.add("20kg");
        expect(newBaggage).toBeDefined();
        expect(baggage.isEmpty()).toBeFalsy();
    });

    it("remove the baggage ", function() {
        baggage.remove(newBaggage);
        expect(baggage.isEmpty()).toBeTruthy();
    });
});
```

Listing 6.44 Baggage Service Test Suite

If we run our unit tests, we'll see that the **add a new baggage** unit test fails, as shown in Figure 6.19. This is no surprise because we haven't implemented any logic.

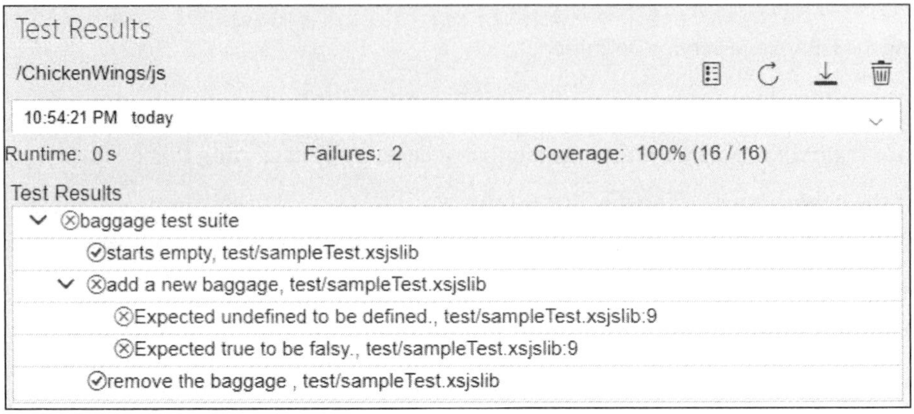

Figure 6.19 First Unit Tests Execution

Let's move on by adding some logic to `isEmpty` and `add` functions, as shown in Listing 6.45.

```
var baggageList = [];

function isEmpty() {
    return baggageList.length === 0;
}
function add(type) {
    baggageList.push(type);
    return baggageList.length;
}
function remove(id) {
}
```

Listing 6.45 Baggage Service First Implementation

If we run our unit tests again, we'll get different results; that is, now the **add a new baggage** test is correct, but **remove the baggage** fails, as shown in Figure 6.20.

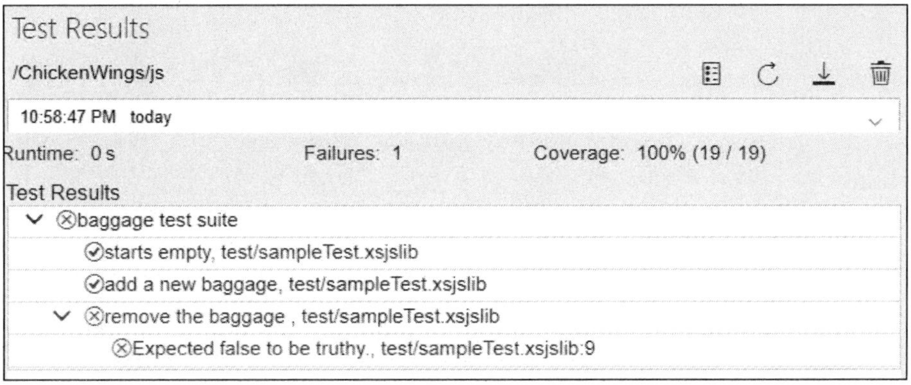

Figure 6.20 Second Unit Tests Execution

So, we still must complete the service implementation to fix all unit tests. Let's add a simple implementation code for the function `remove` in Listing 6.46.

```
var baggageList = [];

function isEmpty() {
    return baggageList.length === 0;
}
function add(type) {
    baggageList.push(type);
    return baggageList.length;
}
function remove(id) {
     baggageList.splice(id-1, 1);
}
```

Listing 6.46 Baggage Service Final Implementation

By running the unit tests again, we now have all tests green, as shown in Figure 6.21.

In this way, we've completed the first development iteration: we started with an empty service definition, then we added the unit tests that we expected the application should pass, and we continued to add implementation logic until all the tests were successful.

Next iterations will follow the same approach, and we can ensure that no side effects are generated when new functionalities are implemented.

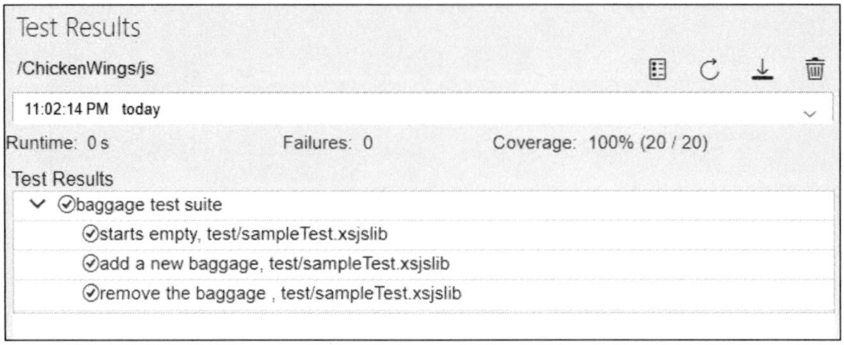

Figure 6.21 Third Unit Tests Execution

6.3 Java as Application Layer

In this section, we'll take a closer look at the development of Java modules with SAP HANA XS Advanced and SAP Web IDE for SAP HANA. We'll reveal useful features such as the code generation support that allows creating OData services from CDS entities, and we'll create a new application layer feature for our Chicken-Wings Airline application. We'll demonstrate how to read data from the SAP HANA database via a Java module with SAP HANA XS Advanced. Furthermore, we'll develop a Java application layer that allows us to maintain the crew information of our Chicken-Wings Airline.

Java, one of the most popular programming languages in the world, is an object-oriented programming language that is intended to run on any platform that supports Java without having to recompile the source code of the application. A Java virtual machine (VM) executes the bytecode of a compiled Java application. The SAP HANA XS Advanced runtime supports the development and execution of application layer logic written in Java. Java is supported as the runtime for SAP HANA XS Advanced since SAP HANA 1.0 SPS 11.

As of SAP HANA 2.0 SPS 0, SAP Web IDE for SAP HANA supports the creation of Java modules. The Java runtime of the SAP HANA XS Advanced platform offers an optimal integration with the SAP HANA database. Standard libraries allow developers to connect to the SAP HANA database and perform create, read, update, and delete operations via the SQL-JDBC (Java Database Connectivity) interface. The SAP HANA XS Advanced runtime takes care of the binding automatically to the correct HDI container of the SAP HANA XS Advanced application during the build and deployment process. Furthermore, the Java runtime option within SAP HANA XS Advanced allows developers to implement proper security mechanisms by leveraging a standard Java library that supports the SAP HANA XS Advanced UAA. We'll go into the details of the SAP HANA XS Advanced security concepts in Chapter 8.

The OData interface in SAP HANA XS Advanced exposes application layer logic written in Java. The SAP HANA XS Advanced platform supports the OData v4 standard for Java modules. It's not possible to create OData v2 services with Java applications in SAP HANA XS Advanced. A set of standard libraries enables developers to expose OData services. A developer can create read access OData services by using SAP Web IDE for SAP HANA wizard when creating a new Java module. The SAP HANA XS Advanced runtime generates read OData services automatically by interpreting the annotations within CDS definitions. The SAP HANA XS Advanced runtime translates OData requests into SQL queries to access data from underlying tables of an HDI container via the JDBC interface when executing an OData service via an OData client, such as an HTML5 application. The OData client retrieves the data via HTTP.

The Java OData libraries within SAP HANA XS Advanced also offer an extension framework for which a developer can program Java logic in case additional operations need to be performed in the Java application layer. Figure 6.22 highlights the architecture of an application deployment built using OData Java libraries within SAP HANA XS Advanced.

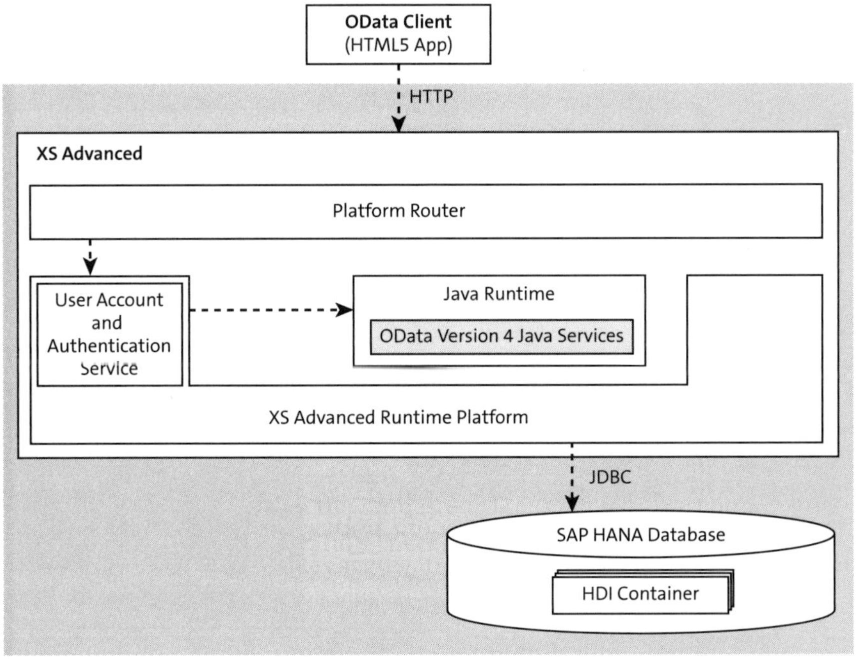

Figure 6.22 Architecture of an OData Java Application Deployment in SAP HANA XS Advanced

We'll reveal the steps to create a read OData service with Java for SAP HANA XS Advanced in Section 6.3.1. In Section 6.3.2, we'll demonstrate how the Java extension framework can be used to implement additional application layer logic that gets exposed via OData. In Section 6.3.3, we'll demonstrate how to overwrite the standard OData read service with the extension framework to add your own OData read logic.

6.3.1 Creating a Java Module to Read Database Content

In this section, we'll demonstrate how to create an OData service that reads data from an SAP HANA database table. We'll expose the information from our `Crew` table of the Chicken-Wings Airline via OData.

The basis for the information that we're going to expose is the table definition in the CDS documents we created in Chapter 5 when we set up the data model for the Chicken-Wings Airline. As a first step, the CDS entity that we want to expose via OData gets annotated with the `@OData.publish` annotation. This annotation allows us to generate a read OData service.

To demonstrate the capabilities of exposing a CDS definition as an OData service via the Java runtime of SAP HANA XS Advanced, we'll create a new CDS definition based on the `Crew` entity that we created in Chapter 5. To begin, follow these steps:

1. Create a new CDS definition file with the name *CrewJavaExample.hdbcds*. This CDS definition will follow the same structure as the `Crew` table in the SAP HANA database module of the ChickenWings application. We'll use this definition to add the OData annotation.
2. Open the *CrewJavaExample.hdbcds* CDS definition file with the **Code Editor** option in SAP Web IDE for SAP HANA. Right-click on the *Crew.hdbcds* file in the Chicken-Wings project, and select the **Open With • Code Editor**. (see Figure 6.23). The source code of this CDS definition will be displayed.

Note: When Using the @OData.publish Annotation

The `@OData.publish` annotation in a CDS definition only supports the creation of OData v4 services. All top-level contexts that a developer defines in a CDS document and that appear under the annotation `@OData.publish` are published as an OData v4 service. There is no restriction on the number of CDS contexts that a developer can annotate. A developer can't use the `@OData.publish` annotation to publish individual CDS entities or a CDS context that includes a subcontext. The SAP HANA XS Advanced runtime can't generate an OData service if the annotated context includes navigation to an external entity or view outside of the annotated context.

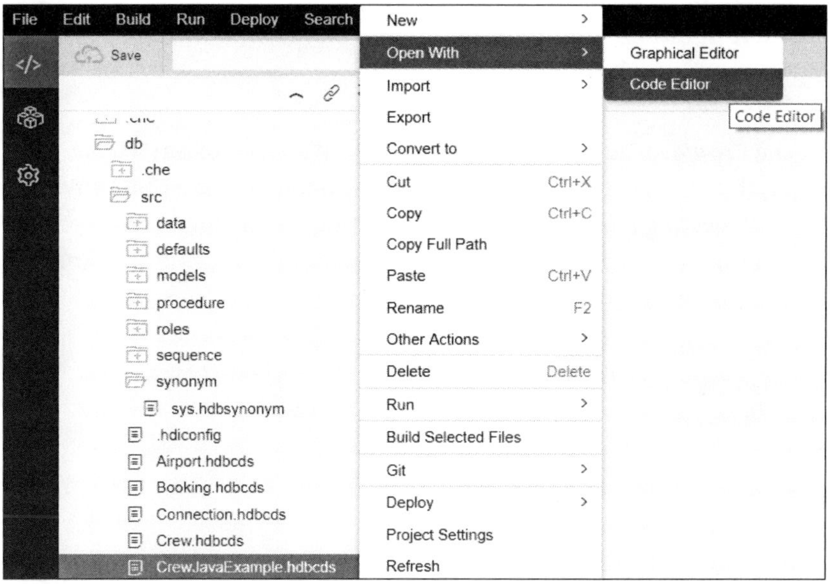

Figure 6.23 Opening the CrewJavaExample.hdbcds Definition File with the Code Editor

3. All top-level contexts that a developer defines in a CDS document and that appear under the annotation `@OData.publish` are published as an OData v4 service. Therefore, we must first adjust our current *CrewJavaExample.hdbcds* file definition and include a CDS context before adding the `@OData.publish` annotation. We'll call this context `ChickenWings` according to the name of our application. Listing 6.47 shows the updated CDS definition, including the context `ChickenWings` definition.

```
context ChickenWings {
  entity CrewJavaExample
  {
    key CREWID : Integer not null; /* Customer ID */
    FNAME : String(20); /* First Name */
    LNAME : String(20); /* Last Name */
    MOBILE : String(20); /* Mobile/Cell Number */
    EMAIL : String(20); /* Email */
    COUNTRY : String(20); /* Country of Residence */
    ROLE : String(20); /* Job Role of Crew */
  };
}
```

Listing 6.47 Context Definition of the CrewJavaExample.hdbcds CDS Definition

4. Now we can add the following OData annotation in the first line of the CDS definition:

```
@OData.publish: true
```

5. Next, build the *CrewJavaExample.hdbcds* file in SAP Web IDE for SAP HANA after implementing this change by right-clicking on the **db** folder of the ChickenWings application and selecting the **Build** menu entry. Listing 6.48 highlights the content of the updated *CrewJavaExample.hdbcds* with the `@OData.publish : true` annotation in line number one of the CDS file.

```
@OData.publish : true
context ChickenWings {
  entity CrewJavaExample
  {
    key CREWID : Integer not null; /* Customer ID */
    FNAME : String(20); /* First Name */
    LNAME : String(20); /* Last Name */
    MOBILE : String(20); /* Mobile/Cell Number */
    EMAIL : String(20); /* Email */
    COUNTRY : String(20); /* Country of Residence */
    ROLE : String(20); /* Job Role of Crew */
  };
}
```

Listing 6.48 Context Definition of the CrewJavaExample.hdbcds CDS Definition

6. As a next step, create a new Java module within SAP Web IDE for SAP HANA. To do that, right-click on the **ChickenWings** project in SAP Web IDE for SAP HANA, and select **New • Java Module** (see Figure 6.24).
7. Define the type of Java module. Since SAP Web IDE for SAP HANA 2.0 SP 00, the application supports the following module types:
   - **Simple web application**: Generates a Java module that contains a primary, ready-to-run "Hello World" application.
   - **Web application with OData V4 support**: Creates a Java module that provides an OData endpoint.
   - **Multi-Module web application:** Generates a Java module with dependencies.
   - **SpringBoot application:** Creates a Java module that brings its own runtime.

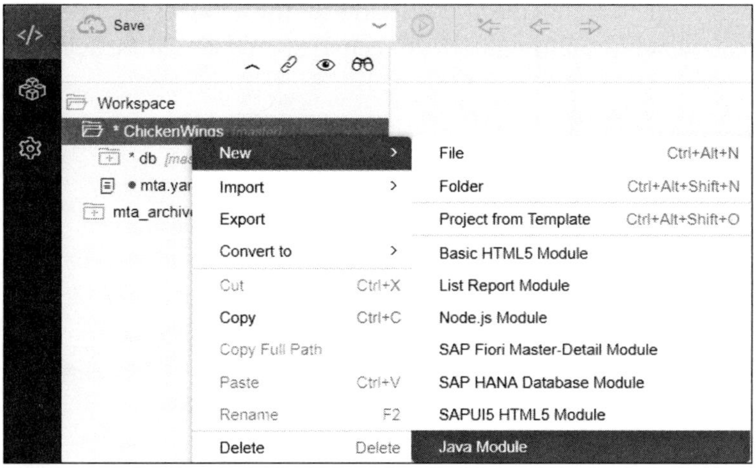

Figure 6.24 Creating a New Java Module in SAP Web IDE for SAP HANA

8. To create an endpoint for OData services, select **Web Application with OData V4 Support**, as shown in Figure 6.25. This option automatically adds all required libraries and settings to connect to the SAP HANA database from the Java module via the JDBC interface.

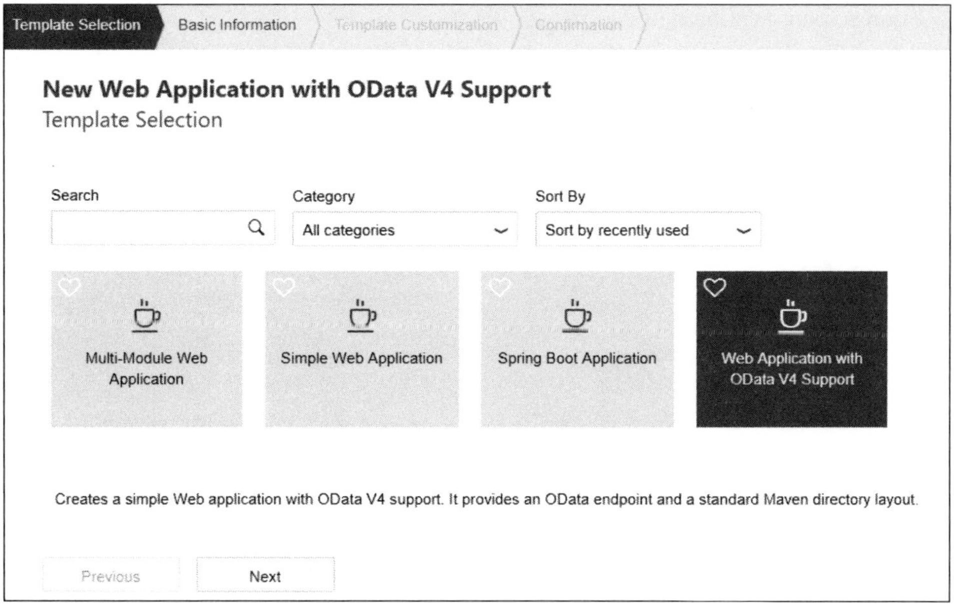

Figure 6.25 Selecting the Java Module Type

9. On the next screen, enter "java" as the **Module Name** for the new Java module (Figure 6.26). Click the **Next** button to get to the screen to open the basic **Module Settings**.

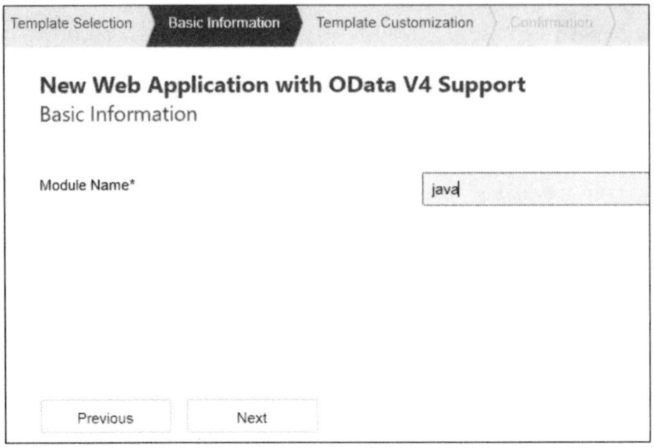

Figure 6.26 Specifying a Module Name for the New Java Module

10. Now we're ready to generate our first Java module with SAP HANA XS Advanced. Complete this step by clicking on the **Finish** button in the **Template Customization** screen, as shown in Figure 6.27.

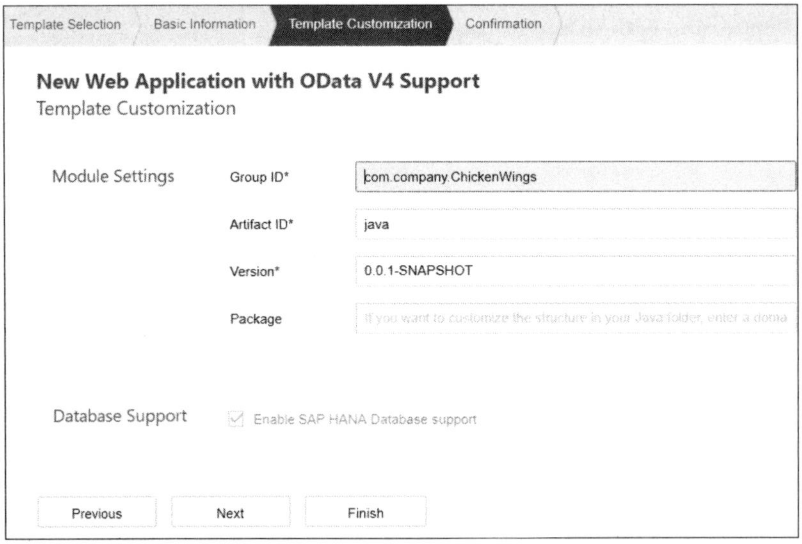

Figure 6.27 Template Customization Screen for a Java Module in SAP Web IDE for SAP HANA

11. After generating the Java module, you can see that SAP Web IDE for SAP HANA produced a new folder named **java** in our **ChickenWings** project folder. This folder contains a full Java application, including a read access OData service and access control. This OData service is now working out of the box. Figure 6.28 highlights the source code structure of the generated Java module within SAP Web IDE for SAP HANA.

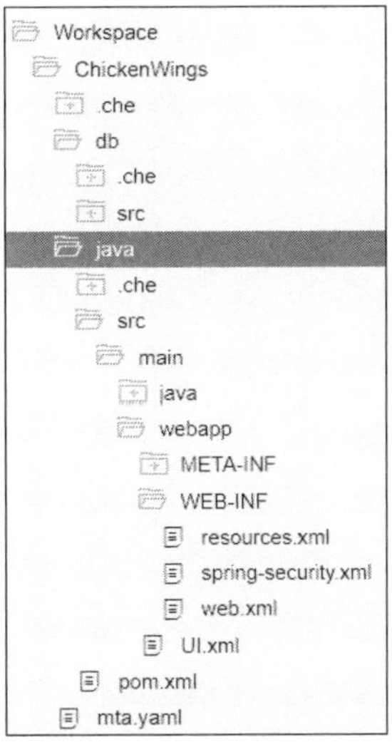

Figure 6.28 Java Module Source Code Structure in SAP Web IDE for SAP HANA

12. To simplify our test case for the read OData service, deactivate the access control settings of the OData service. We'll go into the details of the security mechanisms in Chapter 8 and will activate the access control for OData later.
13. Just like for any web application written in the Java programing language, the generated *web.xml* file is the deployment descriptor of the Java module. It declares how to handle OData requests and how to map URLs, and it defines security constraints, among other things. To disable the auto-generated security mechanism, you must open the generated *web.xml* file, which is available under the **web app** folder, and select the **web-inf** subfolder. Double-click on the **web.xml** file to open it in the source code editor of SAP Web IDE for SAP HANA.
14. After the file is open, scroll down to the XML tag **security-constraint**, as shown in Figure 6.29. Disable the security constraint by commenting out this block.

Figure 6.29 Disabling the Security Constraint in the web.xml File of the Java Module

15. After performing the initial configuration changes, we must build and run the Java module within SAP Web IDE for SAP HANA to activate the Java application. Right-click on the **java** package of our ChickingWings project, and selecting the **Build and Run** option. The console in SAP Web IDE for SAP HANA displays the steps of the build and run process of the application. After the app is available, the console displays an **Application is running** message and the URL of the Java application. Figure 6.30 shows the SAP Web IDE on SAP HANA has successfully built the Java module and it's running.

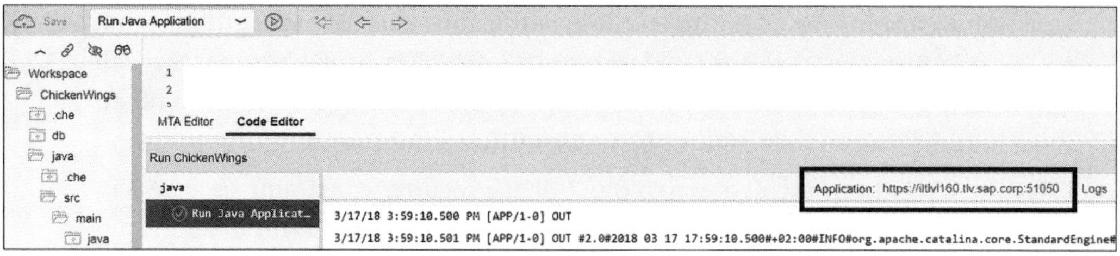

Figure 6.30 The Java Module Successfully Built and Running on SAP Web IDE on SAP HANA

16. Take note of the **Application** URL of the Java module that SAP Web IDE for SAP HANA displays. Add the following OData path at the end of the URL to display the metadata of the initial OData service. The URL should have the following format now:

    https://<servername>:<port>/java/odata/v4/<OuterContext>.<InnerContext>/ $metadata.

    In our example, we didn't use a namespace within the CDS definition of the table. When using a namespace within the CDS definition, a developer also defines this namespace in the OData URL. In such a case, the OData service uses the following URL:

    /java/odata/v4/<namespace>._.<context>.

    In our example, the URL has the following format:

    https://<servername>:<port>/java/odata/v4/CrewJavaExample/$metadata.

    Figure 6.31 shows the metadata of our first OData read service.

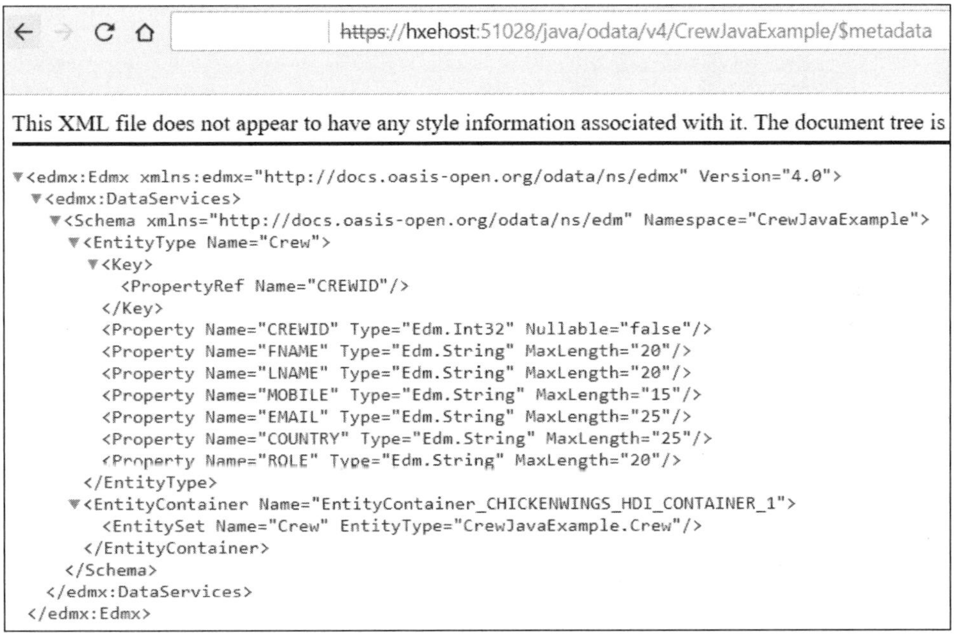
https://hxehost:51028/java/odata/v4/CrewJavaExample/$metadata
This XML file does not appear to have any style information associated with it. The document tree is
<edmx:Edmx xmlns:edmx="http://docs.oasis-open.org/odata/ns/edmx" Version="4.0">
<edmx:DataServices>
<Schema xmlns="http://docs.oasis-open.org/odata/ns/edm" Namespace="CrewJavaExample">
<EntityType Name="Crew">
<Key>
<PropertyRef Name="CREWID"/>
</Key>
<Property Name="CREWID" Type="Edm.Int32" Nullable="false"/>
<Property Name="FNAME" Type="Edm.String" MaxLength="20"/>
<Property Name="LNAME" Type="Edm.String" MaxLength="20"/>
<Property Name="MOBILE" Type="Edm.String" MaxLength="15"/>
<Property Name="EMAIL" Type="Edm.String" MaxLength="25"/>
<Property Name="COUNTRY" Type="Edm.String" MaxLength="25"/>
<Property Name="ROLE" Type="Edm.String" MaxLength="20"/>
</EntityType>
<EntityContainer Name="EntityContainer_CHICKENWINGS_HDI_CONTAINER_1">
<EntitySet Name="Crew" EntityType="CrewJavaExample.Crew"/>
</EntityContainer>
</Schema>
</edmx:DataServices>
</edmx:Edmx>

Figure 6.31 Metadata of the OData Read Service

17. After displaying the metadata of our OData service, we can request the actual data. We can display the data by adding the name of an entity at the end of the

OData URL. Following is an example OData request that retrieves all records from the table in our HDI container:

https://<servername>:<port>/java/odata/v4/<OuterContext>.<InnerContext>/entity

The data gets displayed in the JSON format when opening this URL in a new web browser window. In our example, the URL will look like the following:

https://<servername>:<port>/java/odata/v4/CrewJavaExample/Crew

Figure 6.32 displays the data returned by our read OData service.

https://hxehost:51028/java/odata/v4/CrewJavaExample/Crew
{
@odata.context: "$metadata#CrewJavaExample.Crew",
- value: [
- {
CREWID: 1,
FNAME: "User A",
LNAME: "Last Name A",
MOBILE: "123",
EMAIL: "user@test.com",
COUNTRY: "US",
ROLE: "Pilot"
},
- {
CREWID: 2,
FNAME: "User B",
LNAME: "Last Name B",
MOBILE: "456",
EMAIL: "user2@test.com",
COUNTRY: "US",
ROLE: "Stewardess"
}
],
@odata.nextLink: "https://hxehost:51028/java/odata/v4/CrewJavaExample/Crew?$skiptoken=1000"
}

Figure 6.32 Result of the Read OData Service

18. Because we have a working read OData service for our Java module, we can also leverage the standard parameters of OData. The OData v4 definition allows the use of standard parameters, such as `$select`, `$filter`, `$top`, and `$skip`, for retrieving data. These standard OData parameters are also available within the Java runtime of SAP HANA XS Advanced. Some OData example calls are provided next to demonstrate these capabilities.

You can order the result with the following OData service call:

https://<servername>:<port>/java/odata/v4/<OuterContext>.<InnerContext>/entity

An OData URL can be tested in a web browser window directly by opening the URL. Figure 6.33 displays the data returned by our read OData service where we request one entry via the `$top=1` parameter and sort the result set by the `CREWID` field.

https://hxehost:51028/java/odata/v4/CrewJavaExample/Crew?$top=1&$orderby=CREWID
{
@odata.context: "$metadata#CrewJavaExample.Crew",
- value: [
- {
CREWID: 1,
FNAME: "User A",
LNAME: "Last Name A",
MOBILE: "123",
EMAIL: "user@test.com",
COUNTRY: "US",
ROLE: "Pilot"
}
]
}

Figure 6.33 Ordering the Results of an OData Service Call

6.3.2 Creating an OData Service to Modify Data

In this section, we'll demonstrate how to create an OData service that allows you to create, update, and delete data from an SAP HANA database table. We'll extend our read OData service by adding the capability to modify data of the `Crew` table of the Chicken-Wings Airline via OData. To implement create, update, and delete support for our OData service, we'll make use of the OData extension framework for Java modules in SAP HANA XS Advanced.

Insert, Update, and Delete Operations via OData in Java

Only reading information is supported from a CDS table in SAP HANA XS Advanced via OData. It's not possible to insert, update, or delete data from a CDS table via the default OData services. Custom code extensions are required to support insert, update, and delete operations via OData in the Java runtime of SAP HANA XS Advanced.

Extensions for the Java module OData services in SAP HANA XS Advanced are custom Java code containing methods that implement functionality regarding how to handle the create, update, or delete OData operations. An `extensionTemplate` class gets automatically defined when creating a new Java module with SAP HANA XS Advanced. This `extensionTemplate` class provides the default framework for writing extension methods. We write an extension method for every OData entity set and OData method where custom logic is required. In our example, we'll write an extension method for the Crew entity set, and the OData methods `create`, `update`, and `delete`.

Create a New Java Class

Before implementing the methods, we must create a new Java class in our ChickenWings application. Right-click on the **java** folder under the **src-main-java-com-company-ChickenWings** folder, and select **New • Java Class** (Figure 6.34).

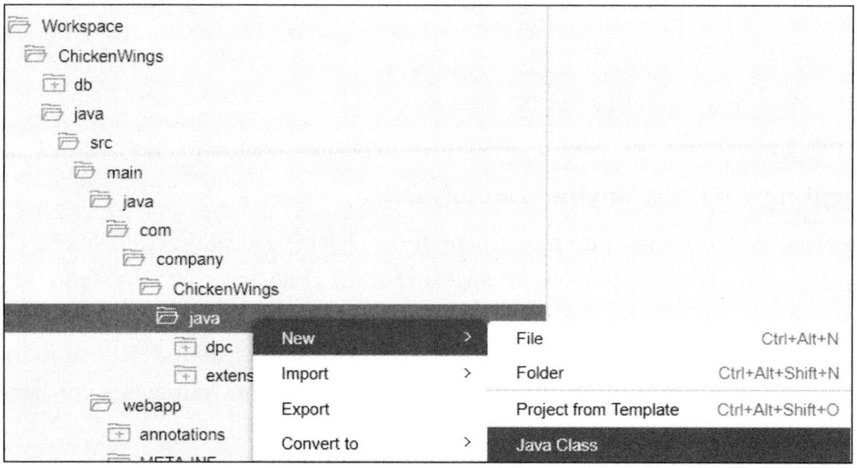

Figure 6.34 Creating a New Java Class

Next, we provide a name for the package and the Java class. We'll use "com.company.ChickenWings" as the **Package** name and "ChickenWingsJavaExtension" as the **Name** of the Java class (Figure 6.35). Select the **Next** and **Finish** buttons to create the template of this new Java class.

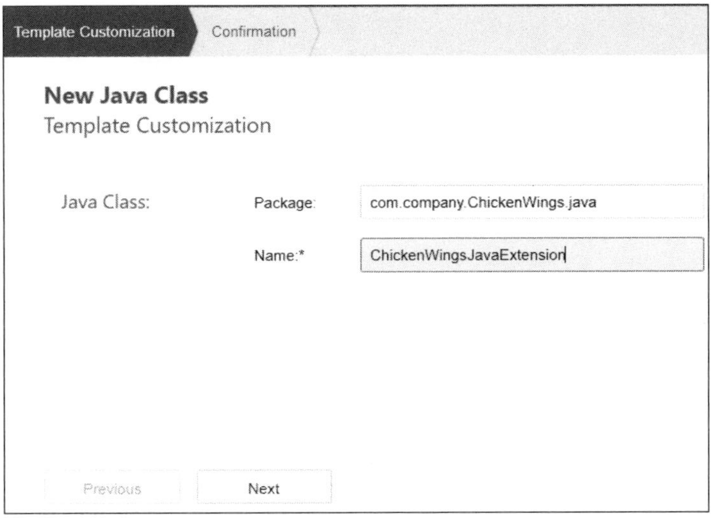

Figure 6.35 Specifying the Package and Java Class Names

SAP Web IDE for SAP HANA automatically creates a new file called *ChickenWingsJavaExtension.java* and the default Java class structure. We'll use this file to implement the logic of inserting, updating, and deleting records in the `Crew` table. Figure 6.36 displays the new *ChickenWingsJavaExtension.java* file in SAP Web IDE for SAP HANA.

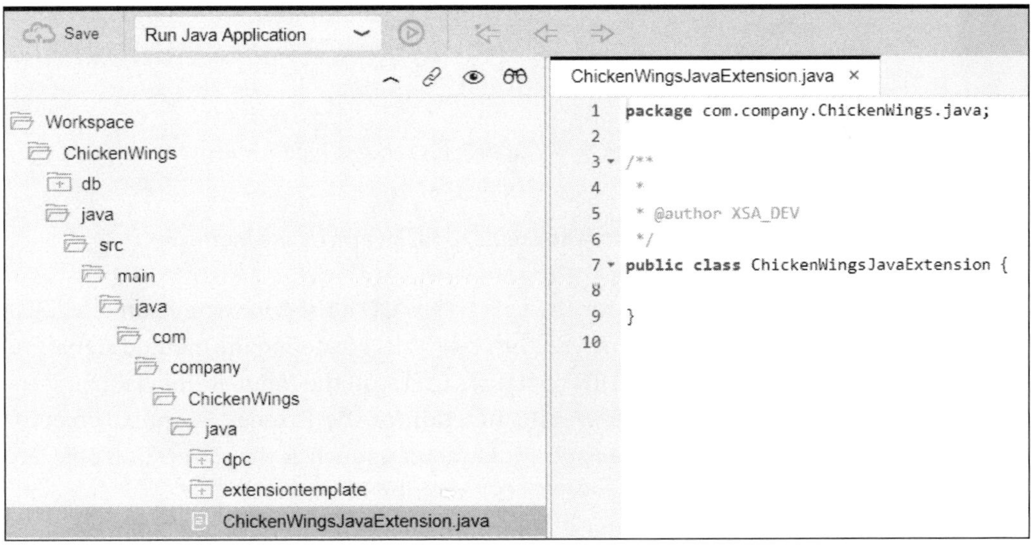

Figure 6.36 ChickenWingsJavaExtension.java File in SAP Web IDE for SAP HANA

Add Methods

The Java methods that implement the custom logic for the create, update, and delete operations get annotated with the `ExtendDataProvider` annotation. As general guidance, we recommend defining the return option void and an input parameter of type `ExtensionContext`. Furthermore, the `ExtendDataProvider` annotation of the method requires the following mandatory parameters:

- `entitySet`
  The name of the OData entity set of the extension.
- `requestTypes`
  The OData service request type, which can be one of the following values: `CREATE`, `READ`, `UPDATE`, or `DELETE`.
- `ServiceName`
  An optional parameter that can be used when it's required to specify the name of the service explicitly. This is the case in scenarios where exposed OData services share the same entity name.

The method signatures for our `Crew` table's create, update, delete feature look like Listing 6.49.

```
@ExtendDataProvider(entitySet = { "Crew" }, requestTypes = RequestType.CREATE)
public void createCrew(ExtensionContext ecx)

@ExtendDataProvider(entitySet = { "Crew" }, requestTypes = RequestType.UPDATE)
public void updateCrew(ExtensionContext ecx)

@ExtendDataProvider(entitySet = { "Crew" }, requestTypes = RequestType.DELETE)
public void deleteCrew(ExtensionContext ecx)
```

Listing 6.49 Method Signatures of the Create, Update, and Delete Methods

Now, we'll write the method for the `createCrew` OData service extension. We'll use this method to create a new entry in the `Crew` table. We define the method signature, establish a connection to the HDI container, and read the input entity via the `ExtensionContext` object. The `getDSParams()` function of the ExtensionContext object is required to retrieve data-source-specific parameters such as the connection object to the HDI container. The `getODataRequest()` function of the `ExtensionContext` object is used to retrieve the OData request object, which can be used for getting the request headers. The `getUriInfo()` method returns the Uniform Resource Identifier (URI) information object that contains information about the URI and query options. This method is mandatory with DELETE and UPDATE where the key predicate is required.

In the method, we read the input values from the entity of the payload of the OData request first via the following method:

```
Entity requestEntity = payload.getEntity();
```

We can read specific values of the OData payload via the getProperty method. An example of how the property CREWID and type cast the value into a numeric datatype is as follows:


```
(Integer)requestEntity.getProperty("CREWID").getValue()
```

Afterward, we can write the records into the Crew CDS table via SQL statements. The prepareStatement method is required to define the prepared SQL statement. The values are set for the prepared SQL statement via the setInt or setString method. Finally, the SQL statement is executed by calling the execute() method. The relevant source code is highlighted in Listing 6.50.

```
private static final String INSERT = "INSERT INTO \"CrewJavaExample.Crew\"
(\"CREWID\",\"FNAME\",\"LNAME\",\"MOBILE\",\"EMAIL\",\"COUNTRY\",\"ROLE\")
VALUES" + " (?,?,?,?,?,?,?)" ;
PreparedStatement pstmt = conn.prepareStatement(INSERT);
    pstmt.setInt(1, (Integer)requestEntity.getProperty("CREWID").getValue());
pstmt.execute();
```

Listing 6.50 Relevant Functions to Insert a New Record in the Crew Table

After inserting the new entry into the Crew table, we'll select this record and return it as a result of the OData call. We achieve this with the method createEntityFromResultSet, and we set the result set as the return value of the OData call by calling the setResultEntity method. The following highlights the relevant function calls:

```
Entity result = rs.next() ? createEntityFromResultSet(rs) : null;
dpCtx.setResultEntity(result);
```

Listing 6.51 shows the source code of the createCrew method.

```
private static final String INSERT = "INSERT INTO \"CrewJavaExample.Crew\"
(\"CREWID\",\"FNAME\",\"LNAME\",\"MOBILE\",\"EMAIL\",\"COUNTRY\",\"ROLE\")
VALUES" + " (?,?,?,?,?,?,?)" ;
```

```
@ExtendDataProvider(entitySet = { "Crew" }, requestTypes =
 { RequestType.CREATE })
public void createCrew(ExtensionContext ectx) throws ODataApplicationException {
  try {
    Connection conn = ((CDSDSParams) ectx.getDSParams()).getConnection();
    DataProviderExtensionContext dpCtx = ectx.asDataProviderContext();
    DeserializerResult payload = dpCtx.getDeserializerResult();
    Entity requestEntity = payload.getEntity();
    PreparedStatement pstmt = conn.prepareStatement(INSERT);
    pstmt.setInt(1, (Integer)requestEntity.getProperty("CREWID").getValue());
    pstmt.setString(2, (String) requestEntity.getProperty("FNAME").getValue());
    pstmt.setString(3, (String) requestEntity.getProperty("LNAME").getValue());
    pstmt.setString(4, (String) requestEntity.getProperty("MOBILE").getValue());
    pstmt.setString(5, (String) requestEntity.getProperty("EMAIL").getValue());
    pstmt.setString(6, (String) requestEntity.getProperty("COUNTRY").getValue())
;
    pstmt.setString(7, (String) requestEntity.getProperty("ROLE").getValue());
    pstmt.execute();
    pstmt = conn.prepareStatement(SELECT);
    pstmt.setInt(1,  (Integer)requestEntity.getProperty("CREWID").getValue());
    ResultSet rs = pstmt.executeQuery();
    Entity result = rs.next() ? createEntityFromResultSet(rs) : null;
    dpCtx.setResultEntity(result);
    conn.close();
    } catch (SQLException sqlException) {
      return;
    }
    finally{
    }
}
```

Listing 6.51 Source Code of the createCrew Method

We use the `setResultEntity` method to specify a return value of the OData service call. The return value is the added data of the table as a JSON object. We use a helper function to create the result object of the return value of the OData service call. We'll use this helper function in our other OData service methods as well. Listing 6.52 shows the implementation of the helper function.

```
private Entity createEntityFromResultSet(ResultSet rs) throws SQLException {
  Entity e = new Entity();
  ResultSetMetaData meta = rs.getMetaData();
  int columnCount = meta.getColumnCount();
  List<String> columns = new ArrayList<String>();
  for (int i = 1; i <= columnCount; i++)
    columns.add(meta.getColumnLabel(i));
    for (String column : columns)
       e.addProperty(new Property(null, column, ValueType.PRIMITIVE,
rs.getObject(column)));
    return e;
}
```

Listing 6.52 Source Code of the Helper Function for Creating the Result Entity Set

Logging

So far, this method doesn't include any logging functionalities. We cover additional concepts of how to add logging output to Java applications in SAP HANA XS Advanced in Chapter 9.

The `updateCrew` method follows a similar concept. Note that the method signature now specifies the `UPDATE` request type. We can implement our custom update logic for the `Crew` table in this method. Listing 6.53 displays the source code of the `update` method.

```
private static final String UPDATE = "UPDATE \"CrewJavaExample.Crew\
" SET " + "\"FNAME\"=?,\"LNAME\"=?,\"MOBILE\"=?,\"EMAIL\"=?,\"COUNTRY\"=?,
\"ROLE\"=? WHERE \"CREWID\"=" + "?";
@ExtendDataProvider(entitySet = { "Crew" }, requestTypes = { RequestType.
UPDATE })
    public void updateCrew(ExtensionContext ectx) {
      DataProviderExtensionContext dpCtx = ectx.asDataProviderContext();
         try {
            Connection conn = ((CDSDSParams) ectx.getDSParams()).
getConnection();
            DeserializerResult payload = ectx.asDataProviderContext().
getDeserializerResult();
```

```
            Entity requestEntity = payload.getEntity();
            UriInfo ui = ectx.getUriInfo();
            UriResourceEntitySet uriResourceEntitySet =
((UriResourceEntitySet) ui.getUriResourceParts().get(0));
            String keyVal = requestEntity.getProperty("CREWID").getValue().
toString();
            List<UriParameter> kp = uriResourceEntitySet.getKeyPredicates();
            PreparedStatement pstmt = conn.prepareStatement(UPDATE);
            pstmt.setString(1, (String) requestEntity.getProperty("FNAME").
getValue());
            pstmt.setString(2, (String) requestEntity.getProperty("LNAME").
getValue());
            pstmt.setString(3, (String) requestEntity.getProperty("MOBILE").
getValue());
            pstmt.setString(4, (String) requestEntity.getProperty("EMAIL").
getValue());
            pstmt.setString(5, (String) requestEntity.getProperty("COUNTRY").
getValue());
            pstmt.setString(6, (String) requestEntity.getProperty("ROLE").
getValue());
            pstmt.setString(7, kp.get(0).getText());
            pstmt.execute();
            ODataRequest request = dpCtx.getODataRequest();
            final Preferences.Return returnPreference = OData.newInstance()
                    .createPreferences(request.getHeaders(HttpHeader.PREFER)).
getReturn();
            if (returnPreference == null || returnPreference == Preferences.
Return.REPRESENTATION) {
                pstmt = conn.prepareStatement(SELECT);
                pstmt.setString(1, keyVal);
                ResultSet rs = pstmt.executeQuery();
                Entity result = rs.next() ? createEntityFromResultSet(rs) :
null;
                dpCtx.setResultEntity(result);
            }
            conn.close();
        }
```

```
        catch (SQLException sqlException) {
    }
}
```

Listing 6.53 Source Code of the updateCrew Method

Finally, we implement the deleteCrew method to remove a crew member from the Crew table. Note that the method signature now specifies the DELETE request type. We can achieve our custom delete logic for the Airport table in this method. Listing 6.54 displays the source code of the update method.


```
private static final String DELETE = "DELETE FROM \"CrewJavaExample.Crew\
"  WHERE \"CREWID\"= ?";
@ExtendDataProvider(entitySet = { "Crew" }, requestTypes = { RequestType.
DELETE })
    public void deleteCrew(ExtensionContext ectx) {
        try {
            Connection conn = ((CDSDSParams) ectx.getDSParams()).
getConnection();
            UriInfo ui = ectx.getUriInfo();
            UriResourceEntitySet uriResourceEntitySet =
((UriResourceEntitySet) ui.getUriResourceParts().get(0));
            List<UriParameter> kp = uriResourceEntitySet.getKeyPredicates();
            PreparedStatement pstmt = conn.prepareStatement(DELETE);
            pstmt.setString(1, kp.get(0).getText());
            pstmt.execute();
            conn.close();
        }
        catch (SQLException sqlException) {
        }
}
```

Listing 6.54 Source Code of the deleteCrew Method

Run and Test the Java Module

After performing the source code changes, we build and run the Java module within SAP Web IDE for SAP HANA. Perform this step by right-clicking on the **java** package of the ChickingWings project and selecting the **Build and Run** option. The SAP Web IDE for SAP HANA console displays the steps of the build and run process of the application. After the app is available, the console displays an **Application is running** message and displays the URL of the Java application (see Figure 6.37).

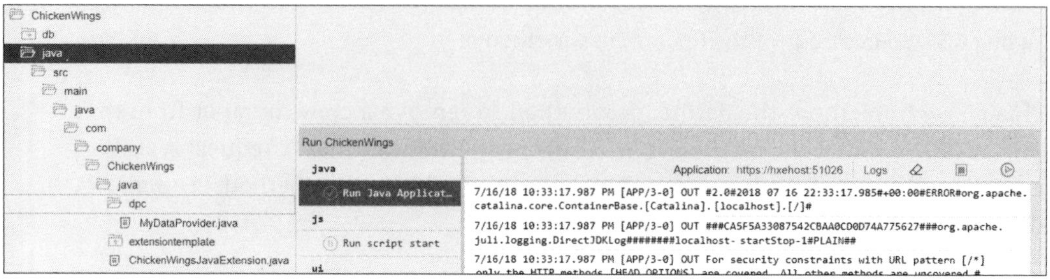

Figure 6.37 The Java Module Successfully Built and Running on SAP Web IDE on SAP HANA

Note the **Application** URL of the Java module that SAP Web IDE for SAP HANA displays. We can now test the create, update, and delete Java service. We'll use the Postman REST client tool to check our custom coding. As highlighted in Chapter 2, where we discussed the SAP HANA development environment, Postman is a tool that allows sending REST-based HTTP calls. This will enable us to test our Java services without having to implement a UI. Postman acts as an OData client in this case. First, we'll check our OData service request to read data. To do that, we specify a new request in Postman with the following details:

- URL: *https://<servername>:<port>/java/odata/v4/CrewJavaExample/Crew*
- HTTP request mechanism: `GET`

We don't have to specify any authentication mechanisms or a user name and password because we haven't enabled security for our OData service yet. Postman sends the request to the OData service after we click on the **Send** button. The result of the OData service call is available in the Postman response screen. Figure 6.38 displays the UI of Postman when sending an OData service request to read data.

Because we've completed an OData read request, we'll now enhance this request to write data. We'll add one record into our `Crew` table. Specify the following details in Postman to write data via OData:

- URL: *https://<servername>:<port>/java/odata/v4/CrewJavaExample/Crew*
- HTTP request mechanism: `POST`
- Body: As shown in Listing 6.55

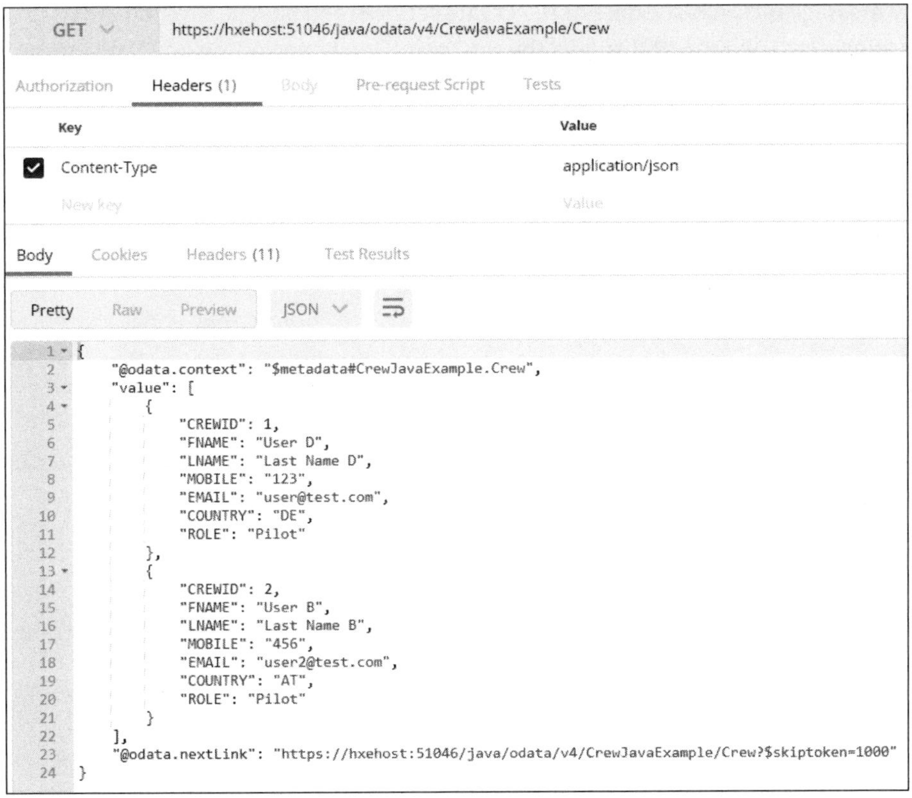
GET
https://hxehost:51046/java/odata/v4/CrewJavaExample/Crew
Authorization
Headers (1)
Body
Pre-request Script
Tests
Key
Value
Content-Type
application/json
New key
Value
Body
Cookies
Headers (11)
Test Results
Pretty
Raw
Preview
JSON
{
"@odata.context": "$metadata#CrewJavaExample.Crew",
"value": [
{
"CREWID": 1,
"FNAME": "User D",
"LNAME": "Last Name D",
"MOBILE": "123",
"EMAIL": "user@test.com",
"COUNTRY": "DE",
"ROLE": "Pilot"
},
{
"CREWID": 2,
"FNAME": "User B",
"LNAME": "Last Name B",
"MOBILE": "456",
"EMAIL": "user2@test.com",
"COUNTRY": "AT",
"ROLE": "Pilot"
}
],
"@odata.nextLink": "https://hxehost:51046/java/odata/v4/CrewJavaExample/Crew?$skiptoken=1000"
}

Figure 6.38 Testing the readCrew OData Service via the Postman Tool

```
{
"CREWID": 2,
"FNAME" : "User B",
"LNAME" : "Last Name B",
"MOBILE" : "456",
"EMAIL" : "user2@test.com",
"COUNTRY" : "AT",
"ROLE" : "Pilot"
}
```

Listing 6.55 Body of the HTTP POST Request to Add a New Crew Member

Postman sends the request to the OData service after we click on the **Send** button. The result of the OData service call is available in the Postman response screen. The body message includes the data of the OData service request. The method `createCrew` gets executed. Figure 6.39 displays the Postman UI when sending an OData service request to write data.

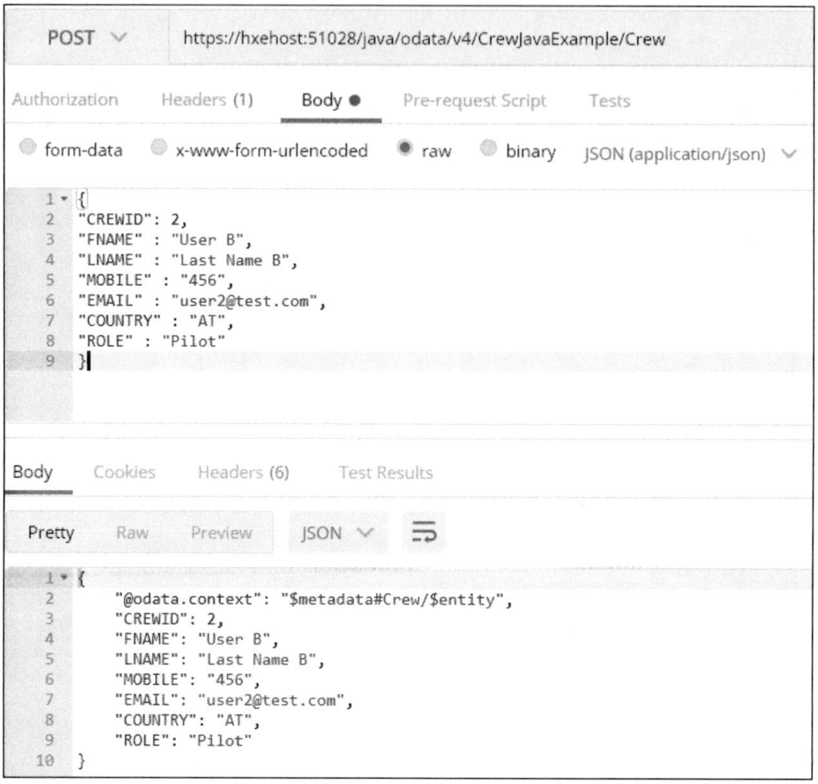

Figure 6.39 Testing the createCrew OData Service via the Postman Tool

Next, we'll test the OData service call to update data. Specify the following details in Postman to update data via OData:

- URL: *https://<servername>:<port>/java/odata/v4/CrewJavaExample/Crew(1)*
- HTTP request mechanism: `PUT`
- Body: As shown in Listing 6.56

```
{
"CREWID": 2,
"FNAME" : "User XYZ",
"LNAME" : "Last Name xyz",
```

```
"MOBILE" : "456",
"EMAIL" : "user2@test.com",
"COUNTRY" : "AT",
"ROLE" : "Pilot"
}
```

Listing 6.56 Body of the HTTP PUT Request to Update an Existing Crew Member

We'll update the record where the `CREWID` has the value `1` in the `Crew` table. Therefore, we specify the `Crew(1)` at the end of the OData URL. Postman sends the request to the OData service after we click on the **Send** button. The result of the OData service call is available in the Postman response screen. The body message includes the data of the OData service request. The SAP HANA XS Advanced Java runtime executes the method `updateCrew`.

Finally, we'll test the OData request to delete data. Specify the following details in Postman to update data via OData:

- URL: *https://<servername>:<port>/java/odata/v4/CrewJavaExample/Crew(3)*
- HTTP request mechanism: `DELETE`

We'll delete the record where the `CREWID` has the value `3` from the `Crew` table. Therefore, we're adding the `Crew(3)` at the end of the OData URL. Postman sends the request to the OData service after we click on the **Send** button. The result of the OData service call is available in the Postman response screen. The body message includes the data of the OData service request. The SAP HANA XS Advanced Java runtime executes the method `deleteCrew`. The data set will be removed from the Crew table. Figure 6.40 displays the Postman UI when sending an OData service request to delete data.

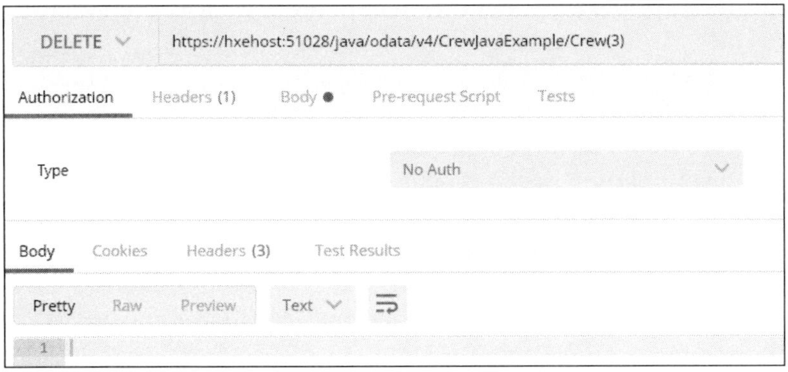

Figure 6.40 Testing the deleteCrew OData Service via the Postman Tool

Overwriting the Standard Read Function

A developer can use the extension framework of OData for Java in SAP HANA XS Advanced to write a custom extension for the OData read operation. This option might be necessary if specific preprocessing or postprocessing in the application layer is required. This custom extension follows the same concept as shown in the previous chapter where we built a custom extension for the create, update, and delete operations.

We annotate the custom read method with the ExtendDataProvider annotation and the request type RequestType.READ. The method takes an input parameter of the type ExtensionContext. The setResultEntity method sets the result. In this example, we create a custom read operation where we select one record via custom SQL as specified in the SELECT string. The value of this prepared SQL statement is specified again via the function call prepareStatement, and the statement gets executed with the executeQuery function. The following highlights the relevant source code of our example to define and execute the SQL statement:

```
PreparedStatement pstmt = conn.prepareStatement(SELECT);
        pstmt.setInt(1,  1);
        ResultSet rs = pstmt.executeQuery();
```

Finally, we use the createEntityFromResultSet function to specify the result set of the OData call. Listing 6.57 displays the source code of our OData service read extension.

```
private static final String SELECT = "SELECT * FROM \"CrewJavaExample.Crew\
" WHERE " + '"' + "CREWID" + '"' + '=' + "?";
@ExtendDataProvider(entitySet = { "Crew" }, requestTypes =
 { RequestType.READ })
public void readCrew(ExtensionContext ectx) throws ODataApplicationException {
    try {
        Connection conn = ((CDSDSParams) ectx.getDSParams()).getConnection();
        DataProviderExtensionContext dpCtx = ectx.asDataProviderContext();
        PreparedStatement pstmt = conn.prepareStatement(SELECT);
        pstmt.setInt(1,  1);
        ResultSet rs = pstmt.executeQuery();
        Entity result = rs.next() ? createEntityFromResultSet(rs) : null;
        dpCtx.setResultEntity(result);
        conn.close();
    } catch (SQLException sqlException) {
        return;
```

```
    }
    finally{
    }
}
```

Listing 6.57 Source Code of the Custom OData Service Read Extension

6.3.3 Connecting Java Services to an HTML5 Frontend

In the previous chapters, we developed OData services for the Java runtime of SAP HANA XS Advanced. We highlighted the different options to create OData services that support read, create, update, and delete operations. In this section, we'll demonstrate how an SAP HANA XS Advanced HTML5 application can consume a Java OData service from SAP HANA XS Advanced.

We'll perform the following configuration steps to consume the Java OData service within an SAP HANA XS Advanced HTML5 module.

- Configure the Java module API and service URL.
- Create a new HTML5 module.
- Add the Java module binding information to the HTML5 module.
- Set up the application router information for the HTML5 module.
- Create a simple SAPUI5 table to consume the Java OData service.

Configure the Java Module API and Service URL

Because SAP HANA XS Advanced follows the concept of microservices, the Java OData services from Section 6.3.2 must be made available for other SAP HANA XS Advanced modules first so that the application router of SAP HANA XS Advanced can route requests from SAP HANA XS Advanced applications correctly to the Java module of the SAP HANA XS Advanced project. The Java module must define that it provides an API and service URL. A developer performs this configuration in the *mta.yaml* file of the SAP HANA XS Advanced project for the Chicken-Wings Airline. A new `provides` tag has to be created under the Java module entry in the *mta.yaml* file.

Furthermore, the name of the new provided service will be `java_api`, the key of the property is `service_url`, and the value is `${default-url}`. This must be specified for the SAP HANA XS Advanced Application router to forward requests correctly. Save the *mta.yaml* file after the changes are made. In Figure 6.41, we highlight the required configuration changes in the *mta.yaml* file.

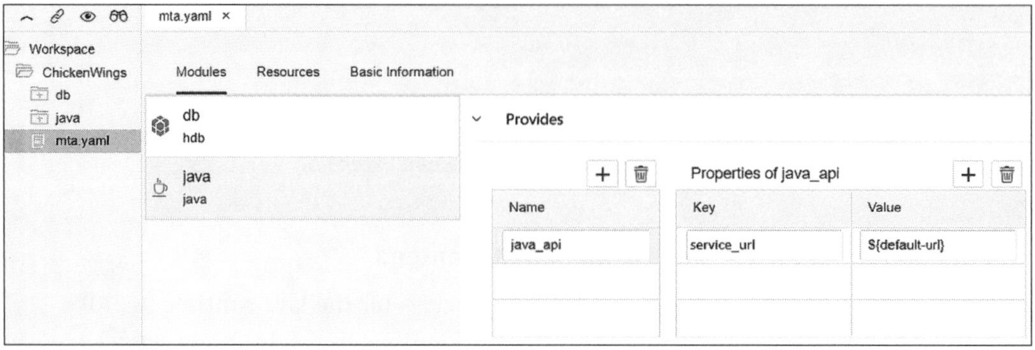

Figure 6.41 Adjusting the mta.yaml File for the Java Module to Expose a service_url

Create a New HTML5 Module

We create a new HTML5 module for the ChickenWings application to develop an HTML5 app that will consume a Java OData service. Because we cover the creation and specifics of SAP HANA XS Advanced HTML5 modules in detail in Chapter 7, we'll only go into details of the required configuration for the integration with a Java module in this section. Refer to Chapter 7 for more detailed information regarding the development of a UI with SAP HANA XS Advanced.

First, select the **ChickenWings** project in SAP Web IDE for SAP HANA, right-click, and select **Basic HTML5 Module**, as shown in Figure 6.42. Specify "ui" as the name of the new module. SAP Web IDE for SAP HANA will create a new HTML5 application within the ChickenWings project. We'll use this HTML5 module later in this chapter to connect to the Java OData service.

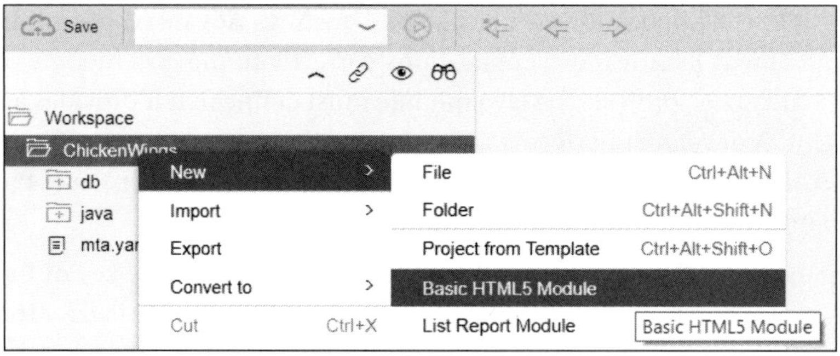

Figure 6.42 Creating a New Basic HTML5 Module

Specify "ui" as the **Module Name**, and click the **Finish** button, as shown in Figure 6.43.

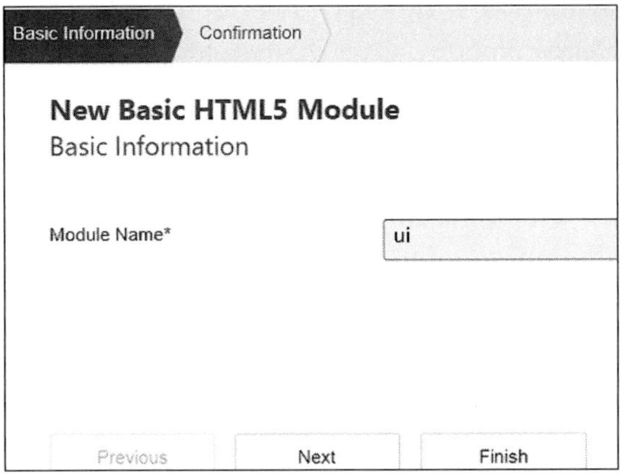

Figure 6.43 Specifying the Name of the New Basic HTML5 Module

SAP Web IDE for SAP HANA generates the HTML5 module in our ChickenWings application. We'll use this HTML5 module to create a UI that consumes our Java OData interface that we've developed in the previous section. Figure 6.44 displays the basic structure of the new HTML5 module.

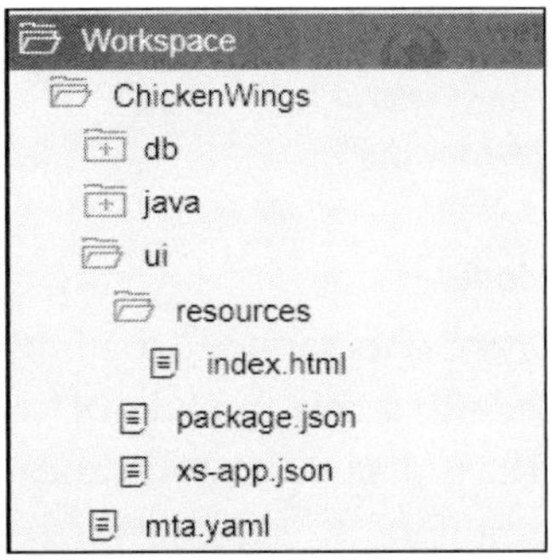

Figure 6.44 Structure of the ui HTML5 Module

Add the Java Module Binding Information to the HTML5 Module

Next, we must configure binding information for the new HTML5 module for the SAP HANA XS Advanced application router to route requests to the correct SAP HANA XS Advanced Java module. We perform this configuration in the *mta.yaml* file of the ChickenWings application. A new property pointing to the Java module's service URL must be specified. We define a new `requires` entry for the `ui` HTML5 module in the *mta.yaml* file.

In the requires entry, we specify the name of the exposed Java API, which we call java_api. For this API, we must define a name property, a service_url, and the forwardAuthToken parameter. The name of the property will be java_be with the value of the forwardAuthToken parameter set to true. This will ensure that the authentication token of the HTML5 module will be forwarded to the Java runtime when the UI requests data from the Java OData service. We'll require this after we enable the security mechanisms for the Java module. Providing this token will ensure that the SAP HANA XS Advanced UAA service will allow us to retrieve data.

Listing 6.58 highlights the configuration change in the *mta.yaml* file for the HTML5 module.

```
- name: ui
  type: html5
  path: ui
  requires:
    - name: java_api
      group: destinations
      properties:
        name: java_be
        url: '~{service_url}'
        forwardAuthToken: true
```

Listing 6.58 Configuration in the mta.yaml File for the HTML5 Module

Set Up the Application Router Information for the HTML5 Module

The new HTML5 module will send HTTP requests to the Java OData service. To submit requests from an SAP HANA XS Advanced HTML5 module to a Java module OData service, we configure a route. This route is required by the SAP HANA XS Advanced application router to forward the requests to the correct module. It's necessary to set the source path to the OData service of the Java module. In our case, we specified the path as /java/odata/v4. This path also must be used later in the HTML5 application when connecting to the OData service.

The configuration has to be performed in the *xs-app.json* configuration file of the HTML5 module. Note that the authentiationType property is set to the value xsuaa. This will trigger a validation of the authentication token when the UI requests data from the Java OData service. (We explain the SAP HANA XS Advanced security mechanisms in Chapter 8.) Listing 6.59 highlights the new route's configuration for the Java OData service.

```
{
  "welcomeFile": "index.html",
  "authenticationMethod": "none",
  "routes": [{
     "source": "/java/odata/v4",
     "destination": "java_be",
     "authenticationType": "none"
  }]
}
```

Listing 6.59 Route Configuration within the xs-app.json Configuration File of the HTML5 Module

We can build and run the HTML5 module after performing the configuration change within the *xs-app.json* file. Trigger the build and run process within SAP Web IDE for SAP HANA. The message **Application is running** will appear in the console within SAP Web IDE for SAP HANA when the HTML5 application is available, along with the URL of the HTML5 app. Figure 6.45 shows SAP Web IDE for SAP HANA with the completed build process of the HTML5 module and the URL to the application in the right corner. In addition, note that our Java application is showing as running in the SAP Web IDE for SAP HANA console. This is required because the Java runtime of SAP HANA XS Advanced will perform the application layer processing in our case.

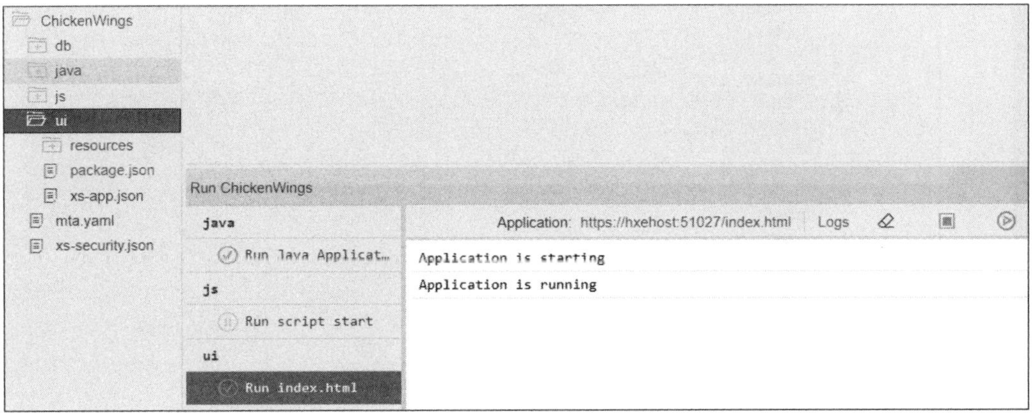

Figure 6.45 Completed Build Process of the HTML5 Module

The initial version of the HTML5 application is now available within the SAP HANA XS Advanced runtime, which is a key part of the successful SAP HANA XS Advanced application router configuration. By specifying the route's configuration in the *xs-app.json* file, the SAP HANA XS Advanced router will now successfully forward requests from the HTML5 module to the Java module of our SAP HANA XS Advanced application. Test the successful routing by using the URL of the HTML5 module as shown in SAP Web IDE for SAP HANA and adding the path to the Java OData service at the end of the URL. In our example, the URL will look like the following:

https://<server>:<port HTML5 module>/java/odata/v4/._./$metadata

It's important to note that the Java OData service URL port and the HTML5 application port are now the same. The application router of the SAP HANA XS Advanced runtime takes care that the requests are routed to the correct application component to process the request.

Open this URL in a new web browser tab to see the metadata of the Java OData service. Figure 6.46 displays a successful OData metadata request from an HTML5 module in a web browser window. This example illustrates how a developer can test an OData web service in a web browser.

://hxehost:51046/java/odata/v4/CrewJavaExample/Crew
{
@odata.context: "$metadata#CrewJavaExample.Crew",
- value: [
- {
CREWID: 1,
FNAME: "User D",
LNAME: "Last Name D",
MOBILE: "123",
EMAIL: "user@test.com",
COUNTRY: "DE",
ROLE: "Pilot"
},
- {
CREWID: 2,
FNAME: "User B",
LNAME: "Last Name B",
MOBILE: "456",
EMAIL: "user2@test.com",
COUNTRY: "AT",
ROLE: "Pilot"
}
],
@odata.nextLink: "https://hxehost:51046/java/odata/v4/CrewJavaExample/Crew?$skiptoken=1000"
}

Figure 6.46 OData Metadata Request from an HTML5 Module

Create an SAPUI5 Table to Consume the Java OData Service

To finalize our example, we'll connect a SAPUI5 table of our HTML5 module to the Java OData service. Because we cover the creation and specifics of SAP HANA XS Advanced HTML5 modules in detail in Chapter 7, we'll only go into details of the required configuration for the integration with a Java module here. Refer to Chapter 7 for more detailed information on creating UIs within the SAP HANA XS Advanced runtime.

The step of connecting an SAP HANA XS Advanced Java OData service to a component in SAPUI5 is the same as with any other backend service of SAP HANA XS Advanced. No specific programming steps are required when connecting to a Java module. We'll make use of the SAPUI5 table component to demonstrate the capability of connecting SAPUI5 to a Java OData service. In our SAPUI5 coding, we'll first initiate the OData model by creating a new instance of the `ODataModel` object. Note that the Java runtime of SAP HANA XS Advanced only allows us to create OData v4 services. This also means that in SAPUI5, we have to use the method `sap.ui.model.odata.v4.ODataModel` to create a compliant `v4` OData model. Listing 6.60 highlights the source code required to create an OData model.

```
var oModel = new sap.ui.model.odata.v4.ODataModel({
                serviceUrl: "/java/odata/v4/CrewJavaExample/",
                synchronizationMode: "None"
            });
```

Listing 6.60 Creating a SAPUI5 v4 OData Model

The rest of the SAPUI5 implementation follows the standard practices of working with the SAPUI5 framework. Listing 6.61 highlights the implementation of the SAPUI5 page.

```
<html>
    <head>
        <title>Table with OData V4 Binding</title>
        <script id='sap-ui-bootstrap'
            src='https://sapui5.hana.ondemand.com/1.40.9/resources/sap-ui-core.js'
            data-sap-ui-theme='sap_belize'
            data-sap-ui-libs='sap.m,sap.ui.table'
            data-sap-ui-xx-bindingSyntax='complex'></script>
        <script>
```

```
            // create an ODataModel from URL
            var oModel = new sap.ui.model.odata.v4.ODataModel({
                serviceUrl: "/java/odata/v4/CrewJavaExample/",
                synchronizationMode: "None"
            });
            var oTable = new sap.ui.table.Table({
                columns : [
                    {label: "CREWID", template: "CREWID", sortProperty: "CREWID" },
                    {label: "FNAME", template: "FNAME", sortProperty: "FNAME" },
                    {label: "LNAME", template: "LNAME", sortProperty: "LNAME" },
                    {label: "COUNTRY", template: "COUNTRY", sortProperty: "COUNTRY" },
                    {label: "ROLE", template: "ROLE", sortProperty: "ROLE" }
                ]
            });
            oTable.setModel(oModel); // set model to Table
            oTable.bindRows({path: "/Crew", $count : true});
// bind the rows to the service
            oTable.placeAt("content"); // place Table onto UI
        </script>
    </head>
    <body id='content' class='sapUiBody'></body>
</html>
```

Listing 6.61 Source Code for the SAPUI5 Table Connecting to a Java OData Service

Build the HTML5 module again within SAP Web IDE for SAP HANA. After the console of SAP Web IDE for SAP HANA displays the status **Application is running**, we can open a new web browser window and open the URL of the HTML5 application. We'll see the SAPUI5 table and the data that is provided by the Java OData service. Figure 6.47 displays the SAPUI5 SmartTable and the data from the Java OData service.

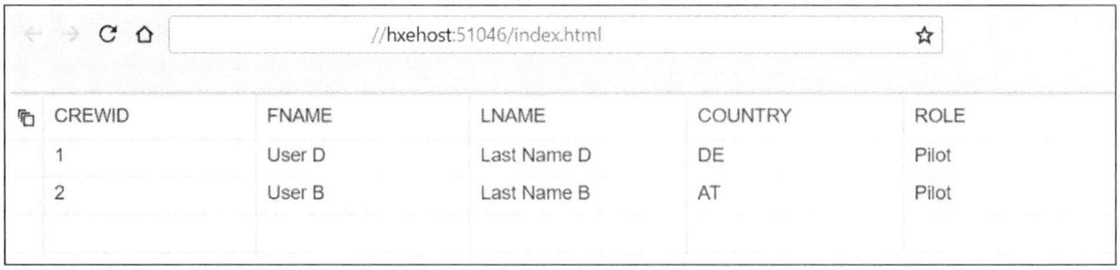

//hxehost:51046/index.html
CREWID
FNAME
LNAME
COUNTRY
ROLE
1
User D
Last Name D
DE
Pilot
2
User B
Last Name B
AT
Pilot

Figure 6.47 SAPUI5 Table Connecting to a Java OData Service

6.4 Summary

In this chapter, we introduced the options to create an application layer in SAP HANA XS Advanced via a Node.js and Java module. First, we explained the general tasks of an application layer and its role in an SAP HANA XS Advanced application. We highlighted the role of an application layer in the context of business applications, which is the link between the data model and the UI. We demonstrated the options for the access tables from an SAP HANA XS Advanced application and exposed this data via the OData interface. Furthermore, we explained the required configuration to implement OData services that support read and write operations in Node.js as well as in Java. Finally, we discussed options to test the implementation of a Node.js application layer and Java application layer.

In the next chapter, we'll explain the options to develop a presentation layer with the mechanisms of SAP HANA XS Advanced.

Chapter 7
Developing a Presentation Layer

When I'm driving, the fewer distractions there are, the better it is to focus on the job in hand. If the engineers could, they'd give you 40 buttons, but . . . it's better to have the ones you really need. The key thing is to make it simpler without getting rid of stuff that I might need to make the car go quicker.
–Lewis Hamilton (BBC Interview)

What Hamilton perfectly describes in the introductory note is the central concept that should be the target for any frontend developer during the creation of an application presentation layer: *provide the right functionality when it's required, without adding anything that would only generate confusion.*

Developing a presentation layer is usually the last part of an application development process, but, at the same time, it's the first contact a user has with the application itself. For that reason, it's extremely important to pay attention to the right things during definition of the presentation layer and to test it as soon as possible, even before development activities begin, with an exhaustive prototyping phase. This will ensure the quality of the software product, its usability, and appeal.

In this chapter, we'll introduce the main concepts behind a presentation layer of an SAP HANA extended application services, advanced model (SAP HANA XS Advanced) application based on the *UI development toolkit for HTML5* (SAPUI5). SAPUI5 is the state-of-the-art technology developed by SAP for building its new set of applications called *SAP Fiori*, where the user experience (UX) has been reimagined in a way that tries to meet as much as possible the design model we introduced at the beginning of the chapter.

SAP Fiori Design Guidelines

SAP provides a full set of guidelines that a developer should follow to deliver SAPUI5 applications in the correct way. These guidelines are available at *https://experience.sap.com/fiori-design-web.*

The SAP Fiori design guidelines describe the general concepts of the SAP Fiori design model and the recommendations that should be used for all the different user interface (UI) elements available in the SAPUI5 library.

This chapter will introduce the essential elements of the SAPUI5 framework. It's quite a complex topic and covering it in its entirety is outside the scope of this book. With the main concepts of SAPUI5 in mind, we'll move on with our application development, and, after having created its data and application layer, we'll create the presentation layer, so that the users can interact with our application. First, we'll see how to define an HTML5 module and the application routes used to address incoming requests to the right microservices to manage them. Then we'll see how the presentation layer consumes the data exposed by the application layer via OData services and how it's possible to define UI elements—*smart controls*—that get the configuration directly specified from the OData metadata information. Finally, we'll introduce application development based on SAP Fiori elements templates.

7.1 SAPUI5 Frontend Development

Some central concepts are essential to get started with SAPUI5:

- **SAPUI5 bootstrapping**
  This refers to how the SAPUI5 libraries are loaded when the application is initialized.
- **SAPUI5 application structuring**
  An SAPUI5 application is structured in reusable components with an application descriptor file (called the manifest file). With component encapsulation, it's possible to reuse an application in different component containers (e.g., SAP Fiori launchpad) that provide an execution framework.
- **Model View Controller (MVC)**
  This is one of the most well-known software architectural patterns.
- **Data binding**
  Data binding keeps the model and the view in synch (i.e., "bound") either one-way (from the model to the view) or two-way.
- **Navigation and routing**
  Because an application developed with SAPUI5 is a single-page application, navigation between the different pages of the application occurs by using some dedicated

JavaScript objects and configuration and not by requesting the pages from the server.

Modern web applications are developed following the *single-page* pattern, so when a user interacts with the web application, the UI is re-rendered directly into the client (usually a web browser) with JavaScript that runs into the engine provided by the browser. SAPUI5 uses three main elements:

- **HTML5**
  The final product of a SAPUI5 application is a web page that uses the latest HTML standard.
- **JavaScript**
  This programming language is used for building the HTML pages, and jQuery is the main JavaScript library used by SAPUI5 for modifying the Document Object Model (DOM). The DOM is an abstraction layer that treats HTML documents as an object with a tree structure.
- **Cascading Style Sheets (CSS)**
  CSS is the standard used for styling the layout of the application and for creating different application themes.

Where to Start

The best starting point for working with SAPUI5 is the SAPUI5 Software Development Kit (SDK) available at *https://sapui5.hana.ondemand.com/*.

The SAPUI5 SDK provides exhaustive documentation, API references, and a set of examples that show the usage of the most important SAPUI5 controls. Another great feature of the SAPUI5 SDK is the availability of many end-to-end demo applications that can be used for analyzing real-life scenarios.

Next let's discuss the core concepts of SAPUI5.

7.1.1 Application Bootstrapping

Bootstrapping is the initial step to load and initialize an SAPUI5 library into your application. For a standalone application, you need to perform the bootstrapping into the HTML of your application. If you're building an application as a component to be used inside the SAPUI5 launchpad, bootstrapping is done by the launchpad.

Listing 7.1 shows an example of standard bootstrapping.

```
<script id="sap-ui-bootstrap"
        type="text/javascript"
        src="resources/sap-ui-core.js"
        data-sap-ui-theme="sap_belize"
        data-sap-ui-libs="sap.m"
        data-sap-ui-compatVersion="edge">
</script>
```

Listing 7.1 SAPUI5 Library Bootstrapping

Of the different bootstrap files you can use, these are the most important:

- *sap-ui-core.js*
  This is the standard bootstrap file that already contains a declaration of the jQuery library and loads a minimal part of library `sap.ui.core`.
- *sap-ui-core-nojQuery.js*
  If your application is already using jQuery, and you don't want to reload it, you can use this variant of the bootstrap file.
- *sap-ui-core-all.js*
  This bootstrap file contains almost all of the resources from library `sap.ui.core`.
- *sap-ui5.js*
  This bootstrap file contains all JavaScript modules from the `sap.ui.core`, `sap.ui.commons`, `sap.ui.table`, and `sap.ui.ux3` libraries. The issue with this bootstrap file is that the set of libraries is predefined, so you can't add additional libraries with parameter `data-sap-ui-libs`.

Most of the time, you'll use standard bootstrap file *sap-ui-core.js*. During the bootstrap phase, the framework synchronously loads the libraries you define in configuration parameter `data-sap-ui-libs` (in our example, we're loading only library `sap-m`) and their dependencies. In some cases, special bootstrap options are required, as discussed in the next two subsections.

Bootstrapping from the Content Delivery Network

SAPUI5 libraries can be loaded from a relative source path from the web server or from a remote content delivery network (CDN) service.

There are two main CDN services available:

- *https://sapui5.hana.ondemand.com/resources/sap-ui-core.js*
  This service can be used to load SAPUI5 libraries.

- *https://openui5.hana.ondemand.com/resources/sap-ui-core.js*
  This service can be used to load the open-source version of SAPUI5 called OpenUI5.

If you want to load a specific version of the framework, you must add it to the path, as shown in Listing 7.2.

```
<script id="sap-ui-bootstrap"
    type="text/javascript"
    src="https://sapui5.hana.ondemand.com/1.42.6/resources/sap-ui-core.js"
    data-sap-ui-theme="sap_belize"
    data-sap-ui-libs="sap.m">
</script>
```

Listing 7.2 CDN Bootstrapping with Library Version Definition

OpenUI5

As the open-source version of SAPUI5, OpenUI5 is free to use, so you don't need the SAP HANA platform license or SAP ERP application license like you do for SAPUI5.

The main difference between SAPUI5 and OpenUI5 is that the latter doesn't provide all the libraries of SAPUI5 (e.g., visualization library `sap.viz` for charts creation isn't available in OpenUI5).

You can get more information on OpenUI5 at *http://openui5.org/index.html*.

Preload Variant for Bootstrapping

We've seen that we can configure the libraries we want to use in our application in parameter `data-sap-ui-libs`. By default, the SAPUI5 framework loads the library's modules on demand when they are requested the first time. However, it's possible to preload the modules for performance reasons in three modalities:

- `async`
- `sync`
- `auto`

`Async` is recommended because it means that the libraries are loaded asynchronously. Because nothing ensures that all the modules are available after the execution of the bootstrap script, it's important that you encapsulate your code that requires the availability of the modules into a callback function with the method `sap.ui.getCore().attachInitEvent`, as shown in Listing 7.3.

```
<script
    id="sap-ui-bootstrap"
       src="/resources/sap-ui-core.js"
       data-sap-ui-theme="sap_belize"
       data-sap-ui-libs="sap.m"
       data-sap-ui-compatVersion="edge"
       data-sap-ui-preload="async" >
</script>
<script>
    sap.ui.getCore().attachInit(function () {
           alert("UI5 is ready");
          });
</script>
```

Listing 7.3 Usage of Method attachInit with Async Libraries Preloaded

Preload modality auto loads the libraries synchronously if optimized sources are requested (that means source libraries are used when the application runs in a productive environment); otherwise, asynchronously loading is used if no optimized libraries are used.

7.1.2 SAPUI5 Application Structuring

If you go to the SAPUI5 SDK and follow the "Hello World" example, you'll see that for creating a simple SAPUI5 application, it's enough to create an HTML document. When more complex application requirements come, this is no longer enough, and the application must be structured in line with best practices. Figure 7.1 summarizes the folder structure of one sample application.

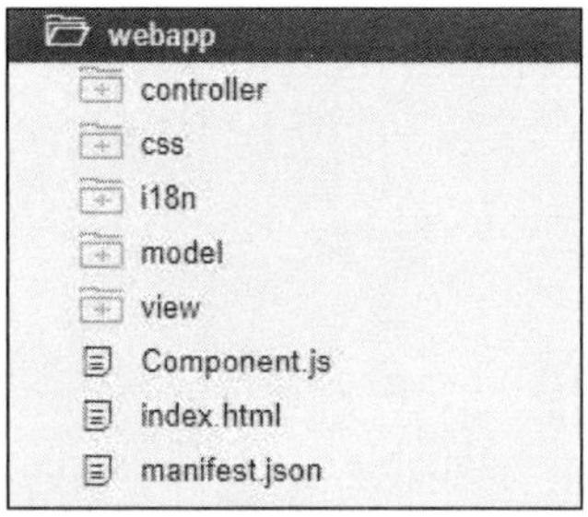

Figure 7.1 Folders Structure

The first concept we must introduce is that each application is a component that can be reused in different scenarios, such as in the SAP Fiori launchpad or as a component integrated into another, more complex, application.

To achieve this, you need to create two files that are the core elements of your application:

- **Component controller**
  A JavaScript file (must be named *Component.js*) that defines an application as a reusable component.
- **Application descriptor**
  A JavaScript Object Notation (JSON) file named *manifest.json* that describes the application metadata as recommended in the W3C Web App Manifest specification (*https://www.w3.org/TR/appmanifest*).

Two kinds of component can be created: faceless components and UI components. The main difference is that faceless component don't have a UI. When we create the application component, we basically extend either the class `sap.ui.core.Component` for the faceless components or the class `sap.ui.core.UIComponent` for the UI components, as shown in Listing 7.4.

```
sap.ui.define([
  'sap/ui/core/UIComponent'
], function(UIComponent) {
  "use strict";
  return UIComponent.extend("my.application.Component", {
    metadata : {
      manifest : "json"
    },
    init : function () {
      // call the parent's init function and create
      // the router and the App view
      UIComponent.prototype.init.apply(this, arguments);
    // create the views based on the URL/hash
      this.getRouter().initialize();
    }
  });
});
```

Listing 7.4 Component Controller Definition

Our sample component has two attributes:

- `init`
  This method is a function that is called automatically when an instance of the component is created; in our example, we're first calling the `init` method of the parent class `UIComponent`. This is mandatory because in the `init` method of the parent, the router and the initial view (we'll see them later) are created. Then, we initialize the router to ensure the creation of the views based on the `URL/hash` path (again keep this in standby for a moment because it will be clear with the introduction of navigation and routing concepts).
- `metadata`
  This property is where we define the metadata of the component. In previous versions of SAPUI5, it was possible to define the component metadata directly inside the *Component.js* file, but with the latest versions, this isn't supported anymore. The `metadata` property should be defined with `manifest: "json"` to indicate that our component uses a *manifet.json* file for metadata definition.

manifest.json is the application descriptor file that is structured in the namespaces where the metadata is organized. The available namespaces are as follows:

- `sap.app`
- `sap.ui`
- `sap.ui5`
- `sap.platform.abap`
- `sap.platform.hcp`
- `sap.fiori`

The most important ones are `sap.app`, `sap.ui`, and `sap.ui5`; `sap.platform.abap` and `spa.platform.hcp` are automatically filled during the deployment of the application either into an ABAP repository or into the SAP Cloud Platform.

In the `sap.app` namespace, we describe the main metadata of the application. The most important properties defined here are as follows:

- **Application ID**
  This corresponds to the component name. When we generate a SAPUI5 application as an HTML5 module of an SAP HANA extended application services, Advanced model (SAP HANA XS Advanced) application, the application ID is defined using a

variable (`${project.artifactId}`) and its value is stored in the file *pom.xml* (Project Object Model [POM]). This file contains information about the project and configuration details.

- **Application Title** and **Description**
  These are reused, for instance, in the SAP Fiori launchpad.
- **Application Type**
  This can be **Application**, **Component**, and **Library**, and refers to the data sources used during the definition the OData models.

Namespace `sap.ui` contains the UI metadata, basically the supported UI technology (currently, it can be only **UI5**), the icons used (for SAP Fiori launchpad, Favorites, and mobile devices), the supported devices (desktop, tablet, and phone), and the theme used.

Namespace `sap.ui5` defines SAPUI5-specific metadata, such as the minimum version of SAPUI5 supported and SAPUI5 library dependencies, navigation-related metadata (the root view and the routing configuration, as you'll see later), the models (JSON and OData) used by the application, and whether the application uses additional resources (e.g., additional CSS or JavaScript files).

7.1.3 Model View Controller

As you saw in Figure 7.1, there are standard structure folders called **Model**, **View**, and **Controller**. MVC is one of the best-known architectural patterns for developing web applications (or applications in general). The idea behind this pattern is that the representation of information should be separate from user interaction. To do this, three components interact with each other:

- **Model**
  This is where the application data is managed. For SAPUI5, there are four kinds of models: OData, JSON, XML, and resource models.
- **View**
  This is the application UI or the representation of information. The main concept is that we can have more views of the same information that can reuse the same application logic. SAPUI5 supports four kinds of views: XML, JSON, HTML, and JavaScript views.

- **Controller**
  This controls how the application should respond to user activities, it receives notifications either from the model or from the view and modifies them consequently.

Model

The model is where the data is stored and managed. The model responds to controller calls for retrieving or modifying the data. There can be a direct connection between the model and the view without the active interaction of the controller; this is called *data binding*. In this case, you can bind a component of the view (e.g., a table or an input field) to a property or aggregation of the model. Doing so directly exposes the model data to the view elements, and the only action of the controller is to set the model when the view is rendered—all the rest is managed by the SAPUI5 framework.

SAPUI5 supports four kinds of models:

- **OData models**
  These are server-side models, which means that all data operations (e.g., sorting, filtering, updating, creating, deleting, etc.) are managed by the server, and the client interacts with the model through OData calls. SAPUI5 supports both OData v2 and v4 specifications (even if v4 isn't completely supported yet because of some incompatibility of the standards between v2 and v4).

  You can do data binding between view controls and OData model entities either with one-way binding (from the model to the view) or two-way binding (both from the model to the view and vice versa). One-way binding is the default for OData v2 models, and two-way binding is the default for OData v4 models; however, you can change it when you define the model. We'll analyze the data binding concept in more detail later.
- **JSON and XML models**
  By default, these models are created with two-way binding support. The most-used kind of client-side model is the JSON model mainly because it's easier to read than XML, and its syntax is like the literal JavaScript object definition. They are intended for small sets of data because performance mechanisms (e.g., data paging and delta loading) aren't supported.
- **Resource models**
  These are mainly used for managing the internationalization (i18n) of the application. You use resource models, for instance, for binding a label of a field to different

texts that the browser loads according to the language defined in the browser settings. Resource models are created with one-time binding, meaning the data is loaded only once when the model is created.

View

The view is the representation of information that contains the UI elements with which the user interacts.

SAPUI5 supports four kinds of view definitions:

- XML views
- JSON views
- HTML views
- JavaScript views

The first three kinds (XML, HTML, and JSON views) follow a declarative approach; in this case, you define the elements of the view using one of those three languages and by indicating the properties of each UI element.

JavaScript views are slightly different because here the approach used is programmatic, so you can create view elements by calling JavaScript functions. The risk here is that you can be tempted to put some application logic inside the JavaScript files used for defining the view elements, breaking the MVC pattern. The recommendation is to use XML, JSON, or HTML views. The most used type of view is XML.

Views can use XML namespaces (`xmlns`) defined in the root node of the XML file. With XML namespaces, we can map SAPUI5 libraries to specific namespaces and use controls defined in one library by prefixing it with the namespace and not with the full library path. In the example, we're mapping libraries `sap.ui.layout` to namespace `l`, `sap.ui.core.mvc` to namespace `mvc`, and `sap.m` to the default namespace.

The last consideration for the view definition is that we can create a view by creating a file with this naming convention:

- *<myViewName>.view.xml* for XML views
- *<myViewName>.view.json* for JSON views
- *<myViewName>.view.html* for HTML views
- *<myViewName>.view.js* for JavaScript views

When we define a view, we also must define the controller file for the view.

Controller

The controller is notified from the view when the user interacts with the application, mainly with an events handler. For instance, when the user clicks a button, the event "press" of the button control is raised, and a function defined in the controller operates as a handler for the event. In the same way, the controller is notified from the model when something changes on the model side (e.g., when the data load is complete).

In SAPUI5, controllers are defined with JavaScript files with this naming convention: *<myControllerName>.controller.js*.

There are some predefined events (called *lifecycle hooks*) that can be used during controller implementation. They are described in the SDK as follows:

- `onInit()`
  Called when a view is instantiated, and its controls (if available) have already been created. This is used to modify the view before it's displayed to bind event handlers and to do other one-time initializations.
- `onExit()`
  Called when the view is destroyed. This is used to free resources and finalize activities.
- `onAfterRendering()`
  Called when the view has been rendered, and, therefore, its HTML is part of the document. This is used to do postrendering manipulations of the HTML. SAPUI5 controls get this hook after being rendered.
- `onBeforeRendering()`
  Invoked before the controller view is re-rendered and not before the first rendering. Uses `onInit()` for invoking the hook before the first rendering.

7.1.4 Data Binding

Data binding is a technique used to connect and synchronize two different data or information sources together. Basically, UI elements (e.g., a text field) are bound to a model property, and when a change happens on the data source, it's immediately reflected on the UI elements.

As we've already seen, we can have three modes of data binding:

- **One-way binding**
  One-way binding is the default for OData v2 models. With this mode of binding, only value changes on the model are reflected to the view.

- **Two-way binding**
  Two-way binding is the default for OData v4, JSON, and XML models. OData v2 models can support two-way binding but with some limitations (e.g., only property binding is supported and not aggregation binding).
- **One-time binding**
  One-time binding means that the data from the model is read only once and not synchronized.

Beside the data binding modes, there are also three types of binding:

- Element binding
- Aggregation binding
- Property binding

Element Binding

Element binding, or context binding, is used to synchronize a UI element with an object of the model. This is the best practice to interact with the view from the controller to dynamically redefine the state of the view in accordance with the state of the controller (e.g., by hiding controls or by changing the state of control properties).

Let's assume that in our controller, we define a JSON model as shown in Listing 7.5 with only the object "input".

```
sap.ui.controller("myController", {
    onInit: function() {
        var oData = {
            "input": {
                "value" : "you can edit me",
              "editable" : true
            }
        };
        var    oModel =
            new sap.ui.model.json.JSONModel(oData);
        this.getView().setModel(oModel);
    }
})
```

Listing 7.5 Element Binding: Controller Definition

To define an element binding for a view element, we must assign the path to the model object or property that we want to use as data source to the binding property of the element, as shown in Listing 7.6.

```
<mvc:View xmlns:core = "sap.ui.core"
    xmlns:mvc = "sap.ui.core.mvc"
    xmlns = "sap.m"
    controllerName = "myController"
    displayBlock = "true" >
  <App>
    <Page>
      <Panel>
        <Input
          binding="{/input}"
          value="{value}"
          editable="{editable}"  />
      </Panel>
    </Page>
  </App>
</mvc:View>
```

Listing 7.6 Element Binding: View Definition

By setting the binding="{/input}", we create a *binding context* for the control sap.m.Input, and we can bind properties of the control (in our example, we're binding properties "value" and "editable") using relative paths (paths that don't start with the slash "/" at the beginning).

Without element binding, we should define the binding using the absolute path, so the code of the view must be changed, as shown in Listing 7.7.

```
<mvc:View xmlns:core = "sap.ui.core"
xmlns:mvc = "sap.ui.core.mvc"
        xmlns = "sap.m"
        controllerName = "myController"
        displayBlock = "true" >
  <App>
    <Page>
      <Panel>
        <Input
```

```
            value="{/input/value}"
            editable="{/input/editable}"  />
        </Panel>
      </Page>
    </App>
</mvc:View>
```

Listing 7.7 Element Binding: View Definition with Absolute Model Binding Paths

The same element binding can be done programmatically inside the controller using functions bindElement and bindProperty, as shown in Listing 7.8.

```
sap.ui.controller("myController", {
onInit: function() {
            var oData = {
                    "input": {
                        "value" : "you can edit me",
                      "editable" : false
                    }
            };
            var oModel =
new sap.ui.model.json.JSONModel(oData);
            this.getView().setModel(oModel);
        var oInput = this.byId("myInput");
         oInput.bindElement("/input");
         oInput.bindProperty("value", "value");
            oInput.bindProperty("editable", "editable");
        }
})
```

Listing 7.8 Element Binding: Controller Definition with Programmatic Binding Instantiation

Aggregation Binding

Aggregation binding is used when the models return an array of objects, and we want to bind them to an aggregation property of a SAPUI5 control. For instance, the sap.m.ListBase class provides aggregation items, and we can use aggregation binding for creating children elements (list items) automatically inside the items aggregation.

How to Find Control Properties and Aggregations

SAPUI5 API Reference (*https://sapui5.hana.ondemand.com/#/api*) provides a complete documentation of the properties and aggregations available for each SAPUI5 control.

We can extend the example introduced for element binding to show how aggregation binding works. Instead of defining only one object inside the JSON model, we can hard-code an array of objects that we'll use for an aggregation binding, as shown in Listing 7.9.

```
sap.ui.controller("myController", {
onInit: function() {
var oData = {
           "inputs": [{
                         "editable": true,
                         "value": "change me!"
                     }, {
                         "editable": false,
                         "value": "sorry you can't change me"
                     }, {
                         "editable": true,
                         "value": "change me!"
                     }, {
                         "editable": false,
                         "value": "sorry you can't change me"
                     }, {
                         "editable": false,
                         "value": "sorry you can't change me"
                     }, {
                         "editable": true,
                         "value": "change me!"
                 }]
};
var oModel = new sap.ui.model.json.JSONModel(oData);
       this.getView().setModel(oModel);
}
});
```

Listing 7.9 Aggregation Binding: Controller Definition

Having defined the model with an array of objects ("inputs"), we can bind this array to the aggregation items of control sap.m.Table. In the XML definition of the view, we can define a template for the items aggregation (in the next example, the template is based on the control sap.m.ColumnListItem) and reuse this template for all objects of the model array, as shown in Listing 7.10.

```
<mvc:View xmlns:core = "sap.ui.core"
    xmlns:mvc = "sap.ui.core.mvc"
    xmlns = "sap.m"
    controllerName = "myController"
    displayBlock = "true" >
  <App>
    <Page>
      <Panel>
        <Table
          items="{/inputs}"
          id="testTable">
          <columns>
            <Column width="12em">
              <Text text="Editable/Not Editable" />
            </Column>
          </columns>
          <items>
            <ColumnListItem>
              <cells>
                <Input
                  value="{value}"
                  editable="{editable}"  />
              </cells>
            </ColumnListItem>
          </items>
        </Table>
      </Panel>
    </Page>
  </App>
</mvc:View>
```

Listing 7.10 Aggregation Binding: View Definition

The attribute items="{/inputs}" binds all the children of aggregation "items" of the sap.m.Table control to the array defined in the model. As we've seen for the element binding, the path for property binding of each aggregation element is relative and not absolute (value="{value}" and not value="{/inputs/value}").

Figure 7.2 is the result of this example code.

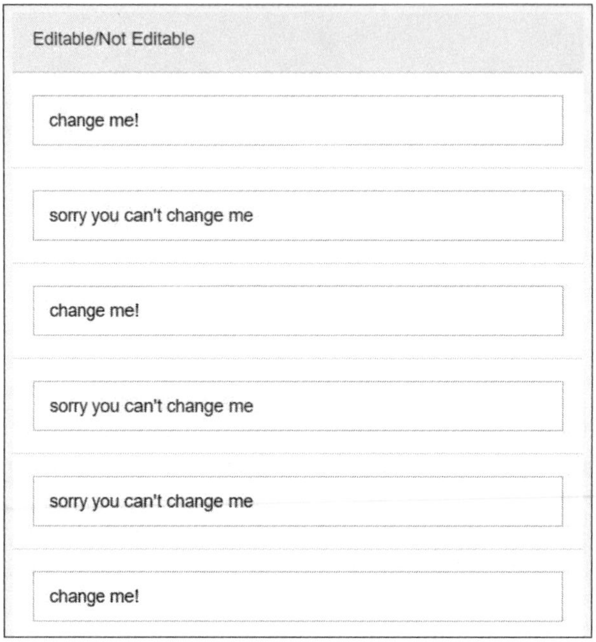

Figure 7.2 Example of Aggregation Binding

As for property binding, we can define aggregation binding programmatically using method bindAggregation. This method requires three input parameters:

- The aggregation we want to bind
- The path of the model property we want to use as the data source
- A *control template* to use as a model during the creation of aggregation elements

Reusing our example, we can create a sap.m.table with aggregation binding programmed directly into the controller file, as shown in Listing 7.11.

```
var oTemplate = new sap.m.ColumnListItem({
    cells : new sap.m.Input({
           value: "{value}",
```

```
                editable: "{editable}"
    })
});
var oTable = this.byId("testTable");
oTable.bindAggregation("items", "/inputs", oTemplate );
```

Listing 7.11 Aggregation Binding: Controller Definition with Programmatic Binding

When you use aggregation binding, you might need to add some logic when a new child is created in the UI. For instance, you must derive some characteristics of the UI element according to some property of the model (e.g., if the model doesn't provide a Boolean variable for the "editable" property, and you must calculate it from other properties of the model). In those cases, you can use a *factory function* for creating controls from model data. A factory function is called during the creation of each child of the aggregation and provides the following parameters:

- sId
  This is the ID of the new control that is added to the aggregation.
- oContext
  The binding context of the new control is basically a member of the array defined on the model for which we're doing the binding. We can access a specific property of the object using function getProperty.

Let's assume that in the previous example, the model isn't returning property "editable", but, instead, it returns a property "status" that can have values "open", "closed", and "re-open", and we must make a table line editable only if the property "status" is "open" or "re-open". We can achieve this by defining a factory function (this isn't the only way, we can also use a formatter function or complex binding, as introduced in the next Note box).

To do this, we have to change the view saying that "items" aggregation of the table control is populated using a factory function, as shown in Listing 7.12.

```
<mvc:View xmlns:core = "sap.ui.core"
    xmlns:mvc = "sap.ui.core.mvc"
    xmlns = "sap.m"
    controllerName = "myController"
    displayBlock = "true" >
  <App>
    <Page>
```

```
      <Panel>
        <Table
          items="{path: '/inputs', factory: '.createContent'}"
          id="testTable">
          <columns>
            <Column width="12em">
              <Text text="Editable/Not Editable" />
            </Column>
          </columns>
        </Table>
      </Panel>
    </Page>
  </App>
</mvc:View>
```

Listing 7.12 Aggregation Binding: View Definition with a Factory Function

Note the "." before the name of the factory function: `factory: '.createContent'`. In this way, we're saying that the function is looked up in the controller of the current view.

Now we must define the factory function inside the controller, as shown in Listing 7.13.

```
sap.ui.controller("myController", {
  onInit: function() {
    var oData = {
          "inputs": [{
                      "status": "open",
                      "value": "change me!"
                  }, {
                      "status": "close",
                      "value": "sorry you can't change me"
                  }, {
                      "status": "open",
                      "value": "change me!"
                  }, {
                      "status": "close",
                      "value": "sorry you can't change me"
```

```
                }, {
                    "status": "close",
                    "value": "sorry you can't change me"
                }, {
                    "status": "re-open",
                    "value": "change me!"
            }]
    };
    var oModel = new sap.ui.model.json.JSONModel(oData);
    this.getView().setModel(oModel);
  },

  createContent: function (sId, oContext) {
    var oColumnListItem = new sap.m.ColumnListItem();
    var oInput = new sap.m.Input();
    oInput.setValue(oContext.getProperty("value"));
    if (oContext.getProperty("status")==="close") {
        oInput.setEditable(false);
      oInput.setValueState(sap.ui.core.ValueState.Error);
    } else {
        oInput.setEditable(true);
      oInput.setValueState(sap.ui.core.ValueState.Success);
    }
    oColumnListItem.addCell(oInput);
    return oColumnListItem;
  }
});
```

Listing 7.13 Aggregation Binding: Definition of a Factory Function within the Controller

Inside the factory function, we're just returning a new `sap.m.ColumnListItem` containing a `sap.m.Input` object that has different properties (we're changing `editable` and `valueState` properties) according to the value of the property "`status`" of the model object. The result is a view like the one you see in Figure 7.3, with only different colors of the input field defined by changing the property `valueState`.

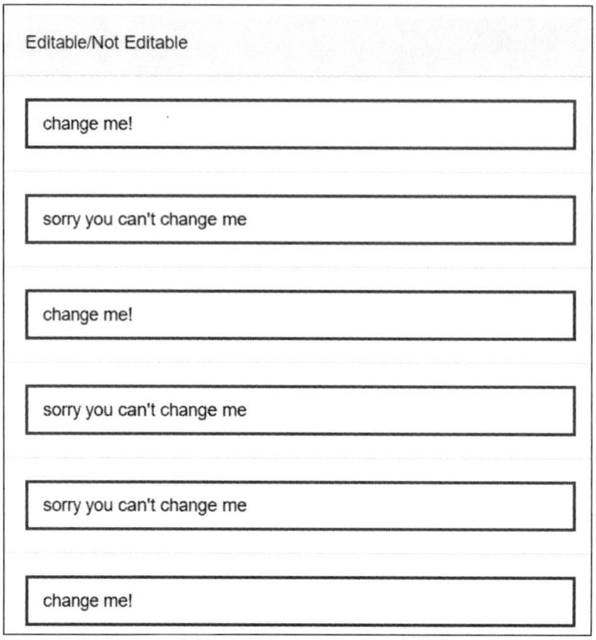

Figure 7.3 Aggregation Binding with a Factory Function

Property Binding

Property binding refers to the binding of a specific property of a view element to a characteristic of the model. We've already used property binding in previous examples when, for instance, we were changing the "editable" property of sap.m.Input with a binding to a model property, as follows:

```
<Input
          value="{/input/value}"
          editable="{/input/editable}"  />
```

Property binding is defined either during the control definition in the XML view or directly in JavaScript by passing the binding setting as an input parameter of the control constructor function, as follows:

```
var oInput = new sap.m.Input({
    value: "{/input/value}",
    editable: "{/input/editable}"
});
```

When we define a property binding, SAPUI5 automatically takes care of parsing the type of the model data so that it's formatted before being displayed in the UI controls.

All types supported by SAPUI5 are defined into classes that inherit from class `sap.ui.model.Type`. Currently, SAPUI5 supports the following simple types:

- `sap.ui.model.type.Boolean`
- `sap.ui.model.type.Date`
- `sap.ui.model.type.DateTime`
- `sap.ui.model.type.Float`
- `sap.ui.model.type.Integer`
- `sap.ui.model.type.String`
- `sap.ui.model.type.Time`
- `sap.ui.model.type.DateTimeInterval`

Each type supports different *format options* (e.g., types `Date` and `DateTime` support format options either based on *Locale Data Markup Language (LDML) syntax* or using predefined output styles (*short, medium, long, or full*) and *constraints* (e.g., for type `Integer`, you can define some constraints to limit the maximum and minimum number supported).

In all previous examples, we've seen simple cases where the UI element properties are bound to the model just with the indication of the path to the model characteristics. But property binding also supports *complex syntax*, where it's possible to define the binding with additional configuration parameters and by defining a data type different from the standard one.

One of the most-used characteristics of complex binding is the *formatter function* when defining the binding. The formatter function is a kind of callback function that is called when the property binding is evaluated, and we can put any arbitrary code in this function to redefine the binding output.

Let's rewrite the example used before and define a formatter function for binding the "`editable`" property of the `sap.m.Input` control, as shown in Listing 7.14.

```
<mvc:View xmlns:core = "sap.ui.core"
    xmlns:mvc = "sap.ui.core.mvc"
    xmlns = "sap.m"
    controllerName = "myController"
    displayBlock = "true" >
```

```
    <App>
      <Page>
        <Panel>
            <Table
          items="{/inputs}"
                id="testTable">
            <columns>
              <Column width="12em">
                <Text text="Check column" />
              </Column>
              <Column width="12em">
                <Text text="Editable/Not Editable" />
              </Column>
            </columns>
            <items>
              <ColumnListItem>
                <cells>
                  <Text text="{editable}" />
                  <Input value="{value}"
                    editable="{
path: 'editable',
formatter: '.editableFormatter'
  }" />
                </cells>
              </ColumnListItem>
            </items>
</Table>
        </Panel>
      </Page>
    </App>
  </mvc:View>
```

Listing 7.14 Property Binding with Formatter: View Definition

In this view, we've defined the binding for the property "editable" of the Input fields of our table using a formatter function that we'll define in our controller (remember that the "." before the function means that the function is looked up in the controller code), as shown in Listing 7.15.

```
sap.ui.controller("myController", {
    onInit: function() {

        var oData = {
            "inputs": [{
                editable: "editable",
                value: "change me!"
            }, {
                editable: "not editable",
                value: "sorry you can't change me"
            }, {
                editable: "editable",
                value: "change me!"
            }, {
                editable: "not editable",
                value: "sorry you can't change me"
            }, {
                editable: "not editable",
                value: "sorry you can't change me"
            }, {
                editable: "editable",
                value: "change me!"
            }]
        };
        var oModel = new sap.ui.model.json.JSONModel(oData);
        this.getView().setModel(oModel);
    },

    editableFormatter: function (value) {
        if (value === 'editable') {
        return true;
      } else {
        return false;
      }
    }
});
```

Listing 7.15 Property Binding with a Formatter Function: Controller Definition

It's also possible to define a custom formatter that uses more than one input parameter. This procedure is defined as a *calculated field*, meaning we can use more than one model property to calculate the value of the view element property.

Listing 7.16 is taken from SAPUI5 SDK and defines the usage of four different model properties in the same formatter.

```
oTxt.bindValue({
    parts: [
        {
            path: "/firstName",
            type: new sap.ui.model.type.String()
        },
        {
            path: "/lastName",
            type: new sap.ui.model.type.String()
        },
        {
            path: "/amount",
            type: new sap.ui.model.type.Float()
        },
        {
            path: "/currency",
            type: new sap.ui.model.type.String()
        }
    ],
    formatter: function(firstName, lastName, amount, currency){
        if (firstName && lastName) {
            return "Dear " + firstName + " " + lastName +
            ". Your current balance is: " + amount + " " +                 currency;
        } else {
            return null;
        }
    }
});
```

Listing 7.16 Calculated Binding

With *expression binding*, it's also possible to use calculated binding without defining a formatter function. This is useful for simple binding derivation rules (e.g., when we just need to derive an element property if the model has one specific characteristic value).

Expression binding is defined with one of following options:

- `{=expression}`
  Expression binding with one-way binding mode.
- `{:=expression}`
  Expression binding with one-time binding mode.

To use model properties in the expression, you must use the syntax `${binding}`, where `binding` can be either simple binding to one property of the model or a complex binding.

In Listing 7.17, we'll rewrite the code of Listing 7.14 using expression binding.

```
<mvc:View xmlns:core = "sap.ui.core"
    xmlns:mvc = "sap.ui.core.mvc"
    xmlns = "sap.m"
    controllerName = "myController"
    displayBlock = "true" >
      <App>
        <Page>
          <Panel>
              <Table items="{/inputs}" id="testTable">
              <columns>
                <Column width="12em">
                  <Text text="Check column" />
                </Column>
                <Column width="12em">
                  <Text text="Editable/Not Editable" />
                </Column>
              </columns>
              <items>
                <ColumnListItem>
                  <cells>
                    <Text text="{editable}" />
                    <Input value="{value}"
               editable="{= ${editable} === 'editable' }"/>
                  </cells>
                </ColumnListItem>
```

```
                </items>
                            </Table>
            </Panel>
        </Page>
    </App>
</mvc:View>
```

Listing 7.17 Expression Binding

For the controller, the code remains the same, with the only difference that we're no longer using the formatter function.

7.1.5 Routing and Navigation

We'll close the introduction of essential SAPUI5 elements by discussing the navigation and routing concept. We've seen that following the MVC pattern, a SAPUI5 application is basically a set of different views that present the application data to the user and a set of controllers that implement the application logic for each view. Now we'll see how it's possible to navigate between the different views within a SAPUI5 application.

SAPUI5 is a framework for client-based applications. SAPUI5 applications are also called single-page applications, meaning that when we're navigating between application views new HTML pages aren't requested from the server. Instead, we're manipulating the same single page using JavaScript functions and requesting asynchronously new data from the server with Ajax calls.

In addition, the navigation is mainly managed by the client and its defined *hash-based navigation*. This is because the URL is split in two parts: the first one identifies the path for getting our application from the server, and the second one is the navigation path managed by the client. The two parts are separated by a hash as follows:

http://site.com/myapp/#/products/id_1

In this example URL, we're displaying a specific product out of one product list, and the URL part after the hash identifies the ID of the product we're displaying (*/products/id_1*).

In this way, we don't have to reload the page from the server if the user wants to display another product, and standard browser functionalities (e.g., back and forward navigation or bookmarking) are still usable.

Navigation is implemented using three elements:

- Router class
- Routes
- Targets

The router class acts as a listener, and when a change on the hash part of the URL occurs, it activates the correspondent route and target. In the same way, the router class provides some navigation methods that can be used programmatically for enabling the navigation.

You must initialize the router class in the component controller `init` method using the code in Listing 7.18.

```
sap.ui.define([
  'sap/ui/core/UIComponent'
], function(UIComponent) {
  "use strict";
  return UIComponent.extend("my.application.Component", {
    metadata : {
      manifest : "json"
    },
    init : function () {
      // call the parent's init function and create
      // the router and the App view
      UIComponent.prototype.init.apply(this, arguments);
    // create the views based on the url/hash
      this.getRouter().initialize();
    }
  });
});
```

Listing 7.18 Router Initialization in the Component Controller

After the initialization of the router, it's possible to access it in the view's controllers for calling navigation methods or for attaching listeners to navigation events. To access the router, you can use this code:

```
this.getOwnerComponent().getRouter();
```

The *routes* match the hash part of the URL to a target, and the *targets* identify the view that must be loaded during the navigation. Initialization of the routing requires its configuration to be defined in the application descriptor.

Routing Configuration

Routing configuration is defined directly in the manifest of the application under the namespace `sap.ui5`, as shown in Listing 7.19.

```
"sap.ui5": {
    …
    "models": {
        …
    },
    "routing": {
      "config": {
        "routerClass": "sap.m.routing.Router",
        "viewType": "XML",
        "viewPath": "sap.ui.demo.wt.view",
        "controlId": "app",
        "controlAggregation": "pages"
      },
      "routes": [
        {
          "pattern": "",
          "name": "overview",
          "target": "overview"
        },
        {
          "pattern": "detail/{id}",
          "name": "detail",
          "target": "detail"
        }
      ],
      "targets": {
        "overview": {
          "viewName": "Overview"
        },
        "detail": {
```

```
          "viewName": "Detail"
        }
      }
    }
  }
```

Listing 7.19 Routing Configuration in the Application Descriptor

The three configuration sections we must define are as follows:

- "config"
- "routes"
- "targets"

The Config section contains the global router configuration such as the router class we're using (class sap.ui.core.routing.Router or any of its subclasses; in our example, we're using subclass sap.m.routing.Router) and the "bypassed" parameter where you can define the default target when all the routes are bypassed (that means the default view that will be shown in case the hash part of the URL the user has inserted isn't a valid value). This section can also contain default values that are valid for all routes and targets if not specified differently in the routes and targets sections (in our example, we're defining as default values the view type and path, the control ID, and the aggregation where the routes and targets will be attached).

The Routes section contains the patterns that match the hash part of the URL. In this section, we can define the following:

- name
  The name of the route; it must be unique for each route.

- pattern
  This is a pattern for the hash part of the URL; when they match, the route is activated. The pattern can contain some parameters. Mandatory parameters are defined with a curly brackets syntax: "pattern": "detail/{mandatory_parameter}"; optional parameters are defined between colons: "pattern": "detail/:optional_parameter:".
- target
  This must identify a target defined into the targets section.
- parent
  This refers to one route being nested under another one. For instance, we can have

pattern parent/{id} on the parent route and pattern children/{id} in the children route. These two routes will be matched if the hash part of the URL is #/parent/01/children/01.

The targets section is where we can define most parameters. The main ones for this section are as follows:

- viewName
  The name of the view that will be displayed.
- viewType
  The type of the view definition (XML, JSON, JavaScript, or HTML).
- controlId
  The ID of the control that acts as a navigation container. During the navigation, the view defined for the target is attached to an aggregation of this control. It depends on the layout of the application we're building, but, in general, there are two kind of application controls we can use: sap.m.App for full-screen applications and sap.m.SplitApp for master-details applications.
- controlAggregation
  The aggregation of the control defined in parameter controlId where the view of the target is attached. For example, for master-details applications, we use the sap.m.SplitApp control, which has two aggregations where we can enable navigation: masterPages and detailPages. In addition, we can define different targets for both aggregations.
- viewPath
  The path to locate the view of the target.

Navigation Methods and Events

The router class, targets, and routes provide some methods and events that can be used to trigger navigation or to execute some application logic when a navigation event happens.

The easy way to navigate to a specific route is to use method navTo of the router class, as follows:

```
var oRouter = this.getOwnerComponent().getRouter();
oRouter.navTo("detail", {
    id: "detail_01
});
```

In this example, we're navigating to the route "detail" and passing a parameter that is defined in the route configuration. To define a route with parameters, you must add a syntax like this {parameter_name} into the pattern configuration of the route, as shown in Listing 7.20.

```
"routes": [
        {
          "pattern": "",
          "name": "overview",
          "target": "overview"
        },
        {
          "pattern": "detail/{id}",
          "name": "detail",
          "target": "detail"
        }
      ],
...
```

Listing 7.20 Definition of a Route That Accepts a Parameter

If a navigation event to a route with parameter happens, most likely in your target view, you'll need to access the parameter values for applying some logic before displaying the data. The route class provides some events to attach some listeners defined in your controller. There are two main events:

- Matched
  This event is raised if one of these conditions is true:
  - The hash part of the URL matches the pattern of the route.
  - The hash part of the URL matches the pattern of one of the route subroutes (it's now deprecated, but it was possible to define subroutes in the configuration of one route).
  - The hash part of the URL matches one of the nested routes (a nested route is defined using the parameter "parent" in the route configuration).
- patternMatched
  This event is raised only when the route pattern is matched and not when it's matched to the pattern of one subroute or nested route.

Listing 7.21 provides an example of how you can create a listener for event "matched" of the route "detail" that we've defined in our routing configuration:

```
sap.ui.controller("MyApp.View1", {
  onInit: function() {
    var oRouter = this.getOwnerComponent().getRouter();
    oRouter.getRoute("detail").attachMatched(function(oEvent) {
    this._routeMatched(oEvent.getParameter("arguments").id);
    }, this);
  },

  _ routeMatched: function(id) {
    //implementation
  }
}
```

Listing 7.21 Creation of a Listener for a Matched Event in a View Controller

7.2 SAP HANA XS Advanced Application Routing

In the previous section, you've seen how SAPUI5 manages navigation inside the different views that comprise an application. When you create an HTML5 module of your SAP HANA XS Advanced application, you also must define how the resources of other microservices are used by your application. For instance, user authentication isn't managed directly by the application, but it's addressed to the right microservice that confirms or denies the user identity.

In the SAP HANA XS Advanced programming model, the routing to the different microservices is managed by the application router ("approuter"), which must not to be confused with the SAPUI5 router class (that, as we've seen, is responsible for addressing the navigation between the views of a single application).

7.2.1 Application Routing Files

Application routing is defined by two main files that are automatically added when you create a new HTML5 module:

- *package.json*
- *xs-app.json*

package.json

The package descriptor file is used to start the application router as the entry point of your application.

Listing 7.22 shows the default *package.json* version that a new HTML5 module automatically generates.

```
{
    "name": "chickenWingsweb-approuter",
    "engines": {
        "node": ">=4.0.0 <7.0.0"
    },
    "dependencies": {
        "@sap/approuter": "2.9.1"
    },
    "scripts": {
        "start": "node node_modules/@sap/approuter/approuter.js"
    }
}
```

Listing 7.22 package.json of an HTML5 Module

As you can see, there is only the dependency defined to module @sap/approuter. This module contains the application router (approuter.js), and the application router is initialized as the entry point of the application in the script section of *package.json*.

xs-app.json

The application descriptor file contains the router configuration. The application router will look at this file to identify the configured routes. It's automatically generated when you add an HTML module to your application, as in Listing 7.23.

```
{
    "welcomeFile": "webapp/index.html",
    "authenticationMethod": "none",
    "routes": []
}
```

Listing 7.23 Generated xs-app.json of an HTML5 Module

By default, a new HTML5 module gets a generated *xs-app.json* file with three sections:

- `welcomeFile`
  The `welcomeFile` contains the web page served by default if the HTTP request doesn't include a specific path (in our case, it will be served the *index.html* file).
- `authenticationMethod`
  The `authenticationMethod` is used to authenticate the user and can be "`route`" or "`none`". If it's "`route`", the authentication method is configured into each defined route.
- `routes`
  The `routes` section is an array that contains the routes served by this application. We'll analyze a route definition in the next section.

Other sections you can add to the application descriptor file are as follows:

- `login`
  The endpoint for OAuth2 authentication with the User Account and Authentication service (UAA). See Chapter 8 for more details on user authentication.
- `logout`
  You can also define a central endpoint for the logout action.
- `destinations`
  You can define additional options for the destinations defined in the application descriptor file (see the next section for more details of routes destinations).
- `compression`
  This configuration defines whether the application router should compress text resources before providing them. By default, resources larger than 1 KB are compressed, but you can change this threshold or disable compression.
- `plug-inMetadataEndpoint`
  You can build a service that returns all the plug-ins used by your application and returns their metadata in JSON format.
- `whitelistService`
  This configuration is used to prevent click-jacking attacks (e.g., attacks where an HTML page is loaded into an invisible iframe, and clicks on visible buttons or keystrokes on visible input fields are redirected to the invisible iframe controlled by the hacker). With this parameter, you can define an endpoint that confirms whether the parent frame can render the application into a frame.

- `websockets`
  You can enable WebSocket communication in your application by setting the property "`enabled`" of the `websockets` section to `true`.
- `errorPage`
  You can set custom pages for the different error statuses that the application router can return (e.g., you can define a custom error page for error 501 and a different one for error 400).

7.2.2 Application Routes and Destinations

In the application descriptor file (*xs-app.json*), the third section automatically generated is called `routes` and should contain all the routes that the application router will serve and their destinations. Listing 7.24 shows an example.

```
{
    "welcomeFile": "index.html",
    "authenticationMethod": "none",
    "routes": [{
        "source": "/xsodata/flightBooking.xsodata/",
        "authenticationType": "xsuaa",
        "destination": "js_be"
    }]
}
```

Listing 7.24 xs-app.json of an HTML5 Module with a Single Route Configuration

A route is an object composed of different properties. The most important properties are listed here:

- `source`
  This regular expression (RegEx) should match the incoming request as a condition for activating the route.
- `destination`
  This is the destination where the incoming request will be forwarded. You'll see later how destinations are defined in the multi-target application (MTA) development descriptor file (*mta.yaml*).
- `target`
  You can define a target path where the application router will forward the request.

- `localDir`
  This is the directory from which the application router should serve static content.
- `httpMethods`
  This is the HTTP methods supported from the route, which is an array with one or more of these supported methods: `DELETE`, `GET`, `HEAD`, `OPTIONS`, `POST`, `PUT`, `TRACE`, and `PATCH`.
- `authenticationType`
  This can contain "`xsuaa`", "`basic`", or "`none`", and the default value is "`xsuaa`". In this case, you must create the `uaa` (User Account and Authentication) service in your application and assign it to the HTML5 module as a dependency (see Chapter 8 for more information). "`basic`" works only with SAP HANA database users.
- `replace`
  When you serve static resources, you can replace placeholders with variables. We'll see an example of its usage later when we load the SAPUI5 library from an MTA service.

The only mandatory property is `source`, but one of `destination`, `target`, and `localDir` must also be defined; otherwise, the application router can't manage the incoming request.

A destination defines a backend service to which a request is forwarded. You define the destination in the MTA development descriptor file (*mta.yaml*) using the code in Listing 7.25.

```
- name: web
  type: html5
  path: test
  requires:
    - name: js_api
      group: destinations
      properties:
        name: js_be
        url: '~{url}'
```

Listing 7.25 Definition of a Destination in a mta.yaml File

You can also define it using the MTA editor, as shown in Figure 7.4.

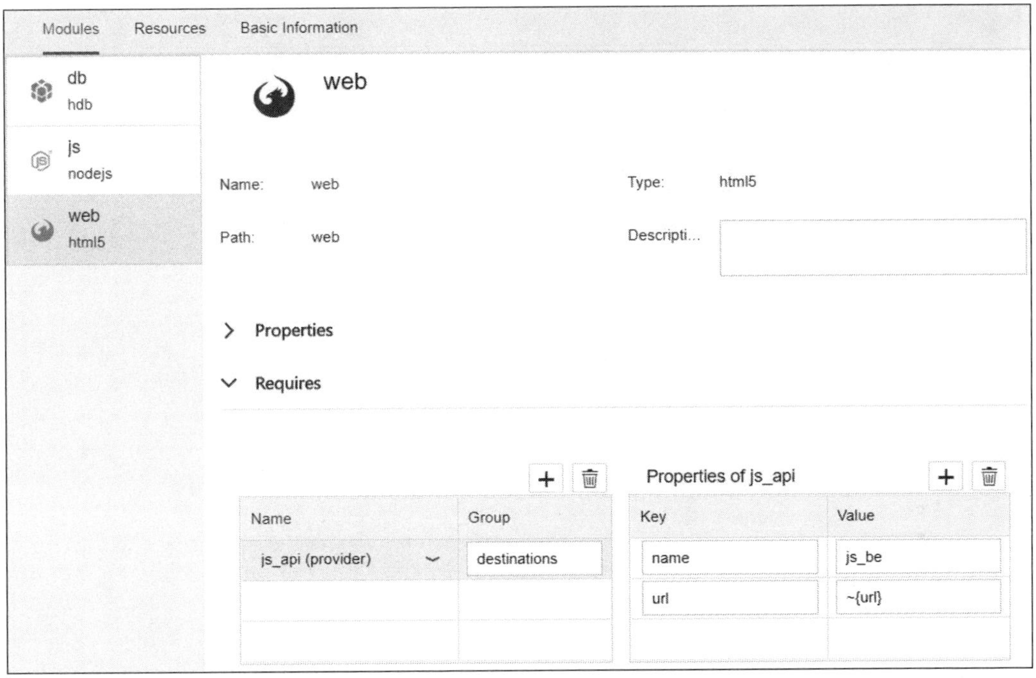

Figure 7.4 Definition of a Destination into a mta.yaml File Using the MTA Editor

When you define a destination, properties "`name`" and "`url`" are mandatory.

7.2.3 SAPUI5 Central Service

When we introduced SAPUI5, we stated that SAPUI5 libraries are loaded during application bootstrap, either from a CDN (e.g., *https://sapui5.hana.ondemand.com/resources/sap-ui-core.js*) or from a local resource on the application service.

With SAP HANA XS Advanced, SAPUI5 libraries are provided as MTA applications, which allow different applications to consume the same copy of SAPUI5 runtime and to use a different version of the libraries without affecting other applications running on the same instance.

You can find available SAPUI5 runtimes in the **XS Advanced Administration** cockpit screen, as shown in Figure 7.5.

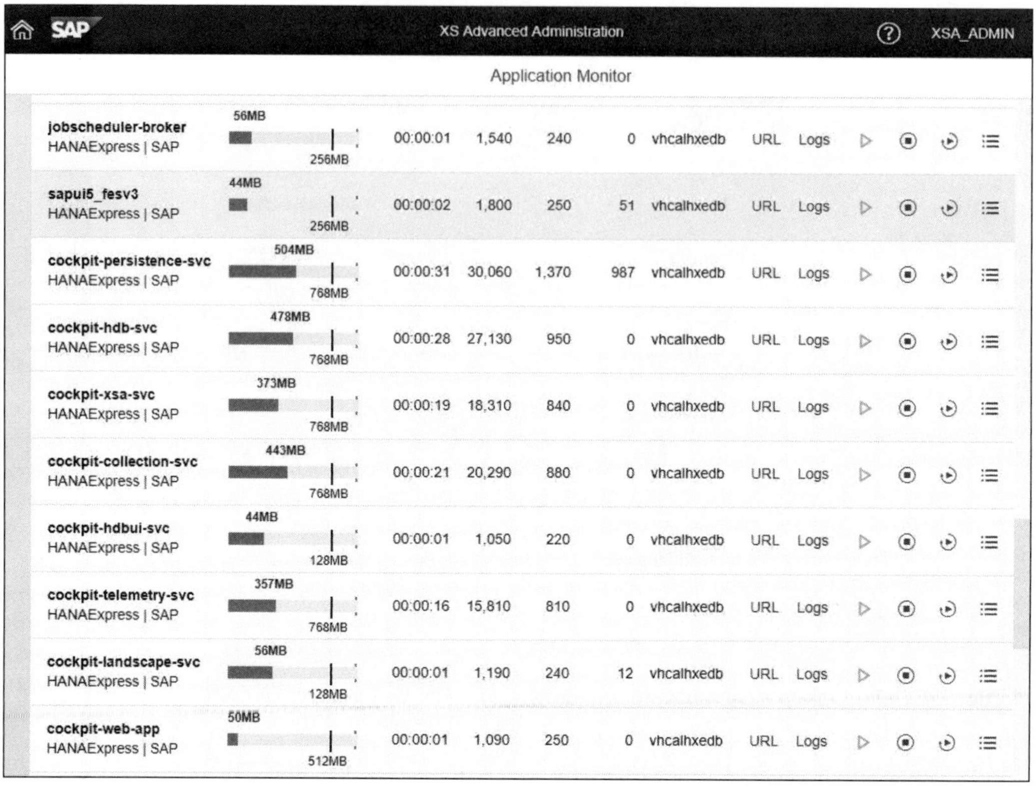

Figure 7.5 SAPUI5 Runtimes as MTA Applications

To use the SAP HANA XS Advanced SAPUI5 runtime, you must declare the usage of the SAPUI5 microservice in your *mta.yaml* file as a resource. Add a new resource (you can call it "ui5-lib"), choose **Configuration** in the **Type** field, and add two parameters, as shown in Figure 7.6:

- **provider-id**: **com.sap.ui5.dist.sapui5-dist-xsa.XSAC_UI5_FESV3:sapui5_fesv3**
- **version**: **>=1.44.23**

When you've defined the new resource, you must assign it as a requirement to your HTML5 module. Add a new requirement with property **ui5liburl** set to **~{url}**, as shown in Figure 7.7.

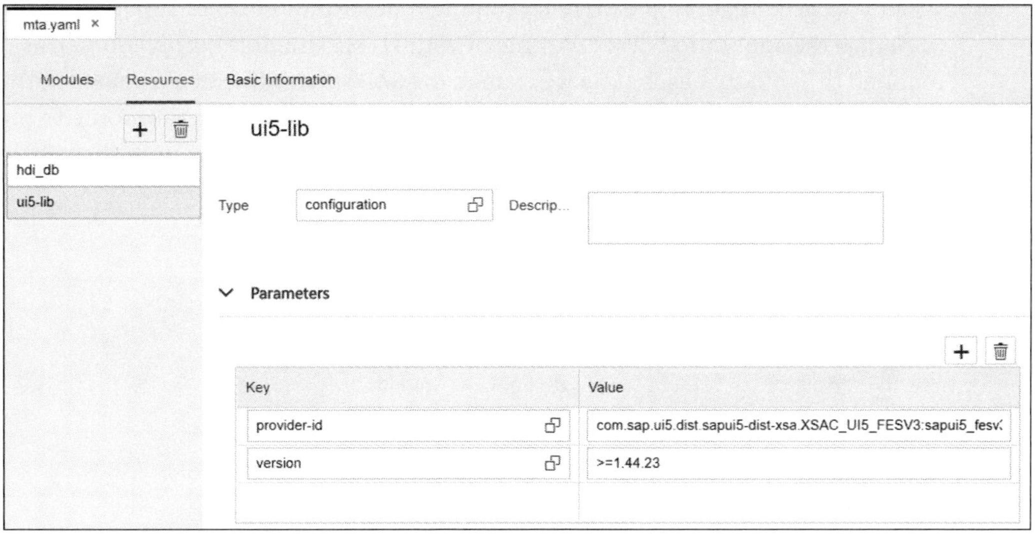

Figure 7.6 New Resource ui5-lib Added to the mta.yaml File

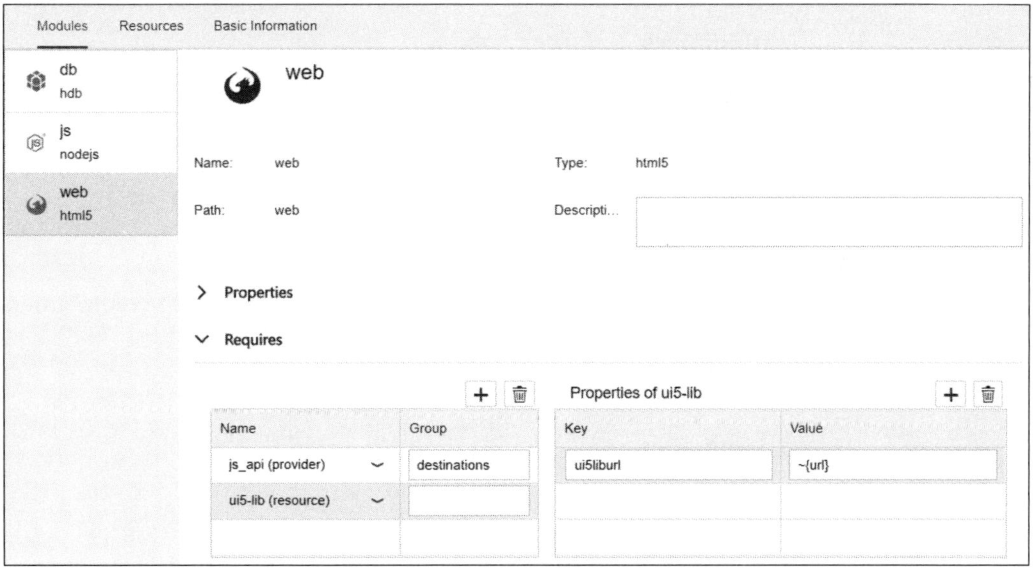

Figure 7.7 New Requirement to Resource ui5-lib Added to the HTML5 Module

When you've configured the MTA development descriptor file (*mta.yaml*), you need to change the application descriptor file of your HTML5 module (*xs-app.json*). This is required to avoid that each time we change the SAPUI5 runtime as a resource in the *mta.yaml*, we also have to replace the SAPUI5 bootstrap URL. Add a new route to the file with this configuration that will replace the variable `ui5liburl` with the URL of SAPUI5 MTA service in the *index.html* file, as shown in Listing 7.26.

```
{
    "welcomeFile": "index.html",
    "authenticationMethod": "none",
    "routes": [{
        "source": "/xsodata/flightBooking.xsodata/",
        "authenticationType": "xsuaa",
        "destination": "js_be"
    }, {
        "source": "/(.*)",
        "localDir": "resources",
        "authenticationType": "xsuaa",
        "replace": {
            "pathSuffixes": ["index.html"],
            "vars": ["ui5liburl"]
        }
    }]
}
```

Listing 7.26 xs-app.json File with Variable ui5liburl Replacement

The final task is to adapt the bootstrap script of file *index.html* with the replacement variable, as shown in Listing 7.27.

```
<!DOCTYPE html>
<html>
<head>
    <meta http-equiv="X-UA-Compatible" content="IE=edge" />
    <meta http-equiv="Content-Type" content="text/html;charset=UTF-8"/>
    <meta name="viewport" content="width=device-width, initial-scale=1.0" />
    <title>Airports</title>

    <!-- Bootstrapping UI5 -->
    <script id="sap-ui-bootstrap"
```

```
            src="{{{ui5liburl}}}/resources/sap-ui-core.js"
            data-sap-ui-libs="sap.m"
            data-sap-ui-theme="sap_bluecrystal"
            data-sap-ui-compatVersion="edge"
            data-sap-ui-resourceroots='{"chickenwings": "."}'
            data-sap-ui-frameOptions="trusted">
    </script>

    <script>
        sap.ui.getCore().attachInit(function () {
            sap.ui.require([
                "sap/m/Shell",
                "sap/ui/core/ComponentContainer"
            ], function (Shell, ComponentContainer) {
                // initialize the UI component
                new Shell({
                    app: new ComponentContainer({
                        height : "100%",
                        name : "chickenwings"
                    })
                }).placeAt("content");
            });
        });
    </script>

</head>

<!-- UI Content -->
<body class="sapUiBody" id="content">
</body>
</html>
```

Listing 7.27 File index.html with the Replacement Variable {{{ui5liburl}}} Used in the src Property of the Bootstrap Script

If we run our HTML5 module and inspect it with the Chrome debug tools, we can see that the source path of the SAPUI5 bootstrap has been changed with the service port of the SAPUI5 MTA service, as shown in Figure 7.8.

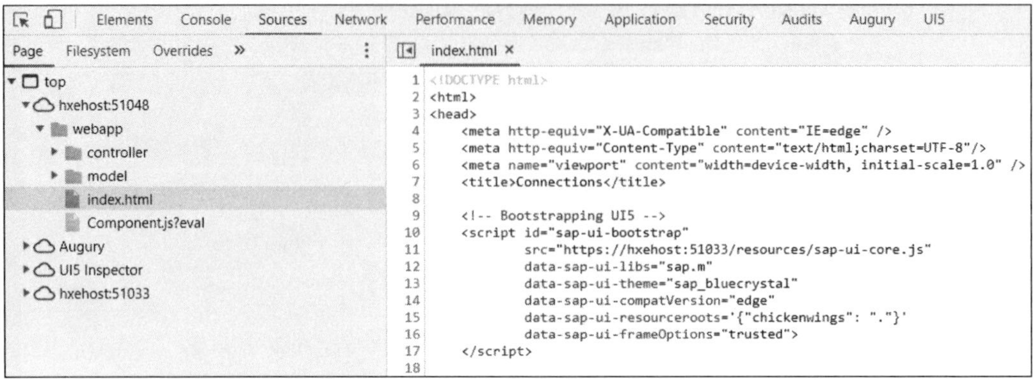

Figure 7.8 Bootstrap Script Using the SAPUI5 MTA Service

7.3 Demo Application

In this section, we'll start to add a simple presentation layer to our demo application. We'll create a simple application based on the master-detail layout that shows the list of the connections and, for each connection, the list of its flights by date.

Before you start following the steps of this demo, make sure you've implemented the database module as introduced in Chapter 5 and that you have a Node.js module with the XSODATA service, as shown in Listing 7.28.

```
service {
    "CVConnection" as "Connections" without ("TO_LOCATION","FR_LOCATION")
key ("FLIGHT")
        navigates ("Connection_flights" as "HisFlights");
    "CVFlight" as "Flights" key ("FLIGHT", "FDATE");
    association "Connection_flights" with referential constraint principal
"Connections"("FLIGHT")
multiplicity "1" dependent "Flights"("FLIGHT") multiplicity "*";
}
```

Listing 7.28 XSODATA Service Definition Required for the Application Demo

This OData service is basically exposing two entity sets:

- `Connections`: the list of the available connections
- `Flights`: the list of the available flights

The two entities are connected using the association "Connection_flights" that allows you to navigate from a connection to all the flights available for that connection. And the Connections entity has a navigation property "HisFlight" to get the list of the flights for a specific connection ID. In the following sections, we'll see how to use this OData service as a model for a frontend view based on the master-detail template, where the master view contains the list of connections, and the detail view contains the flights for a selected connection.

7.3.1 Create the SAP Fiori Master-Detail Module

The first step is to define a new web module; we'll use the *SAP Fiori Master-Detail Module* template that hides most of the complexities related to SAPUI5 application development.

Start the Node.js Module First

Before starting with the SAP Fiori Master-Detail Module creation, remember to start the Node.js module as a prerequisite. The wizard will look for the OData services defined in the current project, and it needs to fetch the service metadata for proposing the available entities to use in the web module.

Otherwise, you'll get the following error message: **Invalid metadata document.**

When the Node.js module is running, you can open the context menu at the project level, and select the **New • SAP Fiori Master-Detail Module**, as shown in Figure 7.9.

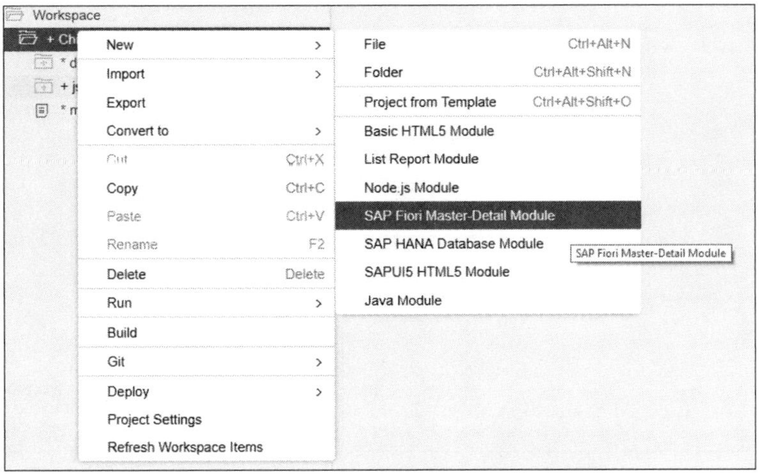

Figure 7.9 Creation of a New SAP Fiori Master-Detail Module

We can call our module whatever we want, but we'll follow the best practices and name it "web", as it will contain all the objects related to the web application (see Figure 7.10).

Type in the name and click on **Next** button to proceed.

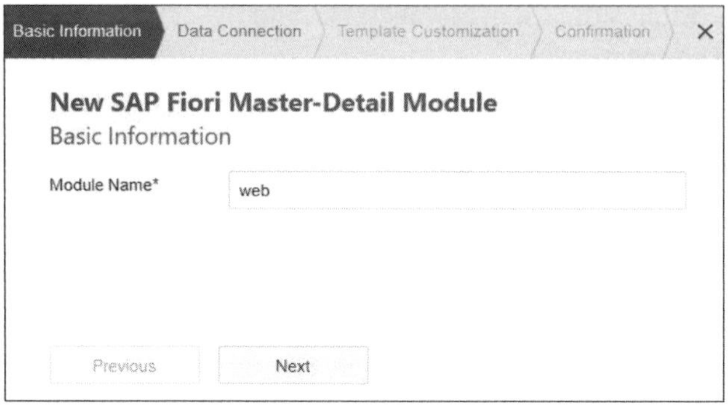

Figure 7.10 Creation of a New Module Named "web"

In the second screen of the wizard, select the OData service to use in the application. In our example, we have only one **Service** named **flightBooking** that exposes the two entities for the **Connections** and the **Flights**, as shown in Figure 7.11.

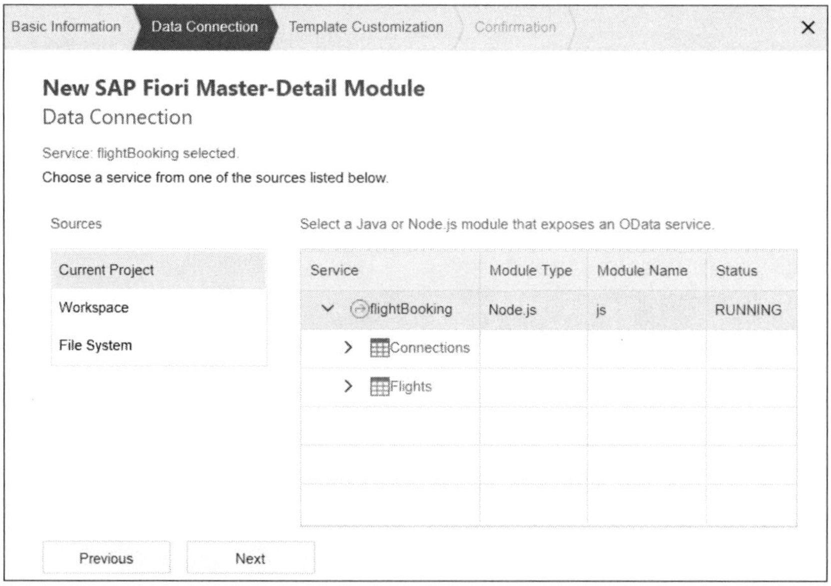

Figure 7.11 Selection of the OData Service in the Wizard

Click the **Next** button to go to the last screen of the wizard to define some application properties (e.g., application title, description, and namespace) and the configuration that will be used to identify how the properties of the OData entities will be bound to the properties of the UI controls.

Namespace property

The namespace property is used by the application wizard to define the property `data-sap-ui-resourceroots` of the bootstrap script.

This property defines the location of all resources (e.g., views and controllers) to address them during a module definition. Having defined the namespace of our application as "chickenwings", we can address all objects of our application using this string as the source path.

We must select two entities from the OData service:

- One for the master list objects collection
- One for the collection of the list items that are shown in the detail view

Both for the master list and list item collections, we can bind the following UI elements to the properties of the OData entity:

- The ID of the object
- The title that will be shown in the list
- A numeric attribute that will be shown close to the title and its unit of measure

For the moment, we'll define only the entities used in the two collections—the `Connections` entity for the master list and the `Flights` entity for the list items that are connected using the "`HisFlights`" navigation property—and we'll define only the following binding properties:

- **Object Collection ID** with the **FLIGHT** property
- **Object Title** with **FR_CITY** (the departure city) property
- **List Item Collection ID** with the **FDATE** (flight date) property

Complete the wizard as shown in Figure 7.12, and click on **Finish**.

When the wizard is complete, a new HTML5 module is created and added to the *mta.yaml* file with the dependency to the Node.js module, as shown in Figure 7.13.

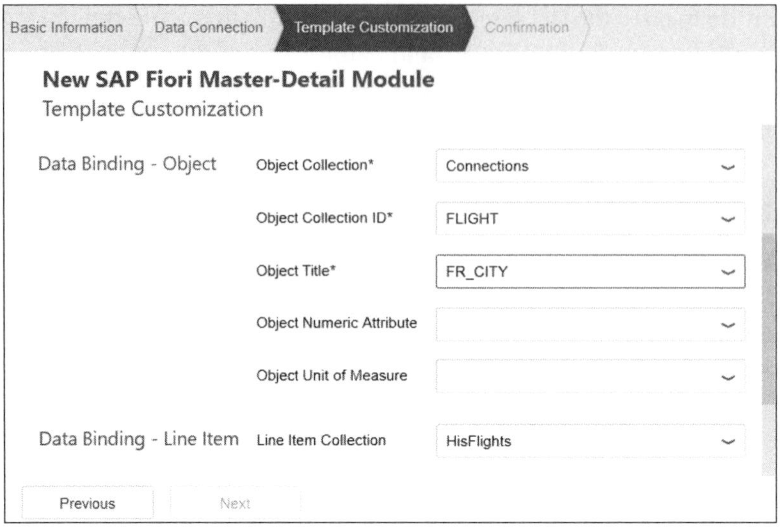

Figure 7.12 Binding OData Properties to the UI Elements

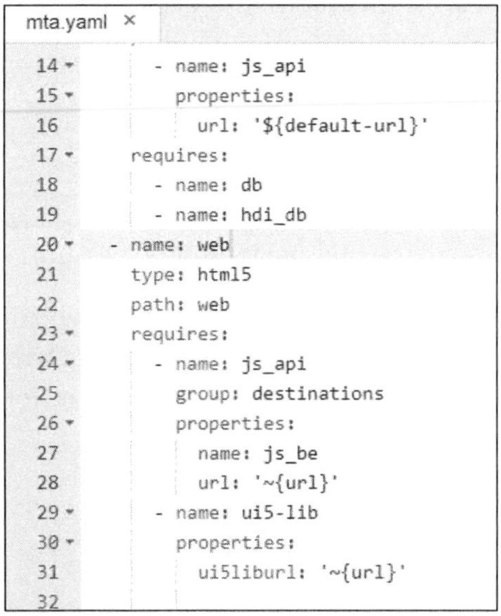

Figure 7.13 mta.yaml File with the New HTML5 Module defined

As soon as we've built our module, we can test our application by right-clicking on the module and selecting **RUN • Run as • Web application**. In the popup shown in Figure 7.14, select **Index.html** as the file to run.

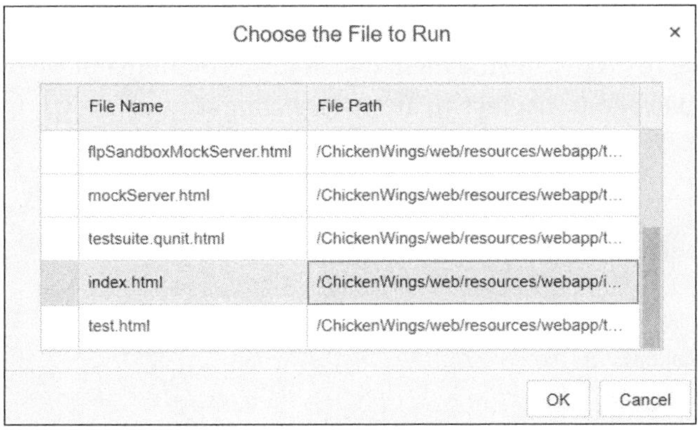

Figure 7.14 Testing the HTML5 Module

If no errors occur, you should see a screen like Figure 7.15 with your first HTML5 application running.

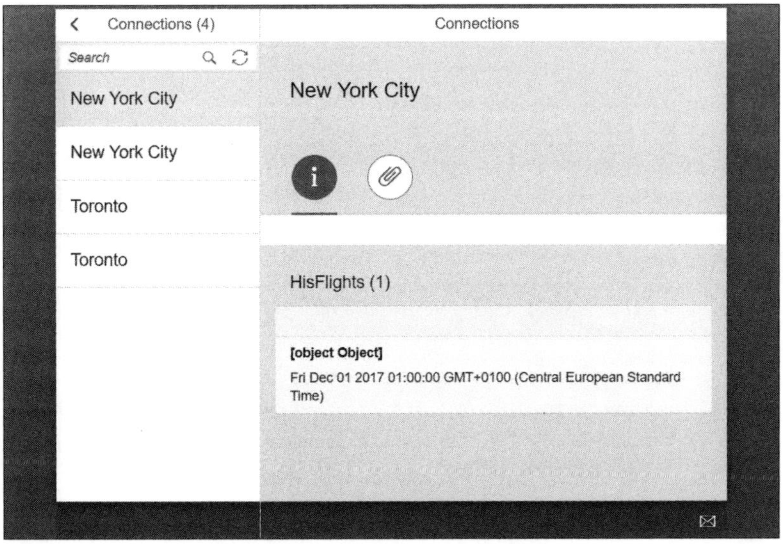

Figure 7.15 Generated SAP Fiori Master-Detail Module Running

7.3.2 Demo Application Layout Adjustments

As you saw in the previous section, the generated application needs some improvements. We'll change it by formatting the layout of the flight's date and adjusting the layout of the connections displayed in the master view list.

Adding a Format Option to Date Fields

Currently, in the flights list, we're just listing the flight date for each of them but we're missing a formatter for the date, so it displays in an unappealing way, as shown in Figure 7.16.

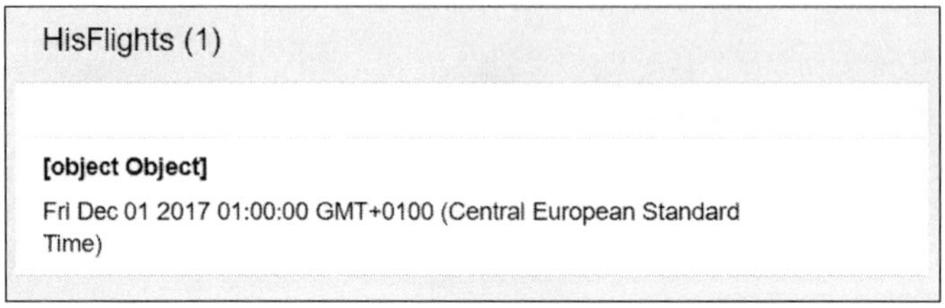
HisFlights (1)
[object Object]
Fri Dec 01 2017 01:00:00 GMT+0100 (Central European Standard Time)

Figure 7.16 Date Field Displayed without a Formatter

Let's change the detail view and try to adjust it. We can use the code editor (right-click **Open with • Code Editor**) to open the file *Detail.view.xml* in the *resources* • *webapp* • *view* folder, as shown in Figure 7.17.

Detail.view.xml ×
<columns>
<Column>
<Text text="{i18n>detailLineItemTableIDColumn}"/>
</Column>
<Column
minScreenWidth="Tablet"
demandPopin="true"
hAlign="Right">
<Text text="{i18n>detailLineItemTableUnitNumberColumn}"/>
</Column>
</columns>
<items>
<ColumnListItem>
<cells>
<ObjectIdentifier
title="{}"
text="{FDATE}"/>
<ObjectNumber/>
</cells>
</ColumnListItem>
</items>
</Table>
</semantic:content>

Figure 7.17 Editing the Detail.view.xml with the Code Editor

We must look for the ObjectIdentifier tag and change following code:

```
<ObjectIdentifier
title="{}"
text="{FDATE}"/>
```

We'll remove the text property and add a new binding for the title property to the FDATE field using a date type definition and a format option, as shown in Listing 7.29.


```
<ObjectIdentifier
title="{
    path: 'FDATE',
    type: 'sap.ui.model.type.Date',
    formatOptions: {
        style: 'medium'
    }
}"/>
```

Listing 7.29 Binding of ObjectIdentifier Changed with the Date Type Definition

If we rebuild the application and run it again, we can see a better flight list, as shown in Figure 7.18.

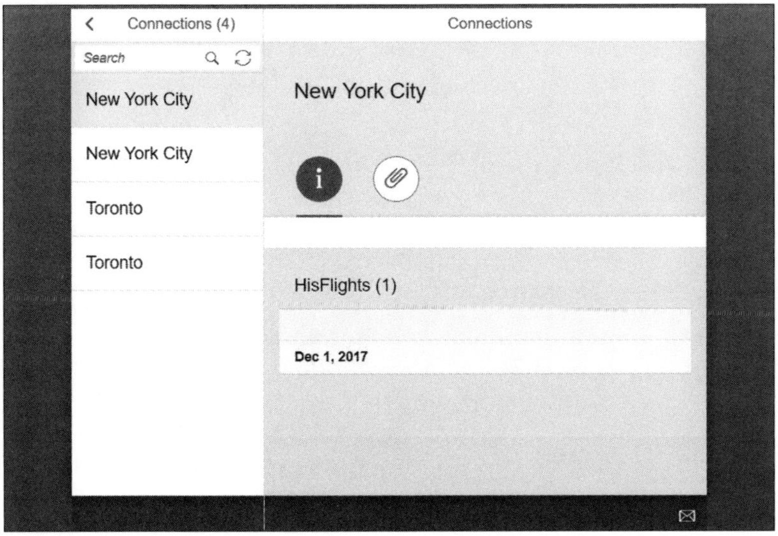

Figure 7.18 Date Field Displayed with a Format Option

Changing the Master List

Now we'll enhance the master list by adding the number of available flights for each connection. To do this, we need to create a new method in the controller file, so let's change the file *Master.controller.js* available under folders *resources* • *webapp* • *controller* by adding the function from Listing 7.30.

```
flightsCount: function(oValue) {
//read the number of flights returned
var flightsCount = 0;
if (oValue) {
flightsCount = oValue.length;
}
return flightsCount;
}
```

Listing 7.30 New Method for Counting the Number of Flights for Each Connection

Now, we need to change the view file (*Master.view.xml*), both for using the function we've just created as formatter in the object list item number binding and for adding a parameter to the `items` binding of the list control.

First, as shown in Listing 7.31, we need to extend the `items` binding of the list control in a way that the binding is "expanded" to the "`HisFlights`" navigation property.

```
<List
id="list"
    items="{
        path: '/Connections',
        parameters: {
            expand: 'HisFlights'
        },
        sorter: {
            path: 'FR_CITY',
            descending: false
        },
        groupHeaderFactory: '.createGroupHeader'
        }"
        busyIndicatorDelay="{masterView>/delay}"
        noDataText="{masterView>/noDataText}"
        mode="{= ${device>/system/phone} ? 'None' : 'SingleSelectMaster'}"
        growing="true"
```

```
        growingScrollToLoad="true"
        updateFinished="onUpdateFinished"
        selectionChange="onSelectionChange">
```

Listing 7.31 Items Aggregation Binding Changed

As you can see, we've added the following parameter to the `items` binding:

```
parameters: {
            expand: 'HisFlights'
        }
```


In this way, when the binding is evaluated, the navigation property "`HisFlights`" is used, and we can access the connections flights array to get the number.

Now we can change the binding for the number property of the object list item. We'll define the binding using the navigation property "`HisFlights`" as the path and define the formatter we've just created into the controller using the code in Listing 7.32.

```
<ObjectListItem
type="{= ${device>/system/phone} ? 'Active' : 'Inactive'}"
press="onSelectionChange"
title="{FR_CITY}"
number="{
path : 'HisFlights',
formatter:'.flightsCount'
}"
>
```

Listing 7.32 Number Binding of Object List Item Using the Formatter

The last change we'll do to the layout of the master list is to add a new binding to the `intro` property of the object list item. Let's change the *Master.view.xml* as shown in Listing 7.33.

```
<ObjectListItem
type="{= ${device>/system/phone} ? 'Active' : 'Inactive'}"
press="onSelectionChange"
title="{FLIGHT}"
intro="From {FR_CITY}"
number="{
path : 'HisFlights',
```

```
formatter:'.flightsCount'
}"
>
```

Listing 7.33 New Intro Binding Added to Object List Item

If you build your app and restart it, you should see something like Figure 7.19.

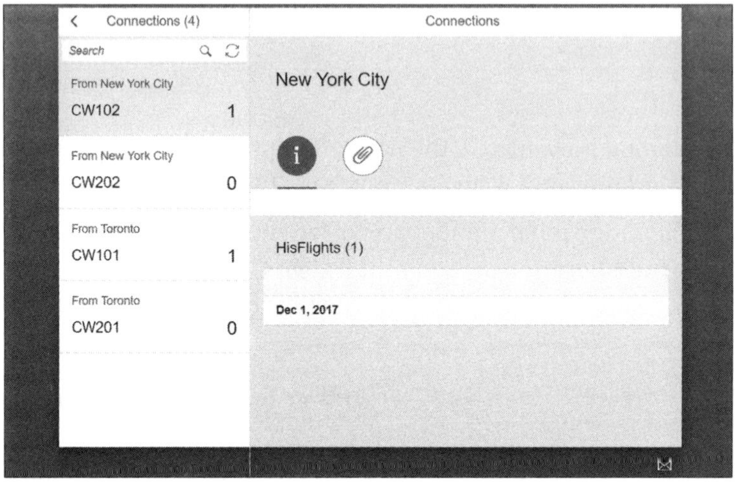

Figure 7.19 The Application after the Layout Adjustments

7.4 Summary

In this chapter, we introduced SAPUI5 as a development framework for building the presentation layer of an SAP HANA XS Advanced application.

We discussed the main concepts behind the SAPUI5 development framework. By adding the presentation layer to our application, we've analyzed how it can interact with different resources defined in the SAP HANA XS Advanced application routing descriptor file and how it can consume them with the data binding technique that makes it easy to integrate data exposed via OData services into the UI elements.

Furthermore, we've seen how, behind the technical implementation of the UI layer, the development phase should be integrated by a deep design activity that makes the usage of the application easy, immediate, and coherent to the end users.

In the next chapter, we'll explain the how to secure your application using SAP HANA XS Advanced functionality.

PART III

Refining the Application

Chapter 8
Securing Your Application

In this chapter, you'll learn how to implement the security mechanisms of SAP HANA XS Advanced in your applications.

Security is one of the primary considerations when implementing an application. We want to ensure that our applications and data are adequately protected. Only authorized users must have access. The SAP HANA extended application services, advanced model (SAP HANA XS Advanced) platform offers functionalities to secure our applications in every layer. In this chapter, we'll explain the different options to configure the security mechanisms in every segment of an SAP HANA XS Advanced application. We'll discuss how to secure the user interface (UI) layer developed with HTML5, the application layer developed with Java or Node.js, and the SAP HANA database layer.

We'll first highlight the security concepts of SAP HANA XS Advanced and explain the different components that must be considered when setting up the security mechanisms of an SAP HANA XS Advanced application. Next, we'll discuss the various authorization concepts that exist in SAP HANA XS Advanced today to make sure that only authorized users can access applications and see only data that they are permitted to access.

We'll then demonstrate practical examples on how to enable the security mechanisms for our ChickenWings application. We'll show how to set up the authentication and authorization mechanisms of SAP HANA XS Advanced in the different modules of the ChickenWings application. We'll discuss the options to maintain users and their roles within SAP HANA XS Advanced, followed by examining the options to grant access to an SAP HANA Deployment Infrastructure (HDI) container of SAP HANA XS Advanced to a classic SAP HANA database user. Finally, we'll give an overview of the default access roles for HDI containers and discuss the permissions for HDI container objects in SAP HANA XS Advanced.

8.1 SAP HANA XS Advanced Security Concepts

An SAP HANA XS Advanced application consists of one or multiple modules. These modules share the same application lifecycle from the development of the app to the deployment in a productive environment. A developer can create modules with different technologies and deploy these modules to various target runtime platforms. Trends in a microservices-based architecture led to the development of applications constructed out of multiple decoupled modules. Typically, the SAP HANA database provides persistence services for SAP HANA XS Advanced applications. The SAP HANA XS Advanced application server is responsible for deploying, running, and monitoring the application. Security-related features, such as authentication and authorization, are enforced in the SAP HANA XS Advanced application server layer.

An SAP HANA XS Advanced application accesses data from the SAP HANA database through a technical database user that the SAP HANA XS Advanced platform automatically generates. Direct access to the database is only intended for database administrators. In SAP HANA XS Advanced, users are classified as business users or administrator users. Business users access applications according to assigned privileges. This user and authorization information is stored in the identity provider (IdP). Business-user-specific authorization information is propagated to the database when the SAP HANA XS Advanced application requests data. An administrator requires a named SAP HANA database user. SAP HANA XS Advanced application developers are designed as business users.

Access Privileges of the Technical SAP HANA XS Advanced Container User

In SAP HANA XS Advanced applications, the SAP HANA XS Advanced runtime assigns roles to the technical database user of the SAP HANA XS Advanced application. A developer can control the access privileges of this technical user with the access role `default_access_role`. We discuss the concept of the default access role in more detail in Section 8.6.

The deployment of database objects in SAP HANA XS Advanced is based on a container model and called SAP HANA Deployment Infrastructure (HDI). In SAP HANA XS Advanced, the development is performed in a database schema-less way because database objects of an SAP HANA XS Advanced application are deployed to an application-specific container. Each container corresponds to a database schema in the SAP HANA database.

Privileges for Accessing Objects in an HDI Container

A developer requires synonyms in SAP HANA XS Advanced to obtain a database object that isn't part of the same SAP HANA XS Advanced application container. The options for a developer to define the privileges of the SAP HANA XS Advanced application container to access external objects are discussed in Section 8.7.

Every object deployed into this database schema, such as stored procedures, tables, and calculation views, is owned by a dedicated technical database user who is created automatically by the SAP HANA XS Advanced platform. For every container deployed, a new technical database user and schema with the same name as the database container are created. Additional schemas and technical users required for metadata and deployment application programming interfaces (APIs) are also produced. The following technical users are generated during the deployment of an SAP HANA XS Advanced application:

- **User** `S`
  Owner of the container schema S.
- **User** `S#DI`
  Owner of the schema S#DI containing metadata and deployment APIs.
- **User** `S#OO`
  Owner of database objects in schema S.
- **Users** `_DI#S#METADATA_COM_SAP_HANA_DI_<metadata>`
  Owners of schemas containing metadata.

These technical users are required internally by HDI only. They are created as restricted database users who don't have any privileges by default. These users can't be used to log on to the SAP HANA database. End users typically don't interact with the technical users because the infrastructure manages them.

Business users or external users aren't bound to any HDI privileges or permissions. These users use the same service to connect to the database backend using the same technical user. The business users are defined, and permissions are assigned to those users by adding role collections to them in the user management of SAP HANA XS Advanced. The authorization concepts of SAP HANA XS Advanced and how to map role collections to end users are discussed in more detail later in this chapter. Figure 8.1 illustrates different users involved in an HDI container.

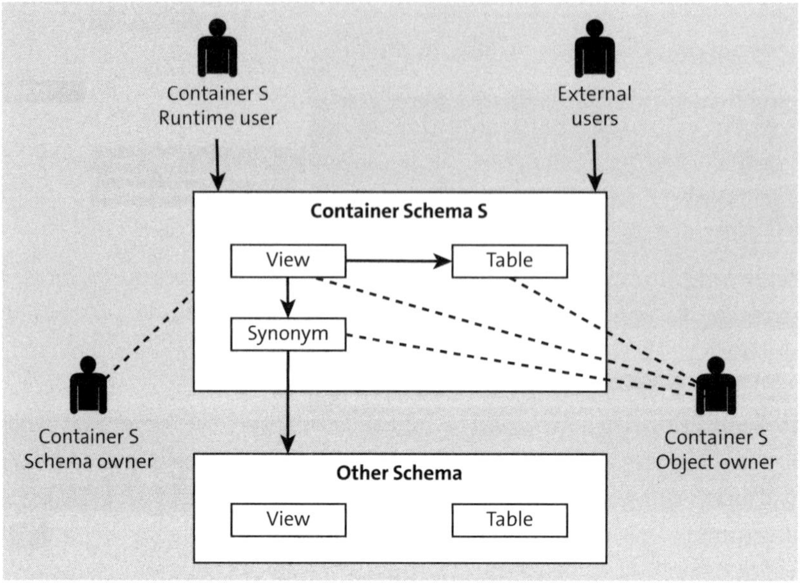

Figure 8.1 Involved users in an HDI Container

End users access an SAP HANA XS Advanced application typically via a web browser. The central entry point for the application is the application router. Each SAP HANA XS Advanced application has its own application router that initiates the authentication and authorization checks of an end user via the User Authentication and Authorization (UAA) service by an IdP. SAP HANA is the default IdP of SAP HANA XS Advanced. However, it's possible to use any other IdP that supports the Security Assertion Markup Language (SAML) 2.0 standard for exchanging authentication and authorization data between security domains. After the user logs in successfully, the UAA service issues an access token that follows the OAuth industry-standard protocol for authorization for the user's session. Subsequent requests use this token for authorization tasks. Figure 8.2 highlights the SAP HANA XS Advanced architecture and components of the initial authentication.

Next, after the OAuth access token for the user's session is generated, the application router triggers requests to the runtimes of the SAP HANA XS Advanced application. The target destination of a specific route is configured in the *manifest.yml* configuration file. The target route is specified in the *xs-app.json* configuration file. The token for the user's session is included in every call to the application containers. The containers validate the token that they receive in specific module libraries. The signature, timeliness, correct recipient (OAuth client and UAA identity zone), and authorizations are validated. The access to the SAP HANA database container of an SAP HANA XS Advanced application is performed via a technical user that gets generated when the SAP HANA database container is created. The privileges of a business user are forwarded to the technical user when the database layer is accessed so that the security mechanisms can be enforced on the database layer.

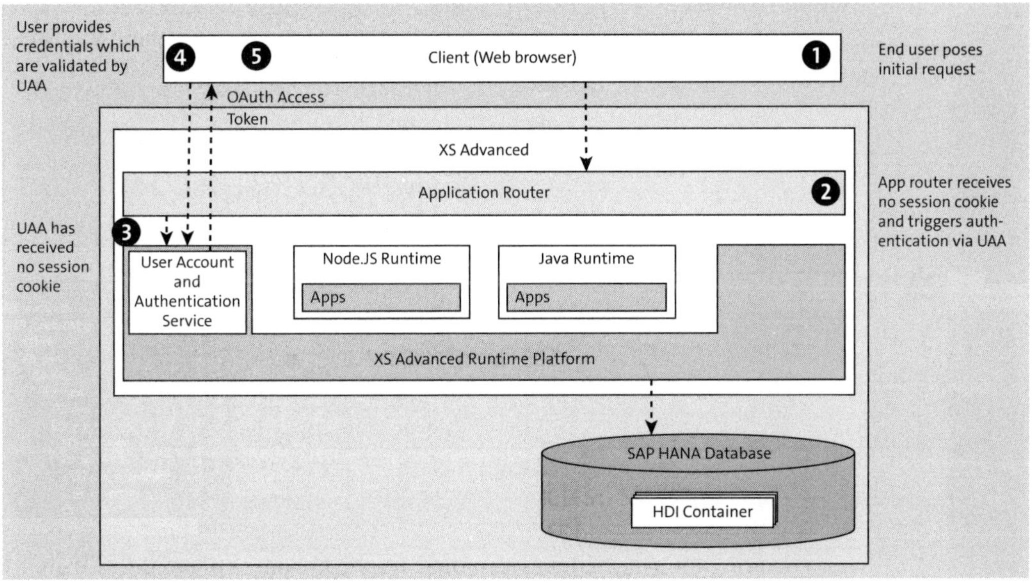

Figure 8.2 SAP HANA XS Advanced Architecture and Security Components

In SAP HANA XS Advanced applications, authorization checks for business users are based on scopes and attributes. *Scopes* are for functional authorizations checks (e.g., the end user is allowed to view cost center data). Thus, a developer can restrict data access to specific objects. *Attributes*, on the other hand, are instance-based authorizations (e.g., the end user is only allowed to see data for cost center XYZ) that would enable the restriction of data on specific records.

Scopes and Attributes

We'll discuss the concept of scopes and attributes in SAP HANA XS Advanced in more detail in Section 8.2.1.

The application router of SAP HANA XS Advanced performs declarative URL-based (and HTTP verb-based) authorization checks based on the privileges that are assigned to an end user. The runtime container security in the Node.js runtime offers the option to perform programmatic authorization checks. The container security features in the Java runtime provides the opportunity to perform declarative authorization checks via the Spring Framework and programmatic authorization checks based on the attributes assigned to an end user.

Practical Examples of Security Checks in Node.js and Java

You'll find practical examples on how to implement security checks in a Node.js and Java module in SAP HANA XS Advanced in Section 8.3.

On the SAP HANA database layer, instance-based authorization checks can be performed via attribute values or the Data Control Language (DCL). We discuss the authorization concept of SAP HANA XS Advanced in detail in Section 8.2. Figure 8.3 highlights the components of an SAP HANA XS Advanced application and the type of authorization checks managed by the components.

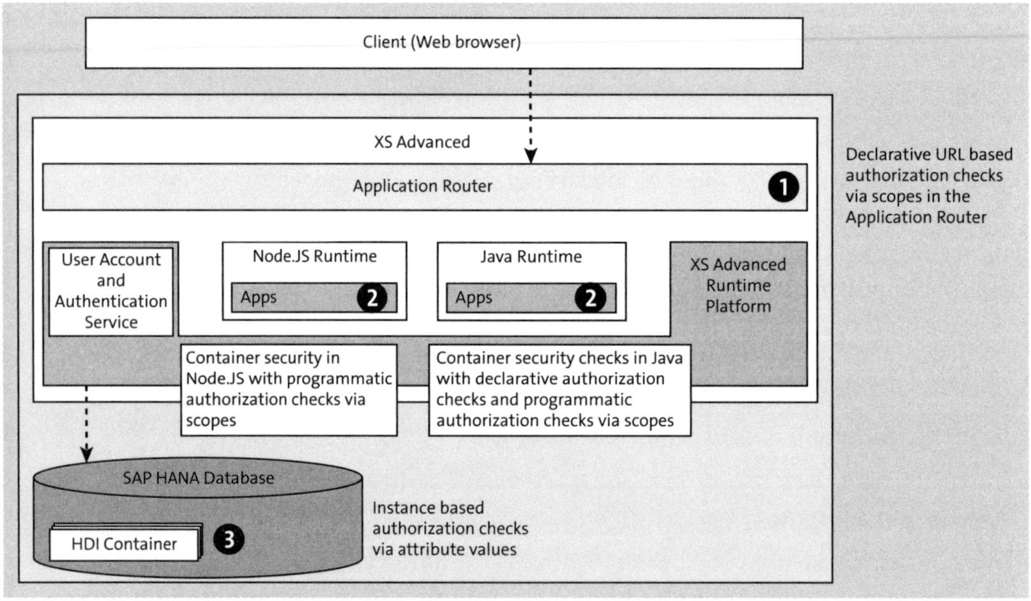

Figure 8.3 SAP HANA XS Advanced Application Components and Authorization Checks Performed by the Component

8.2 Authorization in SAP HANA XS Advanced

The SAP HANA XS Advanced platform allows end users to access applications and services. An authorization concept is required to control the access to applications and functions of the SAP HANA XS Advanced platform. In SAP HANA XS Advanced, end user permissions are derived from roles that are assigned to end users. Furthermore, as already introduced in Chapter 4 when discussing the architecture of SAP HANA XS Advanced, resources from different applications can be isolated by using organizations and spaces. In this section, we'll discuss the following components that enable the implementing and authorization concept for our SAP HANA XS Advanced applications:

- Scopes and attributes
- Defining application security with the application security descriptor
- SAP HANA XS UAA service
- Role collections
- DCL
- Controller roles

8.2.1 Scopes and Attributes

SAP HANA XS Advanced applications can perform authorization checks via scopes and attributes. A scope is a permission that an end user requires for accessing the SAP HANA XS Advanced application or specific services. Scopes define the actions that can be performed within a service, and they are used for authorization checks by the SAP HANA XS Advanced application router and the application's HDI container. Authorization checks can be performed declaratively in the application router or programmatically in an application container such as Node.js or Java.

For declarative authorization checks, URL prefix patterns can be defined, and scope gets associated with each pattern. If one or more matching patterns are found when a URL is accessed, the application router checks whether the access token included in the request contains at least scopes associated with the matching patterns. If not all scopes are found, access to the requested URL is denied. The container security API for programmatic authorization checks includes a `hasScope` method that allows the current authentication token to be checked to determine if it has the appropriate scope. The authentication token that gets issued by the UAA when an end user authenticates contains all scopes and attributes that are granted to the user based on the assigned role collections. An application performs authorization checks based on these scopes and attributes.

Attributes define the application's entities that a user can access. A list of scopes combined with a list of attributes represents a role. A role template describes a role and any attributes that apply to the role. A developer specifies the scopes and attributes in the *xs-security.json* configuration file of the SAP HANA XS Advanced application. This configuration file gets evaluated during the deployment of the SAP HANA XS Advanced application, and role templates get generated. Roles will be created automatically from role templates. We explain the configuration options of the *xs-security.json* configuration file in Section 8.2.2.

In our ChickenWings application, we're going to have two types of users to demonstrate the concept of scopes and attributes of SAP HANA XS Advanced: the Airport-Reader and the Airport-Manager. The Airport-Reader is allowed only to see the list of crew members but not modify them. The Airport-Manager is permitted to alter the list of crew members. To implement this requirement, we'll set up two role templates: the Airport-Reader and the Airport-Manager.

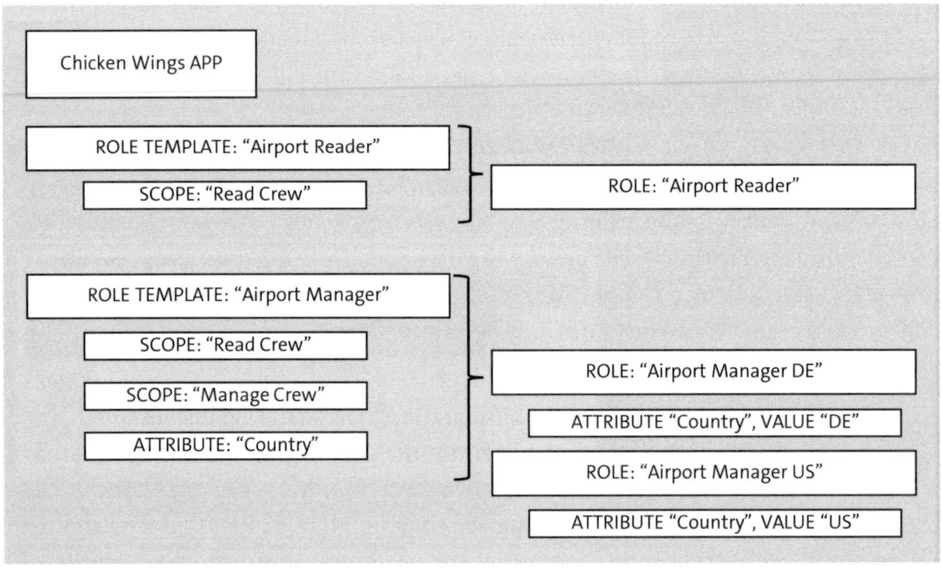

Figure 8.4 Concept of Role Templates in the ChickenWings Application

The Airport-Reader role template contains a scope called `ReadCrew`. This role template will result in one role called `Airport Reader`. The Airport-Manager role template includes a scope called `Read Crew` and `Manage Crew`. Furthermore, the role template includes an attribute called `Country`, which allows us to define for which countries an Airport Manager can make modifications. In our example, we'll have an Airport Manager for `Germany` and one for the `US`. This role template will result in two roles, an `Airport Manager-Germany` and an `Airport Manager-US`. We'll go into the details of how to enable the security checks for the ChickenWings application in Section 8.3. Figure 8.4 highlights how scopes and attributes will be grouped into role templates in the ChickenWings application.

8.2.2 Defining Application Security with the Application Security Descriptor

Application developers in SAP HANA XS Advanced declare scopes, attributes, and role templates in the security descriptor configuration file *xs-security.json* of an SAP HANA XS Advanced application. This file defines the security and deployment options of an application. The information in this file is used at application deployment time. This configuration file must meet some prerequisites. The name of the file must be *xs-security.json*. Furthermore, the location of the file must be in either the root folder of an application (e.g., */path/appname/*) or in the security folder of an application (e.g., */path/appname/security*). The content of the file must follow the JavaScript Object Notation (JSON). The *xs-security.json* file allows the following elements to be defined, and each will be discussed in this section:

- `Xsappname`
- `Scopes`
- `Attributes`
- `role-templates`
- `authorities`
- `foreign-scope-references`
- `oauth2-configuration`
- `tenant-mode`

xsappname

The `xsappname` property in the *xs-security.json* configuration file specifies the name of the SAP HANA XS Advanced application. The maximum length of the name is 128 characters, and the following characters can be used: Aa–Zz, 0–9, -, _, /, and \.

Administrators will work with the xsappname. Therefore, it's recommended that this name be easily recognized. The signature of the xsappname looks like the following:

```
"xsappname" "<app-name>",
```

scopes

A scope is a permission that an end user requires to access the SAP HANA XS Advanced application or specific services. The `scopes` property defines one or multiple security scopes that apply for an SAP HANA XS Advanced application. Each scope has a name and a short description. Typically, a scope is application specific. Such a scope is also called a local scope. The application router of the SAP HANA XS Advanced application checks these scopes. If an SAP HANA XS Advanced application needs access to services from other SAP HANA XS Advanced applications, different scopes have to be configured. Sources outside the context of the current SAP HANA XS Advanced application check the different scopes. Local scopes are prefixed with the variable `<$XSAPPNAME>`, whereas foreign scopes must be prefixed with the name of the foreign SAP HANA XS Advanced application.

The maximum length of the name is 193 characters, and the following characters can be used: Aa–Zz, 0–9, -, _, /, \, and :. Scope names must not start with a leading dot.

When an SAP HANA XS Advanced application grants access to external services, a scope must be defined that specifies a grantable flag. This functionality is helpful to grant authorizations defined in one SAP HANA XS Advanced application's scope to another SAP HANA XS Advanced application to execute actions on behalf of the granting SAP HANA XS Advanced application. This functional behavior can be achieved by using `grant-as-authority-to-apps` with the value of the name of an external application that should get access. Listing 8.1 is an example scope definition in an *xs-security.json* configuration file.

```
"scopes": [
{
"name" : "$XSAPPNAME.Display",
"description" : "display" },
{
"name" : "$XSAPPNAME.Edit",
"description" : "edit" },
{
"name" : "$XSAPPNAME.Delete",
"description" : "delete" },
```

```
{
"name" : "$XSAPPNAME.ForeignCall",
"description" : "Enable calls into other app",
"grant-as-authority-to-apps" : ["RequestingApp"]
 }
]
```

Listing 8.1 Example Scopes Definition in the xs-security.json Configuration File

attributes

The `attributes` property allows specifying one or more attribute configurations in the *xs-security.json* configuration file. An attribute entry requires the name of the attribute, a description, and a `valueType`. Possible values of the `valueType` are `string`, `int`, or `date`. Listing 8.2 is an example attribute definition that defines `Country` and `CostCenter` attributes.

```
"attributes": [
{
"name" : "Country",
"description" : "Country",
"valueType" : "string" },
{
"name" : "CostCenter",
"description" : "CostCenter",
"valueType" : "string" },
]
```

Listing 8.2 Example Attributes Definition in the xs-security.json Configuration File

role-templates

The `role-template` attribute allows specifying one or more roles in the *xs-security.json* configuration file. Each `role-template` entry requires a name, description, `scope-reference`, and an `attribute-reference`. The `scope-reference` can be one or multiple scope names that have been defined earlier in the *xs-security.json* configuration file. Role templates must not contain different scopes. The `attribute-reference` can be the name of one or multiple attributes that were defined earlier. Listing 8.3 is an example of the `role-template` configuration with the name `Editor`, which references the `Edit` and `Delete` scopes, as well as the `Country` and `CostCenter` attributes.

```
"role-templates": [
{
"name" : "Editor",
"description" : "View, edit, delete",
"scope-references" : [
"$XSAPPNAME.Edit", "$XSAPPNAME.Delete"],
"attribute-references" : [ "Country", "CostCenter"]
}
]
```

Listing 8.3 Example Role-Templates Definition in the xs-security.json Configuration File

authorities

Authorities allow the definition of requesting applications that can access specific services of the SAP HANA XS Advanced application. The `authorities` attribute is used to describe the name of one or multiple scopes of the external application. A developer can specify that all authorities flagged as grantable should be accepted by the application. This functionality can be achieved by determining the value `["$ACCEPT_GRANTED_AUTHORITIES"]` or by specifying the name of the scope authorities as follows:

```
"authorities":[
"<GrantingAppName>.ForeignCall", "<GrantingApp2Name>.ForeignCall"]
```

foreign-scope-references

A developer can use this element if an application accepts scopes that were assigned to an end user by another SAP HANA XS Advanced application. A developer specifies the names of the scopes in the value of the `foreign-scope-references` attribute. The SAP HANA XS Advanced application will accept all scopes that are assigned by other applications if a developer specifies the name `$ACCEPT_GRANTED_SCOPES`. The `foreign-scope-references` attribute is typically used when an application integrates multiple different application components where each application has its own *xs-security.json* configuration file. Examples of values of the `foreign-scope-references` attribute are as follows:

```
"foreign-scope-references": ["$ACCEPT_GRANTED_SCOPES"]
"foreign-scope-references": [
"$XSAPPNAME(applicationName,otherAppName).scopeName"]
```

oauth2-configuration

A developer uses the `oauth2-configuration` configuration attribute in the *xs-security.json* file to configure custom values for OAuth 2.0 clients. An example of a custom value is the validity time of an OAuth token. The `xsuaa` service of the SAP HANA XS Advanced application uses this configuration value. Table 8.1 lists the available configuration parameters of the `oauth2-configuration` attribute.

Configuration Parameter	Description
`token-validity`	Validity time of the SAP HANA XS Advanced application JSON Web Token (JWT) in seconds
`refresh-token-validity`	Validity time of the SAP HANA XS Advanced application refresh JWT in seconds
`redirect-uris`	A list that specifies the whitelist of the allowed redirect uniform resource identifiers (URIs)
`grant-types`	A list specifying the grant types with the following possible values: "`password`", "`authorization_code`", "`client_credentials`", "`refresh_token`", and "`urn:ietf:params:oauth:grant-type:saml2-bearer`"
`autoapprove`	Specifies whether the end user must approve the requested scopes or whether the scopes are assigned without approval during the token retrieval
`system-attributes`	List of system attributes to be added to the JWT
`allowedproviders`	List of the allowed IdPs to be used for authentication purposes

Table 8.1 Available Parameters of the oauth2-configuration Attribute

Listing 8.4 demonstrates the usage of the `oauth2-configuration` attribute in the *xs-security.json* configuration file.

```
"oauth2-configuration": {
   "token-validity": 500,
   "refresh-token-validity": 500,
   "redirect-uris": [
                    "http://<host_name1>",
                    "http://<host_name2>"],
```

```
    "grant-types": ["password", "authorization_code"],
    "autoapprove": "false",
    "system-attributes": ["groups", "rolecollections"],
    "allowedproviders": ["useridp1", "useridp2"]
}
```

Listing 8.4 Example Usage of the oauth2-configuration Attribute

tenant-mode

A developer can use the `tenant-mode` attribute in a multitenant environment to specify how the OAuth client of a tenant obtains client secrets. Table 8.2 lists the available configuration parameters of the `tenant-mode` attribute.

Configuration Parameter	Description
`dedicated`	This configuration option is the default value. When this option is selected, the OAuth client receives a specific client secret for every subaccount.
`shared`	A developer must specify this value when an application router is configured for multitenancy applications.
`external`	A developer can use this value for tenants with multiple subscriptions to applications.

Table 8.2 SAP HANA XS Advanced Command-Line Client Tenant Mode Commands

Listing 8.5 demonstrates the usage of the `tenant-mode` attribute in the *xs-security.json* configuration file.

```
{
  "xsappname"   : "<application_name>",
  "tenant-mode" : "shared",
  "scopes"      : [
                   {
                    "name"          : "$XSAPPNAME.Display",
                    "description"   : "display" }
                  ],
[...]
}
```

Listing 8.5 Example Usage of the tenant-mode Attribute

8.2.3 SAP HANA XS Advanced User Account and Authorization Service

The SAP HANA Advanced XS UAA service is the responsible SAP HANA XS Advanced service to authenticate a user of an SAP HANA XS Advanced application. After specifying the security configuration for the ChickenWings application in the *xs-security.json* configuration file, we must create an instance of the SAP HANA XS Advanced UAA service. When creating a new instance of the UAA service, we can specify the *xs-security.json* configuration file as an input parameter. This configuration will ensure that the UAA service leverages our security configurations. The UAA service must be created via the SAP HANA XS Advanced command-line interface (XSA CLI) client. The command follows this syntax:

```
xs create-service <service name> <service plan> <service instance name>
-c xs-security.json
An example command is as follows:
xs create-service xsuaa default authorizationtest-uaa -c xs-security.json
```

Figure 8.5 ❶ highlights the execution of the `create-service` command with the XSA CLI. Because it's important that the XSA CLI has access to the *xs-security.json* configuration file, it's required to copy this configuration file to the computer of the developer that runs this command.

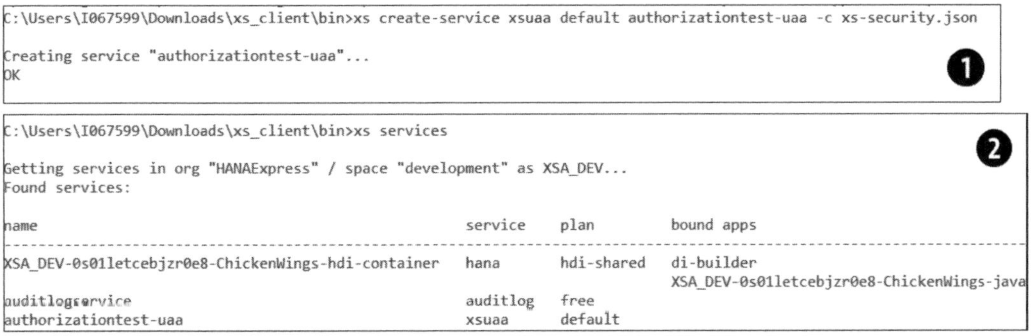

Figure 8.5 Creating the xsuaa Service and Running the xs services Command with the XSA CLI

A developer can confirm the successful creation of the service by running the `xs services` command. Figure 8.5 ❷ highlights the execution of this command in the XSA CLI.

Next, a developer binds the instance of the `xsuaa` service to the SAP HANA XS Advanced application. A developer has to specify the name of the service in the *mta.yaml* configuration file of the SAP HANA XS Advanced application in the `resources` section, add the name of the service instance, and add the path to the *xs-security.json* configuration file as a parameter. We'll go into the details of how to enable the security checks for the ChickenWings application in Section 8.3. Figure 8.6 highlights the *mta.yaml* file with the UAA service instance.

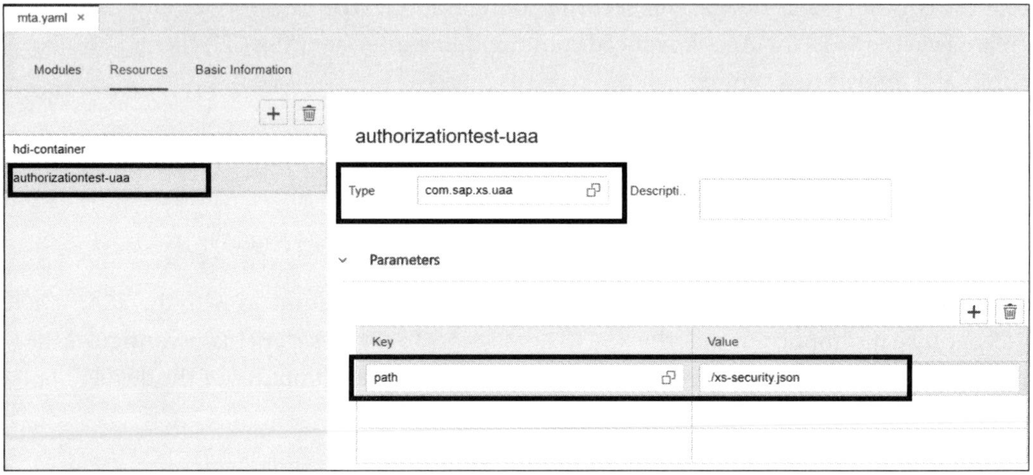

Figure 8.6 mta.yaml File with the xsuaa Service Instance Name

8.2.4 Role Collections

A list of roles in SAP HANA XS Advanced defines a *role collection*. An end user can be assigned to several role collections. Those roles can be grouped into role collections in the Application Role Builder tool of SAP HANA XS Advanced. Multiple roles from different applications can be assigned to a single role collection. Finally, SAP HANA XS Advanced users are assigned to role collections in the User Management tool. An administrator user in SAP HANA XS Advanced performs these activities. Figure 8.7 highlights the concept of role collections in SAP HANA XS Advanced.

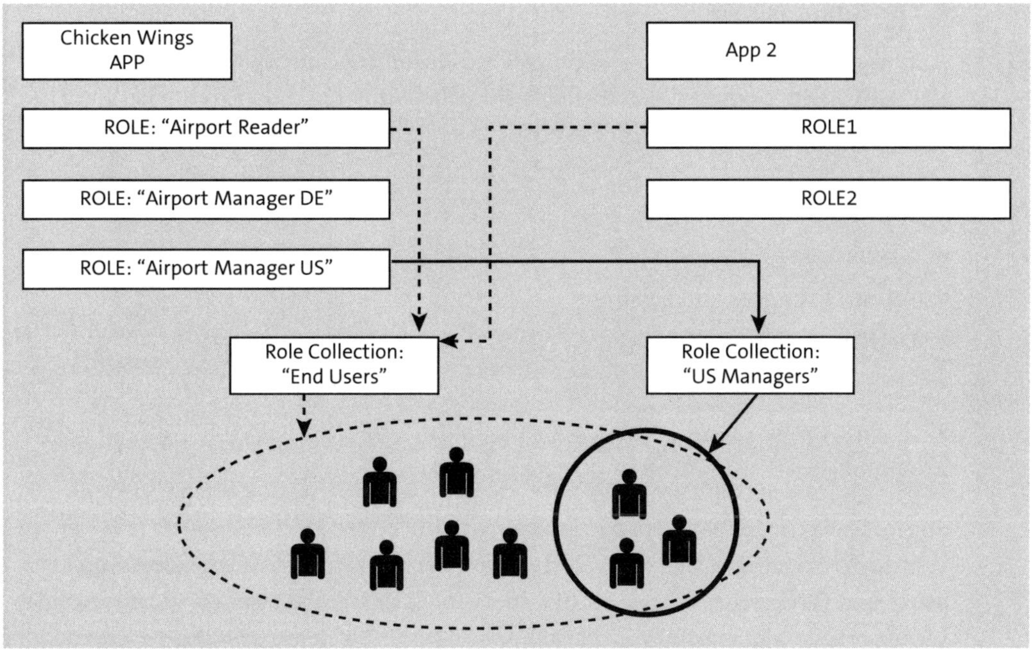

Figure 8.7 Concept of Role Collections in SAP HANA XS Advanced

8.2.5 Data Control Language

DCL is a language used within Core Data Services (CDS) to define instance-based authorization models that enable controlling access to data based on attributes assigned to an end user in SAP HANA XS Advanced. DCL is an extension to SQL and allows privileges to be granted based on attribute values dynamically. DCL uses rules to restrict access to data. The authorization concept of DCL can be used in combination with the concept of scopes, attributes, and role templates or independently of another. The authorization checks with the DCL occur in the SAP HANA XS Advanced application instance. We'll demonstrate a practical example of how to use DCL to configure instance-based authorization checks for our ChickenWings application in Section 8.4.4. Following is an example rule defined in DCL that restricts data on an attribute which is assigned to an end user and available via the session context:

```
grant select on dd.salesOrderView where customerOrgUnit = SESSION_CONTEXT
('XS_ORGUNIT');
```

8.2.6 Controller Roles

A controller role is granted to a controller user for a specific space or organization in SAP HANA XS Advanced. Controller role collections are associated with necessary authorizations, but they don't control the permission for accessing a particular resource of an SAP HANA XS Advanced application. Resources in the controller are entities such as:

- Applications
- Service instances and bindings
- Domains and routes
- Spaces and organizations
- Service broker
- Buildpack

Spaces are a central concept for grouping applications that are tightly coupled and can run in a shared trust zone. Each controller resource has either a reference to a space and is therefore scoped to this space, or it's assigned as a global resource (service broker, buildpacks). Information about which roles are granted to a controller user isn't stored in the UAA but is attached to the space or organization entities in the controller model. The following categories of controller roles are defined:

- `OrgManager`
  An end user with this role is allowed to modify spaces and domains, view the resources of an organization, and grant any controller role to other users.
- `OrgAuditor`
  End users with this role are allowed to view resources of an organization but not make any modifications.
- `SpaceManager`
  An end user with this role is allowed to grant the `SpaceManager`, `SpaceDeveloper`, and `SpaceAuditor` roles to other users.
- `SpaceDeveloper`
  An end user with this role is allowed to make modifications to resources within a specific space such as SAP HANA XS Advanced applications.
- `SpaceAuditor`
  An end user with this role is allowed to view resources within a space but isn't allowed to make any changes.

8.3 Enable Security in your SAP HANA XS Advanced Application

In this section, we'll explain how the security mechanisms of SAP HANA XS Advanced can be implemented for our ChickenWings application. We demonstrated how to develop application layer logic and create a UI for SAP HANA XS Advanced in Chapter 6 and Chapter 7, respectively. Now, we'll further improve our application by making sure we define the appropriate security mechanisms.

First, we'll demonstrate how to create a new user authorization and authentication service for our ChickenWings application. Then, we'll enable the security mechanisms for the different layers of our application. We'll start with enabling the security mechanisms for the SAP HANA XS Advanced Java module. Next, we'll configure the security checks for the Node.js module. In Section 8.3.4, we'll activate the security mechanism for the HTML5 module. Finally, we'll discuss some best practices to secure your application against web-based attacks.

8.3.1 Creating the SAP HANA XS Advanced User Account and Authorization Service

Before we can start setting up the security mechanisms for the different application layers of the ChickenWings application, we must define what type of access and what roles we want to have in our application. In our ChickenWings application, we're going to have two types of users to demonstrate the concept of scopes and attributes of SAP HANA XS Advanced: the Airport-Reader and the Airport-Manager. The Airport-Reader is allowed only to see the list of crew members but not modify them. The Airport-Manager is permitted to alter the list of crew members. However, the Airport-Manager can update the crew members for a specific country.

To implement this requirement, we'll set up two role templates: the Airport-Reader and the Airport-Manager. The Airport-Reader role template contains a scope that is called `Read Crew`. This role template will result in one role called `AirportReader`. The Airport-Manager role template includes scopes called `ReadCrew` and `ManageCrew`. Furthermore, the role template consists of an attribute named `Country`, which allows us to define for which crew members of which countries an Airport Manager can make modifications. We define this setup in the *xs-security.json* configuration file, which is a new file that we have to create in the root folder of our ChickenWings application.

First, create a new file in the ChickenWings application in the SAP Web IDE for SAP HANA with the name *xs-security.json*. We define two security roles, an `AirportReader` role, and an AirportManager role. Furthermore, we'll restrict the AirportManager role on an attribute of the country of the crew member. After we've specified the content of the file, we save the file and build the application in the SAP Web IDE for SAP HANA. Listing 8.6 displays the content of the *xs-security.json* configuration file.

```
{
"xsappname" : "ChickenWings",
"scopes" : [
{
"name" : "$XSAPPNAME.ReadCrew",
"description" : "Read crew" },
{
"name" : "$XSAPPNAME.ManageCrew",
"description" : "Create new or delete existing crew" }
],
"attributes" : [
{
"name" : "Country",
"description" : "Country of crew member",
"valueType" : "string"
} ],
"role-templates" : [
{
"name" : "AirportReader",
"description" : "Template for reading crew members",
"scope-references" : [ "$XSAPPNAME.ReadCrew"]},
{
"name" : "AirportManager",
"description" : "Template for managing crew members",
"scope-references" : [ "$XSAPPNAME.ReadCrew","$XSAPPNAME.ManageCrew" ],
"attribute-references" : ["Country"]}
]
}
```

Listing 8.6 xs-security.json Configuration File of the ChickenWings Application

Figure 8.8 highlights the location of the *xs-security.json* configuration file in the ChickenWings application in the SAP Web IDE for SAP HANA.

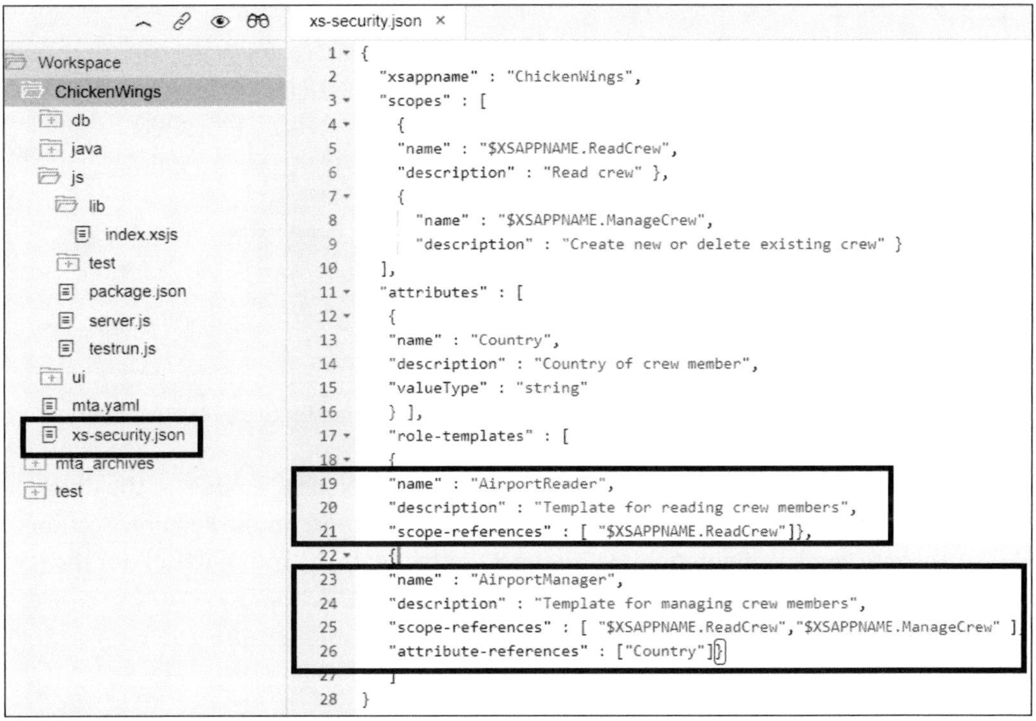

Figure 8.8 xs-security.json Configuration File in the ChickenWings Application

In the previous step, we specified the role concept of our application in the *xs-security.json* file. Next, we create a new xsuaa service for our ChickenWings application by using the process described in Section 8.2.3. This service is responsible for authenticating users and validating that users have the correct authorizations when accessing the ChickenWings application.

Next, a developer has to bind the instance of the xsuaa service to the SAP HANA XS Advanced application using the process described in Section 8.2.3.

We must add the authorizationtest-uaa resource to the different modules of our ChickenWings application in the *mta.yaml* configuration file. In the *mta.yaml* configuration file, select the entry of our **html5** module first. Add a new required entry by clicking on the **+** icon, and set **authorizationtest-uaa (resource)** as the **Name** in the **Requires** area. The **Value** for the **Group** can be empty. Figure 8.9 highlights the configuration in the SAP Web IDE for SAP HANA.

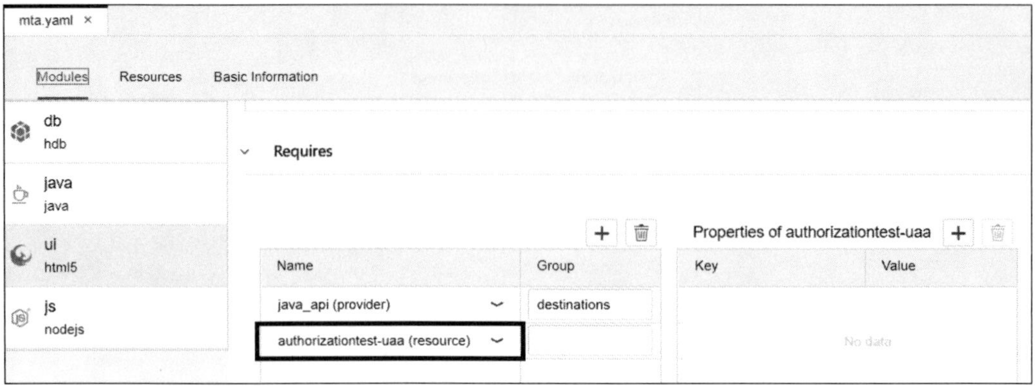

Figure 8.9 Specifying the xsuaa Service in the Requires Area for the HTML5 Module

Perform the same step for the Java module and the Node.js module of the ChickenWings application. Add the **authorizationtest-uaa** service in the **Requires** section of the *mta.yaml* configuration file. Figure 8.10 highlights the configuration for the Java module in the SAP Web IDE for SAP HANA.

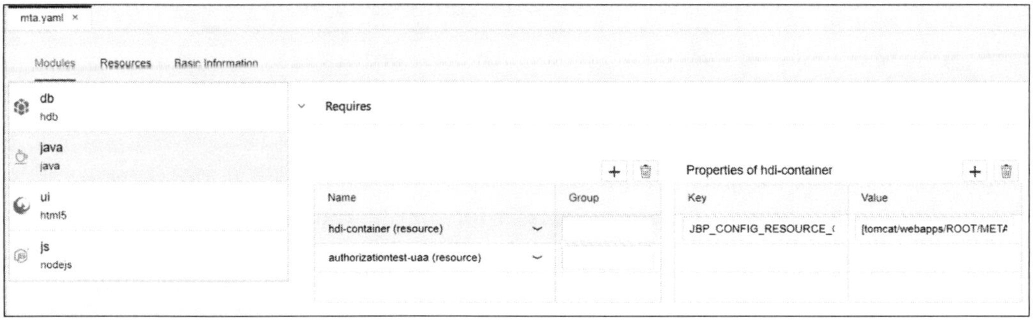

Figure 8.10 Specifying the xsuaa Service in the Requires Area for the Java Module

Click on the **Save** icon in the SAP Web IDE for SAP HANA after performing this configuration change in the *mta.yaml* configuration file. Now we can enable the security checks in the application layer as well as the UI of our ChickenWings application as described in the following sections of this chapter.

8.3.2 Enabling Security for Java Modules

In the previous chapters, we created an OData service to demonstrate the options to create, read, update, and delete data from an SAP HANA database table with the Java runtime of SAP HANA XS Advanced. To simplify our testing efforts, we didn't enable a security mechanism for our OData services. In Chapter 6, Section 8.3.1, we demonstrated how to disable the security constraint within the *web.xml* configuration file of the Java module. In this section, we'll describe how to enable the security constraint and discuss the options for Java modules to perform authentication and authorization checks during the execution of an OData request by leveraging the UAA service of SAP HANA XS Advanced.

First, we'll enable the security constraint in the *web.xml* configuration file of our Java module to activate the authorization check. Open the *web.xml* configuration file of the ChickenWings application by choosing **java • src • main • webapp • WEB-INF** in the SAP Web IDE for SAP HANA to perform this configuration.

Remove the XML comment for the `<security-constraint>` XML tag. By doing this, we leverage the web container-based security mechanism to protect the OData service endpoints. Specify `ReadCrew` as the name of the `role-name` tag in the `auth-constraint` section. This configuration means that an end user will require the `ReadCrew` role to access the Java module of the ChickenWings application. We demonstrate how to assign roles to end users in SAP HANA XS Advanced in Section 8.4. Save the *web.xml* file after performing this configuration change. Figure 8.11 highlights the required configuration in the *web.xml* file.

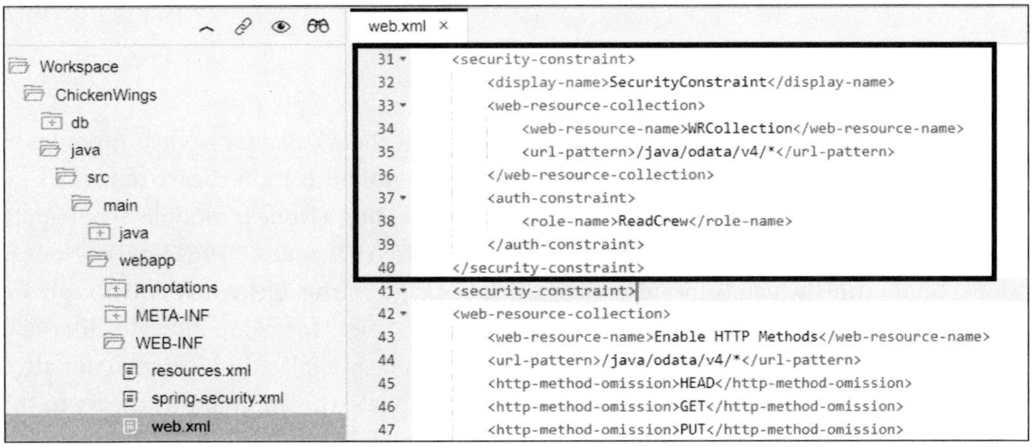

Figure 8.11 Enabling the Security Constraint in the web.xml Configuration File

Build and run the application. The authorization check is now active. We created two roles: `ReadCrew` and `ManageCrew`. Only a user that has the `ReadCrew` role assigned is allowed to read data. For update, delete, and insert operations, an end user requires the ManageCrew role. To achieve that, we add a security constraint to the Java class ChickenWingsJavaExtension. The source code example in Listing 8.7 highlights the ServletSecurity annotation for our Java class, which implements the OData write, update, and delete operations. The ServletSecurity annotation will activate the authorization check for our Java class.

```
import javax.servlet.annotation.*;
import javax.servlet.http.*;
@ServletSecurity(@HttpConstraint(rolesAllowed = {"ManageCrew"})) public class
ChickenWingsJavaExtension {
}
```

Listing 8.7 ServletSecurity in the Java Class Implementing the OData Extension for the Update, Delete, and Insert Operations

Build and run the Java module after adding the ServletSecurity constraint. We're not quite done yet. End users will now get a **Forbidden** error message when trying to perform a delete, update, or insert operation via the ChickenWingsJavaExtension Java class. This error message is expected because we defined that end users will require the ManageCrew role to access this service. We'll have to add the ManageCrew role to our end user. We discuss the options to assign roles to end users in SAP HANA XS Advanced in Section 8.4.

8.3.3 Enabling Security for Node.js Modules

We can enable authentication and authorization checks also for Node.js modules in SAP HANA XS Advanced. Let's first activate the authentication checks to make sure that end users must be authenticated before accessing a Node.js module of our application. To do that, open the *server.js* file in SAP Web IDE for SAP HANA of the Node.js application, which is located under the **js** package. In this file, you'll find an options variable that should have an entry anonymous : true. This value indicates that end users don't have to authenticate to access the Node.js application. Remove this attribute or put a comment // on this line to deactivate the anonymous access to the Node.js module. When you build and run the Node.js module, the end user will be required to authenticate before accessing the module. Figure 8.12 highlights the configuration needed in the *server.js* file.

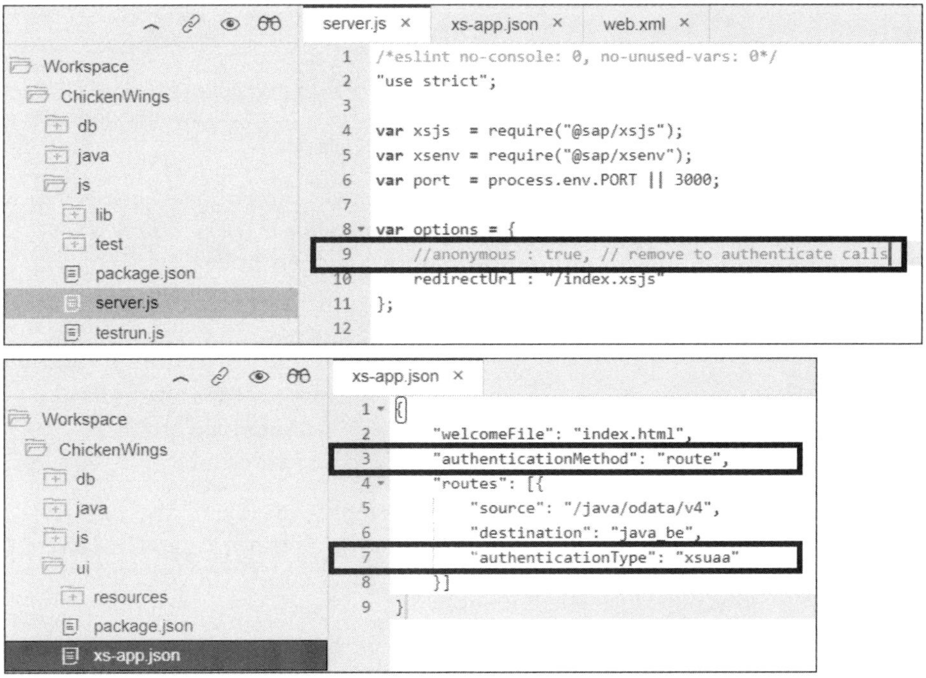

Figure 8.12 Enabling the Authentication Check for the Node.js Module

Next, we want to enable authorization checks in our Node.js application to make sure that only users with a specific role are accessing our application. This scenario can be achieved with the container security API of SAP HANA XS Advanced.

To authenticate a user, the SAP HANA XS Advanced runtime that processes the request receives a JWT from the SAP HANA XS Advanced application router. This token contains information about the end user such as the user's scope information, which will be validated using the SAP HANA XS Advanced container security API. The Node.js application can use this API to validate the values of the scope information that are assigned to an end user. The SAP HANA XS Advanced container security API provides an `XSASecurityContext` object, which is initialized with the JWT. The object provides the functions listed in Table 8.3.

Function	Description
`getUserInfo()`	This function returns `logonName`, `firstName`, `lastName`, and `email` from an end user.

Table 8.3 XSASecurityContext Functions

Function	Description
checkScope(String scopeName)	This function checks a scope that is published by an application. The scopeName must be prefixed by the application's name.
checkLocalScope(String scopeName)	This function checks a scope that is published by the current application in the *xs-security.json* file. The scopeName must not be prefixed.
listAttributes()	This function returns a list of attributes passed during the authentication.
hasAttributes	This function returns true if the token contains any SAP HANA XS Advanced user attributes. Otherwise, this function returns false.
getAttribute (String name)	This function returns the value of the specified attribute, which is contained in the access token.

Table 8.3 XSASecurityContext Functions (Cont.)

In our Node.js implementation, we'll have to use the standard Express module to work with the SAP HANA XS Advanced container security API. Express is an open-source module of Node.js. The Express module form Node.js helps to configure the handling of HTTP request and response objects.

In the new Node.js module of our SAP HANA XS Advanced application, the first step is to declare the Express module via require ('express'). We can instantiate a router object from the Express module via the method express.Router(). This object helps us to handle HTTP request objects and response objects. To validate whether an end user has a specific scope assigned, we can leverage the method req.authInfo.checkLocalScope. This method takes the name of a scope as an input parameter and returns true if the end user has this scope. Otherwise, this method returns false.

For example, in the ChickenWings application, we can use this method to verify whether an end user has the scope ReadCrew assigned by calling req.authInfo.checkLocalScope('ReadCrew'). Listing 8.8 highlights the source code of a Node.js example that validates if the HTTP request authentication information object contains the ReadCrew scope via the container security API of SAP HANA XS Advanced.

```
var express = require ('express');
var router = express.Router();
var chickenWingsManager = require ('./chickenWingsManager');
```

```
router.get('/rest/chickenwings/', function (req,res){
    chickenWingsManager(req.db, function(error, result){
        if(!req.authInfo.checkLocalScope('ReadCrew')){
            res.writeHead(403,{'Content-Type': 'application/json'});
            console.error("User is not authorized");
            res.end('{}');
        }else{
            res.writeHead(200,{'Content-Type': 'application/json'});
            res.end(JSON.stringify({crew: result}));
        }
    });
});
module.exports = router;
```

Listing 8.8 Authorization Check Example with the checkLocalScope Method in Node.js

Finally, we have to add the Express module as a dependency to our Node.js application to ensure that we can use this module in our application. We have to add a new dependency to the `dependencies` section of the *package.json* configuration file of our Node.js application. The *package.json* file is located directly under the root folder of the Node.js module. Add a new dependency "`express`" : "`~4.15`" to the *package.json* file. Build and run the Node.js module after performing this configuration change so that the new authentication and authorization checks become active. Figure 8.13 highlights the configuration in the *package.json* file.

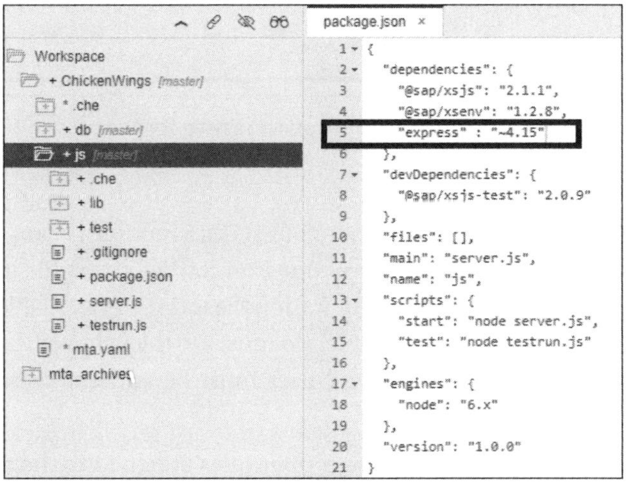

Figure 8.13 Adding the Express Module as a Dependency in the package.json Configuration File

8.3.4 Enabling Security for SAPUI5 Modules

In SAP HANA XS Advanced, it's, of course, possible that an HTML5 module can consume services from a Node.js or Java module. We've already activated authentication and authorization checks for our Node.js and Java modules in previous sections. In this section, we'll demonstrate how to enable the security mechanisms of SAP HANA XS Advanced for an HTML5 module.

Before we can use the SAP HANA XS Advanced UAA service, we have to bind the `authorizationtest-uaa` service, which we created at the beginning of this chapter, to our HTML5 module in the *mta.yaml* configuration file. Open the *mta.yaml* configuration file of our ChickenWings application in SAP Web IDE for SAP HANA, and select the **HTML5** module. Navigate to the required section, and add a new **Requires** entry for the **authorizationtest-uaa** service. Save the changes. This configuration ensures that our HTML5 module can now leverage the SAP HANA XS Advanced UAA service. Figure 8.14 highlights the setting in SAP Web IDE for SAP HANA.

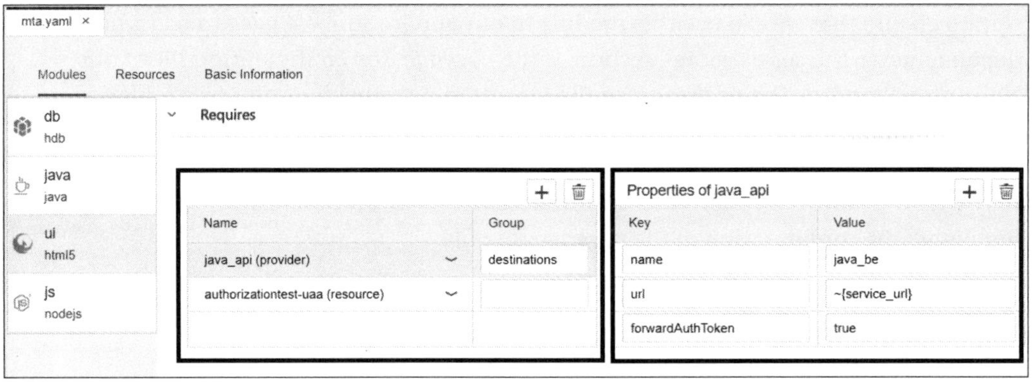

Figure 8.14 Configure the mta.yaml File to Add the Authorization Service for the HTML5 Module

Next, we must enable the authentication mechanism for our HTML5 module because so far, we've set up none. To configure this, open the *xs-app.json* configuration file in the SAP Web IDE for SAP HANA. The *xs-app.json* configuration file is directly available under the root folder of the HTML5 module. In this file, we must set the value of the `authenticationMethod` to `route` to ensure that the end user must be authenticated when accessing the HTML5 application.

Furthermore, we want to ensure that end users have proper roles assigned to them to access the application. This behavior can be achieved by configuring routes in the *xs-app.json* configuration file. The application router of SAP HANA XS Advanced is responsible for checking whether the caller is authorized to call the OData service and for blocking all requests that are involving the OData service in cases the caller isn't permitted. Thus, the application router validates whether the end user has the corresponding scope assigned. The check is performed on the application router level. The application router of SAP HANA XS Advanced will ensure that the SAP HANA XS Advanced UAA service validates the roles of an end user when accessing our application and only grants access when the defined roles are assigned to the end user.

We configure the `/java/odata/v4` entry of our routes configuration by setting the `authenticationType` attribute to the value xsuaa, and we add a new attribute `scope` with the value `$XSAPPNAME.ReadCrew`. This setting ensures that an end user must be authenticated when fetching data from our Java OData service. The end user must also have the `ReadCrew` role to be authorized to access the Java OData service. Additionally, we want to ensure that end users have the `ReadCrew` role when accessing any content of the HTML5 module. Therefore, we also change the existing source entry `"^/(.*.)$"` by adding a scope attribute with the value `$XSAPPNAME.ReadCrew`. By adding this configuration, we ensure that end users must have the `ReadCrew` role to access any content of the HTML5 module via HTTP. Figure 8.15 highlights the configuration in the *xs-app.json* configuration file.

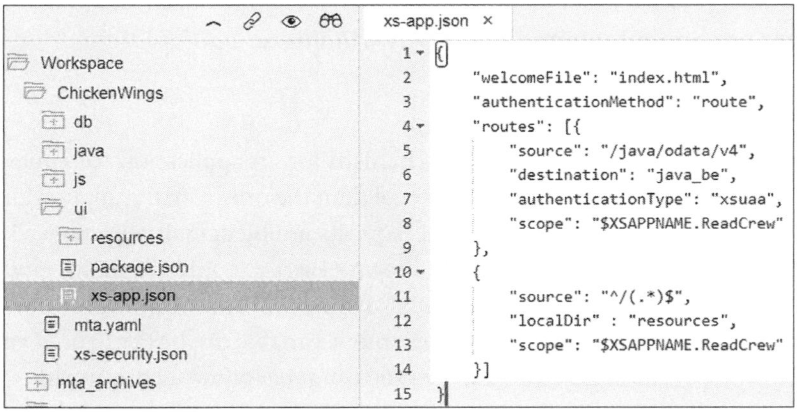

Figure 8.15 Configuring the xs-app.json File of the HTML5 Module for Authentication Checks and Authorization Checks

Build and run the HTML5 module after adding the configuration in the *xs-app.json* and *mta.yaml* configuration files. As in Section 8.3.2, end users will now get a **Forbidden** error message when trying to access the HTML5 application. We'll have to add the

ReadCrew role to our end user. We discuss the options to assign roles to end users in SAP HANA XS Advanced in Section 8.4.

8.3.5 Secure Your Application against Web-Based Attacks

In the previous sections, we explained how to secure an application by enabling the authentication and authorization functionalities of SAP HANA XS Advanced. In this section, we'll discuss some best practices to secure your application against web-based attacks with the mechanisms of SAP HANA XS Advanced.

We'll discuss the following options to enable additional security mechanisms for SAP HANA XS Advanced applications:

- Enable cross-origin resource sharing.
- Protect against cross-site request forgery.
- Protect against click-jacking attempts.
- Protect against cross-site scripting.
- Configure timeouts for application user sessions.
- Perform additional options to secure Node.js applications in SAP HANA XS Advanced.
- Perform additional options to secure Java application in SAP HANA XS Advanced.
- Leverage data privacy and anonymity in SAP HANA Views.

Enabling Cross-Origin Resource Sharing

Cross-Origin Resource Sharing (CORS) is a mechanism for an application to request resources from a different domain, port, or protocol than the one from the application where the request originated from. Such CORS requests are by default automatically refused by the security policy of web browsers. The SAP HANA XS Advanced CORS environment variable enables a developer to provide support for cross-origin requests of SAP HANA XS Advanced applications. The environment variable can be configured via the XSA CLI. A developer can set the variable by executing the following command:

```
xs set-env <AppName> CORS {<CORS_Configuration>}
```

The following command highlights an example configuration of the CORS environment variable for the ChickenWings application and the allowed origin www.test.com:

```
xs set-env ChickenWings CORS '{"uriPattern": "^\route1$", "allowedOrigin":
[ { "host": "www.test.com", "protocol": "https", "port": 443 } ]}'
```

Protect Against Cross-Site Request Forgery

Cross-site request forgery (CSRF) attacks are exploits of a web application where unauthorized commands are executed by a user that the web application trusts. A developer configures CSRF protection in the application router configuration via the csrfProtection attribute and defines which routes need protection against CSRF attacks. Listing 8.9 highlights a CSRF configuration.

```
{
[...]
  "routes": [
      {
        "source": "^/test/app/1(.*)$",
        "target": "$1",
        "destination": "app",
        "csrfProtection": true
      },
[...]
}
```

Listing 8.9 CSRF Configuration in the Application Router

Protect Against Click-Jacking Attacks

In a click-jacking attack, an attempt is made to trick the end user of a web application into clicking on something different from what an end user perceives to click on. This attack tries to reveal confidential information from an end user by tricking them into clicking on a seemingly harmless web application. A developer can avoid this type of attack by enabling a whitelistService in the application router configuration. The whitelistService allows opening endpoints that accept HTTP GET requests. Listing 8.10 highlights the whitelistService configuration in the application router configuration.

```
{
[...]
  "whitelistService": {
    "endpoint": "/whitelist/service"
  }
[...]
}
```

Listing 8.10 whitelistService Configuration in the Application Router

Protect Against Cross-Site Scripting

In cross-site scripting (XSS) exploits, the attacker tries to inject client-side scripts into web pages that are accessed by end users. For example, an attacker might try to overcome access control configurations of a web application. The Node.js package `@sap/xss-secure` from SAP can be used to encode Cascading Style Sheets (CSS), HTML, JavaScript, URLs, or XML code to prevent XSS attacks. The following highlights how to include `@sap/xss-secure` into a Node.js application:

```
var xsssecure = require('@sap/xss-secure');
```

Configure Timeouts for Application User Sessions

A developer can configure an automatic log-out of an end user's session from the SAP HANA XS Advanced `xsuaa` service by configuring the `SESSION_TIMEOUT` environment variable per SAP HANA XS Advanced application. Note that if the `authenticationType` parameter of the application router has the value `xsuaa`, the session timeout value configured by the `xsuaa` service will be considered. A developer can avoid unexpected timeouts of end user sessions by aligning the session timeout values of the `xsuaa` service and SAP HANA XS Advanced applications. The following highlights an option to set the end user session timeout to 20 minutes for the ChickenWings application:

```
xs set-env ChickenWings SESSION_TIMEOUT 20
```

Additional Options to Secure Node.js Applications in SAP HANA XS Advanced

SAP provides a set of standard Node.js packages that enable developers to implement additional security mechanisms for SAP HANA XS Advanced applications. A developer can download the Node.js packages from the SAP node package manager (npm) registry `npm.sap.com`. Additionally, customers who have the appropriate access authorization to the SAP Service Marketplace can also download the Node.js packages from the SAP Service Marketplace. Table 8.4 lists the Node.js packages that offer useful features to secure SAP HANA XS Advanced applications.

Node.js Package Name	Description
`@sap/audit-logging`	This Node.js package enables a developer to leverage the audit-log service of SAP HANA XS Advanced. We'll explain the functionalities of the audit log service in more detail in Chapter 9.

Table 8.4 Node.js Packages with Useful Security Functionalities

Node.js Package Name	Description
@sap/hdbext	This package offers a JavaScript client for Node.js that allows a developer to use the SAP HANA Database SQL Command Network Protocol.
@sap/xsenv	This Node.js package allows a developer to set up environment variables and services for SAP HANA XS Advanced.
@sap/xssec	This Node.js package implements a security API for Node.js modules of SAP HANA XS Advanced.
@sap/xss-secure	This Node.js package provides developers with functionalities to protect the application against XSS attacks.

Table 8.4 Node.js Packages with Useful Security Functionalities (Cont.)

Additional Options to Secure Java Applications in SAP HANA XS Advanced

SAP provides a set of standard Java libraries that enables developers to implement additional security mechanisms for SAP HANA XS Advanced applications. Developers who have the appropriate access authorization to the SAP Service Marketplace can download the Java libraries there. Table 8.5 lists the Java libraries that offer useful features to secure SAP HANA XS Advanced applications.

Java Library	Description
xs-env	This library allows a developer to set up and access environment variables and services of the SAP HANA XS Advanced environment.
audit-java-client-api	This library enables a developer to use the SAP HANA XS Advanced audit log service. We describe the usage of the audit log service in Java applications in more detail in Chapter 9.
java-container-security	This Java library offers access to the security context of an authentication object in SAP HANA XS Advanced.

Table 8.5 Java Libraries with Useful Security Functionalities

Leverage Data Privacy and Anonymity in SAP HANA Views

A developer can anonymize the result sets in view nodes of SAP HANA calculation views. This feature helps a developer to implement anonymity of private data. The graphical modeler of the SAP Web IDE for SAP HANA offers an `anonymize` view node.

A developer can specify an anonymization method in this view node and define a level of privacy for the data set. A developer must configure the anonymize view node as a leaf node in an SAP HANA calculation view.

8.4 Maintaining Users and Roles in SAP HANA XS Advanced

In this section, we'll explain how to create roles in SAP HANA XS Advanced and assign them to end users to enable functional and instance-based authorization checks for our ChickenWings application.

First, we'll demonstrate how to create a new role and assign this role to a new user in SAP HANA XS Advanced with the administration tools. Then, we'll enable functional and instance-based authorization checks for our ChickenWings application to make sure that only end users with the specified roles have access to our application.

8.4.1 Create Roles in SAP HANA XS Advanced

We created an SAP HANA XS UAA service in Section 8.3.1. We used the *xs-security.json* configuration file to define role templates, scopes, and attributes. Now, we'll build roles on top of this role template, which we can later assign to end users. We'll use the **Role** functionality from the **SAP HANA XS Advanced Cockpit** screen to create new roles (Figure 8.16). First, log in to the SAP HANA XS Advanced cockpit web application, and click on the **Role Collections** tool.

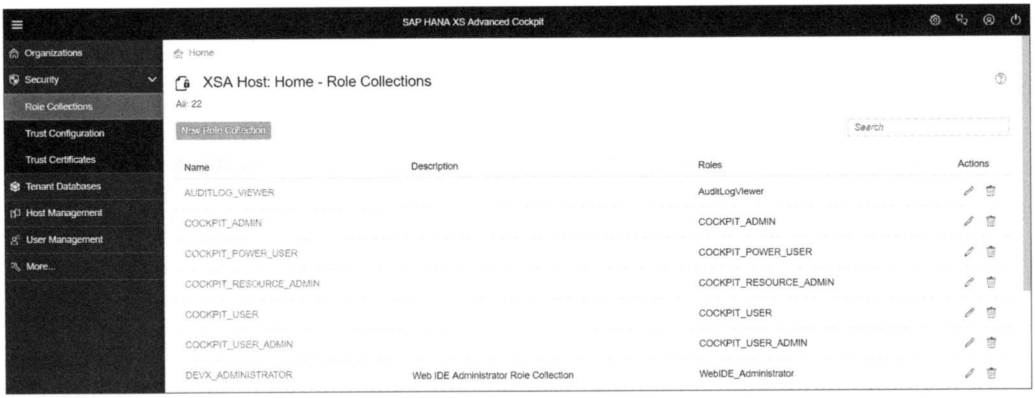

Figure 8.16 Application Role Builder Application in the SAP HANA XS Advanced Administration Application

In SAP HANA XS Advanced, you must distinguish between a role and a role collection. A role is a set of roles, scopes, and attributes that have been configured for an SAP HANA XS Advanced application. In our case, we configured the `role-templates`, `scopes`, and `attributes` in the *xs-security.json* configuration file. In a role collection, we specify the `role-templates` and `roles` that were defined for an SAP HANA XS Advanced application. A role collection will be assigned to an end user in SAP HANA XS Advanced to grant privileges for applications.

You can view the available roles of an application by navigating to an SAP HANA XS Advanced application in the SAP HANA XS Advanced cockpit and selecting the **Role** menu item. Figure 8.17 highlights the application roles of our ChickenWings application.

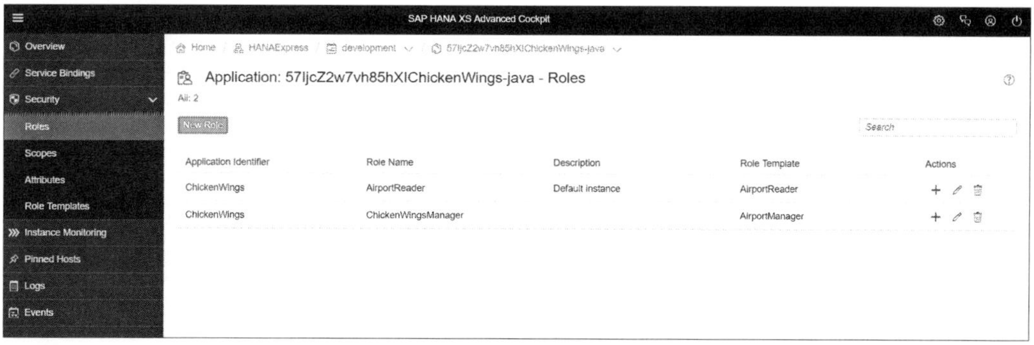

Figure 8.17 Application Roles for the ChickenWings Application

By clicking on the **Scopes** menu item, you can see the scopes that were defined in the *xs-security.json* configuration file. In our case, we set a `ReadCrew` and `ManageCrew` scope for the ChickenWings application. Figure 8.18 displays the available scopes in the SAP HANA XS Advanced application.

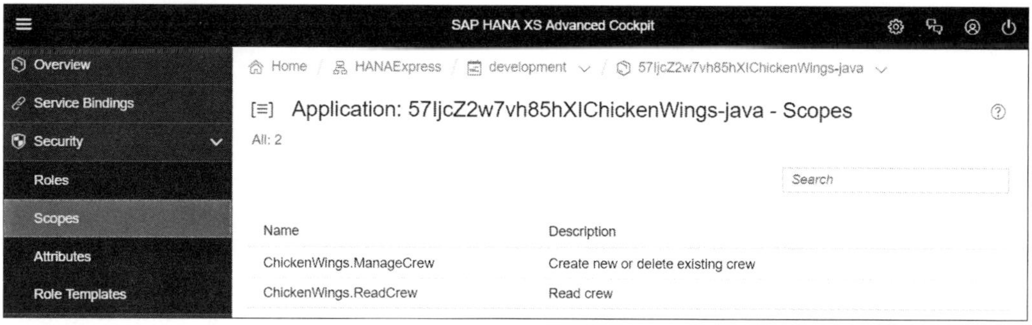

Figure 8.18 Scopes of the ChickenWings Application

Furthermore, we want to restrict the data on a specific attribute of our data set. For the ChickenWings application, we want to give the `ManageCrew` role only the option to view crew members from the United States. Therefore, we had to configure an `attribute` in the *xs-security.json* configuration file. We apply the `attribute` restriction on the `country` field. Click on the **Attributes** menu item to view the `attribute` restrictions that were defined in the *xs-security.json* configuration file. Figure 8.19 displays the attribute restrictions in the **SAP HANA XS Advanced Cockpit** screen.

Figure 8.19 Attributes for the ChickenWings Application

Finally, we specified two `role-templates` in the *xs-security.json* configuration file. A `role-template` combines scopes and attributes. We defined the `AirportReader` and `AirportManager` role templates. This configuration can also be viewed in the SAP HANA XS Advanced cockpit tool by clicking on the **Role Templates** menu item. Figure 8.20 displays the role templates of our ChickenWings application.

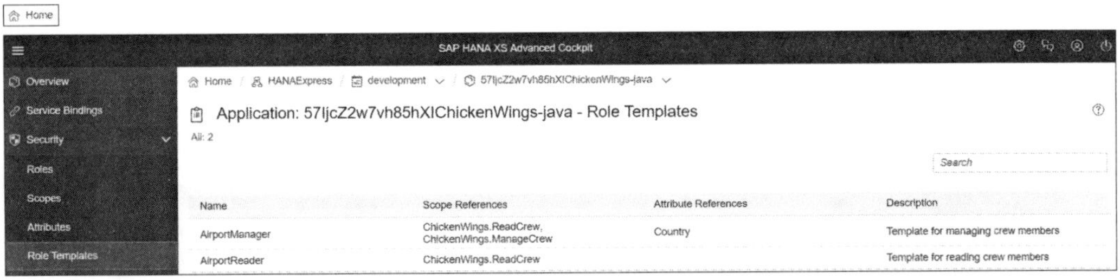

Figure 8.20 Role Templates for the ChickenWings Application in the Application Builder Application

Select the **Roles** menu item again and click on the **edit icon** (pencil) next to the **ChickenWingsManager** role. This functionality will allow us to configure the attribute restriction for this role. We'll select **Static** as the Source for the attribute restriction and assign the value **US**. This configuration means that the `AirportManager` role will only have access to crew members with the country attribute value `US`. Note that it's also possible to specify **SAML** as the **source** of the attribute restriction. This setting allows us to retrieve the attribute value from the end user's SAML token. Click on the **Save** button to confirm and activate your configuration changes.

It's also possible to create new roles to specify different attribute restrictions, for example, a `ChickenWingsManager` for the United States with a `country` attribute restriction of `US`. A new role can be formed by selecting the **New role** button in the menu bar. Figure 8.21 highlights the configuration of an attribute value restriction for the **ChickenWingsManager** role.

8

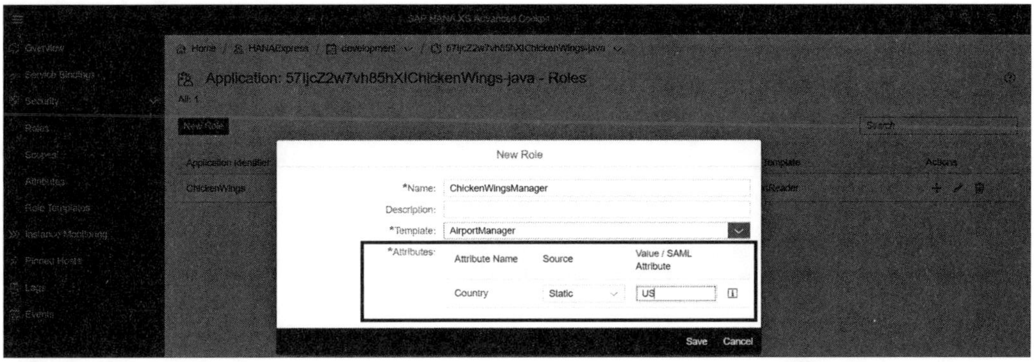

Figure 8.21 Instance-Based Authorization Checks for the ChickenWings Application

Before we can assign a role to an end user in SAP HANA XS Advanced, we must create a role collection. The application roles we've just defined are the basis of the new role collection of our ChickenWings application. As mentioned previously, a role collection combines one or multiple roles of SAP HANA XS Advanced applications and is then assigned to an end user in SAP HANA XS Advanced to grant the user access to a specific application. To build a new role collection, select the **Role Collections** menu item on the **Home** screen of the SAP HANA XS Advanced cockpit (refer to Figure 8.16). All role collections that are currently available in the system will be displayed.

We'll now create a new role collection for our ChickenWings application. Click on the **New Role Collection** button to create a new role collection. In the dialog that appears, specify the name of the new role collection; in this case, enter "ChickenWingsManager" (Figure 8.22). Click on the **Save** button to confirm the creation of a new role collection.

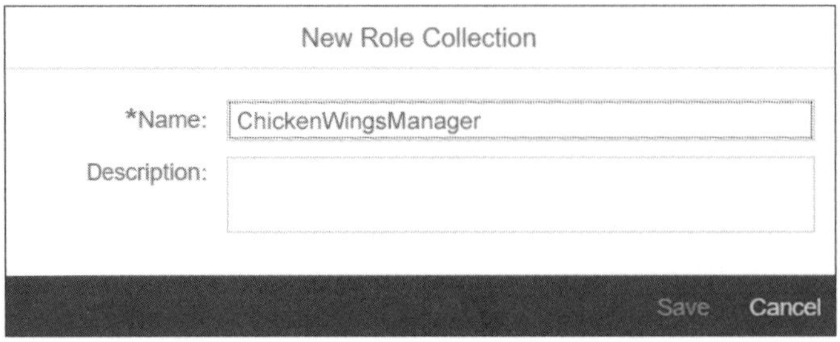

Figure 8.22 Creating a New Role Collection

We can now see that the new role collection `ChickenWingsManager` was created. Next, we must assign an application role to this role collection, as shown in Figure 8.23. Therefore, we'll use one of the application roles that we just created in the previous configuration steps.

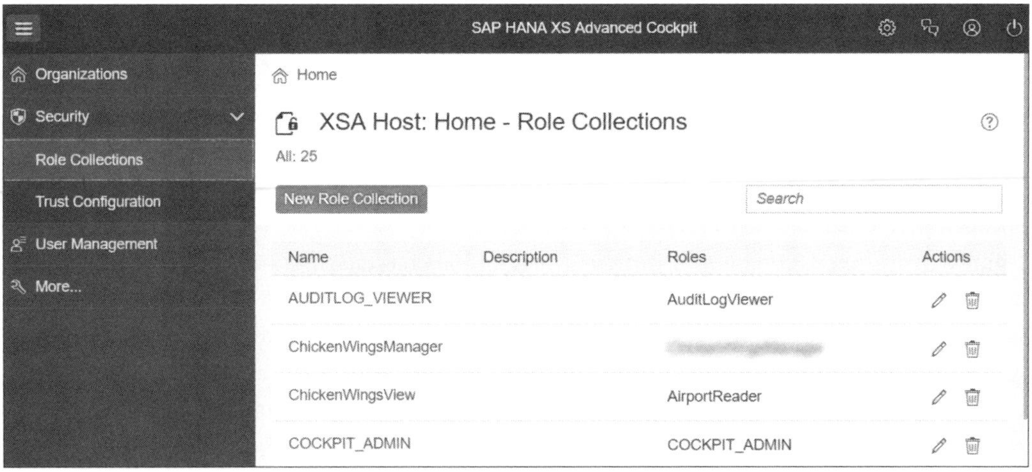

Figure 8.23 New ChickenWingsManager Role Collection

Click on the **ChickenWingsManager** entry in the **Role Collection** list to navigate to the details section of the `ChickenWingsManager` role collection. Click on the **Add Role** button to add a new application role. We'll add privileges based on the `AirportManager` role which we created earlier. Select `ChickenWings` as the **Application Identifier**, AirportManager as the **Role Template,** and `ChickenWingsManager` as the **Role** (Figure 8.24). Confirm this configuration by clicking on the **Save** button.

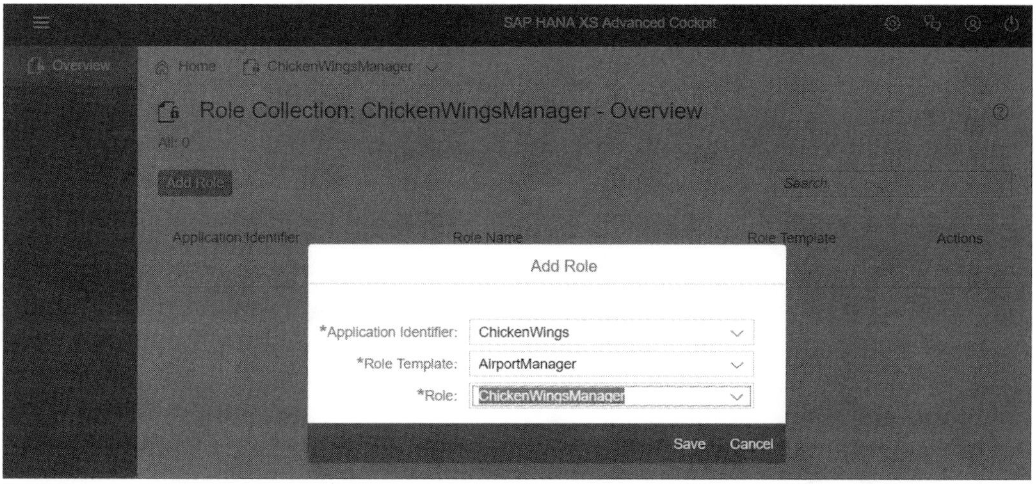

Figure 8.24 Adding a New Application Role to the ChickenWingsManager Role Collection

We've now added a role with the name `ChickenWingsManager` to the role collection `ChickenWingsManager`. This role collection will give an end user read and write privileges to the ChickenWings application. Next, we must assign this role collection to an end user. We'll reveal the required configuration steps in the next section. Figure 8.25 displays the assigned roles to the `ChickenWingsManager` role collection in the SAP HANA XS Advanced Administration application.

Figure 8.25 Updated ChickenWingsManager Role Collection

8.4.2 Create an Application User with the Administration Tools

In this section, we'll demonstrate how to create a new end user in the SAP HANA XS Advanced cockpit. In the next section, we'll then highlight how to assign a role collection to this end user.

First, log on to the SAP HANA XS Advanced cockpit web application, and select the **User Management** menu item. This function displays the list of users and their assigned role collection in the SAP HANA XS Advanced environment. The assigned role collections for this user are shown in the **Role Collections** column (Figure 8.26). The properties of a user can be changed by clicking on the **Edit** icon. The password of a user can be changed by selecting the **Change Password** icon. Furthermore, it's possible to delete an end user by selecting the **Delete** icon from the list.

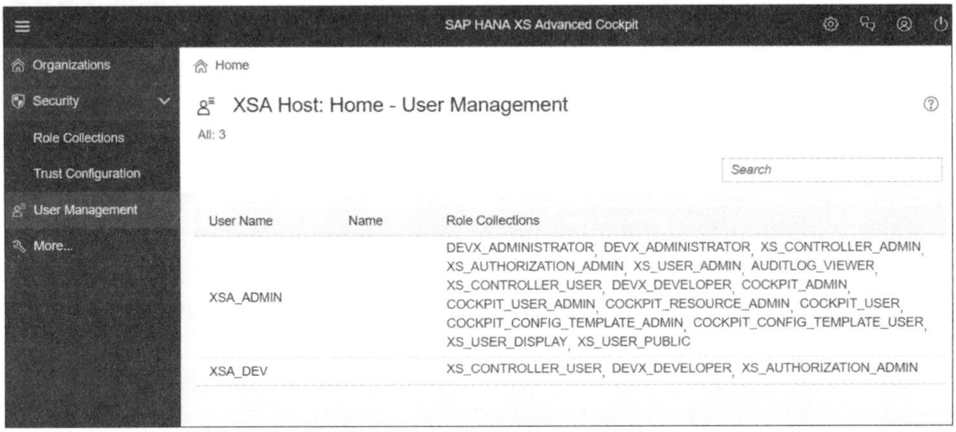

Figure 8.26 User Management Application in SAP HANA XS Advanced Cockpit

Create a new user by clicking on the **New User** button in the User Management tool.

> **Migrate SAP HANA User**
>
> The **Migrate SAP HANA User** functionality of the User Management tool enables an administrator to migrate an existing classic SAP HANA database user to an SAP HANA XS Advanced user.

Specify the **User Name**, **First Name**, **Last Name**, **E-Mail**, and **Password** of the new user and click **Create** to create the new user (Figure 8.27).

Although we've created a new user, the user won't be able to access our ChickenWings application just yet. We still must assign a role collection of the ChickenWings application to the end user. We demonstrate the steps to assign a role collection to an end user in the next section. Now, an end user will get a **Forbidden** error message when trying to access our ChickenWings application without having the proper role collection assigned, as shown in Figure 8.28.

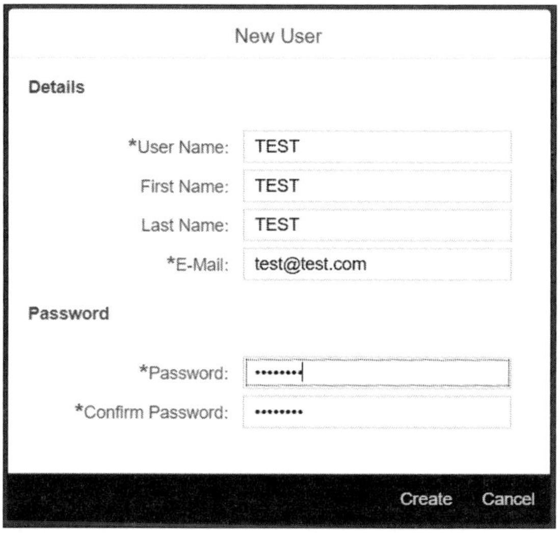

Figure 8.27 New User Dialog in the SAP HANA XS Advanced Cockpit Application

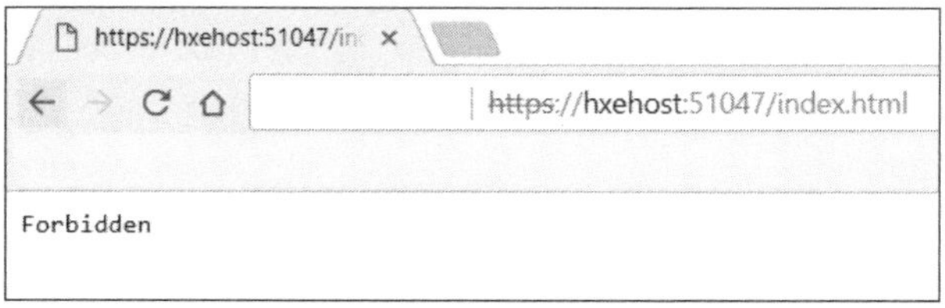

Figure 8.28 Forbidden Error When an End User without the AirportReader Roles Tries to Access the HTML5 Application

8.4.3 Configuring Functional Authorization Checks

We demonstrated how to create a new user in the SAP HANA XS Advanced cockpit tool in the previous section. In this section, we'll reveal how to assign a role collection to an end user so that this user gets access to our ChickenWings application by using the User Management tool.

Click **User Management**, select the user to assign a role collection to, and click on the **Assign Role Collections** icon in the row where the user name is displayed (Figure 8.29). We'll assign a new role collection to the **TEST_USER**, which we created in the previous section.

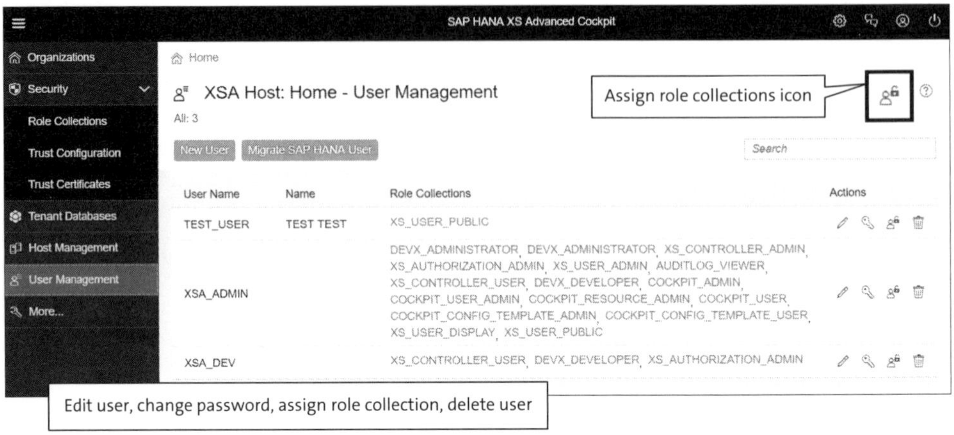

Figure 8.29 Assigning SAP HANA XS Advanced Role Collections to a User

A new dialog window pops up and displays all role collections that are currently assigned to the user. Figure 8.30 shows the assigned role collection of the **TEST_USER**. Because we just created the user, only the **XS_USER_PUBLIC** role collection is currently assigned.

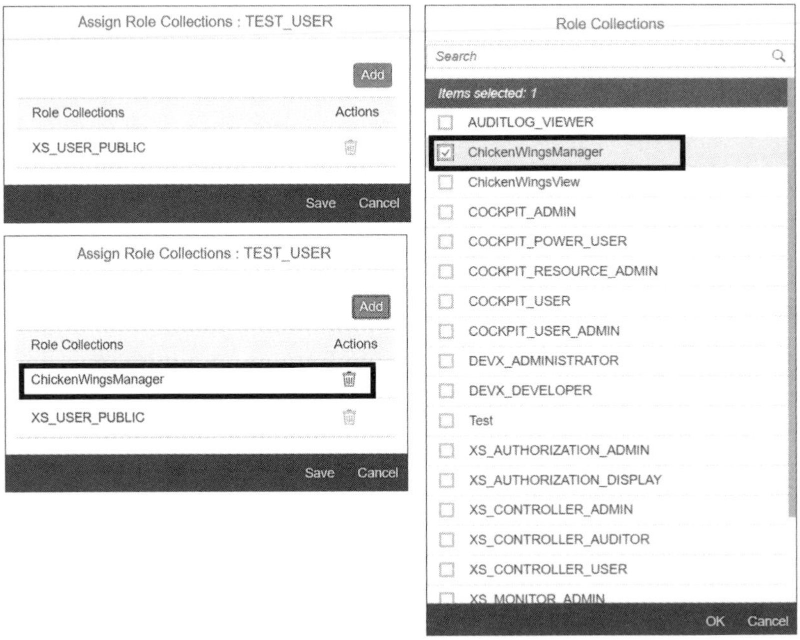

Figure 8.30 Assign Role Collections

To assign a new role collection, click on the **Add** button in the **Assign Role Collections** dialog. A new window pops up that displays all available role collections on the SAP HANA XS Advanced system, including a **ChickenWingsView** and a **ChickenWingsManger** role collection. Select the **ChickenWingsManager** role collection to assign this role collection to our new **TEST_USER** end user (Figure 8.30). Confirm the selection by clicking on the **OK** button.

In the **Assign Role Collections** screen, we can now see that the **ChickenWingsManager** role collection has been added to the end user. This screen also allows you to remove a role collection again from an end user by clicking on the **Delete** icon 🗑 in the row of the role collection. Confirm the assignment of the new role collection by clicking on the **Save** button (Figure 8.30).

8

The new role collection **ChickenWingsManager** is now also visible for the user **TEST_USER** when displaying the list of end users in the **User Management** tool, as shown in Figure 8.31.

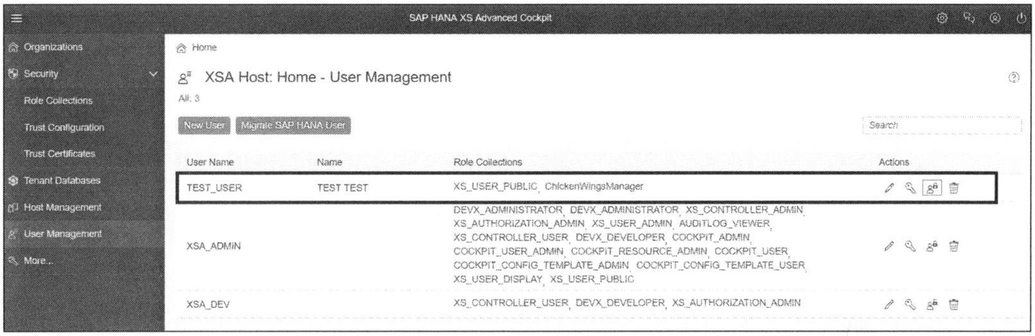

Figure 8.31 Displaying the TEST_USER and Assigned Role Collections in the User Management Tool

Our end user now has all the required roles to access the ChickenWings application. For example, when the end user opens the HTML5 application, the list of crew members will now be displayed. With this configuration, we ensured that users must authenticate when accessing our HTML5 app, as well as that the users require proper roles of the ChickenWings application to be authorized to access the application and retrieve data. Figure 8.32 displays the HTML5 app when a user with the `ChickenWingsView` role accesses the application.

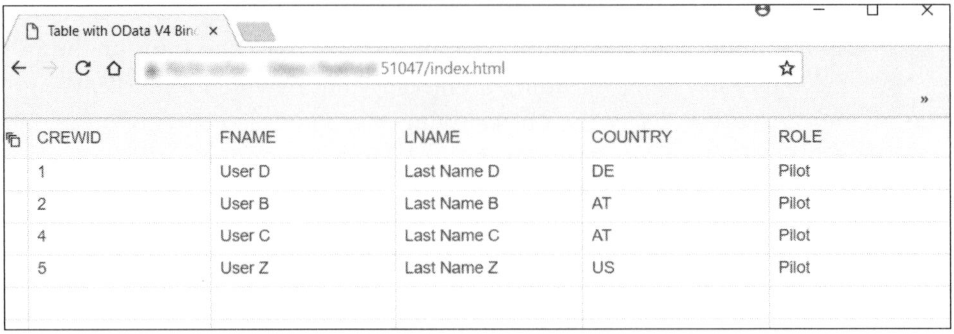

CREWID	FNAME	LNAME	COUNTRY	ROLE
1	User D	Last Name D	DE	Pilot
2	User B	Last Name B	AT	Pilot
4	User C	Last Name C	AT	Pilot
5	User Z	Last Name Z	US	Pilot

Figure 8.32 End User Accessing the HTML5 Application

Remember, in the *xs-security.json* configuration file of our ChickenWings application, we defined the `AirportReader` and `AirportManager` `role-templates`. The `role-templates` reference the `ReadCrew` scope. The `AirportManager` `role-template` also references the `ManageCrew` scope. We already saw the *xs-security.json* configuration file of our ChickenWings application with the `role-templates` configuration in Figure 8.8.

In the *xs-app.json* configuration file of the HTML5 module, we specified that an end user requires the `ReadCrew` scope to access any resources of the HTML5 application, as well as when the end user retrieves data from our Java backend service, which is available at the `/java/odata/v4` source. Figure 8.33 highlights the relevant configuration in the *xs-app.json* configuration file.

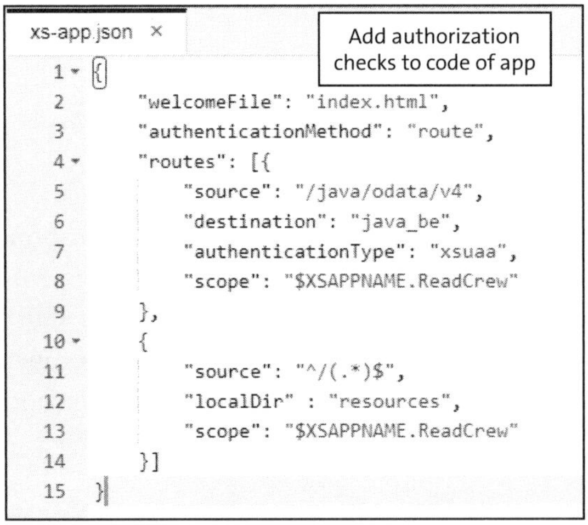


```
{
    "welcomeFile": "index.html",
    "authenticationMethod": "route",
    "routes": [{
        "source": "/java/odata/v4",
        "destination": "java_be",
        "authenticationType": "xsuaa",
        "scope": "$XSAPPNAME.ReadCrew"
    },
    {
        "source": "^/(.*)$",
        "localDir" : "resources",
        "scope": "$XSAPPNAME.ReadCrew"
    }]
}
```

Figure 8.33 Definition of the Required Scopes in the xs-app.json Configuration File

8.4.4 Configuring Instance-Based Authorization Checks

In the previous sections, we've demonstrated how to create roles and new users in SAP HANA XS Advanced. Furthermore, we highlighted how to implement functional authorization checks by assigning role collections to end users, and we discussed the required configuration steps in our SAP HANA XS Advanced application to perform the authorization checks based on roles. In this section, we'll demonstrate how to implement instance-based authorization checks. Configuring instance-based authorization checks means that we want to restrict the data that an end user can see. In our example, we want to limit end users with the `ChickenWingsManager` role collection, to view only crew member information about crew members with the country attribute US. In SAP HANA XS Advanced, instance-based authorization checks are configured via DCL. Required attributes for the instance-based authorization check are extracted from the JWT, which is passed to the SAP HANA XS Advanced runtime.

8

Data Access Control Using SQL Analytic Privileges

SQL analytic privileges are an alternative to manage data security based on a user's attributes and display relevant business data based on a user's role. Typically, SQL analytic privileges are used when working with modeled calculation views in SAP HANA, whereas DCL is an extension of CDS. We discuss the concept of SQL analytic privileges in Chapter 5, Section 5.9.6 , in the context of the data modeling capabilities of SAP HANA XS Advanced.

In the *xs-security.json* configuration file of our ChickenWings application (refer to Figure 8.8), we've already prepared the configuration for an instance-based authentication. We added an attribute with the name `Country` to the `attributes` section in the *xs-security.json* configuration file. Furthermore, we specified this attribute as an `attribute-reference` in the `AirportMangcr rolc-template`. These settings form the basis for the instance-based authorization checks.

Next, we used the SAP HANA XS Advanced cockpit web application to configure the `ChickenWingsManger` role in the previous section. In this role, we specified the attribute restriction on the attribute `Country` with the attribute value `US` (refer to Figure 8.21). This configuration means that we want end users with the `AirportManager` role to only be able to view crew members where the country attribute has the value `US`.

Next, we leverage the DCL to configure instance-based authorizations. First, we'll extend our CDS definition `CrewJavaExample.hdbcds` with the definition of a CDS view. We'll then activate the instance-based authorizations by adding the key words `with structured privilege check` to our new CDS view. Note that it's mandatory to add the keyword `with structured privilege check` to the CDS source to activate the instance-based checks. If the instance-based authorization check is active, and the user doesn't have the privilege to access the object instance, an empty result set is returned. Listing 8.11 highlights the configuration of the CDS views `CrewMemberView` in the *CrewJavaExample.hdbcds* file.

```
view CrewMemberView as select from Crew{
CREWID,
FNAME,
LNAME,
MOBILE,
EMAIL,
COUNTRY,
ROLE} with structured privilege check;
```

Listing 8.11 Extending the CrewJavaExample CDS Definition with the CDS View CrewMemberView, Including Structured Privilege Checks

Next, we define a DCL role. In this DCL role, we define the restriction that should be applied on the SAP HANA database level. First, we have to create a new file in our SAP HANA database module `db` with the name *dcl_role.hdbdd*. In this file, we define the conditions and how to dynamically bind the runtime check to the security attributes that are defined in the *xs-security.json* configuration file. The attribute values are propagated to the variable `$env.user.`<attribute name>.

In our case, we defined the attribute name `country`. Thus, we'll have to use the variable `$env.user.country` to fetch the correct attribute value from the end user. Listing 8.12 shows the source code of the *dcl_role.hdbdd* configuration file. Build the SAP HANA database module after performing this configuration change to activate the instance-based authorization check.

```
using CrewJavaExample as ddl;
AccessPolicy dcl_role {
  role airportManagerUS {
```

```
    grant select on ddl.CrewMemberView
        where COUNTRY = $env.user.country;
  };
};
```

Listing 8.12 DCL Role dcl_role.hdbdd for Instance-Based Authorization Checks

Now, when an end user with the `ChickenWingsManager` role accesses the ChickenWings application, the `Crewmember` data will be filtered according to the attribute restriction. In our case, the `ChickenWingsManager` role will only be able to see data of crew members where the `Country` attribute has the value US. With this configuration, we've successfully implemented an instance-based authorization check for our ChickenWings application. Figure 8.34 displays our HTML5 application, which reads data from the new CDS view `CrewMemberView`. The data set is automatically filtered when a user with the `ChickenWingsManager` role accesses the application.

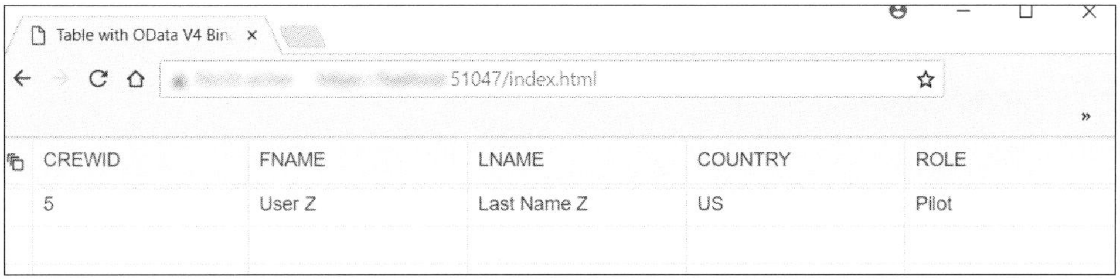

Table with OData V4 Bin
51047/index.html
CREWID
FNAME
LNAME
COUNTRY
ROLE
5
User Z
Last Name Z
US
Pilot

Figure 8.34 Data Restricted to the Defined Attribute Value When the End User Accesses the HTML5 Application

8.5 Assigning HDI Container Roles to Classic Database Users

A scenario that is quite common when developing SAP HANA XS Advanced applications is that SAP HANA database users require access to the database content of the HDI container of an SAP HANA XS Advanced Application. HDI containers are isolated, and access to those HDI containers must be explicitly granted. There are two ways in SAP HANA XS Advanced to grant this access to the HDI container:

- Via schema access
- Via roles

8.5.1 Granting HDI Container Access via Schema Access

With the schema access method, the SAP HANA database user gets access to a database schema level, which allows granting the database user access to tables, stored procedures, or views of the SAP HANA XS Advanced application. To perform this configuration, we first must log in to the SAP Web IDE for SAP HANA and open the SAP HANA database explorer application to connect to the HDI container of our ChickenWings application. Figure 8.35 displays the SAP HANA database explorer and the objects of our ChickenWings application.

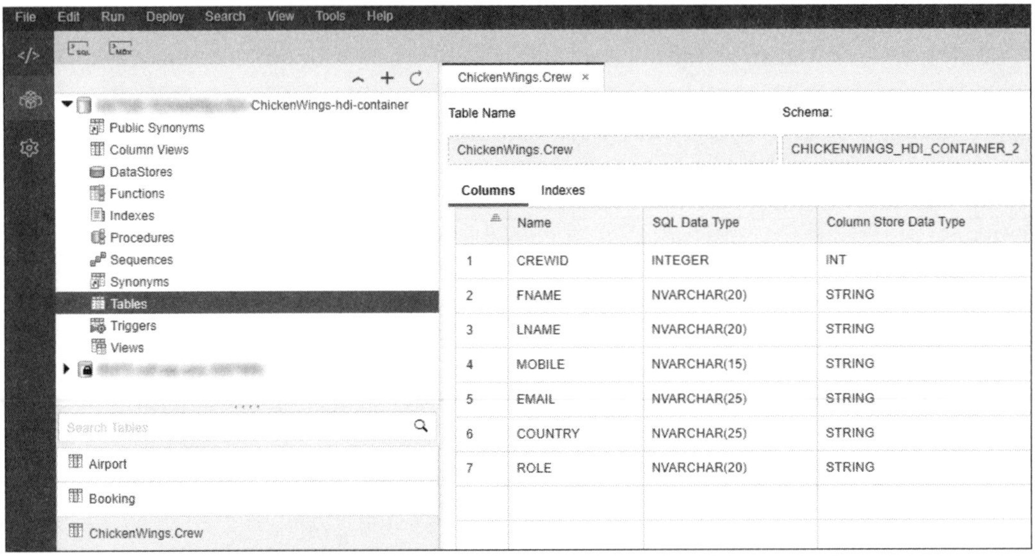

Figure 8.35 Opening the HDI Container in the SAP HANA Database Explorer

Next, we must open the SQL Console to grant the privileges to the classic SAP HANA database user. The SAP HANA database explorer offers a specific mode called SQL Console (Admin) of the SQL Console to perform this operation. Right-click on the name of the HDI container in the SAP HANA database explorer, and select the menu item **Open SQL Console (Admin)** to open a new SQL Console in the admin mode (Figure 8.36). The mode will allow us to grant privileges on the ChickenWings HDI container to classic SAP HANA database users.

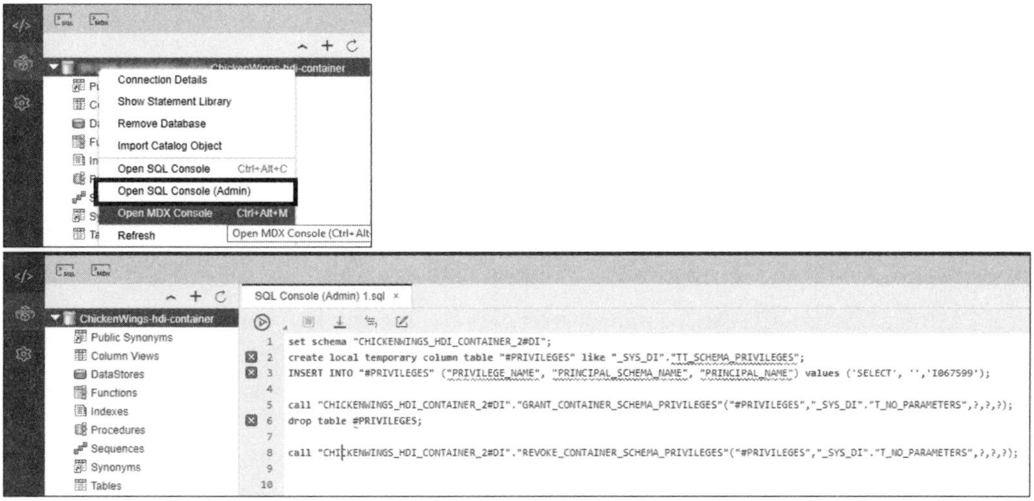

Figure 8.36 Opening the SQL Console in the Admin Mode and Running the GRANT_CONTAINER_SCHEMA_PRIVILEGES Procedure in the SQL Console

Next, we must run several SQL statements to grant privileges. It's possible to issue INSERT, DELETE, UPDATE, and SELECT privileges to tables within HDI containers. Furthermore, it's also possible to give SELECT privileges on views or EXECUTE privileges on stored procedures.

In our example, we'll grant SELECT privileges to the CLASSIC_DATABASE_USER_NAME user via the GRANT_CONTAINER_SCHEMA_PRIVILEGES stored procedure. The relevant SQL statements are highlighted in Listing 8.13.

```
set schema "CHICKENWINGS_HDI_CONTAINER_2#DI";
create local temporary column table "#PRIVILEGES" like "_SYS_DI"."TT_SCHEMA_
PRIVILEGES";
INSERT INTO "#PRIVILEGES" ("PRIVILEGE_NAME", "PRINCIPAL_SCHEMA_
NAME", "PRINCIPAL_NAME") values ('SELECT', '','CLASSIC_DATABASE_USER_NAME');
call "CHICKENWINGS_HDI_CONTAINER_2#DI"."GRANT_CONTAINER_SCHEMA_PRIVILEGES"
("#PRIVILEGES","_SYS_DI"."T_NO_PARAMETERS",?,?,?);
drop table #PRIVILEGES;
```

Listing 8.13 Granting HDI Container Access to a Classic Database User

Execute the SQL statements by clicking on the **Run** icon ⊚ in the menu bar of the SQL Console. Of course, it's also possible to revoke privileges to an HDI schema via the stored procedure REVOKE_CONTAINER_SCHEMA_PRIVILEGES. Following is an example execution of the REVOKE_CONTAINER_SCHEMA_PRIVILEGES stored procedure which will revoke access to a classic SAP HANA database user:

```
call "CHICKENWINGS_HDI_CONTAINER_2#DI"."REVOKE_CONTAINER_SCHEMA_PRIVILEGES"
("#PRIVILEGES","_SYS_DI"."T_NO_PARAMETERS",?,?,?);
```

Refer to Figure 8.36 to see the **SQL Console (Admin)** in the SAP HANA database explorer allowing us to grant or revoke access privileges to an HDI container of SAP HANA XS Advanced to a classic SAP HANA database user.

After a classic SAP HANA database user gets access to an HDI container, this database user can run SELECT statements, for example, on database objects of an HDI container. Figure 8.37 is an example scenario where a SELECT statement on an HDI container table is executed with a classic SAP HANA database user.

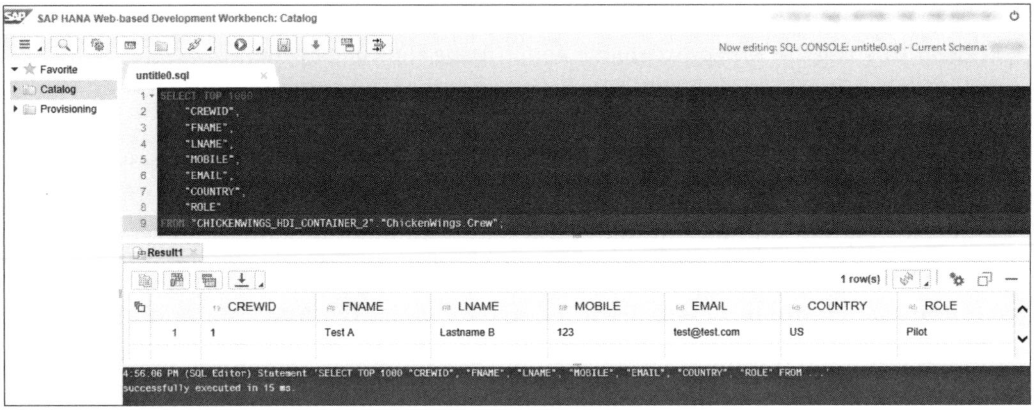

Figure 8.37 Classic Database User with Access to the HDI Container

8.5.2 Granting HDI Container Access via Roles

The roles method of issuing classic SAP HANA database users access to an HDI container of SAP HANA XS Advanced allows the access to an HDI container to be defined on a very granular level. For example, it's possible to grant access privileges only on specific database objects such as tables, views, or stored procedures, rather than to give a classic SAP HANA database user access to all objects within an HDI container. To perform this configuration, we first must log in to the SAP Web IDE for SAP HANA and create a role in our SAP HANA XS Advanced application. This role will then later be assigned to a classic SAP HANA database user. In this role, it's possible to grant schema privileges, object privileges, or analytic privileges. Listing 8.14 is an exemplary role definition with the name `ChickenWings.db::roles.testrole`, which grants `select object_privileges` on the `ChickenWings.Crew` table of our ChickenWings application.

```
{
"role": {
"name": "ChickenWings.db::roles.testrole",
"object_privileges": [
    {
        "name" : "ChickenWings.Crew",
        "type": "TABLE",
        "privileges": ["SELECT"]
    }
]
}
}
```

Listing 8.14 Role for the Classic Database User HDI Container Access

To activate this role, we create a new file called *roles.hdbrole* in our ChickenWings application under the folder **db • src • roles**. Build the db module of our SAP HANA XS Advanced application after you add the new role. Figure 8.38 highlights the *roles.hdbrole* definition in the ChickenWings application.

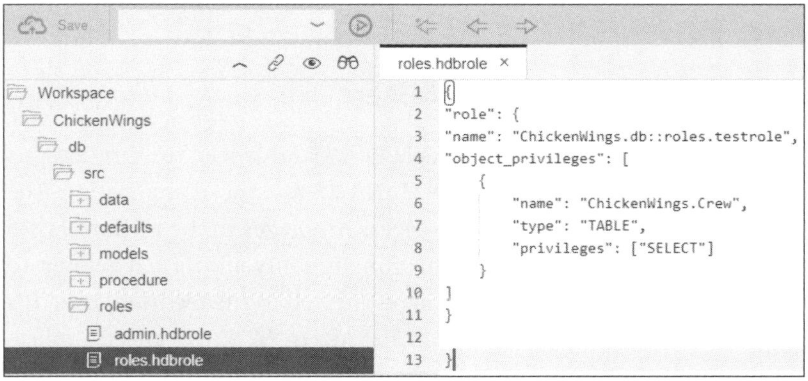

Figure 8.38 Definition of the roles.hdbrole Configuration in SAP Web IDE for SAP HANA

Open the SAP HANA database explorer application, and connect to the ChickenWings HDI container after the build of the database module of the ChickenWings application is successful. Select **Open SQL Console (Admin)** to open the SQL Console in admin mode, as shown previously in Figure 8.36.

Next, we have to run several SQL statements to grant the role ChickenWings.db::roles. testrole to the classic SAP HANA database user. We'll give the role via the GRANT_CONTAINER_SCHEMA_ROLES stored procedure to the classic SAP HANA database user CLASSIC_DATABASE_USER_NAME. The relevant SQL statements are highlighted in Listing 8.15.

```
set schema "CHICKENWINGS_HDI_CONTAINER_2#DI";
create local temporary column table "#ROLES" like "_SYS_DI"."TT_SCHEMA_ROLES";
INSERT INTO "#ROLES" ("ROLE_NAME", "PRINCIPAL_SCHEMA_NAME", "PRINCIPAL_NAME")
values ('ChickenWings.db::roles.testrole', '','CLASSIC_DATABASE_USER_NAME ');
call "CHICKENWINGS_HDI_CONTAINER_2#DI"."GRANT_CONTAINER_SCHEMA_ROLES"
("#ROLES","_SYS_DI"."T_NO_PARAMETERS",?,?,?);
drop table #ROLES;
```

Listing 8.15 Granting the Role ChickenWings.db::roles.testrole to the Classic SAP HANA Database User

Execute the SQL statements by clicking on the **Run** icon ⦿ in the menu bar of the SQL Console. Of course, it's also possible to revoke the role again from the database user via the REVOKE_CONTAINER_SCHEMA_ROLES stored procedure, as shown here:

```
call "CHICKENWINGS_HDI_CONTAINER_2#DI"."REVOKE_CONTAINER_SCHEMA_ROLES"("#
ROLES","_SYS_DI"."T_NO_PARAMETERS",?,?,?);
```

8.6 Default Access Role for HDI Containers

In SAP HANA XS Advanced applications, the SAP HANA XS Advanced runtime assigns roles to the technical database user of the SAP HANA XS Advanced application. The default_access_role is required to control the access privileges to the technical user of the SAP HANA XS Advanced application. This functionality allows a developer to define a role that represents what privileges will be granted to the technical user. It's possible to configure this default_access_role in an SAP HANA XS Advanced application for application access scenarios. Furthermore, the definition of roles enables the setup of specific access privileges for technical users from external applications that require access to the SAP HANA XS Advanced application.

The default role definition file has to be present in the file path location *src/defaults/* and has to have the name *default_access_role.hdbrole*. Furthermore, a developer must define a role with the name default_access_role in this file.

The SAP HANA XS Advanced runtime creates an HDI container that consists of a runtime database schema, an HDI metadata database schema, an API database schema, and an object owner database schema for every new instance of the HDI container service. Additionally, a global access role consisting of the HDI container name and the name `access_role` becomes available. The new access role contains an initial set of permissions on the newly created HDI runtime schema. The initial set of privileges on this database schema include the following access rights:

```
SELECT, INSERT, UPDATE, DELETE, EXECUTE, CREATE TEMPORARY TABLE, SELECT CDS
METADATA
```


Two new database users get created every time the HDI container service instance is bound to an application. The database users are specific to the binding of the application. One technical user is required to access the runtime schema of the HDI container and has the global access_role assigned. This user has the same name as the HDI runtime schema. The other user has privileges for the APIs of the HDI metadata schema and the API schema.

Figure 8.39 highlights the application users of an SAP HANA XS Advanced application that are automatically created, as well as the role of the global access role.

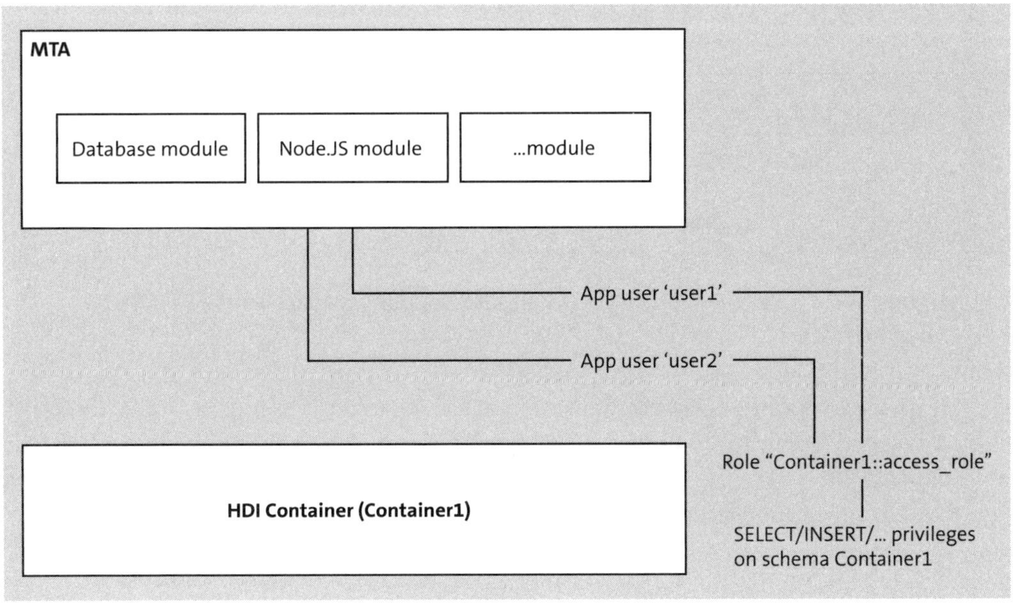

Figure 8.39 Application Users of an SAP HANA XS Advanced Application and the Global Access Role

Roles can be assigned to application-binding-specific users with the assignment of the `default_access_role` role if this role is available in the SAP HANA XS Advanced application. The HDI service grants this role to the service instance global access role with the name access_role during the deployment phase of an SAP HANA XS Advanced application. The default permissions will be revoked from the global access role after the SAP HANA XS Advanced runtime grants the `default_access_role`. Figure 8.40 displays the SAP HANA XS Advanced specific application users and the role of the global access role and the default `access_role`.

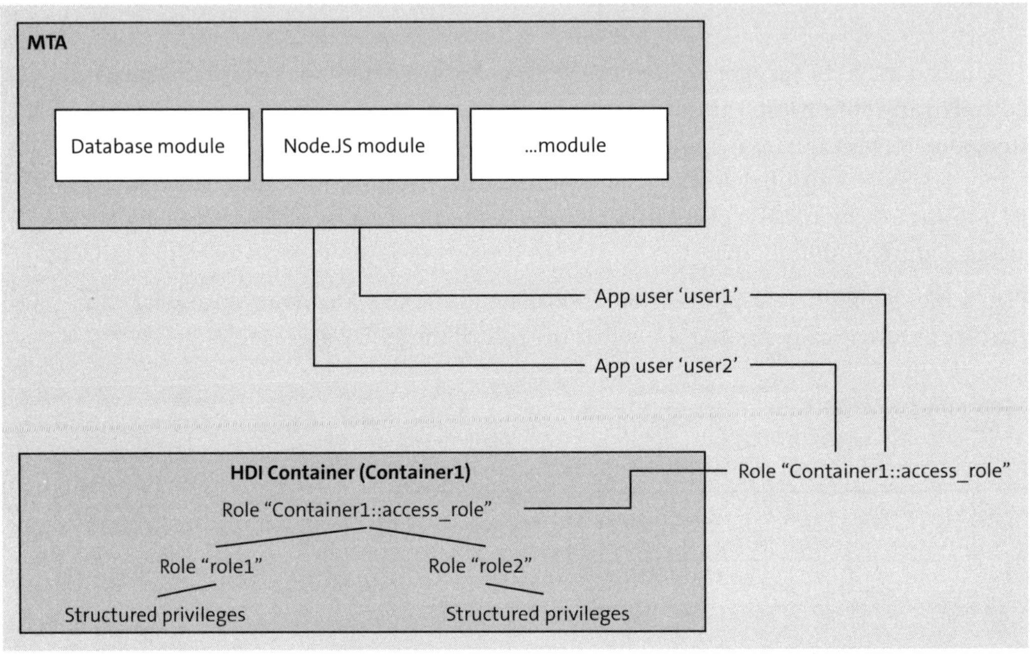

Figure 8.40 Role of the Global Access Role and Default Access Role in SAP HANA XS Advanced

Listing 8.16 is an example configuration of the default access role in an SAP HANA XS Advanced application project. The *default_access_role.hdbrole* configuration file must be present in the */src/defaults/* folder of the database module of the SAP HANA XS Advanced application.

```
{
"role" : {
"name" : "default_access_role",
"schema_roles" : [ {
```

```
"name" : ["user"]
}]
}
}
```

Listing 8.16 Default Access Role Configuration Example

8.7 Permissions for Container Objects

In SAP HANA XS Advanced, the development is performed in a database schema-less way because database objects of an SAP HANA XS Advanced application are deployed to an application-specific container that is a system-generated database schema. A developer requires synonyms in SAP HANA XS Advanced to access a database object that isn't part of the same SAP HANA XS Advanced application container. We discussed the usage of synonyms and a practical example for our ChickenWings application already in Chapter 5 when designing and implementing the data model of our application. In this section, we'll focus on the options for a developer to define privileges of the SAP HANA XS Advanced application container to access external objects.

As highlighted in the previous section when discussing the default access roles, the technical SAP HANA XS Advanced container user is assigned only a few database privileges by default. The technical user of the SAP HANA XS Advanced application requires additional rights to access database objects within other database schemas. Use the *hdbgrants* configuration file to assign privileges to the technical owner of the synonym objects and application users of the target object of a synonym. Additional rights are granted to these users then via the *hdbgrants* configuration file. Listing 8.17 highlights the basic structure of an *hdbgrants* file.

```
{
  "granting-service": {
    "object_owner": {
      <privileges>
    },
    "application_user": {
      <privileges>
    }
  }
}
```

Listing 8.17 Structure of an hdbgrants File

The top-level entries define the grantors, that is, the names of the bound services which grant the privileges. This is `granting-service` in the preceding code example.

In the next level, a developer defines the users to whom the privileges are granted. These are the grantees:

- `object_owner`
  The HDI container's object owner.
- `application_user`
  The application users who are bound to the application modules. The `application_user` refers to the technical user associated with the global `access_roles` required to access the SAP HANA XS Advanced application's runtime container.

With Grant Option Privileges

If a role name ends with the # character, the role definition is allowed to include `'WITH GRANT OPTION'` privileges as well as references to other roles whose names end with the # character.

The `schema_roles` property is used to specify one or more schema roles to be assigned to users via the grantor service.

In SAP HANA XS Advanced, a developer enables access to the synonym's target object by assigning an HDI container role that grants the container's object owner access to the target object in the external schema. The role must also have privileges with the grant option, and for this reason, the role name must end with the # character. The roles property specifies the role or roles to be assigned to the object owner and application user by the grantor service. If the role name doesn't end with the # character, a developer can only include privileges without grant options. Otherwise, the with grant option is added when the # character completes the name of the role.

The third level defines the set of privileges to grant using a structure that is similar to the format used in a *.hdbrole role-definition* file. On startup, the HDI Deployer service looks for files with the *.hdbgrants* suffix and processes them in the following way: For each grantor specified in the *.hdbgrants* file, the HDI Deployer service first looks up a bound service with the specified name (subject to service replacements). Then, the HDI Deployer service connects to the database with the service's credentials and grants the specified privileges to the grantees.

Listing 8.18 highlights privileges defined in an *hdbgrants* configuration file. We use the `schema_roles` property to specify the schema role with the name `Role1#` to be assigned to users. Furthermore, we define `select` privileges on table database objects and view database objects in the SAP HANA database schema SYS.

```
{
  "SYS-access": {
    "object_owner": {
"schema_roles":[
    "roles": "Role1#"],
      "object_privileges":[
        {
          "schema": "SYS",
          "name": "VIEWS",
          "privileges": ["SELECT"]
        },
        {
          "schema": "SYS",
          "name": "TABLES",
          "privileges": ["SELECT"]
        } ]
    },
    "application_user": {
      "object_privileges":[
        {
          "schema": "SYS",
          "name": "VIEWS",
          "privileges": ["SELECT"]
        },
        {
          "schema": "SYS",
          "name": "TABLES",
          "privileges": ["SELECT"]
        }
      ]
    }
  }
}
```

Listing 8.18 Privileges Defined in an hdbgrants Configuration File

8.8 Summary

In this chapter, we described the security mechanisms of SAP HANA XS Advanced and gave practical examples of how a developer can protect applications and data in every layer of an application. First, we provided an overview of the security concepts of SAP HANA XS Advanced and explained the different components that allow configuring security for an SAP HANA XS Advanced application. We revealed the authorization concepts and explained the purpose of scopes, attributes, and role collections in the context of SAP HANA XS Advanced applications. We provided practical examples to demonstrate how to secure our ChickenWings application. Furthermore, we discussed the options to grant access to an HDI container in SAP HANA XS Advanced. Finally, we explained the concept of the default access roles for HDI containers and described the permissions for HDI container objects.

In the next chapter, we'll explain the tools and methods to troubleshoot and debug the different layers of an SAP HANA XS Advanced application.

Chapter 9
Troubleshooting Your Application

In this chapter, you'll learn about methods to troubleshoot and debug SAP HANA XS Advanced applications.

9

A very important part of a software developer's day is devoted to troubleshooting applications and finding the cause of application errors. Finding the cause of application errors is, of course, critical to making sure that specific bugs can be adequately resolved, thus increasing the quality of an application. While creating the Chicken-Wings application, we had to troubleshoot our source code and iron out software bugs. Luckily, the SAP HANA extended application services, advanced model (SAP HANA XS Advanced) platform offers tools and functionalities to review log files of applications, as well as to debug the source code.

This chapter gives an overview of the debugging and logging functionalities of SAP HANA XS Advanced. We'll first highlight the options to debug database content such as calculation views or stored procedures. Furthermore, we'll reveal how Java application code, Node.js application code, and HTML5 application code can be debugged. Next, we describe where log files can be found and how a developer can write log file entries from an SAP HANA XS Advanced application. In addition, we'll explain how to retrieve and read trace files from the SAP HANA database. Finally, we'll discuss options to optimize the performance of your applications.

9.1 Debugging

In this section, we give an overview of the different options for a developer to debug an SAP HANA XS Advanced application. We'll first highlight the possibilities to debug calculation views and stored procedures. Then, we'll go into detail regarding the debugging capabilities of application layer logic written in Node.js and Java. Finally, we'll describe the options to debug HTML5 code.

9.1.1 Debugging Calculation Views

SAP Web IDE for SAP HANA provides a debugging editor for calculation views that can help analyze the runtime behavior of the calculation view to make necessary changes to improve query performance.

To debug a calculation view, open the calculation view in the view editor, and select the **Debug this View** icon in the editor toolbar. Select the **Semantic** node of the calculation view, and proceed to the **Debug Query** tab, as shown in Figure 9.1 ❶. The editor will propose a default query with all the attributes and measures defined for the calculation view. You can use the default query, but it's easier to debug with a query that has a smaller number of fields. You can use the **Reset the Query** option to display the default query again. Select the **Execute** option to start the debugging process.

Columns that aren't part of the debug query and nodes that are pruned during execution (e.g., **P_PY** of the **Union** node) will be grayed out, as shown in Figure 9.1 ❷.

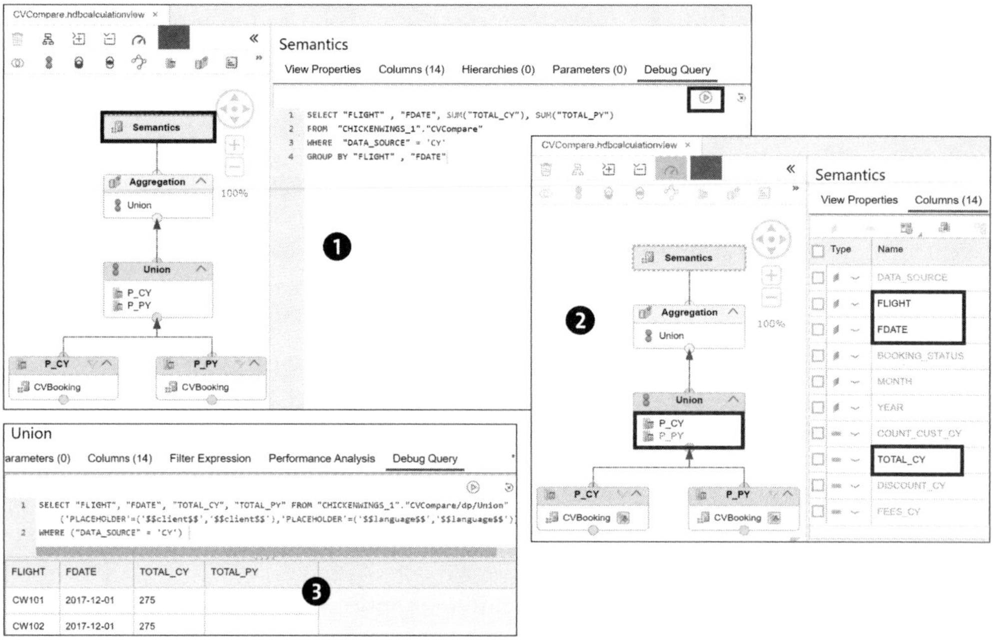

Figure 9.1 Debugging Calculation Views

Click each of those engaged nodes on the left side of the editor, and check the **Debug Query** tab on the right to see the actual query executed for that node to retrieve data. The query at the individual nodes can be checked to see the list of columns requested and if filters are being pushed down correctly. As an example, the debug query for the **Union** node is shown in Figure 9.1 ❸.

All referenced data sources that are part of the calculation view can be drilled down to analyze their performance. Select the option in the debugger editor to drill down to the underlying data source in a new debugger editor. Proceed to perform similar debugging operations on the underlying data source as well.

9.1.2 Debugging Stored Procedures

SAP HANA stored procedures can be debugged using the SAP HANA database explorer tool in SAP Web IDE for SAP HANA. To do so, connect to the SAP HANA Deployment Infrastructure (HDI) container in SAP HANA database explorer, locate the stored procedure in the HDI container, and select **Open for Debugging** in the context menu, as shown in Figure 9.2 ❶.

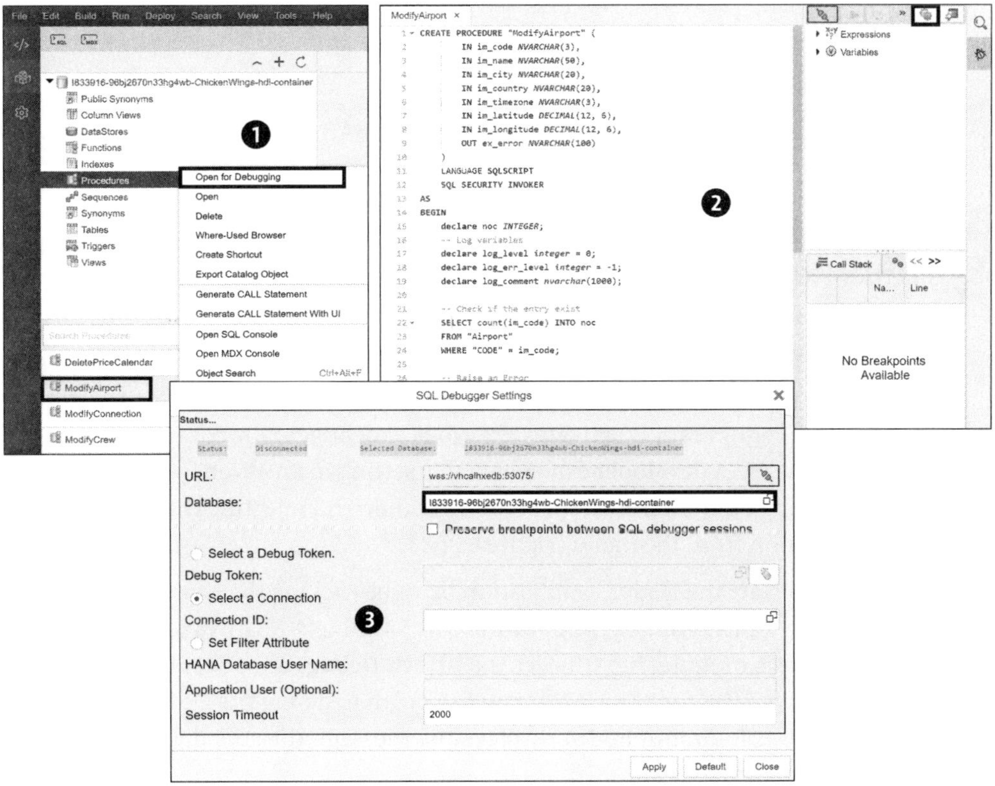

Figure 9.2 Debugging Stored Procedures

The stored procedure will be opened in an editor along with the SQL debugger pane, as shown in Figure 9.2 ❷.

Select the **Settings** option from the SQL debugger toolbar to choose a **Database** to debug, as shown in Figure 9.2 ❸. Choose the **Toggle Connection** button from the **URL** field to create a connection to the database for debugging. The status of the connection will change to **Connected**. Select **Apply** and **Close** to proceed. The setup is complete and ready for debugging.

Set one or more breakpoints in the stored procedure code by clicking the line number in the editor. Run/call the stored procedure with appropriate parameters (if any) to proceed with debugging.

The debug session begins, and the status of the session is shown in the SQL debugger pane. The debugger stops at the first breakpoint, and the session is suspended until it's resumed using the **Resume** button or the code execution is stepped through using the **Step Over** button.

9.1.3 Debugging a Node.js Application

In this section, we'll highlight the functionality of SAP Web IDE for SAP HANA that allows you to debug source code of a Node.js module. In Chapter 6, we demonstrated how to develop an application layer in SAP HANA XS Advanced with the Node.js technology in SAP Web IDE for SAP HANA. SAP Web IDE for SAP HANA allows debugging SAP HANA XS JavaScript (XSJS) source code files, as well as JavaScript source code files of Node.js modules.

The debugging mode within SAP Web IDE for SAP HANA has to be enabled by configuring a run configuration with the debugger enabled before starting the Node.js module. This configuration activates the Node.js debugging mode within SAP Web IDE for SAP HANA. A developer can enable this setting in SAP Web IDE for SAP HANA by right-clicking on the name of the Node.js module and selecting the **Run • Run Configuration** option from the menu (Figure 9.3).

Next, you can start the Node.js application by right-clicking the Node.js module and selecting **Run • Run as • Node.js Application**. The SAP HANA XS Advanced runtime will start the Node.js module. Next, select the **Attach Debugger** option in the debugger panel in SAP Web IDE for SAP HANA. You can begin to debug the Node.js application after SAP Web IDE for SAP HANA displays the message that the application is running, as shown in Figure 9.4.

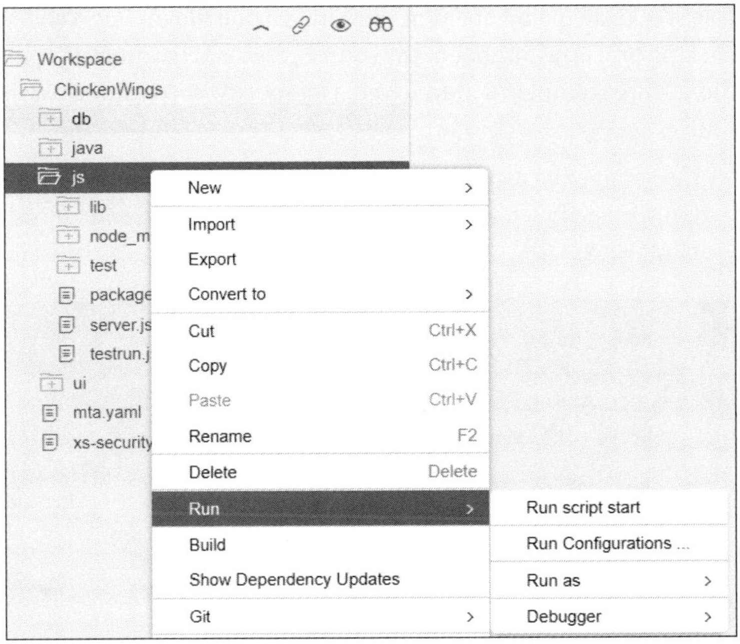

Figure 9.3 Specifying the Run Configuration When Starting a Node.js Module in SAP Web IDE for SAP HANA

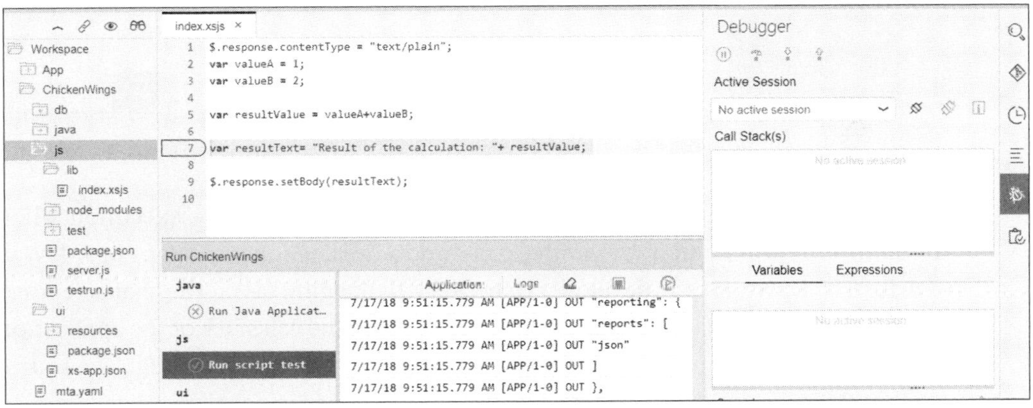

Figure 9.4 Node.js Module Started in Debugging Mode in SAP Web IDE for SAP HANA

As a developer, it's possible to specify breakpoints within source code files (either **.XSJS* or **.js* files) of the Node.js module to start debugging the application. A breakpoint can be enabled within a source code file by opening the source code file in SAP Web IDE for SAP HANA and clicking on a line number in the source code. Furthermore, it's possible to use conditional breakpoints. A developer can specify a condition when enabling a breakpoint.

The debugger pauses the script execution only when it's meeting the condition. Figure 9.5 shows the option to specify a conditional breakpoint in a **.XSJS* source code file in SAP Web IDE for SAP HANA.

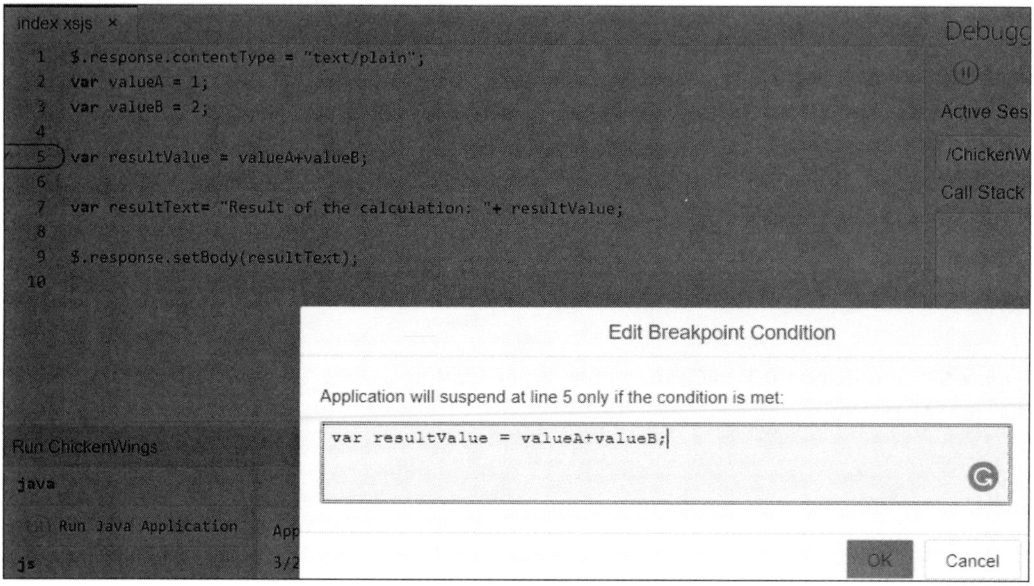

Figure 9.5 Conditional Breakpoint in SAP Web IDE for SAP HANA

When the Node.js runtime executes the script, it will pause the execution when reaching the breakpoint in the source code, and a debugger panel opens in SAP Web IDE for SAP HANA for the developer to perform debugging tasks. The available functionality of the debugging functions include viewing the call stack of the application execution, evaluating variables in the source code, and stepping through the source code and into function calls. Furthermore, the debugger panel allows developers to evaluate JavaScript code, which they can specify during the debugging session. Figure 9.6 shows the debugger panel during a paused script execution, along with the available debugging features.

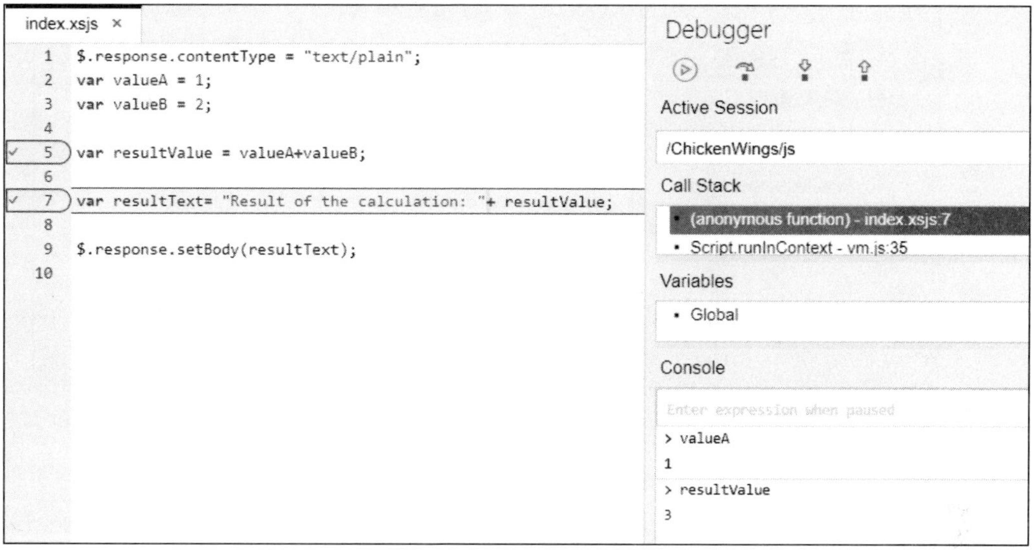

Figure 9.6 Debugging Panel in SAP Web IDE for SAP HANA

9.1.4 Debugging a Java Application

In this section, we highlight the functionality of SAP Web IDE for SAP HANA that allows you to debug the source code of a Java module. In Chapter 6, we demonstrated how to develop an application layer in SAP HANA XS Advanced with the Java technology in SAP Web IDE for SAP HANA.

SAP Web IDE for SAP HANA supports an integrated debugging functionality of Java source code. This functionality is like the debugging capabilities of Node.js modules discussed in the previous section. The debugging mode within SAP Web IDE for SAP HANA must be enabled by configuring a run configuration with the debugger enabled before starting the Java module.

This setting will activate the Java debugging mode within SAP Web IDE for SAP HANA. To enable this setting, right-click on the name of the Java module and select **Run Configurations** from the menu. It's important to select the **Enabled** checkbox in the **Debug** area when starting this run configuration, as shown in Figure 9.7.

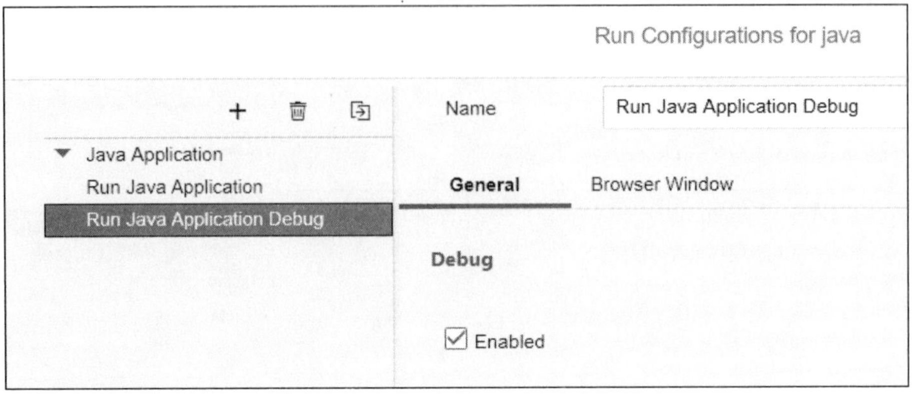

Figure 9.7 Specifying the Run Configuration When Starting a Java Module in SAP Web IDE for SAP HANA

It's possible to debug the Java application after SAP Web IDE for SAP HANA is started in debugging mode. Like the debugging option of Node.js modules, a developer can specify breakpoints in Java modules within Java source code files (**.java* files) of the Java module to start debugging the application. A breakpoint can be enabled by opening the source code file in SAP Web IDE for SAP HANA and selecting a line in the source code. Like the Node.js debugging capabilities, it's also possible to leverage conditional breakpoints when debugging a Java module. The debugger will pause the script execution only when the condition is met. Figure 9.8 shows the option to specify a conditional breakpoint in a **.java* source code file in SAP Web IDE for SAP HANA.

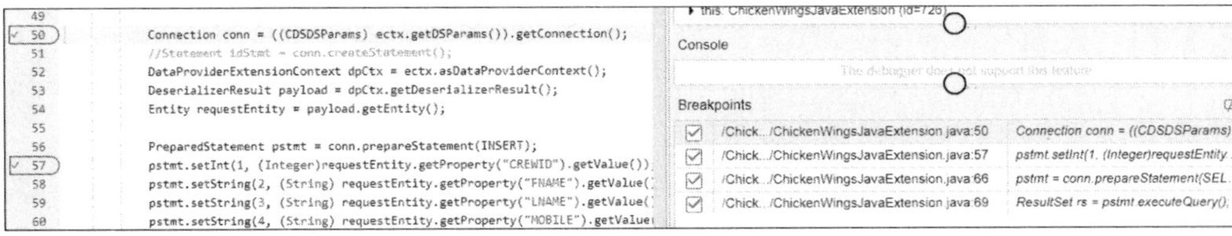

Figure 9.8 Conditional Breakpoint in a Java Source Code File in SAP Web IDE for SAP HANA

When the Java runtime executes the source code, it will pause the execution when reaching the line in the source code where the breakpoint is set. A debugger panel opens in SAP Web IDE for SAP HANA when the breakpoint is reached in which a developer can perform debugging tasks. The available functionality of the debugging functions include viewing the call stack of the application execution, evaluating variables that are used in the source code, and stepping through the source code and into function calls. Figure 9.9 highlights the debugger panel during a paused source code execution, along with the available debugging features.

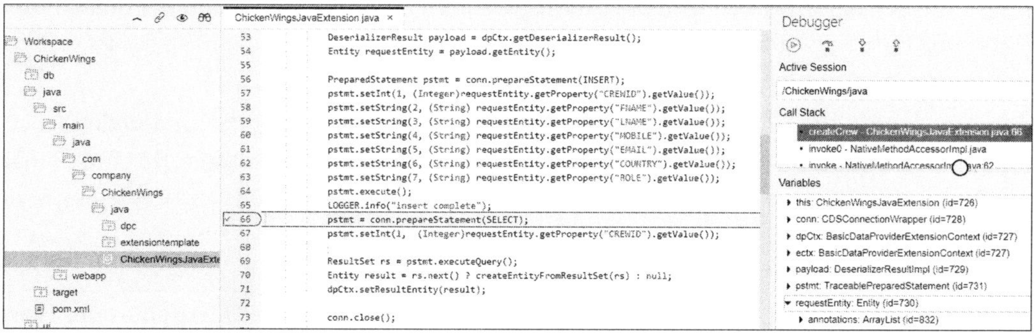

Figure 9.9 Debugging Panel while Debugging a Java Application in SAP Web IDE for SAP HANA

9.1.5 Debugging a SAPUI5 Application

In Chapter 7, we demonstrated how to develop a presentation layer in SAP HANA XS Advanced with the SAPUI5 technology in SAP Web IDE for SAP HANA. In this section, we'll highlight some of the options to debug the presentation layer of an SAP HANA XS Advanced application created with SAPUI5.

Note

We're giving an overview of the debugging capabilities of SAPUI5 applications in this section. A more detailed reference is available in the *SAP Fiori and SAPUI5: Debugging the User Interface* SAP PRESS E-Bite (*www.sap-press.com/4305*).

SAPUI5 applications can be debugged via the following methods, which we'll discuss in this chapter:

- Google Chrome developer tools
- SAPUI5 debugging tools

Google Chrome Developer Tools

The Google Chrome web browser offers compelling capabilities when it comes to debugging a SAPUI5 application. When running a SAPUI5 app in the Google Chrome web browser, the Google Chrome debugger tools can be opened from the context menu of the web browser by selecting **More Tools • developer Tools** (or press `Ctrl`+`Shift`+`I`).

The Google Chrome developer tools panel offers the following options to analyze a SAPUI5 application:

- **Elements**
  This option allows developers to inspect and manipulate the underlying Document Object Model (DOM) of the SAPUI5 application. For example, this functionality can be used to investigate the generated HTML source code and Cascading Style Sheets (CSS) information of the SAPUI5 application.
- **Console**
  The console displays messages, which are logged by the SAPUI5 application. These messages can include error or warning messages, as well as notifications that an application developer displays in the SAPUI5 code. Furthermore, the console can interpret JavaScript code that is entered in the console.
- **Sources**
  This option displays the structure and JavaScript source code of the SAPUI5 application. With this functionality, it's also possible to set breakpoints within the JavaScript source code and debug the SAPUI5 application. The available features of the debugging tasks include viewing the call stack of the application execution, evaluating variables that are used in the source code, and stepping through the source code and into function calls.
- **Network**
  The Google Chrome developer tools capture all HTTP requests that the SAPUI5 application initiates. These requests include the source code files of the application but also requests for backend services to fetch data. For example, it's possible to capture OData service requests with this functionality as well to understand what requests the SAPUI5 application sends to retrieve or modify data.
- **Timeline**
  This functionality records the runtime performance of the SAPUI5 application. It reveals how long it took to load specific resources, as well as in which order the resources of a SAPUI5 application were loaded. This functionality is especially necessary when investigating the runtime performance of a SAPUI5 application.
- **Profiles**
  This functionality is helpful when investigating the performance of a SAPUI5 application. It provides information about the efficiency of JavaScript code, including, for example, hints for memory leaks.

- **Application**
  This functionality highlights information about the resources that a SAPUI5 application stores on the web browser client. This information includes cookies, local storage, and caches.
- **Security**
  This feature reveals findings of the security mechanisms of the SAPUI5 application. For example, this includes problems with certificates when consuming resources via HTTPS.
- **Audits**
  This feature analyzes the SAPUI5 application when it's loading. The function then provides recommendations for improving the performance of the SAPUI5 application.

SAPUI5 Debugging Tools

The SAPUI5 framework offers the following useful debugging capabilities that can be activated by developers:

- **`sap-ui-debug` parameter**
  It's a good practice to increase the loading time of a SAPUI5 application by using a minified version of the SAPUI5 source libraries. However, this configuration to enhance the performance of the application makes it more difficult to debug the source code of a SAPUI5 application. Therefore, debugging resources can be loaded on demand in SAPUI5 by adding the URL parameter `sap-ui-debug=true` and the URL of the SAPUI5 application or by activating them with the keyboard combination [Ctrl]+[Alt]+[Shift]+[P]. Reload the app in the web browser after the debugging mode for SAPUI5 is activated. Use the source functionality of the Google Chrome developer tools as described in the previous section to debug to the uncompressed source code of the SAPUI5 application. Figure 9.10 highlights this debugging option for SAPUI5.
- **SAPUI5 support diagnostics tool**
  SAPUI5 offers a support diagnostics tool that can be activated with the keyboard combination [Ctrl]+[Alt]+[Shift]+[S] when running a SAPUI5 application in a web browser. The tool provides information about the structure and controls of the SAPUI5 application. Developers can set breakpoints and leverage a debugging functionality. Furthermore, the tool provides information about the technical bindings from the SAPUI5 controls to backend resources and status of attributes. Figure 9.11 shows the SAPUI5 support diagnostics tool.

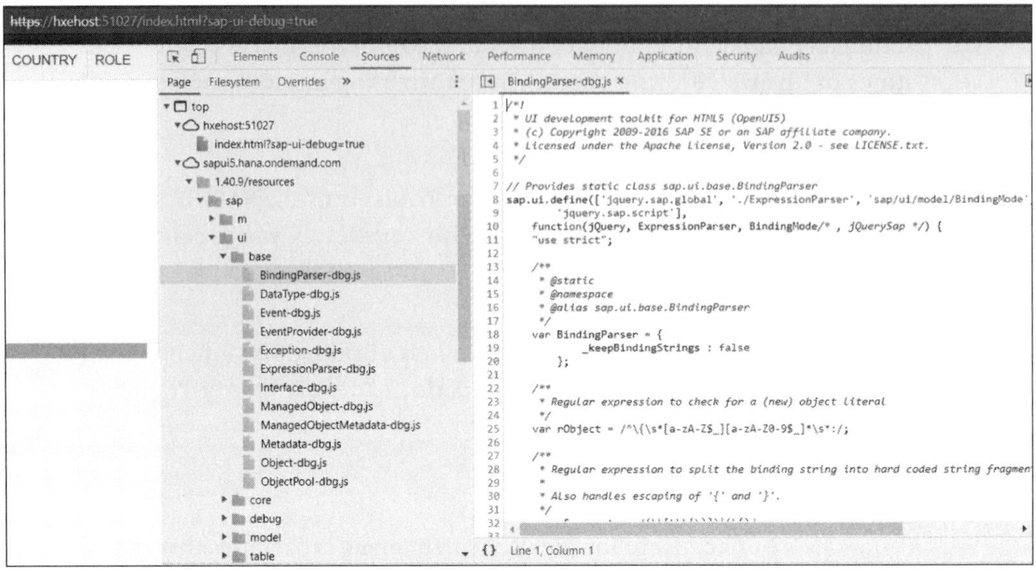

Figure 9.10 SAPUI5 Debugging Parameter

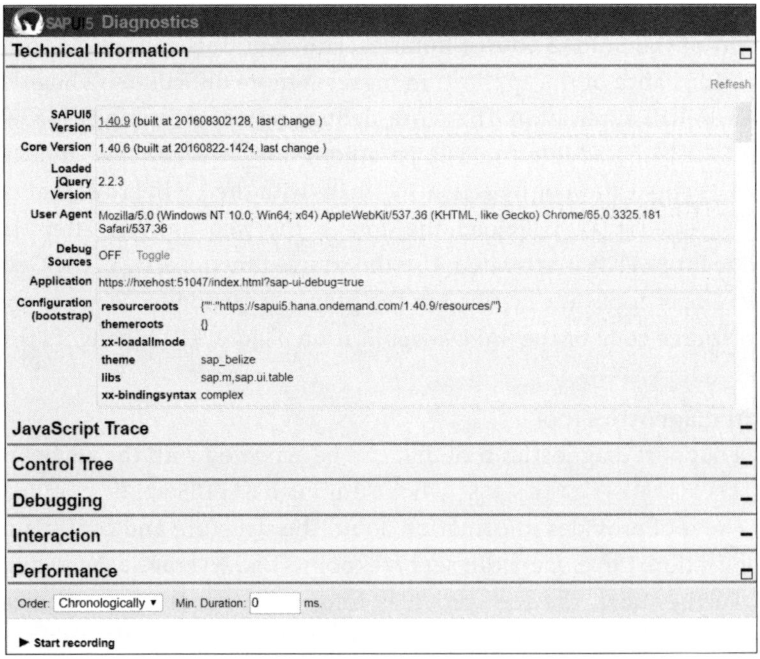

Figure 9.11 SAPUI5 Support Diagnostics Tool

9.2 Application Logs and Logging

In this section, we give an overview of the options for an administrator or developer of SAP HANA XS Advanced applications to write log file entries. Furthermore, we highlight how and where these log files can be retrieved. We'll first explain how to log data changes, as well as how to log actions within stored procedure executions. We'll explain where log files of SAP HANA XS Advanced can be retrieved. Finally, we'll reveal how events can be logged in application layer logic written in the Node.js or Java runtime of SAP HANA XS Advanced.

9.2.1 Logging Data Changes

Several strategies available to track changes at the database table level depending on the type of data and business requirements, as follows:

- **Last change**
  At as basic level, two *nonkey* technical fields `Last Changed Timestamp` and `Last Changed By User` can be added to all database tables to record the timestamp and user details of the last change. Using this approach, only the most recent change is available, and changes before the last change are lost. This may be enough for most common scenarios as businesses are typically interested to know the event surrounding the latest changes.

  For our example, we've used the `CHANGE.TIMESTAMP` and. `CHANGE.USER` fields to store the latest changes in the tables.

- **Slowly changing/moving dimension**
  For business analysis, it's certainly useful to keep track of all changes or changes to certain business-critical attributes of key business entities. As the name suggests, changes are made to these data sets during certain events (e.g., name change of an employee or manager of an organization, etc.). Using this approach, a new record is created for any changes to the data set.

  This can be achieved using the following approaches:

  - Add an auto-increment technical column (e.g., version `1`, `2`, `3`) part of the primary key.
  - Add two timestamps fields, `FromTimestamp` and `ToTimestamp`, as part of the primary key to store the validity of the data record. This can also be simplified further using two date fields, `FromDate` and `ToDate`, to store only one and the latest change per day.

- **Fast-changing data set**

  For fast-changing high-frequency and high-volume data sets, only an auto-increment technical column or timestamp is used as the primary key.

  SAP HANA history tables can be used to store fast-changing data sets, and time travel reporting (status as of a given timestamp) against the historical state of the data set is possible with history tables.

9.2.2 Logging Stored Procedure Actions

A logging table can be used to store execution logs of stored procedures. As an example, we've created the `SPLogs` table and a simple `CreateLog` procedure to store execution logs of all procedures in our application. The structures of the `SPLogs` and `CreateLog` stored procedure are shown in Listing 9.1 and Listing 9.2, respectively.

Filename: /src/data/SPLogs.hdbcds

```
/* Plane Details
*  Used for loggings in Stored Procedure
*/
entity SPLogs
{
    TIMESTAMP : UTCTimestamp;     //Timestamp
    USER      : String(100);     //User name
    SPNAME    : String(250);     //Procedure Name
    LOGLEVL      : Integer;         //Logging steps, starting from 1
    COMMENT      : String(1000);     //Log comment
    RECORDS      : Integer;        //Record Count info (if any)
}
technical configuration {
    column store;        //Column Table
    auto merge;        //Enable auto merge
    unload priority 5;      //Standard settings
    group type app group subtype ChickenWings group name logs;
};
```

Listing 9.1 SPLogs.hdbcds

Filename: /src/procedure/CreateLog.hdbprocedure

```
/*
* Create log entries
```

```
*/
PROCEDURE "CreateLog" (    IN im_spname NVARCHAR(250),
    IN im_level integer,    --1: Error, 0 >= Information
    IN im_comment NVARCHAR(1000),
    IN im_record integer)
LANGUAGE SQLSCRIPT SQL
SECURITY DEFINER AS
BEGIN
    -- Insert record
    BEGIN AUTONOMOUS TRANSACTION
        INSERT INTO "SPLogs" (TIMESTAMP, USER, SPNAME, LOGLEVL, COMMENT, RECORDS)
        VALUES (CURRENT_TIMESTAMP,
            CURRENT_USER,
            im_spname,
            im_level,
            im_comment,
            im_record
        );
    END;
END
```

Listing 9.2 CreateLog.hdbprocedure

The CreateLog procedure can be called from other procedures using the following code

```
call "CreateLog" (::CURRENT_OBJECT_NAME, log_level, log_comment, log_rec_count);
```

In this syntax, the following is true:

- log_level: –1 for errors and > 0 for logging steps (e.g., step 1, step 2, etc.).
- log_comment: Error logs or comments for the logging step.
- log_rec_count: –1 or actual number of records affected in the logging step.

The entries in the SPLogs table can be analyzed for errors in procedure execution and aid in troubleshooting. They can also be used to track performance of stored procedure execution over time.

9.2.3 SAP HANA XS Advanced Transaction Logs

The SAP HANA XS Advanced runtime supports functionalities to log events of the different runtime components. These application logs can be retrieved via the SAP HANA XS Advanced cockpit web application. We introduced this application in Chapter 3 when describing the development tools of SAP HANA XS Advanced. In this section, we'll highlight the options to analyze log files of the SAP HANA XS Advanced application components.

The SAP HANA XS Advanced cockpit web tool offers the application monitor as functionality to view application logs. Navigate to the space where your SAP HANA XS Advanced application is deployed. Click on the **Applications** menu item on the left-hand side to view all available applications within this space (Figure 9.12).

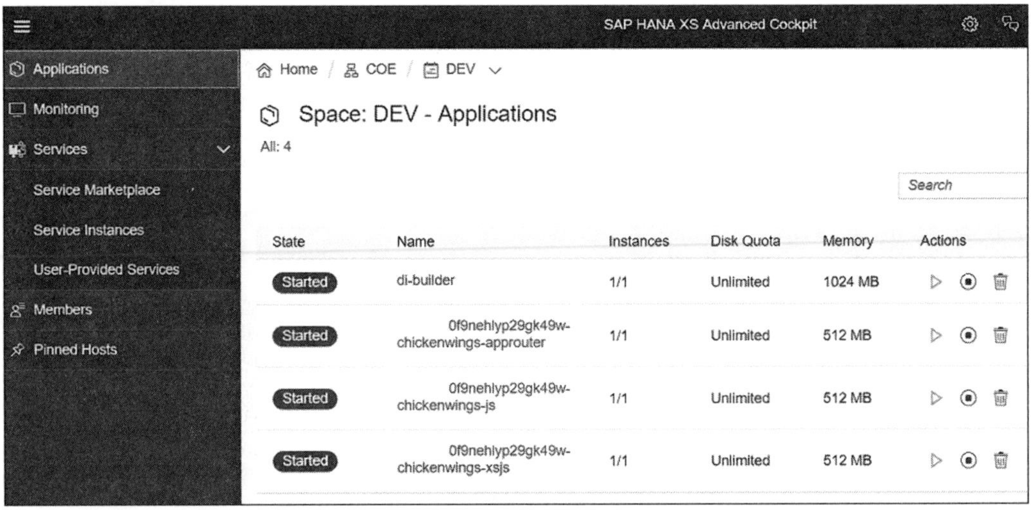

Figure 9.12 Applications in an SAP HANA XS Advanced Space in the SAP HANA XS Advanced Cockpit

The application displays the different runtime components of SAP HANA XS Advanced in a list that highlights the name of the application, the application's status, the reserved memory, number of instances, disk quota, and actions. The **Actions** icons allow you to start, stop, or delete an application.

Log files of the different applications can be displayed by clicking on the application's name in the row. A new window appears that shows more detailed information about the status of an application (Figure 9.13). Click on the **Logs** menu item on the left-hand side to display the logs of the application. Furthermore, you can change the log level of the application (e.g., to activate detailed tracing, select **Change Log Level**), or to download the log files to the client by clicking on the **Download** icon ⤓ in the menu.

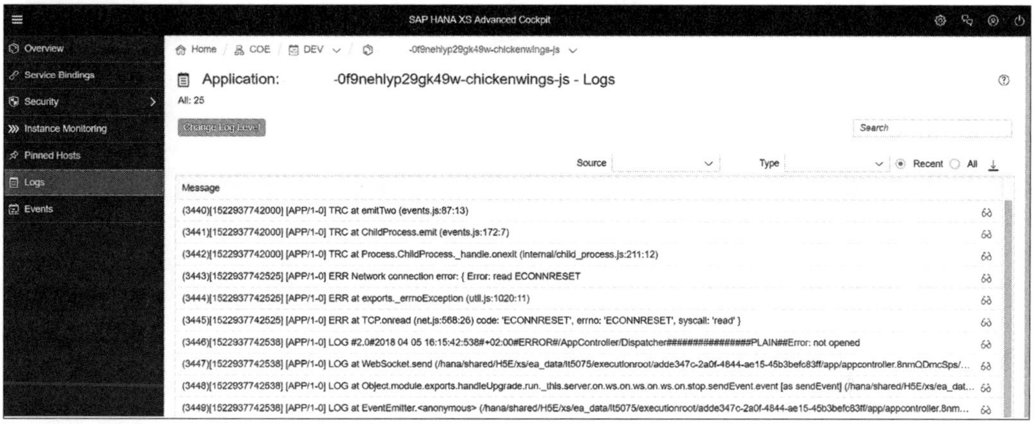

Figure 9.13 Log File Window of an Application in the SAP HANA XS Advanced Cockpit Web Application

9.2.4 Logging in Node.js Applications

We introduced the concepts of implementing an application layer with the Node.js technology in Chapter 6. In this section, we'll highlight an option to include logging capabilities within a Node.js application.

Logging entries within a Node.js application can be created via the JavaScript function `console.log`. The function takes an input parameter and prints the parameter to the application log of the SAP HANA XS Advanced application. Listing 9.3 displays a JavaScript code where information is printed to the standard log of SAP HANA XS Advanced via the `console.log` function.

```
const count = 5;
console.log('count: %d', count);
// Prints: count: 5, to stdout
console.log('count:', count);
// Prints: count: 5, to stdout
```

Listing 9.3 Log File Window of an Application in the SAP HANA XS Advanced Cockpit Web Application

The log entries can be displayed in the SAP HANA XS Advanced cockpit web application log files.

Furthermore, developers can also leverage the audit-logging capabilities of SAP HANA XS Advanced within Node.js. The `sap-audit-logging` library provides an audit-logging application programming interface (API) for Node.js applications. With the help of this audit-logging feature, application-logging entries can be written in a specific format to the SAP HANA XS Advanced log storage. Typically, the SAP HANA XS Advanced audit log is used to capture security, data access, or system configuration change events.

To enable the audit log service for SAP HANA XS Advanced, create an instance of the audit log service in the SAP HANA XS Advanced space of your application via the SAP HANA XS Advanced client tool. You have to execute the `create-service` audit log command, as follows:

```
xs create-service auditlog free <my-service-instance>
```

The `xs create-service` command highlights the creation of the `auditlog` service via the SAP HANA XS Advanced command-line interface tool (XSA CLI).

Next, you have to add the `auditlog` service as a resource in the *mta.yaml* file of the SAP HANA XS Advanced application, as shown in Figure 9.14. Therefore, select the **Resources** tab in the *mta.yaml* file, and add a new entry called **auditlog**. Specify **com.sap.xs.auditlog** as the **Type**. Add a new parameter to this new resource with **service** as the **Key** and **auditlogservice** as the **Value**.

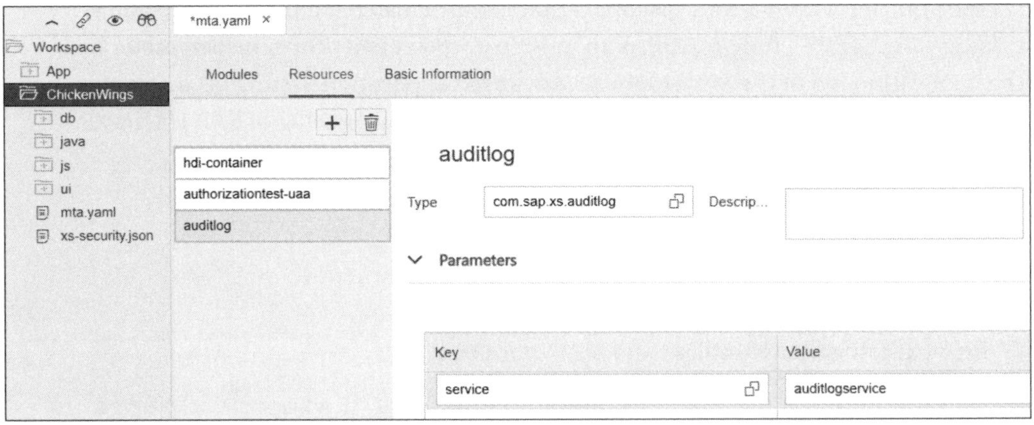

Figure 9.14 Adding the auditlog Service as a New Resource to the mta.yaml File

Next, add the new resource to the application module of the SAP HANA XS Advanced application that should make use of the `auditlog` service. Therefore, add the new service under the **Requires** section of the relevant module, and specify the name **auditlog**, as shown in Figure 9.15.

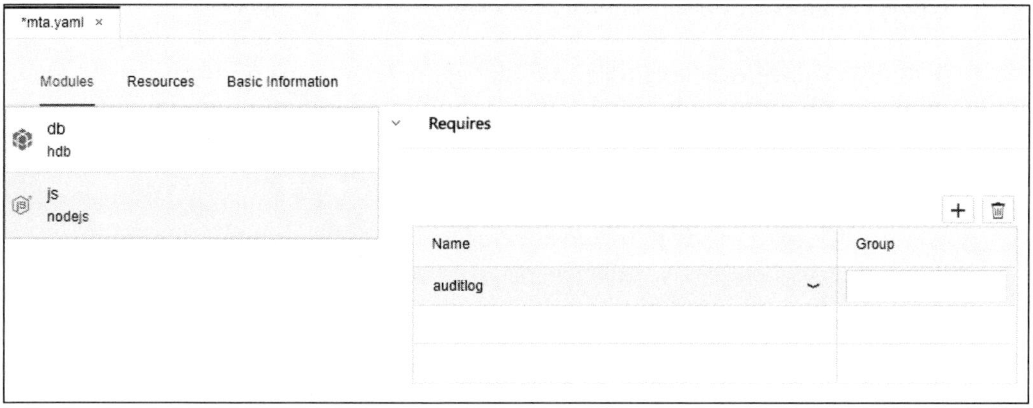

Figure 9.15 Adding the auditlog Service to an Application Module

Import the `audit-logging` library first in the Node.js application before using this API via the following command:

```
var auditLog = require('@sap/audit-logging')
```

The `auditLog` object contains the following functions listed:

- `create`
  This function writes an entry in the audit log for a create operation.
- `read`
  This function writes an entry in the audit log for a read operation.
- `update`
  This function writes an entry in the audit log for an update operation.
- `delete`
  This function writes an entry in the audit log for a delete operation.
- `securityMessage`
  This function writes a security message in the audit log.

The `auditLog` object is used to call the different methods, such as `securityMessage` or `create`, of the audit log library. Listing 9.4 highlights how to create a general security message in the audit log in a Node.js application.

```
auditLog.securityMessage('%d unsuccessful login, 1).by('User name').
customAttribute('user status', 'not authenticated');
auditLog.create('123456', 'application configuration') .category('configuration')
.by('Application Admin') .log(function (err) {});
```

Listing 9.4 Creating a Security Message Log Entry in a Node.js Application

A Node.js source code example that highlights how to log an unsuccessful logon attempt in a SAP HANA XS Advanced application is provided in Listing 9.5. The example makes use of the securityMessage function to record an unsuccessful login attempt and returns an HTTP 500 status code.

```
  var auditLog = require('@sap/audit-logging');
app.get("/ChickenWings", function(req, res) {
      var ip = req.headers['x-forwarded-for'] || req.connection.remoteAddress;
      if (req.headers['x-forwarded-for']) {
          ip = req.headers['x-forwarded-for'].split(",")[0];
      } else if (req.connection && req.connection.remoteAddress) {
          ip = req.connection.remoteAddress;
      } else {
          ip = req.ip;
      }
      auditLog.securityMessage('%d unsuccessful login attempt', 1).by(req.user
.id).externalIP(ip).log(function(err, id) {
          if (err) {
          res.type("text/plain").status(500).send("ERROR: " + err.toString());
              return;
          }
  res.type("application/
json").status(200).send(JSON.stringify('Log Entry Saved as: ' + id));
      });
  });
```

Listing 9.5 Audit Log securityMessage Example with Node.js

9.2.5 Logging in Java Applications

We introduced the concepts of implementing an application layer with the Java technology in Chapter 6. In this section, we'll highlight the options to leverage the standard logging capabilities for Java in the SAP HANA XS Advanced runtime.

The SAP HANA XS Advanced runtime offers standard services to include logging capabilities in Java modules. In this section, we'll highlight the following options:

- Simple Logging Facade for Java (SLF4J)
- Audit log service for Java

Simple Logging Facade for Java

The SLF4J is a framework to write log files from Java applications and is supported within Java modules of SAP HANA XS Advanced. A developer creates an instance of the `org.slf4j.Logger` class to use this framework within a Java SAP HANA XS Advanced application. The framework allows the generation of log files and setting the logging level for an application.

To start using the framework within a Java application, the framework must first be initialized within the SAP HANA XS Advanced Java module and configured in the *pom.xml* file, as shown in Figure 9.16.

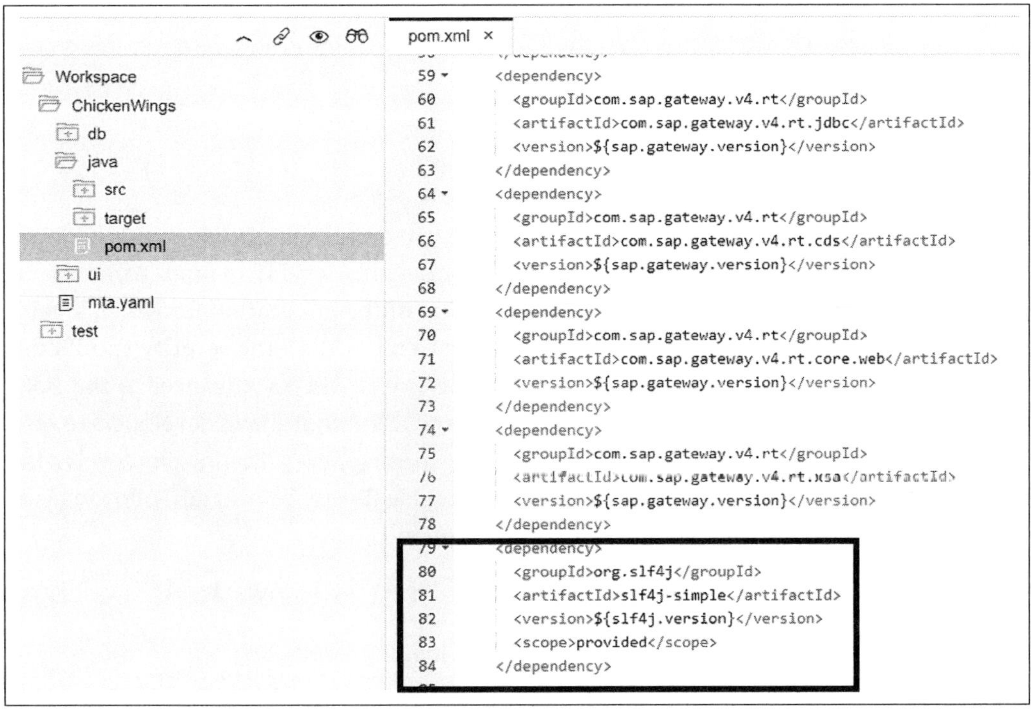

Figure 9.16 Initializing the SLF4J Framework in the Java Module

The SLF4J class can be instantiated in the Java module after initializing the framework in *pom.xml*. Import the `org.slf4j.Logger` and `org.slf4j.LoggerFactory` libraries in the Java class where the logging capabilities are required. Then, you can start writing log entries via the debug function or info function, for example. Listing 9.6 shows the first example of how the logging function can be used in Java code via the `LOGGER.info` function.

```
import org.slf4j.Logger;
import org.slf4j.LoggerFactory;
public class ChickenWingsJavaExtension {
    private static final Logger LOGGER =
 LoggerFactory.getLogger(ChickenWingsJavaExtension.class);
    @ExtendDataProvider(entitySet = { "Crew" }, requestTypes =
 { RequestType.CREATE })
   public void createCrew(ExtensionContext ectx) throws ODataApplicationException {
        try {
            LOGGER.info("Entered the method createUser");
        }catch{Exception e}
    }
}
```

Listing 9.6 Calling SLF4J Functions in a Java Code

Next, specify a log level for the application via the SAP HANA XS Advanced client tool with the command `xs set-logging-level`. The severity level is an input parameter of the command. Furthermore, specify the name of the application for which logging will be activated. Log entries will then be written based on the severity specified in the command. The default logging level for SAP HANA XS Advanced is the `ERROR` level. Furthermore, the SAP HANA XS Advanced client tool allows developers to reset the logging level via the command `xs unset-logging-level`. The logging levels of all applications can be listed with the `xs list-logging-levels` command. Following is an example SAP HANA XS Advanced client command:

```
xs set-logging-level <applications name> <logger path> <log level>
```

The SLF4J framework supports the following logging levels:

- `ALL`
  All logging levels are enabled.

- DEBUG
  With this log level, DEBUG, INFO, WARN, ERROR, and FATAL messages will be displayed.
- INFO
  With this log level, INFO, WARN, ERROR, and FATAL messages will be displayed.
- WARN
  This log level displays WARN, ERROR, and FATAL messages.
- ERROR
  This log level displays ERROR and FATAL messages.
- FATAL
  This log level displays FATAL messages.
- OFF
  This log level deactivates the logging functionality.

The `set-logging-level` command requires the name of the SAP HANA XS Advanced Java application as an input parameter. A developer can retrieve this name by running the `xs apps` command with the XSA CLI. The result of this command returns all the names of the apps that are running in the current SAP HANA XS Advanced space.

Now, you can copy the name of the Java application and use it in the command for the SAP HANA XS Advanced client tool. In our example, the command will look like the following to set the INFO log level for our Java application, which is located in the `com.company.ChickenWings` package:

```
xs set-logging-level XSA_DEV-0s01letcebjzr0e8-ChickenWings-java
com.company.ChickenWings INFO
```

Figure 9.17 displays the result when running this command in the XSA CLI.

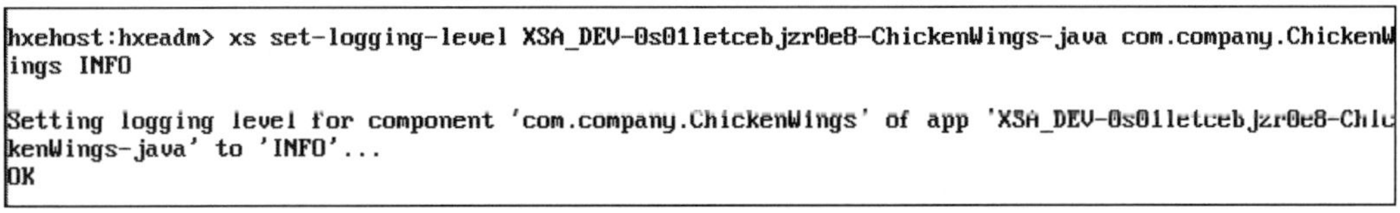
hxehost:hxeadm> xs set-logging-level XSA_DEV-0s01letcebjzr0e8-ChickenWings-java com.company.ChickenW
ings INFO
Setting logging level for component 'com.company.ChickenWings' of app 'XSA_DEV-0s01letcebjzr0e8-Chic
kenWings-java' to 'INFO'...
OK

Figure 9.17 Setting the Logging Level of a Java Application via the XSA CLI

We can confirm that the logging level is set correctly by running the `xs list-logging-levels <app name>` command. Figure 9.18 displays the result of the `xs list-logging levels` command.

```
hxehost:hxeadm> xs list-logging-levels XSA_DEV-0s01letcebjzr0e8-ChickenWings-java

Retrieving configured logging levels for app 'XSA_DEV-0s01letcebjzr0e8-ChickenWings-java'...

Component                    Logging Level
com.company.ChickenWings     INFO
```

Figure 9.18 Result of the xs list-logging-levels Command

Finally, the new logging level of the Java application is active, and an administrator of the SAP HANA XS Advanced system can view the log information in the application log screen in the SAP HANA XS Advanced cockpit application. The tool lists all available applications. Select the Java application, and click on the **Logs** link of the application. The log information that we added to our Java application, for example, via the function call `LOGGER.info("Entered the method createUser")`, is now displayed in this log file. Figure 9.19 highlights the logging information from the Java application.

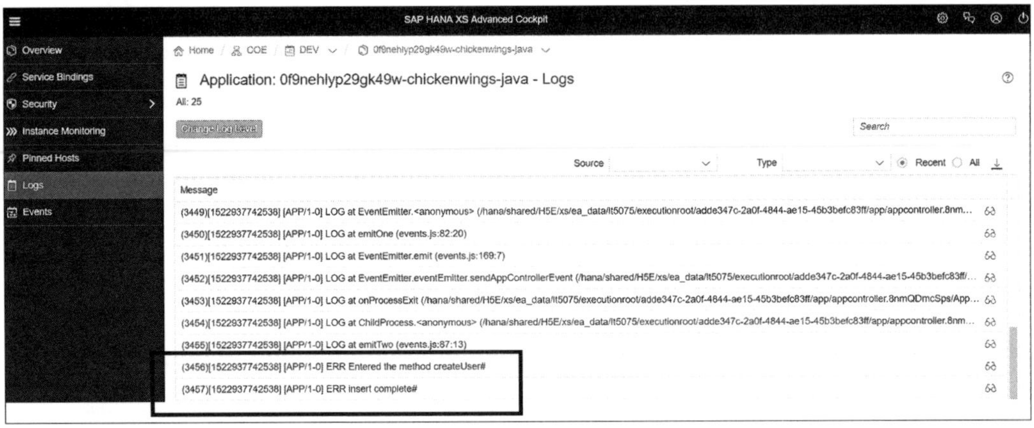

Figure 9.19 Logging Information from the Java Application

It's also possible to remove the logging level of a Java application again by running the `xs unset-logging-level <applications name> <logger path>` command in the SAP HANA XS Advanced client tool. The `<applications name>` parameter is the name of the Java application. The `<logger path>` parameter indicates the name of the Java package. It's recommended to restart the Java application after executing the `xs unset-logging-level` command for the changes to take effect. This can be achieved either via the SAP HANA XS administrator web application or by running the command <logger path> in the SAP HANA XS Advanced client tool. Figure 9.20 displays the results of running the xs unset-logging-level command.

```
hxehost:hxeadm> xs unset-logging-level XSA_DEV-0s01letcebjzr0e8-ChickenWings-java com.company.Chicke
nWings

Unsetting logging level for component 'com.company.ChickenWings' of app 'XSA_DEV-0s01letcebjzr0e8-Ch
ickenWings-java'...
OK
TIP: Use 'xs restart XSA_DEV-0s01letcebjzr0e8-ChickenWings-java' to ensure your logging level change
s take effect
```

Figure 9.20 Executing the xs unset-logging-level Command in the SAP HANA XS Advanced Client Tool

Audit Log Service for Java

The audit log service for Java web applications of SAP HANA XS Advanced allows you to capture and persist audit events. Furthermore, the SAP HANA XS Advanced cockpit web application offers functionalities to review the recorded audit events from applications. The Java runtime of SAP HANA XS Advanced supports functionalities that allow developers to register auditing events when users access Java web applications or Node.js applications. This audit functionality of SAP HANA XS Advanced allows capturing security, data access, and configuration change events.

To enable the audit log service for SAP HANA XS Advanced, create an instance of the audit log service in the SAP HANA XS Advanced space of your application via the SAP HANA XS Advanced client tool with the create-service auditlog command, as follows:

```
xs create-service auditlog free <my-service-instance>
```

Next, add the auditlog service as a resource in the *mta.yaml* file of the SAP HANA XS Advanced application. Therefore, select the **Resources** tab in the *mta.yaml* file, and add a new entry called **auditlog**. Specify **com.sap.xs.auditlog** as the **Type**. Add a new parameter with the **service** as the **Key** and **auditlogservice** as the **Value** for this new resource, as shown in Figure 9.21.

Next, we need to add the new resource to the application module of the SAP HANA XS Advanced application that should make use of the auditlog service. Therefore, add the new service under the **Requires** section of the relevant module, and select **auditlog** as the **Name**, as shown in Figure 9.22.

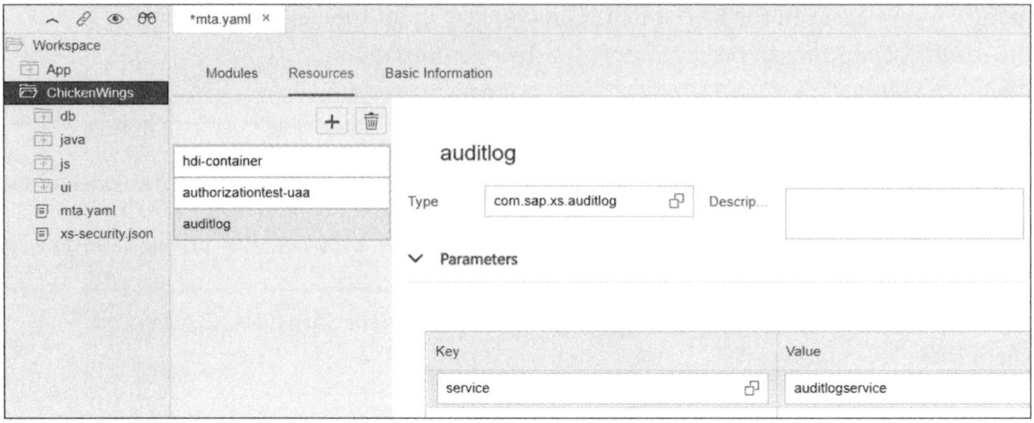

Figure 9.21 Adding the auditlog Service as a New Resource to the mta.yaml File

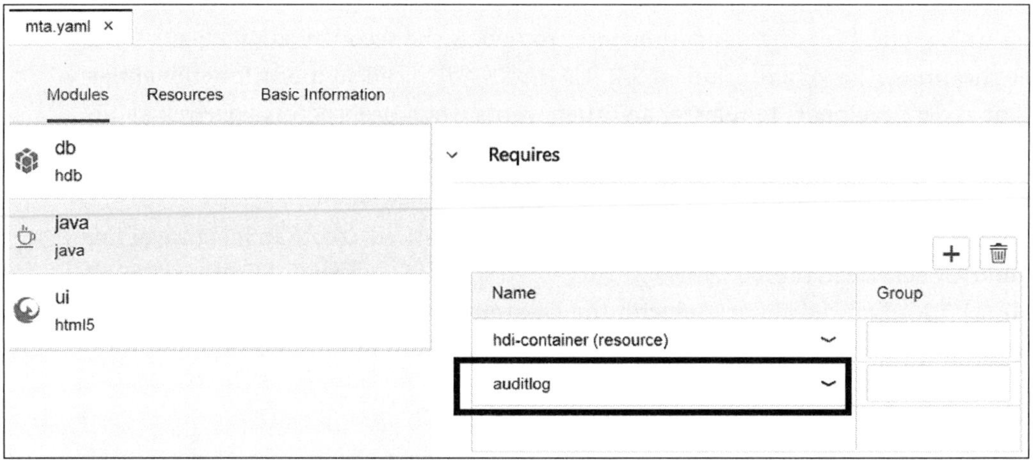

Figure 9.22 Adding the auditlog Service to an Application Module

For a Java module in SAP HANA XS Advanced, include the `auditlog` service of SAP HANA XS Advanced in the *pom.xml* configuration file of the Java module as a new dependency to start using the audit service. Listing 9.7 highlights the configuration in the *pom.xml* file.

```
<dependency>
        <groupId>com.sap.xs.auditlog</groupId>
    <artifactId>audit-java-client-api</artifactId>
```

```
        <version>0.0.1-SNAPSHOT</version>
        <scope>provided</scope>
    </dependency>
```

Listing 9.7 Audit Log Service Configuration in the pom.xml File

Next, configure the integration of the application *audit* service for the SAP HANA XS Advanced Java runtime. When you use a TomEE Java runtime, add the resource entry in the *WEB-INF\resource.xml* file of the Java module.

```
<Resource name="audit" auth="Container" type=
"com.sap.xs.audit.api.AuditLogMessageFactory" factory=
"com.sap.xs.XSObjectFactory" singleton="true" />
```

Figure 9.23 highlights the configuration of the *resource.xml* configuration file.

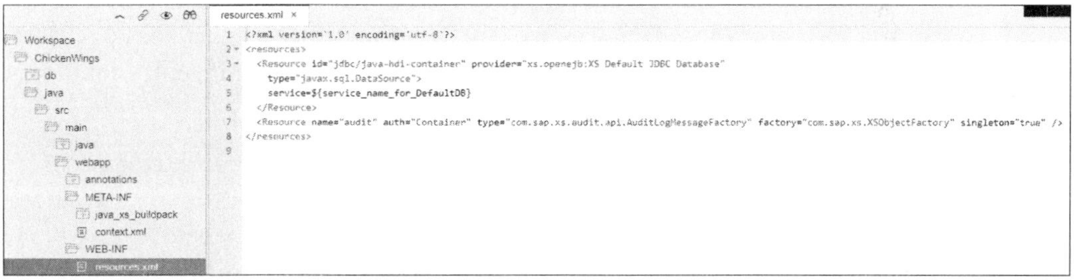

Figure 9.23 Adding the auditlog Resource to the resource.xml Configuration File

When you use a Tomcat Java runtime, add the following resource entry in the *META-INF\context.xml* file of the Java module:

```
<Resource name="audit" auth="Container" type=
"com.sap.xs.audit.api.AuditLogMessageFactory" factory=
"com.sap.xs.XSObjectFactory" singleton="true" />
```

Next, instantiate the `AuditLogMessageFactory` in the Java class to make use of the `auditlog` service. The `auditlog` message function can either be initiated via the Java Naming and Directory Interface (JNDI) lookup or via resource injection. A source code example of how to access the `AuditLogMessageFactory` via JNDI is as follows:

```
Context ctx = new InitialContext();
AuditLogMessageFactory auditlogMesageFactory = (AuditLogMessageFactory)
ctx.lookup("java:comp/env/audit");
```

A source code example of how to access AuditLogMessageFactory via resource injection is as follows:

```
@Resource(name="audit") private AuditLogMessageFactory mesageFactoryInj;
```

To create a log entry for a configuration change event, use the ConfigurationChangeAuditMessage class. Listing 9.8 shows an example of how to create a new audit log entry for a configuration change event.

```
ConfigurationChangeAuditMessage message =
mesageFactory.createConfigurationChangeAuditMessage();
message.setUser("<user>"); message.setObjectId("logger.com.sap.xs.test");
message.addValue("severity", "error", "warn");
message.logSuccess();
```

Listing 9.8 Create an Audit Log Entry for a Configuration Change

To create a log entry for a data access event, use the DataAccessAuditMessage class. Listing 9.9 shows an example of how to create a new audit logging entry for a data access event.

```
DataAccessAuditMessage message = mesageFactory.createDataAccessAuditMessage();
message.setUser("<user>");
message.setObjectId("class=com.sap.example.ChickenWingsJavaExtension");
message.addAttribute("crew", true);
message.log ();
```

Listing 9.9 Create an Audit Log Entry for a Configuration Change

To create a log entry for a security event (e.g., an end user accessing an application), use the SecurityEventAuditMessage class. Listing 9.10 shows an example of how to create a new audit log entry for a security event.

```
SecurityEventAuditMessage message =
mesageFactory.createSecurityEventAuditMessage();
message.setUser("<user>"); message.setIp("10.10.10");
message.setData("successful logon”);
message.log ();
```

Listing 9.10 Create a Security Log Entry

To log audit events in a Node.js application, a developer has to import the relevant library into the application first. The following example shows how the audit log library can be imported in a Node.js application:

```
var credentials = { "user": "user", "password": "password", "url": "https://
host:port" };
var auditLog = require('@sap/audit-logging')(credentials);
```

After the library is imported, a developer can log audit events in the Node.js application. Listing 9.11 shows an example source code that highlights how audit log events can be captured in a Node.js application.

```
var xsenv = require('@sap/xsenv');
xsenv.loadEnv();
var credentials = xsenv.getServices({ auditlog: 'auditlog-instance-name'
}).auditlog;
var auditLog = require('@sap/audit-logging')(credentials);
auditLog.securityMessage('%d unsuccessful login attempts',
3).by('<user>').externalIP('123.0.0.1').log(...);
```

Listing 9.11 Creating an Audit Log Event in a Node.js Application

Now, we can restart the Java application or Node.js application. The audit logging service is active, and the logging entries can be accessed via the **View Audit Log** functionality of the SAP HANA XS Advanced cockpit web application. Open the SAP HANA XS Advanced cockpit web application in a web browser, and select **More** from the main menu to access this log. Click on the **View Audit Logs** link to display the audit logs of the SAP HANA XS Advanced environment, as shown in Figure 9.24.

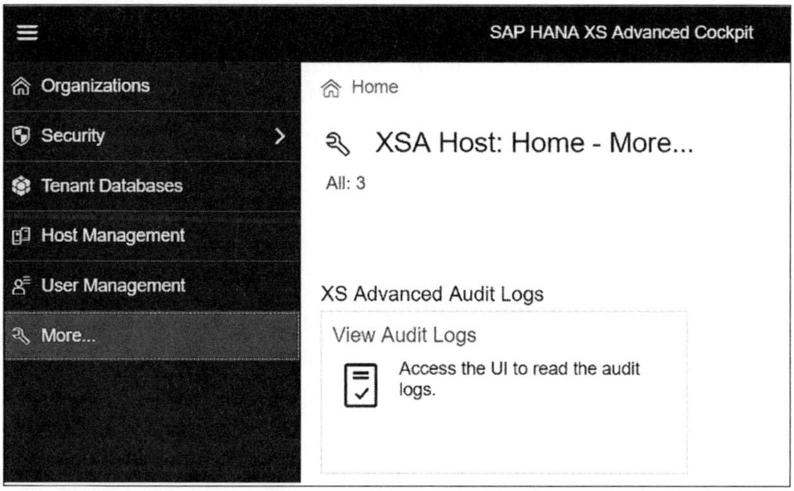

Figure 9.24 Audit Log Functionality of the SAP HANA XS Advanced Cockpit Web Application

9.3 Database Traces

Various types of traces can be enabled in the SAP HANA database to monitor and obtain detailed information about the database system processing.

These traces can be enabled using the **Trace Configuration** tab in the **SAP HANA Administration Console** perspective in SAP HANA Studio. Traces can also be enabled using the **Traces** option in the SAP HANA Web-Based Development Workbench (based on SAP HANA extended application services, classic model [SAP HANA XS]).

> **Note**
>
> SAP Web IDE for SAP HANA currently doesn't have options to enable trace or downloading trace files. These features may be available in future releases of the tool.
>
> Database traces can also be enabled using SAP HANA cockpit 2.0, which needs to be downloaded and installed separately. For more information, refer to *https://help.sap.com/viewer/p/SAP_HANA_COCKPIT*.

System privilege `TRACE_ADMIN` is required to configure traces in the SAP HANA database. All traces except the database trace is inactive by default. Let's discuss the various types of traces available and their usage:

- **Database trace**
  The database trace records detailed information about activities of the internal components of the SAP HANA database. Each service of the SAP HANA database records its own trace file (e.g., *indexserver_host.port.000.trc*); these files are available in the **Diagnosis Files** tab of the administration editor. Database trace is enabled by default, and the trace files are used by system administrators to diagnose/debug errors and analyze the performance of the SAP HANA database.
- **SQL trace**
  As the name suggests, the SQL trace is used to record information about all executed SQL statements in the SAP HANA database. The information recorded includes execution time, execution time of each statement, the number of records affected, and potential errors (if any, e.g., unique constraint violations). SQL trace is disabled by default and can be enabled for all/specific database users. We'll discuss the SQL trace configuration in detail in Section 9.3.1.
- **User-specific trace**
  As the name suggests, this is used to trace activity through the available components (i.e., index server and name server) for a specific application or database user.

- **Performance trace**
  This is the one of the most important traces from an application development perspective to analyze, understand, and troubleshoot performance issues for a given query. The performance trace records performance indicators for individual query processing steps in the database, including processing time, data size read and written, network communication, and information specific to the operator or processing step (e.g., number of records used as input and output). The performance trace is disabled by default and can be enabled for a specific database user for a specific duration. We'll discuss performance trace configuration in detail in Section 9.3.2.
- **End-to-end traces**
  The end-to-end traces are used by applications to trace activity through all the available components (i.e., all services, index server, and the SAP HANA XS server or XS Advanced server).
- **Expensive statements trace**
  All SQL statements with execution times exceeding configured threshold limits (e.g., 30 seconds) are recorded for further analysis and are available by choosing **Performance • Expensive Statement Trace** in the Administration editor.
- **Kernel profiler**
  The kernel profiler is a sampling profiler used to analyze performance issues that aren't accessible by the performance trace. This trace is meant for SAP HANA development support for troubleshooting uncommon performance issue. The standard SAP HANA role `SAP_INTERNAL_HANA_SUPPORT` is required to enable the kernel profiler trace.

As discussed, database traces can be configured in tools –such as SAP HANA Studio and SAP HANA Web-Based Development Workbench. We'll discuss enabling various database traces using SAP HANA Studio in the following sections.

9.3.1 Configuring SQL Traces

Click the **Trace Configuration** tab in the SAP HANA administration console perspective in SAP HANA Studio. Select the **Edit Configuration** button for **SQL Trace** to configure tracing. Select the appropriate tracing options, and then click the **Finish** button to enable/disable SQL tracing as, illustrated in Figure 9.25. The generated SQL trace file will be available in the **Diagnosis Files** tab of the administration editor.

Available options for enabling SQL trace are as follows:

- **Trace Status**
  Select **Active/Inactive** to enable/disable tracing.

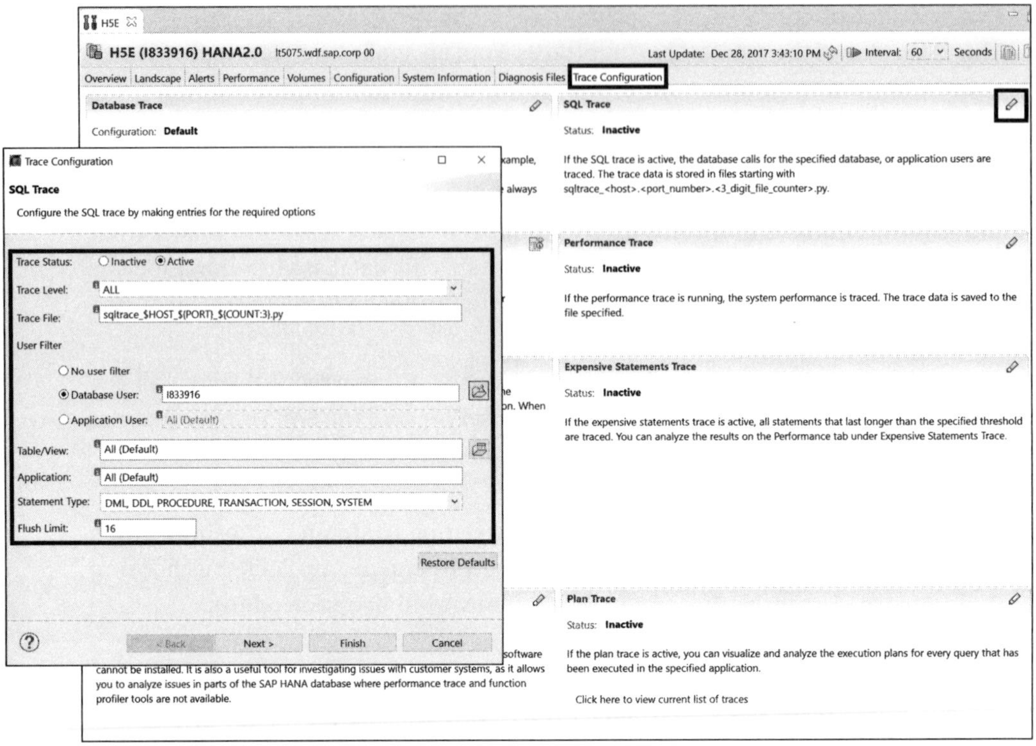

Figure 9.25 Configuring SQL Trace

- **Trace Level**
  Different levels of tracing are available that record detailed information about the SQL statement execution, including executed timestamp, thread ID, connection ID, and statement ID. The trace level options are as follows:
  - **NORMAL**: Only successfully executed SQL statements are recorded.
  - **ERROR**: Only SQL statements that failed with errors are recorded.
  - **ERROR_ROLLBACK**: Only SQL statements that failed and are rolled back are recorded.
  - **ALL**: All executed SQL statements (status of **Normal**, **Error**, and **Rollback**) are recorded.
  - **ALL WITH RESULTS**: All executed SQL statements along with the result of `SELECT` statements are recorded.
- **Trace File**
  Select the appropriate name of the SQL trace file. The default name is `DB_<dbname>/sqltrace_$HOST_${PORT}_${COUNT:3}.py`, as detailed here:

- DB_<dbname> is the subdirectory for the tenant database.
- $HOST is the hostname of the service (e.g., indexserver).
- $PORT is the port number of the service.
- $COUNT:3 is an automatically generated three-digit number starting with 000.

- **User Filter**
  Filters to restrict traced SQL statements for specific database users or application users
- **Table/View**
  Filters to restrict traced SQL statements for specific tables and views.
- **Application**
  Filters to restrict traced SQL statements for specific applications.
- **Statement Type**
  Filters to restrict traced SQL statements for certain statement types.
- **Flush Limit**
  This is the buffer setting. Traced SQL statements are written to the trace file in batches of flush limit (or if the connection is closed).

9.3.2 Configuring Performance Trace

Select the **Edit Configuration** button for **Performance Trace** to configure tracing. Select the appropriate tracing options, and click the **Finish** button to enable/disable SQL tracing, as illustrated in Figure 9.26. The generated SQL trace file will be available in the **Diagnosis Files** tab of the administration editor.

Available options for enabling performance trace are as follows:

- **Trace Status**
  Status of the performance trace. Select **Start Tracing** to enable the performance trace. If the performance trace is active, it can be stopped using the **Stop Tracing Manually** option.
- **Trace Mode**
  Two options, **Standard Trace** and **Extended Trace**, are available to collect detailed information.
- **Trace File**
  Name of the trace file. Select an appropriate and unique file name.
- **Database User/Application User/Application Name**
  Filters to restrict traced details for specific database users, application users, or

applications. It's recommended to use appropriate filters to collect relevant details and to limit the size of the trace file.

- **Passport Trace Level**
  Relevant for the Process Monitoring Infrastructure (PMI) in SAP ABAP and SAP BusinessObjects stacks.
- **Trace execution plans**
  Collect additional details such as trace execution plans.
- **Activate function profiler**
  Collect additional details about the individual processing steps in the database kernel.
- **Duration (min)**
  Duration of the performance trace in minutes. The trace duration value should be greater than the time it takes to execute the scenario.

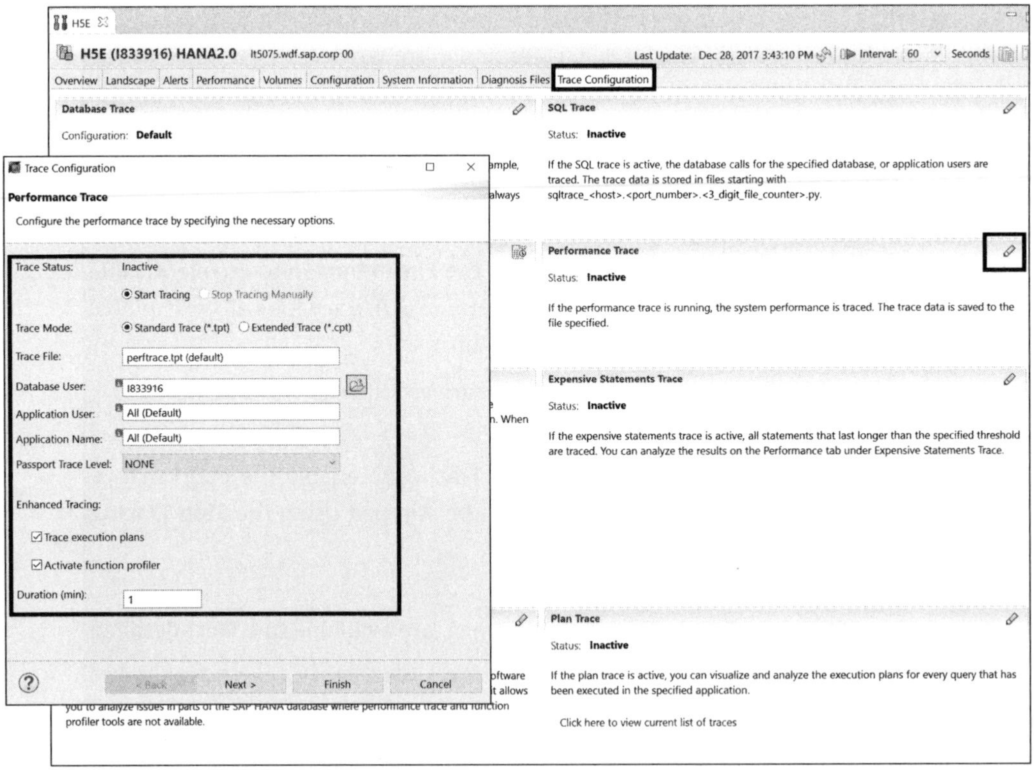

Figure 9.26 Configure Performance Trace

9.4 Performance Optimization

In this section, we explain how the performance of your application can be analyzed and optimized. We explain the usage of some standard functionalities in SAP HANA application development such as the EXPLAIN PLAN feature and the Plan Visualizer (commonly called PlanViz). Furthermore, we give examples of how the SQL query execution can be analyzed with SAP Web IDE for SAP HANA.

9.4.1 Execution of SQL Queries on Calculation Views

The SQL Engine in SAP HANA is responsible for processing SQL queries on database tables/views as well as SAP HANA calculation views. Starting with SAP HANA 1.0 SPS 09, additional SQL optimizations are implicitly enabled for all graphical calculation views (see SAP Notes 1857202 and 2291812 for details). These optimization and execution behaviors of a SQL query against a graphical calculation view can be described as follows:

1. Based on the selected fields in the SQL query, SAP HANA composes a single execution model from all included graphical calculation views. All graphical calculation views (part of the queried calculation views) are unfolded to the table/database objects, and any table/database objects not contributing to the SQL execution are eliminated to build a single acyclic data-flow graph for the SQL query, as shown Figure 9.27.
2. Rule-based optimizations (e.g., applying filters at the lowest level to narrow the intermediate result sets, combining multiple aggregations into one operation, and similarly combining multiple join operations into one operation) are applied to optimize the acyclic data-flow graph.
3. All column store operations are then converted to equivalent SQL operators to create a single SQL statement for the complete data-flow graph. The SQL statement is then passed to the SQL optimizer.
4. The SQL optimizer can apply further optimizations, such as join reordering across the complete data flow graph. The SQL optimizer applies a cost-based estimate for each operation and may generate multiple execution plans (based on the best order of operations and best choice operator variants for optimal performance). The most cost-effective execution plan will be then forwarded to the SQL executor.
5. The SQL executor will forward the database operations to the best SAP HANA column store engines (e.g., execution of a star-join node will be forwarded to the Online Analytical Processing [OLAP] engine) for efficient execution.

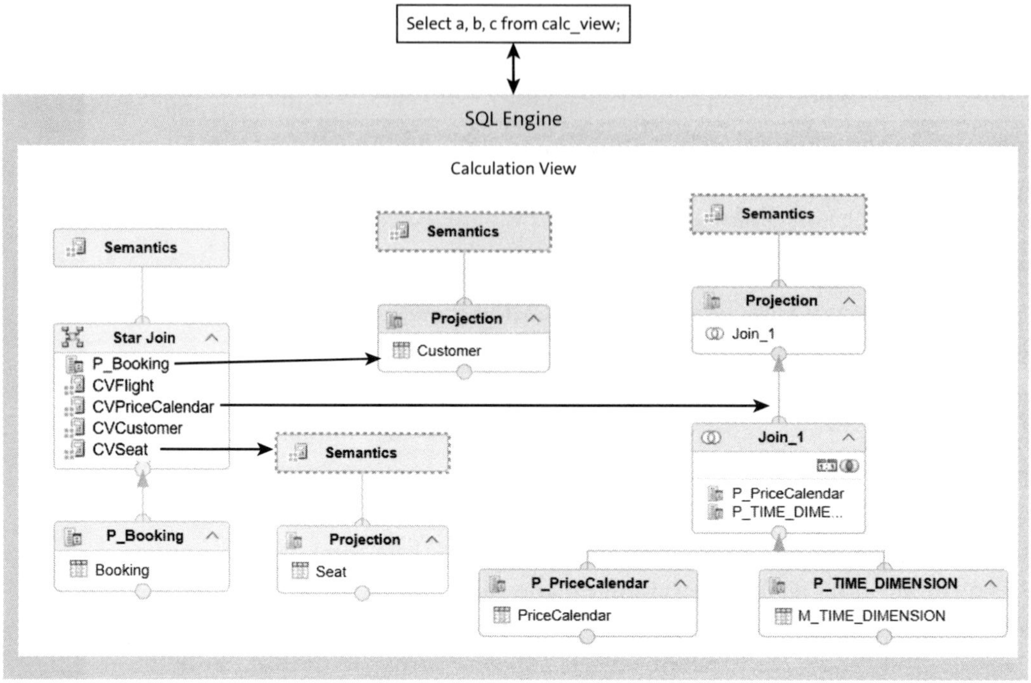

Figure 9.27 Calculation View Unfolding

9.4.2 Analyze SQL in SAP Web IDE for SAP HANA

As the name suggests, the Analyze SQL tool in SAP Web IDE for SAP HANA executes the SQL query and displays its execution plan. The execution plan provides significant insight into each process to determine performance bottlenecks and can be used for performance optimization.

To use the Analyze SQL tool, open the SQL editor in SAP Web IDE for SAP HANA, and select **Analyze SQL**, as shown in Figure 9.28. The query is executed, and the details of the executed plan are displayed in a new tab with various detailed views, as follows:

- **Overview**
  Displays the summary/overview of the executed plan in various tiles, as illustrated in Figure 9.28.
  - **Time** tile: Displays timing detail of the query execution.
    - **Compiled**: Time taken to compile the SQL query.
    - **Executed**: Time taken to execute the query (excluding compile time).

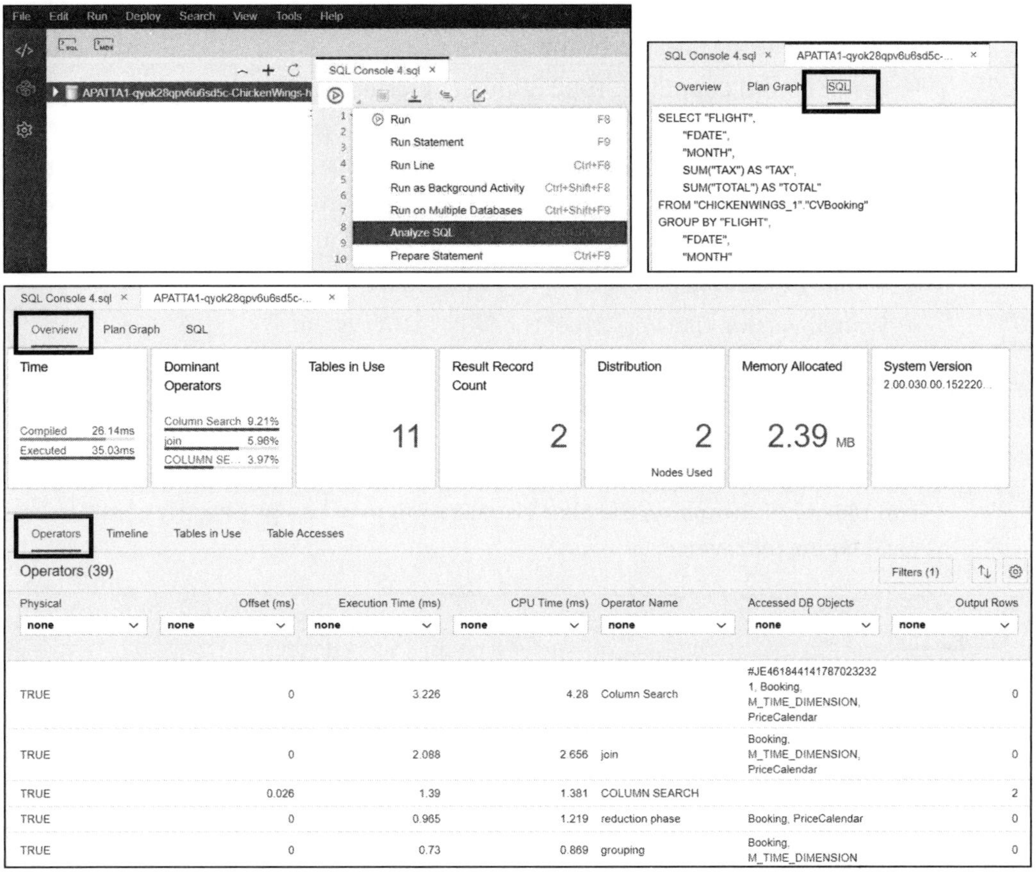

Figure 9.28 Analyze SQL Tool in SAP Web IDE for SAP HANA

- **Dominant Operators** tile: The top three dominant operators based on execution time. These operators should be analyzed for potential performance improvements. Clicking the operators will display additional details in the execution plan. The name of the operators describes the underlying database engine used and the operation they perform, as follows:
  - Operators beginning with `ce` are executed in the Calculation Engine.
  - Operators beginning with `BwPop` are executed in the OLAP engine.
  - Operators beginning with `JE` are executed in the Join Engine.
  - Operators beginning with `Sql` are executed in the SQL Engine.

- **Tables in Use** tile: Total number of database table, including temporary tables, accessed during query execution.
- **Result Record Count** tile: Total number of result records returned during query execution.
- **Distribution** tile: Total number of nodes/hosts involved in the query execution. For a single node system, it will be **1**; for a distributed system, it will depend on the physical location of the tables or table partitions in the scale-out system.
- **Memory Allocated** tile: Total dynamic memory used for query execution.
- **System Version** tile: Version of the SAP HANA system.

■ **Plan Graph**
Graphical network representation of the executed plan for the SQL query. The plan can be traversed from top to bottom to explore plan details and expand each node to seek further details about them, as illustrated in Figure 9.29. Depending on the complexity of the query, the plan visualization may be significantly complex and challenging to traverse.

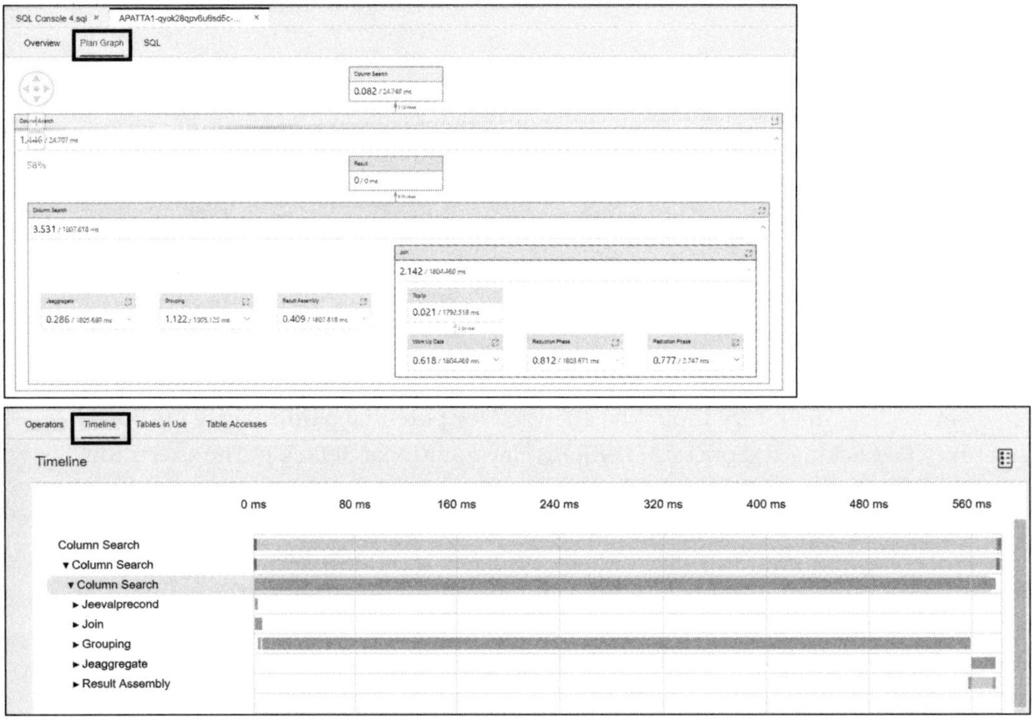

Figure 9.29 Plan Graph and Timeline View

- **Timeline**: Displays the sequence of operations as occurred during the plan execution with the X-axis displaying the execution time and the Y-axis displaying the list of operators in a tree structure.

  Plan operations that are executed in parallel will also be displayed as parallel bars in the graphical view, while plan operations executed in serial will appear sequentially in the graphical view. This gives a hint about the degree of parallel execution of a specific query.

  Some plan operations are executed on single CPU cores, while other plan operations are executed on multiple CPU cores in SAP HANA. Plan operations that have "parallel" in their POP method name are automatically executed on multiple CPU cores and tend to use all available CPU cores. By looking at the **Timeline** view, you can find out the following:

  - The list of operators executing in parallel (or serial) and the interdependency between these operators may be a pointer to inefficiency (if serial) in the model.
  - The size of the operator is also an indicator of the bottleneck. Focus should be on the top five big blocks (operator) in the plan visualization.

- **Tables in Use**: Provides an overview of the list of tables, including temporary tables, used during query execution and can be used to cross-check business understanding if certain tables are needed to fulfill a given SQL statement. The view displays three pieces of table information and three metrics, as illustrated in Figure 9.30:

  - **Table Name**: Name of the table.
  - **Location**: The host and port of the table's partition.
  - **Partition**: The partition number of the table's partition.
  - **Max. entries processed**: The overall output cardinality of any processing step on that table in the statement execution.
  - **Number of Accesses**: How often a table has been accessed during statement execution.
  - **Max. processing time (ms)**: The maximum processing time across possibly multiple table accesses.

- **Table Accesses**: Provides the list of table accesses by various plan operators, as illustrated in Figure 9.30. This is very useful because the same table may be accessed multiple times for very specific purposes in the overall execution plan. The view displays the following details:

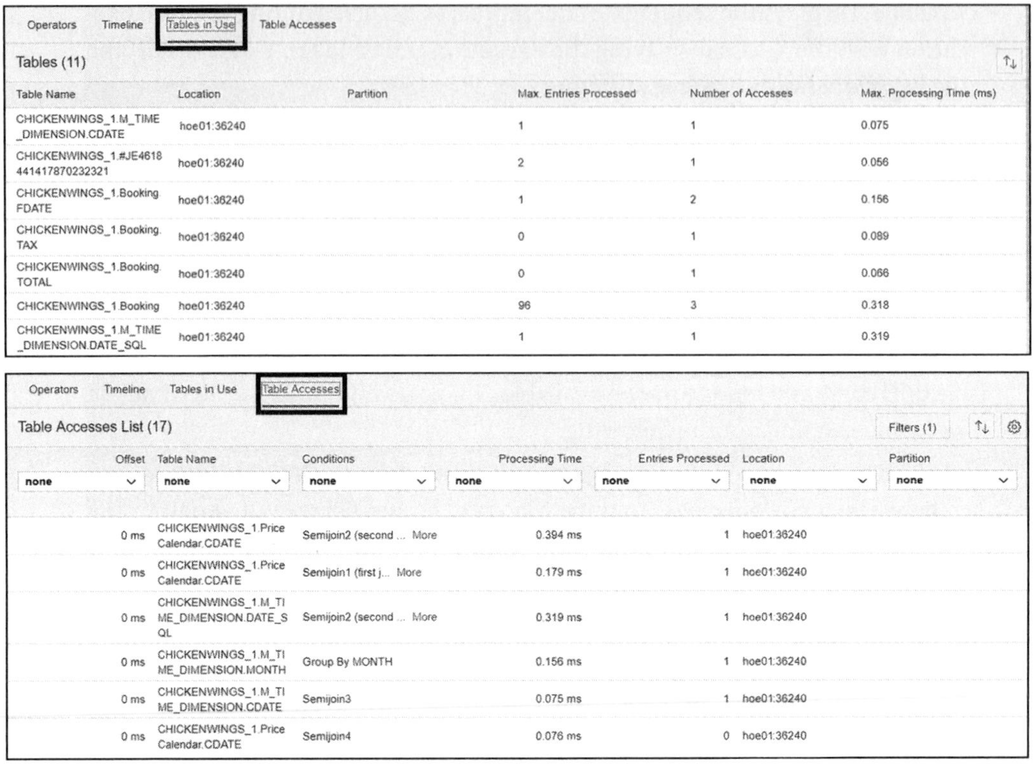
Operators
Timeline
Tables in Use
Table Accesses
Tables (11)
Table Name
Location
Partition
Max. Entries Processed
Number of Accesses
Max. Processing Time (ms)
CHICKENWINGS_1.M_TIME_DIMENSION.CDATE hoe01:36240 1 1 0.075
CHICKENWINGS_1.#JE4618441417870232321 hoe01:36240 2 1 0.056
CHICKENWINGS_1.Booking.FDATE hoe01:36240 1 2 0.156
CHICKENWINGS_1.Booking.TAX hoe01:36240 0 1 0.089
CHICKENWINGS_1.Booking.TOTAL hoe01:36240 0 1 0.066
CHICKENWINGS_1.Booking hoe01:36240 96 3 0.318
CHICKENWINGS_1.M_TIME_DIMENSION.DATE_SQL hoe01:36240 1 1 0.319
Operators
Timeline
Tables in Use
Table Accesses
Table Accesses List (17)
Filters (1)
Offset
Table Name
Conditions
Processing Time
Entries Processed
Location
Partition
none
0 ms CHICKENWINGS_1.PriceCalendar.CDATE Semijoin2 (second ... More 0.394 ms 1 hoe01:36240
0 ms CHICKENWINGS_1.PriceCalendar.CDATE Semijoin1 (first j... More 0.179 ms 1 hoe01:36240
0 ms CHICKENWINGS_1.M_TIME_DIMENSION.DATE_SQL Semijoin2 (second ... More 0.319 ms 1 hoe01:36240
0 ms CHICKENWINGS_1.M_TIME_DIMENSION.MONTH Group By MONTH 0.156 ms 1 hoe01:36240
0 ms CHICKENWINGS_1.M_TIME_DIMENSION.CDATE Semijoin3 0.075 ms 1 hoe01:36240
0 ms CHICKENWINGS_1.PriceCalendar.CDATE Semijoin4 0.076 ms 0 hoe01:36240

Figure 9.30 Tables in Use and Table Accesses View

- **Offset**: Table access as an offset for the overall plan.
- **Table Name**: Name of the table.
- **Conditions**: Operator/operations that accessed the table.
- **Processing Time**: Time table for processing the table access.
- **Entries Processed**: The output cardinality of the processing step on the table.
- **Location**: The host and port of the table's partition.
- **Partition**: The partition number of the table's partition.

- **SQL**
  Displays the SQL query executed for the analyze plan, as illustrated in Figure 9.28.
- **Operators**
  The operator list view provides detailed characteristics of all operators within a current query plan. It can be used to dynamically explore the operator set along user-defined filters to pinpoint specific operators of interest.

The view displays various key performance indicators (KPIs), for example, **Physical** (whether an operator is a real, physically executed one), **Offset** time for the overall plan, **Execution Time**, **CPU Time**, and **Input Rows/Output Rows**, as illustrated in Figure 9.28. The operator list reveals whether filters are pushed down to the table and/or if desired tables are engaged in joins.

9.4.3 Explain Plan in SAP HANA Studio

As discussed in the previous section, the SQL Engine may create one or more execution plans for a given SQL query, and the most cost-efficient execution plan is forwarded to the SQL executor.

`EXPLAIN PLAN` in SAP HANA Studio can be used to evaluate the execution plan (only for Data Manipulation Language [DML] statements) generated by the SAP HANA SQL optimizer. The result of the evaluation is also temporarily persisted in the `EXPLAIN_PLAN_TABLE` and can be queried.

Note

The SAP HANA database explorer in SAP Web IDE for SAP HANA currently doesn't support `EXPLAIN PLAN`. It may be available in future releases.

To use `EXPLAIN PLAN`, open the SQL editor in SAP HANA Studio, and enter the SQL query to evaluate. Right-click the SQL query, and select **Explain Plan** in the context menu to generate and display the plan, as shown in Figure 9.31.

The most important columns in `EXPLAIN PLAN` are subtree cost and operator name. After analyzing the `SUBTREE COST` of each operational steps in `EXPLAIN PLAN`, the operator name(s) contributing to higher subtree costs deserves our utmost attention and are the candidates for further tuning. For two SQL queries on an identical set of tables and producing identical results, the SQL query with the lower subtree cost is more efficient. The list of columns returned as part of the `EXPLAIN PLAN` are as follows:

- `OPERATOR NAME` and `OPERATOR DETAILS`
  Explains the actions of each step in the query execution plan. Depending on the SQL query, some of the following common operators may be part of the `EXPLAIN PLAN`:
  - `COLUMN SEARCH`: Starting position of column engine operators. `OPERATOR_DETAILS` lists the projected columns.
  - `ROW SEARCH`: Starting position of row engine operators. `OPERATOR_DETAILS` lists the projected columns.

- COLUMN TABLE: Operator for scanning the column table. OPERATOR_DETAILS may provide additional details, such as filter condition.
- LIMIT: Operator for limiting the number of output rows (e.g., TOP 10).
- ORDER BY: Operator for sorting output rows.
- GROUP BY: Operator for grouping and aggregation.
- HAVING: Operator for filtering with predicates on top of grouping and aggregation.
- JOIN: Operator for joining two or more tables. Join type suffix (e.g., INNER) may be added.
- DISTINCT: Operator for duplicate elimination.
- FILTER: Operator for filtering with predicates (e.g., WHERE conditions).
- MERGE AGGREGATION: Operator for merging the results of multiple parallel groupings and aggregations.
- UNION ALL: Operator for producing union-all of input relations.
- MATERIALIZED UNION ALL: Operator for producing union-all of input relations with intermediate result materialization.
- BTREE INDEX JOIN: Operator for joining input relations through B-tree index searches. Join type suffix can be added.
- CPBTREE INDEX JOIN: Operator for joining input relations through CPB-tree index searches. Join type suffix can be added.
- HASH JOIN: Operator for joining input relations through probing hash tables built on the fly. Join type suffix can be added.
- NESTED LOOP JOIN: Operator for joining input relations through nested looping. Join type suffix can be added.
- MIXED INVERTED INDEX JOIN: Operator for joining an input relation of row store format with a column table without format conversion using an inverted index of the column table. Join type suffix can be added.
- BTREE INDEX SEARCH: Table access through a B-tree index search.
- CPBTREE INDEX SEARCH: Table access through a CPB-tree index search.
- TABLE SCAN: Table access through scanning.
- AGGR TABLE: Operator for aggregating the base table directly.
- MONITOR SEARCH: Monitoring view access through search.
- MONITOR SCAN: Monitoring view access through scanning.

- SUBTREE_COST
  Weighted cost of the operation in the execution plan.

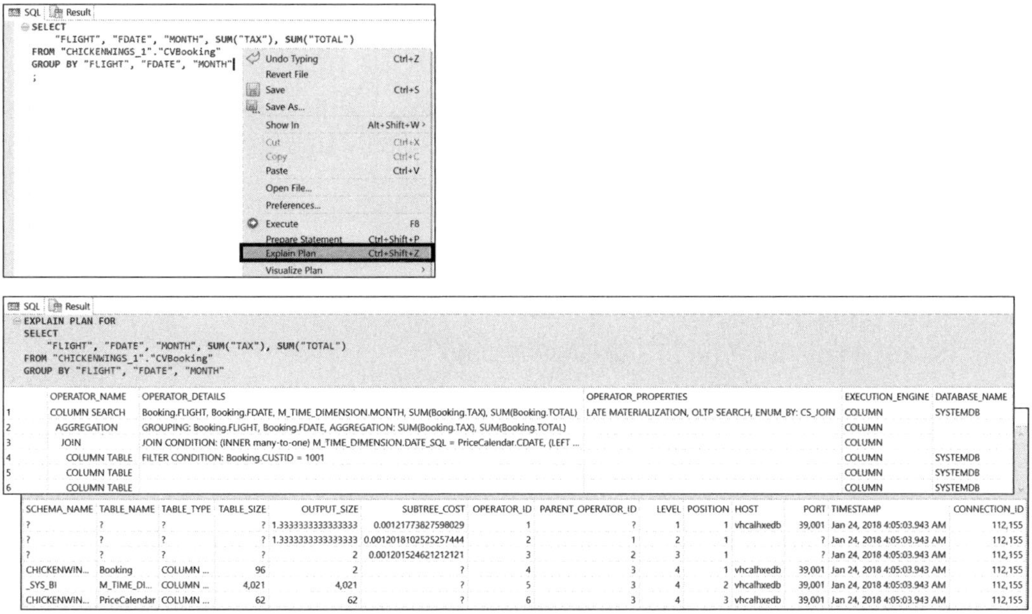

Figure 9.31 Explain Plan

The other columns that are part of EXPLAIN PLAN are as follows:

- EXECUTION ENGINE
  Row or column database engine used to perform the operation. Note that certain SQL operations may be available only in row or column engines.
- DATABASE NAME
  Name of the tenant database (relevant for multitenant databases).
- SCHEMA NAME, TABLE NAME & TABLE TYPE
  List of database tables accessed by the SQL query.
- TABLE TYPE
  Type of the database table (row-store or column-store tables).
- HOST
  SAP HANA node (host), where the table is physically located depending on table partitions.
- TABLE SIZE
  Total number of records in the table.

- `OUTPUT SIZE`
  Total number of result records for the step.
- `OPERATOR ID`
  Sequential number for the steps.
- `PARENT OPERATOR ID`
  Parent in the tree structure. For example, step 3 is the parent of steps 4, 5, and 6, which also means that step 3 can be executed only after steps 4, 5, and 6 are completed.
- `LEVEL`
  Level of the steps in the tree structure.

9.4.4 Plan Visualizer in SAP HANA Studio

As the name suggests, PlanViz in SAP HANA Studio displays the actual plan executed for the SQL query and provides significant insight that is valuable for performance optimization.

> **Note**
>
> The Analyze SQL option in SAP HANA database explorer discussed in Section 9.4.2 is a replacement for the PlanViz tool in SAP HANA Studio. However, as of SAP HANA 2.0 SP 03, the PlanViz tool has more options (e.g., network data transfers) for performance analysis.

To use the PlanViz tool, open the SQL Editor in SAP HANA Studio, and enter the SQL query to evaluate. Right-click on the SQL query, and choose **Visualize Plan • Execute** to generate and display the graphical representation of the SQL query execution plan, as shown in Figure 9.32.

> **Note**
>
> If you're not in the **SAP HANA PlanViz** perspective, it will prompt you to switch to this perspective.

PlanViz displays the performance summary and graphical representation of the executed plan as discussed next.

The **Overview** tab provides a summary of the executed plan with the following details:

- **Time**
  - **Compilation**: Time taken to compile the SQL query.
  - **Execution**: Time taken to execute the query (excluding compile time).
- **Context**
  - **SQL Query**: Executed SQL query.
  - **System**: SAP HANA host/node where the SQL query was executed (relevant for multinode scale-out systems).
  - **Memory Allocated**: Total dynamic memory used for query execution.

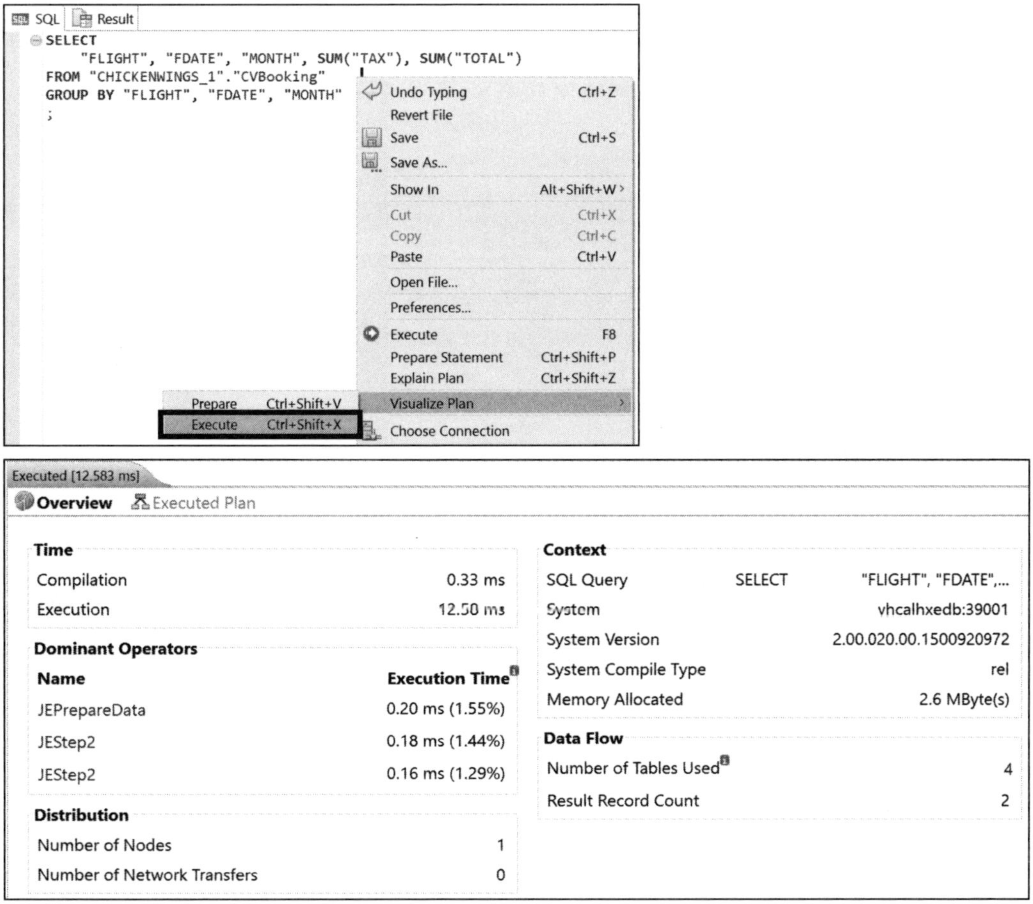

Figure 9.32 Plan Visualization in SAP HANA Studio

- **Dominant Operators**
  The top three dominant operators based on execution time. These operators should be analyzed for potential performance improvement. Clicking the operators will display additional details in the execution plan.
- **Data Flow**
  - **Number of Tables used**: Total number of database tables engaged during SQL query execution. Click on the number of tables to display the **Tables Used** screen, as shown in Figure 9.33. The list of tables accessed includes temporary tables created during query execution. Double-clicking on the table name displays the data access operations for the table in the **Operator List** tab, which reveals whether filters are pushed down to the table and/or whether desired tables are engaged in joins.

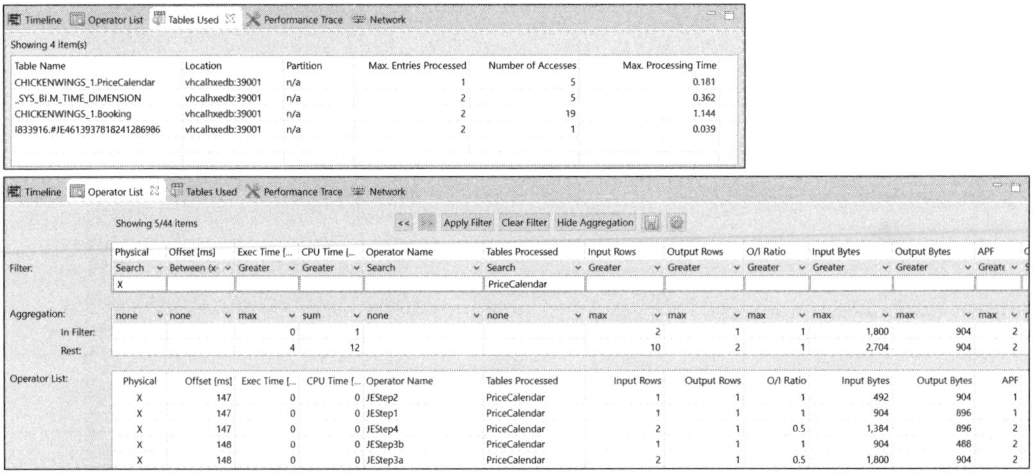

Figure 9.33 Plan Visualization: Tables Used

  - **Maximum Rows Processed**: The maximum number of rows processed by the query. This is usually the maximum number of rows fetched from a table, unless there is a Cartesian product of two tables, which may produce more records than the two tables.
  - **Result Record Count**: Total number of result records returned during query execution.
- **Distribution**
  - **Number of Nodes**: Total number of nodes/hosts involved in the query execution. For a single node system, it will be **1**; for a distributed system, it will depend on the physical location of the tables or table partitions in the scale-out system.

- **Number of Network Transfers**: Amount of data transfer between the SAP HANA nodes/hosts in a distributed system. This usually occurs for operations (e.g., join) between tables/table partitions physically stored in different SAP HANA nodes.

Details of the network transfers are available in the **Network** display. Pay attention to the network transfers with high runtime and/or high memory. Network transfers can be eliminated by co-locating the tables/table partitions in the same SAP HANA host.

The **Executed Plan** tab displays the graphical representation of the executed plan for the SQL query. The plan can be traversed from top to bottom to explore plan details, and expanding each node reveals further details about them. Depending on the complexity of the query, the plan visualization may be significantly complex and challenging to traverse.

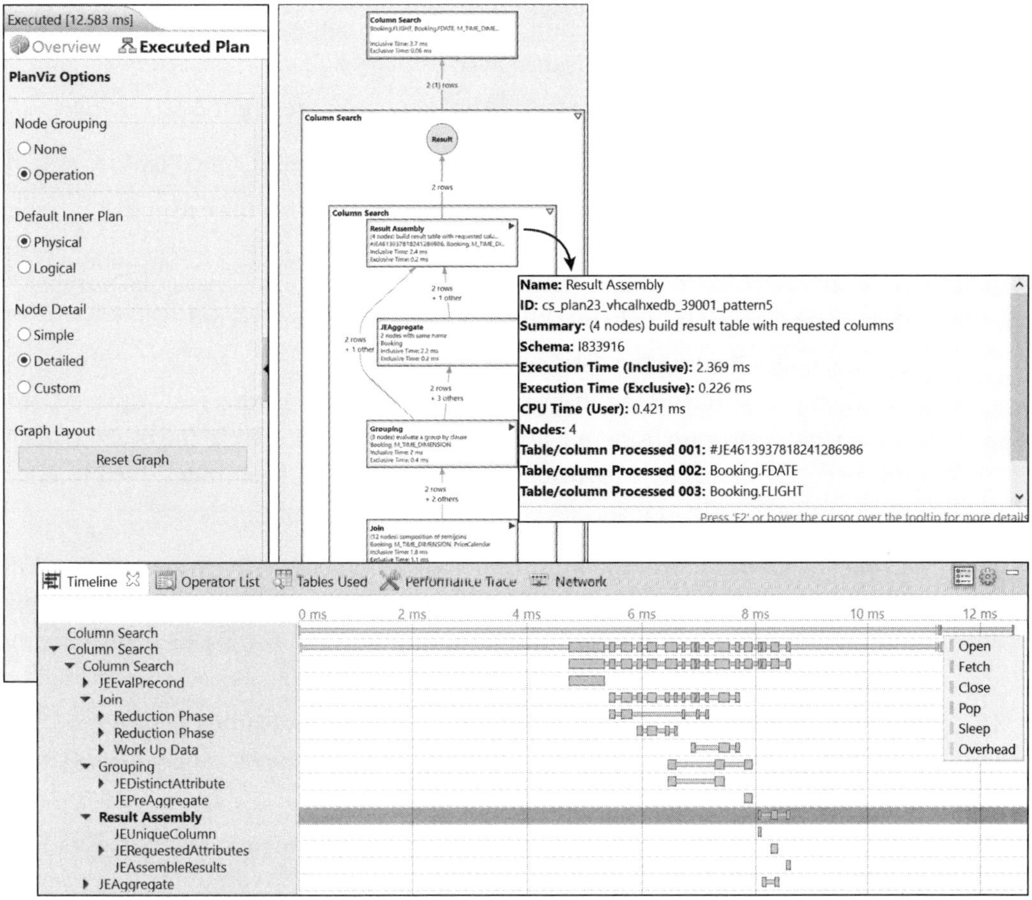

Figure 9.34 Plan Visualization: Executed Plan

Several **PlanViz Options** are available on this tab to simplify visualization and to help in understanding the plan better:

- **Node Grouping**
  - **None**: No grouping. All nodes are displayed.
  - **Operation**: Grouping of nodes by various operations.
- **Default Inner Plan**:
  - **Physical**: Displays the actual operations that occurred during the query execution and contains in-depth information about the runtime behavior.
  - **Logical**: Displays a high-level logical view of the estimated plan.
- **Node Detail**:
  - **Simple**: Only the operation name is displayed.
  - **Detailed**: Detailed information, such as table names, inclusive and exclusive operation time, and so on, is displayed.
  - **Custom**: Display can be customized based on user preferences.

There are two other important pieces of information to understand PlanViz:

- **The actual number of records flowing between nodes vs. the estimated number of records flow**
  For example, as illustrated in Figure 9.34, if you see 2(1), then the actual number of records transferred is 2, whereas the estimated number of records was 1
- **Parallel nodes feeding the data set**
  For example, as illustrated in Figure 9.34, if 2 rows + 1 others is displayed, this means that 2 rows are from one node and 1 row is coming from the other. Usually this occurs if the table is partitioned and no filter has been mentioned to effectively prune the partitions.

The **Timeline** view is one of the most useful views to analyze the executed plan. The **Timeline** view displays the sequence of operations that occurred during the plan execution with the X-axis displaying the execution time and the Y-axis displaying the list of operators in a tree structure, as shown in Figure 9.34.

The timeline display is available as part of the SAP HANA **PlanViz** perspective. This can also be enabled in SAP HANA Studio by choosing **Windows • Show View • Other**, searching for “timeline”, and then selecting **OK** to proceed.

By looking at the **Timeline** view, you can find out the following:

- List of operators executing in parallel (or serial) and the interdependency between these operators. This may be a pointer to inefficiency (if serial) in the model.
- The size of the operator is also an indicator of the bottleneck. Focus should be on the top five big blocks (operator) in the plan visualization.
- In addition, look for the time spent on the network data transfer node.

9.5 Summary

In this chapter, we explained the approach and tools to debug source code, analyze performance bottlenecks, and troubleshoot applications. We started with debugging database objects, such as calculation views and stored procedures, followed by debugging Java, Node.js, and HTML5 application code. Next, we discussed the process of enabling SQL and performance traces in the SAP HANA database. These database trace files and SAP HANA tools, including Analyze SQL, `EXPLAIN PLAN`, and PlanViz, can be used to figure out the actual bottleneck before modifying queries or models.

In the next chapter, we'll move on to discuss the deployment of SAP HANA XS Advanced applications and promoting/transporting applications from a development to a production system landscape.

Chapter 10
Deploying Your Application

In this chapter, you'll learn how to deploy an application and transport it though a system landscape.

Now that you have a working SAP HANA application, the tests you wrote are all running green, and extensive testing is complete, you're ready to unleash the destructive creativity of the end users onto the app.

For our example, we used the SAP Web IDE for SAP HANA to build the database module and to run the application and frontend modules, which resulted in a personal version of the application being deployed on the platform for you to test. To make the application productively available we can either first build a multi-target application (MTA) archive (*.mtar*) and then deploy it to a target space, or we can deploy the application directly from a folder structure. In both cases, we can choose to deploy from a local file system or from a Git repository. As the deployment from a folder structure requires the (manual) preparation of the deployment descriptor and the *MANIFEST.MF* file, which we'll look at more closely later, let's first discuss the MTAR build process, which automatically creates them for us.

10.1 Building the Multi-Target Application Archive

Before building the MTA archive, you should review the version number that has been defined in the application development descriptor (*mta.yaml*), as this will be reflected in the build result. As the version number isn't incremented automatically, you should change it manually for subsequent versions of your application. Nevertheless, the adjustment isn't mandatory for every deployment, so you can fix errors and still build and deploy an MTAR with the same version number.

In SAP Web IDE for SAP HANA, click on the root folder of your project, and choose **Build** from the context menu, as shown in Figure 10.1.

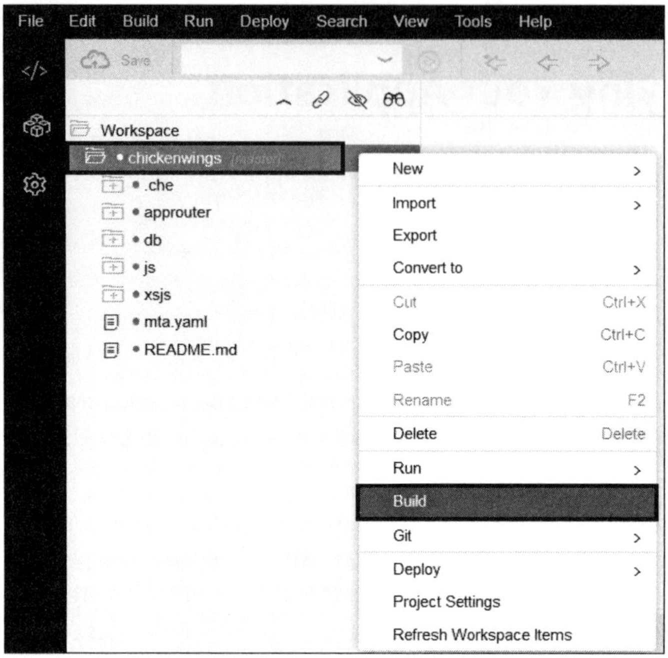

Figure 10.1 Building the MTAR from the SAP Web IDE for SAP HANA

Depending on the size of the application, the build process may take a while as, for example, dependencies must be downloaded. You can follow the progress in the console at the bottom of the screen, which should return a message such as **(Builder) Build of /<projectName> completed successfully.**

As soon as the build finishes successfully, you can find the MTAR file in the **mta_archives** folder in the SAP Web IDE for SAP HANA, as shown in Figure 10.2.

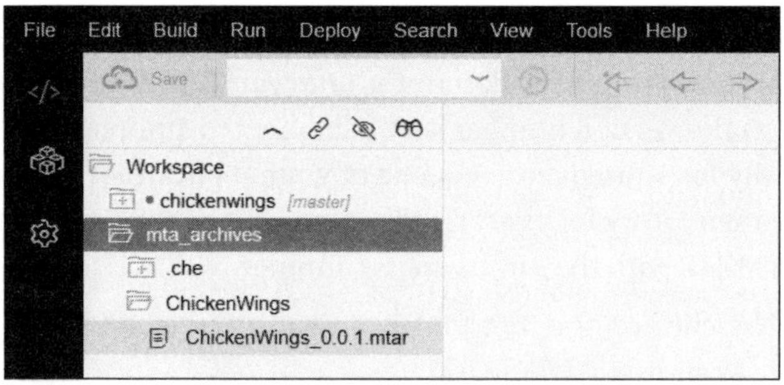

Figure 10.2 MTARs in the Project Folder Structure

The build MTARs are basically renamed Java archives (*.jar*), containing a folder for each module in the MTA, which holds the deployable module archives. For SAPUI5/Node.js applications, you find a *.zip* archive containing the application code, and for Java modules, you find a web application archive (*.war*) file.

In addition to the module archives, the *.mtar* file contains a *META-INF* folder with the following metadata information, necessary for the deployment:

- First, we have the *MANIFEST.MF* file (see Listing 10.1), which contains a list of the application's modules and the corresponding resource configuration files that hold the service creation or service binding information.

  ```
  Manifest-Version: 1.0
  Created-By: SAP WebIDE

  Name: js/data.zip
  MTA-Module: js
  Content-Type: application/zip
  [...]
  ```

  Listing 10.1 MANIFEST.MF Content Example

- Second, the MTA *deployment descriptor* (*mtad.yaml*) is generated out of the *development descriptor* (*mta.yaml*) during the build process. In principle, both descriptors contain the same information (e.g., the MTA version number and ID) as the contained modules and their dependencies as well as the services that have to be created and/or bound to the application modules. The development descriptor might contain build parameters and different types of information that are only used during the build process, whereas the deployment descriptor is used with the translated information by the deploy service to correctly execute the deployment process.

Building without the SAP Web IDE for SAP HANA

If you decide to develop MTAs with another development environment, you can use the MTA archive builder to build the *.mtar* file out of your development sources.

You can download the builder from the SAP Download Center (MTA Archive Builder) and see how it's used in the official documentation: *https://bit.ly/2ydfQ4E*.

10.2 Deployment Process

Now that we've prepared the MTAR for deployment, let's explore how the deployment process works and what options are available to deploy the application.

Regardless of the tool used to deploy the application archive, the following deployment process is done by the `deploy-service`, which is present by default in the `SAP` space:

1. The `deploy-service` receives an *.mtar* file.
2. The *.mtar* files consistency is checked.
3. The existence of referenced services is validated, and new or missing ones are created.
4. The deployment order of the contained modules is determined via the configured dependencies in the deployment descriptor (*mtad.yaml*).
5. The modules are deployed (pushed) in the determined order.
6. The required services are bound to the deployed modules, and the environment variables are populated.

We'll now see how this is done in the SAP Web IDE and using the SAP XS Advanced Command-Line Interface (XSA CLI).

10.2.1 Deployment via the SAP Web IDE for SAP HANA

As mentioned before, the easiest way to deploy the MTAR is the use of the SAP Web IDE for SAP HANA. Clicking on the *.mtar* file, you can proceed directly to the deployment by choosing a **Deploy** option from the context menu or from SAP Web IDE's menu bar, as shown in Figure 10.3.

You can either deploy the application to the current SAP HANA XS Advanced system or to a Cloud Foundry tenant in the SAP Cloud Platform. In both cases, you're required to choose the organization and space to which the applications get pushed.

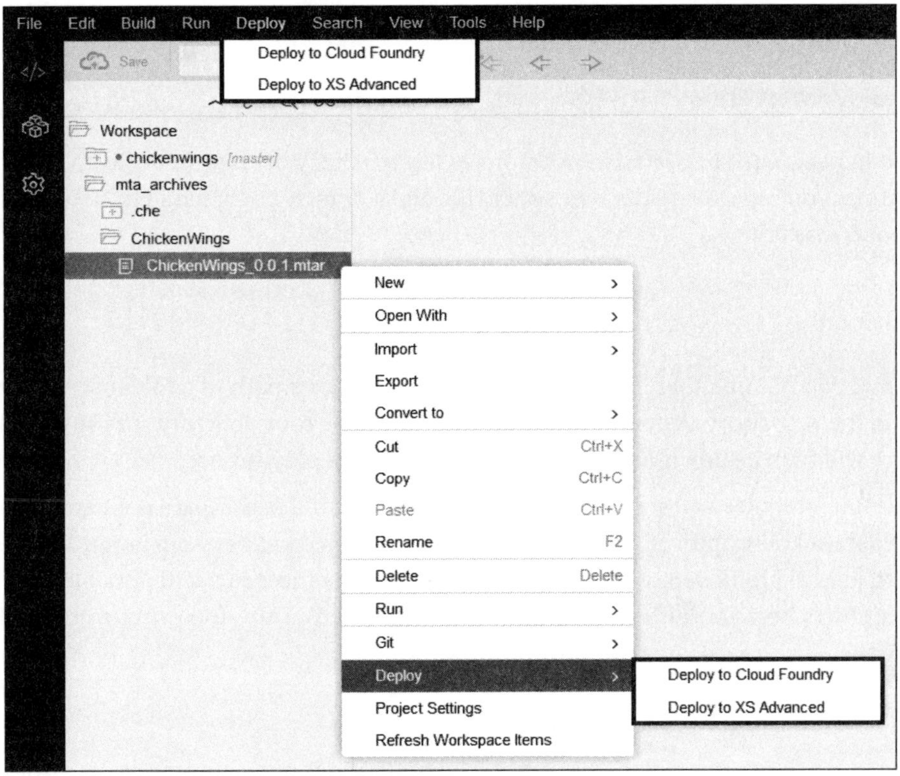

Figure 10.3 Deploying the MTAR from SAP Web IDE for SAP HANA

10.2.2 SAP HANA XS Advanced Command-Line Interface

To have more control over the deployment process and to get better feedback about the progress, we recommend downloading the *.mtar* file (choose **Export** from the context menu) and using the XSA CLI for the deployment activities. In this section, besides the deployment, we'll also discuss how to manage and analyze failed deployments, how to use a deployment extension descriptor and finally how to undeploy an application.

Deploy

The `xs deploy` command offers additional options and output when deploying the MTAR to an SAP HANA XS Advanced system. After you've downloaded the file from SAP Web IDE, make sure that you're logged in (`xs login`) and that you target the space in which you want to deploy the application (xs target). The basic deployment is then started with the following command:

```
xs deploy <mtarFile>
```

If you instead want to use an MTAR from a Git repository or want to deploy a folder structure, you can specify the repository URL and a branch or tag name to be used as the source, as follows:

```
xs deploy <sourcePath> --git-uri https://chickengit.corp/chickenwings.git --
git-ref 1.0
```

The sourcePath can either be the location of an MTAR or a path to a folder structure within the repository. A dot (.) refers to the repository's root directory. The specified source will then be downloaded and deployed by the deploy service.

By default, modules and services are deployed without the namespace defined in the development descriptor (ID). Depending on how crowded your system is, it might be a good idea to prefix deployed modules and service instances to avoid possible naming conflicts between different MTAs as demonstrated in the following command using the --use-namespaces option:

```
xs deploy <mtarFile> --use-namespaces
```

When using the --use-namespaces option, the prefixing is done automatically during the deployment for modules and for services, unless you use the --no-namespaces-for-services option in addition to exclude the created service instances.

During the deployment, the XSA CLI will output the process status and hopefully terminate with a success message of **Process finished**, as shown in Figure 10.4. In that case, you can test the deployed application components and services.

```
 Application "ChickenWings.approuter" staged
 Starting application "ChickenWings.approuter"...
 1 of 1 instances running (1 running)
 Application "ChickenWings.approuter" started and available at "https://hana.chickenwings.corp:51143"
 Publishing public provided dependencies for application "ChickenWings.approuter"...
 Creating subscriptions...
 Registering service URLs...
 Deleting discontinued subscriptions...
 Deleting discontinued published dependencies...
 Unregistering discontinued service URLs...
 Creating service brokers...
 Updating subscribers...
Process finished
```

Figure 10.4 Successful Deployment

Manage and Analyze Failed Deployments

If anything went wrong during the deployment, the deploy service will stop the process and give you the following options for troubleshooting (see Figure 10.5):

- Retry the deployment
- Abort the deployment
- Download logs

```
Unexpected error: Async execution has failed
Use "xs deploy -i 78254 -a retry" to retry the process
Use "xs deploy -i 78254 -a abort" to abort the process
Use "xs dmol -i 78254" to download the logs of the process
```

Figure 10.5 Failed Deployment

To interact with the deployment process, you need the deploy operation ID, which is either returned by the deploy service in case of an issue, or you can find your process in the list of all stopped deployments via the following command:

```
xs mta-ops
```

The output would look similar to the one in Figure 10.6.

```
$ xs mta-ops

Getting active multi-target app operations in org "CHW" / space "BCN" as MASTER...
Found active operations:

id     type     mta id         status   started at                    started by
-----------------------------------------------------------------------------------
78254  DEPLOY   ChickenWings   ERROR    Apr 1, 2018 23:59:59 PM       FILIPPO
```

Figure 10.6 Active Deployment Operations

You can retry the deployment as well, which is useful, for example, if you forgot to create a service instance up-front that the application depends on. Create the missing service instance, and then use the following command:

```
xs deploy -i <operationId> -a retry
```

If you want to restart the whole deployment, the ongoing process that has been stopped has to be aborted first. If you issue a new deployment command, you'll be asked by the deploy service if you want to abort the ongoing process. Alternatively, you can use the following abort option manually:

```
xs deploy -i <operationId> -a abort
```

In any case, you want to look at what exactly went wrong during the deployment. If the output of the deploy service isn't very helpful, you can download the full deploy logs to your local workstation using this code:

```
xs download-mta-op-logs -i <operationId>
```

By default, the logs are placed in the current folder, but you can change that using the `-d <directory>` option.

Deployment Extension Descriptor

An important advantage of the XSA CLI deployment is that we can influence the application's configuration by providing an *extension descriptor* (*.mtaext*) to the deploy service.

Usually there are parameters for your application that change according to the environment they are deployed in. For example, application resources, such as memory disk space or active application instances, are different if the app runs in the development system or in production. In addition, some information simply shouldn't be stored in a code repository, such as application programming interface (API) keys or connection credentials.

With a deployment extension descriptor, we can change already-defined parameters and properties of modules and services to provide sensitive data exclusively during the deployment of an application.

The used *.mtaext* file has basically the same syntax and structure as the deployment descriptor. In the header, we specify the deployment descriptor ID we're planning to extend using the `extends` keyword. Subsequently, we specify the parameters and properties we want to overwrite with new values or create new ones. Let's look at the example in Listing 10.2.

```
_schema-version: '2.0'
ID: ChickenWings
version: 0.0.1
modules:
 - name: WeatherService
   type: nodejs
   properties:
     externalAccessToken: <DUMMY>
```

Listing 10.2 Development Descriptor (mta.yaml) Defining an External API Key

The `WeatherService` module uses an external API key, which is defined as a property with a dummy value. The extension file to overwrite the value would look like Listing 10.3.

```
_schema-version: '2.0'
ID: ChickenWings.productionConfiguration
extends: ChickenWings
modules:
 - name: WeatherService
   properties:
     externalAccessToken: 42
```

Listing 10.3 Deployment Extension Descriptor 42.mtaext with the Actual API Key

Protected Parameters and Properties

Properties and parameters can be defined as protected in the deployment descriptor metadata. If you observe that a value in the deployment extension descriptor doesn't get applied, check whether the parameter or property is marked with overwritable: false in the corresponding metadata section.

The extension is then applied by using the `-e` parameter together with the deploy command:

```
xs deploy <mtarFile> -e <extionsionFile>
```

Undeploy

You may want to get rid of an old or faulty MTA. In this case, the best strategy is to first look at all the installed MTAs in the current space (`xs mtas`), and then use the following command to undeploy a complete application:

```
xs undeploy <mtaId> --delete-services
```

The `--delete-services` is necessary to remove all created services, such as User Account and Authorization (UAA) and user-provided services. It also removes any SAP HANA Deployment Infrastructure (HDI) containers from the database that have been created by the deployment process.

Forgot to Delete the Services?

If you forgot to use the --delete-services option to remove the HDI containers of the MTA, you can still manually delete the service instances using xs services to individuate the HDI container and xs delete-service <serviceId> to remove it.

10.3 Transporting SAP HANA XS Advanced Applications

The process of bringing a developed application from the development environment to the test environment and later into the production environment is usually referred to as application transport or application lifecycle management. In the following sections, we'll look at the options available for transporting your application.

10.3.1 Manual Transport

What we defined in this chapter until now can be defined as the manual transport process, as shown in Figure 10.7. When you're happy with the application, you first initiate a build to compile the whole application into an MTAR, which is then manually deployed to the target environment using the SAP Web IDE for SAP HANA or XSA CLI.

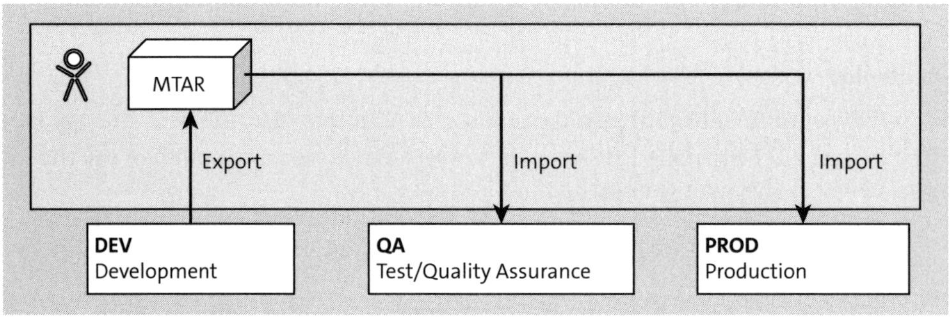

Figure 10.7 Manual Transport

As the name suggests, the steps are manual and suitable up to a certain number of deployments. If the development of an SAP HANA XS Advanced application increases, you might want to evaluate the usage of one of the options discussed in the following sections.

10.3.2 Transport Using the Change and Transport System

The Change and Transport System (CTS) is usually used in an SAP system landscape to transport ABAP objects from the development environment to the corresponding quality and test systems. It can also be configured to support the transport of generated MTAR files, as shown in Figure 10.8, to defined SAP HANA XS Advanced target systems. In principle, this works as follows:

1. Manual export of the MTAR file from the development environment.
2. Manual upload and assignment to a transport request in the CTS system.
3. Release the transport request.
4. Trigger the import to the target system, which starts an automatic deployment.

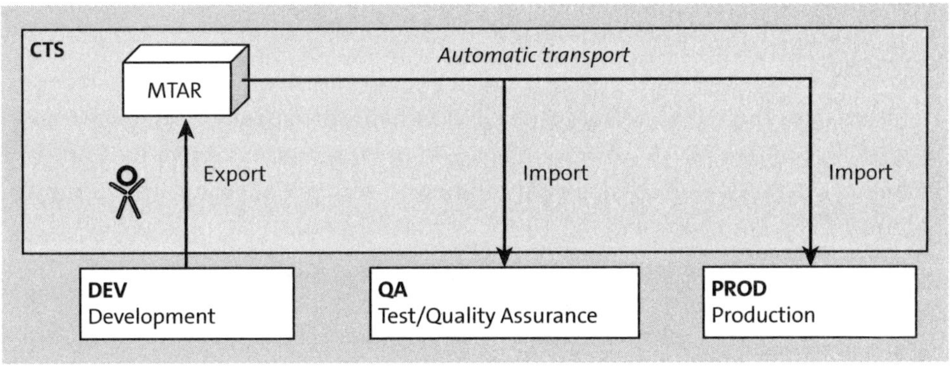

Figure 10.8 CTS Transport

With the CTS-based approach, the transport follows the previously defined routes from one system to another and can be centrally monitored, and the release of transports can be controlled before they are executed.

A drawback is the manual MTAR export from the development system and attachment to a transport request. However, we expect to see an automated integration of those steps in the future, which will make this solution even more interesting and worthy to consider, especially if you already have a CTS system in your landscape to manage ABAP-related transports.

To give a high-level idea of the configuration of the CTS system, the steps include the creation of HTTP(s) destinations from the CTS system to the target SAP HANA XS Advanced systems, configuring the transport organizer Web UI, enabling SAP HANA XS Advanced as an application type, creating the transport landscape with development, test, and production, and defining the transport route the application should take.

You can find a detailed step by step guide here: *https://bit.ly/2MldHah*.

10.3.3 Continuous Integration

Well, we could probably start writing a second book about Continuous Integration (CI), but we'll give you a short overview of the topic and how you can use it not only for transportation purposes but also for the whole development process of native SAP HANA XS Advanced applications.

The idea behind the CI process is to regularly merge software changes and new functions made by different team members for the same application and automate the build, test, and deployment processes to give the developer quick feedback about the code quality.

Unfortunately, there is no ready-made environment that already implements the CI process for SAP HANA XS Advanced, but SAP provides an extensive best practice, including a detailed step-by-step guide on how to set up the technical environment at *https://bit.ly/2JXoJUy*.

Let's take a brief look at how it works, as demonstrated by Figure 10.9.

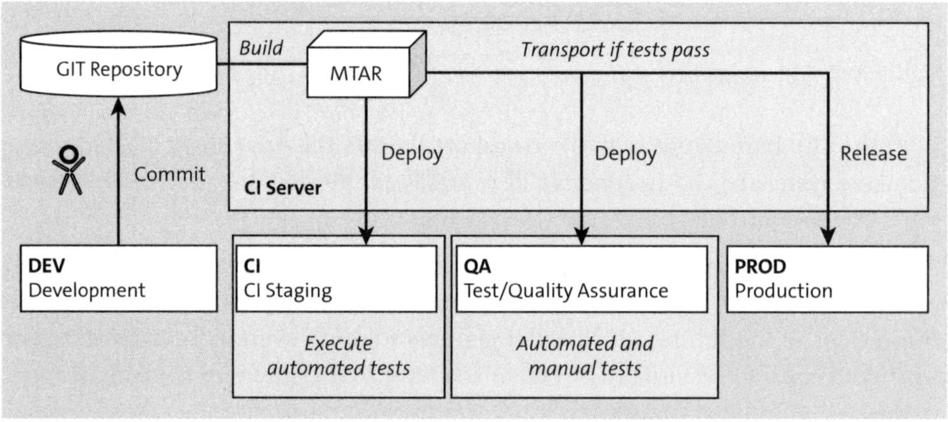

Figure 10.9 CI Process

The first step is to establish a common code repository where the application code is stored and to which all changes are committed by the developers. For MTAs, we use the already-introduced Git repository.

If we want to contribute to the application, we check out a working copy of the baseline, which is the common code base currently under development. In Git terms, this would correspond to the development or feature branch. In the local environment, which, in our case, could be the SAP Web IDE for SAP HANA, we hack the new functionality, bug fix, Easter egg, or whatever.

Once finished, the code is tested in the local environment by executing the unit tests and running the application.

If we're convinced by the test results, the code can be committed back to the central Git repository. Before the code is actually merged into the baseline, a code review can be enforced using Gerrit, so the test results must also convince the reviewer. If so, the code is merged into the baseline.

After our code reaches the baseline, a build is automatically executed from there by a CI server that watches the code repository. In the best practice guide, a Jenkins server is used in conjunction with the scriptable MTA archive builder introduced earlier. Besides the automation aspect, using a dedicated build server also ensures independence from the development environment, which might be "contaminated" with special configuration.

After the build is successful, the *.mtar* file is automatically transported to a test or quality assurance (QA) environment for automated and manual tests, ideally under production conditions. The test environment can be a separate space on the same SAP HANA system or a dedicated server.

If the tests are again successful, the application transport to the production environment can be triggered. This can happen again automatically after all tests are passed or manually by a delivery manager. In addition, the released version can be archived in a repository for later reference and distribution.

10.3.4 Outlook: Native Transport

The last option we want to bring to your attention is the possibility of a native application transport between different SAP HANA XS Advanced systems, as shown in Figure 10.10.

For the SAP HANA extended applications, classic model (SAP HANA XS) application, SAP HANA application lifecycle management offers the possibility to automatically export, transport, and import an application without the need for an external system such as CTS. Especially for SAP HANA-only landscapes, this seems to be an easy and straightforward transportation solution.

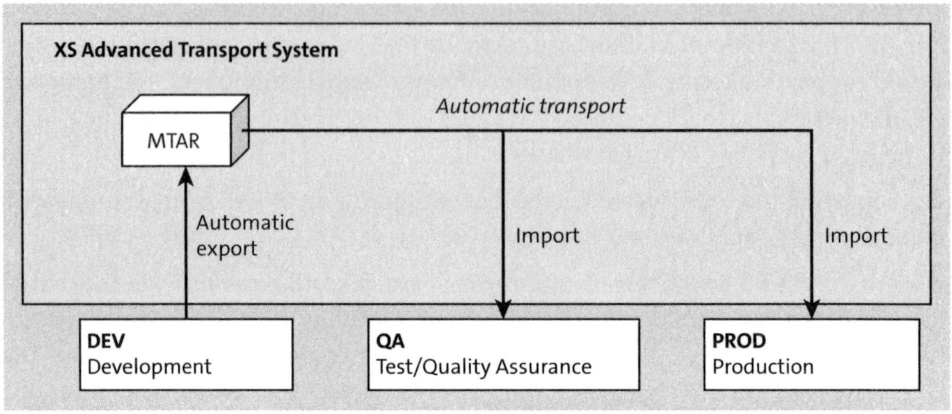

Figure 10.10 Native SAP HANA XS Advanced Transport

Unfortunately, at the time of writing (Q1, 2018), the support for SAP HANA XS Advanced applications is still under development, but we think it's worth taking a look at this option as soon as it's released as an out-of-the-box transport option without the need for a dedicated transport system.

10.4 Summary

In the first part of this chapter, we discussed how to prepare an application for deployment and transportation by using the build function of the SAP Web IDE for SAP HANA and which options are available to deploy the MTAR. The deployment with SAP Web IDE for SAP HANA can be done directly after the build, but using the XSA CLI provides more control over the deployment process and a better output for troubleshooting.

Finally, we discussed the different options to transport an SAP HANA XS Advanced application from the development environment through the system landscape. Besides the manual process, we covered the possibility of using a CTS system, a CI setup, and the planned native transport mechanism.

Appendices

A Migrating an SAP HANA XS Application to SAP HANA XS Advanced 573

B Additional Resources 593

C The Authors 595

Appendix A
Migrating an SAP HANA XS Application to SAP HANA XS Advanced

This appendix introduces the tools for migrating an SAP HANA extended application services, classic model (SAP HANA XS) application to the SAP HANA extended application services, advanced model (SAP HANA XS Advanced). But first, we should ask ourselves this question: *Why migrate?*

SAP HANA XS has been available since SAP HANA SPS 05 for SAP HANA 1.0 (Q1 of 2013). SAP HANA XS Advanced became available with SAP HANA SPS 11 for SAP HANA 1.0 (Q4 of 2015). If you've developed using the SAP HANA XS engine model, you may wonder why you should move your application to SAP HANA SAP HANA XS Advanced.

There are different reasons to consider:

- **New functionalities**
  New SAP HANA applications and development features will only be delivered now for SAP HANA XS Advanced.
- **New security model**
  With the SAP HANA XS Advanced model, there is no more direct connection between application user and database user. Instead, SAP HANA XS Advanced uses a technical user for consuming database artifacts.
- **New deployment model**
  The multi-target application (MTA) in the *.mtar* format is used instead of delivery units.

Besides the last one in the list, which has more technical impact, the first two points also have business relevance. In these times of accelerated digitalization of business processes, not being able to enhance our application because we can't take advantage of the new application framework features can be critical. In the same way, it's fundamental to make sure that our application follows the security standards that best practices recommend.

The last motivation for migrating our application is to answer this question: *How long will SAP support SAP HANA XS?*

SAP HANA XS was deprecated in July 2017 with the release of SAP HANA 2.0 SPS 02. It's now in maintenance mode, probably for the next four to five years, which means we should start to think how and when to migrate our application now (see SAP Note 2465027 for more information).

There are two main tools for supporting the migration of an SAP HANA XS application into an SAP HANA XS Advanced application:

- Migration tool of SAP HANA Studio
- SAP HANA XS Advanced Migration Assistant

In the next sections, we'll discuss those two tools in detail and the steps required to migrate an application.

A.1 Migration Steps

Migrating an SAP HANA XS application to SAP HANA XS Advanced is a multistep process. Although tools are available to support some of the steps, there isn't a tool that can automatize all the steps, so some manual activities are required.

We can organize the migration steps in three macro categories:

- **Preparation steps**
  The main activity for the preparation steps is the manual migration of the following artifacts using SAP HANA Studio:
  - Script-based calculation views
  - Attribute views
  - Analytic views
  - Analytic privileges
  - Application function library (AFL) models (*.aflpmml*)
  - Decision tables (*.hdbruldec*)

  Script-based calculation views, attribute views, and analytic views must be converted into graphical calculation views (**.calculationview*). AFL models must be converted into `AFLLang` procedures (**:hdbafllangprocedure*), and decision tables must be converted into graphical calculation views or equivalent SQL artifacts such as procedures (decision tables have been replaced by the *SAP HANA Rules Framework* in SAP HANA XS Advanced).

We'll see later the tool that SAP has made available for converting these artifacts using SAP HANA Studio.

- **Migration steps**
  Migration steps can be performed with the help of the *SAP HANA XS Advanced Migration Assistant*. This tool will convert the delivery unit of the old SAP HANA XS application into the new SAP HANA XS Advanced format. It also provides a report that helps during the migration project by creating a list of required manual activities to perform.
- **Adjustment steps**
  Unfortunately, the SAP HANA XS Advanced Migration Assistant can't automatize all the migration steps. Some manual activities are required, mainly for the migration of the security concept that is completely different between the two application models. However, the SAP HANA XS Advanced Migration Assistant will support the application development team with the guidelines for performing these manual activities.

A.2 SAP HANA Studio Migration Tool

If you want to move an SAP HANA XS application to SAP HANA XS Advanced, you first need to convert script-based calculation views, attribute views, and analytic views to graphical calculation views.

> **Note**
>
> The steps from this section are summarized in a document available with SAP Note 2325817.

You can use the tool with SAP HANA Studio when the SAP HANA version is at least on SP 11. To begin, follow these steps:

1. Open SAP HANA Studio, and display the **Quick View** (**Window • Show View • SAP HANA • Quick View**), as shown in Figure A.1.

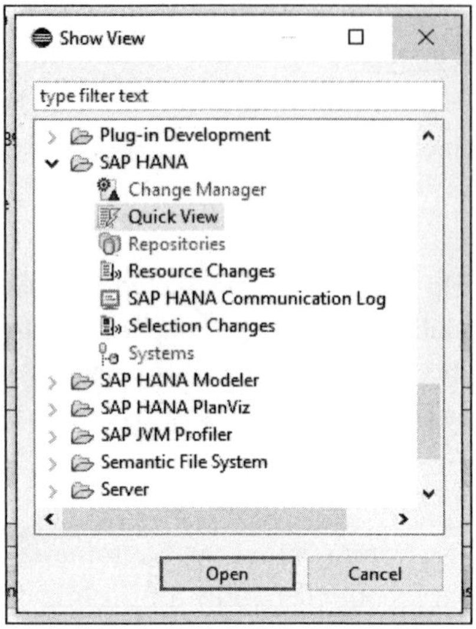

Figure A.1 Opening Quick View in SAP HANA Studio

2. In the **Quick View** functions available, select the **Migrate**, as shown in Figure A.2.

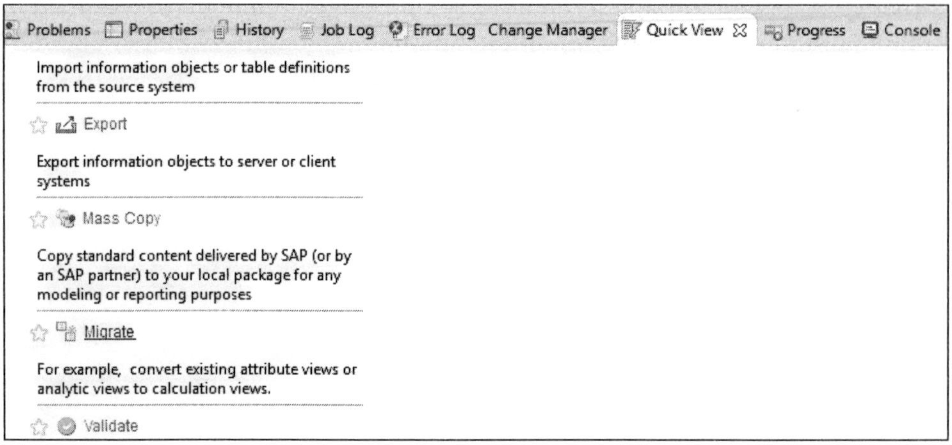

Figure A.2 Migrate Function in Quick View

3. SAP HANA Studio opens a popup where you can select the migration type you want to perform (see Figure A.3):
   - **Attribute views and analytic views to calculation views**.

- **Script-based calculation views to graphical calculation views and table functions.**
- **Classical XML-based analytic privileges to SQL analytic privileges.**

Note

SQL analytic privileges are available since SAP HANA 1.0 SPS 10, and you can maintain both XML and SQL analytic privileges in SAP HANA XS applications, but SAP HANA XS Advanced with SAP Web IDE for SAP HANA supports only SQL analytic privileges.

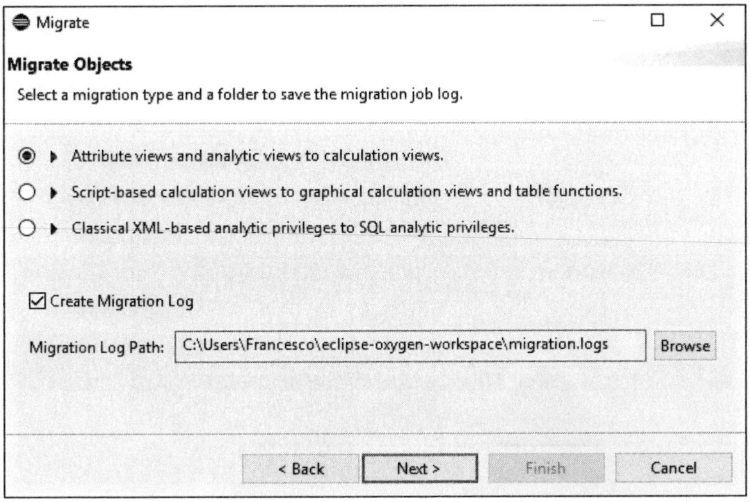

Figure A.3 Migration types in SAP HANA Studio Migrate Function

4. For our example, we'll convert one attribute view to a graphical calculation view, so select **Attribute views and analytic views to calculation views**.
5. The wizard opens a new screen, where you can drag and drop the artifacts that you want to migrate.
6. You can convert the views directly into the source package (the wizard will delete the attribute or analytic view and create a new graphical calculation view), or you can select a new target package for the migrated objects.
7. You also can define the join order for attribute views:
   - **Outside in**: Joins are executed outside in, that is, from the fringes of the star schema to the inside (fact table).

  - **Inside out**: Joins are executed from the central table (the table containing the key fields) to the outside.
  - **Default:** The system will determine the most suitable join order.

8. In the **Inside Out** joins approach, the Join Engine is used, and in the **Outside In** approach, the OLAP engine is used. For conversion of attributes views not used in analytic views, the **Inside Out** approach should be used.
9. By selecting the **Activate objects after migration** checkbox, the new views will be activated automatically; otherwise, you must activate them manually (see Figure A.4). If you want to activate them manually, you'll have to activate the full package because the deletion of the converted attribute/analytic views must be activated as well to avoid the error related to the activation tentative of objects with the same name.

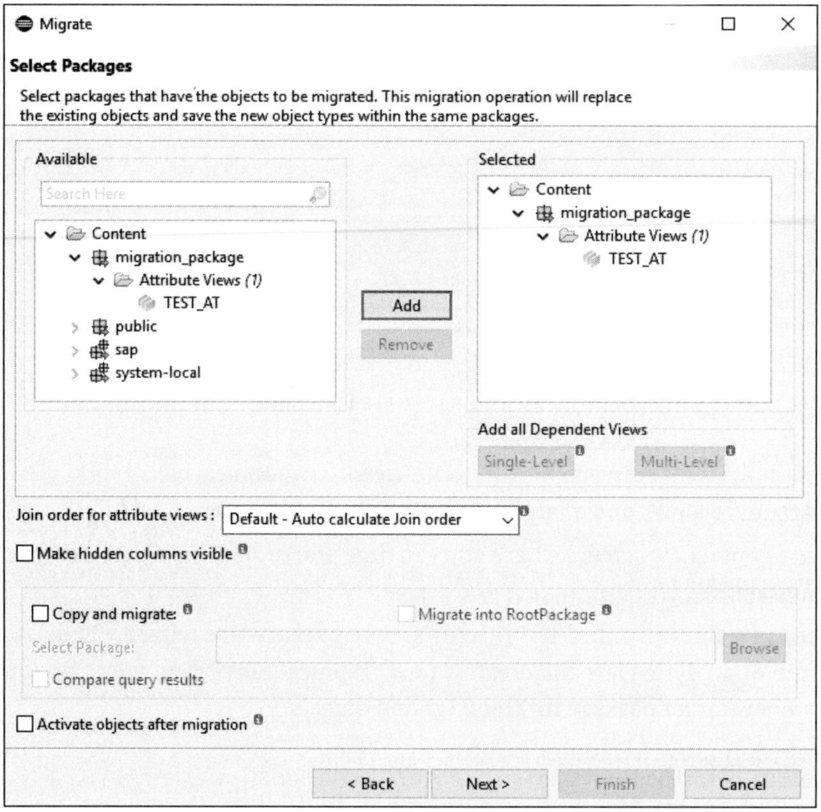

Figure A.4 Views Selection in SAP HANA Studio Migrate Function

A.3 SAP HANA XS Advanced Migration Assistant

The *SAP HANA XS Advanced Migration Assistant* is a client tool that you can install either on the SAP HANA appliance or on your local client (Windows or Linux), if it can connect to the SQL port of the SAP HANA system. This tool allows you to analyze one delivery unit to check the steps required for its migration to SAP HANA XS Advanced. It provides a report with the check results and automatically converts all the objects that it can process in a target package (MTA project) that you can install in the SAP Web IDE for SAP HANA of the system where you want to import the migrated application.

If your source SAP HANA system (the system that contains the delivery unit you want to migrate) has SPS 11 or higher, you can run the SAP HANA XS Advanced Migration Assistant with only the connection to the source SAP HANA system. If your source system has SPS 10 or SPS 09, you need an external SAP HANA system with SPS 11 or higher that acts as an *external parse system*.

You can download the SAP HANA XS Advanced Migration Assistant from the software download area of the SAP One Support Launchpad. Go to *https://launchpad.support.sap.com/#/softwarecenter/*, and search for "*XSAC MIGRATION*" (see Figure A.5).

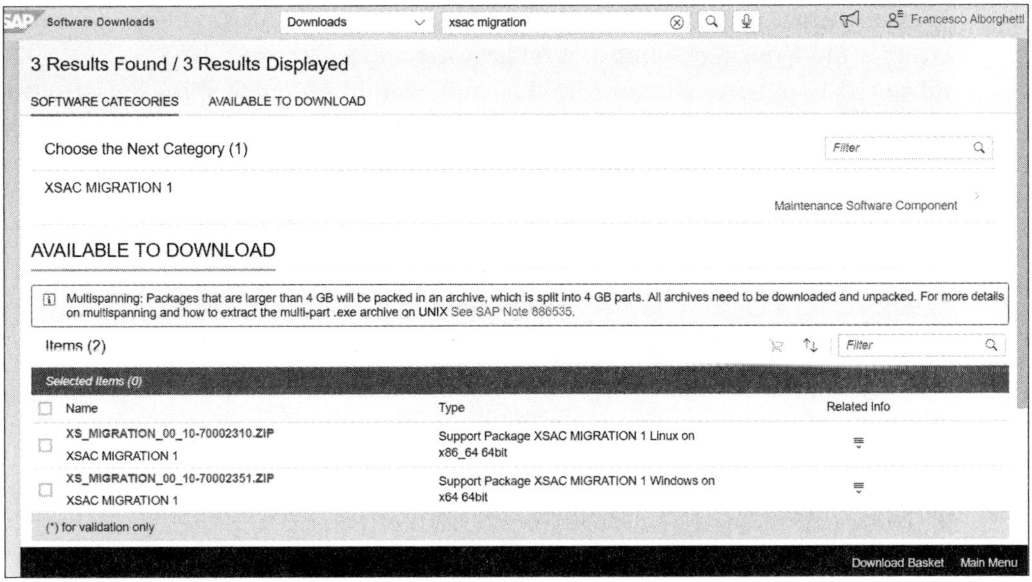

Figure A.5 SAP HANA XS Advanced Migration Assistant Installation Packages

There are two installation packages available: one for Windows and one for Linux. We'll use the package available for Windows. Let's see now how to install the SAP HANA XS Advanced Migration Assistant, the report that it provides to support a delivery unit migration, and the main options available when you execute it.

A.3.1 SAP HANA XS Advanced Migration Assistant Installation

To install the SAP HANA XS Advanced Migration Assistant, you must download the ZIP file and extract it in one folder of your client (e.g., *C:\XS_MIGRATION*).

To execute it, you need to perform the following setup activities:

- Configure the connection to the SAP HANA source system and to the external SAP HANA parse system (if used).
- Define a user in the SAP HANA systems with the required authorizations.
- Enable the SAP HANA parse system (or the source system if you aren't using a parse system) to execute the procedure **"SYS"."GET_OBJECTS_IN_DDL_STATEMENT"**.

Configure the Connection

To configure the connection to the source and parse SAP HANA systems, you must create a file named *.env* into the folder where you extracted the SAP HANA XS Advanced Migration Assistant with the configuration parameters. The downloaded package provides a file (*.env-template*) with template parameters. These parameters are required:

- `HANA_HOST=<HANA hostname>`
- `HANA_SQL_PORT=<HANA SQL port>`
- `HANA_USER=<HANA user>`
- `HANA_PASSWD=<HANA password>`
- `HANA_CERTIFICATE=</path/to/HTTPS/certificate/file>`

If you also need an external SAP HANA parsing system, you need to define the connection parameters for this system as well:

- `HANAEXT_HOST=<XSA hostname>`
- `HANAEXT_SQL_PORT=<HANA SQL port>`
- `HANAEXT_USER=<HANA username>`

- HANAEXT_PASSWD=<HANA password>
- HANAEXT_CERTIFICATE=</path/to/HTTPS/certificate/file>

Define a User with Authorizations

The database user for the SAP HANA XS Advanced Migration Assistant must have the privileges listed in Table A.1.

Privilege Type	Privileges
Object privileges	▪ _SYS_REPO.ACTIVE_CONTENT_TEXT: SELECT ▪ _SYS_REPO.ACTIVE_CONTENT_TEXT_CONTENT: SELECT ▪ _SYS_REPO.ACTIVE_OBJECT_TEXT: SELECT ▪ _SYS_REPO.ACTIVE_OBJECT_TEXT_CONTENT: SELECT ▪ _SYS_REPO.ACTIVE_TAGS: SELECT ▪ _SYS_BI.M_SCHEMA_MAPPING: SELECT ▪ _SYS_REPO.CATALOG_OBJECTS_CREATED_BY_REPOSITORY_ACTIVATIONS: SELECT ▪ SYS.SYNONYMS: SELECT ▪ SYS.GET_OBJECT_DEFINITION: EXECUTE ▪ SYS.TABLE_COLUMNS: SELECT ▪ SYS.TABLES: SELECT ▪ SYS.OBJECT_DEPENDENCIES: SELECT ▪ SYS.M_DATABASE: SELECT ▪ SYS.GRANTED_PRIVILEGES: SELECT ▪ SYS.GRANTED_ROLES: SELECT ▪ SYS.PROCEDURES: SELECT ▪ SYS.OBJECTS: SELECT ▪ SYS.REPOSITORY_REST: EXECUTE
System privileges	▪ CATALOG READ
Package privileges in migrated delivery unit	▪ REPO.READ

Table A.1 User Privileges for Executing the SAP HANA XS Advanced Migration Assistant

Enable GET_OBJECTS_IN_DDL_STATEMENT

To be able to use the SAP HANA XS Advanced Migration Assistant, you must add the following entry in the *indexserver.ini* SQLScript configuration group of your SAP HANA source or parsing system (if you need an external system):

```
enable_builtin_procedure_get_objects_in_ddl_statement = True
```

Figure A.6 shows the configuration entry in SAP HANA Studio.

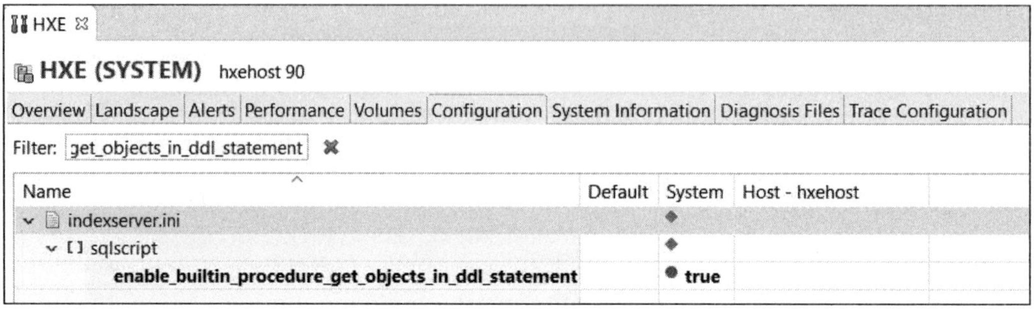

Figure A.6 Configuration Parameter: enable_builtin_procedure_get_objects_in_ddl_statement

If your SAP HANA system runs in a multitenancy scenario, you must change the *nameserver.ini* configuration file.

You also have to grant the EXECUTE privilege to the SAP HANA user for the SAP HANA XS Advanced Migration Assistant on the built-in procedure GET_OBJECTS_IN_DDL_STATEMENT:

```
GRANT EXECUTE ON "SYS"."GET_OBJECTS_IN_DDL_STATEMENT" TO <user>
```

A.3.2 SAP HANA XS Advanced Migration Assistant Report

The SAP HANA XS Advanced Migration Assistant can generate a report that will guide when you plan a migration of an application to SAP HANA XS Advanced.

We'll test the SAP HANA XS Advanced Migration Assistant report using the SAP HANA demo model (the SAP HANA Interactive Education package [SHINE]) delivery unit. You can download it from the SAP support portal software download center by looking for "*HCO Democontent*", as shown in Figure A.7.

You can also download it from this repository on GitHub: *https://github.com/SAP/hana-shine* (see Figure A.8).

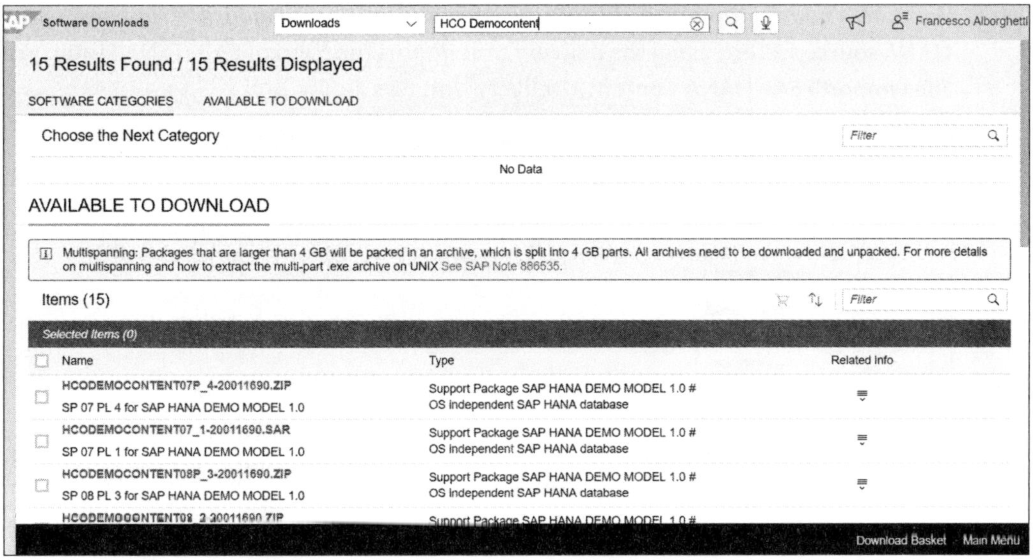

Figure A.7 SAP HANA Demo Model Available on SAP Support Portal

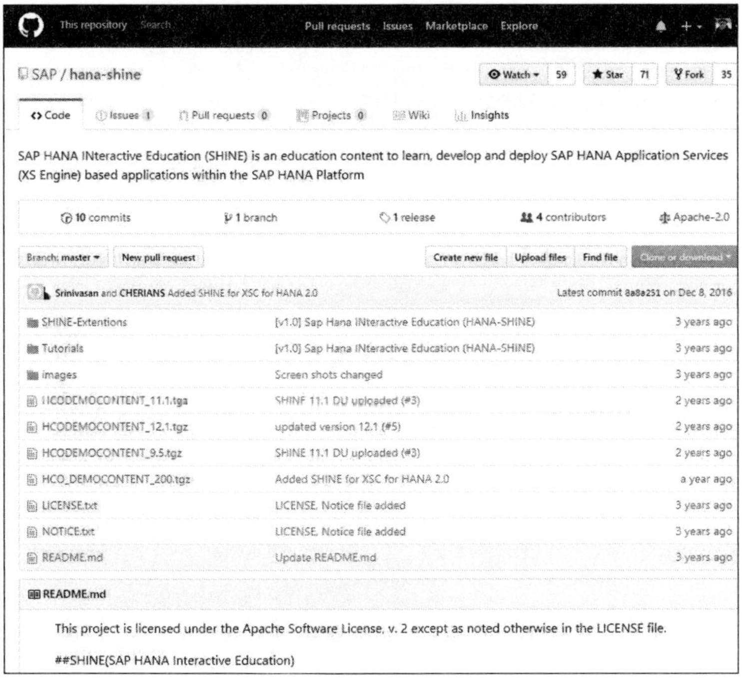

Figure A.8 SHINE Available on GitHub

As soon as you've downloaded the SHINE delivery unit, you can install it on your SAP HANA source system using the delivery unit import function of SAP HANA Studio via **File • Import • SAP HANA Content • Delivery Unit** (see Figure A.9).

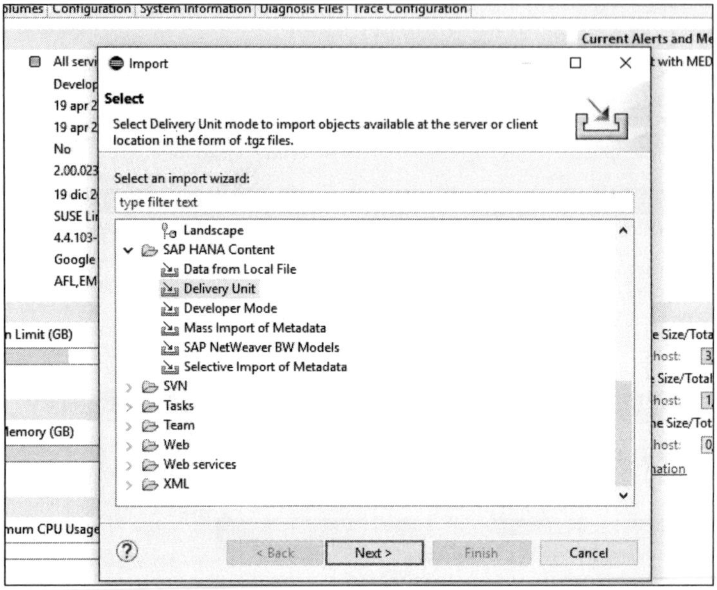

Figure A.9 Importing a Delivery Unit in SAP HANA with SAP HANA Studio

To import it, you must select the file with extension *.tgz*, as shown in Figure A.10.

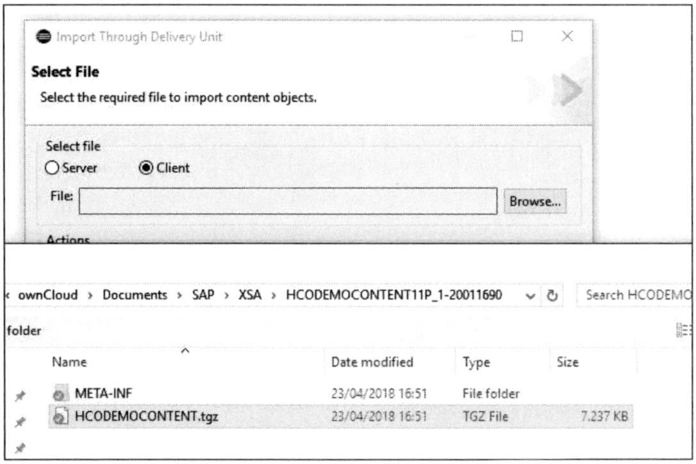

Figure A.10 Importing the HCODEMOCONTENT.tgz File into Your SAP HANA Source System

When you've installed the SHINE delivery unit in your source SAP HANA system and configured the SAP HANA XS Advanced Migration Assistant, you can run it from the folder where you've unzipped the SAP HANA XS Advanced Migration Assistant. Open a console in your client, and write this command (this is for Windows shell):

```
.\xs-migration.bat HCO_DEMOCONTENT
```

It will run for a while and then provide the report at the end in folder *results*. Double-click on the *report.html* file to open it (see Figure A.11).

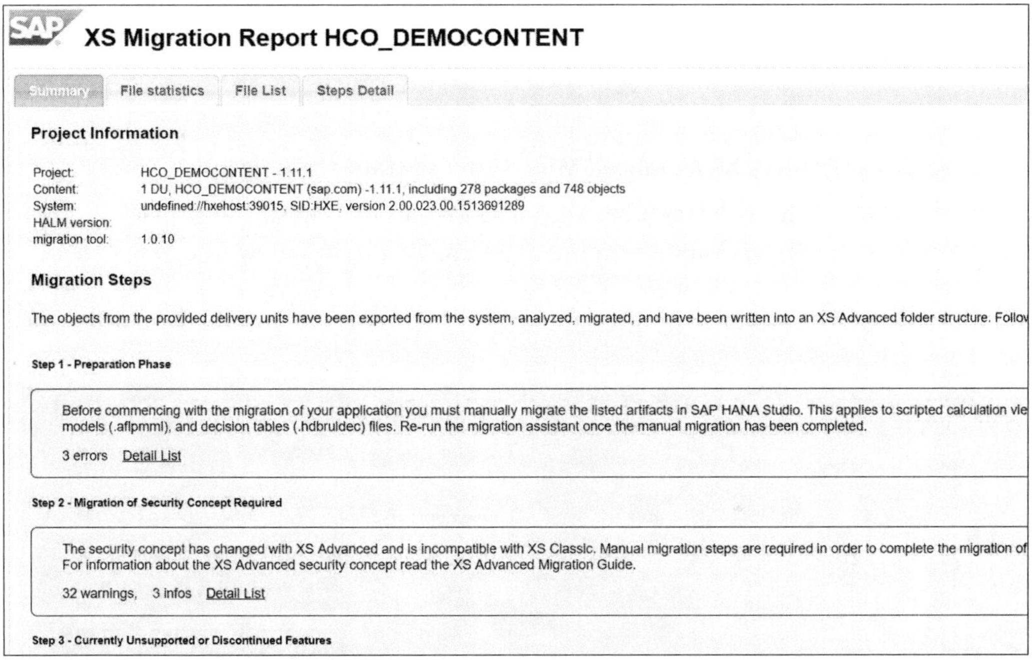

Figure A.11 SAP HANA XS Advanced Migration Assistant Report for the SHINE Delivery Unit

The report is structured in four tabs:

- **Summary**
- **File statistics**
- **File List**
- **Steps Detail**

The most important one is the **Steps Detail** tab that describes all the steps required for migrating the application to SAP HANA XS Advanced, as described here:

- **Preparation Phase**
  The first step, as you've already seen, is related to all the objects (e.g., attribute views or analytic views) that we must convert in the source system.
- **Migration of Security Concept Required**
  Then the security concept is analyzed. In Section 1.4, you'll see the main changes for the security concept that a migration to SAP HANA XS Advanced requires.
- **Currently Unsupported or Discontinued Features**
  The next steps identify a list of unsupported or discontinued objects or a list of objects that the SAP HANA XS Advanced Migration Assistant can automatically migrate but needs a manual review to ensure that they will work correctly after the migration.

A.3.3 SAP HANA XS Advanced Migration Assistant Options

You can run the SAP HANA XS Advanced Migration Assistant with many different options. To get the complete list (see Figure A.12), run the following command:

```
.\xs-migration.bat -help
```

Figure A.12 SAP HANA XS Advanced Migration Assistant Options

The SAP HANA XS Advanced Migration Assistant help provides enough explanation for all the options, so we'll only analyze the following two options:

- `--synonym-target-provider <path-to-configuration-file>`
  The `--synonym-target-provider` option starts a staged migration using a configuration file where you define the target provider's definition criteria.
- `--generate-providers`
  The `--generate-providers` option starts a staged migration with a generated target provider configuration.

Those options are relevant when you want to perform a *staged migration*. A staged migration is used when you want to separate semantic units (e.g., calculation views) in different SAP HANA Deployment Infrastructure (HDI) containers. In this case, the views can access their data sources using synonyms, and the synonyms target providers are either generated automatically by the SAP HANA XS Advanced Migration Assistant or defined in a configuration file.

A.4 Migration of the Security Concept

The migration of the security concept is probably the step that requires the most significant manual effort for an application migration because the SAP HANA XS and SAP HANA XS Advanced infrastructures use quite different security models.

In SAP HANA XS, application users get SAP HANA database module (HDB) privileges with the definition of design-time artifacts (*.hdbroles*), and these roles are owned by system user `_SYS_REPO` and granted/revoked with `_SYS_REPO` database procedures (e.g., `CALL_GRANT_ACTIVATED_ROLE`). In SAP HANA XS Advanced, instead, business users aren't bound to any HDI privileges; they use the same technical user to connect to the HDI container. Therefore, you must review the SAP HANA XS JavaScript (XSJS) coding to check the user authorization before sending any request to HDI.

The SAP HANA XS Advanced Migration Assistant still supports you with following automatic conversion of SAP HANA XS artifacts:

- Application access (*.xsaccess*)
- Roles (*.hdbrole*) and privileges (*.xsprivileges*)
- Analytic privileges (*.analyticprivilege*)

For analytic privileges, we've seen in Section A.2 that they can be converted in SAP HANA Studio using the migrate function of the SAP HANA Modeler perspective. We'll see now how the SAP HANA XS Advanced Migration Assistant converts the application access file and the application privileges and roles files.

A.4.1 Application Access

Application accesses (*.xsaccess*) are converted using the SAP HANA XS Advanced application descriptor. Listing A.1 shows the SHINE application access file.

```
{
    "exposed": true,
    "authentication": [
{ "method": "LogonTicket" },
{ "method" : "Form" }
],
    "authorization": [ "sap.hana.democontent.epm::Basic" ],
    "prevent_xsrf" : true
}
```

Listing A.1 SHINE .xsaccess

As you can see, the application access for the SHINE application requires that the user has the privilege `sap.hana.democontent.epm::Basic`. The SAP HANA XS Advanced Migration Assistant converts this file into SAP HANA XS Advanced application descriptor (*xs-app.json*), preventing the application access to business users with a role that contains the scope `$XSAPPNAME.sap.hana.democontent.epm.Basic`, as shown in Listing A.2.

```
{
    "welcomeFile": "index.html",
    "authenticationMethod": "route",
    "routes": [
        {
            "source": ".*\\.xsjs.*",
            "destination": "xsjs"
        },
        {
            "source": ".*\\.xsodata.*",
            "destination": "xsjs"
        },
        {
```

```
            "source": "^/sap/hana/democontent/epm/(.*)$",
            "localDir": "resources",
            "scope": [
                "$XSAPPNAME.sap.hana.democontent.epm.Basic"
            ]
        },
        {
            "source": "^/sap/hana/democontent/epm/admin/(.*)$",
            "localDir": "resources",
            "scope": [
                "$XSAPPNAME.sap.hana.democontent.epm.Admin"
            ]
        }
    ]
}
```

Listing A.2 .xsaccess Converted into xs-app.json File of SAP HANA XS Advanced

There are some considerations to remember when the application access properties are converted with the SAP HANA XS Advanced application descriptor:

- `Exposed`
  This property isn't relevant for SAP HANA XS Advanced. By default, XSJS packages are exposed, and HDI packages aren't exposed.
- `Authentication`
  SAP HANA XS Advanced supports authentication mechanisms with the SAP HANA XS User Account and Authentication service (UAA). SAP HANA XS Advanced has only two authentication mechanisms that you can define in the SAP HANA XS Advanced application descriptor (`route` and `none`).
- `anonymous_connection` and `default_connection`
  These options aren't required for SAP HANA XS Advanced because of the different database access model. If you need them, you can create a user-defined service.

A.4.2 Roles and Privileges

The conversion of roles and application privileges is the most challenging task because SAP HANA XS Advanced acts in a different way for HDI-related privileges and for user access application control.

In SAP HANA XS, you can grant both catalog object privileges and application privileges in the same *.hdbrole* file. Figure A.13 shows an example from the SHINE delivery unit.

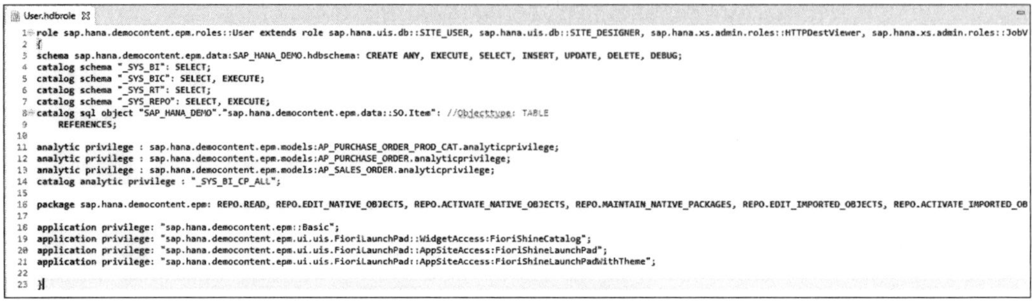
User.hdbrole
role sap.hana.democontent.epm.roles::User extends role sap.hana.uis.db::SITE_USER, sap.hana.uis.db::SITE_DESIGNER, sap.hana.xs.admin.roles::HTTPDestViewer, sap.hana.xs.admin.roles::JobV
{
schema sap.hana.democontent.epm.data:SAP_HANA_DEMO.hdbschema: CREATE ANY, EXECUTE, SELECT, INSERT, UPDATE, DELETE, DEBUG;
catalog schema "_SYS_BI": SELECT;
catalog schema "_SYS_BIC": SELECT, EXECUTE;
catalog schema "_SYS_RT": SELECT;
catalog schema "_SYS_REPO": SELECT, EXECUTE;
catalog sql object "SAP_HANA_DEMO"."sap.hana.democontent.epm.data::SO.Item": //Objecttype: TABLE
REFERENCES;
analytic privilege : sap.hana.democontent.epm.models:AP_PURCHASE_ORDER_PROD_CAT.analyticprivilege;
analytic privilege : sap.hana.democontent.epm.models:AP_PURCHASE_ORDER.analyticprivilege;
analytic privilege : sap.hana.democontent.epm.models:AP_SALES_ORDER.analyticprivilege;
catalog analytic privilege : "_SYS_BI_CP_ALL";
package sap.hana.democontent.epm: REPO.READ, REPO.EDIT_NATIVE_OBJECTS, REPO.ACTIVATE_NATIVE_OBJECTS, REPO.MAINTAIN_NATIVE_PACKAGES, REPO.EDIT_IMPORTED_OBJECTS, REPO.ACTIVATE_IMPORTED_OB
application privilege: "sap.hana.democontent.epm::Basic";
application privilege: "sap.hana.democontent.epm.ui.uis.FioriLaunchPad::WidgetAccess:FioriShineCatalog";
application privilege: "sap.hana.democontent.epm.ui.uis.FioriLaunchPad::AppSiteAccess:FioriShineLaunchPad";
application privilege: "sap.hana.democontent.epm.ui.uis.FioriLaunchPad::AppSiteAccess:FioriShineLaunchPadWithTheme";
}

Figure A.13 File user.hdbrole of the SHINE Delivery Unit

In SAP HANA XS Advanced, the concepts are separated: HDI-related privileges remain in the *.hdbrole* files that secure the HDI container objects access. As for the application privileges (*.xsprivileges*), they are, instead, converted in SAP HANA XS Advanced *scopes*, and the application privileges definition of the SAP HANA XS *.hdbrole* files are converted in *role templates* that contain the scopes. At the end, you secure the application privileges by assigning roles to the business users.

The target file for scopes and role-templates definition is the *xs-security.json* file. Listing A.3 shows the *xs-security.json* file generated by the SAP HANA XS Advanced Migration Assistant for the SHINE application.

```
{
    "xsappname": "HCO_DEMOCONTENT",
    "scopes": [
        {
            "name": "$XSAPPNAME.sap.hana.democontent.epm.Basic",
            "description": "Basic usage privilege"
        },
        {
            "name": "$XSAPPNAME.sap.hana.democontent.epm.Admin",
            "description": "Administration privilege"
        },
        ...
    ],
    "role-templates": [
        {
```

```
            "name": "sap_hana_democontent_epm_roles_Admin",
            "scope-references": [
                "$XSAPPNAME.sap.hana.democontent.epm.Admin"
            ]
        },
        {
            "name": "sap_hana_democontent_epm_roles_User",
            "scope-references": [
                "$XSAPPNAME.sap.hana.democontent.epm.Basic",
                ...
            ]
        }
    ]
}
```

Listing A.3 Generated file xs-security.json of an SAP HANA XS Advanced Application

As you can see, the application privileges have been converted in scopes and the application privileges of the SAP HANA XS *.hdbroles* have been converted into role-templates.

Separating the HDI-related object privileges from the application-related privileges means that to migrate the SAP HANA XS application, you need to review the XSJS coding to ensure that the application privileges are evaluated as they were before. The SAP HANA XS Advanced Migration Assistant highlights this manual activity in the migration report, as shown in Figure A.14.

Step 2: Migration of Security Concept Required

description area

Warning (32)

type	category	file
WARNING	SECURITY	migration\orig-src\sap\hana\democontent\epm\.xsaccess Features in xsaccess can only be partially migrated to new XS Advanced security concept (xsjs/xs-app.json). Check migration guide for detail. Check the security migration guide
WARNING	SECURITY	migration\orig-src\sap\hana\democontent\epm\admin\.xsaccess Features in xsaccess can only be partially migrated to new XS Advanced security concept (xsjs/xs-app.json). Check migration guide for detail. Check the security migration guide
WARNING	SECURITY	xsjs\lib\sap\hana\democontent\epm\admin\DataGen.xsjs (in line: 29) Role access privileges must be checked when using $.hdb.getConnection. check migration guide for detail.
WARNING	SECURITY	xsjs\lib\sap\hana\democontent\epm\admin\checkDG.xsjs (in line: 1) Role access privileges must be checked when using $.hdb.getConnection. check migration guide for detail.

Figure A.14 SAP HANA XS Advanced Migration Assistant Warning Messages for XSJS Required Manual Activities

For all the reported XSJS coding, you must use `$.session.hasAppPrivilege()` or `$.session.assertAppPrivilege()` before sending requests to HDI.

For the same reason, you must add routes with scope checks to *xs-app.json* for all XSODATA-like objects (objects that go through the application router to the HDI, without the possibility to check this in XSJS code).

Appendix B
Additional Resources

Following is a list of some additional resources that may be of use to you:

- **Text analysis**
  - SAP HANA Text Analysis Developer Guide
    https://help.sap.com/doc/7064d9cce146477Obcb38158ff318dc9/2.0.03/en-US/SAP_HANA_Text_Analysis_Developer_Guide_en.pdf
  - SAP HANA Academy – Text Analysis: 1. Introduction
    https://youtu.be/nH968kGfBlA
  - Open SAP Course
    https://open.sap.com/courses/hstal
- **Presentation layer**
  - UI Development Toolkit for HTML5
    https://sapui5.hana.ondemand.com
  - SAP Fiori Design Guidelines
    https://experience.sap.com/fiori-design
  - SAPUI5: The Comprehensive Guide (Goebels, Christiane, Seidel), Rheinwerk Publishing, 2016
    https://www.sap-press.com/sapui5_3980/
- **General SAP HANA native development**
  - SAP HANA Developer Guide
    https://help.sap.com/viewer/4505d0bdaf4948449b7f7379d24d0f0d/2.0.03/en-US
  - Multi-Target Application Concept Guide
    www.sap.com/documents/2016/06/e2f618e4-757c-0010-82c7-eda71af511fa.html
  - SAP HANA Interactive Education (SHINE) Application
    https://github.com/SAP/hana-shine-xsa
  - Official OData Website
    www.odata.org/

- **Database layer and security**
  - Best practices and recommendations for role developing for SAP HANA XSA
    https://www.sap.com/documents/2018/04/fe086f0d-fa7c-0010-87a3-c30de2ffd8ff.html
  - Open SAP Course, Software Development on SAP HANA (Update Q4/2016 & Q4/2017)
    - *https://open.sap.com/courses/hana5*
    - *https://open.sap.com/courses/hana6*
  - SAP HANA Academy: Modeling and Design with SAP HANA
    https://www.youtube.com/watch?v=j-LFppxTIJo&list=PLkzo92owKnVz9hgx4CzWONc2ocU7riEMr
- **Node.js**
  - Comprehensive Node.js Tutorials for Beginners
    https://nodeschool.io/
  - *Node.js Design Patterns*, Mario Casciaro
    https://books.google.it/books/about/Node_js_Design_Patterns.html?id=55WqDQAAQBAJ&source=kp_cover&redir_esc=y
- **Martin Fowler on continuous integration**
  - *www.martinfowler.com/articles/continuousIntegration.html*

Appendix C
The Authors

Francesco Alborghetti is the cofounder of and a managing partner for Inquaero, an innovative consulting company with a focus on SAP lean data management solutions. He is an expert SAP consultant who has developed his wide expertise for more than 15 years, working for major SAP system integrators and SAP itself, where he was the principal consultant for the SAP HANA EMEA CoE (Centre of Excellence). In his current role, he helps drive and support his customers in SAP HANA and SAP S/4HANA adoption and transformation projects.

Jonas Kohlbrenner is a senior SAP HANA engineer and architect. Since 2012, he has supported SAP customers and partners as they implemented the SAP HANA platform by providing holistic architectural guidance and practical implementation skills across the full platform. His areas of focus include SAP HANA Basis technology topics like data center integration and operations, SAP HANA application architecture and development (SAP HANA modeling, SQLScript programming, application layer design, and security concept definition), as well as SAPUI5 application architecture design and development.

Abani Pattanayak has more than 15 years of experience in data warehousing, and has been working with SAP in-memory technology since 2007. As a principal architect at SAP and an SAP HANA Distinguished Engineer, he has helped implement and performance-tune SAP HANA for multiple customers. He is a frequent contributor to SAP Community and a regular speaker at events like SAP TechEd.

Dominik Schrank is a principal consultant for SAP HANA and SAP analytics solutions at SAP Deutschland SE & Co. KG. Dominik has more than ten years of experience in designing and implementing large business analytics and native SAP HANA applications based on the SAP HANA, SAP BusinessObjects BI, and the SAP Cloud Platform solution portfolio for global customers. Dominik focus is on building innovative solutions based on the latest SAP analytics technologies. He regularly shares his knowledge on various SAP analytics topics in blogs and articles.

Primo Sboarina is a technical developer and consultant at SAP.

Index

@OData.publish annotation ... 360
12-Factor Apps ... 123

A

Access privileges ... 450
  HDI container ... 451
ACID-compliant (atomicity, consistency, isolation, durability) ... 26
Admin processes ... 127
Administration application ... 487
Aggregation binding ... 407
  controller definition ... 408
  defining within the controller ... 413
  example ... 410
  factory function ... 412
  programmatic ... 411
  view definition ... 409
Analysis view ... 243
Analytic privileges ... 274, 577
Analyze SQL tool ... 542–543
ANSI SQL ... 159
API key ... 565
Application concepts ... 140
Application deployment ... 557
Application descriptor ... 399
Application design ... 38
Application layer ... 289, 291
  tasks ... 290
Application logs ... 519
Application monitor
  viewing application logs ... 522
Application package descriptor ... 294
Application privileges ... 590–591
Application programming interface (API) ... 31, 564
  container security ... 473
Application Role Builder tool ... 464
Application router ... 135, 452, 477
  authorization checks ... 454
  files ... 426
Application Security Descriptor ... 457
approuter ... 426
Architecture ... 119, 122
  advanced ... 453
  deploying and executing ... 131
  microservices ... 119
  organization ... 129
  runtime components ... 133
Async library ... 326
  further information ... 330
Asynchronous function ... 320
  parallel processing ... 321
Asynchronous programming model ... 316
Attribute view ... 577
Attributes ... 137, 152, 453, 456
  authorities ... 460
  foreign-scope-references ... 460
  oauth2-configuration ... 461
  property ... 459
  restricting ... 484
  role-templates ... 459
  tenant-mode ... 462
Audit log ... 524
Audit log service for Java ... 531
  accessing logging entries ... 535
  adding ... 532
  creating log entries ... 534
auditLog object ... 525
Audit-log service ... 139
Authentication token ... 455
Authorization ... 455, 581
  defining application security ... 457
  scopes and attributes ... 455
  setting up role templates ... 456
  user account and authorization service ... 463
Authorization checks ... 452
  configuring ... 489
  configuring instance-based ... 493–494
  declarative ... 455
  instance-based ... 454
  Java modules ... 471
AWS ... 54
Azure ... 54

B

Backing services ... 124
Binary Linux installation ... 48
Binding context ... 406
Blob store ... 132–133
commands ... 95
Blocking ... 317
Bootstrapping ... 394–395
content delivery network ... 396
files ... 396
preload variant ... 397
Breakpoint
conditional ... 514
Java application ... 514
Node.js application ... 511
Build, release, run phases ... 125
Building MTAR ... 557–558
Buildpacks ... 132
commands ... 94
Business users ... 451
authorization checks ... 453
Business view ... 243

C

Calculated binding ... 418
Calculated field ... 418
Calculation column ... 261
Calculation views ... 33, 102
advanced properties ... 250
creating ... 245
data preview ... 250
debugging editor ... 508
properties ... 249
unfolding ... 542
Callback convention ... 307
Callback method ... 318
Cardinality ... 152
Cascading Style Sheets (CSS) ... 395
CDS associations ... 222
CDS editors ... 208
graphical editor ... 209
text editor ... 209
CDS entities ... 211
structure ... 211
CDS extensions ... 226
steps ... 227
CDS view ... 224
parameters ... 225
Certificates ... 92
Change and Transport System (CTS) ... 567
Click-jacking attacks ... 479
Cloud Foundry ... 60–61, 68
basics ... 127
environment ... 128
organization ... 129
setting up ... 61
Cloud Foundry Router ... 134
Codebase ... 123
Column tables ... 166
Columnar aggregation operations ... 167
Command-line interface (CLI) ... 71
Complex syntax ... 415
Component controller ... 399
definition ... 399
Concurrency ... 126
Configuration ... 124
commands ... 98
Container objects
permissions ... 503
Container schema ... 191
Content delivery network (CDN) ... 396
Continuous Integration ... 568
Control flow logic ... 291
Control template ... 410
Controller ... 402, 404
Controller roles ... 466
categories ... 466
resources ... 466
Core Data Services (CDS) ... 208, 360
CreateLog procedure ... 521
Cross-Origin Resource Sharing (CORS) ... 478
Cross-schema access ... 237
enabling ... 239
mta.yaml file ... 239
Cross-site request forgery (CSRF) ... 479
Cross-site scripting (XSS) ... 480
Cube calculation views ... 272
key features ... 267
Cube calculation views with star joins ... 264
input parameters ... 271

Cube calculation views with star joins (Cont.)
restricted columns 269
variables 270
Custom read method 382

D

Data binding 394, 402, 404
Data Control Language (DCL) 465
Data Definition Language (DDL) 31
Data extensions 275
Data foundation 265
Data model 152
defining 151, 167
demo application 154
Data model design 159
Data temperature 27
Database artifacts 281
deployment infrastructure 286
supported HDI artifacts 286
Database Explorer 160
Database explorer tool 509
Database layer 291
Database persistence 196
Database sequence 281
Database traces 536
Database view 282
Debugger panel 512, 515
Debugging 507
calculation views 508
enabling 510
integrated functionality 513
Java application 513
Java applications 514
Node.js application 510
SAPUI5 application 515
specifying breakpoints 511
stored procedures 509
Decision tables 575
Default calculation views 263
Delivery unit 183, 584
Denormalization 166
Dependencies 124, 301
Deploy app 305
Deploy MTAR 560–561
abort deployment 563
command line interface 561

Deploy MTAR (Cont.)
download deploy logs 564
restart deployment 563
retry deployment 563
SAP Web IDE 560
Deploy with namespaces 562
Deployed file system 193
Deployed runtime objects 182
Deployment extension descriptor 564
Deployment phases 131
Design-time artifacts 189
Design-time container (DTC) 190
Design-time definitions 182, 184
Destinations 135, 429
defining 430
Detail.view.xml 442
Dev/Ops 126
Dev/prod parity 126
Development (DEV) tier 43
Development environment 43
Development perspective 114
Development tools 83, 113
DevOps methodology 45
support 46
Dimension view 243, 251
column view 258
XML contents 255
Dispatcher 134
Disposability 126
Distinct count 269
Document Object Model (DOM) 395
Domain 91
Download Manager 49–50
Droplet 133
Droplets 132

E

Element binding 405
absolute model 407
programmatic 407
view definition 406
End user 452
accessing HTML5 application 491
assigning role collection 488
assigning roles 476
creating 487

End-to-end traces ... 537
Enterprise information management
(EIM) ... 35
Entities ... 152, 156
Entity modifiers ... 217
Entity-relationship (ER) diagram ... 152
Error messages
forbidden ... 472, 488
Expensive statements traces ... 537
Explain plan ... 547
columns ... 547
Express application
creating ... 334
Express framework ... 334
application port listening ... 337
further inforamtion ... 338
mount middleware ... 338
route path ... 335
Express module ... 474
adding as a dependency ... 475
Express security middleware ... 315
Expression binding ... 418, 420
Extended store server ... 36
External buildpack processes ... 71
External parse system ... 579

F

Factory function ... 411
Failed deployment ... 563
File-based module ... 298
File-system storage ... 139
flight-rectoder.js ... 299
Flowgraph editor ... 202
Folder-based module ... 298
Formatter function ... 415
Functional extensions ... 275

G

Geo-spatial features ... 34
Gerrit ... 46, 74, 569
Git ... 46, 74, 145–146
Git repository ... 74, 78, 146, 291, 562, 569
cloning ... 79
git pane ... 78
GitHub ... 75
Global temporary tables ... 219
Google Chrome developer tools ... 515
Grantable flag ... 458
Graph database features ... 34
Graphical calculation view ... 577
gulpfile.js ... 296

H

Hash-based navigation ... 420
HDB module ... 196
artifacts ... 202
building artifacts ... 203
creating ... 199–200
folder structure ... 203
hdbgrants ... 503
.hdbrole file ... 283
.hdbschema file ... 185
.hdbsequence file ... 188
.hdbtable file ... 185
.hdbtabledata ... 229
building ... 234
.hdbview file ... 187
HDI API ... 193
HDI client ... 194
HDI container ... 137, 189–190, 501
assigning roles ... 502
database users ... 501
default access role ... 500
deployer ... 192
deployment ... 193, 195
granting access ... 497
granting access via roles ... 498
involved users ... 451
plug-ins ... 195
proxy library ... 195
roles ... 495
runtime database objects ... 204
server ... 195
technical users ... 205
.hdiconfig file ... 280
Helper function ... 374
Hierarchy
properties ... 254
Hostname-based routing ... 134

HTML5 395
HTML5 module 384
setting up router information 386
Hypertext Transfer Protocol (HTTP) 31
Hypervisors 49

I

Identity provider (IdP) 450
index.html file 434
adapting the bootstrap script 434
INF 153
Information Access (InA) 31
init method 400
Inner join 246
Intel Virtualization Technology 49
Internet of Things (IoT) 27

J

Jasmine 348
expectations 351
standard matchers 351
Java 358
Java libraries 481
Java methods 372
Java modules
creating 360
creating a new class 370
creating in SAP Web IDE 363
disabling security constraint 366
generating 364
running and testing 377
selecting 363
source code structure 365
Java Naming and Directory Interface (JNDI) 533
Java OData libraries 359
Java services
API and service URLs 383
configuring binding information 385
connecting to HTML5 frontend 383
connecting to SAPUI5 table 389
creating HTML5 module 384
Java virtual machine (VM) 358
JavaScript 292, 395
Job Scheduler 138
Join Engine 578
Join order 577
JSON model 402
JSON Web Token (JWT) 135, 315

K

Kernel profiler 537
Key attributes 152

L

Left outer join 246
Level hierarchy 253
Lifecycle hooks 404
Logging 519
audit-logging 524
displaying log files 522
fast changing data set 520
Java applications 526
last change 519
Node.js application 523
severity level 528
slowly changing/moving dimension 519
stored procedure actions 520
table 520
unsuccessful logon 526
Logs 126

M

Maintaining users and roles 482
Managed associations 222
Managing asynchronous control flow 320
manifest.json 400
Manual transport 566
Master.controller.js 444
Master.view.xml 444
Matcher function 351
MDX console 105
metadata property 400
Microservices 32, 121
Microservices architecture 119, 121
advantages 122
Middleware 338

Migration ... 576
Migration Assistant ... 575, 579, 585
intallation ... 580
options ... 586
report ... 582, 585
Model ... 401
Model view controller (MVC) ... 394, 401
Modeled views ... 33
Modeler perspective ... 114
Modules ... 297
notations ... 300
XSJS support ... 314
Monolithic architecture ... 120
MTA applications ... 431
MTA deployment descriptor ... 196
MTA editor
defining destinations ... 430
mta.yaml ... 559
mtad.yaml ... 559
.mtaext ... 564
Multidimensional (cube) view ... 243
Multidimensional expressions (MDX) ... 30
Multi-target applications (MTA) ... 46, 66, 123, 196, 573
architecture ... 144
archive ... 143, 145
archive builder ... 559, 569
Build tool ... 144
building an archive ... 205–206
concept ... 141–142
creating a project ... 197–198
deployer ... 143
deploying an archive ... 207
deployment descriptor ... 143, 559
development descriptor ... 142, 559
development workflow ... 146
node module ... 293
UAA ... 142

N

N and N+1 system landscape ... 44
Name server ... 36
Namespace property ... 439
Native data types ... 217
Native transport ... 569
Neo ... 61, 66
Node database access ... 338
Node DB access
calling database procedure ... 344
connection pooling ... 341
database query ... 343
environment variables ... 340
Express middleware ... 342
Node ID ... 254
Node.js ... 292, 299, 318
connecting ... 338
exposing data ... 330
Node.js event loop ... 319
Node.js module ... 293, 297, 437
debugging ... 510
Node.js security packages ... 480
Node.js unit testing ... 348
choosing code to test ... 354
matchers ... 351
run unit test ... 349
test results ... 349
Normalization ... 153
npm repository ... 297
local npm repository ... 301

O

OAuth access token ... 136
Object definition ... 162
Object privileges ... 581, 590
OData ... 31, 330
associations ... 332
deleting data ... 381
exposing CDS definition ... 360
functionality ... 331
Java ... 359
models ... 402
modifying data ... 369
object name ... 331
parameters ... 368
read service ... 367
service extension ... 372
updating data ... 380
One-time binding ... 405
One-way binding ... 404
Online analytical processing (OLAP) ... 27

Online transaction processing (OLTP) ... 27
On-premise SAP HANA ... 128
OpenUI5 ... 397
Operator list ... 546
Organization ... 129
managing ... 71
Organizations ... 69
cockpit ... 111
commands ... 90

P

Package privileges ... 581
package.json ... 294–295, 298, 427
scripts ... 296
Parallel processing ... 325, 328
Parent-child hierarchy ... 254
Path callback ... 336
Performance analysis tools ... 102
Performance optimization ... 541
analyzing SQL ... 542
executing SQL queries ... 541
explaining plan in SAP HANA Studio ... 547
Performance traces ... 537
configuring ... 539
options ... 539
Persistence database ... 124
Plan Visualizer ... 541, 550, 554
executed plan tab ... 553
overview tab ... 551
using ... 550
Platform controller ... 130
Platform services ... 135
Plug-ins
commands ... 99
Port binding ... 125
Portal service ... 139
Port-based routing ... 134
Postman ... 117, 378
Postman REST client tool ... 378
Preload modalities ... 397
Presentation layer ... 291
adding format option ... 442
changing the master list ... 444
developing ... 393
layout adjustments ... 441
Principle propagation ... 67
Privileges ... 283
defining ... 503
TRACE_ADMIN ... 536
with grant option ... 504
Procedural extensions ... 275
Process ... 125
Production (PRD) tier ... 43
Projection node ... 252
Promises ... 321
further information ... 326
Promisifying an API ... 323
.properties file ... 235
Property binding ... 414
controller definition ... 417
format options ... 415
view definition ... 416
Protected parameters and properties ... 565
PuTTY ... 51
PuTTYgen ... 59

Q

Quality (QAS) tier ... 43
Queueing service ... 124

R

Referential join ... 247
Reporting view ... 243
Resource models ... 402
Return value ... 374
Right outer join ... 246
Role collections ... 464, 483
assigning ... 490
assigning application role ... 486
assigning to end user ... 487
creating ... 485
Role templates ... 484, 590
Roles ... 283, 483
creating ... 482
creating instance-based ... 485
viewing ... 483
Route path ... 335
Router class ... 421
initializing ... 421

Routes ... 422, 429
commands ... 93
HTML5 module ... 386
matched event ... 425
navigating ... 424
pattern matched event ... 425
properties ... 429
Routing ... 130
Routing configuration ... 422
defining parameters ... 423
Rule-based optimizations ... 541
rungulp.js ... 296
Runtime container (RTC) ... 190, 291
Runtime tools ... 37

S

SAP Cloud Appliance Library ... 54
accessing SAP HANA, express edition ... 59
create instance ... 56
instance details ... 58
registrations ... 55
SAP HANA, express edition post-configuration ... 58
SAP HANA, express edition setup ... 56
SAP Cloud Platform ... 60
registrations ... 61
SAP Cloud Platform cockpit ... 63
SAP Enterprise Performance Management ... 34
SAP Event Stream Processor ... 35
SAP Fiori ... 393
SAP Fiori launchpad ... 139
SAP Fiori Master-Detail Module ... 437
binding OData properties ... 440
creating ... 437
running ... 441
selecting OData service ... 438
testing ... 440
SAP HANA ... 159
application business cases ... 25
application layers ... 39
application services ... 32
architecture ... 29, 38
cloud-based deployment ... 27
components ... 29
database ... 39
database services ... 32
SAP HANA (Cont.)
demo model ... 582
development platform ... 25
in-memory database ... 26
integration services ... 35
interfaces ... 30
parsing system ... 580
platform ... 30
platform innovations ... 28
programming model ... 40
technical services ... 36
SAP HANA administration console ... 114
SAP HANA cockpit ... 37, 116
SAP HANA database container ... 106
SAP HANA database explorer ... 104, 106
SAP HANA Deployment Infrastructure (HDI) ... 37, 128, 189, 450, 590
containers ... 565, 587
technical users ... 191
SAP HANA development perspective ... 183
SAP HANA Interactive Education package (SHINE) ... 582, 588
SAP HANA Platform cockpit ... 64
SAP HANA Repository ... 44, 74, 182
design-time objects ... 182
SAP HANA Rules Framework ... 575
SAP HANA Secure Store ... 138
SAP HANA Service Broker ... 137, 191
SAP HANA service Instance
provisioning ... 61
SAP HANA service instance ... 60
creating ... 62
SAP HANA services ... 137
SAP HANA smart data integration (SDI) ... 35
SAP HANA smart data quality (SDQ) ... 35
SAP HANA Studio ... 113, 574
accessing Cloud Foundry ... 65
creating design-time objects ... 183
database objects ... 162
EXPLAIN PLAN ... 547
migration tool ... 575
migration type ... 576
SAP HANA views ... 481
SAP HANA Web-Based Development Workbench ... 37, 115
functionalities ... 115
traces ... 536

SAP HANA XS 53, 122, 182, 569, 574
artifacts 587
migration 573
SAP HANA XS Advanced 400
application routing 426
migration 573
overview 32
SAPUI5 runtime 431–432
SAP HANA XS Advanced Admin tool 109
SAP HANA XS Advanced cockpit 109
displaying applications 112
functionalities 110
opening 111
SAP HANA XS Advanced cockpit web application
creating end users 488
roles 482
SAP HANA XS JavaScript (XSJS) 587
SAP HANA, express edition 47
checking application status 54
excluded features 47
installing VM images 48
on-premise installation 48
organization and space 71
post-installation checks 52
prerequisites 49
SAP Node.js modules 303
@sap/hdi-deploy 305
@sap/textanalysis 305
@sap/textbundle 308
@sap/xsenv 310
@sap/xsjs 312
@sap/xssec 314
application environment variables 310
application router 303
container security API 314
database client 304
HDI Deployer 305
internationalization 308
SAP HANA Database Client 304
SAP HANA XS compatibility layer 312
SAP HANA-based text analysis 305
SAP Web IDE 60, 101, 508
accessing 59, 102
creating Java module 362
full-stack development 66
preferences 103
SAP Web IDE for SAP HANA 37, 560, 579
sap.app namespace 400
sap.ui namespace 401
sap.ui5 namespace 401
SAPUI5 393
application structuring 398
central service 431
debugging tools 517
frontend development 394
routing and navigation 420
SmartTable 390
Scalar functions 277–278
Schema 138
Schema access 496
Scopes 136, 453, 455
defining 458
property 458
viewing 483
Search and text analysis 33
Security 449, 587
application access 588
concepts 450
enabling 467
Java modules 470
Node.js modules 472
roles and privileges 589
SAPUI5 modules 476
web-based attacks 478
Security Assertion Markup Language (SAML) 2.0 standard 452
Security constraint
enabling 471
Semantic versioning 300
Semantics 266
Sequential processing 324, 326
server.js 296
Server-side application 120
Service broker 70, 130, 136
Service instance 130
Service plan 129
Service query object 310
Services 88, 129
Simple Logging Facade for Java (SLF4J) 527
initializing 527
logging information 530
logging levels 528
removing logging levels 530

Single-page pattern ... 395
Smart controls ... 394
Software Development Kit (SDK) ... 395
Source code ... 145–146
Space Enablement tool ... 73
Spaces ... 69–70, 129, 466
adding users ... 73
cockpit ... 112
commands ... 90
creating ... 72
enabling ... 73
managing ... 71
SQL ... 32, 159
SQL analytic privileges ... 493
SQL analyzer ... 105
SQL commands
executing ... 160
SQL Console ... 37, 105, 160
SQL Console (Admin) ... 496
SQL debugger ... 105
SQL Engine ... 541
execution plans ... 547
SQL executor ... 541
SQL optimizer ... 541
SQL processor ... 194
SQL queries ... 541
dominant operators ... 543
optimizing behaviors ... 541
plan graphs ... 544
SQL statements ... 163
ALTER TABLE ... 165
COMMENT ON ... 164
CREATE SCHEMA ... 163
CREATE TABLE ... 164
INSERT INTO ... 165
SELECT ... 166
SET SCHEMA ... 163
SQL traces ... 536
configuring ... 537
levels ... 538
options ... 537
SQLScript ... 32, 102
best practices ... 275
stored procedures ... 275
Staging process ... 133
Star join ... 264–265
Stored procedure
loading and calling ... 345
Stored procedures ... 276
Structure data type ... 220
Structured Query Language (SQL) ... 30
Synchronous programming model ... 316
Synonym editor ... 238
Synonyms ... 237, 503
System database ... 62
System landscape ... 43, 46
System privileges ... 581

T

Table accesses view ... 545
Table data
attributes ... 231
generating time data ... 236
loading ... 228
using plug-in ... 229
using properties ... 235
Table functions ... 277
Tables
AIRPORT ... 168
BOOKING ... 179
CONNECTION ... 175
CREW ... 173
CUSTOMER ... 171
FLIGHT ... 177
PLANE ... 169
PRICE_CALENDAR ... 174
SEAT ... 175
Tables in use view ... 545
Technical users ... 451
Tenant database ... 62
Test driven development ... 354
Text analysis
example ... 308
parameters ... 306
Text bundles ... 308
Text join ... 247
Time data ... 236
generating ... 236
Timeline view ... 545, 554
Timeouts
configuring ... 480

Tomcat Java runtime ... 533
Transaction logs ... 522
Transport using CTS ... 567
Transporting SAP HANA XS Advanced applications ... 566
Troubleshooting ... 507
Two-way binding ... 405

U

Undeploy MTA ... 565
- *delete services* ... 566

undeply.json ... 204
Uniform Resource Identifier (URI) ... 372
Union node ... 273
Unit testing ... 348
Unmanaged associations ... 223
Upstream repository ... 302
User acceptance (UAT) tier ... 43
User Account and Authentication Service (UAA) ... 135–136, 314, 463, 565
- *binding* ... 476
- *creating* ... 467

User Management tool ... 464
- *migrating SAP HANA user* ... 488

User-defined data types ... 220
User-defined structures ... 220
User-provided services ... 140, 144
Users ... 70, 129
User-specific traces ... 536

V

View ... 401, 403
- *JavaScript* ... 403

Virtual data models ... 243
VM image ... 48

W

WebSocket communication ... 429
Work file system ... 193

X

XML for Analysis (XMLA) ... 31
XML namespaces ... 403
XS Engine ... 122
XS runtime ... 36
XSA CLI ... 83, 529, 561–562
- *application management* ... 86
- *buildpacks* ... 94
- *certificates* ... 92
- *configuration* ... 98
- *domains* ... 91
- *getting* ... 84
- *help functionality* ... 84
- *organizations and spaces* ... 90
- *other commands* ... 100
- *plug-ins* ... 99
- *routes* ... 93
- *runtime environments* ... 95
- *services management* ... 88
- *setting up* ... 85
- *tasks* ... 96
- *user administration* ... 97

xs-app.json ... 427
- *sections* ... 428

XSASecurityContext functions ... 473
xsenv module ... 310
XSODATA ... 330
- *associations* ... 333
- *further information* ... 333

XSODATA service ... 436
xs-security.json ... 457, 468
- *xsappname property* ... 457